Jerusalem's Rise to Sovereignty

Zion and Gerizim in Competition

Ingrid Hjelm

T & T CLARK INTERNATIONAL
A Continuum imprint
LONDON • NEW YORK

Copyright © 2004 T&T Clark International
A Continuum imprint

Published by T&T Clark International
The Tower Building, 11 York Road, London SE1 7NX
15 East 26th Street, Suite 1703, New York, NY 10010

www.tandtclark.com

British Library Cataloguing-in-Publication Data
A catalogue record for this book is available from the British Library

Typeset and edited for Continuum by Forthcoming Publications Ltd
www.forthcomingpublications.com

Printed on acid-free paper in Great Britain by Antony Rowe Ltd

ISBN 0-5670-8085-4 (hardback)

CONTENTS

PREFACE

An ancient text is like an orphan.

—Paul Ricoeur

The present monograph is a revised version of my doctoral thesis, 'Jerusalem's Rise to Sovereignty in Ancient History and Tradition', which was submitted for PhD defence at the Theological Faculty, University of Copenhagen, in December 2002. I want to thank Professor Graeme Auld, University of Edinburgh, Professor Thomas Römer, University of Lausanne, and Lecturer Arne Munk, University of Copenhagen, for their very useful comments and objections, some of which have been incorporated and, I think, integrated in a way that conceals their origin in the present work as additions.

I want to thank the Danish Research Council for the PhD grant and the Department of Biblical Exegesis, University of Copenhagen, for housing me and supporting my work. Special thanks to the members of the department's senior seminar for fruitful discussions. I owe the *Société d'Études Samaritains* many thanks for accepting me as member. I am especially grateful to Dr Ruairidh Bóid, Melbourne, and Benyamim Tsedaka, director of the A.B. Institute of Samaritan Studies in Holon, both of whom have been very helpful in regard to Samaritan literary traditions.

Professor Niels Peter Lemche, University of Copenhagen, to whom I dedicate this book, I want to thank for his continual encouragement, support and insistence on academic integrity: 'Do it your way and do it convincingly'. I can say for sure that 'I did it my way', but I must admit that my work has been directed by two principles: Niels Peter Lemche's maximalist approach to research illuminating the insight of Blaise Pascal—'Knowledge is like a balloon, the more you fill into it, the larger is the area you do not know'—and Karl Popper's theories of falsification, which does not allow to stand what might fall.

Deeply felt are my thanks to my husband, colleague, soul mate and editor of the Copenhagen International Series, Professor Thomas L. Thompson for never-ending interest, encouragement and care taking. I will not resort to saying 'without you', because that probably is not true, but I will say 'with you' this book has become a more interesting and challenging book; a reception of thoughts and ideas, we have discussed for many hours.

I also thank my children and family, who have so fully sacrificed your own needs on the altar of scholarship.

Finally, I thank the Press for accepting this manuscript and for fruitful cooperation in the process of editing. Special thanks to Dr Duncan Burns, whose keen eye caught all my mistakes. Those left, I intended for the reviewers to catch.

21 June 2004
Copenhagen

ABBREVIATIONS

AAR	American Academy of Religions
AASF	Annales Academiae Scientiarum Fennicae
AB	Anchor Bible
ABD	David Noel Freedman (ed.), *The Anchor Bible Dictionary* (New York: Doubleday, 1992)
ACEBT	Amsterdamse cahiers voor exegese en bijbelse theologie
AF	P. Stenhouse, 'The Kitāb al Tarīkh of Abū 'l-Fath: New Edition' (unpublished PhD dissertation, University of Sydney, 1980); ET in *idem*, *The Kitāb al Tarīkh of Abū 'l-Fath: Translated into English with Notes* (Sydney: The Mandelbaum Trust, University of Sydney, 1985). (Chapter and page numbers refer to the Arabic manuscript in the 1980 dissertation according to its arrangement in 1985 published edition.)
AHw	Wolfram von Soden, *Akkadisches Handwörterbuch* (Wiesbaden: Harrassowitz, 1959–81)
ANET	James B. Pritchard (ed.), *Ancient Near Eastern Texts Relating to the Old Testament* (Princeton: Princeton University Press, 1950)
AOAT	Alter Orient und Altes Testament
Aq.	Aquila
ATANT	Abhandlungen zur Theologie des Alten und Neuen Testaments
ATD	Das Alte Testament Deutsch
BARev	*Biblical Archaeology Review*
BASOR	*Bulletin of the American Schools of Oriental Research*
BETL	Bibliotheca ephemeridum theologicarum lovaniensium
Bib	*Biblica*
BJRL	*Bulletin of the John Rylands University Library of Manchester*
BKAT	Biblischer Kommentar: Altes Testament
BWANT	Beiträge zur Wissenschaft vom Alten und Neuen Testament
BZ	*Biblische Zeitschrift*
BZAW	Beihefte zur *ZAW*
CAD	Ignace I. Gelb *et al.* (eds.), *The Assyrian Dictionary of the Oriental Institute of the University of Chicago* (Chicago: Oriental Institute, 1964–)
CANE	J.M. Sasson (ed.), *Civilizations of the Ancient Near East* (4 vols.; New York, NY: Charles Schribner's Sons, 1995)
CB	*Cultura bíblica*
CBOTS	Coniectanea Biblica: Old Testament Series
CBQ	*Catholic Biblical Quarterly*
CBQMS	*Catholic Biblical Quarterly*, Monograph Series
CBR	*Currents in Biblical Research*
CIS	Copenhagen International Seminar
CRB	*Currents in Biblical Studies*
CRBS	*Critical Reviews in Biblical Studies*
CR:BS	*Currents in Research: Biblical Studies*

CRINT	Compendia rerum iudaicarum ad Novum Testamentum
DBAT	*Dielheimer Blätter zur Archäologie und Textüberlieferung der Antike und Spätantike*
DDD¹	K.van der Toorn, B. Becking and P.W. van der Horst (eds.), *Dictionary of Deities and Demons in the Bible* (Leiden: E.J. Brill, 1995)
DDD²	K.van der Toorn, B. Becking and P.W. van der Horst (eds.), *Dictionary of Deities and Demons in the Bible* (Leiden: E.J. Brill, 1999)
DBSup	*Dictionnaire de la Bible, Supplément*
DJD	*Discoveries in the Judaean Desert*
DTT	*Dansk teologisk tidsskrift*
EBib	Etudes bibliques
EPRO	Etudes préliminaires aux religions orientales dans l'empire romain
ESHM	European Seminar in Historical Methodology
FAT	Forschungen zum Alten Testament
FBE	Forum for bibelsk eksegese
FOTL	The Forms of the Old Testament Literature
FRLANT	Forschungen zur Religion und Literatur des Alten und Neuen Testaments
HANE/S	History of the Ancient Near East/Studies
HKAT	Handkommentar zum Alten Testament
HSM	Harvard Semitic Monographs
HTR	*Harvard Theological Review*
HUCA	*Hebrew Union College Annual*
ICC	International Critical Commentary
IDB	George Arthur Buttrick (ed.), *The Interpreter's Dictionary of the Bible* (4 vols.; Nashville: Abingdon Press, 1962)
IEJ	*Israel Exploration Journal*
Int	*Interpretation*
JB	Jerusalem Bible
JBL	*Journal of Biblical Literature*
JPOS	*Journal of the Palestine Oriental Society*
JQR	*Jewish Quarterly Review*
JRAS	*Journal of the Royal Asiatic Society*
JR(G)	The John Rylands Library (Manchester), Moses Gaster Collection
JSOR	*Journal for the Society of Oriental Research*
JSOT	*Journal for the Study of the Old Testament*
JSOTSup	*Journal for the Study of the Old Testament*, Supplement Series
JSP	*Journal for the Study of the Pseudepigrapha*
JTS	*Journal of Theological Studies*
KJV	King James Version
LXXᴬ	LXX Codex Alexandrius
LXXᴸ	LXX Codex Lucianic
LXXᴹˢˢ	LXX Greek Manuscripts
LXXᴼ	LXX Codex Origenes
MT	Masoretic Text
NCB	New Century Bible
NorTT	*Norsk Teologisk Tidsskrift*
NRSV	New Revised Standard Version
OBO	Orbis biblicus et orientalis

OIP	*Oriental Institute Publications* (Chicago: University Press)
*OIP*²	D.D. Luckenbill, *The Annals of Sennacherib* (1924)
Or.	Oriental Manuscripts
OT	Old Testament
OTL	Old Testament Library
OTP	James Charlesworth (ed.), *Old Testament Pseudepigrapha*
OTS	*Oudtestamentische Studiën*
PEFQS	*Palestine Exploration Fund, Quarterly Statement*
PEQ	*Palestine Exploration Quarterly*
POT	De Prediking van het Oude Testament
RB	*Revue biblique*
REJ	*Revue des études juives*
Sam.	Samaritan
SBL	Society of Biblical Literature
SBLDS	SBL Dissertation Series
SBLMS	SBL Monograph Series
SBLTT	SBL Texts and Translations
SBS	Stuttgarter Bibelstudien
SBT	Studies in Biblical Theology
SEÅ	*Svensk exegetisk årsbok*
SHANE	Studies in the History of the Ancient Near East
SJLA	Studies in Judaism in Late Antiquity
SJOT	*Scandinavian Journal of the Old Testament*
Sym.	Symmachus
SP	Samaritan Pentateuch
ST	Samaritan Text
TANZ	Texte und Arbeiten zum neutestamentlichen Zeitalter
TBAT	Teologische Bücherei Altes Testament
Theo.	Theodotian
ThR	*Theologisches Rundschau*
ThWAT	G.J. Botterweck and H. Ringgren (eds.), *Theologisches Wörterbuch zum Alten Testament* (Stuttgart: W. Kohlhammer, 1970–)
VT	*Vetus Testamentum*
VTQ	*Vetus Testamentum Quarterly*
VTSup	*Vetus Testamentum*, Supplements
WBC	Word Biblical Commentary
WMANT	Wissenschaftliche Monographien zum Alten und Neuen Testament
ZAW	*Zeitschrift für die alttestamentliche Wissenschaft*
ZDMG	*Zeitschrift der deutschen morgenländischen Gesellschaft*
ZDPV	*Zeitschrift des deutschen Palästina-Vereins*
ZRGG	*Zeitschrift für Religions- und Geistesgeschichte*

Chapter 1

INTRODUCTION: CREATING THE CASE

This study takes its point of departure from questions left unanswered in my study, *The Samaritans and Early Judaism: A Literary Analysis.*[1] Concluding that Jewish and Samaritan conflicts were not caused by the Samaritans' move to Shechem in the fourth century BCE (as the first-century Jewish-Roman writer Josephus wanted us to believe), but rather had developed from conflicts over political supremacy in Persian-Hellenistic times culminating in the second to first century BCE as a result of the Maccabaean success, it still needed to be examined why this success included a centralization of religious and secular power in a single place (Jerusalem). Both Jewish and Samaritan tradition agree that Jerusalem's cult moved from north to south, reflected literarily in the abolishment of former cult places, most of which lay to the north of Jerusalem, David's move of the ark to Jerusalem and the division of the united monarchy. Thereafter, traditions begin to diverge. While Jewish tradition struggles to place Samaritans within a heretical sphere, Samaritan tradition claims that Jews had left their old heritage, the tradition of the fathers, and had developed a Judaism which, in a reinterpretation of the Pentateuch carried out by prophets and teachers, changed the common doctrines so as to cause a split between the two groups.

Whatever historical reality lay behind these traditions, they have 'movement' as a very central motif. I am not here thinking of the motif of going on pilgrimage—which also forms part of the ideology, and functions as a confirmation of where one pays one's allegiance (cf. Jeroboam's erection of the calves in Dan and Bethel in order to prevent the people from going to Jerusalem [1 Kgs 12] or John Hyrcanus' wish to go to Gerizim after his quarrel with the Pharisees in Samaritan tradition[2] [*AF*, ch. XXIX, p. 113]). I am rather thinking of 'movement' from one ideal place to another, as a necessary step to secure independence and integrity. An important motif belonging to this movement from periphery to centre is the competition with places left, as expressed in Judges–2 Kings' denigration of 'former' cult places: Shechem, Bethel, Gilgal, Shiloh, Nob and Gibeon. The denigration serves the promotion of David's move to Jerusalem and of Jerusalem's struggle for sovereignty. While in biblical tradition *all* Israel participated in the transference of the cult to

---

1. I. Hjelm, *The Samaritans and Early Judaism: A Literary Analysis* (CIS, 7; JSOTSup, 303; Sheffield: Sheffield Academic Press, 2000).
2. See further below, Chapter 4, pp. 179-84, 216.

Jerusalem, in Samaritan tradition most Samaritans never took part in that move-ment. Having established the cult in Shechem and Gerizim-Bethel in the second year after their entrance into the Promised Land, Samaritans remained in that place continuously, except when forced into exile, from whence they returned more than once.

With the traditions of the Pentateuch, both Jews and Samaritans place their origins in the ancient world's cultural and political clashes between the kingdoms and peoples of the Euphrates and the Nile. Coming out of Mesopotamia and Egypt, Abraham and Jacob's descendants are given the task of making fruitful the home-land given to them, the fertile soil of Palestine, inhabited with various indigenous people with whom they can choose either to live in harmony or in conflict. While the fathers seek peaceful solutions, their sons and their children are minded to drive out these people, whom they call 'foreigners of the land'. Based on the Penta-teuchal laws on ethnic and religious purity, biblical narratives in Joshua–2 Kings about the life within the land are characterized by seemingly never-ending internal and external conflicts over sovereignty. The internal conflicts result in civil wars between the tribes and develop a north–south opposition between Israel/Ephraim and Judah, which in biblical tradition finds its solution in Yahweh's removal of Israel/Ephraim at the Assyrian king Shalmaneser's conquest of Samaria. While this sad solution has given impetus to later Jewish interpretations (especially those of Josephus), which explain why the Samaritans should be regarded as foreigners, the Latter Prophets and Chronicles expose an ambivalence which argues for the status of Judah (and Benjamin) as rightful heirs to Yahweh's promise to Abraham,[3] while at the same time admitting Israel/Ephraim's role as firstborn.[4] It is in that role as firstborn that the Samaritans claim to be the true descendants from the Pentateuchal traditions about Jacob's son Joseph and his sons Ephraim and Manasseh, already in Josephus' time.[5] At that time, the Samaritans, whose home had for long been the central highlands of Palestine with its holy institutions—Mt Gerizim, the ancient traditions about Shechem, Bethel and Gilgal, the burial places of the Patriarchs, as well as Shechem's position as capital city and home for the Samaritans at least since the fourth century BCE[6]—had numbered as many as the Jews, with whom they

---

3.   I. Hjelm, 'Brothers Fighting Brothers: Jewish and Samaritan Ethnocentrism in Tradition and History', in T.L. Thompson (ed.), *Jerusalem in Ancient History and Tradition* (CIS, 13; JSOTSup, 381; London/New York: T. & T. Clark International, 2003), pp. 197-222.

4.   Most explicitly argued in 1 Chron. 5.1-3's statement that although the birthright belongs to Joseph, Judah is given the role of being the chief ruler, which places this book in close connection with similar argumentation in second- to first-century BCE extra-biblical literature's struggle for Judaean hegemony based on the biblical concept of the twelve tribes of Israel.

5.   Josephus, *Ant.* 11.340-41; cf. also 4Q372 presented by E. Schuller, '4Q372.1 A Text about Joseph', *Revue de Qumran* 14 (1990), pp. 349-76; Ḥ. Eshel, 'The Prayer of Joseph: A Papy-rus from Masada and the Samaritan Temple in Argarizin', *Zion* 56 (1991), pp. 125-36 (Hebrew); U. Rappaport, 'Reflections of the Origins of the Samaritans', in Y. Ben-Artzi, I. Bartal and E. Reiner (eds.), *Studies in Geography and History in Honour of Yehoshua Ben-Arieh* (Jerusalem: Magnes Press, 1999), pp. 10-19.

6.   N. Schur, *History of the Samaritans* (Beiträge zur Erforschung des Alten Testamentes und des antiken Judentums, 18; Frankfurt: Peter Lang, 1989), p. 38.

shared many ancient traditions and belief. They did not share, however, the opinion that Jerusalem was the proper place for Yahweh's dwelling or that any other books than the Pentateuch should be given canonical status.

While discussions over cult places are presented in a variety of extra-biblical sources as taking place in post-exilic times, biblical narratives anachronistically place the north–south competition in a pre-exilic divided Israel, mirrored against the ideal Israel of David (and Solomon), in which Jerusalem plays the role as 'the place Yahweh has chosen'. The double movement created thereby—the monarchic establishment of Jerusalem as the elected cult place, where the ark finally found rest, and the implicit challenge to its status, which in the biblical north–south competition has the purpose of confirming Yahweh's choice—are the parameters, which place Jerusalem in its mythic chrono-spatial centre. The literary and historical tensions created thereby are pertinent to problems raised in the present study.

Contrasting these 'historical' and geographical 'movements' is 'conversion' theology's move through a purgative process to make Yahweh's people holy. This movement, which is mainly expressed in Prophets and Psalms, serves a similar purpose of elevating Jerusalem, now set within Zion-ideology's idealization of Jerusalem-Zion as Yahweh's abode, from where teaching shall go forth. The impact of this ideology in biblical and extra-biblical literature and modern interpreters' attempts at creating an ephemeral tenth-century BCE ideal Davidic kingdom by harmonizing these strands of tradition, have created scenarios fitting neither the literature nor the history of the period. As texts reflect other texts, however, not just supplement or agree with them, a thematically and linguistically driven examination of various strands of literary tropes and tradition will help place each book and tradition in its own context. The goal of the examination is a clearer picture of internal and external dialogues inherent in our biblical texts. That extra-biblical texts often compete with biblical texts is well known, but do our biblical texts compete with each other? Is the Bible's chronological succession of the Patriarchs, Moses and David representative of a literary succession, supersessionism or something else?

1. *Preliminary Remarks on Contextual Problems Regarding the Zion Metaphor*

The biblical Zion metaphor and ideology has been dealt with extensively within historical-critical scholarship during the past three generations. Most of these works are based on an effort at historical interpretation of the biblical stories about David's move of the cult to Jerusalem, Zion's legendary inviolability in the reign of Hezekiah and, finally, the destruction of Jerusalem in the Babylonian period and its restoration in the Persian period. J.J.M. Roberts' article 'The Davidic Origin of the Zion Tradition'[7] offers a good introduction to some of the problems involved in establishing the Zion tradition as pre-Davidic and lists some of the relevant

---

7.   J.J.M. Roberts, 'The Davidic Origin of the Zion Tradition', *JBL* 92 (1973), pp. 329-44.

literature on the subject.[8] Roberts' conclusion, that the formation of the Zion tradition 'is best understood as a product of Zion's most glorious days, the golden age of David and Solomon' without any influence of a pre-Davidic Jebusite tradition, has gained few supporters.[9] Clements' suggestion that the specific tradition about Zion's inviolability was a late addition to the Zion ideology intended to establish the preaching of Isaiah as authentically and historically related to the events of 701 BCE.[10] In contrast, G. von Rad[11] and S. Mowinckel[12] argued that the preaching of Isaiah was reflective of an already established Jerusalem cult tradition. Mowinckel,

---

8. H. Schmid, 'Jahwe und die Kulttraditionen von Jerusalem', *ZAW* 26 (1955), pp. 168-98; A.R. Johnson, *Sacral Kingship in Ancient Israel* (Cardiff: University of Wales Press, 1955); E. Rohland, 'Die Bedeutung der Erwählungstraditionen Israels für die Eschatologie der alttestamentlichen Propheten' (unpublished PhD dissertation, University of Heidelberg, 1965), p. 142; H.-J. Kraus, *Psalmen* (BKAT 15/1; Neukirchen–Vluyn: Neukirchener Verlag, 2nd edn, 1961), pp. 197-201; G. von Rad, *Old Testament Theology* (2 vols.; New York: Harper, 1962–65), I, pp. 46-47; II, pp. 156-58; J. Schreiner, *Sion-Jerusalem, Jahwes Königssitz: Theologie der heiligen Stadt im Alten Testament* (StANT, 7; Munich: Kösel, 1963); J.H. Hayes, 'The Traditions of Zion's Inviolability', *JBL* 82 (1963), pp. 419-26, who rejected J. Bright's argument that 'some marvelous deliverance of Jerusalem (in the time of Hezekiah) must be assumed, if only to explain the dogma of the inviolability of Zion' (cf. J. Bright, 'Isaiah I', in M. Black and H.H. Rowley [eds.], *Peake's Commentary on the Bible* [London: Thomas Nelson, 1962], p. 514, and *A History of Israel* [Philadelphia: Westminster Press, 1959], pp. 282-87); W. Schmidt, 'Jerusalemer El-Traditionen bei Jesaja, ein religionsgeschichtlicher Vergleich zum Vorstellungskreis des göttlichen Königtums', *ZRGG* 16 (1964), pp. 302-13; H.-M. Lutz, *Jahwe, Jerusalem und die Völker: zur Vorgeschichte von Sach 12,1-8 und 14,1-5* (WMANT, 27; Neukirchen–Vluyn: Neukirchener Verlag, 1968); F. Stolz, *Strukturen und Figuren im Kult von Jerusalem, Studien zur altorientalischen vor- und frühis-raelitischen Religion* (BZAW, 118; Berlin: W. de Gruyter, 1970).

9. R.E. Clements, *Isaiah and the Deliverance of Jerusalem: A Study of the Interpretation of Prophecy in the Old Testament* (JSOTSup, 13; Sheffield: JSOT Press, 1980), pp. 72-81, who understood the motif as such to have been part of Israel's own heritage and part of a genuine development in the Davidic–Solomonic court, while the 'doctrine of the inviolability of Jerusalem' developed as a result of the events in 701 BCE; B.C. Ollenburger, *Zion the City of the Great King: A Theological Symbol of the Jerusalem Cult* (JSOTSup, 41; Sheffield: JSOT Press, 1987), *passim* (especially pp. 17, 134-36, 140-44); T.N.D. Mettinger, *The Dethronement of Sabaoth: Studies in the Shem and Kabod Theologies* (CBOTS, 18; Lund: C.W.K. Gleerup, 1982), p. 37; J.D. Levenson, 'Zion Traditions', in *ABD*, VI, pp. 1098-102, arguing against Clements' partly eighth century dating (*Isaiah*) and G. Wanke's fifth- to fourth-century dating in his *Die Zionstheologie der Korachiten: In ihrem traditionsgeschichtlichen Zusammenhang* (BZAW, 97; Berlin: Alfred Töpelmann, 1966).

10. Clements, *Isaiah*, pp. 72-89 (84): 'The doctrine of the inviolability of Jerusalem, therefore, which several scholars have come to regard as a central feature of the so-called "Zion tradition", must rather be understood as a particular adaptation of the interpretation placed upon what happened in 701. It was not an original part of the Jerusalem cultic tradition, but rather a belief that came to be introduced into it at a particular time by a very distinctive circle... The doctrine of Jerusalem's inviolability, therefore, emerged, not as an adaptation of an ancient myth, but as an interpretation of a series of historical events, and focused most directly upon Hezekiah's confrontation with Sennacherib'.

11. Von Rad, *Old Testament Theology*, I, p. 159.

12. S. Mowinckel, *Psalmenstudien* (3 vols.; Oslo: A.W. Brøggers Bogtrykkeri, 1921), II, p. 65.

especially, understood the cult-mythological theme of Jerusalem to have led to the highly elaborated and largely unhistorical account of what had happened to the city when it was confronted by Sennacherib's armies. Placing the flourishing of the Hezekiah narrative alongside a 'development of the faith in Jerusalem's especially privileged position among the cities of Israel' in Josianic time, Clements[13] distanced himself from those who understood tenth- to ninth-century events as creative of the ideology, as well as from those who dated the ideology to the fifth–fourth century BCE based on the combined motifs of *Völkerkampf* and eschatology in the so-called Zion Psalms.[14] Following A.R. Johnson[15] and S. Mowinckel,[16] Clements rejected a late dating for these psalms, since 'the content of these psalms is not a general doctrine of Jerusalem's inviolability, nor yet an affirmation of the final eschatological victory of Yahweh. Rather, they express in a very distinctive fashion the hopes and aspirations for a kingdom of peace and righteousness, which was associated with the Davidic dynasty.'[17]

13. Clements, *Isaiah*, p. 97: 'Certainly by the time that the Deuteronomistic History came to be written no hesitation existed about openly identifying the sanctuary which the law demanded with Jerusalem (cf. 1 Kgs 11.13 etc.). Our own investigation into the Josianic redaction of the book of Isaiah and the origin of the narrative of Jerusalem's deliverance show that a very clear historical and prophetic witness was thought to exist to show why Jerusalem was to be singled out in this fashion. Yahweh had himself "chosen" Jerusalem by establishing his dwelling there (cf. Ps. 76.2) and he had revealed the consequences of this choice by protecting Jerusalem from the Assyrians'.

14. Wanke, *Die Zionstheologie der Korachiten*, p. 112: 'Damit gehören also nicht nur die korachitischen Zionslieder und hier besonders Psalmen 46, 48 un 87 in eine sehr späte Zeit, sondern auch die in ihnen repräsentierte "Überlieferung" spiegelt eine späte Entwicklung der an Zion-Jerusalem entstanden Vorstellungen wider, wofür das Völkerkampfmotiv einen unübersehbaren Beweis liefert'; and p. 113: 'Durch ihre Übertragung auf Zion-Jerusalem vor allem seit Ezechiel bildete sich an der Gottesstadt ein Vorstellungskomplex, der bis ins Neue Testament (Vgl. Apc 21.10; 22.1f) Zeugnisse seiner Überlieferung aufweisen kann. Die Basis zur Ausbildung dieses Vorstellungskomplexes wurde in der vorexilischen Zeit gelegt. Die Erhebung des Jerusalemer Heiligtums zum Staatsheiligtum durch die Davididen, die Ausweitung des Heiligkeitscharakters vom Tempel auf den Zion und in einem letzten Stadium auf die ganze Stadt, die Hervorhebung Jerusalems durch die Kultuszentralisation, wie sie das Deuteronomium forderte, die durch Jesajalegenden ins Wunderhafte gesteigerte Bewahrung Jerusalems vor dem Angriff der Assyrer 701 und schliesslich die Vorstellung vom Wohnen Jahwes auf dem Zion bereiteten den Boden für die in der exilisch-nachexilischen Zeit zu beobachtende grossartige Ausgestaltung der an Zion-Jerusalem haftenden Vorstellungen, vor allem in der eschatologischen Prophetie. Eine am zweiten Tempel wirkende Tempelsängergruppe konnte an dieser Entwicklung freilich nicht vorübergehen, da sie ihr zentrales Anliegen und Interesse betraf. Die korachitischen Zionspsalmen repräsentieren als die Lieder dieser Sängergruppe nicht eine schon aus vorisraelitischer Zeit stammende Kulttradition, sondern vertreten eine an den in exilisch-nachexilischer Zeit um die Gottesstadt entstandenen Vorstellungen orientierte Zionstheologie.' See also G. Fohrer, 'Zion-Jerusalem im Alten Testament', in *idem, Studien zur alttestamentliche Theologie und Geschichte (1949–1966)* (Berlin: W. de Gruyter, 1969), pp. 195-241 (214-19).

15. Johnson, *Sacral Kingship in Ancient Israel*, p. 31.

16. S. Mowinckel, *The Psalms in Israel's Worship* (2 vols.; trans. D.R. Ap-Thomas; Oxford: Basil Blackwell, 1962), I, pp. 181-88.

17. Clements, *Isaiah*, pp. 87-88.

Whatever other differences these datings might imply, they implicitly hold the opinion in common that Jerusalem had gained its first importance during the biblical David's united monarchy. The struggle for Jerusalem's independence and sovereignty, as reflected in the narratives of the Bible, is seen as a description of past events which had been compiled sometime between the rise of this monarchy and the return from exile. Based on the Bible's own chronology and course of events, the Zion ideology has been separated from the narrative structure of the texts in which it occurs, as if it were an established ideology behind the texts.[18] However, if the ideology is not merely creative, but created by the texts, then we need to look for some other historical context for its origin and development. Moreover, we need to ask whether the whole of the Zion and Jerusalem ideology belongs to a specific program established at a time later than the literary chronology implied by its purported origin story, since it has left various imprints on—and perhaps has even determined—that story. We are challenged here by the complex problem that we are induced to read the Zion ideology of Psalms and Prophets into both the Deuteronomistic and the Chronistic Histories,[19] although none of these

18.   Roberts' recent reassertion of his 1973 argument (J.J.M. Roberts, 'The Zion Tradition in Solomon's Temple' [unpublished paper delivered at the SBL National Meeting, Boston, 1999]) fully demonstrates this. In a discussion about a possible later dating of Solomon's reign (Finkelstein) and the doubts about an ever existent biblical Davidic Empire ('the radical minimalists') he concludes: 'In short, all the elements of the Zion tradition are present in the work of Isaiah of Jerusalem in a way that suggests he was making use of a pre-existing tradition. He does not argue for this theology so much as he presupposes it. He simply calls upon his audience to take this royal Zion theology, long cultivated in Jerusalem's court and temple, with utmost seriousness... But even if one rejects an early date for this [Ps. 68] and other relevant psalms, one cannot so easily dismiss the evidence of the eighth century prophets by a late dating. In the prophetic literature from the last half of the eighth century, one finds references to the house of David and other historical allusions that suggest an acquaintance with just such historical traditions as are found in the books of Samuel and Kings. This is less than 200 years from the end of Solomon's purported reign.' The circularity of the argument speaks for itself. G. von Rad, *Theologie des Alten Testament* (2 vols.; Munich: Chr. Kaiser Verlag, 1957–60), II, pp. 166-79 (p. 167): 'aber die Vermutung legt sich dringend nahe, dass sowohl die Form wie die einzelnen Vorstellungsinhalte bei dieser Sprücheeinheit vom Propheten nicht ad hoc geschaffen wurden, sondern dass Jesaja hier von einer Überlieferung abhängig ist. Bei der Frage, um welche Überlieferung es sich handeln könnte, wäre zunächst an die Gruppe der sogenannten Zionlieder zu denken (Ps 46; 48; 76), weil sich in ihnen eine spezifisch jerusalemische—und das hiesse: eine ganz unamphiktyonische—Tradition ausspricht'. For the possibility of seeing a Canaanite origin of traditions reflected in these psalms, see von Rad, *Theologie des Alten Testament*, I, pp. 54-55.

19.   The terms are used conservatively as a designation of the Masoretic text corpora: (Deuteronomy,) Joshua–2 Kings and Ezra–Nehemiah–Chronicles, regardless of authorial, editorial or linguistic inter-dependency (or lack of such) or of the possibility of 'Deuteronomistic' influence in almost all parts of the Old Testament; cf. the survey in R.J. Coggins, 'What Does "Deuteronomistic" Mean?, in L.S Shearing and S.L. McKenzie (eds.), *Those Elusive Deuteronomists: The Phenomenon of Pan-Deuteronomism* (JSOTSup, 268; Sheffield: Sheffield Academic Press, 1999), pp. 22-35; see also, in the same volume, R.R. Wilson 'Who Was the Deuteronomist? (Who Was Not the Deuteronomist?): Reflections on Pan-Deuteronomism', pp. 67-82. In the following discussion, 'Deuteronomic' describes that which pertains to the book of Deuteronomy and 'Deuteronomistic' that which pertains to scholars' Masoretic Deuteronomistic History as a text corpus. The

works reveal any comprehensive explicit trace of such an ideology.[20] That the primary goal of Old Testament authors hardly was to give an objective account of history's events should warn us that, in using history as an interpretative matrix for a theological discussion, Old Testament scriptures, as we have them, need to have been written somewhat later than the implied history itself. This becomes crucially clear when compared with the royal propaganda found in, for example, Assyrian and Babylonian inscriptions, much of which is played with in the Old Testament. The decline of the Assyrian empire, predicted in the Hezekiah narrative's anticipation of the Babylonian rise (2 Kgs 20.12-19), forms part of the narrative's structure, as does the prediction of Judah's fall in the Manasseh and Josiah stories (21.10-16; 23.26-27). Whether redacted or not, the story as we have it cannot be separated from its own structure. Judging from its implicit distance, Old Testament narrative is not about Israel's history as such.[21] It is not about any Israelite world of gods or religion. Placed within an interim between the Israel of the past and the Jerusalem/Zion of the future, the 'Writings' and 'Prophets' of the Old Testament serve as theological treatises, discussing how its audience should understand itself and its God.

Recently, A. Laato, in a thorough study of the composition of the book of Isaiah,[22] demonstrates that the author behind the present form of the book cannot be earlier than the Persian (or perhaps Hellenistic) period. The book was written with the purpose of establishing Jerusalem as a religious centre for the entire world (Jews and non-Jews). The righteous group, following the preaching of Isaiah, considered itself to be the saved remnant who would guarantee the fulfilment of these expectations. Using the ideology of Zion's inviolability in the eighth century (Isa. 1–39) as a driving force, the reader should be persuaded that 'as Yahweh saved his city in the past, he also can do it again'.[23] Although Laato touches upon problems of election,

rabbinic term 'Former Prophets' appears as more neutral than 'Deuteronomistic History', but one must be aware that it implies a rabbinic assertion of the books of Joshua, Judges and Samuel, and 1 and 2 Kings to have been written by Joshua, Samuel and Jeremiah respectively. As such, the rabbinic term refers to the traditions of books, which we know from 'lower criticism' were pluriform in antiquity, and not to the later Masoretic (Deuteronomy) Joshua–2 Kings, which text is the basis of Noth, Cross and the Göttingen schools' assertion of a Deuteronomistic History.

20. See Chapters 2 and 3 below.

21. Against H.M. Barstad, 'The Strange Fear of the Bible: Some Reflections on the "Bibliophobia" in Recent Ancient Israelite Historiography', in L.L. Grabbe (ed.), *Leading Captivity Captive: The 'Exile' as History and Ideology* (ESHM, 2; JSOTSup, 278; Sheffield: Sheffield Academic Press, 1998), pp. 120-27.

22. A. Laato, *About Zion I Will Not Be Silent: The Book of Isaiah as an Ideological Unity* (CB OTS 44; Stockholm: Almqvist & Wiksell, 1998).

23. Laato, *About Zion I Will Not Be Silent*, p. 207: 'Therefore the "Assyrian invasion" paradigm is mentioned at the beginning (1.2-9) and at the end of the book of Isaiah. This indicates that the "Assyrian paradigm" in Isa. 1–39 is a central key to understand the message of the whole book. It shows that the marvellous fate of Zion promised in the book of Isaiah is more than merely utopian visions of the future. *Yhwh saved his city in the past and he can do it again in future*.' So also, R.E. Clements, 'Isaiah 14.22-27: A Central Passage Reconsidered', in J. Vermeylen (ed.), *The Book of Isaiah: Le Livre d'Isaïe: Les Oracles et leurs relectures. Unité et complexité de l'ouvrage*

he seems to be operating within the same spectrum of presuppositions about Jerusalem's sovereignty as former works have: Jerusalem was saved because Yahweh had once elected his city and had found a faithful remnant there.[24] It is not within the scope of Laato's work to question whether the traditions of Zion's inviolability form part of a program that leaves Jerusalem as the only place left after the destruction of the Northern Kingdom and the Judaean cities in the vicinity of Jerusalem. Did Yahweh spare Jerusalem because of its importance, or did Jerusalem interpret the events in order to make a theological statement about its special status? Is the fall of the Northern Kingdom, which is so closely connected to this Zion tradition,[25] a necessary paradigm for the documentation of Yahweh's election not only of the city, but also of the teaching delivered there (e.g. Isa. 2.3)? Here we will have to keep in mind that Isaiah was not merely delivering a message given to the people through Moses, but rather actively interpreting the message which the Northern Kingdom is accused of having rejected. If Josiah's reform had left other places fit for the Yahweh cult, would they then have been saved?[26] Did Sennacherib abstain from conquering the city because of its importance and divine protection? Or did he leave Judaea after having conquered those sites, necessary for his purpose, of which Lachish seems to have had greatest importance?

From extra-biblical literature we know of Jewish expectations and hopes in the second to first century BCE. We know of an increasing argumentation for the establishment of a 'national' state, comprising the twelve tribes with Jerusalem as its capital.[27] 1 Maccabees gives an account of a return to Zion in the time of Judas and Jonathan, a rebuilding of the temple and a declaration of independence in the first year of the reign of Simon. Josephus tells of conquests and extensions of Judaea's borders during the reigns of Jonathan, Simon, John Hyrcanus and Alexander Jannaeus. He tells us about a centralization program which forced Jerusalem's

---

(BETL, 81; Leuven: Leuven University Press, 1989), pp. 253- 62; *idem*, 'The Prophecies of Isaiah to Hezekiah Concerning Sennacherib: 2 Kings 19.21-34//Isa. 37.22-35', in R. Liwak and S. Wagner (eds.), *Prophetie und geschichtliche Wirklichkeit im alten Israel: Festschrift für Siegfried Hermann zum 65 Geburtstag* (Cologne: W. Kohlhammer, 1991), pp. 65-78.

24. The book of Isaiah's overall concern for this righteous remnant encouraged Laato to conclude (*About Zion I Will Not Be Silent*, p. 210): 'the Book of Isaiah contains the *roots of the Second Temple Jewish eschatological and apocalyptic expectations centered around Zion*. The apocalyptic milieu is particularly visible in Isaiah 24–27 and 65–66. Furthermore, the present form of the Book of Isaiah provides evidence of the development within the Jewish community during the Second Temple period. *The division between the righteous and the ungodly in the Jewish society* is typical of the Jewish writings of this period, as for example, in the Psalms of Solomon and the Qumran writings. The Book of Isaiah is one of the earliest documents to describe such an internal dichotomy in the Jewish society. Indeed, we go so far as to suggest that the presentation of the division between the righteous and sinners in the Qumran texts may have its origin in the community's pesher interpretations of the Book of Isaiah.'

25. See below, Chapter 2.

26. Hjelm, *Samaritans and Early Judaism*, p. 149.

27. D. Mendels, *The Land of Israel as a Political Concept in Hasmonean Literature* (Tübingen: J.C.B. Mohr, 1987), and *idem*, *The Rise and Fall of Jewish Nationalism* (Garden City, NY: Doubleday, 1992).

neighbours to submit to belief and practice performed at the temple in Jerusalem. He also tells us of serious conflicts within Judaism, between Jews and Samaritans and among various Jewish groups. We are thus given a potential *a quo* date for the program presented in Isaiah. The main question, however, is still lacking. Can we also establish an *a quo* date for the development of the ideology about Zion's inviolability as part of the 'national' as well as religious program presented above? As Laato rightly points out, the expectations raised in Isaiah 55–65 have not found their fulfilment within the book's own chronology. This fits well the lack of closure of the books of Ezra and Nehemiah. Will the saved remnant succeed in realizing their temple-state in Jerusalem? Although there are certain similarities in the programs presented in Ezra–Nehemiah and in Isaiah, the reform program presented in Ezra and Nehemiah as a possible *Sitz im Leben* for the composition of the book of Isaiah does not offer itself as an easy solution.[28] Not only do these books not have an explicit Zion ideology, they do not have an explicit David ideology, any Messianism, or a program for the centralization of the cult in Jerusalem, as opposed to any other centre in Judaism.[29] The discussion with *am ha-aretz* in Ezra 4 is not a discussion about whether the temple in Jerusalem is Judaism's temple *par excellence*, but rather whether Jerusalem should be rebuilt. Depending on Persian authority, the returnees are left—'historiographically'—with no possibility of developing a national ideology. Under the auspices of the foreign ruler, the remnant community in Jerusalem has the defence and security of its own holiness as its goal.

---

28. Laato, *About Zion I Will Not Be Silent*, p. 165, with reference to: J. Blenkinsopp, *A History of Prophecy in Israel: From Settlement in the Land to the Hellenistic Period* (Philadelphia: Westminster Press, 1983), pp. 250-51; *idem*, *Ezra–Nehemiah: A Commentary* (OTL; Philadelphia: Westminster Press, 1988), pp. 178-79, and *idem*, 'The Servant and the Servants in Isaiah and the Formation of the Book', in C.C. Broyles and C.A. Evans (eds.), *Writing & Reading the Scroll of Isaiah: Studies of an Interpretive Tradition* (VTSup, 70/1; Leiden: E.J. Brill, 1997), I, p. 169; M.A. Sweeney, *Isaiah 1–39, with an Introduction to Prophetic Literature* (FOTL, 16; Grand Rapids: Eerdmans, 1996), pp. 51-54; and W.A.M. Beuken, *Jesaja IIIA* (POT; Nijkerk: Callenbach, 1989), pp. 9-10.

29. I do not here join the 'customary view among scholars that Ezra rejected all eschatological (including messianic) hopes and expectations preserved in the prophetic literature in favour of establishing a theocracy in the Jewish community'; cf. A. Laato, *A Star is Rising: The Historical Development of the Old Testament Royal Ideology and the Rise of the Jewish Messianic Expectations* (Atlanta: Scholars Press, 1997), pp. 221-30 (221). This tradition, albeit based on Wellhausen's distinction between the Pentateuch and the Prophets, basically follows the explicit chronology in Prophets, which places these books prior to the books of Ezra and Nehemiah, which, furthermore, are assumed to have originated from a 'canonical' line of development. Laato's own speculation about whether Ezra and Nehemiah toned down royal expectations, because of Persian dependency (p. 223) is based on *eisegesis* from such an anachronistic canonical tradition and does not take seriously that in both books, the 'David' references are related either to the cult (Ezra 3.10; 8.20; Neh. 12.36) or to geography (Neh. 3.15-16; 12.37). In Nehemiah, David is called 'man of God' (איש האלהים). References to one of David's descendants, Hattush, in Ezra 8.2 is not given any special weight. He is not called a 'Davidic prince', and Zerubbabel son of Shealtiel, is nowhere called a Davidic scion (Ezra 2.2; 3.8; 4.2, 3; 5.2; Neh. 7.7; 12.1, 47; Hag. 1.1, 14; 2.2, 4, 21, 23; Zech. 4.6, 7, 9, 10). Our possibilities of creating genealogies do not prove that such knowledge or intention is implied in the Ezra and Nehemiah narratives.

Yahweh's protection and the safeguarding of Jerusalem for the sake of his 'servant David' (2 Kgs 19.34; 20.6c) have no impact on the confession given in Nehemiah 9. It is not 'the fallen booth of David' (Amos 9.11) which is rebuilt, but a city and a wall (גדר, Ezra 9.9)[30] for a faction of the people whose main task it is to keep the ordinances put down in the Law of Moses. Therefore, Ezra–Nehemiah's request for ethnic purity and regionalism must be considered in contrast to Isaiah's 'universalism'.[31] Placed between these two extremes, we find Jeremiah's wish for a reconciliation of Israel's tribes in Jerusalem (Jer. 30–31) without reference to the foreign nations. Although, in a Christian context of 'New Covenant Theology', this move is interpreted as having universalistic perspectives, the text itself does not bear such an understanding. The people brought from the north, gathered from the farthest parts of the earth (31.8) and listening to the word of Yahweh on far away islands (31.10) is, in fact, Israel's remnant, scattered by Yahweh himself (31.10). They are those with whom Yahweh will renew his covenant (31.31-37) and rebuild his city (31.6, 38-40). Combining themes of Ephraim as firstborn and the mountain of Ephraim with themes of movement to Zion, 31.1-20 offers a fulfilment of attempts at reconciliation, with which Hezekiah had been so unsuccessful (2 Chron. 30.6-12). The promise to plant vineyards on the mountain of Samaria (Jer. 31.5) does not refer to Samaria's cultic past. The vineyard is for profane use (חלל).[32] By the initiating כי in the following verse a contrast is set between a Samaria of the past and a Zion of the future. How do we fit this book into the 'Zion'-ideology, which is given such disparate orientation in the Bible as well as within extra-biblical literature?

2. *Biblical Chronology and Historical Reconstruction*

Taking the Bible's own chronology as a point of departure for its composition and redaction has not proven to be a valid working hypothesis. The various attempts to use that chronology in support of a history of authorship or redaction, including the establishment of a 'Deuteronomistic' tradition of scribes and schools, have been based on circular arguments. Dating the whole of the so-called Deuteronomistic History to one author in the exilic period, shortly after 562 BCE (the date of Jehoiachin's release from prison), as Noth did in his *Überlieferungsgeschichte*, is merely

---

30. The term signify a defensive wall (Ezek. 13.5; 22.30) and a protective border (Isa. 5.5; Mic. 7.11; Ps. 80.13; Prov. 24.31).

31. See M.A. Sweeney, 'The Book of Isaiah as Prophetic Torah', in R.F. Melugin and M.A. Sweeney (eds.), *New Visions of Isaiah* (JSOTSup, 214; Sheffield: Sheffield Academic Press, 1996), pp. 50-67 (56-58, 65).

32. It is, of course, a moot point whether the text is so explicitly polemical or rather uses the language of Deut. 20.6, in which the vineyard cannot be nursed because of war, or Deut. 28.30 (Amos 5.1), in which the vineyard is taken away from its owner because of apostasy. It seems, however, probable that the text has an implicit reference to the critique of Samaria in, for example, Mic. 1.6, in which Yahweh 'turns Samaria into a heap of rubble in the field, a place for planting vines' (למטעי כרם), and Yahweh's breaking his covenant with the city in the reference to his laying 'bare her foundations' (יסדיה אגלה); cf. the covenant in Jer. 31.37 and the judgement in Mic. 6.2, both of which take the foundations of the world (מוסדי־ארץ) as witness.

arguing for the first possible *a quo* dating on the basis of the story's own chronology.[33] However fitting this dating might appear, it does not tell us anything that is not part of the story. Noth's perception of that story as negative (that the Israelites were without any hope for the future), von Rad's perception of the story as positive (that the story expressed hope of a restoration of the Davidic monarchy),[34] and H.W. Wolff's criticism of both perceptions (arguing that the story balanced in virtue between these extremes in a demonstration of the choice given to the exiles of salvation through repentance),[35] are all deeply rooted in the story's composition.

Positing a primary edition of the Deuteronomistic History (Dtr[1]) in the time of Josiah,[36] because of its focus on Josiah as 'good king David', is an implicit demonstration of the persuasiveness of that story. Since the story presupposes the decline, it is hard to see how it could have functioned as an exhortation to believe in a restoration of the Davidic kingdom during a time when the real decline belongs to an unknown future. Cross' conclusion that the 'omission of a final, edifying discourse on the fall of chosen Zion and the Davidic crown is better explained by attributing these final terse paragraphs of the history to a less articulate Exilic editor',[37] conflicts with his own portrait of the creative work of this 'Exilic hand' as having 'overwritten and contradicted the original theme of hope, namely the expectation of the restoration of the state under a righteous Davidide to the remembered greatness of the golden age of David'.[38] Cross' assignment of 'exilic passages' in Deuteronomy, Joshua, 1 Samuel and 1 and 2 Kings to this author[39] is based only on his chronology of redaction. It falls apart if this cannot be upheld. The circularity in the argument: that the story arose in Josiah's court because it was needed there (based on its first possible *a quo* dating) can hardly be said to be valid, since this opinion is derivative of the interpreted narrative as we have it.[40] Why should the Dtr[1] story be

---

33. M. Noth, *Überlieferungsgeschichtliche Studien: Die sammelnden und bearbeitenden Geschichtswerke im Alten Testament* (Tübingen: Max Niemeyer, 3rd edn, 1967 [1943]), p. 12; although Noth regarded 2 Kgs 25.27-30 as an addition to the original account, his dating is directed by its existence.

34. G. von Rad, *Deuteronomium-Studien* (FRLANT, 58; Göttingen: Vandenhoeck & Ruprecht, 1948), pp. 52-64, based on the influence from prophetic sayings, which formed the structure of Deuteronomistic History as a 'history of Yahweh's word at work'.

35. H.W. Wolff, 'Das Kerygma des deuteronomistichen Geschichtswerk', *ZAW* 73 (1961), pp. 171-86.

36. F.M. Cross, *Canaanite Myth and Hebrew Epic: Essays in the History of the Religion of Israel* (Cambridge, MA: Harvard University Press, 1973), pp. 274-89.

37. Cross, *Canaanite Myth*, p. 288.

38. Cross, *Canaanite Myth*, p. 288. Attributing the despair to the exilic layer, Cross is able to give credit to Noth's negative perception as well as von Rad's positive perception, based, however, not on the release of Jehoiachin but on the glory of the Josianic era.

39. Cross, *Canaanite Myth*, pp. 286-87: Deut. 4.27-31; 28.36-37, 63-68; 29.27; 30.1-10; Josh. 23.11-13, 15-16; 1 Sam. 12.25; 1 Kgs 2.4; 6.11-13; 8.25b, 46-53; 9.4-9; 2 Kgs 17.19; 20.17-18; 21.2-15 (probably only vv. 7-15 are meant); 22.15-20; 23.25–25.30. (In question: Deut. 30.11-20; 1 Kgs 3.14.)

40. S.L. McKenzie, *The Trouble With Kings: The Composition of the Books of Kings in the Deuteronomistic History* (VTSup, 42; Leiden: E.J. Brill, 1991), p. 149: 'Attempts to retain the

necessary if conditions were good and no immediate threat demanded a return to Mosaic piety. Ascribing the pronouncement of doom in 2 Kgs 17.19, 20.17 and 21.7-15 to the exilic Dtr², the reason for Josiah's fear of Yahweh's wrath (22.11-13) seems somewhat arbitrary. What 'disaster' should be 'postponed', and what 'new possibility of salvation' should be 'rallied',[41] when we are still in the seventh century and nobody could have imagined a fall of Jerusalem some decades later?

The historical problems arising from failing to consider such basic methodological issues, are demonstrated even more clearly by I.W. Provan's work on the Hezekiah narrative.[42] Provan's conclusion that the high place, the במות theme in the judgment formulae of the books of Kings points to a double redaction, assuming an early pre-exilic conclusion of the work, with the Hezekiah narrative written at the beginning of Josiah's reign, and an exilic redaction, which added the chronologically later material and reworked some of the older version, merely assumes the chronology required by his scenario.[43] If Provan were right in his assumptions, then cult centralization took priority over cult control and the prohibition against idolatrous places reflected only in his exilic material.[44] If this were true, however, why would this later redaction blame the kings before Josiah for not having removed the idolatrous places? Would he not have known that this was without historical basis? Furthermore, why would he praise Hezekiah for having removed the pillars (מצבת) and the *Asherah* (האשרה, 2 Kgs 18.4aβ), in a clear reference to the accusation in 2 Kgs 17.10a, if his primary intention had been to make the Josiah narrative the conclusion of the raids against idolatry? Provan's handling of this problem, as well as his argument for the 'missing' information about Manasseh and Amon, is unconvincing.[45] If for any reason the historical Josiah had intentions of expanding his

exilic date for DH and to explain away these two themes (David and Manasseh) have not been very convincing, and it seems better to date the initial composition of the DH to the reign of Josiah, recognizing that the evidence for this decision comes entirely from Kings'.

41. Cross, *Canaanite Myth*, p. 285.

42. I.W. Provan, *Hezekiah and the Books of Kings: A Contribution to the Debate about the Composition of the Deuteronomistic History* (Berlin: W. de Gruyter, 1988).

43. Provan, *Hezekiah and the Books of Kings*, pp. 82-90, 171-72; Provan's exilic material comprises 1 Kgs 12.31–13.34; 2 Kgs 14.22-24; 17.7aβ-17; 18.4αβ; 20–25. For a review of the validity of Provan's redaction-critical conclusions, see P.S.F. van Keulen, *Manasseh Through the Eyes of the Deuteronomists: The Manasseh Account (2 Kings 21.1-18) and the Final Chapters of the Deuteronomistic History* (OTS, 38; Leiden: E.J. Brill, 1996), pp. 44-48. The circularity of Provan's argument, based as it is on his construction of both presuppositions and results and lacking a *tertium comparationis*, constantly forces him to ascribe 'non-fitting' material to one or other redactor on indeed very weak grounds.

44. Provan, *Hezekiah and the Books of Kings*, pp. 65, 67, 69-70: 'A clear distinction is made between Yahwistic and idolatrous worship, with references to worship at the במות in general occurring only within the context of the former. Another view of the במות is also to be found in Kings, however, and requires our attention at this point... [p. 73]: A quite different view of במות then, from that to be found in the Judaean judgement formulae is apparent in 2 Kgs 17.9-11 [Cross' Dtr¹]. A later editor, reviewing the history of Israel and Judah from an exilic perspective, understood the two kingdoms to be equally guilty of idolatry, and saw the worship at the במות in Judah as indicative of Judah's participation in this.'

45. Provan, *Hezekiah and the Books of Kings*, p. 154.

kingdom, the Hezekiah event certainly was a bad example, since, after his encounter with the Assyrians, all he had left was Jerusalem and the status of a vassal.[46] In a comparison of both kings one must conclude: as Hezekiah's rebellion had lost him his kingdom, so in fact did Josiah's encounter with the Egyptians lead to his kingdom's vassalage to the Egyptians.[47] It is only in the biblical rendering that their attempts at independence are judged virtuous. Even more serious, the purported finding of the Deuteronomic Law in Jerusalem as expressed in the Josiah narratives and attributed by Provan to an exilic redaction,[48] could not have taken place before the reforms of Hezekiah. However, Hezekiah is not only removing high places, but also the copper serpent (2 Kgs 18.4b) that belongs to Provan's exilic material. Conflicting as it is with the rule given in the Tetrateuch (cf. Num. 21.8-9), how should this step be understood as 'keeping the commandments of Yahweh given by Moses' (2 Kgs 18.6)? In what Provan defines as pre-exilic material, the doom of Samaria would be a result of not having accepted moving the cult to Jerusalem to pay worship to Yahweh there. As stated by Provan,

> It is the Davidic dynasty, and the presence of Yahweh in the Jerusalem Temple, which in his [the historian's] view makes the difference between the two states. While it is certainly true, therefore, that a pre-exilic Kings containing these themes might have functioned as a propaganda document for that dynasty, intent on re-establishing suzerainty over the north after the events of 722–721 BCE, it is very difficult to see how it could at the same time have functioned as a call to obedience to the law... Josiah in particular avoids the wrath of Yahweh because of his own obedience, and not because of David (22.14-20). David's role in these chapters is only as a model of righteousness to be imitated (22.2), and even then, as Friedman's observations[49] about the parallelism between Moses and Josiah imply, he is not the primary model.[50]

Provan's redaction-critical conclusions inevitably lead to the historical conclusion that the first move, prompting a centralization of the Yahwist cult during the reign of Hezekiah, had been a political move, while the second move, prompting control of the entire cult in a removal of idolatry from Israel during the reign of Josiah, was a religious move. However, this is not what is claimed in the Hezekiah narrative—

---

46. D.D. Luckenbill, *Ancient Records of Assyria and Babylonia* (Chicago: University of Chicago Press, 1927 [reprint: New York: Greenwood Press, 1968]), II, §§ 239-40, 309-12.

47. J.A. Soggin, *An Introduction to the History of Israel and Judah* (London: SCM Press, 1999 [3rd edn of *idem, A History of Israel: From the Beginnings to the Bar Kochba Revolt, AD 135* (London: SCM Press, 1984); translated from the Italian: *Introduzione alla Storia d'Israele e di Guida* (Brescia: Paideia Editrice, 1998)]), p. 277.

48. Provan, *Hezekiah and the Books of Kings*, pp. 147-51: 'It is unlikely that the *Reformbericht* was ever present in Kings without the *Auffindungsbericht* and the *Auffindungsbericht* is an exilic entity which shares the same perspective as 23.26-27 on the inevitability of the judgement on Judah. There is little reason to suppose from the evidence of 2 Kgs 22.1–23.30 then, that the original edition of Kings was revised and updated in the pre-exilic period.'

49. R.E. Friedman, 'From Egypt to Egypt: Dtr[1] and Dtr[2]', in B. Halpern and J.D. Levenson (eds.), *Traditions in Transformation: Turning Points in Biblical Faith* (Winona Lake, IN: Eisenbrauns, 1981), pp. 167-92 (171-73).

50. Provan, *Hezekiah and the Books of Kings*, p. 28, in his critique of Cross.

whether redacted or not. The narrative has the primary goal of establishing Yahweh in Jerusalem as the only living god, contrasting the gods of the nations, to whom also the Northern Kingdom is said to have paid allegiance in a dismissal of Yahweh's covenant (2 Kgs 18.12). It was not Hezekiah who had removed these apostate northerners. They were removed by Yahweh for not having been loyal clients.

So, did Hezekiah centralize Yahweh's cult in Jerusalem? Or did Yahweh confirm Jerusalem as the chosen place because Hezekiah had shown himself worthy of being Yahweh's messiah? Who saved Jerusalem, Yahweh, Hezekiah or Sennacherib? Could it, in fact, be more likely that the collection of narratives introduced cult centralization as its primary theme in order to make the Hezekiah narrative the climax of the book and the point of departure for its theology. With the narrative's historical setting in the context of Assyrian royal ideology, this interpretation lay right at hand for further exploitation. Having established Jerusalem as the central Yahwist shrine with the Hezekiah narrative, this theme should occur in the later narrative chronology only insofar as it is opposed, exactly as it functions in the Josiah narrative. Cult centralization in this narrative takes measures against both idolatrous shrines and Yahwist shrines[51] as well as Jeroboam's competing cult in the north, all of which are presented as sinful acts in the Jeroboam–Rehoboam segments of Kings. The absence of the theme in the chapters following the Josiah story should not lead to the false conclusion that these chapters belong to a later editor.[52] The author's awareness of Josiah's removal of the idolatrous cult necessitated that the accusation be limited to 'Manasseh's sins', without specification, and especially to 'the blood, he had shed' (2 Kgs 24.4 par. 21.16; 23.26). The continuation of the rebellion and the vassalage themes in 2 Kings 23–24 displays a similar consciousness. As Hosea's revolt (17.3-4) against the Assyrians cost him his kingdom, so did Jehoiakim's against the Babylonians (24.1-2). Linguistically, the two episodes share so many similarities that assigning 17.3 to a pre-exilic author and 24.1 to a post-exilic author[53] contradicts linguistic and thematic principles of source analysis. Imitation does not explain the case. As Noth pointed out regarding the vassalage theme, it is not introduced in the post-Josianic chapters by sheer imitation. The decline of the Judaean Kingdom is also a decline of its wealth.[54] While Rehoboam had items of his forefather (Solomon) taken away together with the gold and silver in the treasuries of temple and palace (1 Kgs 14.26), Asa gave away the silver and

51. Erected by Manasseh (2 Kgs 21.3).

52. Cf. G. Vanoni, 'Beobachtungen zur deuteronomistischen Terminologie in 2 Kön 23,25–25,30', in N. Lohfink (ed.), *Das Deuteronomium: Entstehung, Gestalt und Botschaft* (Leuven: Leuven University Press, 1985), pp. 357-62. Vanoni's use of H.-D. Hoffmann, *Reform und Reformen: Untersuchungen zu einem Grundthema der deuteronomistischen Geschichtsschreibung* (ATANT, 66; Zürich: Theologischer Verlag, 1980), to prove his case should not lead to any conclusion that Hoffmann is in agreement with Cross' double redaction theory. Hoffmann's intention was a reassertion of Noth's thesis about the creative deuteronomistic author against the theories of the 'Göttingen School': 'Die unterschiedliche Akzentuierung eines der zahlreichen Hauptthemen der dtr Schule ist nicht Argument genug, diese auf je einen anderen Redaktor aufzuteilen' (*Reform und Reformen*, p. 20).

53. Provan, *Hezekiah and the Books of Kings*, pp. 71-72, 144.

54. Noth, *Überlieferungsgeschichtliche Studien*, pp. 75-77.

gold *that was left* (הנתרים) in the treasuries of temple and palace (15.18). With Jehoash wealth had once more been accumulated, so he also had items of his forefathers (Jehoshaphat, Jehoram and Ahaziah) to give away together with all the gold and silver in the treasuries of both temple and palace (2 Kgs 12.19). Ahaz had only the silver and the gold *that was found* (הנמצא) in the temple and in the treasuries of the palace (16.8). Hezekiah found silver only in the temple and in the treasuries of the royal palace. The gold he stripped off the doors of the temple, which he himself had overlaid (18.15-16).[55] Finally we find Jehoiakim taxing the land and the people in order to pay the assigned taxes (23.35). Closely following this decline in wealth, we find an intensification of the threats behind the payments, from paying or bribing the overlords to a regular taxation, indicated by the terms ערך and נגש in 2 Kgs 23.35.[56] What is here implied, of course, creates a problem not only for Provan's chronology, but for any dating of the books of Kings prior to their literary chronological closure. If we depart from this biblical chronology, however, it would be quite possible to assert a Josiah narrative which aimed at arguing for a removal of both idolatrous and Yahwist shrines. Such an argumentation would conflict with northern interests as well as the interests of 'foreigners' in the country. I will return to these considerations in the closing part of Chapter 2.

3. *The Value of Form and Redaction Criticism*

However tempting it is to search for different sources and layers of redaction in the Deuteronomistic History, as so many ideological and literary contradictions can be depicted in that History, it turns out that the contradictions depicted expose a great dependency on already established hypotheses about what might be expected. Each scholar, in fact, has created inconsistency on the basis of his or her own expectations.[57] The methodological principles for source analysis of the Deuteronomistic

---

55.   The shift in gold and silver to silver and gold here clearly demonstrates that we are not dealing with pre- or post-exilic Biblical Hebrew's preference for one or another form, such as has been argued by A. Hurwitz, ' "Diachronic Chiasm" in Biblical Hebrew', in B. Uffenheimer (ed.), *Bible and Jewish History: Studies in Bible and Jewish History Dedicated to the Memory of Jacob Liver* (Tel Aviv: University of Tel Aviv Press, 1971 [Hebrew]), pp. 248-55. When there is wealth in the country gold comes first.

56.   On this, see further Chapter 2.

57.   B. Gieselmann, 'Die sogenannte josianische Reform in der gegenwärtigen Forschung', *ZAW* 106 (1994), pp. 223-42. M. Weinfeld, *Deuteronomy and the Deuteronomic School* (Oxford: Clarendon Press, 1972), p. 8, in an answer not to Cross' book (which was published in 1973) but to an earlier article: 'we have no fixed criterion by which we may differentiate between the two editorial stages'. Weinfeld attacked the problems from a different angle and ascribed to his 'Deuteronomic School': Deuteronomy, composed in the latter half of the seventh century; the Deuteronomic edition of Joshua–Kings, which received its fixed form in the first half of the sixth century; the Deuteronomic prose sermons in Jeremiah, which were apparently composed during the second half of the sixth century (p. 7). Contemporaneously with these scribal activities rooted in ancient wisdom literature and driving its inspiration from the political-national sphere, went a priestly activity which result is the Priestly document (P) rooted in temple ideology and driving its inspiration from the divine sphere (pp. 183-89).

History—so closely associated with Wellhausen's Documentary Hypothesis of an Elohist, a Priestly and a Deuteronomist redaction of the Hexateuch and, in fact, with O. Eissfeldt's syntheses of form and source criticism—created a division of the Deuteronomistic History into two or more layers, named DtrG, DtrP and DtrN.[58] The authors of the work, Smend called DtrG (*der deuteronomistische Geschicht-screiber*). The term was later changed to DtrH (*der deuteronomistische Historiker*). On the basis of their interest in either prophecy or law, successive redactors, named DtrP (Prophetic) and DtrN (Nomistic) redactors, re-edited DtrG/DtrH, correcting it and adding new material. Assigning a variety material to these redactors who worked within a relatively short range of time, contradictions could be explained rationalistically. The assignment, however, created more problems. While A. Jepsen's work from 1939[59] had laid a foundation for most works, almost nobody followed Jepsen's results. While the 'Göttingen School' agreed on the basic principles for a division, they disagreed on the perspectives of each strand, for which they did not give a clear profile. In fact, the positions of both DtrG and DtrN in Dietrich's work[60] were so weak that DtrP tended to take over the control of the material.[61]

While Cross' thematically based double redaction theory has attracted quite a number of scholars, they have disagreed on the division of the material.[62] While

---

58. This was the interest of the 'Göttingen School' (also called the 'Smend School'), represented by R. Smend, 'Das Gesetz und die Völker: Ein Beitrag zur deuteronomischen Redaktionsgeschichte', in H.W. Wolff (ed.), *Probleme biblischer Theologie: Gerhard von Rad zum 70. Geburtstag* (Munich: Chr. Kaiser Verlag, 1971), pp. 494-509. Smend's article sought to explain some of the redactional problems left aside by Noth by assigning those passages (Josh. 1.7-9; 13.1bβ-6, 23, and Judg. 1.1–2.9; 2.17, 20-21, 23) to a later nomistic redactor. It was Smend's belief that DtrN could be found in all parts of Deuteronomistic History. W. Dietrich, *Prophetie und Geschichte: Eine redaktionsgeschichtliche Untersuchung zum deuteronomistischen Geschichtswerk* (FRLANT, 108; Göttingen: Vandenhoeck & Ruprecht, 1972), argued for two redactions of DtrG, all within around twenty years from 580–560 BCE. T. Veijola, *Die ewige Dynastie. David und die Entstehung seiner Dynastie nach der deuteronomistischen Darstellung* (AASF B, 193; Helsinki: Academia Scientiarum Fennica, 1975), and *idem, Das Königtum in der Beurteilung der deuteronomischen Historiographie* (AASF B, 198; Helsinki: Academia Scientiarum Fennica, 1977), had special interest in the various ideologies about the kingship and the Davidides represented by his assumed redactors. The basic principles of the Göttingen School have laid the foundation for quite a number of articles, monographs and introductions, all of which have their own interests and perspectives. Detailed summaries can be found in E. Eynikel, *The Reform of King Josiah and the Composition of the Deuteronomic History* (OTS, 33; Leiden: E.J. Brill, 1996), pp. 7-31, and van Keulen, *Manasseh Through the Eyes of the Deuteronomists*, pp. 14-22.

59. Which was not, however, published before 1953: A. Jepsen, *Die Quellen des Königbuches* (Halle: Max Niemeyer, 1953).

60. Dietrich, *Prophetie und Geschichte*, especially pp. 107-109, 138-39.

61. Cf. the discussions in Provan, *Hezekiah and the Books of Kings*, pp. 15-31 (22-27); S.L. McKenzie, 'Deuteronomistic History', in *ABD*, II, pp 160-68, and van Keulen, *Manasseh Through the Eyes of the Deuteronomists*, pp. 20-22.

62. Cf. Provan, *Hezekiah and the Books of Kings*, pp. 11-14; Eynikel, *The Reform of King Josiah and the Composition of the Deuteronomic History*, pp. 12-20; G.N. Knoppers, *Two Nations Under God: The Deuteronomistic History of Solomon and the Dual Monarchies* (HSM, 52; 2 vols.; Atlanta: Scholars Press, 1993), I, pp. 46-54.

form-critically[63] and thematically based analyses pointed to various strains of ideologies, none of the results adequately challenged Noth's fundamental thesis that the Deuteronomistic History formed a coherent linguistic, compositional, chronological and theological work.[64]

O'Brien's work succeeded well in demonstrating the basic hypotheses of the 'Göttingen School'; it confirmed, however, that this kind of analysis is not able to break the circularity of the arguments that 'it is necessary that the structure, conceptual plan and text of the history be clearly established. It is only when this has been done that a clear perception of the course of later redaction can be gained.'[65] Closing the primary document with the Josiah narrative, of which O'Brien left out the closing remarks (2 Kgs 23.26-30) in order to make the Josianic reform the closure of the promotion of the Deuteronomic code,[66] he had to invent a first stage of successive redaction for the last chapters of Kings.[67] From here decline not only belongs to biblical Israel, but also to O'Brien's interpretation of that decline in a series of successive redaction of the tripartite composite story about Israel's past.[68] In a plot-driven examination, O'Brien does not convincingly provide the literary and linguistic analysis of the text he intended to give[69] but merely a contextual analysis of the authors' diverging opinions based on his own perceptions of how each strand should appear. The striking absence of applying the 'Deuteronomic code' to his material[70] certainly undermines his basic assumption about the function of this code. A thorough analysis of this code at work in, for example, the accusations of sin and utterances of doom in the books of Kings would have made it clear that those utterances are closely related linguistically and thematically to the laws of the Pentateuch (see later, Chapter 2). Furthermore, confusing biblical history with history, of which he shows little interest (note the lack of references to historical works in his bibliography, with not a single reference to extra-biblical sources), his interpretation of history's course for the development of his successive redactions is based solely on the story he attempts to place within reality's chronology.

However, Noth's criteria *can* be understood as part of the work's superstructure and the question of possible sources underlying a final redaction of the work may still be open to discussion. Since Noth's thesis about a single author was based on his inclination to accept the existence of ancient sources—collected, selected and theologically interpreted[71]—it still needs to be questioned whether any source can

---

63. The methodological principles for the work of the Göttingen School were not literary-critical in a modern sense of the term (against McKenzie, 'Deuteronomistic History', p. 163). They rather worked on the basis of form and redaction criticism applied to a plot-driven examination.

64. Cf. M.A. O'Brien, *The Deuteronomistic History Hypothesis: A Reassessment* (OBO, 92; Göttingen: Vandenhoeck & Ruprecht, 1989), pp. 6-10 and *passim*.

65. O'Brien, *Deuteronomistic History Hypothesis*, p. 272.

66. O'Brien, *Deuteronomistic History Hypothesis*, pp. 24-26, 44.

67. O'Brien, *Deuteronomistic History Hypothesis*, pp. 272-73.

68. O'Brien, *Deuteronomistic History Hypothesis*, pp. 273-87.

69. O'Brien, *Deuteronomistic History Hypothesis*, pp. 22-23.

70. O'Brien, *Deuteronomistic History Hypothesis*, pp. 67-271.

71. Noth, *Überlieferungsgeschichtliche Studien*, p. 11. For an overview of Noth's divisions of his Deuteronomistic History, see A.F. Campbell, 'Martin Noth and the Deuteronomistic History', in

be considered to be neutral in regard to its own purpose. Even a king-list undergoes redaction when kings are added or left out for political reasons. R. Rendtorff clearly understood these implications of Noth's thesis.[72]

It was this obvious contradiction in Noth's one author thesis which forced scholars such as B. Peckam and H.-D. Hoffmann to suggest, on the one hand, that the Deuteronomistic History had undergone various revisions at the hand of tradents, rewriting the stories they inherited,[73] and, on the other, that an exilic (post-exilic) author wrote the history as political propaganda on the basis of oral traditions in an effort to admonish the returnees to re-establish the Davidic kingdom, using Josiah and his reign as ideal.[74] Both suggestions undermined the historical value of the Deuteronomistic History and relegated it to a relatively fictitious status.[75]

The discussion reiterates well earlier debates about the historicity of the Pentateuch. Already in 1901, H. Gunkel, making a sharp distinction between Wellhausen's source criticism and his own form criticism, had used the expression 'historicized fiction' for the patriarchal narratives.[76] It was H. Gressmann, however (a student of Wellhausen and a colleague of Gunkel), who brought the question into a larger context through his comparative studies of the traditions of the ancient Near East and the Old Testament.[77] Arguing for an underlying oral tradition, which came into written form first in the period of the monarchy, the collection of legends and folk traditions took priority over historiography, authorship and editorial activity. The work of O. Eissfeldt sought to combine these alternatives.[78] Arguing

---

S.L. McKenzie and M.P. Graham (eds.), *The History of Israel's Traditions: The Heritage of Martin Noth* (JSOTSup, 182; Sheffield: Sheffield Academic Press, 1994), pp. 31-62.

72.   R. Rendtorff, 'Martin Noth and Tradition Criticism', in McKenzie and Graham (eds.), *The History of Israel's Traditions*, pp. 91-100 (94): 'Before Noth's day, the term "redactor" was regularly used in a depreciatory sense. Noth gave it a new connotation by redefining the work of the person responsible. Thus the "Deuteronomist" was born.'

73.   B. Peckham, 'The Composition of Deuteronomy 5–11', in C.L. Meyers and M. O'Connor (eds.), *The Word of the Lord Shall Go Forth: Essays in Honor of David Noel Freedman in Celebration of His Sixtieth Birthday* (Winona Lake, IN: Eisenbrauns, 1983), pp. 217-40, and *The Composition of the Deuteronomistic History* (HSM, 35; Atlanta: Scholars Press, 1985).

74.   Hoffmann, *Reform und Reformen*.

75.   So also A.G. Auld's radical reinterpretation of both Chronicles and Samuel–Kings as alternative or competing appropriations of an earlier story of Judah's kings in his *Kings Without Privilege: David and Moses in the Story of the Bible's Kings* (Edinburgh: T. & T. Clark, 1994).

76.   H. Gunkel, *Genesis: übersetzt und erklärt* (Göttinger Handkommentar zum Alten Testament, I.1; Göttingen: Vandenhoeck & Ruprecht, 1901), p. 19.

77.   H. Gressmann, 'Sage und Geschichte in den Patriarchenerzählungen', *ZAW* 30 (1910), pp. 1-34, 'Ursprung und Entwicklung in den Patriarchenerzählungen', in H. Schmidt *et al.* (eds.), *Eucharisterion: Festschrift Hermann Gunkel* (FRLANT, 36; Göttingen: Vandenhoeck & Ruprecht, 1923), pp. 1-55, *Altorientalische Bilder zum Alten Testament* (Berlin: W. de Gruyter, 1926), and *Altorientalische Texte zum Alten Testament* (Berlin: W. de Gruyter, 1927).

78.   O. Eissfeldt, 'Stammesage und Novelle in den Geschichten von Jakob und von seinen Söhnen', in Schmidt *et al.* (eds.), *Eucharisterion*, pp. 56-77; further references to Eissfeldt's works are to be found in T.L. Thompson, *Early History of the Israelite People: From the Written and Archaeological Sources* (Leiden: E.J. Brill, 1992), p. 8 n. 15.

for an underlying historicity reflected in various forms of 'fictionalized history', Eissfeldt

> established the immensely influential doctrine that originating events lay behind
> the early biblical traditions wherever more than a single variant or account of a
> tradition was extant in the received text. An original historical event, which was
> thought to have given rise to such a complex tradition, could be recovered, so Eiss-
> feldt argued, by discounting and removing the later, secondary accretions, until
> ultimately one discovered the historical nucleus that was hidden in all significant
> early traditions.[79]

It is not difficult to see the influence of this theory in the 'Göttingen' and 'Cross' Schools, which went even further than Eissfeldt had by claiming a historicity for each of the various editorial levels as well.

The opposition to Eissfeldt's theory took several directions, all of which challenged the question of historicity. One direction was introduced by T.L. Thompson's 1974 book on the patriarchal narratives. In this book, Thompson argued on the basis of the theories of Wellhausen and Gressmann that these narratives were: 'historically determined expressions about Israel and Israel's relationship to its God, given in forms legitimate to their time'.[80] This conclusion, together with a constant request for historical evidence in biblical scholarship, has determined Thompson's work ever since. With his 1992 book[81] the debate reached its nadir, and in the aftermath of the 'deconstruction' movement[82] many works and debates have sought to place the biblical books within ideologies of post-exilic Judaism.[83] In Thompson's work, *The Bible in History: How Writers Create a Past*,[84] the transition from an historical to a theological interpretation of the biblical tradition set the stage for renewed studies in the intellectual world of the ancient Near East. Returning to the main interest of the *Religionsgeschichtliche Schule*—namely, the intellectual

---

79. Thompson, *Early History*, p. 9.

80. T.L. Thompson, *The Historicity of the Patriarchal Narratives: The Quest for the Historical Abraham* (Berlin: W. de Gruyter, 1974), p. 330.

81. Thompson, *Early History*.

82. The term should not be confused with J. Derrida's literary criticism. It relates to the historical criticism, which since the 1970s has challenged the historiographic value of our biblical texts and raised doubt about biblical archaeology's relevance for historical reconstruction. Although this has been the work of several international scholars, the 'movement' is now mostly identified with the 'Copenhagen School'; cf. below, n. 91.

83. The literature reflecting these debates and the paradigm shift in Old Testament Studies must be sought in updated bibliographies in relevant literature; for example, G.W. Ramsey, *The Quest for the Historical Israel* (London: SCM Press, 1981), who gives a summarized overview of the implications for biblical scientism; Thompson, *Early History*, pp. 77-126, who presents an annotated introduction to this new paradigm and its implications for historical research; D.V. Edelman (ed.), *The Fabric of History: Text, Artefact and Israel's Past* (JSOTSup, 127; Sheffield: JSOT Press, 1991); L.L. Grabbe (ed.), *Can a History of Israel Be Written?* (ESHM, 1; JSOTSup, 245; Sheffield: Sheffield Academic Press, 1997).

84. T.L. Thompson, *The Bible in History: How Writers Create a Past* (London: Jonathan Cape, 1999) (published in America as *The Mythic Past: Biblical Archaeology and the Myth of Israel* [New York: Basic Books, 1999]).

history of the ancient Near East and its interaction with the biblical material—
Thompson has recently devoted several articles to that subject in an explicit effort
to answer his own question from 1974: 'what then, if not history?'[85] Thompson's
conclusion that the Bible is a collected, secondary tradition, however, does not
solve the problem between reference and referent. Even if one argues on the basis
of this secondary tradition and the literary world referenced, one still needs to
consider how the tradition interacts with the non-literary world behind the composition. The basic problem is not whether there are cores of historical truth in our
tradition (there probably are several), but whether the tradition is operating within
such a 'protestant' *ad fontes* mode of authentic objective presentation. Using stories
and traditions in an interpretative act of narrative creation is in itself an expression
of realities that begs for attention.

Another direction of criticism was introduced by J. Van Seters' 1975 book on
Abraham, which was strongly expanded in his 1983 book on the Deuteronomistic
History.[86] Albeit Van Seters argued for the biblical genre as being 'fictional historiography', he claimed it to be 'a historical account to Israel of its past', created by
an ancient historian in exilic time.[87] Van Seters' claim for that history as national
and canonical, preceding 'the work of the Yahwist's universalist story of the Pentateuch, as well as the Chronicler's "Kingdom of God" story of the Books of Chronicles',[88] has served as a basic premise in all his following works.[89] Using the

---

85.   Thompson, *Historicity of the Patriarchal Narratives*, pp. 325-30 (330). See also the
following works by Thompson: 'Text, Context and Referent in Israelite Historiography', in
Edelman (ed.), *The Fabric of History*, pp. 65-92; 'Why Talk about the Past? The Bible Epic and
Historiography', in P.R. Davies (ed.), *The Origins of the Jewish People and Contemporary Biblical
Scholarship* (forthcoming); the double article 'Historiography in the Pentateuch: Twenty-Five
Years After Historicity', *SJOT* 13/2 (1999), pp. 258-83, and 'Kingship and the Wrath of God: or
Teaching Humility', *RB* 109 (2002), pp. 161-96; 'A Testimony of the Good King: Reading the
Mesha Stela' (ESHM, 6; London/New York: T. & T. Clark International, forthcoming). Thomp-
son's work should not be confused with traditional biblical form criticism, since it rather follows
the direction of 'formalistic studies' and motif analysis; cf. the distinction made in his *The Origin
Tradition of Ancient Israel: The Literary Formation of Genesis and Exodus 1–23* (JSOTSup, 55;
Sheffield: JSOT Press, 1987), p. 48.
86.   J. Van Seters, *Abraham in History and Tradition* (New Haven: Yale University Press,
1975), and *In Search of History: Historiography in the Ancient World and the Origins of Biblical
History* (New Haven: Yale University Press, 1983).
87.   Van Seters, *In Search of History*, pp. 320-21.
88.   Van Seters, *In Search of History*, pp. 361-62.
89.   J. Van Seters, *Prologue to History: The Yahwist as Historian in Genesis* (Louisville, KY:
Westminster/John Knox Press, 1992), p. 330: 'It is no longer the particular ethic of a national code
reflected in Deuteronomy but a universal morality that is in view, and this constantly informs the
Yahwist's perspective throughout Genesis... If the DtrH corresponds to the nationalistic, prophetic
view of Israel's history up to the exile, then the Yahwist is more akin to the broader universalistic
concerns of Second Isaiah'. See also Van Seters' *The Life of Moses: The Yahwist as Historian in
Exodus–Numbers* (Kampen: Kok Pharos, 1994), pp. 1-3, 33-34: 'J reconstructs his story of origin
from the older DtrH, the prophetic tradition, and "old poems" to produce what was likely to have
happened... Yet the work was never intended as an independent, self-contained history; it was
meant to be an introduction to the national history of DtrH' (p. 457). In contrast to his 1975 book,

chronology of the books of Kings, supported by the evidence of the existence of history writing in the Levant (especially Herodotus' work), Van Seters' *terminus a quo* established the Deuteronomist as the first true historian in Western civilization. This argumentation is hardly distinguishable from Josephus' claim that Jewish history traced back to creation surpasses all competing histories of his time. Referring to a glorious past with the purpose of making it known in the Greek world, Josephus, surpassing Dionysius of Halicarnassus, carried his story, 'pure of that unseemly mythology current among others' (*Ant.* 1.15) past the mythological world of Roman origin to creation.[90]

Thompson and Van Seters' works have had and still have strong influence on the scholarly debates about the historicity of the Bible's narratives. The tension between Van Seters' claim for the Deuteronomistic History as fictional historiography and Thompson's claim that it is theology have attracted each their own supporters among historical-critical and literary exegetes as well as quite a number of opponents, who, with increasing intensity, have argued for the credibility of the Bible based on its historical affirmation. While those agreeing with Van Seters—bypassing his views on historicity—still found his reassessment of Noth's *Überlieferungsgeschichtliche* context in exilic time useful, those accepting Thompson's perspective had to look for other contexts, chronological and historical. The increasing criticism of Noth's thesis of the amphictyony had not only removed the foundation for a premonarchic 'nation' of Israelites, it had removed the foundation for the Deuteronomistic History's presentation of that 'nation', which subsequently could not have been led into exile as a people or have returned from that exile as anything other than characters of narrative.[91]

he now further argues (*The Life of Moses*, p. 458): 'J is not the result of a long traditio-historical process, such as Noth and R. Rendtorrf believed. I have argued that neither in terms of the major themes nor in the individual units do we possess much evidence of a long process of tradition transmission or of a repository of ancient tradition. The innovation of the Yahwist himself has been greatly underestimated.'

90. Hjelm, *Samaritans and Early Judaism*, pp. 191-92. Van Seters' conclusion about the similarity of DtrH and Herodotus should not lead to the false assumption that he thereby implied that DtrH depends on Herodotus; cf. the failure to take into consideration that Van Seters dates DtrH a whole century before Herodotus in F.A.J. Nielsen, *The Tragedy in History: Herodotus and the Deuteronomistic History* (CIS, 4; JSOTSup, 251; Sheffield: Sheffield Academic Press, 1997), pp. 14-15, 89-90, 163.

91. Noth's amphictyony thesis—a central argument for both Noth's understanding of Israel's historical origins and his reconstruction of the Bible's original composition—was rejected indisputably in the 1960s by scholars, who later became known as the 'Copenhagen School': H. Friis, who wrote her prize essay on the subject in 1968 (unfortunately not published until 1986 as *Die Bedingungen für die Errichtung des Davidischen Reichs in Israel und seiner Umwelt* [Dielheimer Blätter zum Alten Testament Beiheft, 6; Heidelberg: B.J. Diebner & C. Nauerth, 1986]); see also Friis' 'Eksilet og den israelitiske historieopfattelse', *DDT* 38 (1975), pp. 1-16, and N.P. Lemche, *Israel i Dommertiden: En oversigt over diskussionen om Martin Noths 'Das system des zwölf Stämme Israels'* (Tekst og Tolkning, 4; Copenhagen: G.E.C. Gad, 1972). The consequence of this deconstruction of the Bible as history found far-reaching expression in Lemche's monographs, *Early Israel: Anthropological and Historical Studies on the Israelite Society Before the Monarchy* (Leiden: E.J. Brill, 1985) and *The Canaanites and Their Land: The Idea of Canaan in the Old*

Van Seters' claim for DtrH as primary national history and Thompson's claim for that history as theology and identifiable 'with the theologized world of the biblical tradition, within which Israel itself was a theologumenon and a new creation out of tradition'[92] are challenging conclusions. They must be given further investigation in both coming reconstructions of Judaean history and in this history's interaction with Samaritan history. I have suggested elsewhere that, based on extra-biblical evidence, the Pentateuchal narratives must be dated within the Persian-Hellenistic period.[93] This, however, does not automatically relegate them to a secondary relationship to the Deuteronomistic History as we have it since so much of that material cannot be dated earlier. Van Seters' conclusion, based on comparative literary studies and the acceptance of his story's own dating of its authoritative prophets,[94] does not take into consideration any historical context that is not itself part of his literary world of near-contemporary historiographies.[95] Further, it does not consider the religio-political circumstances for the writing of that literature. Still further, it does not address the challenge of his basic argument that the historiography is fictional, which, if taken seriously, would require that not only his history be understood as fiction, but also the roles of his prophets. Any scholarly claim of redaction history regarding the Latter Prophets, in fact, holds implicit the literary and non-historical character of these figures and their purported writings.[96] As

Testament (JSOTSup, 110, Sheffield: JSOT Press, 1991), as well as in P.R. Davies' *In Search of 'Ancient Israel'* (JSOTSup, 148, Sheffield: Sheffield Academic Press, 1992), respectively arguing that neither the biblical Canaanites nor the biblical Israelites were historical. A less noticed forerunner of many of the arguments brought forward in these disputes about the *Sitz im Leben* for the biblical books was B.J. Diebner from Heidelberg, who, since 1974, had published several articles in *DBAT*, opting for a post-exilic dating in the Persian and Hellenistic periods for most of the biblical material; see T. Römer, 'Bernd-Jörg Diebner und die "Spätdatierung" der Pentateuch—und der historischen Traditionen der Hebräischen Bibel', *DBAT* 30 (eds. C. Nauerth and R. Grieshammer, *Begegnungen Bernd Jörg Diebner zum 60. Geburtstag am 8. Mai 1999*) (1999), pp. 151-55. See O. Bächli, *Amphiktyonie im Alten Testament: Forschungsgeschichtliche Studie zur Hypothese von Martin Noth* (Theologische Zeitschrift Sonderband, 6; Basel: Fr. Reinhart Verlag, 1977), for references to the early discussion.

    92.   Thompson, *Early History of the Israelite People*, p. 423.

    93.   Hjelm, *Samaritans and Early Judaism*, p. 283.

    94.   See further in Chapter 4, pp. 169-84, below. So also H.H. Schmid, *Der sogenannte Jahwist: Beobachtungen und Fragen zur Pentateuchforschung* (Zürich: Theologischer Verlag, 1976), p. 175: 'Die Prophetie ist nicht nur älter als das (deuteronomische und priesterschriftliche) Gesetz, sondern auch älter als die (vor allem in den sog. geschichtlichen Büchern des Alten Testamentes zum Ausdruck gebrachte) Erkenntnis der theologischen Basisfunktion der Geschichte. Die prophetische Verkündigung ist nicht die Konzequenz alttestamentlicher Geschichtstheologie, sondern deren Vorläufer und Voraussetzung.'

    95.   N.P. Lemche, 'Good and Bad in History: The Greek Connection', in S.L. McKenzie and T. Römer (eds.), *Rethinking the Foundations: Historiography in the Ancient World and in the Bible: Essays in Honour of John Van Seters* (Berlin: W. de Gruyter, 2000), pp. 127-40, and, in the same volume, T.L. Thompson, 'Tradition and History: The Scholarship of John Van Seters', pp. 9-21.

    96.   N.P. Lemche, 'The God of Hosea', in E. Ulrich, J.W. Wright, R.P. Carroll and P.R. Davies (eds.), *Priests, Prophets and Scribes: Essays on the Formation and Heritage of Second Temple Judaism in Honour of Joseph Blenkinsopp* (JSOTSup, 149; Sheffield: Sheffield Academic Press, 1992), pp. 241-57.

argued by Robert Carroll regarding Jeremiah, 'there is no outside the text',[97] by which he meant that deducing from text to reality is a hazardous enterprise. Since it is claimed in Samaritan historiography that the prophets wrote false stories and told lies to the people, the validity of the Deuteronomistic History as a historical account must be qualified and supported by independent argument. Furthermore, since it is told within that history that the cult moved from north to south, abandoning all the former cult places, it must be asked why that part of the Deuteronomistic History was understood to be necessary. Why would a Jerusalem-oriented author place the original cult in the north only thereby to be forced to argue for the authenticity of his own cult in Jerusalem, unless unavoidable circumstances had demanded such a story to be written?

Singling out the various thematic elements dealt with in the Deuteronomistic History, we find at least five which are recurrent: (1) north–south conflict, (2) cult centralization, (3) Mosaic Law and prophetic interpretation, (4) the status of the Davidic kingship and (5) loyalty. These issues also lay at the centre of Jewish–Samaritan disputes.[98] In the various examinations of the Deuteronomistic History, the possibility that the work might have more than one audience has been ignored. The polemical character of the work implies that the primary themes are under discussion and that alternative voices stand outside the work. Stories do not simply reflect or give an account of reality. Whether intentionally or not, they hide and distort reality. An analysis of redaction needs not simply to ask the question of 'how' a text came to be, it also needs to ask 'why', 'by which means' and 'for what purpose'. What situation demanded that a 'new' story be written? Noth's enduring problem: the incoherence of passages in Joshua and Judges, with his claim for conceptual unity based on his so-called Dtr reflections (Josh. 1; 12; 23; Judg. 2.11-12; 1 Sam. 12; 1 Kgs 8.14-15; 2 Kgs 17.7-23), must be judged in the light of extra-biblical material. It needs to be taken seriously that the Samaritan Chronicles present variant traditions to those of the Masoretes, which should not be rejected *a priori* as anachronistic.[99] Considering the preaching of Isaiah as normative for his time is just as tendentiously misleading as assuming, for example, that the Dead Sea Scroll text 4QMMT belongs to a sectarian circle. The discussion about what is to be given normative status had not ended in the Maccabaean period, if we are to believe Josephus. In fact, the question has not yet found resolution in regard to Jewish–Samaritan disputes. The thematic elements of 'rejection of the prophets' does not belong to some unknown pre-exilic past of scribes or schools. It forms part of an ongoing discussion about the criteria for emerging normative Judaisms, in which early Christianity took its part.[100] In this context, the possibility of a 'prophetic' redaction or authorship behind the Former Prophets becomes far more interesting, since it raises questions about the identity and self-interest of these

---

97. R.P. Carroll, *Jeremiah* (Sheffield: JSOT Press, 1989 [repr. 1993, Sheffield: Sheffield Academic Press]), p. 81.

98. Hjelm, *Samaritans and Early Judaism*.

99. Hjelm, *Samaritans and Early Judaism*, Chapters 3 and 6.

100. Hjelm, *Samaritans and Early Judaism*, Chapters 4 and 6.

'prophets'.[101] In the first place one recalls that in rabbinic tradition Joshua wrote the book of Joshua, Samuel wrote the books of Judges and Samuel, while Jeremiah wrote the books of Kings (*b. Bat.* 14b-15a). Similarities between the books of Jeremiah and Kings have long been recognized, however, without firm conclusion regarding interdependency.[102]

4. *Concluding Remarks Regarding Form and Redaction Criticism*

In bringing together the various problems and themes this introduction has raised, we must conclude:

(1) 'Higher criticism' gives and can give only limited answers to questions that are restricted essentially to form- and redaction-critical issues. If we do not apply 'lower' criticism's methods, based on the analysis of ancient Hebrew and Greek manuscripts and given further perspective in extra-biblical material among the Pseudepigrapha, Apocrypha, and other early Jewish authors as well as Samaritan material, we have no hope of establishing historical contexts for our material. Nor do we have any criteria for breaking the circularity of source criticism's dependence on its own interpretation of the material when a *tertium comparationis* is not applied to the material. In the following examination, the focus of interest will therefore not be oriented so much to questions of whether we can detect pre-exilic or post-exilic layers in the Former Prophets, but rather to what is the relationship between Masoretic and non-Masoretic texts. This question forces us to operate with three *a quo* datings: the earliest, based on the narrative chronology in biblical stories, the second in the second–first century BCE, based on Dead Sea Scrolls and extra-biblical issues of centralization, and the third in the sixth–tenth century CE's Masoretic redaction of biblical texts. It is the tensions between such dates that set the parameters for the exegetical questions raised throughout the study.

Scholars usually regard the pointed Hebrew text, whether published by the Deutsche Gesellschaft on the basis of the Codex Leningradensis from the hand of Aaron Ben-Asher of the Tiberian group from 1008 CE, or on other editions, based on tenth–eleventh century Masoretic manuscripts, as the primary 'biblical' text. I attempt to call these publications by their proper origin, namely as *Masoretic texts*, which developed over a 400 year period from the sixth–tenth century CE.[103] Prior to that time, some standardization was attempted. Comparative analyses of Hebrew and Greek variants of Old Testament traditions in Pseudepigrapha, Apocrypha, Dead Sea Scrolls, New Testament, Josephus and Samaritan text traditions such as the Samaritan Pentateuch (SP), the Samaritan book of Joshua, Genealogies and Chronicles have revealed that the Masoretic traditions and texts should not be given

---

101. R. Polzin, *Moses and the Deuteronomist: A Literary Study of the Deuteronomic History* (New York: Seabury Press, 1980); Hoffmann, *Reform und Reformen*.

102.   Auld, *Kings Without Privilege*, pp. 167-70, who is in favour of a relationship from Jeremiah to Kings rather than the other way around.

103.   E. Tov, *Textual Criticism of the Hebrew Bible* (Minneapolis: Fortress Press, 1992), *passim* (especially pp. 22-39, 77-79).

priority—*a priori*—against these other traditions, since the Masoretic text (MT) represents a final, rather than a formative product.[104] The consonantal proto-MT form was one among other forms in pre-Christian times, and only in the course of rabbinic revision and preservation did it become a standard text for most groups in Judaism.[105]

(2) Theories about redaction criticism must take historical implications into consideration. The persuasiveness of a biblical narrative belongs to the narrative. The intention of creating a persuasive story, however, lies outside the story and must be qualified by an analysis of discussion and commentary on that story and its material in extra-biblical material.

Using the methods and insights gained from literary criticism we will be able to move once again to historical criticism. Lacking the 'why' and 'how' of literary critique's search for a text's persuasiveness[106] must inevitably lead back to a more qualified request for a historical setting. Who wrote the text? For whom was it written? What was the purpose of the text? What is the message or anti-message of the text? We are not asking here about the historicity of *our* 'biblical history', but rather about the identification of a 'story' given by those to whom it belonged. Identifying 'ownership' of the Bible with what the Bible presents has brought historical-critical scholarship into a fruitless situation of defending a story. Hermeneutics has basically concentrated on searching out the meaning of a text as related to its explicit narrative chronology, while neglecting the search for the identity of those who wrote the story. As it is now, we do not even know if the biblical authors presented what they believed to be a factual history. We do not know what purpose their stories served: whether they had an interest in recounting history or in hiding it for the purpose of defending or promoting theological or other ideological interests. We do not know how such disparate books as those of the Pentateuch (Hexateuch) and of Judges–Samuel–Kings have been brought into the same canon.[107]

---

104.   Tov, *Textual Criticism*, p. 22: 'As a rule the term *Masoretic Text* is limited to a mere segment of the representatives of the textual tradition of MT, namely, that textual tradition which was given its final form by Aaron Ben Asher of the Tiberian group of the Masoretes. Since all the printed editions and most manuscripts reflect this Ben Asher tradition, the term *Masoretic Text* is imprecise, since it is actually used only for part of the Masoretic tradition, *viz.*, that of Ben Asher'. In spite of this imprecision the term has gained conventional use and in the mind of most scholars it is equated with R. Kittel's *BH* (until 1951: *BHK*) or K. Elliger's *BHS*, both of which are, in fact, products of the nineteenth–twentieth century! The anachronisms implied hereby might be diminished by replacing MT with *BH*, *BHS* or whatever edition is used when reference is made to a specific text and retain MT for *Masoretic texts* or *tradition*.

105.   Tov, *Textual Criticism*, pp. 24-29.

106.   M. West, 'Looking for the Poem: Reflections on the Current and Future Status of the Study of Biblical Hebrew Poetry', in P.R. House (ed.), *Beyond Form Criticism: Essays in Old Testament Literary Criticism* (Winona Lake, IN: Eisenbrauns, 1992), pp. 423-32; see also, in the same volume, M. Sternberg, 'The Bible's Art of Persuasion: Ideology, Rhetoric, and Poetics in Saul's Fall', pp. 234-71.

107.   P.R. Davies, *Scribes and Schools: The Canonization of the Hebrew Scriptures* (Louisville, KY: Westminster/John Knox Press, 1998); Hjelm, *Samaritans and Early Judaism*. The new trend in scholarship labelled 'Pan-Deuteronomism', seeks to answer just such questions, however

Lemche's recent attempt to revive Noth's thesis about the amphictyony as a literary construct from late Persian and Hellenistic times, creating an ideological claim for heritage to all Israel,[108] operates paradigmatically with only one set of problems: that of Israel against 'the nations'. But what if Israel is not against 'the nations' but against 'itself'? What if the story presented as an *all* Israel 'national' epic[109] is a propagandistic work serving rather narrow 'nationalistic' interests? The question lingers in the background of Lemche's work, but is not incorporated in any dynamic way. Being loyal to Yahweh in Samuel–Kings is not a matter of religious piety, but rather about paying allegiance to the God in Jerusalem.

The purpose of the ark stories in Joshua–2 Kings might serve just such an ideology, implicitly answering the question: Which was Yahweh's 'chosen place' before the building of the temple? It certainly was not any Yahwist sanctuary in Shechem, Bethel or Shiloh, all of which are denigrated in the course of the story of Yahweh's move to Jerusalem. In the non-Pentateuchal Masoretic tradition, diversity, not unity, is the characteristic of the time between the entrance into the Promised Land and the establishment of the kingship in Jerusalem. Judges' 'patronage vs. chaos' narrative—'that in those days there was no king in Israel and everyone did what was right in his own eyes'—strongly confirms the lack of such a central shrine in its attempt to prepare the reader for the blessings of kingship, the establishment of justice and order, the joining of the tribes around a central shrine and a central government.[110] In fact, Judg. 20.27 is the only mention of an assemblage of *all* Israel around the ark in Bethel; this, however, without the participation of the Benjaminites and the Gileadites (Judg. 21.8), with whom they wage war. In all its occurrences in Joshua–1 Kings, we find that references to the ark and the people seeking Yahweh in front of the ark implicitly designate unity (Josh. 3; 4; 6; 8; 1 Sam. 14; 2 Sam. 6; 7; 11; 1 Kgs 3; 6; 8) or lack of unity (Judg. 20; 1 Sam. 4–7; 2 Sam. 15; 1 Kgs 2). Attention should be drawn to 1 Sam. 7.2 and 14.18's anticipation of 'Samuel's (ch. 7) and Saul's (ch. 14) victories over the Philistines, which in both cases imply that Israel achieves peace within its own borders. The constant antagonism between Israel's tribes in the book of Judges becomes even clearer when Masoretic tradition is compared to Samaritan tradition. Here the good conditions established during the time of Joshua and Eleazar continue. Kings elected by the people in Shechem under the conduct of the high priest do their royal duties and are succeeded by other kings similarly elected. High priests are all unproblematic successors of their fathers. We find no apostasy or punishment, nor any deceitful kings similar to Judges' Abimelech. The Israelites' careless moving around with

creating a many-headed monster in regard to the traditional use of the term 'deuteronomistic' and the composition of biblical books; cf. Shearing and McKenzie (eds.), *Those Elusive Deuteronomists, passim.*

108.   N.P. Lemche, *The Israelites in History and Tradition* (London: SPCK; Louisville, KY: Westminster/John Knox Press, 1998), pp. 104-107, 130.

109.   Lemche, *The Israelites in History and Tradition*, pp. 130-31.

110.   K.W. Whitelam, *The Just King: Monarchical Judicial Authority in Ancient Israel* (JSOTSup, 12; Sheffield: JSOT Press, 1979), p. 60. See also Lemche's critique of the amphictyony thesis in his earlier works (e.g. *Early Israel*, pp. 291-305).

the ark in the opening of the books of Samuel, leading to the departure of the 'glory' from Israel (1 Sam. 4.21) and to the end of the house of Eli (1 Sam. 4.17-18), the continuous unrest until the ark has been properly installed in Jerusalem in the presence of the multitude of Israel (2 Sam. 6.17-19; 7.1) and the planning of the building of the temple (2 Sam. 7), all expose a purposeful literary composition which must have had a complex audience as its implied reader. The ark's metaphorical function as a symbol of Israel's relationship with itself and with its god Yahweh suggests that the ark narratives have little to do with any cult item in Palestine's history of religion. This is not to say that there might not have been such an item, about whose form and function we can speculate, but the author's interest lies first and foremost in the possibilities of creating its literary symbolic meaning as a way of binding the tribes together before any central cult had become established literarily (and historically?). In this respect, we might agree with McCormick that 'the DtrH version of the ark as the repository box for the covenant that was placed in the *debir* of Solomon's temple' is the starting point for the ark tradition.[111] Not so agreeable, however is McCormick's understanding of this narrative as a literary starting point 'which underwent various modifications and supplementations by P', thereby implying a chronological order related to exilic and post-exilic communities. It could well be that we are operating with a mental and paradigmatic starting point that gave shape to the narratives.

(3) Van Seters' claim for DtrH as the primary history with a prologue in the Hexateuchal Yahwist strand must be qualified through an examination of its dissonance with Jewish and Samaritan claims that the cult had moved from north to south. An affirmation of Van Seters' claim must imply considerations about the relationship between Samaria and Judaea before the Judaean claim for hegemony in the second century BCE. It must be considered whether there ever had been such a move in history. Placed in the narrative world's tenth-century united monarchy, we must conclude that such a 'move' was never successfully accomplished within the Bible's own literary world. In the extra-biblical world, the attempts to force such a move at a much later time in the second century BCE were formed rather on Josianic models of conquest than upon Hezekian models of election.

(4) The possibility of the existence of two competing strands in the Hezekiah and the Josiah material must be qualified within a tradition historical setting. The assumed linkages between David–Hezekiah,[112] David–Josiah[113] and Moses–Josiah[114]

111. C.M. McCormick, 'From Box to Throne: A New Study of the Development of the Ark Tradition' (unpublished paper delivered at the SBL National Meeting, Nashville, 2000). Van Seters, *In Search of History*, p. 310, made a similar suggestion regarding Dtr's account of Solomon's reign: 'The whole account is composed from this perspective and scarcely reflects any other document source'.

112. Provan, *Hezekiah and the Books of Kings*.

113. Cross, *Canaanite Myth*.

114. Provan, *Hezekiah and the Books of Kings*. This was the proposal also of Friedman, 'From Egypt to Egypt: Dtr[1] and Dtr[2]', who reasserting Cross' two-redaction hypothesis, however, argued for a coherence of the final Deuteronomistic History by the hand of Dtr[2] as a work written in Egyptian exile with the purpose of telling the 'story of Israel from Egypt to Egypt' (p. 191).

must be brought into a larger religio-political context, including Jewish–Samaritan conflicts.

(5) The role of prophets in the shaping of Joshua–2 Kings needs to be given new evaluation in view of the work's polemical character.[115] If Lemche's basic contention that the 'historical books are supported by the prophetic books and *vice-versa*'[116] is affirmable, then we need not look for any explicit pan-Deuteronomistic traits in the prophetic literature, but rather for common ideologies.[117] Since it is claimed in Samaritan historiography that the prophets wrote false stories and told lies to the people, the validity of the Deuteronomistic History as a historical account needs also to be qualified. Special attention needs to be given to Josephus' treatment of the biblical narratives in comparison with the Septuagint (LXX) as well as Samaritan variants. Samuel–Kings' claim that the Yahweh cult should be centralized in Jerusalem and that idolatrous shrines be removed needs to be compared to the Zion ideology in its variant expressions in the Prophets and the Writings.

(6) Biblical literature's character as reiterative history, 'reused' in the second to first-century BCE extra-biblical writings related to the Hasmonaean uprising, seriously challenges the historicity of ancient traditions. These reiterations not only relate to themes, but also to composition, in which each hero faces his own set of problems; problems which nevertheless expose great similarities with those of his predecessors with whom our author establishes comparability. Ascribing historicity to all these variants is unscientific and sorting out degrees of credibility is hazardous. How then do we handle the problems that biblical heroes imitate each other and that, for example, the stories in 1 Maccabees and Josephus stories about the Hasmonaean uprising, formation and decline of the Jewish nation follow closely biblical narrative? Can they all be historical?

5. *Outline of the Investigation*

In an attempt to answer some of the problems just raised, I will first examine the composition of the Deuteronomistic History (the books of Kings), using the Hezekiah narrative in 2 Kings 18–20 as focus. The function of the judgment formulae as thematic will be scrutinized against scholarly assertions of their editorial character (Chapter 2). As the Hezekiah story also appears in Isaiah, its relevance for both books will be examined independently. The Hezekiah narrative's connection with Isaianic Zion ideology suggests that it is used in Kings with a specific purpose. Establishment of provenance and compositional relevance of the Hezekiah narrative for the book of Isaiah and scholarly assumptions of a Davidic Yahweh Zebaoth

115. Auld, *Kings Without Privilege*, pp. 162-63.

116. Lemche, 'The God of Hosea', p. 247 (my emphasis).

117. Auld, *Kings Without Privilege*, p. 163: 'The Chronicler and the Deuteronomist both breathed the same post-exilic air. And their interests in prophets as actors, doers, healers, and intercessors, overlap with the concerns of those who developed the (strictly) prophetic books. The prose narratives of Jeremiah are replete with precisely these concerns—and were written in a similar period.'

cult in an eleventh–tenth century BCE Zion-Jerusalem will be the basic themes dealt with in Chapter 3. In Chapter 4, questions about text traditions in the light of Van Seters' late dating of the Yahwist will lead to an examination of Jewish–Samaritan discussions about text traditions. Shiloh's intermediary function as a divider between Shechem and Jerusalem in these traditions will be treated separately. The tension which our traditions have set between Moses and the prophets and prophets and kings leads to an examination of the roles of Moses and David in competition and supplement: 'With whom does Yahweh speak?' Having established that Yahweh speaks with both Moses *and* David, our further questions concern the function of the Law *and* the prophets; that is, 'Zion's predicted heritage to the legacy of Sinai'[118] (Chapter 5). In Chapter 6, a search for a realization of Zion expectations will bring us to examine extra-biblical sources in the Apocrypha and Pseudepigrapha in order to follow datable traces of this ideology. As no realization of these expectations takes place within the biblical corpus, our concern will be whether the second-century BCE struggle for independence has been influential in the formation of a specific Jerusalem oriented ideology, claiming heritage to all Israel. In Chapter 7, results from Chapters 2–6 will be evaluated in the light of my previous work on Samaritans and Early Judaism. Are the traditions of the Patriarchs offered as a return or a departure? Which place has Yahweh chosen?

---

118.   J.D. Levenson, *Sinai and Zion: An Entry into the Jewish Bible* (San Francisco: Harper-SanFrancisco, 1987), p. 187.

Chapter 2

THE HEZEKIAH NARRATIVE AND THE COMPOSITION
OF THE DEUTERONOMISTIC HISTORY

It was not David's moving of the ark to Jerusalem (2 Sam. 6) that gave the city and its temple their special status. The struggle for sovereignty had only begun. It was not until much later—half a century after Yahweh's election of the city during the reign of Hezekiah (2 Kgs 18–20)—that competing cult places were finally destroyed and Jerusalem appears as the only place fit for the worship of Yahweh (2 Kgs 23). We are dealing here with a literary construction, which writes 'history' about a people within a paradigm of 'diversity' and 'unity' in a constant *movement* between these concepts. Thus, the exodus narrative is also the beginning of the dispersion of the people after their entrance into the Promised Land. Co-operation and commitment to one central leadership is nearly disastrous. Because there was no king, 'everyone did what he saw fit in his own eyes'. However, kingship did not solve this problem. The dominant position given to the tribe(s) of Judah (and Benjamin) rather increased the antagonism. Though the narrative seeks to give the impression that the Davidic kingship finally united the tribes, such 'unity' is not created by a removal of former disagreements. Solomon's peaceful reign from Dan to Beersheba was one of exception (1 Kgs 5.4-5) rather than of normality. It did not secure Israel and Judah shading branches of either fig or wine for long. Divisiveness lay in wait. The rejection of Rehoboam in Samaria (1 Kgs 12 [especially v. 16]) and the election of Jeroboam make the motif clear that the house of David had been primarily supported by the tribe of Judah, while the remaining tribes had paid their allegiance elsewhere.[1] The judgment of a faithless Israel is dramatically spelled out and made paradigmatic for the narrative as a whole. In the centre of this narrative cycle (1 Kgs 11.1–2 Kgs 23.15)—thematically designed as *'he walked in[2] all the way of Jeroboam the son of Nebat and in the sins with which he made Israel to sin, provoking Yahweh, God of Israel to anger by their idols'*—is the narrative about Ahab the son of Omri, who sinned even more by marrying the daughter of the Sidonian king Ethbaal and by raising an altar to Baal in Samaria (1 Kgs 16.30-32). The reiteration of this theme[3] relates the narratives to each other and predicts the

---

1. It should not go unnoticed that the division of the tribes follows the division and antagonism played out in the return narrative of Ezra (1.5; 2.1; 4.1, 12, 23; 5.1, 5; 6.7-8, 14) and of Nehemiah (3.34; 4.6; 13.23).

2. Or 'did not turn away from'; see further below.

3. 1 Kgs 15.34; 16.19, 26, 31; 22.53; 2 Kgs 3.3; 10.29, 31; 13.2, 11; 14.24; 15.9, 18, 24, 28; 17.22; 23.15.

fate of the Northern Kingdom. It is contrasted to the reforms of Josiah, which, in a final reiteration of both Solomon and Jeroboam's sins and the defilement of their cult places (2 Kgs 23.13-20), mark every place outside the walls of Jerusalem as unclean. Reiterating the Passover from the time of the Judges (23.22), Israel and Judah's unified and diverse royal pasts are made parenthetical, and Judah has proved its sovereignty as the chosen tribe with Jerusalem as the chosen place. Since no Passover is mentioned in the book of Judges, the authors might have the Passover after the crossing of the Jordan in mind (Josh. 5.10). The intention of the reform is not so much unification as selection between alternatives, in the transformation of a pre-monarchic past's hope to a new beginning. In the Josiah story's 'transfer' of the Law of Moses to Jerusalem, the reforms of Josiah not only signify that Israel's glorious past centred in the north is over, but also that Jerusalem has been chosen to bring it forward in a new beginning.[4] As argued by Provan, Josiah in 2 Kings 22–23 is presented as the figure of Moses rather than that of David, whom he 'actually leaves behind (23.21-23)'[5] in his statement that 'no such Passover was held from the days of the Judges…nor the days of the kings of Israel, nor the kings of Judah'. Denigrating the rule of Solomon as a period of apostasy (23.13) and completely 'forgetting' Hezekiah's faithfulness,[6] Josiah is announced as the only king to have followed in the paths of Moses (23.25), however, without benefiting much from it. The beginning was doomed to failure even before it had begun in an unfaithful pre-exilic Jerusalem (23.27). It is not 2 Kings, which informs us that, just as Moses had led the *Benei Ysrael* through the desert to the Promised Land, so Ezra would reiterate this and inaugurate a New Jerusalem in post-exilic times, similarly threatened to fall because of 'Solomon's sin' (Ezra 9 and Neh. 13).

In contrast to the books of Kings, the Chronicler's portrayal of Josiah presents him as a follower of both David and Moses (2 Chron. 34.3, 14; 35.3-6, 12-15). Reiterating the time of the prophet Samuel (35.18), the building of the Solomonic temple, the transfer of the ark and the directions for temple service (35.3-5), the Chronicler 'recreates' the foundation for a successful return to Israel's glorious past before the division of the kingdom.[7] In an imitation of Moses and Samuel's mediating roles in Yahweh's rejection of the people in Jeremiah 15 and his forgiveness in Psalm 99's hymn of his exultation on Zion, the Chronicler's Josiah is given the role of delaying Yahweh's wrath (2 Chron. 34.26-28). In a like manner, Hezekiah's Passover celebration (2 Chron. 30) reiterates the time of the common monarchy. In a reconciliatory context Hezekiah celebrates the Passover twice. This suggests that he meets the calendar disagreements with the northern tribes (those from Ephraim,

---

4. It hardly is coincidental that the term 'Lord, God of Israel' (יהוה אלהי ישראל) disappears in the Judaean parts of Kings' narrative after Solomon's reign, not to be taken up again before the Northern Kingdom has been removed from the scene (2 Kgs 18.5; 19.15, 20; 21.12; 22.15, 18).

5. Provan, *Hezekiah and the Books of Kings*, p. 116. So also Friedman, 'From Egypt to Egypt: Dtr[1] and Dtr[2]', p. 173.

6. Cf. the similar structure, from David to Moses in Kings' Hezekiah narrative (2 Kgs 18.3-6).

7. Auld, *Kings Without Privilege*, p. 139: 'Along with David, Solomon is for them ["the shared source" and "the Chronicler"] simply part of the ideal beginnings of monarchy (and state and religion?)'.

Manasseh, Issachar and Zebulon; cf. 2 Chron. 30.18-20). The aim is the unity of the people, expressed in the statement that 'since the time of Solomon, the son of David, king of Israel, there had been nothing like this in Jerusalem' (2 Chron. 30.26; cf. 2 Chron. 7.8-10; 1 Kgs 8.65-66). By placing Hezekiah's reform before Sennacherib's invasion, with its demonstration of Jerusalem's inviolability, the author of 2 Chronicles creates a rationalistic basis for Jerusalem's election in a reconciliatory gesture towards the northern tribes, who are thereby given reason to identify themselves with Jerusalem's surviving remnant. The initiative is received without much enthusiasm.

1. *2 Kings 17–20: A Survey*[8]

The biblical rendering of the saving of Jerusalem is put in contrast to the fall of Samaria at the hands of Shalmaneser. Samaria fell and Israel[9] was taken into exile because 'they did not obey the voice of Yahweh their God, but transgressed his covenant—all that Moses the servant of Yahweh had ordered' (2 Kgs 18.10-12). 2 Kings 17 does not have this explicit reference to Moses. Israel's transgression of laws and commandments is combined with a neglect of the warning of the prophets (2 Kgs 17.13-14, 23) and a separation from the house of David (17.21-22).[10] These theological explanations of the invasion and fall do not differ from the rationalistic 'historical' one that Hoshea, the king of Israel, had allied with the king of Egypt, revolted against the king of Assur and not paid the tribute (17.3-5). At the core of both renderings lies a question of loyalty. The immigrants, settled in Samaria by the Assyrian rulers, are made paradigmatic for this theme of loyalty: they feared Yahweh, but they worshipped other gods from their homelands (17.33, 41), which means that they in fact did not fear Yahweh, since they did not follow the Law given to the sons of Jacob (v. 34). Similarly, Hezekiah is said to have revolted against the king of Assur and refused to be his vassal (18.8). On a rationalistic level, the political situations cannot be seen to differ and yet, that is exactly what is claimed in the narrative.

8.   The exegesis of the text will not take into consideration any possibility of multiple sources behind the text. As argued in the introductory chapter, source criticism has come to a point where further text examination confuses matters; cf. also the discussion in B.O. Long, *2 Kings* (FOTL, 10; Grand Rapids: Eerdmans, 1991), pp. 200-201. Questions of 'lower criticism' will be taken up in Chapter 3 as part of discussions of provenance. I consciously use the term 'author' to imply, that, *a priori*, I consider the work to have a coherent thought and plotline, until proven otherwise.

9.   LXX: Σαμάρειαν in 18.11, but Ισραηλ in the variant account in 17.6. The distinction might be well founded, since only 17.5 (LXX and MT) mentions that the Assyrian king went against the whole country. According to Assyrian inscriptions, it was Sargon II who took the city in the first year of his reign (721 BCE), removed its population (which consisted of 27,290 people), rebuilt the city 'more splendid than before', repopulated it with people of his conquered lands and placed one of his officials as governor there. Samaria had thus become the capital of the Assyrian province *Samerina*; cf. *ARAB*, II, §§ 4, 92, 99. See, however, the discussion of the chronological problems and of the number of deportees and repopulation in B. Becking, *The Fall of Samaria: An Historical and Archaeological Study* (Leiden: E.J. Brill, 1992), Chapters 3-5.

10.   We will deal with questions about relationship between Law, Prophets and David in Chapter 5 below.

The threat against Jerusalem is set in perspective by Sennacherib's siege of Lachish, which leads Hezekiah to seek a peaceful solution. Not satisfied by the given offer—the trifling wealth of the temple as well as the palace—implicitly putting not only Hezekiah but also his patron Yahweh under siege,[11] Sennacherib sends his commander-in-chief to Hezekiah in Jerusalem in order to 'persuade' him to submit. Here follows what might be termed a biblical interpretation of 'events'.[12] Before we deal with this interpretation (2 Kgs 18.17–19.19), we need to look briefly at some Assyrian sources.

In the Bull Inscription[13] and the Taylor Prism,[14] Sennacherib's account of his third campaign is described as a campaign against 'Hittiteland'. Having taken all the coastal cities from Sidon to Ashkelon (whose king Sidqa did not immediately submit to the kings yoke and was well punished for it), Sennacherib advances to settle Judaean affairs. According to the Assyrian Annals, the cause for Sennacherib's campaign against the cities of the Shephelah and the southern coastal plain was their disloyalty. Having revolted against Padi, the king of Ekron, who was an Assyrian vassal taken into captivity by Hezekiah, the nobles of Ekron, who had sided with Hezekiah in his revolt against the Assyrians, called upon Egyptian military forces, 'the bowmen, chariots and horses of the king of Meluhha [Ethiopia]', to aid them in their struggle. They were finally defeated by Sennacherib in a fight, which began at Eltekeh, north of Ekron, and ended in a conquest of 46 of Hezekiah's strong walled cities as well as the small cities in their vicinity. Some 200,150 people were carried away as spoil, together with their belongings.

2. *What Happened to Jerusalem and Hezekiah?*

Himself, like a caged bird, I shut up in Jerusalem, his royal city. Earthworks I threw up against him,—the one coming out of his city gate I turned back to his misery. The cities of his, which I had despoiled, I cut off from his land and to Mitinti, king of Ashdod, Padi, king of Ekron, and Silli-bel, king of Gaza, I gave them. And thus I diminished his land. I added to the former tribute, and laid upon them as their yearly payment, a tax (in the form of) gifts for my majesty. As for Hezekiah, the terrifying splendor of my majesty overcame him, and the Arabs and his mercenary troops which he had brought in to strengthen Jerusalem, his royal city, took leave. (*ARAB*, II, § 240)

11. The parallel story in 2 Chron. 32.1-19 does not mention this act, but rather portrays Hezekiah as a vigorous king who, from the time of the threat, mobilizes his army and takes measures to counter the siege.

12. It is a moot point whether the author of the Hezekiah narrative interprets events or traditions. His familiarity with Assyrian traditions (cf. Chapter 3 below) and the story's parallelism with Babylonian and Seleucid siege of Jerusalem narratives (cf. Chapter 6 below) make it quite possible that the author has created this narrative from a variety of events and sources.

13. Found in Sennacherib's palace at Nineveh, and published in H.C. Rawlinson, *The Cuneiform Inscriptions of Western Asia* (5 vols.; London: n.p., 1861–84), III, Plates 12-13; *ARAB*, II, §§ 309-12.

14. Dated to 691 BCE and now in the British Museum, published in Rawlinson, *The Cuneiform Inscriptions*, I, Plates 37-38; *ARAB*, II, §§ 239-40; *ANET*, pp. 287-88.

In addition to thirty talents of gold and 800 talents of silver, various treasures as well as daughters, harems and musicians, were brought to Sennacherib in Nineveh. Does this account imply a victory for Hezekiah? Or was Jerusalem spared or left because a 'caged bird' is controlled already? According to Assyrian sources the 'cage' was not made of Assyrian troops laying siege to the city, albeit the siege language of this narrative indicates that. It was formed by the conquered Judaean cities (of which Lachish posed a severe threat [cf. the Assyrian reliefs in Sennacherib's palace in Nineveh]) as well as by the conquered areas from the Phoenician border in the north to Edom in the south, comprising all of the petty kingdoms on both sides of the Jordan. Seen in a long-term historical perspective, the conquest of Palestine had begun half a century earlier. During the reign of Tiglath-pileser III (745–727 BCE), Azariah of Judaea sought to unite the coastal areas as far north as Hamath in an attempt to revolt against the Assyrians. Moving from north to south, waves of Assyrian armies suppressed the revolt, and over years, made the various regions subject to the Assyrian Empire as vassal kingdoms, or incorporated them into the provinces of Samerina, Magiddu, Gal'aza, Du'ru and Asdudu.[15] In this perspective, the 'victorious' outcome of Hezekiah's unsuccessful revolt spared him a potential loss of his kingship, though not of his kingdom, most of which was given over to his neighbours.

In the biblical text, the 'cage' is interpreted as that which saves the remnant and gives them protection under Yahweh's power. In a 'contest' with other Yahwist shrines, Jerusalem is 'proved' to have been the chosen one. Hezekiah's disloyalty is presented as a virtue, that he would not serve the Assyrian king and that he smote the Philistines as far as Gaza: from watchtower to fortified city (2 Kgs 18.7-8). In the sermon put into the mouth of the Assyrian commander, Hezekiah is not said to have sided with the Egyptians, or to have sought strength by establishing friendship with the people of Judah, whose altars and high places he had just destroyed; that lies only implicitly in the *Rabshaqeh*'s mocking speech (18.20-25) and in the *rumour* that Tirhakah, king of Ethiopia is advancing (19.9).[16] That Hezekiah should

---

15. *ARAB*, I, § 770; N. Na'aman, 'The Kingdom of Judah under Josiah', *Tel Aviv* 18 (1991), pp. 3-71 (3-4); G.W. Ahlström, *The History of Ancient Palestine from the Palaeolithic Period to Alexander's Conquest* (ed. D.V. Edelman; JSOTSup, 146; Sheffield: JSOT Press, 1993), pp. 635-37; J. Strange, *Bibelatlas* (Copenhagen: Det Danske Bibelselskab, 1998), Maps 17, 42 and 43.

16. That 2 Kings here mentions Tirhakah, who did not become king before at least 699 BCE, should not lead to the assumption that the narrative (2 Kgs 18.17–19.37) reflects two campaigns instead of one, a view revived by J. Bright, *The History of Israel* (London: SCM Press, 2nd edn, 1972), pp. 298-308; W.H. Shea, 'Sennacherib's Second Palestinian Campaign', *JBL* 104 (1985), pp. 401-18; reasserted in *idem*, 'Jerusalem Under Siege: Did Sennacherib Attack Twice?', *BARev* 25/6 (1999) pp. 36-44, 64. The theory has been refuted by several scholars because of lack of 'evidence'; cf. the discussion in H.H. Rowley, *Men of God: Studies in Old Testament History and Prophecy* (London: Thomas Nelson, 1963), pp. 120-22; F.J. Gonçalves, *L'expédition de Sennachérib en Palestine dans la littérature hébraïque ancienne* (Paris: J. Gabalda, 1986), pp. 129-31; B. Becking, 'Chronology: A Skeleton without Flesh? Sennacherib's Campaign as a Case-Study', in L.L. Grabbe (ed.), *Like a Bird in a Cage: The Invasion of Sennacherib in 701 BCE* (ESHM, 4; London: Sheffield Academic Press, 2003), pp. 46-72. Assyrian inscriptions do not give any name to the Egyptian king nor do they mention the siege of Lachish in the 'accounts' of Sennacherib's

rely on such uncertain human powers is set in contrast to his trust in Yahweh as the only real power (18.22; 19.15-19). With the *Rabshaqeh*'s speech, the Bible sets the stage for the theological discussion in a highly ironic play on the might of the Egyptian and Assyrian gods. The *hubris* of the Assyrian commander, who himself relies on the powers of this world—gods made by men's hands, of wood and of stone—marks the Assyrian attack as a theological contest rather than a political one. This is the message given in Isaiah's song (2 Kgs 19.21-34). As in Psalm 2, Yahweh laughs at the mighty *Rabshaqeh*s of the world. Following closely this narrative of the *hubris* of the Assyrian general, the story—anticipating Jerusalem's fall—finds Hezekiah himself falling victim to this same *hubris*. Relying on the powers of this world, he offers *Babylonian* envoys whatever is in his treasure house they want. In this narrative (2 Kgs 20.12-19), the critical voice is put in the mouth of the prophet Isaiah.

Second Chronicles is even more cautious not to mention any Egyptian connection, but shares the view of 2 Kings that it was Judah's king Ahaz that had first brought in the Assyrians (Tiglath-pileser [III]; 2 Chron. 28.16-21; 2 Kgs 16.7-9), as well as that Hezekiah had separated himself from such worldly support. The weight given to the fall of Samaria by the books of Kings—that Shalmaneser conquered Samaria because Hoshea had revolted, not paid tribute and had furthermore gone into a coalition with the Egyptian king (2 Kgs 17.3-6)—is missing from Chronicles, which does not deal with the fall of Samaria at all. Contrasting with this biblical picture are the Assyrian inscriptions from Sargon II (721–705 BCE), Sennacherib (705–681 BCE) and Esarhaddon (680–669 BCE). During the time of Sargon II, the kings of Philistia, Judah, Moab and possibly Edom are claimed to have trusted their own strength, revolted against the Assyrian king and tried to bribe the Egyptian king to become their ally.[17] The Sennacherib case we have seen already. The later Esarhaddon inscription concludes that Esarhaddon conquered the Egyptian–Ethiopian king Tirhakah and his heir Ushanahuru in Egypt at Memphis and that he had subdued Ba'lu, king of Tyre, who had put his trust in his friend Tirhakah, king of Ethiopia.[18] According to these inscriptions, Egyptian presence in Palestine was a recurrent threat to the Assyrian Empire also in Hezekiah's time.

So, did Hezekiah rely on any of these powers[19] or did he have aspirations of establishing a strong independent kingship in Judaea, incorporating Israel in his kingdom?[20] Certainly, in both narratives, he challenged the patron–client system on

campaign against Judaea. In 2 Kings these 'names' set the stage for the threat against Hezekiah: the fall of mighty Lachish and the *absence* of the Kushite king, who is only advancing (2 Kgs 19.8-9).

17. *ARAB*, II, § 195.

18. *ARAB*, II, § 556.

19. Soggin, *An Introduction to the History of Israel of Judah*, p. 265: 'The coalition also relied on Egyptian help, despite the contrary that the biblical tradition attributes to the prophet Isaiah (30.1-5; 31.1-3)'.

20. M. Lubetski, 'King Hezekiah's Seal Revisited', *BARev* 27/4 (2001), pp. 44-51, 59: Hezekiah relied on Egypt and sought to placate Egyptian desire for a 'reunification' of Upper and Lower Egypt, which took place 'towards the end of the seventh century BCE [*sic*]' (cf. Lubetski's n. 22). See further the critique of Lubetski in R. Deutsch, 'Lasting Impressions: New Bullae Reveal Egyptian-Style Emblems on Judah's Royal Seals', in *BARev* 28/4 (2002), pp. 42-51, 60-62.

which Assyrian policy was based and, like Sidqa, was strongly rebuked for this. Petty kingdoms were not supposed to fight each other, rely on their own strength or make alliances if that conflicted with Assyrian interests.

In the Bible's theological interpretation, with its constant critique of reliance on the great powers of the past, which the text knows all fell one after the other, we are placed at a great distance from the events recounted. We are far from any historical event referred to as an example of how Israel's fate turned disastrous every time it relied on one or another of the empires of the world. In contrast to Hoshea, king of Israel, who put his trust in the Pharaoh of Egypt,[21] from whom Yahweh had saved them ([*sic*] 2 Kgs 17.4, 7), Hezekiah is presented as the just king, who trusted in no-one save Yahweh alone. Realizing that the gods of the nations are human works, he is ready to pronounce Yahweh as the only God (19.18-19). This is what the fight is about. Although the narrative is presented as a narrative about Jerusalem against the empires of the world, its more specific purpose is related to the unsettled question of the fallen Samaria and the saved Jerusalem. In his saving of a remnant, Yahweh has affirmed his centre.[22] The problem is not whether the gods of Hamath, Arpad, Sephar-vaim, Hena and Ivvah saved their areas, but whether they saved Samaria! (18.34). Lacking all consideration for chronological consistency (these gods were first brought into the area after the fall of Samaria; cf. 17.24), the author of 2 Kings has demonstrated that his theological interest takes priority over historiographic consistency.

The demonstration of the emptiness (הבל) and nothingness (ויהבלו) of the people, who follow such gods is made explicit in 2 Kgs 17.15-17's removal of the Israelites as a consequence of having acted thus וילכו אחרי ההבל ויהבלו ('and they went after emptiness and they became nothing'). Following the empty gods that can be cast into the fire (19.18), the unavoidable fate has manifested itself. In a variant story of this motif, it is the house of Baasha which is destroyed (שמד) after the word of the prophet Jehu, because they provoked (כעס) Yahweh to anger with their empty gods (בהבליהם, 1 Kgs 16.13). Sharing the fate of the house of Baasha, the narrative about the house of Omri is initiated by characterizing his gods as empty (הבל, 1 Kgs 16.26). In a threefold narrative structure, Israel's fate has been intensified through narrative chronology to form a climax of what ultimately happens to those following empty gods. Within this narrative (1 Kgs 16.23–2 Kgs 10.30), the Israelite king Jehu plays the role of usurper, seizing the throne from the house of Ahab in accordance with Yahweh's command (2 Kgs 10.30). Breaking the curse pattern related to the houses of Jeroboam, Baasha and Omri, the kings succeeding Jehu are not accused of this lethal sin, until it is introduced again in the narrative of Israel's

---

21. As did the nobles of Ekron and Hezekiah (*ARAB*, II, § 240) and the Philistines of Ashdod (Isa. 20.1-6). Both demonstrate that the Egyptian aid is futile. For a correlation of Assyrian inscriptions with Isaiah's condemnation of reliance on Egypt, see Laato, *About Zion I Will Not Be Silent*, pp. 68-74 (70).

22. 2 Sam. 24's narrative about Yahweh's pestilence, which kills 70,000 of the people 'from Dan to Beer-sheba', but spares Jerusalem, is another variant of the election theme, which establishes Arunah as the sacred place for the building of the Solomonic temple (cf. 1 Chron. 21.28–22.1; 2 Chron. 3.1). See further below Chapter 5.

fall.[23] In a much larger tradition, we find the same setting: the fallen generation in the desert, the fallen Israel and finally the fallen Judaea, all of which are represented in 2 King's midrash on Samaria's fall (17.7-23 [especially vv. 14-15, 19-20]).

The affirmation of Jerusalem becomes a constant conflict in Old Testament theology. Anticipating the fall of Jerusalem, Hezekiah is later placed in the role of the unjust king who secures his own peace by making treaties with the Babylonians (2 Kgs 20.12-19). Led to believe that Yahweh protects his city, we are immediately reminded that the city itself has no importance. When Yahweh's remnant is removed from the city, the city is cast into ruins. Using Manasseh as a connecting cue name,[24] Samaria and Jerusalem's fates are combined (21.12-15). In Yahweh's doom over Jerusalem, references are not only given to the fall of Samaria in the mention of Ahab (2 Kgs 21.13), but also to Israel's first sin from the time of the wandering in the desert: the making of the golden calf. In a fulfilment of the prophecy—'the day I punish, I will punish their sin upon them' (Exod. 32.34)—Yahweh no longer worries about the judgment of the Egyptians (Exod. 32.12), but predicts bringing 'such evil upon Jerusalem and Judah that the ears of every one who hears it will tingle' (2 Kgs 21.12). As the doom was pronounced over Samaria in 2 Kings 17, it is now pronounced also over Judah and Jerusalem, because they have 'provoked me to anger (כעס),[25] since the day when their fathers came out of Egypt and to this day' (21.15).

3. *Biblical Narrative and Historical Reality: Some Remarks*

Considering that the author of 1 and 2 Kings shows no interest in Judaean history as such, but only in its comparison with Israelite history, we must realize that his historiographic perspective does not belong to history but ideology. Knowing that for the centuries under consideration Israel and Judaea did not form a coherent state,[26] we can not but wonder why the author of the books put such great effort into convincing his reader that the Northern Kingdom had more to do with the petty state of Jerusalem, than had, for example, Gezer, Ashkelon, Lachish, Tyre, Sidon, and so on.[27] It is not the two-kingdom (or, in fact, many-'kingdom') structure that

23. We will return to this theme below, pp. 70-78.

24. Hjelm, *Samaritans and Early Judaism*, pp. 193, 227, 254.

25. For this term's thematic implications, see below p. 77.

26. I. Finkelstein and N.A. Silberman, *The Bible Unearthed: Archaeology's New Vision of Ancient Israel and the Origin of Its Sacred Texts* (New York: Free Press, 2001), pp. 149-50: 'As we have seen, there is no compelling archaeological evidence for the historical existence of a vast united monarchy, centered in Jerusalem, that encompassed the entire land of Israel. On the contrary, the evidence reveals a complex demographic transformation in the highlands, in which a unified ethnic consciousness began only slowly to coalesce.' See also Thompson, *Early History*, pp. 407-12.

27. Finkelstein and Silberman, *The Bible Unearthed*, p. 159: 'There is no doubt that the two Iron Age states—Israel and Judah—had much in common. Both worshipped YHWH (among other deities). Their peoples shared many legends, heroes, and tales about a common [*sic*] ancient past. They also spoke similar languages or dialects of Hebrew ("West Semitic" is a better term for the language spoken also by Ugarites, Edomites, Moabites, Ammonites and Aramaeans), and by the

creates the problem for biblical exegesis. This situation is a testified historical fact from as early as late Bronze–Iron I transition, and at least from the ninth century BCE onwards.[28] It is the 'utopian' unified state, with its single-people structure, that creates the problem. As stated by Gary Knoppers: 'Historically, factionalism among the tribes may have been the norm, but the Deuteronomist upholds Israel as an "organism", whose unity is quite apparent during the first period of Solomon's rule'.[29] Contrary to Knoppers' more historicist reading of the biblical material, I do not think that we can use biblical 'evidence' for '(dis)unity' as 'a vital issue in the pre-exilic era' or as a witness to any historical reality at that time of 'factionalism among the tribes', since these 'tribes' are part of the paradigmatic biblical narrative.

The unity of Iron Age Palestine in extra-biblical sources is not a given and occurs only fragmentarily in references to various sorts of coalitions during the Assyrian period. Without the paradigmatic use of this idealized past of the first period of Solomon's rule,[30] we would not have had a biblical monarchic (or perhaps also pre-monarchic) history.[31] We might instead have had more objective stories about Palestine's petty kingdoms[32] and about the ways they interrelated in their various dealings with internal and external enemies. We might have had stories about the highly developed Philistine culture, as well as of the impact of the Aramaean culture far beyond its own borders.[33] We might have had stories about life in the Assyrian province *Samerina* for the four-fifths of the indigenous population, which had remained there.[34] Contrary to what the Bible purports and what scholars

eighth century BCE, both wrote in the same script. But they were also very different from each other in the demographic composition, economic potential, material culture and relationship with their neighbours. Put simply, Israel and Judah experienced quite different histories and developed distinctive cultures. In a sense Judah was little more than Israel's rural hinterland' (sparsely populated and with a significant pastoral segment until the seventh century BCE; cf. pp. 154, 159).

28. Finkelstein and Silberman, *The Bible Unearthed*, pp. 153-59. Thompson, *Early History*, pp. 412-15.

29. Knoppers, *Two Nations Under God*, I, 6, see also p. 4: 'Indeed, there is evidence in a variety of biblical sources and within the Deuteronomistic History itself that (dis)unity was a vital issue in the preexilic era'.

30. Knoppers, *Two Nations Under God*, I, pp. 54-56.

31. Van Seters, *In Search of History*, pp. 316-17, 320: 'While the record of the monarchy in Kings focuses on evaluating the progress of people and their kings from the time of Solomon until the end, this appraisal does not make sense without the story of the rise of the monarchy, the enunciation of the divine promise to David, and the establishment of the true cult center in Jerusalem under Solomon. The author must first set out these constitutional elements of the Israelite state by which all the "reforms" must be judged.'

32. Or larger ones, such as the Omride dynasty; cf. Finkelstein and Silberman, *The Bible Unearthed*, pp. 169-95.

33. P.-E. Dion, *Les Araméens à l'âge du fer: histoire politique et structures sociales* (EBib, NS 34; Paris: J. Gabalda, 1997); P.M.M. Daviau, J.W. Wevers and M. Weigl (eds.), *The World of the Aramaeans: Studies in Honour of Paul-Eugène Dion* (JSOTSup, 324-36; 3 vols.; Sheffield: Sheffield Academic Press, 2001). This lack of biblical as well as scholarly interest in Syria-Palestine's history, which do not serve biblical interests, was the concern of K.W. Whitelam, *The Invention of Ancient Israel: The Silencing of Palestinian History* (London: Routledge, 1996).

34. Finkelstein and Silberman, *The Bible Unearthed*, p. 221.

deceptively have concluded,[35] Samaria's population did not cease to exist after the Assyrian conquest.[36] It might not be wrong to understand this paradigm as mirroring the 'cessation' of Judah and Jerusalem after the Assyrian and Babylonian conquests, which in literature did not lead to a repopulation of Jerusalem, but to the myth of the empty land.[37]

How did these remaining people—citizens of Assyria—with their priesthood, royal houses, and so on, function and interact with the rest of Palestine, most of which came under Assyrian dominion in less than one generation after the fall of Aram, Samaria and the Transjordan? How did they interact with the new settlers under Assyrian and Babylonian dominion with Samaria and Megiddo[38] as provincial capitals and Bethel as an important cult site from the seventh century until well into the Persian period?[39] What opposition was created by the status given to

35. Even some of those scholars most critical towards the biblical presentation; for instance, Thompson, *Early History*, p. 415: 'By the end of the sixth-century, the *Jerusalem* and *Judah* of the Assyrian period had ceased to exist as thoroughly as had the *Samaria* and *Israel* of the eighth-century'; see, however, *idem*, 'A History of Palestine: The Debate', *The Journal of Palestinian Archaeology* II/1 (2001), pp. 18-24; *idem*, 'Introduction: Can a History of Ancient Palestine and Jerusalem be Written?', in Thompson (ed.), *Jerusalem in Ancient History and Tradition*, pp. 1-15; N.P. Lemche, *Ancient Israel: A New History of Israelite Society* (The Biblical Seminar, 5; Sheffield: JSOT Press, 1988), p. 128; *idem*, *The Israelites in History and Tradition* (Louisville, KY: Westminster/John Knox Press, 1998), p. 85, arguing, however, also for a continuation of the material culture: 'The local population might have received a massive contribution of foreigners in the Assyrian period, something that should be reflected in the material remains, but most of it remained stable, tilling their farmland, breeding children, and living a peasant's uneventful life'.

36. B. Oded, *Mass Deportations and Deportees in the Neo-Asyrian Empire* (Wiesbaden: Reichert, 1979), pp. 26-32, 116-35, clearly shows that while Phoenicia, lower Galilee, Judaea and the southern coastal areas were highly affected by several deportations, especially from the time of Sennacherib onwards, only the town of Samaria itself had its population removed. In central Palestine most of its population remained unchanged. Interestingly, 2 Kgs 18.11 of the LXX witness this against the MT (cf. n. 9 above). See I. Eph'al, 'The Samarian(s) in Assyrian Sources', in M. Cogan and I. Eph'al (eds.), *Ah, Assyria, Studies in Assyrian History and Ancient Near Eastern Historiography Presented to Hayim Tadmor* (Jerusalem: Magnes Press, 1991), pp. 36-45; *idem*, 'The "Samaritans" in the Assyrian Sources', in E. Stern and H. Eshel (eds.), *The Samaritans* (ספר השומרונים) (Jerusalem: Yad Ben-Zvi Press, 2002 [Hebrew]), pp. 34-44; N. Na'aman, 'Population Changes in Palestine Following Assyrian Deportations', *Cathedra* 54 (1988), pp. 43-63 (Hebrew).

37. H.M. Barstad, *The Myth of the Empty Land: A Study of the History and Archaeology of Judah During the 'Exilic' period* (Oslo: Scandinavian University Press, 1996); Hjelm, *Samaritans and Early Judaism*, pp. 16, 149-51.

38. Finkelstein and Silberman, *The Bible Unearthed*, pp. 216-17.

39. Finkelstein and Silberman, *The Bible Unearthed*, pp. 221-22: 'In the hill country around the city of Samaria, which was destined to serve as the hub of the new Assyrian province, the deportation was apparently minimal... In the northern valleys, the Assyrians destroyed the Israelite administrative centers but left the rural population (which was basically Canaanite, Phoenician, and Aramean in tradition) unhurt... Indeed, surveys and excavations in the Jezreel valley confirm the surprising demographic continuity. And about half of the rural sites near Samaria continued to be occupied in subsequent centuries...a significant number of Israelites were still living in the hill country of Samaria, including the southern area of Bethel, alongside the new populations brought by the Assyrians'.

Samaria as an administrative and political centre for Assyrian interests in central Palestine? 2 Kings 17.24-41 offers an ironic play on tendencies of Assyrian dominion and cultural assimilation when Samaria's replaced population worships Yahweh rather than Ashur. We might have had documents to support these stories, rendering information, inscriptions memorializing the grandeur of, say, Philistine, Aramaean, Israelite and Judaean kings. Did it all vanish after the writing of the biblical narratives?[40] Did the Josianic scribes' attempt 'to authorise massive royal reforms', in order to 'reverse the outstanding transgressions committed by both his [Josiah's] southern and his northern predecessors',[41] eliminate competing stories?[42] Or does this authorization also belong to the mythic past, which in literature only came to life again in the second century BCE's extra-biblical documentation of the Maccabaean state.[43]

The argumentation in Judges–2 Kings is not descriptive, but prescriptive. Moving backwards, we learn that when Israel was finally united under one ruler with its centre in Jerusalem, everyone lived in peace from the Euphrates to Gaza, from Dan to Beer-sheba (1 Kgs 5.4-5). This is exactly what the Assyrian cupbearer, the *Rab-shaqeh*, offers (2 Kgs 18.31-32) and what Isaiah prophesies (19.29-31) to Jerusalem's remnant. This, however, is a literary and not a historical departure. History is used and created.[44] Both Van Seters and Knoppers fail to recognize that the

---

40. G. Garbini, *History & Ideology in Ancient Israel* (London: SCM Press, 1988), pp. 17-20, rightly asks (p. 17): ' "where are the Hebrew inscriptions of the Iron Age?", not one of the forty kings from Saul to Zedekiah has left a direct trace of his name'; and (p. 19): '[where are] "the documents of the Persian period?": the epigraphic and archaeological remains are reduced to a tiny quantity until well into the Hellenistic period'.

41. Knoppers, *Two Nations Under God*, I, p. 56.

42. Finkelstein and Silberman, *The Bible Unearthed*, p. 167: 'It was Josiah's ambition to expand to the north and take over the territories in the highlands that once belonged to the northern kingdom. Thus the Bible supports that ambition by explaining that the northern kingdom was established in the territories of the mythical united monarchy, which was ruled from Jerusalem; that it was a sister Israelite state; that its people were Israelites who would have worshipped in Jerusalem; that the Israelites still living in these territories must turn their eyes to Jerusalem; and that Josiah, the heir to the Davidic throne and to YHWH's eternal promise to David, is the only legitimate heir to the territories of vanquished Israel. On the other hand the authors of the Bible needed to delegitimize the northern cult—especially the Bethel shrine—and to show that the distinctive religious traditions of the northern kingdom were all evil, that they should be wiped out and replaced by the centralized worship at the Temple of Jerusalem. The Deuteronomistic History accomplishes all this'. Further (p. 223) they state: 'Had Israel survived, we might have received a parallel, competing, and very different history. But with the Assyrian destruction of Samaria and the dismantling of its institutions of royal power, any such competing histories were silenced.' Needless to say, it is the biblical narrative that informs us that such a competition ever existed in the Iron Age!

43. Garbini, *History & Ideology in Ancient Israel*, pp. 174-75.

44. Auld, *Kings Without Privilege*, pp. 172-73, argues for a construed 'all Israel' ideology in Samuel–Kings on the basis of an earlier Judaean history represented in his 'Shared Text' of Chronicles and Samuel–Kings. Auld's Shared Text should, however, be used with great caution as it is not a source and not representative of common material in Kings and Chronicles, but Auld's establishment of what he thinks might have been a common source.

creation of the idealized David–Solomonic past cannot have been modelled upon the biblical Josianic period of the books of Kings. In this book, the northerners are not invited to participate in the cult reforms or in the Passover celebration (2 Kgs 23). Unification is not within the scope of the narrative, and Josiah's reign does not signify the recreation of Great Israel, but rather an election of Judah and Jerusalem after the disappearance of the Northern Kingdom. It is the books of Chronicles which offer us allusions to the warranted scenario (2 Chron. 34.9, 21; 35.4, 18).[45] If for any reason Josiah's court dreamt of extending Judah's borders or perhaps succeeded in doing so—as has most often been maintained in biblical scholarship[46]— its 'royal archives', supposedly represented in Kings' narrative, are rather negligent of such idealistic political efforts.[47] Biblical scholars have deceptively filled in the gaps and read into the biblical narrative hopes and longings deduced from the 'false similarity' between Josiah's reign and the days of the United Monarchy.[48] Similarly, the often-argued expansion of Jerusalem (partly based on archaeological findings) and its increased importance in seventh-century BCE Palestine as the sole kingdom of the southern Levant, lacks consideration of the political dynamics of the entire region, in which especially the Philistine and later also the Phoenician areas shared Jerusalem's status as Assyrian vassals.[49]

4. *Motifs and Themes in the Hezekiah Narrative's Zion Ideology*

To speak about a Zion ideology in the Deuteronomistic history, or for that matter in the Chronistic history, is a kind of *eisegesis* which takes its content from the Prophets and Psalms. The lack of any conscious Zion terminology in the historical books, which prefers the term עיר־דוד to ציון—occurrences of the latter term are found only in the prophetic material of the Hezekiah story and in the mention of the move of the ark from 'the city of David, the same as Zion' to the temple in 1 Kgs 8.1 par. 2 Chron. 5.2 (cf. 2 Sam. 5.7 par. 1 Chron. 11.5)—forms a sharp contrast to the term's numerous occurrences in, for example, the book of Isaiah. This book, on the other hand, only mentions עיר־דוד once (Isa. 22.9). Not only does the specific term not occur often in the Deuteronomistic History, neither does its associated

---

45. Auld, *Kings Without Privilege*, p. 125, leaves the false impression that 2 Kgs 23.22 shares with 2 Chron. 35.18 an 'all Israel' participation in Josiah's Passover celebration.

46. See the critique of such interpretations in N. Na'aman, 'The Kingdom of Judah under Josiah', pp. 3-71; Ahlström, *The History of Ancient Palestine*, pp. 764-81; W.B. Barrick, 'On the Meaning of בית־ה/במות and בתי־הבמות and the Composition of the Kings History', *JBL* 115 (1996), pp. 621-42; Finkelstein and Silberman, *The Bible Unearthed*, pp. 347-53 (Appendix F).

47. Ahlström, *The History of Ancient Palestine*, p. 766: 'It is inconceivable that the biblical writer would not mention anything about Josiah's extension of his kingdom, had it occurred, for such military–political success would have been a very important factor in the glorification of Josiah as the most important king after David. There was simply no space for Josiah to play a grand political role.'

48. Na'aman, 'The Kingdom of Judah under Josiah', pp. 55-60.

49. E. Stern, *Archaeology of the Land of the Bible*. II. *The Assyrian, Babylonian and Persian Periods (732–33.2 BCE)* (Anchor Bible Reference Library; New York: Doubleday, 2001).

terminology of trust (root בטח)[50] and salvation (root ישׁע). The latter is a frequent term in Judges and the books of Samuel. Almost half of its occurrences refer to Yahweh's acts as saviour of his people or of David.[51] Child's distinction between בטח as Deuteronomistic rather than Isaianic and between ישׁע as Isaianic rather than Deuteronomistic[52] cannot be confirmed. Both terms clearly belong to prophetic and psalmodic literature. Both terms occur nowhere in the books of Kings except in the Hezekiah story's testimony of whom to trust (2 Kgs 18.5, 19, 20, 21, 22, 24, 30; 19.10) and from whom to expect salvation (18.29, 30, 32, 33, 34, 35; 19.11, 12; 20.6). The similar use of these terms in Chronicles' Hezekiah narrative and their remarkably few occurrences outside this narrative[53] give reason to believe that we are not only dealing with a specific theme, but also with a specific narrative. While the patronage motif of 'my people—your god', such as expressed in the covenantal language of Deuteronomy 28, is a kind of pre-supposition for the Deuteronomistic History as a whole, its adherence to the 'threat–salvation' motif of prophetic and psalmodic literature is strikingly absent in Kings' part of the Deuteronomistic History. In the books of Kings, Hezekiah is the only example of a king praying to Yahweh in the temple in a critical situation, which could not be solved by paying off the oppressive foreign rulers. In similar narrative compositions, Hezekiah's predecessors had treasures of temple and palace with which to avert threatening disaster from neighbouring rulers: Rehoboam to the Egyptian Pharaoh Shishak (1 Kgs 14.25-26);[54] Asa to the Aramaean king Ben-hadad (1 Kgs 15.18-20; cf. 2 Chron. 16.2-4); Jehoash to the Aramaean king Hazael (2 Kgs 12.18-19);[55] and Ahaz to the Assyrian king Tiglath-pileser (2 Kgs 16.7-9; cf. 2 Chron. 28.21[56]). Both Asa and Ahaz bribed their future overlords to protect them against minor enemies: the Israelite king Baasha in the Asa narrative (1 Kgs 15.16-22); the Aramaean king Rezin together with the Israelite king Pekah (and perhaps also the king of Edom) in the Ahaz narrative (2 Kgs 16.5-9). None of these four kings 'cried to the Lord';

---

50. Deut. 28.52; Judg. 9.26; 18.7, 10, 27.

51. Judg. 6.9; 8.34; 1 Sam. 7.3; 10.18; 12.11; 17.37; 2 Sam. 12.7; 22.1, 49.

52. B.S. Childs, *Isaiah and the Assyrian Crisis* (SBT, 2/3; London: SCM Press, 1967), pp. 84-85.

53. 1 Kgs 5.5; 2 Kgs 17.39; 1 Chron. 5.20; 11.14; 16.35 and 25.15 (belonging to a similar theme).

54. The pattern in this narrative is slightly different from the other examples, since Shishak goes into Jerusalem and '*takes* the treasures from the temple and palace' (cf. also 2 Chron. 12.9-10), as do also Jehoash of Israel (2 Kgs 14.14; 2 Chron. 25.24) and Nebuchadnezzar (2 Kgs 24.13; 25.13-17; 2 Chron. 36.18). 2 Chron. 12.2-9's thematic variant of the Hezekiah narrative, has Shishak conquer all the fortified towns of Judah on his way to Jerusalem, the king and the people humbling themselves, spare of the city, vassalage and despoliation (v. 9 par. 1 Kgs 14.25-26).

55. The counterpart to this in 2 Chron. 24 does not follow Kings' bribe pattern. Auld's Shared Text (*Kings Without Privilege*, pp. 116, 127 n. 1) is directed by Kings' narrative and does not take into consideration that Chronicles is telling a different story, one in which Aram plunders Judah and Jerusalem and defeats Jehoash (2 Chron. 24.23-25; cf. also 25.24: Jehoash of Israel's defeat of Judah's king Amaziah son of Jehoash of Judah).

56. Against Auld, *Kings Without Privilege*, p. 119 n. 1: 'There is no counterpart in Chronicles to what follows in Kings (v. 8)'. There is, in fact, though it is not fashioned in Kings' language.

they paid their way out of the danger. The foreign rulers either went away (Shishak and Hazael) or they 'listened to them' (שמע), which means they accepted the bribe (Ben-hadad [1 Kgs 15.20] and Tiglath-pileser [2 Kgs 16.9]) and conquered the minor enemies.[57] In three of these four narratives the threat is set against Jerusalem.[58] In ABABA structure, we finally find Hezekiah not bribing put paying tribute to the Assyrian king Sennacherib (2 Kgs 18.14-16).[59] Moving a step further than in the previous stories, the Assyrian king does not accept the payment and there is no mighty king to bribe. Hezekiah is check-mated and his belief in Yahweh is put to the test.[60]

The test is not given in the voice of the prophet, but in that voice of the Assyrian commander. The language of this commander, however, is indistinguishable from the language of the biblical prophets.[61] Playing with the motif of threat–salvation,

57. In Chronicles, only Asa benefits from the bribe action, but is rebuked for having trusted Aram's king rather than Yahweh (2 Chron. 16.2-7).

58. Israel's king Baasha's rebuilding of Ramah in the Asa narrative (1 Kgs 15.16-22) is in order to prevent people from going to Asa of Judah and does not explicitly mention Jerusalem.

59. The verses are missing in Isa. 36.1-2 and in 2 Chron. 32. Kings' wider compositional pattern of treasure transference is, in fact, an ABCABCA pattern having Rehoboam, Amaziah and Zedekiah robbed of treasures (A); Asa and Ahaz bribing overlords to protect them against minor enemies (B) and Jehoash and Hezekiah paying their enemies (C).

60. F.J. Gonçalves, '2 Rois 18.13–20.19 par. Isaïe 36–39. Encore une fois, lequel des deux livres fut le premier?', in J.-M. Auwers and A. Wénin (eds.), *Lectures et relectures de la Bible* (Festschrift P.-M. Bogaert; BETL, 144; Leuven: Leuven University Press, 1999), pp. 27-55 (31): 'En rapportant la conquête de toutes les villes de Juda, ce verset souligne la gravité de la situation supposée par 2 R 18.17–19.37 par. Is 36.2–37.38 et, du fait même, met en lumiére la grandeur de la confiance d'Ézéchias en Yahvé'. The possibility of reading 2 Kgs 18.13a, 14-16, together with 2 Kgs 20, 2 Chron. 32 and Isa. 22 and based on the Azekah inscription as an account reflecting Sargon II's retributive action against Hezekiah's conquests of Philistine areas before 712 BCE might be historically justified; cf. J. Goldberg, 'Two Assyrian Campaigns against Hezekiah and Later Eighth Century Biblical Chronology', *Bib* 80/3 (1999), pp. 360-90. Reading 2 Kgs 18.14-16 as reflecting Sennacherib's Campaign in 701 BCE and 2 Kgs 18.17–19.37 as reflecting Sargon II's *possible* campaign against Judah (and Jerusalem) in 715 BCE (not to be confused with his campaign against Ashdod in 712 BCE), as Becking ('Chronology: "A Skeleton Without Flesh?"') has recently argued, partly following A.K. Jenkins ('Hezekiah's Fourteenth Year: A New Interpretation of 2 Kings XVIII 13–XIX 37', *VT* 26 [1976], pp. 284-98 [296]), is equally possible, although both proposals raise considerable problems. The redactor of 2 Kings' Hezekiah narrative, however, seems not to have had the intention of rhetorically separating events and thereby diminishing the threat faced by Hezekiah—a matter Becking is well aware of. The repetitive וישלח (2 Kgs 18.14, 17) together with a repetition of מלך אשור (vv. 16, 17) indicates the continuity of the paragraphs.

61. K.A.D. Smelik, 'Distortion of Old Testament Prophecy: The Purpose of Isaiah xxxvi and xxxvii', *OTS* 24 (1986), pp. 70-93 (86): 'Rabshakeh is a literary figure who plays the opposite to Isaiah and has to speak in a similar way'. E. Ben Zvi, 'Who Wrote the Speech of Rabshakeh and When?', *JBL* 109 (1990), pp. 79-92; Long, *2 Kings*, pp. 219-20, following the argument of Childs, *Isaiah and the Assyrian Crisis*, pp. 84-85, but without accepting Child's argument for historical veracity based on comparative studies and redaction criticism: 'At best we may assert that the biblical writer's presentation of the Rabshakeh's disputation accords with literary convention found in other types of contemporary historiography (e.g., royal inscriptions) and historical materials (e.g., letters). The scene may or may not have been fictionalized in ways familiar to us from a few

the *Rabshaqeh* offers the Judaeans listening on the wall a patronage-solution. As Yahweh is said to have been with Hezekiah (2 Kgs 18.7) because of his faithfulness towards Yahweh (expressed in the terms שמר and לא־סר, דבק, בטח, 18.5-6), the people are promised a future life in a land flowing with wine, olive and honey if they will abandon their former patron (18.31-32) and 'be with' the king of Assur. Using the covenantal language of the Pentateuch (especially Deut. 28), the narrative is the sole example in the books of Kings of a fulfilment of the 'my people—your Lord' relationship expressed in Solomon's prayer in the temple inauguration narrative (1 Kgs 8.23-53). The *Rabshaqeh's* speech is set to contrast with Yahweh's promise to Moses' people: a land flowing with milk and honey, if they had the courage to go in and fight with giants (Num. 14.8-9, 24). Just so, the *Rabshaqeh* takes the role of trying to seduce the people into believing that they can have their milk and honey without fighting (the Assyrian giant), that they shall live and not die in a land 'as their own land, a land of grain and wine, of bread and vineyards, of olive trees and honey' (2 Kgs 18.32 [Isa. 36.16 does not mention 'olive trees and honey']). While the Israelites in the desert did not have the courage to fight against the giants (which the spies had said lived in the country) but cried, complained, rebelled[62] and died (Num. 14.1-12,[63] 21-24, 28-30; 16.12-15; 26.64; Deut. 1.26)— and while only Caleb and Joshua stood the test to become this story's surviving remnant (Num. 14.24, 30; 26.65; Deut. 1.36; Josh. 14.6-14)—the people on Jerusalem's wall remain silent to the *Rabshaqeh's* promise of survival. Obedient to the king's command—'do not answer him'—they demonstrate their allegiance (2 Kgs 18.36). And good for them; for it is not Assur's but Yahweh's vineyards that are prophesied a flourishing future in Isaiah's song (19.29-31).

Demonstration of power belongs to the structure of patronage. Who is the mightier? The giants of the land flowing with milk and honey or Yahweh, who had promised the people a secure future in that land. Mistrust in Yahweh's ability to fulfil his promise was disastrous. The language employed to express the range and consequence of such a mistake belongs to the realm of pride. With words like despise (נאץ/נאצה, 2 Kgs 19.3), mock (חרף, 2 Kgs 19.4, 16, 23) and scorn (גדף, לעג, בוז, 19.6, 21, 22), the *Rabshaqeh* is judged to have despised the living god. As

---

Greek and Roman historians, who invented credible speeches for their literary personages (see Montgomery, *Kings*, p. 487)'. So also, G.H. Jones, *I and II Kings* (2 vols.; Grand Rapids: Eerdmans, 1984), II, p. 570; D. Rudman, 'Is Rabshakeh also Among the Prophets? A Rhetorical Study of 2 Kings XVIII 17-35', *VTQ* 50/1 (2000), pp. 100-10.

62.   Caleb's admonition to the people, not to rebel (מרד) against Yahweh, further confirms the relationship between these narratives, as the word's rare occurrences in Kings are found in Hezekiah's rebellion against Assyria (2 Kgs 18.7, 20) and in Jehoiakim's and Zedekiah's rebellion against the Babylonians (24.1, 20). While only Hezekiah's rebellion is judged positively, Israel's rebellion against Yahweh and Judah's rebellion against the Babylonians is doomed to fail. In this light, the author's judgment of Hezekiah's co-operation with the Babylonians (20.12-19) seems ambiguous.

63.   In Num. 14.1-12 they are slain by Yahweh with plague (נכה בדבר), as were the Israelites in Exod. 32.35 (נגף) and the Assyrians in 2 Kgs 19.35 par. Isa. 37.36 (נכה). Whether the last act involves a plague or something else (cf. the discussion in various commentaries) seems to have been without interest to the author, who stresses the fact that the Assyrians were slain by Yahweh.

Yahweh did not allow the Israelites to enter the Promised Land because of their contempt for him (נאץ, Num. 14.11, 23), so Sennacherib shall not enter the city (2 Kgs 19.28). The role of the giants—a play of comparables—is the role played by the mighty king of Assur.

The argument implicit to this comparison is given in Hezekiah's prayer. Although the kings of Assur had fought against people, countries and gods, they nevertheless had not demonstrated superior power, since 'these were not gods, but the work of men's hands, wood and stone' (2 Kgs 19.17-18). The emptiness of such man-made gods is comparable to the emptiness of the all-too-feared giants whose 'shadow has left them' (מעליהם[64] סר צלם, Num. 14.9). Of all the possibilities for using this metaphor (cf. Pss. 102.12; 109.23; 144.4), we find its only occurrence in the books of Kings in Hezekiah's illness narrative. His shadow did not leave him but was delayed for another 15 years, because of his tears (2 Kgs 20.5, 9-11). This life–death (emptiness) metaphor is given further expression in the designation of Yahweh's qualities: that he is a living God (אלהים חי, 2 Kgs 19.4, 16) and the only one (אתה יהוה אלהים לבדך, 2 Kgs 19.19). In Number's rebellion story, Yahweh's anger is a consequence of the challenge to his sovereignty: חי אני וימלא כבוד־יהוה את־כל־הארץ ('As I live and the Glory of Yahweh fills the earth', Num. 14.21, 28) and a demonstration of his capacity to punish whom he wishes.[65] As with Israel's tears in the Josiah narrative, so did the people's tears come much too late. Moses' plea for mercy, because of Egypt's embarrassing judgment—that Yahweh might not have had the power to lead the people into the Promised Land (Num. 14.16)— forms a striking contrast to the Exodus narrative's demonstration of Yahweh's absolute power in front of Pharaoh—אין כמני בכל־הארץ ('there is none like me in the whole world', Exod. 9.13-16; cf. 14.4)—and to the Hezekiah narrative's demonstration of that power in front of Sennacherib. In biblical theology, salvation and punishment are problems both of narrative composition and of dogma. Obliteration is not total. Having been expelled twice—in the desert and in the exile tradition— hope is still awaiting the day of Yahweh's bringing home his scattered remnant as king of the whole world, and he is one, and his name is one (Zech. 14.9). The Hezekiah narrative's anticipation of this theme, which carries the weight of the whole world's submission to this god, connects it with the Zion ideology of the Prophets and Psalms.

Another matter, which needs to be dealt with, is the composition of the threefold narrative: the Assyrian threat, Hezekiah's illness and the Babylonian envoys. Contrasting Hezekiah's faithfulness in the Sennacherib narrative, Hezekiah's unfaithfulness in the Babylonian narrative seems to follow as a critical anti-climax, extinguishing all hopes for a future survival. The problems of dating the narrated event and Hezekiah's relationship with the Babylonian king Merodach-baladan (Marduk-apla-Idinna), who reigned from 721–710 and again from 705–702 BCE, are due to 2 Kings' placement of this narrative after the Sennacherib invasion. In a

---

64. LXX: ὁ καιρός.

65. The thematic reiteration of Moses' plea for mercy and God's steadfast anger in the Pentateuch (Exod. 32.30-34; Num. 14.11-45; Deut. 28–30) forms a contrast to Solomon's confidence in Yahweh's mercy, 'since there is no man who does not sin' (1 Kgs 8.31-40, [46-]51).

world of stories, however, this is fully justified, as is Tirhakah's advance only, which in a world of reality would have given the Assyrian armies enough time to conquer Jerusalem. With the placement of Hezekiah's cure from his illness between these narratives, the author of 2 Kings made a compromise between his wish for portraying Hezekiah as a king relying on Yahweh only, without neglecting Hezekiah's dependence on Babylonian support, however indirect that may have been. The key to the understanding lies in the movement of the shadow. Moving Hezekiah's shadow ten steps backwards, future fate became changeable. With the involvement of the saving of Jerusalem in the promise of cure (2 Kgs 20.5-6), the author's intention has become visible.[66]

In 2 Kings' rearrangement of the Hezekiah sickness narrative, the sign signifying a 'delay of disaster' leads right over to the Babylonian envoy narrative. The reader is left to consider whether Hezekiah is still sick (חלה), or whether he has recovered as Isa. 39.1 explicitly states (חלה ויחזק). The ambiguity invites an interpretation of the event both as having taken place before Hezekiah's encounter with the Assyrians and as being a sign of 'delayed judgment',[67] anticipating the Babylonian conquest. The chronological possibilities are further indicated in the imprecise 'at that time' (בעת ההיא).[68] If the Assyrians had had the intention of destroying Jerusalem, their troubles with the Babylonians prevented this act from being carried out. Compared with similar settings in the books of Kings, the narrative should have presented Hezekiah as bribing the Babylonians before or during the Assyrian invasion as did Asa to the Aramaean king Ben-hadad (1 Kgs 15.18-20) and Ahaz to the Assyrian king Tiglath-pileser (2 Kgs 16.7-9). This would have placed the Hezekiah narrative within the compositional pattern of the books of Kings. Placed within the authorship of the book of Isaiah, however, the narrative follows a different pattern: threat against Jerusalem, Yahweh's salvation of the city, sign of life or death, salvation by the hand of a mighty king (cf. the Ahaz narrative, Isa. 7.1–8.4, and the Hezekiah narrative, Isa. 36–39).[69]

---

66.   While Long (*2 Kings*, pp. 238-39) does not make this interpretation, he argues for the temporal relationship, in the author's paratactic mode of composition as a way of expressing his 'thematic concerns all the more forcefully'. The incompatibility of Hezekiah's giving away the temple treasures to Sennacherib (2 Kgs 18.15-16) and still being able to show all his riches to the Babylonians (20.13) made Long suggest that the incidents took place during Jerusalem's siege (p. 191). The incompatibility only relates to the version in the books of Kings, not in Isaiah. This is a fact overlooked by J.D.W. Watts (*Isaiah 34–66* [WBC, 25; Waco, TX: Word Books, 1987], p. 64), who suggests that Hezekiah's illness in the Babylonian envoy narrative might be a metaphor for Hezekiah's vassalage to Assyria (714–705 BCE) and that his recovery of strength refers to his announcement that he was throwing off that yoke at the time of Sargon's death. This would put Hezekiah on an equal footing with the Babylonian leader and place the event in 705–703 BCE, 'a period when Hezekiah still had treasures to show'.

67.   Watts, *Isaiah 34–66*, p. 65.

68.   E. Würthwein, *Die Bücher der Könige 1. Kön. 17–2. Kön. 25: Übersetzt und erklärt* (ATD, 11.2; Göttingen: Vandenhoeck & Ruprecht, 1984), pp. 435-37.

69.   The discussion about the provenance of the common Hezekiah narrative from Kings or Isaiah (2 Kgs 18.13 + 18.17–20.19; Isa. 36–39 [except 38.9-20]) will be taken up in Chapter 3. For now I simply assume that it belongs primarily to the book of Isaiah.

While 2 Kings' Ahaz and Hezekiah portraits are set in contrast to each other, Isaiah's portrait of these kings demonstrates their similarities. As Ahaz received a sign of salvation (Isa. 7.11-16) so did Hezekiah.[70] In both narratives the sign is signifying Jerusalem's salvation. In Isaiah's setting, it is not Ahaz who brings in the Assyrians—they were brought in by Yahweh (Isa. 8.7; 10.6), but it is Hezekiah, who opens his doors for the Babylonians. Confirming the *Rabshaqeh*'s question— 'Were it without Yahweh's consent that I went up against this land' (Isa. 36.10 and 2 Kgs 18.25)—Isaiah's absolute monotheism[71] could not allow any other interpretation.

In a paratactic setting, the author of 2 Kings made use of the Babylonian envoy narrative to include hope and despair, and to present Hezekiah as relying on Yahweh alone in a strong contrast to the Assyrian king Sennacherib's reliance on worldly gods. Interpretation of the Babylonian event as an anticipation of Jerusalem's fate[72] is based on the historical knowledge expressed by the prophet, whose closure of the narrative leads right over into the story's end in exile (Isa. 40.2). 2 Kings' use of the narrative, however, might serve quite another purpose. Having defeated the Assyrians, signified by the slaying of Assur's 185,000 warriors, the road is prepared for the Babylonians to take over. It was not the Babylonians, however, who slew the Assyrians. They were slain by Yahweh because of Hezekiah's faithfulness. In 2 Kings this is further qualified in the 'disappearance' of the Assyrians from the following narrative, although in history Hezekiah, Manasseh and Josiah had to submit to the Assyrians.[73] In Na'aman's view the Deuteronomistic author sought to avoid presenting Judaea and especially Josiah as 'subordinate to foreign rulers for most of his days—a subordination perceived in the Deuteronomistic outlook as unfitting the righteous king'.[74] However fitting such an interpretation is, it needs to explain the accusation of idolatry related to the Manasseh and Amon narratives. The close connection between cult and policy in Old Testament narratives makes it extremely difficulty to make a certain distinction between the language of making alliances and the language of subordination. While submission forced upon a client avoids condemnation, the making of treaties and alliances becomes comparable to idolatry and harlotry as violation of patronage relationship.

70. Josephus, *Ant.* 10.25, ascribes Hezekiah's illness to severe distemper and melancholy, caused by the lack of an heir to the throne: 'he was childless'. The modern reader, of course immediately brings into mind the Abraham narrative, which neither Josephus nor the author of the Hezekiah narrative 'refer to'. The tragedy of the Hezekiah narrative that his descendants shall be taken into captivity forms the climax in Josephus' narrative.

71. Ben Zvi, 'Who Wrote the Speech of Rabshakeh?', p. 85: 'There is no doubt that the idea is in the Isaianic tradition (see Isa. 10.5-6); however, it is a *sine qua non* in any theological system that claims that YHWH governs human history, or at least Judean history'.

72. Watts, *Isaiah 34–66*, p. 65; Sweeney, *Isaiah 1–39*, pp. 508-11.

73. *ARAB*, II, § 690 (during Esarhaddon) and II, § 876 (during Ashurbanipal). 2 Chronicles does not share in this implicit ideological interpretation of Sennacherib's defeat, but accords with Assyrian annals on Manasseh's submission (2 Chron. 33.10-12). See further, Na'aman, 'The Kingdom of Judah under Josiah', pp. 35, 40-41, 55. E. Ben Zvi, 'Malleability and Its Limits: Sennacherib's Campaign Against Judah as a Case Study', in Grabbe (ed.), *Like a Bird in a Cage*, pp. 73-105.

74. Na'aman, 'The Kingdom of Judah under Josiah', p. 41.

5. *Hezekiah and the Function of the Judgment Formulae*
in the Books of Kings

Most of the northern and southern kings, mentioned in the books of Kings, are presented with a judgment formula, which in a dense summary of the religious conduct of each king, characterizes him as either good or bad. Since these repetitive formulae have played such a considerable role in attempts of creating a redaction history of the books of Kings,[75] we will here examine their specific forms in relation to each formula's narrative context and look for its symbolic, rather than editorial value. The judgment formulae will be presented in their entirety, since just phrasing part of them does not reveal the narrative interest of the author. Aligning glossary fashioned utterances to one or another author on the basis of parts of the utterances only, such as has been common in studies on the judgment formulae, seems too negligent of their dynamic function as creative.[76]

Of the judgment formulae, within the synchronized story about the Israelite and Judaean kingdoms, Judaean kings are generally evaluated positively, while Israelite kings are evaluated negatively. Exceptions from this pattern relate primarily to relationship and secondarily to conduct. Judaean kings independent of the northern kingship are said to have done right in the eyes of Yahweh (ויעש הישר בעיני יהוה) although none of them was as righteous as David had been, and none of them had removed the high places. Judaean kings related to the northern kingship are said to have done evil in the eyes of Yahweh (ויעש הרע בעיני יהוה). The Judaean king Ahaz appears as a significant exception as the only Judaean king who is given a negated form of the southern formula: ולא־עשה הישר בעיני יהוה אלהיו כדוד אביו ('and he did not do right in the eyes of Yahweh his god as had David his father done', 2 Kgs 16.2). After the cessation of the Israelite kingdom, the negative judgment formula reserved for these kings and their associates becomes transferred to the Judaean kings, all of whom 'do evil in the sight of Yahweh—all except Hezekiah and Josiah, that is, who both did right according to all that David had done.

Let us first look at the characterization of the Judaean kings *related to* the Northern Kingdom or kingship:

75. E.g. H. Weippert, 'Die "deuteronomistischen" Beurteilungen der Könige von Israel und Juda und das Problem der Redaktion der Königsbücher, *Bib* 53 (1972), pp. 301-39; R.D. Nelson, *The Double Redaction of the Deuteronomistic History* (JSOTSup, 18; Sheffield: JSOT Press, 1981); A. Lemaire, 'Vers l'histoire de la rédaction des livres des Rois', *ZAW* 98 (1986), pp. 221-36; A.F. Campbell, *Of Prophets and Kings: A Late Ninth-Century Document (1 Samuel 1–2 Kings 10)*, (CBQMS, 17; Washington: The Catholic Biblical Association of America, 1986); Provan, *Hezekiah and the Books of Kings*.

76. Note Van Seters' criticism, *In Search of History*, p. 315: 'The judgments cannot be viewed in isolation, but are closely related to a number of thematic speeches and episodes'. So also Hoffmann, *Reform und Reformen*, p. 366. S.L. McKenzie, 'The Books of Kings in the Deuteronomistic History', in McKenzie and Graham (eds.), *The History of Israel's Traditions*, pp. 281-307 (303): 'it is unnecessary to resort to different hands as an explanation for these patterns. The balance, symmetry and uniformity of the message seem to bear the imprint of a single composer, Dtr, especially in the light of the deuteronomistic language that Campbell [*Of Prophets and Kings*] notes, but limits to the pattern for the first eight kings.'

Solomon (1 Kgs 3.3):

ויאהב שלמה את־יהוה ללכת בחקות דוד אביו רק בבמות הוא מזבח ומקטיר

And Solomon loved Yahweh and walked in the statutes of David his father, but he offered and burned incense at the high places.

Solomon (1 Kgs 11.6-7):

ויעש שלמה הרע בעיני יהוה ולא מלא אחרי יהוה כדוד אביו:
אז יבנה שלמה במה לכמוש שקץ מואב
בהר אשר על־פני ירושלם ולמלך שקץ בני עמון[77]

And Solomon did evil in the eyes of Yahweh and he was not wholly with Yahweh as his father David. At that time, Solomon built on the mountain opposite Jerusalem a high place [shrine] to Chemosh, the abomination of Moab, and to Molech, the abomination of the Ammonites.

Solomon's rule over Great Israel, from the Euphrates to Gaza, from Dan to Beersheba (1 Kgs 5.4-5; 8.65), is characterized by an increasing apostasy. While the people still offered at the high places, since the temple had not yet been built (3.2), Solomon should have known better than to continue offering at the במות. This, however, is judged ambiguously, in a way similar to the judgment of Asa, grandson of Absalom through his mother, who is said to have done right according to what David did, but, not having removed the high places (15.11-15). Solomon's real sin, for which he is judged to have done evil in the sight of Yahweh, is his marriage with foreign women, leading to erection of cult places for foreign gods (11.7).[78] Being a king for *all* Israel and given the role as a transition character, the negative evaluation of Solomon anticipates symbolically Yahweh's rejection of *all* Israel because of idol worship, which in the figures of Ahaz and Manasseh anticipates the transition that leads to a rejection also of Judah.

The two Judaean kings, who in the synchronized narrative are given the negative formulation reserved for Israelite kings, are

Jehoram of Judah son of Jehoshaphat, married to Ahab's daughter (2 Kgs 8.18):

וילך בדרך מלכי ישראל כאשר עשו בית אחאב כי בת־אחאב היתה־לו לאשה ויעש
הרע בעיני יהוה

And he walked in the way of the kings of Israel according to what the house of Ahab did, for he was married to Ahab's daughter, and he did evil in the eyes of Yahweh.

Ahaziah of Judah son of Athaliah, granddaughter of Omri (2 Kgs 8.27):[79]

וילך בדרך בית אחאב ויעש הרע בעיני יהוה כבית אחאב כי חתן בית־אחאב הוא[80]

---

77. LXX, harmonizing the verse with 11.5 and 2 Kgs 23.13, adds καὶ τῇ Ἀστάρτῃ βδελύγματι Ζιδωνίων.

78. Cf. Neh. 13.26.

79. 2 Chron. 22.2 reads 'daughter of Omri', which confirms the Syriac and Arabic readings of 2 Chron. 21.6 that Jehoram's wife was sister rather than daughter of Ahab.

80. The LXX* and MT 2 Chron. 22.2-4 do not mention marriage, but states that Ahaziah did wrong because his mother and the house of Ahab became his advisers after the death of his father.

> And he walked in the way of the house of Ahab and he did evil in the eyes of
> Yahweh as did Ahab's house, for he was related by marriage to Ahab's house.

Related to the Northern Kingdom through marriage, both Jehoram and Ahaziah
followed the practices of the Israelite kings. Their sins are not further characterized
and we have no mention of religious practice.[81] It thus seems that, as Solomon's
marriages with foreign women led to his condemnation, so also Jehoram and Ahaziah's. A variant of this motif is found in the characterization of the northern king
Ahab son of Omri, who sinned even more than Jeroboam (ויהי הנקל לכתו בחטאות
ירבעם בן־נבט ויקח אשה את־איזבל, 'And as if it were not enough for him to walk
in the sins of Jeroboam son of Nebat, he even married Jezebel', 1 Kgs 16.30) by
marrying the daughter of the Sidonian king Ethbaal and raising an altar for Baal in
Samaria (16.30-32).[82]

As the negative judgment of Solomon anticipates the curse which will lead to a
cessation of all Israel, so Jeroboam's kingdom is marked throughout as the kingdom that will not remain. Apart from the last king, Hoshea (and Elah and Shallum,
who are not supplied with judgment formulae), all kings succeeding Jeroboam
receive a judgment formula, which incorporates his sin as ultimate curse:

Nadab of Israel son of Jeroboam (1 Kgs 15.26):

ויעש הרע בעיני יהוה וילך בדרך אביו ובחטאתו אשר החטיא את־ישראל

> And he did evil in the eyes of Yahweh and he walked in the way of his father and
> in his sin with which he made Israel to sin.

Baasha of Israel in Tirzah (1 Kgs 15.34):

ויעש הרע בעיני יהוה וילך בדרך ירבעם ובחטאתו אשר החטיא את־ישראל

> And he did evil in the eyes of Yahweh and he walked in the way of Jeroboam and
> in his sin with which he made Israel to sin.

Zimri of Israel in Tirzah (1 Kgs 16.19):

על־חטאתו אשר חטא לעשות הרע בעיני יהוה ללכת בדרך ירבעם ובחטאתו אשר
עשה לחטיא את־ישראל

> Because of the sin he had committed by doing evil in the eyes of Yahweh and
> walk in the way of Jeroboam and his sin, which he committed in order to make
> Israel to sin.

While the characterization of the sin of these three kings is linked exclusively to
Jeroboam, the next three kings, Omri, Ahab and Ahaziah are characterized as adding to Jeroboam's sin, albeit Omri's transgressions are not presented as different
from those of Jeroboam's, which provoked Yahweh to anger:

---

81. See, in contrast, 2 Chron. 21.11-13.

82. It is indeed striking that the theme of marrying foreign women does not appear at all
in Chronicles, but plays the most pertinent role in Ezra and Nehemiah as well as in the Latter
Prophets.

Omri of Israel in Samaria (1 Kgs 16.25-26):

ויעשה עמרי הרע בעיני יהוה וירע מכל אשר לפניו:
וילך בכל־דרך ירבעם בן־נבט ובחטאתיו אשר החטיא את־ישראל
להכעיס את־יהוה אלהי ישראל בהבליבם

And Omri did evil in the eyes of Yahweh and he did worse than anyone before
him. For he walked in all the way of Jeroboam son of Nebat and in his sins with
which he made Israel to sin, provoking Yahweh God of Israel to anger by their
idols.

In an eponymous line of succession, paralleling the David–Solomon narratives,
Omri buys Mt Samaria,[83] builds the city of Samaria on the mountain (16.24), while
his son Ahab builds a temple and an altar for Baal (16.32). In a further imitation of
Solomon's violation of his patronage relationship with Yahweh by marrying foreign women, Ahab marries a Sidonian woman (16.31). This leads him to worship
Baal, the male counterpart to the Sidonian goddess Ashtoreth, whom Solomon
worshipped:

Ahab of Israel in Samaria son of Omri (1 Kgs 16.30-32):

ויעש אחאב בן־עמרי[84] הרע בעיני יהוה מכל אשר לפניו:
ויהי הנקל[85] לכתו בחטאות ירבעם בן־נבט ויקח אשה את־איזבל בת־אתבעל מלך צידנים
וילך ויעבד את־הבעל וישתחו לו: ויקם מזבח לבעל בית הבעל אשר בנה בשמרון

And Ahab son of Omri did evil in the eyes of Yahweh more than anyone before
him. And as if it were not enough for him to walk in the sins of Jeroboam son of
Nebat, he even married Jezebel the daughter of Ethbaal king of the Sidonians, and
he went and served Baal. And he erected an altar for Baal in the temple of Baal
which he had built in Samaria.

The similarly syncretistic character of his cult, violating both the first and the second commandment, is indicated by the *Asherah*, Yahweh's female counterpart and
consort[86] which Ahab makes (16.33):

ויעש אחאב את־האשרה ויוסף אחאב לעשות להכעיס את־יהוה אלהי־ישראל
מכל מלכי ישראל אשר היו לפניו

And Ahab made an *Asherah* and Ahab did more to provoke Yahweh god of Israel
to anger than had any of Israel's kings before him.

---

83. Cf. 2 Sam. 24.24 where David purchases Aruna's threshing floor.
84. בן־עמרי is missing in the LXX*.
85. Niphal infinitive of קלל; cf. a similar usage in Ezek. 8.17's close thematic parallel regarding Judah's idol worship in the temple and Isa. 49.6's pronouncement regarding Jacob, whose
eponymous function will not be limited to the tribes of Jacob, but will become extended to the
whole world.
86. J. Day, 'Asherah in the Hebrew Bible and Northwest Semitic Literature', *JBL* 105 (1986),
pp. 385-408; R. Albertz, *Religionsgeschichte Israels in alttestamentlicher Zeit* (Göttingen: Vandenhoeck & Ruprecht, 1992), pp. 131-35; T. Binger, *Asherah, Goddesses in Ugarit, Israel and the Old
Testament* (CIS, 2; JSOTSup, 232; Sheffield: Sheffield Academic Press, 1997), p. 132.

The transgressions are continued by Ahab's son Ahaziah forming the third in a line of increasing sin comprising those of his father, his mother and Jeroboam:

Ahaziah of Israel in Samaria son of Ahab (1 Kgs 22.53-54):

ויעש הרע בעיני יהוה
וילך בדרך אביו ובדרך אמו ובדרך ירבעם בן־נבט אשר החטיא את־ישראל:
ויעבד את־הבעל וישתחוה לו ויכעס את־יהוה אלהי ישראל ככל אשר עשה אביו

And he did evil in the eyes of Yahweh and he walked in the way of his father and in the way of his mother and in the way of Jeroboam son of Nebat, who made Israel to sin. And he served Baal and he worshiped him and he provoked Yahweh God of Israel to anger according to all his father had done.

At this climax of violation, we find the first transitional figure in a succession of three, Jehoram of Israel in Samaria son of Ahab, who removes the sin of his parents, however not that of Jeroboam (2 Kgs 3.2-3):

ויעשה הרע בעיני יהוה
רק לא כאביו וכאמו ויסר את־מצבת הבעל אשר עשה אביו:
רק בחטאות ירבעם בן־נבט אשר החטיא את־ישראל דבק לא־סר ממנה

And he did evil in the eyes of Yahweh, however, not like his father and his mother, for he removed the pillar of Baal, which his father had made. But he cleaved to the sins of Jeroboam son of Nebat with which he made Israel to sin; he did not depart from it.

The second transitional figure is Jehu, who is the only Israelite king to be characterized as having done good and right in the eyes of Yahweh, as did all the Judaean kings before Hezekiah, except Rehoboam, Abijam, Ahaz and the former mentioned kings—Solomon, Jehoram and Ahaziah. Jehu removed the Baal cult from Israel, but he did not turn away from the sins of Jeroboam and thus continued the practice of his successors:

Jehu of Israel in Samaria (2 Kgs 10.28-29):

וישמד יהוא את הבעל מישראל:
רק חטאי ירבעם בן־נבט אשר החטיא את־ישראל לא־סר יהוא מאחריהם
עגלי הזהב אשר בית־אל ואשר בדן

And Jehu wiped out Baal from Israel. But Jehu did not turn away from the sins of Jeroboam son of Nebat with which made Israel to sin; the golden calves which are in Bethel and Dan.

He is nevertheless accredited a positive evaluation and the kingship of Israel for his sons in four generations (10.30):

ויאמר יהוה אל־יהוא יען אשר־הטיבת לעשות הישר בעיני ככל אשר בלבבי עשית לבית
אחאב בני רבעים ישבו לך על־כסא ישראל

And Yahweh said to Jehu, because you have done well in carrying out what is right in my eyes and have done to the house of Ahab according to all that is in my heart, your descendants to the fourth generation shall sit on the throne of Israel.

As Jehu's behaviour is not distinguishable from that of Israel's king Jehoram, who removed the pillar of Baal, other reasons must lie behind the judgment of both. The third transitional figure is

Jehoahaz of Israel in Samaria son of Jehu (2 Kgs 13.2):

ויעש הרע בעיני יהוה
וילך אחר חטאת ירבעם בן־נבט אשר החטיא את־ישראל לא־סר ממנה

And he did evil in the eyes of Yahweh, and he walked after the sin of Jeroboam son of Nebat with which he made Israel to sin; he did not turn away from it.

With these three kings as transitional figures, the judgment has shifted from *walking in the way of* Jeroboam (וילך בדרך ירבעם) to having *not turned away from* Jeroboam's sin (לא סר מן־חטאות ירבעם).[87] Thus we find the next six kings stereotypically characterized as were also the first three kings:

Jehoash of Israel in Samaria son of Jehoahaz (2 Kgs 13.11):

ויעשה הרע בעיני יהוה
לא סר מכל־חטאות ירבעם בן־נבט אשר־החטיא את־ישראל בה הלך

And he did evil in the eyes of Yahweh; he did not turn away from all the sins of Jeroboam son of Nebat with which he made Israel to sin, he walked in it.

Jeroboam of Israel in Samaria son of Joash of Israel (2 Kgs 14.24):

ויעש הרע בעיני יהוה
לא סר מכל־חטאות ירבעם בן־נבט אשר החטיא את־ישראל

And he did evil in the eyes of Yahweh; he did not turn away from all the sins of Jeroboam son of Nebat with which he made Israel to sin.

Zechariah of Israel in Samaria son of Jeroboam (2 Kgs 15.9):

ויעש הרע בעיני יהוה כאשר עשו אבתיו
לא סר מחטאות ירבעם בן־נבט אשר החטיא את־ישראל

And he did evil in the eyes of Yahweh as his fathers had done; he did not turn away from the sins of Jeroboam son of Nebat with which he made Israel to sin.

Menahem of Israel in Samaria son of Gad (2 Kgs 15.18):

ויעש הרע בעיני יהוה
לא סר מעל חטאות ירבעם בן־נבט אשר החטיא את־ישראל כל־ימיו

And he did evil in the eyes of Yahweh; he did not turn away from (all) the sins of Jeroboam son of Nebat with which he made Israel to sin all his days.

Pekahiah of Israel in Samaria son of Menahem (2 Kgs 15.24):

ויעש הרע בעיני יהוה
לא סר מחטאות ירבעם בן־נבט אשר החטיא את־ישראל

---

87. With slight rhetorical differences.

And he did evil in the eyes of Yahweh; he did not turn away from the sins of
Jeroboam son of Nebat with which he made Israel to sin.

Pekah of Israel in Samaria son of Remaliah (2 Kgs 15.28):

ויעש הרע בעיני יהוה
לא סר מן־חטאות ירבעם בן־נבט אשר החטיא את־ישראל

And he did evil in the eyes of Yahweh; he did not turn away from the sins of
Jeroboam son of Nebat with which he made Israel to sin.

Hoshea, the last Israelite kings marks the final change of the Northern kings:

Hoshea of Israel in Samaria son of Elah (2 Kgs 17.2):

ויעש הרע נביני יהוה
רק לא כמלכי ישראל אשר היו לפניו

And he did evil in the eyes of Yahweh; however, not as the kings of Israel, who
were before him.

The utterance is ambiguous, but the comparison of him with Israel's kings points
to the judgment of Ahab as he is the only king given a similar characterization.
Both kings are accused of violating patronage loyalty by marriage or alliance with
foreigners.

McKenzie's eight plus eight pattern[88] might thus better be explained as a six plus
three plus six pattern (leaving Jeroboam and Hoshea as framework), since we find
that Jehoahaz received a double judgment, as did Jehoram. The disappearance of the
provocation theme (כעס את־יהוה, 'provoke Yahweh to anger')—causing the curse
on the houses of Jeroboam, Baasha and Omri—after Ahaziah (1 Kgs 22.54, the last
mention) and its reappearance in the interpretations of the falls of Israel and Judah
(2 Kgs 17; 21; 22; 23) suggest that the author wanted to signify that ultimate curse
had been delayed. This places Jehu right in the middle,[89] and we shall see later why
that could have been the author's intention. First, we need to look at the characterizations of the Judaean kings, who are said to 'have done right' (ויעש הישר). The
characterization includes various comments, of which references to the high places,
the במות, are the most consistent.[90]

Asa of Judah son of Abijam (1 Kgs 15.11-12):

ויעש אסא הישר בעיני יהוה כדוד אביו:
ויעבר הקדשים מן־הארץ ויסר את־כל־הגללים אשר עשו אבתיו

88.　McKenzie, 'The Books of Kings in the Deuteronomistic History', p. 302: 'The first eight
kings, Jeroboam through Joram (Jehoram), have the same basic evaluation (with Jehoram being
somewhat transitional): they walk in the way of Jeroboam and provoke Yahweh to anger. The next
eight, Jehu through Pekah, share a different pattern: they do not depart (לא־סר) from the sin of
Jeroboam. The last king, Hoshea, does evil but not like his predecessors.'

89.　Also when we count the two kings who are not supplied with a judgment formula—Elah
and Shallum, Jehu is still in the middle.

90.　The books of Chronicles treat this theme differently and it will confuse matters to bring in
comparative material here.

And Asa did right in the eyes of Yahweh, as his father David had done. And he removed the male cult prostitutes from the land and removed all the idols that his fathers had made.

In addition, Asa dethroned his mother because she had made an abominable image to Ashera. And Asa destroyed her image and burned it at the brook of Kidron. As Jehu did not remove Jeroboam's sin, Asa and successive Judaean kings did not remove the high place.

Asa of Judah son of Abijam (1 Kgs 15.14):

והבמות לא־סרו רק לבב־אסא היה שלם עם־יהוה כל־ימיו

But the high places were not removed, although Asa's heart was wholly with Yahweh all his days.

Jehoshaphat of Judah son of Asa (1 Kgs 22.43-45):

וילך בכל־דרך אסא אביו לא־סר ממנו לעשות הישר בעיני יהוה:
אך הבמות לא־סרו עוד העם מזבחים ומקטרים בבמות:
וישלם יהושפט עם־מלך ישראל[91]

And he walked in all the way of Asa, his father; he did not turn away from it, doing what was right in the eyes of Yahweh. But, the high places were not removed; the people continued to sacrifice and burn incense at the high places; and Jehoshaphat made peace with the king of Israel.

Jehoash of Judah son of Jehoshaphat, instructed by the priest Jehoiada (2 Kgs 12.3-4):

ויעש יהואש הישר בעיני יהוה כל־ימיו
אשר הורהו יהוידע הכהן:
רק הבמות לא־סרו עוד העם מזבחים ומקטרים בבמות

And Jehoash did right in the eyes of Yahweh all his days according to what Jehoiada instructed him. However, the high places were not removed; the people continued to sacrifice and burn incense at the high places.

Amaziah of Judah son of Joash (2 Kgs 14.3-4):

ויעש הישר בעיני יהוה רק לא כדוד אביו ככל אשר־עשה יואש אביו עשה:
רק הבמות לא־סרו עוד העם מזבחים ומקטרים בבמות

And he did right in the eyes of Yahweh, but not as David his father; he did according to everything his father Joash had done. However, the high places were not removed; the people continued to sacrifice and burn incense at the high places.

Azariah of Judah son of Amaziah (2 Kgs 15.3-4):

ויעש הישר בעיני יהוה ככל אשר־עשה אמציהו אביו:
רק הבמות לא־סרו עוד העם מזבחים ומקטרים בבמות

And he did right in the eyes of Yahweh according to everything his father Amaziah had done. However, the high places were not removed; the people continued to sacrifice and burn incense at the high places.

---

91. In 2 Chron. 18.1 he married into (the house of) Ahab (ויתחתן לאחאב); cf. LXX.

Jotham of Judah son of Uzziah (2 Kgs 15.34-35):

וַיַּעַשׂ הַיָּשָׁר בְּעֵינֵי יהוה כְּכֹל אֲשֶׁר־עָשָׂה עֻזִּיָּהוּ אָבִיו עָשָׂה׃
רַק הַבָּמוֹת לֹא־סָרוּ עוֹד הָעָם מְזַבְּחִים וּמְקַטְּרִים בַּבָּמוֹת
הוּא בָּנָה אֶת־שַׁעַר בֵּית־יהוה הָעֶלְיוֹן

And he did right in the eyes of Yahweh according to everything his father Uzziah
had done. However, the high places were not removed; the people continued to
sacrifice and burn incense at the high places. He built the upper gate of the temple
of Yahweh.

Hezekiah of Judah son of Ahaz (2 Kgs 18.3-4):

וַיַּעַשׂ הַיָּשָׁר בְּעֵינֵי יהוה כְּכֹל אֲשֶׁר־עָשָׂה דָּוִד אָבִיו׃
הוּא הֵסִיר אֶת־הַבָּמוֹת וְשִׁבַּר אֶת־הַמַּצֵּבֹת וְכָרַת אֶת־הָאֲשֵׁרָה וְכִתַּת נְחַשׁ הַנְּחֹשֶׁת אֲשֶׁר־עָשָׂה
מֹשֶׁה כִּי עַד־הַיָּמִים
הָהֵמָּה הָיוּ בְנֵי יִשְׂרָאֵל מְקַטְּרִים לוֹ וַיִּקְרָא־לוֹ נְחֻשְׁתָּן

And he did right in the eyes of Yahweh, according to everything his father David
had done. He removed the high places and he smashed the pillars and cut down the
Asherah and broke into pieces the bronze serpent which Moses had made, for until
these days the Israelites had burned incense to it; and he called it Nehushtan.

Josiah of Judah son of Amon (2 Kgs 22.2):

וַיַּעַשׂ הַיָּשָׁר בְּעֵינֵי יהוה וַיֵּלֶךְ בְּכָל־דֶּרֶךְ דָּוִד אָבִיו וְלֹא־סָר יָמִין וּשְׂמֹאול

And he did right in the eyes of Yahweh and he walked in all the way of David his
father and he did not turn to the right or the left.

A quick glance at the positive characterizations will reveal that they all did well,
but some with reservation, as indicated by the modifying clauses אַךְ and רַק (Asa,
Jehoshaphat, Jehoash, Amaziah, Azariah and Jotham): they did not remove the high
places, the במות, so the people still made offerings there.[92] While we might understand this to belong to the negative characterization of these kings, I think the
author was much more concerned with placing Hezekiah and Josiah (with David) in
the outstanding position of being the only kings whose appraisal is without reservation. Even this is a bit ambiguous, since David sinned in the Uriah case (cf. the
judgment of Abijam; 1 Kgs 15.5). Hezekiah probably sinned in the Babylonian and
Josiah in the Pharaoh Neco case.

The three and six pattern has also influenced the composition of the judgments of
the Judaean kings, but in a different way: before Hezekiah, we find that six kings
did evil (Solomon, Rehoboam, Abijam, Jehoram, Ahaziah and Ahaz), however,
only Jehoram, Ahaziah and Ahaz were entirely evil. Six kings did right, although it

---

92. For a thematic anticipation of the books of Kings' במות theme in David's lamentation of
Saul and Jonathan's deaths as having taken place 'upon your high places' (2 Sam. 1.19, 25), see
R. Polzin, *David and the Deuteronomist: A Literary Study of the Deuteronomic History* (Bloomington: Indiana University Press, 1993), pp. 15-23: 'the high places not only recall the particular
circumstances of Saul's death (upon the heights of Gilboa) but also foreshadow the Deuteronomist's devastating critique of the idolatry that will characterize Israel's monarchic history after the
temple is built' (p. 15).

was with reservation (Asa, Jehoshaphat, Jehoash, Amaziah, Azariah and Jotham). After Hezekiah, we once more find six kings doing evil without reservation (Manasseh, Amon, Jehoahaz, Jehoiakim, Jehoiachin and Zedekiah).[93] Of these, Manasseh and Amon's transgressions are told with great details:

Manasseh of Judah son of Hezekiah (2 Kgs 21.2):

ויעש הרע בעיני יהוה כתועבת הגוים אשר הוריש יהוה מפני בני ישראל

And he did evil in the eyes of Yahweh according to the abominable practise of the foreigners, whom Yahweh had driven out before the Israelites.

In the description of Manasseh's reign (2 Kgs 21.3-7), the author brings together northern and southern transgressions in Manasseh's replacing of the high places, which his father Hezekiah removed (וישב ויבן את־הבמות אשר אבד חזקיהו אביו, v. 3) and establishing altars for Baal (ויקם מזבחת לבעל) and making an *Asherah* as Ahab, king of Israel had done (ויעש אשרה כאשר עשה אחאב מלך ישראל). He furthermore worshipped the host of heaven (וישתחו לכל־צבע השמים ויעבד אתם). Similar to Ahaz, he made altars (for Yahweh?) in the temple (ובנה מזבחת בבית יהוה, v. 4), but, surpassing Ahaz, he brought the idolatrous cult *into* the temple area by building altars for all the host of heaven in the two courts of the temple (ויבן מזבחות לכל־צבע השמים בשתי חצרות בית יהוה, v. 5) and placing the *Asherah* in the temple (וישם את־, פסל האשרה אשר עשה בבית, v. 7) chosen by Yahweh such as he had said to David. In addition, he made his son pass through fire; he practised soothsaying and augury, and dealt with mediums and with wizards in doing evil in the eyes of Yahweh to provoke him to anger (והעביר את־בנו באש ועונן ונחש ועשה אוב וידענים הרבה לעשות הרע בעיני יהוה להכעיס, v. 6). In an increasing line of transgressions from Ahaz' violation of the Yahweh cult over Manasseh's syncretistic cult, we find his son Amon worshipping the idols and leaving Yahweh completely (2 Kgs 21.21-22):

Amon son of Manasseh (2 Kgs 21.20-22):

ויעש הרע בעיני יהוה כאשר עשה מנשה אביו:
וילך בכל־דרך אשר־הלך אביו ויעבד את־הגללים אשר עבד אביו וישתו להם:
ויעזב את־יהוה אלהי אבתיו ולא הלך בדרך יהוה

And he did evil in the eyes of Yahweh as his father Manasseh had done. And he walked in all the way of his father and served the idols his father had served and he worshipped them. And he left Yahweh the God of his fathers and he did not walk in the way of Yahweh.

93. According to Auld's 'common text' (*Kings Without Privilege*, p. 136), eight of the Judaean kings did 'evil'. The phrase appears in 2 Chron. 12.14 (Rehoboam); 21.6 (Jehoram); 22.4 (Ahaziah); 33.2, 6 (Manasseh); 33.22 (Amon); 36.5 (Jehoiakim); 36.9 (Jehoiachin); and 36.12 (Zedekiah). In 2 Chron. 29.6-7, Hezekiah utters the accusation against 'our fathers' with implicit reference to Ahaz (cf. 2 Chron. 28.24). The doing evil clause thus appears in Chronicles with equal subject frequency (nine times each) as the doing (non-doing) right clause (2 Chron. 14.1 [Asa]; 20.32 [Jehoshaphat]; 24.2 [Jehoash]; 25.2 [Amaziah]; 26.4 [Uzziah]; 27.2 [Jotham]; 28.1 [Ahaz (did not)]; 29.2 [Hezekiah]; and 34.2 [Josiah]).

The situation that precedes the reign of Josiah hardly could be worse. Josiah's re-instatement of the Yahweh cult and removal of idolatry were not reversed by his sons and grandson as was Hezekiah's reforms by Manasseh. It is not their sins but Manasseh's (2 Kgs 23.26; 24.3, 4, 20) that lead to a rejection of Judah. However, as Judah now takes on the role of being the cursed kingdom, we find that the northern judgment formula is applied to these last four kings of Judah, albeit that no specific transgressions are mentioned and the Yahweh cult seems not to have been vio-lated.[94]

Jehoahaz of Judah son of Josiah (2 Kgs 23.32):

ויעש הרע בעיני יהוה ככל אשר־עשו אבתיו

And he did evil in the eyes of Yahweh according to everything his fathers had done.

Jehoiakim of Judah son of Josiah (2 Kgs 23.37):

ויעש הרע בעיני יהוה ככל אשר־עשו אבתיו

And he did evil in the eyes of Yahweh according to everything his fathers had done.

Jehoiachin of Judah son of Jehoiakim (2 Kgs 24.9):

ויעש הרע בעיני יהוה ככל אשר־עשה אביו

And he did evil in the eyes of Yahweh according to everything his father had done.

Zedekiah of Judah son of Josiah (2 Kgs 24.19):

ויעש הרע בעיני יהוה ככל אשר־עשה יהויקים

And he did evil in the eyes of Yahweh according to everything Jehoiakim had done.

It was mainly this claimed stereotypical form contrasting with a more elaborate style, which had led scholars to assume a Josianic redaction for the part of the narrative chronology prior to Josiah and an exilic redaction for the chronologically later narratives.[95] Stereotype, however, seems to be the norm for both the northern and southern judgments.

The non-application of the כדוד ('as David') motif to the kings following Josiah and the insertion of the father motif is not as thoughtless as Friedman sees it: 'an unthoughtful choice of wording if the writer who described these kings was the same writer who had just described the career of their father Josiah'.[96] The first two kings after Josiah are not compared with Josiah, their father, but with their (fore-) fathers (plural, אשר־עשו אבתיו, 2 Kgs 23.32, 37), whose sins are recurrently made paradigmatic for the fall of the southern kingdom (2 Kgs [17.14;] 21.8, 15, 22;

---

94. Contrasting 2 Chron. 36.12-16's accusation of violation of covenant and cult.
95. E.g. Cross, *Canaanite Myth*, p. 288; Nelson, *Double Redaction*, p. 38.
96. Friedman, 'From Egypt to Egypt: Dtr[1] and Dtr[2]', p. 174.

22.13). Jehoiachin son of Jehoiakim, is rightfully compared with his father (singular, אשר־עשה אביו), while Zedekiah is compared with his brother Jehoiakim, thus implicitly returning to the forefather theme and avoiding any comparison with Josiah, who is contrasted to the fathers (2 Kgs 22.18 [13]).

Counting all Judaea's kings gives nine kings before and after the four kings, Jehoash, Amaziah, Azariah and Jotham, who are all given the same modified judgment. Immediately before and after these four kings, we find Jehoram, Ahaziah and Ahaz, who are the three kings doing evil completely. In a hierarchic construction, we are led to place Yahweh first, the three best kings next (David, Hezekiah, Josiah),[97] the six second best kings third (Asa, Jehoshaphat, Jehoash, Amaziah, Azariah and Jotham), the three not so good kings fourth (Solomon, Rehoboam and Abijam) and finally the nine really bad kings fifth (Jehoram, Ahaziah, Ahaz, Manasseh, Amon, Jehoahaz, Jehoiakim, Jehoiachin and Zedekiah).[98]

The first in line after David for a positive appraisal is Asa,[99] who is said to have removed (root סור) the idolatrous cult, the קדשים and the גללים, however, not the במות. The במות were referred to in the judgment of Solomon, but where did the idolatrous cult come from? Is it the sin of Solomon which is removed by Josiah (2 Kgs 23.13)?

In a very composite and complex story, the author avoids confusing matters by offering another origin for what Asa removed in the judgments of the Judaean kings following Solomon. The judgment of Rehoboam is brought indirectly in the judgment of his son Abijam who walked in the sins of his father:

Abijam of Judah son of Rehoboam (1 Kgs 15.3-5):

וילך בכל־חטאות אביו אשר־עשה לפניו ולא־היה לבבו שלם עם־יהוה אלהיו כלבב
דוד אביו:
כי למען דוד נתן יהוה אלהיו[102] לו ניר בירושלם[101] להקים את־בנו אחריו ולהעמיד[100]
את־ירושלם:

97. If we include Saul, we might think of the four best kings, but since he is not mentioned in the books of Kings, we can as well leave him aside.

98. The pattern of length of reign for the Judaean kings up to the reign of Jehoash exposes some consistency based on the number of 40 years for each of the cult reforming kings: David, Solomon, Asa and Jehoash. Dispersed among these four kings we find the not so good and bad kings (Rehoboam, Abijam, Jehoshaphat, Jehoram and Ahaziah (Athaliah), whose total counts 60 years, with 20 years before and 40 years after Asa. See N.P. Lemche, 'Prægnant tid i Det Gamle Testamente', in G. Hallbäck and N.P. Lemche (eds.), *Tiden' i bibelsk belysning* (Copenhagen: Museum Tusculanum, 2001), pp. 29-47. Auld, *Kings Without Privilege*, p. 158: 'Solomon had nineteen successors in each of Judah and Israel; yet those in Israel reigned on average only three years each for every five of their counterparts in Jerusalem'.

99. Asa is fourth in line after David, while the next reform king, Jehoash, is eighth; Hezekiah, the third reform king, is thirteenth and finally Josiah is sixteenth. We would have liked to see Hezekiah as twelfth, wouldn't we? On this place, we find another, cult reformer, King Ahaz, who is in favour of foreign cults.

100. Missing in the LXX.

101. Missing in the LXX.

102. The phrase refers to Shishak's attack on Jerusalem, however, anachronistically implying a saving of Jerusalem for the sake of David in the Hezekiah narrative.

אשר עשה דוד את־הישר בעיני יהוה
ולא־סר מכל אשר־צוהו כל ימי חייו *רק בדבר אוריה החתי*[103]

And he walked in all the sins which his father had committed before him and his heart was not wholly with Yahweh his God as was the heart of David his father. But for David's sake, Yahweh his God gave him a lamp in Jerusalem, to establish his son after him and let Jerusalem remain; because David had done right in the eyes of Yahweh and had not turned away from anything that he commanded him all the days of his life, except in the matter of Uriah the Hittite.

What, however was the sin of his father? In the *BHS* it is not Rehoboam who is said to have done evil in the eyes of Yahweh, it is Judah[104] (1 Kgs 14.22-24):

ויעש יהודה הרע בעיני יהוה ויקנאו[105] אתו מכל אשר עשו אבתם בחטאתם אשר חטאו:
ויבנו גם־המה להם במות ומצבות ואשרים על כל־גבעה גבהה ותחת כל־עץ רענן:
וגם קדש היה בארץ עשו ככל התועבת הגוים אשר הוריש יהוה מפני ישראל

And Judah did evil in the eyes of Yahweh and they provoked him to jealousy more than their fathers had done with the sins they committed. For they also built to themselves high places and pillars and *Asherim* on every high hill and under every green tree. There were even male cult prostitutes in the land, who did everything according to the abominable practise of the foreigners, whom Yahweh had driven out before Israel.

The reason for the negative judgment of Rehoboam is comparable to Ahijah's accusation directed against Jeroboam in 1 Kgs 14.9 that he has made other gods and molten images and turned his back on Yahweh:

ותרע לעשות מכל אשר־היו לפניו ותלך ותעשה־לך אלהים אחרים ומסכות להכעיסני
ואתי השלכת אחרי גוך

And because you have done evil worse than anyone before you, and you have gone and made for yourself other gods and images to provoke me to anger and you have turned your back on me.

and his curse of Israel in 14.15-16:

והכה יהוה את־ישראל[106] כאשר ינוד הקנה במים ונתש את־ישראל מעל האדמה הטובה
הזאת אשר נתן

---

103.   The words between asterisks are missing in the LXX.

104.   There is a confusion of names here. LXX* has Ροβοαμ and LXX-A has singular for plural יקנא, while LXX-B has singular for plural אבתם. Josephus seems to have had some awareness of this confusion and rather defends the people for having followed the practice of their king (*Ant.* 8.251-53). The confusion might, however relate to the judgment formula, that they did evil in the eyes of Yahweh, which (except for this one, the three kings related to the Northern Kingdom and the six kings succeeding Hezekiah and Josiah) is related exclusively to Israelite kings. If we think in broader terms of relationship, Rehoboam's sin is comparable to Jeroboam's sin, indicated by the initiating גם, and foreshadows the גם יהודה in 2 Kgs 17.19 and Manasseh's and Judah's inclusion in the accusations of betrayal in 2 Kgs 21.2.

105.   Qal with hiphil meaning 'making someone angry, provoke to jealousy'; cf. Deut. 32.16, 21; Ps. 78.58.

106.   Prob. ins. והתנודדו.

לאבותיהם וזרם מעבר לנהר יען אשר עשו את־אשריהם מכעיסים את־יהוה:
ויתן את־ישראל בגלל חטאות ירבעם אשר חטא ואשר החטיא את־ישראל

And Yahweh shall smite Israel as a reed is shaken in water and he shall root up Israel out of this good land, which he gave to their fathers, and he shall scatter them beyond the river (i.e. the Euphrates), because they have made their *Asherim*, with which they have provoked Yahweh to anger. And he shall give up Israel because of the sins, which Jeroboam committed and also made Israel to sin.

While Jeroboam's sin in 1 Kgs 12.31–13.34 is exclusively related to the temples of the high places and the altar in Bethel, this passage in 1 Kgs 14.9 links it with the idolatry, which also Judah is accused of having committed. The pronouncement of Israel's fate in the closure of Ahijah's message links it with its fulfilment in 2 Kings 17. It is not only Jeroboam's house which shall be cut off, but certainly also all of Israel, because of the making of images of *other gods*, with which they provoked Yahweh to anger (כעס, 1 Kgs 14.9, 14-16). It was this ambiguity in the judgment formulae which made Provan suggest a double redaction of the books of Kings: one generated around the במות theme related to cult centralization and reaching its climax in the Hezekiah narrative, the other centred on the idolatry theme which comes to a conclusion in the Josiah narrative.[107] Our investigation in the judgment formulae thus far has not supported Provan's conclusion, although the double theme is apparent. The variations of the judgment formulae seem to be much more specifically related to a north–south relationship and directed by interests of composition and theme. The following three examples, judgments of Ahaz, Jehu and Jehoram, further demonstrate this.

The judgment of Ahaz is puzzling. Acting as the Israelite kings—וילך בדרך מלכי ישראל ('and he walked in the way of the kings of Israel, 2 Kgs 16.3a)—we should expect a judgment formula similar to the characterization of such behaviour: ויעש הרע בעיני יהוה ('and he did evil in the eyes of Yahweh'). However, fighting against Israel's king Pekah son of Remaliah, Ahaz did not associate with Israelite kings as did Jehoram and Ahaziah. Thus, the author avoided confusing genealogic relationships by negating the southern formula ולא־עשה הישר בעיני יהוה אלהיו כדוד אביו ('and he did not do right in the eyes of Yahweh hid God as has David his father', 2 Kgs 16.2)—rather than attributing a northern judgment formula to Ahaz. Compositionally the characterization forms a strong contrast to the four kings after the negative evaluation of Ahaziah: Jehoash, Amaziah, Azariah and Jotham, who all are said to have done right—however, not completely so. Increasing Judah's sin by adding the practice of the foreigners, whom Yahweh had driven out before the Israelites—וגם את־בנו העביר באש כתעבות הגוים אשר הוריש יהוה אתם מפני בני ישראל ('and he also made his sons pass through the fire according to the abominable practice of the foreigners, whom Yahweh had driven out before the Israelites, 2 Kgs 16.3b)—and offering on the high places and under the green trees ויזבח ויקטר בבמות ועל־הגבעות ותחת כל־עץ רענן ('And he offered and burned incense on the high places and on the hills and under every green tree', 2 Kgs 16.4)—Ahaz' sin is comparable to that of Judah (1 Kgs 14.23-24) and 'Israel' (2 Kgs 17.9-11).

107. Provan, *Hezekiah and the Books of Kings*, pp. 97-98.

While Israel is rejected because of that sin, Hezekiah's doing right and cleaving to Yahweh alone (2 Kgs 18.3-6) introduces a delay of Judah's fate, which thereby forms the strongest contrast to the removal of the Northern Kingdom.

The characterization of Jehu confirms the 'genealogical' use of the regnal formulae. As the only Israelite king, he is said to have done good and right in the eyes of Yahweh (2 Kgs 10.30):

ויאמר יהוה אל־יהוא יען אשר־הטיבת לעשות הישר בעיני ככל אשר בלבבי עשית
לבית אחאב

> And Yahweh said to Jehu, 'Because you have done well in carrying out what is right in my eyes and have done to the house of Ahab according to all that is in my heart.

Why did he do right? Because he slew the house of Ahab as Yahweh had wanted him to (2 Kgs 9.6-10; 10.9-14, 17, 30)? Because he exterminated the worshippers of Baal (10.18-29)? No, simply by being a son (or grandson?) of Jehoshaphat (9.2, 14)[108] he had family ties with the Judaean royal house, and therefore received a judgment imitating the judgment formulae for Judaean kings.[109] The arbitrariness of this genealogical relationship is demonstrated in 1 Kgs 19.16, which does not mention Jehoshaphat, but calls Elisha son of Shaphat. Placed in the 'right' genealogy, Jehu's conduct, however, still imitates that of Israelite kings. If the formulae were governed by conduct rather than genealogy, the added judgment that 'he did not turn away from the sins of Jeroboam' (2 Kgs 10.29, 31) and thus 'did not walk in the Law of Yahweh, God of Israel, with *all* his heart', should have accredited Jehu a negative evaluation. Being an Israelite king, he could not obtain a judgment similar to the Judaean kings—Asa, Jehoshaphat, Jehoash, Amaziah, Azariah and Jotham—who also did what was right in the eyes of Yahweh, but did not remove the high places: רק הבמות לא־סרו עוד העם מזבחים ומקטרים בבמות ('but the high places were not removed; the people still offered and burned incense at the high places').[110]

Jehu's sin has nothing to do with the high places, but with the sin of Jeroboam, 'the golden calves in Bethel and Dan'[111] (2 Kgs 10.29), which added to the division of the centralized cult. The judgment of Asa further confirms this ideology behind the judgment formulae. Having acted in a way similar to Jehu, but having not

108.   Jehu is called son of Nimshi, however also called son of Jehoshaphat son of Nimshi (2 Kgs 9.2, 14 and the LXX parallel). Josephus, LXX-L and Syriac omit any reference to a relationship to Jehoshaphat. In J. Macdonald, *Samaritan Chronicle No. II (or: Sepher Ha-Yamim) From Joshua to Nebuchadnezzar* (Berlin: W. de Gruyter, 1969), ST 2 Kings–2 Chronicles §B and C, he is called 'son of Jehoshaphat son of Manasseh'.

109.   I strongly disagree here with Provan (*Hezekiah and the Books of Kings*, p. 61) that the 'omission' of the 'doing evil' clause for Jehu is stylistic. The author certainly had the intention of judging Jehu positively, as can be seen in the modifying clause רק, indicating that 'he did right', even though he did not deviate from the sins of Jeroboam (10.29). The author's confirmation of the judgment by introducing Yahweh as pronouncing it (2 Kgs 10.30) further demonstrates that he had troubles with it.

110.   The slight variations in the formulae are due to narrative interests.

111.   The doubt whether this specific reference is an addition (*BHS*) seems unnecessary, since Josephus also refers to the 'worship of the golden heifers' (*Ant.* 9.139) and the LXX agrees with MT.

removed the high places, the במות in his area, although his heart was fully with Yahweh all his days, he is not accused for not removing the sin of Jeroboam. The situation for the Israelite king Jehu is different. Removing the sin of Jeroboam would have meant submitting to the altar in Jerusalem (cf. Jeroboam's reason for building the בית־במות [1 Kgs 12.26-27, 31-33] and Josiah's reason for removing them [2 Kgs 23.19]). Being an Israelite king, Jehu is not presented as having any intention of removing his own cult places, but only of removing idolatry within his borders.[112] The judgment of Jehu not only links him with the righteous Judaean kings, it also links him with Solomon, who similarly is said to have loved Yahweh, but still made his offerings at the high places, the במות (1 Kgs 3.3). The formulaic use of עוד העם מזבחים ומקטרים בבמות ('the people still offered and burned incense at the high places') refers to the situation before the building of the Solomonic temple in Jerusalem (cf. 1 Kgs 3.2) and anticipates the change introduced with Hezekiah's reform: הוא הסיר את־הבמות ('he removed the high places', 2 Kgs 18.4).

Finally, we have to consider Jehu's removal of the idolatrous kings: Jehoram in Israel and Ahaziah in Judah (2 Kgs 9). The judgment of Jehoram is the *tertium comparationis* of the system behind the judgment formulae. Certainly he is doing evil (he is after all a son of Ahab); this evil is not, however, as bad as that which his parents did. Removing the pillar of Baal (2 Kgs 3.2) credited him with some goodwill. It placed him within the nine Israelite kings whose transgression does not belong to idolatry, but to disloyalty against the purported law of cult centralization. As Jehu, he did not remove Jeroboam's sin. Being as faithful to Yahweh as Jehu is said to have been, he could well have received a judgment formula similar to Jehu's. He did not because he belonged to the cursed house.

Jehu's removal of Ahaziah prepares for Jehoash to become king in Judah at the age of seven in Jehu's seventh year of reign (2 Kgs 12.1). As Jehu's reign, the years of Jehoash's reign are divisible by four: Jehu 28 years (2 Kgs 10.36) and Jehoash 40 years (2 Kgs 12.1). As Jehu is the ninth Israelite king (the tenth if we include Elah), Jehoash is the ninth Judaean king according to the judgments (the tenth, if we include Athaliah, whose reign is not evaluated). Related to him, however, carried out by the priest Jehoiada, is a cult reform imitating Jehu's similar reform (2 Kgs 10.25-26) in reverse order: destruction of Baal's temple, altars, images and the killing of Baal's priest (2 Kgs 11.18).[113] Although we have no explicit mention of a Baal cult in the Southern Kingdom, the two preceding Judaean kings followed the practice of Israel's kings, because of their family ties with the Northern Kingdom: Jehoram, who is said to have 'walked in the way of Israel's kings', and Ahaziah, who is said to have 'walked in the way of Ahab'. Athaliah, granddaughter

---

112. My argument relates to narrative logic and not to a historicist reading such as is found in, for example, Finkelstein and Silberman, *The Bible Unearthed*, p. 197: 'In other words, though he eliminated the Baal cult, Jehu failed to abolish the rival northern cult centers that challenged the religious supremacy of Jerusalem'.

113. Hoffmann, *Reform und Reformen*, pp. 42-43, 112-113: 'Durch eine überaus geschichtliche Parallelkonstruktion zweier Berichte aus Israel und Juda gelingt es Dtr, das Motiv "Baalskult", das bislang ausschliesslich ein Thema der Nordreichs-Kultgeschichte war, nun auch im Südreich einzuführen und von nun an in der Kultberichterstattung über Juda fest zu verankern'.

of Omri, might have continued this practice;[114] however, no mention is made thereof. Neither is it said that she instituted it.[115] The hiding of Jehoash for six years in Yahweh's temple (11.3), the revolt against Athaliah in that temple (11.4-15), the removal of the Baal cult after her death (11.17-18) and the restoration of Yahweh's temple (12.5-17) are the author's implicit argumentation for her support of the Baal worship.

Jehoash's restoration of Jerusalem's temple has no parallel in the Jehu narrative. Literarily, no central temple exists in the Northern Kingdom. With both kings, a return to the cultic situation at the division of the kingdom is indicated. With both kings, the accusation of idolatrous practice, after the habits of the foreigners, disappears temporarily from the narrative in the books of Kings. In history, that would have counted more than a hundred years of contact with the neighbouring Transjordanian, Aramaean and Phoenician kingdoms as well as the more remote Assyrian Empire, from the mid-ninth century BCE to the Assyrian conquests of the area in the last part of the eighth century![116]

The three Judaean kings succeeding Jehoash are all accused of not having removed the high places, the במות (2 Kgs 14.4; 15.4, 35). With the fourth king, Ahaz, a turning point is introduced (16.3). In a reiteration of Judah's sin of 1 Kgs 14.23, Ahaz is given the role of increasing that sin, by combining the idolatry (2 Kgs 16.3) with the offering at the high places (16.4), formerly done only by the people.[117] With Manasseh, the follow-up of this new era in Judaean history combines both Judah and Israel's sins in its reiteration of Ahab's deeds (21.2-3).

The seven Israelite kings, succeeding Jehu, are accused only of not turning away from the sins of Jeroboam. The only exception is the first king, Jehoahaz, who also allowed the *Asherah* to be placed in Samaria (2 Kgs 13.6). No accusation of idolatry appears in 2 Kings before it is taken up again as a thematic explanation of the fall of the Northern Kingdom (ch. 17).[118] So what had the eighth king, Hoshea, done?[119]

114.   Cf. 2 Chron. 22.3.

115.   Against Hoffmann, *Reform und Reformen*, p. 112: 'Die dtr Darstellung hat daraus, da sie Athalja wegen ihrer Abstammung dem Baalskult zuordnete, einen religiösen Grundgegensatz zwischen Baal-und Jahwe-Priestertum gemacht'.

116.   Finkelstein and Silberman, *The Bible Unearthed*, p. 200: 'As was the case with the archaeological study of the Omrides, the post-Omride era of Israel's independent history was not considered formative or particularly interesting from an archaeological point of view. In an unconscious echoing of the Bible's theological interpretations, archaeologists depicted a rather monotonous continuity followed by inevitable destruction... The 120 years of Israelite history that followed the fall of the Omrides was, in fact, an era of dramatic social change in the kingdom, of economic ups and downs and constantly shifting strategies to survive the threat of empire.'

117.   M. Gleis, *Die Bamah* (BZAW, 251; Berlin: W. de Gruyter, 1997), p. 63; D.V. Edelman, 'The Meaning of *qitter*', *VT* 35 (1985), pp. 395-404 (403-404).

118.   Cross' assignment of 'these final terse paragraphs of the history to a less articulate Exilic editor', regarding the kings following Josiah (Cross, *Canaanite Myth*, p. 288), could as well apply to the kings following Jehu and Jehoash.

119.   In Josephus (*Ant.* 9.258) he is 'a wicked man and contemptuous of his duty to God'; in the Lucianic reading of the LXX he is 'the worst king'.

Of the descendants of Jehu, three are under Yahweh's mercy and protected from the Aramaean threat (2 Kgs 13.4, 23; 14.26-27). After the short reigns of Jehu's fourth successor, Zechariah (which lasted six months, 15.8) and his assassin, Shallum (which lasted one month, 15.13), the stage is set for a change in Israel's conditions. With the Assyrian threat (15.19-20, 29), no protection and no delays are introduced; however, neither is any curse. Being an Assyrian vassal seems to be acceptable, when the king is an Israelite king (15.19-20; 17.3). Revolting, as Hezekiah did, is of course better (18.7), but returning to Egypt, as Hoshea did, seems to have been the ultimate sin (2 Kgs 17.4, 7; cf. Num. 14.1-12; Deut. 17.16), which carried with it all other sins. The alliance is comparable to marriage with foreign women. It leads to idolatry.

The reiterative accusation of acting like the foreigners whom Yahweh had driven out (עשו ככל התועבות הגוים אשר הוריש יהוה מפני בני ישראל, with slight variations: 1 Kgs 14.24; 21.26;[120] 2 Kgs 16.3; 17.8;[121] 21.2, 11), is another metaphorical expression comparable to returning to Egypt or Assyria or Babylonia. In three of the five cases, the expression is explicitly linked with either marriage (Ahab 'with the Amorites': 1 Kgs 21.26) or political alliances (Ahaz with the Assyrians, 2 Kgs 16.3, 7-18, and Hoshea with the Egyptians, 17.4). In two cases no alliance is mentioned (Rehoboam, 1 Kgs 14.24; Manasseh, 2 Kgs 21.2, 11), but Egypt and Babylonia linger in the background. Invoking the Amorites and their empty gods (2 Kgs 21.11), Manasseh and Judah's sin is comparable to that of Ahab's. Invoking the Egyptians, Hoshea's sin is comparable to Jeroboam's making of the golden calves (1 Kgs 12) in yet another reiteration of Israel's mental return to Egypt (Exod. 32).

It is of course an open question whether the heifer symbol relates to Syrian, Mesopotamian or Egyptian bull worship, since this was a widespread cult figure in the entire Levant from the Neolithic to at least well into the Roman period.[122] The lack of orientation in the Exodus golden calf story, which only states that Israel had departed from the way (סרו...מן־הדרך) Yahweh had ordered them to follow (Exod. 32.8; Deut. 9.12, 16), opens up a variety of choices. The reiteration of the motif 'returning to Egypt' throughout Exodus–Numbers (Exod. 14.12; 16.3; Num. 11.4; 14.2-4; 20.5), might suggest that Egypt is intended.

The use of the calf motif as characteristic of both Ephraim and Egypt in Jer. 31.18 and 46.20-21 supports an assumed Egyptian orientation. Hosea's reference to Bet Aven's calves (עגלות בית און),[123] which Samaria fears (Hos. 10.5), has its parallel in Hos. 7.11's Ephraim, who, silly as a dove (כיונה פותה) without heart (אין לב),[124] calls at Egypt and goes to Assyria.[125] Both these verses are initiated with

120. Ahab erred by walking after the empty gods as did the Amorites, whom Yahweh had driven out before the Israelites: ויתעב מאד ללכת אחרי הגללים ככל אשר עשו האמרי אשר הוריש יהוה מפני בני ישראל.

121. The Israelites walked after the statutes of the nations: בחקות הגוים.

122. N. Wyatt, 'Calf', in *DDD*[2], pp. 180-82.

123. LXX: τοῦ οἴκου Ὤν and singular 'calf'.

124. Cf. Ps. 78.36-37.

125. For the dove as a divine symbol and the goddess Astarte-Semiramis in Assyrian and Syrian religion and Jewish allegations (*b. Ḥul.* 2a; *y. ʾAbod. Zar.* 4.5) of Samaritan worship of a

allusions to Israel's alliances (7.8-9 and 10.3-4), and both pronounce the exile of Ephraim.[126] Psalm 68's mockery of Israel for lying in the cattle pen, a dove clad in silver and gold (v. 14), and Egypt and Nubia's submission to Yahweh in Jerusalem after the dispersion of the cattle (vv. 31-32) similarly allude to Israel's Egyptian connection.

It is the prophets however, who have given the most expressive voice to the political alliances in terms of a marriage metaphor, when they call Samaria and Jerusalem 'wives of Yahweh'. They are unfaithful wives because they follow the practice of the foreigner, that is, they pay their allegiance to foreign gods and to powerless empires doomed to annihilation: the Egyptians, the Assyrians and the Babylonians (Hos. 1–2; 5.13-15; 7.11; 8.9; 12.2; Ezek. 16.26-31; 23.5-27 [especially vv. 22-23]; Jer. 2.33-3, 13; 11.9-17).[127] Expressed in terms of observing or violating Yahweh's cult, mundane affairs have become interpreted in dogma's claim for Yahweh's people to become a holy people. The king should never go to Egypt for horses, never marry foreign women and never amass wealth (Deut. 17.16-17).[128] But can that be? Is that not what a successful king should do, and for what reason Solomon was so greatly praised? Implicitly repeating the snake's authority-challenging question, 'Can it really be?' (Gen. 3), Hoshea's sin is comparable to the sins of Saul (1 Sam. 15.18-26; 28.18; cf. Lev. 27.28-29), Solomon (1 Kgs 11.4-10, 33) and Ahab (1 Kgs 20.27-43).

6. *Jeroboam's Sin: The High Places and the Temples*

In 1 Kgs 12.26-33, Jeroboam is said to have introduced competing cult places in Bethel and Dan in order to prevent his people from going on pilgrimage to Jerusalem. The political agenda underlying Jeroboam's act is made clear in the statement

dove image on Mt Gerizim as 'a misunderstanding or deliberate distortion of the Samaritan cult of *Šemâ*, the name, i.e. Yahweh', which, however, might be a reference to the goddess Ashima, mentioned in 2 Kgs 17.29-30, see J. Fossum, 'Dove', in *DDD*[1], pp. 500-504; *idem*, 'Samaritan Demiurgical Traditions and the Alleged Dove Cult of the Samaritans', in R. van den Broeck and M.J. Vermaseren (eds.), *Studies in Gnosticism and Hellenistic Religions* (EPRO, 91; Leiden: E.J. Brill, 1981), pp. 143-60; M. Mor, 'The Samaritans and the Bar-Kokhbah Revolt', in A.D. Crown (ed.), *The Samaritans* (Tübingen: J.C.B. Mohr [Paul Siebeck], 1989), pp. 19-31 (26).

126.   Cf. Hos. 8.13 and 9.3. The return to Egypt is interpreted by several scholars together with 2 Kgs 25.26 as a fulfilment of Deut. 28.68 and an indication of a 'Deuteronomistic History' or an Exodus tradition's 'from Egypt to Egypt'. One must, however, not fail to notice that Egypt is given as a punishment in Deut. 28.68, while in 2 Kgs 25.26 and Jer. 41.17-18 it is given as refuge 'for fear of the Chaldeans'. In contrast *AF*, ch. XVI, p. 64, regards Egypt as exile and a fulfilment of Deut. 28.68.

127.   J. Galambush, *Jerusalem in the Book of Ezekiel: The City as Yahweh's Wife* (SBLDS, 130; Atlanta: Scholars Press, 1992); Thompson, *The Bible in History*, pp. 369-74; Schwartz, *The Curse of Cain*, pp. 69-76, 132-42. Regarding Egyptian use of this metaphor, see I. Hjelm and T.L. Thompson, 'The Victory Song of Merneptah, Israel and the People of Palestine', *JSOT* 27.1 (2002), pp. 3-18.

128.   It should not go unnoticed that the items of the forefathers given away by Rehoboam were accumulated by Solomon (1 Kgs 14.26) and those by Jehoash were accumulated by Jehoshaphat, Jehoram and Ahaziah (2 Kgs 12.19), all of whom transgress borders of patronage.

that he feared that the kingship would return (שוב) to the house of David, and the people pay their allegiance to Rehoboam (vv. 26-27). Reiterating the Exodus golden calf episode,[129] Jeroboam made two golden calves to be placed each at the northern and southern borders of his kingdom. This was further aggravated by his appointment of priests from among the people (ויעש כהנים מקצות העם אשר לא־היו מבני לוי, 'And he appointed priests from among all the people, who did not belong to the Levites') and the implicit break with the priestly class of Jerusalem, the Levites.[130] The mentioning of the Levites here implies their role in the golden calf story as those who were with Yahweh (Exod. 32.26-27).[131] As such, they are characters in a narrative, which is not to be confused with a history report on what an otherwise unknown Jeroboam did in the past.[132] The crucial point is not that Jeroboam appointed priests, but that the priests he appointed could not have been the Levites since they opposed the calf worship; at least after Moses had destroyed the calf (Exod. 32.26; cf. 32.20). The priests appointed by Jeroboam were installed by him to officiate at the temples of the high places, the בית־במה, and at the altar, the מזבח in Bethel (vv. 31-32).[133] These temples and the altar in Bethel are the leading motif in the characterization of Jeroboam's sin. It is reiterated in the closure of the man of God's judgment and curse against the altar in Bethel and against the temples of the high places (1 Kgs 13 [especially vv. 2, 32-33]). It is not idolatry which caused the severe judgment, it is disloyalty, made clear in the prophet tale's warning against returning (שוב) to the way he came from (1 Kgs 13.7-10, 16-22).

The consequence of returning is made explicit in the burial formulae that 'your body shall not be buried in the tomb of your fathers' (13.22). This is not simply a metaphorical death sentence. It is a statement of where the man of God belonged after he had demonstrated his disloyalty—namely, in the tomb of the old prophet, who calls him 'brother' (13.30) and with whom he becomes united in death (13.31; 2 Kgs 23.18). The lion motif further specifies the divine[134] and royal authority[135]

129.   M. Aberbach and L. Smolar, 'Aaron, Jeroboam, and the Golden Calves', *JBL* 86 (1962), pp. 129-40, noticed thirteen points of identity or contact between the two accounts. For the possibility that the Jeroboam tradition is prior to Exod. 32's golden calf narrative, see, M. Noth, *Das zweite Buch Mose: Exodus* (ATD, 5; Göttingen: Vandenhoeck & Ruprecht, 5th edn, 1973 [1959]), pp. 202-203; Van Seters, *Life of Moses*, pp. 295-301.

130.   For the quite ambiguous treatment of the Levites in the Pentateuch compared to a high reverence for the same group in other parts of biblical and extra biblical literature, see Hjelm, *Samaritans and Early Judaism*, pp. 152-70.

131.   Aberbach and Smolar, 'Aaron and Jeroboam', p. 131.

132.   Cf. the historicist reading in Aberbach and Smolar, 'Aaron and Jeroboam', who miss the point that the author of the narrative worked from a pro-Jerusalem view and therefore portrayed Jeroboam's cult as the opposite of Jerusalem's.

133.   For a conflation of Bethel and Gerizim in Samaritan literature and the possible conflation of these names in Masoretic literature, see, A.D. Crown, 'Redating the Schism between the Judaeans and the Samaritans', *JQR* 82 (1991), pp. 17-50 (31); Hjelm, *Samaritans and Early Judaism*, pp. 56, 240-41.

134.   Cf. 1 Kgs 20.36; Yahweh is referred to as a lion in Isa. 31.4; Jer. 49.19; 50.44; Amos 3.8.

135.   Cf. the lion as a euphemism for Babylonia (Isa. 35.9; Jer. 4.7; Joel 1.6; Nah. 2.12-14; Dan. 6; 7.4; *1 En.* 89.56, 66); related to Judah (Gen. 49.9; Isa. 31.4; Ezek. 19.2-9); 'remnant of Jacob' (Mic. 5.7); David (2 Sam. 17.10).

behind the curse and brings the old prophet to realize that the doom uttered by the man from Judah against Jeroboam's competing cult is divinely sanctioned (cf. the reference to 'the altar and *all* the temples in the cities of Samaria', 1 Kgs 13.32; 2 Kgs 23.19).[136] In a mutual agreement that the doom of Jeroboam's sin justifies Josiah's act, both prophets are recognized as true Yahweh prophets and, accordingly, their bones are spared desecration (2 Kgs 23.17-18).

While it is obvious that this story belongs to the Josiah narrative, I see no evidence that it has not originally been written in its entirety together with that part of the Josiah narrative. Neither do I find any reason to see a break between 1 Kgs 12.30 and 31.[137] Provan fails to recognize that 12.31 does not speak of במות but of בית־במות. Gleis also argues for a late insertion of 12.31-32, however much it reflects *historisch verwertbare Informationen* [*sic*].[138] It is, however, the building of the temples, the בית־במות and the appointment of priests which 1 Kgs 13.32-34 declares to be *the* sin of Jeroboam's house, which carries with it ultimate rejection of that house.[139] The calf motif is only an additional characterization, aiming at conveying an implicit message, the meaning of which we can only speculate on. The author made a clear distinction in his dual characterization of Jeroboam's cult, the calves, the altar in Bethel and the temples, which not only Jeroboam builds, but which in 2 Kgs 23.19 are referred to as made by 'Israel's kings'. The rejection does not relate to idolatry, but to transgression of the statutes about cult centralization and cult control. As we saw in the Jehu case, having removed Israel's sin, he still followed in the paths of Jeroboam.

If for any reason, one would make chronological divisions of the material, the sections dealing with the calves (2 Kgs 12.28-29, 32) are those that can be separated from the narrative as a whole (and from the Deuteronomistic History) without any loss of meaning. This can be seen from the lack of reference to them in the narrative about Josiah's reform, and a possible allusion to them in 1 Kgs 14.9, which does not deal with the altar and the temples at all.[140] It would, however, have

136.   Barrick, 'On the Meaning of בית־ה/במות', pp. 624-25, 636-37, seems to be mistaken by mixing the altar in Bethel with the temples. There is no mention of any *bamoth*-house in Bethel, only of an altar, which is consistent with other references in Kings (1 Kgs 12.29, 32, 33; 13.1-5, 32; 2 Kgs 23.17). (Amos 7.13's mention of מקדש־מלך in Bethel and 7.9's מקדשי־ישראל further suggests that the distinction should be upheld.) The Bethel reference in 2 Kgs 17.28 can be to either a cultic institution or to a place, from where the teaching is given, and thus could be an allusion to the Gerizim tradition. Whether this included a temple is a moot point, see further Chapter 4 below. The mention of a high place in 2 Kgs 23.15 and the lack of such a reference in 23.17 confirm that the בית־ה/במות of 1 Kgs 12 and 13 does not refer to Bethel. However, the Deuteronomistic author might have wanted to avoid mentioning any structure, which could be compared to Jerusalem's temple, a highly problematic issue in Jewish writings.

137.   Provan, *Hezekiah and the Books of Kings*, pp. 78-81.

138.   Gleis, *Die Bamah*, pp. 122-23: 'Die Sünde Jeroboams besteht nun nicht mehr im Aufstellen der Stierbilder in Dan und Betel, das heisst in der Etablierung eines eigenen Staatskultes des Nordreiches, sondern in einem weitreichenden Eingriff in den Lokalkult'.

139.   Hoffmann, *Reform und Reformen*, p. 60.

140.   Grammatically, one can as easily combine 2 Kgs 12.27 with 12.31 as with 12.28, since their grammatical forms are identical. The lack of explicit subject in 12.31 and the shift of subject

given the author great difficulties in arguing that Jeroboam's cult was related to apostasy rather than policy.[141] The ambiguity related to the calf-motif, which does not signify non-Yahwistic traits,[142] but which, however, could be associated with foreign cults as symbols of 'gods made by men's hands' as were the empty gods of empires, seems to be the implicit theological argumentation.[143] Linking these themes together gives reason for the doom of Jeroboam's administrative measures, which determines that his house become effaced (הכחיד) and annihilated (השמיד) from the surface of the earth (1 Kgs 13.34; 15.29; 16.12; 2 Kgs 10.17, 28).

The altar and the temples are literary consequences of the division of the Davidic kingdom. It was not the cult, but Jeroboam and his kingdom which were threatened by the competing cult in Jerusalem (אם־יעלה העם הזה לעשות זבחים בבית־יהוה בירושלם ושב לב העם הזה אל־אדניהם אל־רחבעם מלך יהודה והרגוני ושבו אל־רחבעם מלך־יהודה, 'if this people go up to offer sacrifices at the temple of Yahweh in Jerusalem, then the heart of this people will turn again to their lord, to Rehoboam king of Judah, and they will kill me and return to Rehoboam king of Judah', 1 Kgs 12.27). The consequence of not establishing an independent cult in the north would have been a re-unification of the kingdoms! (1 Kgs 12.26-27). Linked thematically to the rejection of Israel and to the reforms of Josiah, the focus of the narrative is not so much centred on a characterization of the Northern Kingdom as it is on the legislation of the Jerusalemite cult as having the proper temple, priesthood and festivals.[144]

from Jeroboam to 'the king' in 12.28 might suggest that v. 31 belongs to vv. 26-27. It is v. 32, rather than v. 31, which initiates a narrative beginning ('ein erzählerische Neuinsatz' [Gleis, *Die Bamah*, p. 122]).

141.   Cross, *Canaanite Myths*, pp. 74-75: 'Apparently, Jeroboam's real sin was in establishing a rival to the central sanctuary in Jerusalem, not in the introduction of a foreign god or a pagan idol'.

142.   Van Seters, *In Search of History*, p. 313, argues that the calves are representations of Yahweh, the God of Israel. Hoffmann, *Reform und Reformen*, p. 66: 'zugleich eine Übertretung des *ersten* wie des *zweiten* Gebotes'. Lemche, 'The God of Hosea', p. 253: 'Hosea seemingly rejects this worship, but when he tries to formulate his image of Yahweh, it is a Yahweh who carries with him most of the traits associated with bull worship'; Barrick, 'On the Meaning of בית־ה/במות', p. 636: 'At the *bamoth*-house in Bethel they worshipped Yahweh in "the proper manner" established by Jeroboam's establishment (2 Kgs 17. 25-28+32). This is consistent with 1 Kgs 12.26-32, which represents Jeroboam's establishment as entirely Yahwistic.' J.M. Sasson, 'Bovine Symbol in the Exodus Narrative', *VT* 18 (1968), pp. 380-87; G.W. Coats, *Moses, Heroic Man, Man of God* (JSOTSup, 57; Sheffield: JSOT Press, 1988), p. 174; and J. Zsengellér, *Gerizim as Israel: Northern Tradition of the Old Testament and the Early History of the Samaritans* (Utrechtse Theologische Reeks, 38; Utrecht: University of Utrecht Press, 1998), p. 79, argue for some conflation of Yahweh and Moses in the Exodus golden calf tradition, ascribing to Moses divine traits otherwise related to Yahweh.

143.   J. Pakkala, 'The Original Meaning of Jeroboam's Calves' (unpublished paper delivered at the SBL International Meeting, Rome, 2001); *idem, Intolerant Monolatry in the Deuteronomistic History* (Publications of the Finnish Exegetical Society, 76; Göttingen: Vandenhoeck & Ruprecht, 1999), pp. 156, 159.

144.   Hoffmann, *Reform und Reformen*, p. 73: 'So stellt 1 K 12,26-32 als ganzes eine dtr Fiktion dar. Das Ergebnis der Kumulation von Kultfreveln mit sämtlich antijerusalemischer, gegen

The calves and the festival are used metaphorically as a designation of a return to the desert situation, and we might infer that the narrator indirectly argues that Israel claims to have been led astray when Judah's Yahweh told them to go to Jerusalem.[145] The competing priests resemble the Korahite rebellion in Numbers 16.[146] As the 250 leaders of the congregation were consumed (root אכל) by Yahweh's burning anger, when they wrongly offered incense (איש מקריבו הקטרת, Num. 16.35–17.5), the offering priests (כהני־הבמות) should be slaughtered (root זבח) and burned (root שרף, 1 Kgs 13.2; 2 Kgs 23.20) on the altar on which Jeroboam lit the offering (להקטיר, 1 Kgs 12.33b; 13.1). Anticipating the fate of the Northern Kingdom, the man of God becomes an illustration of what later is to happen to the north, when first Ahab's house (1 Kgs 20.35-43) and later Samaria was given to the 'Lion' because of their disobedience to the word of Yahweh.[147]

The בית־הבמות and the priests of the people theme occurs in the books of Kings as a specific theme related to the sin of Jeroboam in (1) the story about Jehu, who did not remove Jeroboam's sin; (2) the story about the fall of the Northern Kingdom (2 Kgs 17), where the settled peoples from Babylon, Cuthah, Avva, Hamath and Sephar-vaim used the בית־במות the Samaritans had made (v. 29), and appointed their own priests (v. 32); and finally (3) in Josiah's reform (2 Kgs 23.19-20), where he removed (root סור) the בית־במות in the towns of Samaria (v. 19) and slaughtered and burned the bones of the priests of the high places on the altar in Bethel (v. 20). While this theme is related to the sin of the Northern Kingdom, a second stratum brings in the element of *both* Israel *and* Judah's sin.

7. *The High Places,* הבמות, *and the Habits of the Foreigners*

Based on the Laws of the Pentateuch (Exod. 23.24; 34.13-17; Num. 33.52; Deut. 7.1-5, 25; 12.2-3), this common sin is characterized as being related to the cult

---

das Zentralisierungsgebot gerichteter Tendenz ist ein in seiner einseitig negativen Tendenz verzerrtes Bild des historischen Jeroboam, das aber gerade dadurch geeignet ist, eine klare "*Definition*" der "Sünde Jeroboams" zu liefern als Basis für alle folgenden Rückverweise bis hin zur "Erfüllung" (2 K 17) und zur endlichen Beseitigung (2 K 23, 15-20).' Van Seters, *In Search of History*, p. 314: 'The story about Jeroboam and the golden calves is so thoroughly anachronistic and propagandistic that we must suspect it of being a complete fabrication. It is the literary creation of Dtr and functions in much the same way for the account of the northern kingdom as 2 Sam. 7 does for Judah'.

145.   J. Debus, *Die Sünde Jeroboams: Studien zur Darstellung Jeroboams und der Geschichte des Nordreichs in der deuteronomistischen Geschichtsschreibung* (FRLANT, 93; Göttingen: Vandenhoeck & Ruprecht, 1967), pp. 37-47 (45-47).

146.   Aberbach and Smolar, 'Aaron and Jeroboam', p. 134: 'the two eldest sons of Aaron—Nadab and Abihu—and the two recorded sons of Jeroboam—Nadab and Abijah—bear virtually similar names'.

147.   A variant of the motif is found in Esarhaddon's invocation of the god Bethel and the goddess Anat-Bethel to 'give you over to the claws of a devouring lion' in his vassal treaty with King Ba'lu of Tyre (*ANET*, p. 534); cf. M. Cogan and H. Tadmor, *II Kings: A New Translation With Introduction and Commentary* (AB, 11; 2 vols.; Garden City, NY: Doubleday, 1988), II, p. 210. For further references to the Bethel cult, see W. Röllig, 'Bethel', in *DDD*[1], pp. 331-34.

practice of foreigners, whom Yahweh had driven out (הוריש) before the Israelites. The cult symbols related to the cult of the foreigners are the *massebot* (מצבת), the altar (מזבח), the *Asherim* (אשרה/אשרים) and the carved idols (פסילי־אלהים), which should be destroyed (שבר), torn down (נתץ), cut down (כרת) and burned (שרף). In addition to this, the high places (במות) shall be trod upon (דרך, Deut. 33.29) or devastated (השמיד, Num. 33.52). The vocabulary of Numbers is different from that of Exodus and Deuteronomy and employs terms like משכית and צלמי־מסכת for the cult symbols and images, which should be destroyed (אבד in piel). The destruction of the high places using the hiphil form of שמד has a close parallel to Leviticus 26's anticipation of Yahweh's destruction of the Israelite people's high places and images, when they do not obey his commandments: והשמדתי את־במתיכם והכרתי את־חמניכם ('and I will destroy your high places and I will cut down your incense altars', Lev. 26.30). Completing the list of the idolatrous acts of the foreigners, we must add multiple cult places for their gods, 'upon the high mountains, upon the hills, and under every green tree' (על־ההרים הרמים ועל־הגבעות ותחת כל־עץ רענן, Deut. 12.2).

We must now proceed to examine the characteristics of Israel and Judah's sin mentioned in the judgment formulae, the judgments and the dispersion of במה. In the schematic presentation below (Chart 1), underlined numbers signify references to במה. Of these, some are marked with an asterix, signifying a reference to temples of the high places בית־במות. All the italicized and underlined לא־סר occurrences refer to the six Judaean kings, who did not remove the high places: Asa, Jehoshaphat, Jehoash, Amaziah, Azariah and Jotham. Uncommented לא־סר refer to the nine Israelite kings, who did not turn away from Jeroboam's sin: Jehoram, Jehu, Jehoahaz, Jehoash, Jeroboam, Zechariah, Menahem, Pekahiah, Pekah. Its last occurrence (2 Kgs 17.22) refers to Israel's lack of turning away from Jeroboam's sin. As the judgment of not removing the במה is given exclusively to Judaean kings, one might rightly suggest that the necessity of removing these is related to question of cult centralization.[148] Combined with the verbs כעס, חטא, בנה, סור, עשה and noun חטאה, we find the distribution simplified in Chart 1 (see next page).

From the chart, it becomes clear that the provocation theme (כעס) related to Israel's sin does not refer to Jeroboam's establishment of a competing cult, but to Israel's sin claimed in 1 Kings 14. It disappears after Ahaziah and reappears in 2 Kgs 17.11. It is 'transferred' to Judah in the transgressions of Manasseh and Judah in 2 Kings 21 and appears as combining Israel's sin with Judah in 2 Kings 23. The theme of idolatry, designated as walking after the habits of the foreigners, can now be separated from the cult centralization theme related to the high places and the temples of the high places. While Israelite kings are said to have sinned according to the sin of Jeroboam and their forefathers, Judaean kings (and people) are said to have made transgressions either according to the sin of their forefathers (1 Kgs 14.22; 2 Kgs 23.32, 37)[149] or according to the abominations of the nations

148. Provan, *Hezekiah and the Books of Kings*, p. 65.
149. A father reference in the singular is always a specific reference and therefore not included in the list.

Chart 1. *Israel and Judah's Sin, and the Distribution of* במה *and* כעס (חטא)

אלהים	במה	כן	חטא ה/חטאת חטאה	חטא	כעס
3.2-4 (Solomon offered at...)					
	11.7		11.7 (Solomon)	8.31-50 (Solomon's prayer)	
	12.31*,32; 13.2,32*,33		12.31*,32; 13.2,32*,33 (Jeroboam)	12.30; 13.34	
				14.16 (Jeroboam)	14.9, 15 (Jeroboam, Israel)
	14.22		14.23 (Judah)	14.22	
15.5 (David did not turn away from Yahweh's commandments)				15.3 (Abijam of Judah)	
15.14 (Asa of Judah)	15.14				
				15.26, 30, 34 (Nadab, Baasha	15.30
				16.2, 13, 19, 26, 31 (Baasha, Baasha and Elah, Zimri, Omri, Ahab)	16.2, 7, 13, 26, 33
				21.22 (Ahab)	21.22
22.44 (Jehoshaphat of Judah)	22.44				
				22.53 (Ahaziah)	22.54

1 Kings

2 Kings

אשרה	מצבה	פ	בתי הבמות / עבדה	מצבא	כמר
3.3 (Jehoram)		3.2 (Jehoram removed the pillar of Baal)		3.3	
10.29, 31 (Jehu)				10.29, 31	
12.4 (Jehoash of Judah)	12.4				
13.2, 6 (Jehoahaz)				13.2, 6	
13.11 (Jehoash)				13.11	
14.4 (Amaziah of Judah)	14.4				
14.24 (Jeroboam)				14.24	
15.4 (Azariah of Judah)	15.4				
15.9, 18, 24, 28 (Zechariah, Menahem, Pekahiah, Pekah)				15.9, 18, 24, 28	
15.35 (Jotham of Judah)	15.35				
	16.4 (Ahaz of Judah offered at…)				
	17.9, 11		17.9 (Israel)	17.7 (Israel)	17.11, 17
17.22 (Israel)				17.22	
	17.29*, 32*		17.29*, 32* (Samaritans)		
18.6 (Hezekiah of Judah, did not turn away from Yahweh)	18.4, 22	18.4, 22 (Hezekiah)			
	21.3		21.3 (Manasseh of Judah)	21.17	21.6 (Manasseh), 15 (Judah and Jerusalem)
22.3 (Josiah of Judah, did not turn to the right or the left)	23.8, 9 (defiled by Josiah), 13, 15, 19*	23.19* (Josiah)	23.13 (Solomon), 15 (Jeroboam of Israel), 19* (Kings of Israel)	23.15	22.17 (Jerusalem); 23.19* (Kings of Israel), 26 (Manasseh of Judah)

(1 Kgs 14.24; 2 Kgs 16.3; 21.2)[150] and not followed the instructions of the Law. This sin we can now characterize (1 Kgs 14.23-24) as:

ויבנו גם־המה להם במות ומצבות ואשרים על כל־גבעה גבהה ותחת כל־עץ רענן׃
וגם קדש היה בארץ עשו ככל התועבת הגוים אשר הוריש יהוה מפני ישראל

For they also built to themselves high places and pillars and *Asherim* on every high hill and under every green tree. There were even male cult prostitutes in the land, who did everything according to the abominable practice of the foreigners, whom Yahweh had driven out before Israel.

With slight variations, we find the same judgment given of Ahaz' reign (2 Kgs 16.3b-4):

וגם את־בניו העביר באש כתעבות הגוים אשר הוריש יהוה אתם מפני בני ישראל׃
ויזבח ויקטר בבמות ועל־הגבעות ותחת כל־עץ רענן

...and he also made his sons pass through the fire according to the abominable practise of the foreigners, whom Yahweh had driven out before the Israelites. And he offered and burned incense on the high places and on the hills and under every green tree.

Ahaz, however, did not build במות (they were there already), but only replaced the old bronze altar (מזבח) with a Damascene altar (2 Kgs 16.10-14).

Manasseh's reign (2 Kgs 21.2-7) is provided with the most elaborate description bringing together northern and southern transgressions:

(2) ויעש הרע בעיני יהוה כתועבות הגוים אשר הוריש יהוה מפני בני ישראל׃
(3) וישב ויבן את־הבמות אשר אבד חזקיהו אביו ויקם מזבחת לבעל ויעש אשרה כאשר
עשה אחאב מלך ישראל וישתחו לכל־צבע השמים ויעבד אתם׃
(4) ובנה מזבחת בבית יהוה אשר אמר יהוה בירושלם אשים את־שמי׃
(5) ויבן מזבחות לכל־צבע השמים בשתי חצרות בית יהוה׃
(6) והעביר את־בנו באש ועונן ונחש ועשה אוב וידענים הרבה לעשות הרע בעיני
יהוה להכעיס
(7) וישם את־פסל האשרה אשר עשה בבית אשר אמר יהוה אל־דוד ואל־שלמה בנו
בבית הזה ובירושלם אשר בחרתי מכל שבטי ישראל אשים את־שמי לעולם׃

And he did evil in the eyes of Yahweh according to the abominable practise of the foreigners, whom Yahweh had driven out before the Israelites. For he rebuilt the high places, which his father Hezekiah had destroyed and he erected altars for Baal and made an Asherah as Ahab, the king of Israel had done, and he worshiped all the host [lit. army] of Heaven and served them. And he built altars in the temple of Yahweh, of which Yahweh had said: 'In Jerusalem will I place my name'. And he built altars for all the host of Heaven in the two courts of the temple of Yahweh. And he let his sons pass through the fire and he practised soothsaying and augury and dealt with mediums and wizards in doing evil in the eyes of Yahweh to provoke him to anger. And he placed the graven image of *Asherah* that he had made

---

150. Cf. Ahaz: Deut. 18.9; 2 Chron. 28.3; Manasseh: 33.2; the leaders, the priests and the people: 36.14 (without אשר הוריש יהוה מפני בני ישראל); the leaders of Judah, the priests and the people of the land: LXX 2 Chron. 36.14 and *3 Esd.* 1.47.

in the temple, of which Yahweh had said to David and his son Solomon: 'In this temple and in Jerusalem, which I have chosen among all the tribes of Israel will I place my name forever'.

From Ahaz' violation of the Yahweh cult over Manasseh's syncretistic cult, we finally find his son Amon worshipping the idols and leaving Yahweh completely (2 Kgs 21.21-22):

וילך בכל־דרך אשר־הלך אביו ויעבד את־הגללים אשר עבד אביו וישתו לחם:
ויעזב את־יהוה אלהי אבתיו ולא הלך בדרך יהוה

And he walked in all the way of his father and served the idols his father had served and he worshiped them. And he left Yahweh the God of his fathers and he did not walk in the way of Yahweh.

Comparing these accusations with the characterization of the sin of the Northern Kingdom in 2 Kgs 17.7-17, we find that it contains both strata and reflects most of the Pentateuchal language of what the people should not do, or what cult objects they should destroy:[151]

v. 7b	they feared other gods (ויראו אלהים אחרים, cf. Exod. 23.24; 34.13; Deut. 7.4; 12.2)
v. 8	walked after the regulations of the people (בחקות הגוים) Yahweh had removed (הוריש) in front of them (cf. Lev. 20.23; Deut 18.9)
v. 9a	ascribed matters (ויחפאו דברים) which were not from Yahweh
v. 9b	built high places in all their towns (ויבנו להם במות בכל עריהם; cf. Num. 33.52; Deut. 33.29) from watchtower to fortified town (ממגדל נוצרים עד־עיר מבצר)
v. 10	erected pillars and *asherim* (ויצבו להם מצבות ואשרים; cf. Exod. 34.13; Lev. 26.1; Deut. 7.5; 12.3; 16.21-22) on all high hills and under all green trees (ותחת כל־עץ רענן על כל־גבעה גבהה; cf. Deut. 12.2)
v. 11	burned incense on all the high places like the nations (ויקטרו שם בכל־במות כגוים)
v. 12	served the idols (ויעבדו הגללים; cf. Lev. 21.30; 26.30; Deut. 29.16[152])

Of the first part, vv. 10, 11 and 12, reflect, in fact, Judah's sin as narrated about the reigns of Rehoboam, Ahaz and Manasseh. Verse 8 deceptively leads one to regard the imitation of the nations as being the same as Rehoboam, Ahaz and Manasseh's כתעבות הגוים. This, however, is not the case. It is not the abominations but the regulations (בחקות הגוים)—that is, the 'law' of the foreigners—Israel followed, thus ascribing matters which were not from Yahweh (v. 9a). To walk after or to observe the statutes (חקות) is a legalistic term, which in Kings is exclusively connected with the narratives about Solomon's reign, the fall of the Northern Kingdom and Josiah's reform. The conditional promise, related to the behaviour of David, and the immediate judgment (1 Kgs 3.3; 6.12; 9.6; 11.11, 33, 34) leads to a similar conditional promise given to Jeroboam (1 Kgs 11.38). In 2 Kgs 17.13-15, the conditional covenant is invoked in the accusation of having walked after the statutes of the foreigners (v. 8), as Judah would also imitate (v. 19). Josiah's institution of

---

151. For a detailed analysis, see Hoffmann, *Reform und Reformen*, pp. 127-33, 327-66.

152. These are the only three occurrences of גללים in the Pentateuch. In Kings it appears in 1 Kgs 15.12; 21.26; 2 Kgs 21.11, 21; 23.24, and in Ezekiel it appears 38 times.

Yahweh's statutes (2 Kgs 23.3) leads to a reversal of Solomon's sin. Verse 9b bears allusions to Hezekiah's removal of the foreigners (2 Kgs 18.8).

The framework vv. 7b and 12 conflates Judah's and Israel's sins. To *fear* other gods (יראו אלהים אחרים) occurs in Kings in this chapter only. We must therefore regard the expression as functioning as a framework for ch. 17's closing theme: the foreigners, who did not fear Yahweh (17.25). They ended up fearing Yahweh, but not in a proper manner, because this cult was mixed with serving their own gods also (17.32, 33, 41). Restricted as this theme is, we find that such behaviour is indistinguishable from Israel's walking in the paths of Jeroboam [*sic*].[153] The newcomers feared Yahweh after their own habits because they followed the practice of the people (כמשפט הגוים, v. 33) from among whom they had been deported. This practice is declared to be in accordance with the former 'law' (הם עשים כמשפטם הראשנים, vv. 34, 40), and not the ordinances (Law) of Yahweh, given to Israel (v. 34):

> אינם יראים את־יהוה ואינם עשים כחקתם וכמשפטם
> וכתורה וכמצוה אשר צוה יהוה את־בני יעקב אשר־שם שמו ישראל

They do not fear Yahweh and they do not behave according to the statutes or the ordinances or the Law or the commandment which Yahweh has commanded the children of Jacob, whom he named Israel.

Consequently, they did not fear Yahweh. While Israel's empty gods mostly are termed ההבלים, we find in 17.12 the term הגללים used about the idols Asa removed (1 Kgs 15.12), the idols served by Ahab (1 Kgs 21.26), Manasseh and Israel (2 Kgs 21.11) and Amon (2 Kgs 21.21), and removed by Josiah (2 Kgs 23.24). Whether intentionally or not, the term functions as a bridge to the next set of accusations, mostly related to Israel and Judah's sins as narrated in the stories of the reigns of Jeroboam, Ahab, Ahaz and Manasseh. According to these accusations they:

v. 15b   walked after empty gods and became nothingness (וילכו אחרי ההבל ויהבלו; cf. Deut. 32.21)

v. 16b   made for themselves images (מסכה; cf. Exod. 34.17; Lev. 19.4; Num. 33.52; Deut. 4.21-28; 9.12; 27.15), two calves (שני עגלים; cf. Exod. 32; Deut. 9.16),[154] and Asherah (אשירה)

v. 16c   worshipped the host of Heaven (וישתחוו לכל־צבע השמים; cf. Deut. 17.3)

v. 16d   and served Baal (ויעבדו את־הבעל)

v. 17a   made their sons and daughters pass through fire (ויעבירו את־בניהם ואת־בנותיהם באש; cf. Deut. 18.10)

---

153.   Hoffmann's interpretation (*Reform und Reformen*, p. 138), that vv. 24-33 deviates from the theme of 'Jeroboam's sin' and belong to 'die scharf abgrenzende polemische Verurteilung der Samaritaner für alle Zeit, die Festschreibung des Samaritanischen Schismas', is based on his historical-critical reading of the material. Thematically, vv. 24-33 are as much a 'preparation' for 2 Kgs 23.15-20, as is 1 Kgs 12.26–14.16, whether written before, after or in connection with the Josiah narrative.

154.   The two calves might be a late insertion (*BHS*). As the accusation, however, is preceded by the statement that they have left all Yahweh's commandments (ויעזבו את־כל־מצצת יהוה, 17.16aα), a conflation of Jeroboam's idolatrous sin with transgression of prohibition against images seems to be intentional and speaks against a late insertion.

v. 17b they used sorcery (יקסמו קסמים; cf. Deut. 18.10) and divination (ינחשו; cf. Lev. 19.26; Deut. 18.10)

v. 17c and they sold themselves (יתמברו) to do evil in the eyes of Yahweh to provoke him to anger (לעשות הרע בעיני יהוה להכעיסו; cf. Deut. 4.25; 9.18; 31.29; 32.16, 21)[155]

Of these accusations, only vv. 15b, 16b, 16d and 17c relate to *Israel*'s sin which in other texts of 1 and 2 Kings is said to have provoked Yahweh to anger (כעס). In all occurrences of this verb in Deuteronomy and the books of Kings, the reader is given an explicit or implicit message of future annihilation because of this provocation.[156] With increasing intensity, we find that Moses' attempt to save the fallen desert generation (Deut. 9.13–10.5) is nothing but a short-termed relief from total annihilation[157] pronounced in the closure of Deuteronomy (Deut. 31.29; 32.15-25). In a five-step move we find that first Israel and later Judah have provoked Yahweh to such anger that annihilation is the ultimate outcome. While both the Israelites and Judaeans often sinned (חטא), the sin only becomes lethal when provocation (כעס) lies behind. Thus we find the verb's occurrences first in a characterization of Jeroboam's sin that he made 'images' of *other* gods (1 Kgs 14.9, 15), which in 1 Kgs 15.29-30 led to a total annihilation of his house by the hand of Baasha because of the pronouncement given by the prophet Ahijah in 1 Kings 14. When Baasha, however, did not live up to the requirements, we find the author's reiterative play with the pattern of promise–fall–doom, which in 1 Kings 16 increases the sin of Jeroboam by the successive acts of Ahab son of Omri, pronouncing annihilation of his house also (1 Kgs 21.20-21). In all these instances, the references are not to Jeroboam's temples or to the altar in Bethel, but to the idolatry claimed in 1 Kings 14 and 15, the foreign gods which are empty.[158] That Israel had sold itself to do these evil things (1 Kgs 21.20; 2 Kgs 17.17c) implies a severe violation of its

155. The verb כעס appears in the Pentateuch only in Deuteronomy. Its occurrences in the books of Kings belong primarily to the judgment formulae structure, and it is significant that it disappears after the mention of Ahaziah (1 Kgs 22.54), who is the last of the apostate northern kings before the reforms of Jehoram and Jehu. In the intermediary period down to the fall of Israel, no apostasy is mentioned; this makes the judgment in 2 Kgs 17.11 and 17 appear to refer to this 'old sin'.

156. Auld, *Kings Without Privilege*, pp. 84-85, notes that only two instances of the seventeen occurrences of the term in Kings have parallels in Chronicles (2 Kgs 21.6 par. 2 Chron. 33.6; 2 Kgs 22.17 par. 2 Chron. 34.25), while additional use is found in Chronicles' Ahaz narrative (2 Chron. 28.25). On this basis and other occurrences of stereotyped language and themes in Kings, he raises the questions '[Is it that the] often clichéd language used to scold the north has been derived and generalized from the pre-existing narrative about the south? Or is Manasseh the southern scoundrel dressed in northern colours? The issue is nicely focussed as we evaluate the Kings "plus" in 21.3. This links Manasseh's altar-building for Baal and Asherah with the practices of Ahab, king of Israel—has Chronicles omitted this note along with the whole story of the north, or Kings added it along with that whole story?'

157. While Exodus employs the verb אכל (Exod. 32.10; 33.5), Deuteronomy employs the verb שמד similar to the books of Kings.

158. Van Seters (*In Search of History*, pp. 313-14), who rightly understood Jeroboam's cult of 1 Kgs 12–13 as Yahwistic, failed to see that 1 Kgs 14 brings in another theme of idolatry, which adds to the 'original' sin, but which is not to be mixed with it.

patronage relationship with Yahweh (cf. 1 Kgs 9.6, 9; 11.4, 10; 2 Kgs 22.17). It must be noticed that none of the accusations listed above refers to the altar and the temples. The explicit reference to Jeroboam (17.21-22) offers an implicit reference to the golden calf motif (חטאה גדולה, v. 21; cf. Exod. 32.21, 30, 31)[159] and alludes to the cultic edifices only (חטאת ירבעם, v. 22; cf. 1 Kgs 13.34). In contrast, Josiah's reforms only relate to the altar and the temples, which now are declared to be the 'lethal sin' (להכעיס,[160] 2 Kgs 23.19). Although several scholars conflate the northern בית־במות with the southern במות[161]no text in Kings narrates the building of במות in the north. The word occurs only in its connection with the priests of the high places (כהני־הבמות) and then in connection with the בית־במות. It is 2 Kgs 17.9's thematic anticipation of Hezekiah's reform which brings in the במות theme in the 'southern' section. In Josiah's removal both of the altar (המזבח) and the high place (הבמה, 2 Kgs 23.15) at Bethel, the conflation of accusations of southern and northern violation has become explicit.

The fourth step of the move is the threatening of doom over Israel given in 2 Kings 17's *inclusio* of a future invalidation of the division of the monarchy when Israel and Judah's fates become united (17.18-20) and given their own narrative course of promise, fall and doom initiated by Solomon, Rehoboam and Ahijah's sin and fulfilled in the acts of Manasseh. The implementation of the 'Israelite' judgment formula, that they did evil in the eyes of Yahweh (ויעש הרע בעיני יהוה) to the Judaean kings following Hezekiah, clarifies to the implicit reader that it is no longer possible to make any distinction between the two kingdoms.

Between these two last steps we find the reforms of Hezekiah and Josiah. We are now able to make conclusions about the character of these reforms.

8. *Hezekiah as Moses' Successor? The* Nehustan *Motif*

In the judgment of Hezekiah (2 Kgs 18.4), it is said that he removed the high places, broke the pillars, cut down the *Asherah* and broke into pieces the bronze serpent, the *Nehustan*, Moses had made:

הוא הסיר את־הבמות ושבר את־המצבת וכרת את־האשרה וכתת
נחש הנחשת אשר־עשה משה

He removed the high places and smashed the pillars and cut down the *Asherah* and broke into pieces the bronze serpent which Moses had made.

---

159. Van Seters, *Life of Moses*, p. 300.

160. LXX, Syriac and Vulgate insert את־יהוה.

161. See Barrick, 'On the Meaning of בית־/במות', p. 642, and Gleis, *Die Bamah*, pp. 63-64, who might be right that the distinction does not relate to architecture, but wrong when, in a historicist reading of Kings, he fails to acknowledge the author's rhetorical distinction, based on the ideology that no central cult 'exists' in the north, while in the south any cult outside Jerusalem's temple must be inferior to that and could not be termed 'house' or 'temple'—a fact which Van Seters (*In Search of History*, pp. 313-14) was partly aware of. See also Hoffmann, *Reform und Reformen*, pp. 67, 72-73, who however fails to distinguish the terms in his German translation of the Hebrew.

The high places refer to Judah's (Rehoboam's) sin in 1 Kings 14, ויבנו גם־המה להם במות ('they also built high places for themselves'), which Judah's kings did not remove and thereby violated the Deuteronomic command of centralizing the cult.[162] The centralization, which Hezekiah performed, took place within Judah and Jerusalem's borders, as expressed in the *Rabshaqeh*'s speech (18.22) and Manasseh's acts of replacement (21.2, 11). Hezekiah's cult centralization had nothing to do with the Northern Kingdom, where he had no jurisdiction. It did not extend beyond his own borders and the competing Samaritan cult of the north belongs to another narrative stratum, concluded in the Josiah narrative.

The pillars and the *Asherim* relate to the idolatry which Asa removed (1 Kgs 15.12-13), and which does not occur literally in Judah before Manasseh introduces the *Asherah* (2 Kgs 21.3 and 7). As a stock motif, however, they are needed here in a characterisation of the cult practice of the foreigners: the Philistines, whom Hezekiah smote (הכה, hiphil of נכה) from watch tower to fortified town (2 Kgs 18.8). In an inter-textual play on Israel's allegiance to the foreigners, whose regulations they imitated (בחקות הגוים) 'from watchtower to fortified town' (2 Kgs 17.8-9), Hezekiah removed these foreigners from his country.

The removal of the bronze serpent has several purposes. The most obvious is related to the prohibition of making images of 'Yahweh'.[163] The implicit reference in the Hezekiah narrative, however, relates to the reason for the erection of the serpent in Num. 21.4-9.[164] When the Israelites once again revolted against Yahweh and against Moses in the desert, complaining that they were to die from hunger and thirst and that they had got tired of the poor food (הלחם הקלקל), Yahweh sent snakes (הנחשים השרפים) against them. After the people's repentance, Yahweh orders Moses to make a serpent (שרף) and to put it on a stake so that everyone who looks at the serpent will survive from the snakebite. The play with motifs of die and live and bread and water, evokes allusions to the 'eat and drink' motif in the *Rabshaqeh*'s speech, that the people shall drink their own urine and eat their own dung if they do not surrender (2 Kgs 18.27). Comparing Hezekiah's people with Moses' people, Hezekiah has no need for the *Nehustan*; his people will not complain! Deuteronomy 8.14-16's interpretation of the event as Yahweh's test of his people's faithfulness, reiterated throughout Deuteronomy as the purpose of the wandering in the desert (Deut. 4.34; 8.2, 16; 13.4; 33.8), marks the act as a confirmation of Hezekiah and his people's allegiance to Yahweh. They will not follow other gods as did the Israelites, when they sold themselves to doing evil (2 Kgs 17.17). The linguistic interplay between נחש and divination (piel of נחש), which is not allowed (cf. Lev. 19.26; Deut. 18.10) and which did not save Israel (2 Kgs 17.17) as it will not save

---

162. Hoffmann, *Reform und Reformen*, pp. 336-37.
163. Hoffmann, *Reform und Reformen*, pp. 148-49.
164. Historical-critical scholarship's efforts to explain this cult symbol within Israelite history of religion is of no interest here. It is the thematic use of the motif which helps interpret the implications of the statement. Whether Moses actually made the serpent or not is of no concern to the author of Kings! In the Pentateuchal tradition, Moses made the serpent and that is what the author is referring to.

Judah (2 Kgs 21.6), should not go unnoticed. In a wider examination, we should neither fail to notice that Hezekiah's destruction (כתת) does not allude to the golden calf narrative in Exodus, but to the summary of this narrative in Deuteronomy 9 (v. 21). This is important since in that passage of Deuteronomy we also find a reference to the fearful Israelites of Numbers 14, who did not trust Yahweh and did not listen when he told them to go and take the country (Deut. 9.23).

Finally, we need to consider the possibility that Hezekiah's act functions as an inter-textual play with Isaiah's euphemistic reference to the Assyrians in Isa. 14.29 and with Jeremiah's similar reference to the Babylonians, whom the people cannot charm (root נחש, Jer. 8.17).[165] No less likely does Deut. 32.33's reference to Israel's enemies—who in Mic. 7.17 and Ps. 72.9 shall find themselves licking the dust of the soil as if they were snakes—echo throughout 2 Kings' exaltation of Hezekiah. Yahweh's crushing (root כתת) of David's enemies (Ps. 89.24) must also be kept in mind here. Within a royal creation mythology, the fighting and binding of snakes belong to the creation of a peaceful reign.[166] As Solomon had peace in his time, so had Hezekiah (2 Kgs 20.19). The Hezekiah narrative's discourse on Genesis 3's powerful biting snake, which is involved in humanity's never-ending struggle for daily bread, promises a secure future for Jerusalem's remnant (2 Kgs 19.29 par. Isa. 37.30) similar to that of Yahweh's people in Isa. 14.30 and Psalm 23. We will examine this further in Chapter 3's discourse on motifs and themes in Old Testament Zion ideology.

Summing up, we must conclude that Hezekiah removed the foreigners from the country. As the Jebusites were not removed from Jerusalem before David's removal of them (Josh. 15.63; Judg. 1.21; 2 Sam. 17.25-26), so the foreigners were still in the country until Hezekiah finally removed them. Playing the David–Goliath duel (1 Sam. 17.19-27), Hezekiah not only removed (הסיר) the במות but also the reproach with which the *Rabshaqeh* had mocked (root חרף) the living God (2 Kgs 19.16; 1 Sam. 17.26 [Goliath]). Totally surrounded by his enemies, Hezekiah is presented as the only Judaean king who successfully did not submit to their gods. While his success was short-lived—as was Ahab's in a similar narrative pattern (1 Kgs 20)—the stage is set for a second attempt of a removal of iniquity in the Josiah narrative.

9. *Josiah's Acts as a Variant Tradition? How Do We Fit this Narrative into the Ideology of the Books of Kings?*

In a close follow-up on the Hezekiah narrative, Josiah is said to have removed (הסיר) the temples of the high places, the בית־במות, which Israel's kings had made and which provoked Yahweh to anger (כעס, 23.19). Framing the Josiah narrative with the verbs סור and כעס, totality is achieved in the message that Josiah did not turn aside to the right or the left (22.2). The description of his cult reform which

---

165. W.S. McCullough, 'Serpent', in *IDB*, III, pp. 289-91.
166. Mettinger, *Dethronement of Sabaoth*, pp. 69-72; Thompson, 'Kingship and the Wrath of God', p. 190.

includes removal, destruction and desecration (יצא, שבת, נתץ, שרף, דקק, טמא) of several items and places, reiterating all the sins of 'the kings of Judah' (23.5, 11, 12), Ahaz and Manasseh (v. 12), 'Solomon, king of Israel' (v. 13), finds its climax in the destruction of Jeroboam's altar in Bethel and the removal (הסיר) of the temples of the high places made by the kings of Israel (vv. 15-18). Verses 4-7 deal with idolatry, vv. 8-9 with the irregular local cult at the high places, which are not destroyed, but defiled (טמא). Verses 10-13 deal more specifically with idolatry related to one or another of Judah's kings. Ending the southern section with a reference to Solomon's idolatry in v. 13, v. 14's bridging summary, employing the language of the Pentateuch's cutting down (כרת) the *Asherah*[167] and breaking into pieces (שבר) the pillars[168]—although no pillars are said to have been erected after Asa's removal of them[169]—combines Solomon's sin with Jeroboam's and both places become defiled by human bones (vv. 14, 20). While the northern cult places are all destroyed (סור, דקק, שרף, נתץ), the southern places are defiled (טמא).

Although 2 Kings 23 closes the accusations of cult critique—based on the laws of the Pentateuch (Leviticus and Deuteronomy)—raised throughout Kings,[170] it also includes issues and items not referred to earlier. Of these, the mention of the idolatrous priests (כמרים, v. 5)[171] and their linguistic (root שבת) and thematic (לשמש) connection with Judah's horses (v. 11), not mentioned in other texts, allow us to separate the Judaean priests of the high places (v. 8) from the Israelite priests (v. 20). While the first-mentioned are spared—however, they are subordinated to the priests in Jerusalem—when their high places become defiled (טמא, v. 8), the latter are slaughtered and burned on their altars at the destruction of their temples (v. 20). The burning motif (שרף) opens and closes the whole section (vv. 4, 20) and links together the accusations of idolatry[172] in the north—the *Asherah* (v. 15) and the priests (v. 20)—with the idolatry in the south—the vessels (v. 4), the *Asherah* (v. 6) and the horses (v. 11). The transport of the ashes to Bethel (v. 4) combines both sections of cult reforms in the single theme: destruction and desecration of the northern cult (vv. 15-16, 19), which hereby has become the main target of the whole reform.[173] Compositionally, the narrative begins and ends antithetically in Jerusalem (vv. 4, 20) and in Bethel (vv. 4, 19). The narrative pattern of mentioning Jerusalem four times (vv. 5-13) and Bethel or Samaria four times (vv. 15-19) strengthens the impression of antithetic fates that cult 'items' are brought *out from* Jerusalem (מחוץ לירושלם, vv. 4, 6) or are already *outside* of Jerusalem (בערי־יהודה ובמסבי ירושלם [the idolatrous priests], v. 5; [Solomon's altars], v. 13). In contrast,

---

167. Cf. Exod. 34.13.

168. Cf. Exod. 23.24; 34.13; Deut. 7.5; 12.3.

169. Both Ahaz and Manasseh built altars (2 Kgs 16.11; 21.3, 4) and Manasseh built high places and erected *Asherim* (21.3, 7).

170. Hoffmann, *Reform und Reformen*, pp. 239-40. Hoffmann's analysis led scholars, including Friedman ('From Egypt to Egypt', pp. 171-73) and McKenzie (*The Trouble With Kings*, pp. 128-34, 149-50), to conclude a Josianic dating for Dtr[1].

171. See Zeph. 1.4 (Judaean priests) and Hos. 10.5 (Israelite priests).

172. Hoffmann, *Reform und Reformen*, p. 225.

173. Hoffmann, *Reform und Reformen*, pp. 243-44.

cult places are built *in* Bethel (בבית־אל, v. 15) or *in* Samaria (בערי שמרון, v. 19) and defilement is brought *to* them (vv. 4, 16-17, 19).

Conflating Jeroboam's sin with the idolatrous cult of which both Israel and Judah is accused, the author has solved his basic problem that Jeroboam's original sin relates to the division of the kingdom. To sin even more as Ahab did (1 Kgs 16.30-31) and not remove Jeroboam's sin as Jehu did not, although he removed the Baal worship (2 Kgs 10.28-29), indicate that the author of the books of Kings did not intend to confuse these matters.[174] Contrary to Provan's conclusion that the sin of Jeroboam belongs to idolatry because of its similarity with Canaanite Baal symbolism,[175] I find no indication that this aspect refers to the primary theme of the northern cult. It rather belongs to the author's defence of the obvious illogical ambiguity in the narrative cycle (1 Kgs 11.26–14.18), that Yahweh gives Jeroboam the northern kingship for the purpose of punishing the Davidic house (1 Kgs 11.35-39) and then punishes Jeroboam for establishing his own cultic administration! In a defence of cult reforms far beyond one's own border in the Josiah narrative, the northern violation had to be classified as more than a violation of a new convention about cult centralization.[176] The polemic is not only expressive of Jerusalem's hatred against the competing cult place in Bethel,[177] it also belongs to the theme of 'Jerusalem's rise to sovereignty'. Within this thematic narrative, we are told that, after the fall of Shiloh (1 Sam. 4), David established his centre in Jerusalem, confirmed by Hezekiah and Josiah after the fall of the Northern Kingdom. With these examples and the continuity of the Davidic line, which Jeroboam broke for the northern part, Jerusalem's story-telling created the literary foundation for this sovereignty. Contrary to Israel's discontinuities of cult places (from Shiloh to Bethel and Dan), of kingship and of priesthood, Judah's story is presented in a continuous chain of kings and priests from Davidic time.[178] Whether faithful or unfaithful, they held to their line and their centre. As we are not dealing mainly with a historical-critical but a literary analysis in this chapter, it suffices to say that this story-writing has not much to do with Judah and Israel of the Iron Age.

However, as tragedy's fate is inevitable, so is Judah's. Josiah's reforms did not bring Yahweh to turn away from his divine wrath. As he had formerly removed (הסרתי) Israel, so Yahweh will also remove Judah (גם את־יהודה אסיר)[179] because of Manasseh's provocations (כל־הכעסים, 2 Kgs 23.26-27). The turning point for Judah's decline in fact came much earlier, when the Judaean kings Jehoram and Ahaziah brought upon the Davidides the curse of Ahab's house (1 Kgs 21.17-22).

174. So also Hoffmann, *Reform und Reformen*, pp. 41-42.

175. Provan, *Hezekiah and the Books of Kings*, pp. 64-65.

176. Hoffmann, *Reform und Reformen*, pp. 71-73, 260.

177. Debus, *Die Sünde Jeroboams*, p. 46.

178. Van Seters, *In Search of History*, p. 314: 'the one dynasty of Judah and the many dynasties of Israel'. Auld, *Kings Without Privilege*, pp. 156-59.

179. This echo of common fate is signified by the threefold use of גם: in Judah's building of במות in 1 Kgs 14.23 (גם המה), in the pronouncement of doom in 2 Kgs 17.19 (גם יהודה) and the conclusion to this narrative (גם את־יהודה).

From here, the divine favour was taken away and, although the succeeding kings are judged positively, their reigns are characterized by murder (Jehoash, 2 Kgs 12.21), defeat and murder (Amaziah, 14.8-14, 19), leprosy (Azariah, 15.5) and war with Syria and Israel (Jotham, 15.37).[180] The fourfold punishment of the children for the sin of the father is broken with the fifth ruler Ahaz, who created his own sin. So, in fact, did Amaziah with his reckless challenge of war with Jehoash, king of Israel, grandson of Jehu (14.8-14). In a conscious demonstration of an abandonment of the former law (2 Kgs 14.6; cf. Deut. 24.16), the author had to compose his story in such a way as to create the foundation for the turning point indicated with the reigns of Ahaz and Hezekiah.

10. *Patronage and Idolatry, or How to Characterize 'the Way of David'?*

The characterization of some Judaean kings as followers or non-followers of the 'way of David' can now be given a clear definition. In the David narrative of 1 and 2 Samuel, the 'centralization of the cult' in Jerusalem (the story of moving the ark in 2 Sam. 6) marks the emergence of the Davidic kingship. The opposite to this 'centralization' is illustrated in Yahweh's comparative reference to the unsettling period for the name of Yahweh as moving around (מתהלך) in a tent and a tabernacle (באהל ובמשכן, 2 Sam. 7.5-29 [especially vv. 6-7, 13]). Compositionally, the centralization is linked to the 'fall' of 'Israel', the disappearance of the honour (כבוד) from Israel (1 Sam. 4 [especially v. 22]) in the Philistine war, David's election by all Israel (2 Sam. 5.1-5), the conquest of Jerusalem (5.6-12) and the defeat of the Philistines (5.17-25). Having proved himself worthy (5.1-2), David's moving the ark is narrated as a common act for all Israel (6.1). Any possible opposition to this move is hidden in the reference to Uzza's stretching his hand out to grasp the ark (6.6-8). Yahweh's confirmation of the move in his killing of Uzza (עזא/עזה), might be an implicit reference to the Samaritan high priest (Uzzi son of Baghi, עזי בן בקחי), who according to Samaritan tradition was in office at Gerizim in the time of Eli's move to Shiloh.[181] The blessing given to the house of Obed-Edom (2 Sam. 6.11-12), whose name bears allusions to the Edomites[182] accentuates the opposition, when the Philistines (1 Sam. 5.6-12) and the 'Samaritans' were cursed by contact with the ark.

While David's rise to power is paved with the corpses of internal and external enemies, he is never blamed for his successful removal of rivals and he never takes

180. F.A.J. Nielsen, *The Tragedy in History*, pp. 147-48. One might in fact suggest that the turning point came with Jehoram's father Jehoshaphats's peace with Israel (וישלם יהושפט עם־מלך ישראל, 1 Kgs 22.45), which led to intermarriage with the Israelite royal house. In contrast, his father Asa had peace with Yahweh (לבב־אסא היה שלם עם־יהוה כל־ימיו, 1 Kgs 15.14).

181. *AF*, ch. IX, p. 41, see further Chapter 4; Josephus (*Ant.* 5.361-62) supports the Samaritan tradition that Eli, being of the Ithamar line, usurped the high priesthood and accordingly broke the Eleazar line to which Uzzi belonged.

182. A variant of the Gerizim/Shechem–'Edom' contrast is found in Josephus' narrative about the 'destruction' of the Samaritan temple on Gerizim (*Ant.* 13.254-58); cf. Hjelm, *Samaritans and Early Judaism*, pp. 215-16.

credit for it—quite the contrary.[183] It was not David who removed the house of Saul. This house was removed because of Saul's infidelity (1 Sam. 15.11-29; 28.18). Neither did he remove Saul's son Ish-bosheth from his throne in Israel (2 Sam. 2.8-10; 4.1-12) or Abner his general (3.30-37). David's tears over the death of Saul (2 Sam. 1.11-16) certainly extend to Abner's death (3.31-34) as do his immediate and pronounced revenge for the deaths of the three of them, of which he declares himself innocent (2 Sam. 1.14-16; 3.28-29; 4.9-11). So much for cult centralization, which has the double purpose of both raising a common leader for Israel and of establishing Jerusalem as the capital.

The acts of David, for which he is praised, however, do not belong to cult or to centralization, but to his conquest of the foreigners, none of whom he spares (cf. the various conquest stories in 2 Samuel and 'David's song' in the closure of the David narrative, 2 Sam. 22). This motif is closely linked to his dependence on Yahweh, expressed in psalmodic terms of 'cry' and 'listen', and Yahweh's successive acts of salvation (2 Sam. 22.4, 7-20, 29-51). It should not go unnoticed that all occurrences of 'Yahweh being with David' (1 Sam. 16.18; 18.12, 14; 2 Sam. 5.10) refer explicitly or implicitly to his 'success' in wars (1 Sam. 16.18; 18.14-15, 30; 2 Sam. 5.2, 10; 8.14-15). His success was closely related to his active participation in the wars as the rational reason for his election as king (1 Sam. 16.18; 2 Sam. 2.1-4; 5.2). Only 16.18 summarizes all his qualities, calling him a skilled player, a brave man, a soldier, eloquent[184] and good looking. Having succeeded so well in being faithful to his obligations as a warrior, it is hardly a surprise that David's fall from grace is connected with his non-participation in the war with the Ammonites (2 Sam. 11.1). It is only Joab's magnanimous offer which saves him from possible further disgrace (2 Sam. 12.28) of following in the steps of Saul's displacement by his own chief commander.

Without specification, David is said to[185]

> have kept the ways of Yahweh (שמרתי דרכי יהוה) and not to have wickedly departed from his God (לא רשעתי מאלהי). To have had all his ordinances before him (משפטיו לנגדי) and not to have turned aside from his statutes (חקתיו לא־אסור), to have been blameless before him (אהיה תמים לו) and kept himself from iniquity (אשתמרה מעוני), to have been found righteous (וישב יהוה כצדקתי) and pure (כברי לנגד עיניו). (2 Sam. 22.22-26).

The reward for this behaviour is further expressed in Solomon's prayer at Gibeon (1 Kgs 3.6), that Yahweh had shown great and steadfast love (חסד גדול) to David according to his behaviour (כאשר הלך) that he walked before Yahweh in faithfulness (באמת), in righteousness (בצדקה) and with upright heart (בישרת לבב). The reciprocity of the relationship that Yahweh was with David because David 'stayed with' Yahweh (cf. 2 Sam. 22.26-28) sets the condition for his success and pronounces the fate of the Davidic house: 'if you walk in my ways, keeping my

---

183.   Whitelam, *The Just King*, pp. 104-18; *idem*, 'The Defence of David', *JSOT* 29 (1984), pp. 61-87.

184.   נבון דבר, might better be translated 'understanding' (cf. Deut. 1.13; 4.6).

185.   The text is in first person singular.

statutes (חקי) and my ordinances (מצותי) similar to what your father David did
(כאשר הלך דוד אביו), then will I lengthen your days' (1 Kgs 3.14). 1 Kings 2.3-4
and 6.12 both have references to Yahweh's everlasting promise to David and 2.3
explicitly states that it is Yahweh's statutes, commandments, ordinances and
testimonies (חקתיו מצותיו ומשׁטיו ועדתיו) written in the Law of Moses (ככתוב בתרת
משׁה), which shall be kept in order to succeed (השׂכיל) in everything. This *leitmotif*
of the books of Kings—most explicitly stated in 1 Kgs 11.38—sets the premise
both for Judah *and* for Israel.[186] While Israel is cursed because of Jeroboam's lack
of imitating David (1 Kgs 14.8), Judah is credited with David's behaviour in spite
of Abijam and Jehoram's similar non-imitation of Davidic practice (1 Kgs 15.4;
2 Kgs 8.19). The characterisation of Jehoram (2 Kgs 8.18-19) gives explicit voice
to this pro-Davidic theology of the books of Kings. In spite of Jehoram's imitation
of the deeds of Ahab, Yahweh would not destroy (שׁחת[187]) Judah, because of his
'everlasting' promise to David (למען דוד עבדו כאשׁר אמר־לו לתת לו ניר לבניו כל־
הימים, 'for the sake of David his servant, to whom he had said that he would give to
him a lamp for his descendants all days', 2 Kgs 8.19).[188] In all instances, the implementation of the promise is related to threatening situations in which Judah and
Jerusalem could have been destroyed, were it not for Yahweh's promise. Literarily,
it 'predicts' the salvation and, theologically, it interprets the outcome of the wars
(1 Kgs 11.12-39; 15.4-7; 2 Kgs 8.19-22; 18.17–20.6).[189] The non-occurrence of the
gloss in the Josiah narrative is due to such specific usage. Of O'Brien's reward and
retribution scheme in the Deuteronomistic History—which is linked to (1) fidelity
to the exclusive worship of Yahweh, (2) fidelity to centralized worship and (3) fidelity to the prophet–king relationship[190]—only the first is explicitly stated in the
characterizations of David in the books of Samuel. Invoked in the books of Kings'

---

186. This is taken as secondary by Noth and others because of the David reference (cf.
McKenzie, *The Trouble With Kings*, pp. 46-47). Provan's interpretation (*Hezekiah and the Books of
Kings*, p. 105; supported by McKenzie) that the oracle proclaims a twofold message—'that the
Davidic dynasty is to have Judah "forever" because of David (11.36), and that Jeroboam's dynasty
will similarly possess Israel if Jeroboam behaves like David (11.38)'—nicely solves this problem
and accords with the comparison of succeeding Israelite kings with Jeroboam and not with David.
Provan's redaction-historical division of the material, assigning vv. 34bβ, 35bβ and 39 to an exilic
editor, however, distorts the literary tension of the oracle, that whatever happens to David's house
the humiliation will not be forever. We do not need any pre- or post-exilic editions to explain the
tension—it forms part of the composition. That vv. 38bβ-39 are missing in the LXX might point to
some edition (in either the Greek or the Hebrew versions), but cannot be taken for evidence of pre-
exilic 'knowledge' and post-exilic 'hopes' (cf. the discussion in McKenzie, *The Trouble With
Kings*, pp. 39-47).

187. Hiphil, as in 2 Kgs 13.23 and 18.25. One is tempted to insert a 'yet' (עד־עתה), as in
2 Kgs 13.23's delay of Israel's rejection, because of the Abraham, Isaac and Jacob covenant, when
threatened by the Aramaean Hazael.

188. The mention of descendants is missing in several non-MT manuscripts; cf. *ad loc.* in the
BHS apparatus. The only citation of this gloss in Chronicles (2 Chron. 21.7) is in striking contrast
to the conditional promise given to Solomon (1 Chron. 28.7-10; 2 Chron. 1.8-12; 6.16-17; 7.17-18).

189. For linguistic differences between the Hezekiah narrative and the rest of the books of
Kings, see Chapter 3.

190. O'Brien, *Deuteronomistic History Hypothesis*, p. 35.

interpretation of the divine promise given to David in 2 Samuel 7, the unconditioned promise has become transformed through narrative discourse to fit the agenda of the Deuteronomistic narrative as a whole: 'can they keep the Law?'[191] And if not, how do they deal with Yahweh's anger?

Within the כדוד ('as David') motif of the books of Kings, the negative judgment of Solomon relates to his violation of the patron–client relationship established with his god Yahweh, whom he forsook to follow other gods (1 Kgs 11.4-6, 33). The motif is applied positively to the Judaean kings Asa, Hezekiah and Josiah, negatively to Amaziah and Ahaz and positively *and* negatively to Solomon, who 'walked in the statutes of David' (בחקות דוד [*hapax*], 1 Kgs 3.3) and did well in the eyes of Yahweh as long as he realized that the promise given to him in Gibeon included a 'command' to centralize the worship in Jerusalem.[192] Solomon's violation of his relationship is termed in a glossary fashion as not having walked in the ways (the statutes and ordinances)[193] of Yahweh as his father David had (v. 33). Bringing back the foreigners, with whom Yahweh had said he should not mingle, makes him comparable with Ahaz, Hoshea and Manasseh, who did likewise, while Hezekiah removed the foreigners. Although Asa and Josiah are not said to have removed any foreigners, their cult reforms relate to the removal of foreign practice.

The judgment of Amaziah (2 Kgs 14.3) poses a riddle. Suggesting a secondary insertion of the David reference[194] only intensifies the problem by raising the question of what the author intended to signify by this insertion? While it seems reasonable that Jehoshaphat was not compared with David, since he established amicable relations with the king of Israel (Ahab, 1 Kgs 22.45),[195] which lead to his son and grandson's marriages with women of that house, Amaziah's story gives no immediate clue to why he deserved the comparison. The reference to David is set in comparison to Amaziah's father Jehoash who did right 'as long as the priest Jehoiada instructed him' (cf. 2 Kgs 12.3). None of them is said to have behaved like David. For Amaziah, no immediate comparison is at hand. If it were said that he acted like his father, would this have meant that he did right as long as a priest instructed him, but fell behind after the priest's death? But no such priest is mentioned in the Amaziah narrative and such a comparison would not make any sense. The author picked up the David theme in order to avoid confusion about how he did right precisely and applied the father reference to the following kings: Azariah and Jotham. With the Ahaz case, it would not have made sense to apply such a reference to his father; for what would it have meant if Ahaz were said not to have done right as his

191.   Von Rad, *Deuteronomium-Studien*, p. 61: 'Die eigentliche Geschichtserzählung von David ist in bemerkenswerter Weise frei von dtr. Zusäzen. Dieser Befund ist verwunderlich angesichts der fortgesezten Erwähnung Davids als des Urbildes eines Jahwe wohlgefälligen Königs im Fortgang der weiteren Geschichtsdarstellung.'

192.   Cf. the tension between 1 Kgs 3.3 and 3.15 and the story's parallelism to David's 'fight' with Saul's house at Gibeon (2 Sam. 2) leading to the establishment of his kingship.

193.   The syntax is broken here and the LXX* deletes both statutes and ordinances. Their occurrence in the MT version might be related to the author's wish to clarify the term: ולא הלכו* בדרכי, לעשות הישר בעיני *, LXX, Syriac, Vulgate: sg.

194.   Provan, *Hezekiah and the Books of Kings*, p. 93.

195.   Not with Yahweh as his father Asa had done.

father had? His father had not done right, though he had not acted as badly as Ahaz, who walked in the paths of the kings of Israel. That means that he had followed the abominable habits of the foreigners (כתעבות הגוים), whom Yahweh had driven out before Israel (2 Kgs 16.3). In a grand chiastic move, Ahaz is given the role of mirroring Solomon's disgrace.[196] With Hezekiah in the role of a new David, a harmonious story is created. The cult is reformed and the foreigners are thrown out.

However, this was not the author's intention. From the story's beginning, we are told that the Hezekiah narrative could not itself close that story. Expulsion is to become the inevitable experience of Yahweh's people (Lev. 26.33-40; Deut. 4.27-28; 11.17; 28.36-37, 64-68; 29.27; Josh. 23.13, 16; 1 Kgs 8.46; 2 Kgs 17.18-20; 21.14-15).[197] As all tragedies, also this story has its turning points, which, however, do not reverse fate. So the conclusion of the tragedy, that Manasseh's sin extends far beyond his own time (2 Kgs 23.26),[198] regardless of Josiah's acts,[199] is as irreversible as is the promise to David of an eternal kingship. That the forcefulness of this promise comes to a climax in the Hezekiah narrative (2 Kgs 19.34; 20.6) does not point to a so-called Hezekian or Josianic redaction of the Deuteronomistic History.[200] It rather belongs to a programmatic claim for Jerusalem's and the Davidide's inviolability, in spite of what happened to the city and its king.[201] While Israel's kingship had been rejected forever, Judah's kingship and the royal city did not suffer everlasting deportation or devastation. This was rather an interim in their 'glorious history'.[202] With the return from exile, both the city and the Davidic kingship had 'remnants' left for a new era to begin.[203] 2 Kings' closure in the pardon of Jehoiachin serves such a purpose of continuity, however insignificant this may seem.[204] He is placed at the top of the king's table, he is not wearing a prisoner's suit and the Babylonian king takes care of his maintenance (2 Kgs 25.28-30). The promise to David and succeeding kings should not be seen in the light of a long-gone pre-exilic Israel. The books of Kings do not offer such a simple interpretation. We do not have to turn to the language of Near Eastern 'royal legitimation' documents[205] to explain the programmatic claim that David's house should

196. This is even more striking when compared to the book of Isaiah's Ahaz.

197. F.A.J. Nielsen, *The Tragedy in History*, pp. 120-21.

198. It extends, in fact, to four generations, since Jehoahaz, Eliakim/Jehoiakim and Mattaniah/Zedekiah all are sons of Josiah, which makes Jehoiachin son of Jehoiakim, the fourth generation.

199. This is one of the obstacles of the Cross School's interpretation of the Josiah narrative as presenting 'an optimistic outlook for the future'; cf. McKenzie, *The Trouble With Kings*, pp. 143 and 149; Friedman, 'From Egypt to Egypt: Dtr1 and Dtr2'.

200. Cf. the discussion in Provan, *Hezekiah and the Books of Kings*, pp. 117-31; McKenzie, *The Trouble With Kings*, pp. 117-34.

201. Clements, 'The Prophecies of Isaiah to Hezekiah', p. 74.

202. E.g. 2 Chron. 36.18-21; Ezra 1.1-4; Jer. 4.23-27; 29.10-14; Hos. 3.4-5; Joel 4; Zech. 1.12-17.

203. Cf. Isa. 4.1-6; Jer. 22.30–23.6; 30–33; Zech. 3–4; 8.6; Hag. 1–2; Amos 9.11; 1 Chron. 3.17-24.

204. D.F. Murray, 'Of All the Years, the Hopes—or Fears? Jehoiachin in Babylon (2 Kgs 25.27-30)', *JBL* 120/2 (2001), pp. 245-65.

205. B.O. Long, *1 Kings* (FOTL, 9; Grand Rapids: Eerdmans, 1984), pp. 16-17.

stand forever. This is the message of Psalms and Prophets throughout the Old Testament.[206] Neither do we have to turn to linguistic explanations of the hyperbolic significance of עד־עולם as being 'for a long time' (למרחוק), as in 2 Sam. 7.19.[207] McKenzie is quite right here in his criticism of Long. However, he is not right when he asks: 'if Dtr saw the Davidic covenant as grounds for hope in the exile, as in Jer. 33.14-26, why did he fail to refer to it as a source of hope in 2 Kings 23–25?'[208] McKenzie's question relates to redaction rather than literary criticism. One simply must ask: What would have become of the sincerity of Kings' tragic tale if the exile had been presented as nothing but an unfortunate interim within its own narrative composition? What would have become of Jeremiah's recalling of Yahweh's everlasting promise to both Israel and Judah (Jer. 33.14-26) when the people in frustration claim that 'Yahweh has rejected the two families (the Levites and the Davidides) he has chosen' (שתי המשפחות אשר בחר יהוה בהם וימאסם, Jer. 33.24)?[209] In its didactic setting, the closure of the Josiah narrative, that also Jerusalem should be rejected (מאס) belongs to the narrative discourse of books of Kings, but not to the perspective of the books.[210]

While the Josiah narrative lies well within the authorship and narrative discourse of the books of Kings—that both Israel and Judah sinned—the Hezekiah narrative opposes this view.[211] In continuing to examine the Hezekiah narrative's relationship with the book of Isaiah, questions of provenance will be important for interpreting the narrative's literary context within both traditions. If the narrative has its origin within the Isaianic corpus, its potential purpose of functioning as a disruptive epitome rather than part of the narrative discourse of the books of Kings, must be considered. The comparison of Hezekiah and Josiah with successive and previous kings (2 Kgs 18.5-6):

ביהוה אלהי ישראל בטח ואחריו לא־היה כמהו בכל מלכי יהודה ואשר היו לפניו:
וידבק ביהוה לא־סר מאחריו וישמר מצותיו אשר צוה יהוה את־משה

---

206.   E.g. Pss. 89; 132; 144; Isa. 55.3; Jer. 33.14-26; Ezek. 37.20-28.

207.   Long, *1 Kings*, pp. 16-17.

208.   McKenzie, *The Trouble With Kings*, p. 133. Further, S.L. McKenzie, 'The Books of Kings in the Deuteronomistic History', p. 303: 'I cannot believe that an exilic writer who knows that there is no Davidide on the throne in Jerusalem would include and stress such a promise'.

209.   McKenzie's problem with a late post-exilic dating of the Deuteronomistic History, because 'the story ends where it does instead of continuing to the writer's time' ('The Books of Kings in the Deuteronomistic History', p. 303), lacks a similar notion of distinction between history and literature. The book ends with the deportation of the southern kingship, not its disappearance. The period of the governors (Persian, Greek, Ptolemaic and Seleucid), an interim of nearly 400 years (539–141) which spanned between the Iron Age kingship and the Hasmonaean 'kingship', is not viewed as belonging to Israel's glorious past, as can be inferred from, for example, the books of Ezra and Nehemiah, *1 Enoch* and *Eupolemus*.

210.   The didactic function of the tragic tale of the Children of Israel can bee found in such books as Ezra, Nehemiah and Judith, which warn against reiterating the fate of the ancestors.

211.   Laato, *About Zion I Will Not Be Silent*, p. 66, says that the narratives are 'diametrically opposed to each other'.

He trusted in Yahweh God of Israel and among all the kings of Judah none was like him, neither after or before him. For he cleaved to Yahweh; he did not turn away from him, but he kept the commandments, which Yahweh had commanded Moses.

(2 Kgs 23.25):

וכמהו לא־היה לפניו מלך אשר־שב אל־יהוה בכל־לבבו ובכל־נפשו
ובכל־מאוד בכל תורת משה ואחריו לא־קם כמהו

And there was no king before him who turned to Yahweh with all his heart and all his soul and with all his might, according to all the Law of Moses; and nobody arose like him after him.

would support such a hypothesis, since Hezekiah was the only king who saved his 'kingdom', albeit both kings walked in the way of David *and* followed the instructions of Moses. The Josiah story does not contain any immediate motif of threat, and it is only the final outcome of Kings' narrative as a whole that allows his acts to be interpreted within a perspective of temporary salvation. In fact, it is not Josiah's reform but his tears which bring salvation for *him* (2 Kgs 22.19-20). Reconsidering the discussion between Noth, von Rad and Wolff (see above, Chapter 1), we might conclude that the turning point in the books of Kings does not belong to the books as such, but came from the outside, from the 'prophetic' interruption of that story, one which pronounces future salvation of Jerusalem within an Isaianic 'setting'.[212] It is in a voice of the new Israel that the old Israel, as presented in Judges–2 Kings, is dismissed as not worthy of Yahweh's mercy. Solomon's plea for mercy—'since there is no man who does not sin' (1 Kgs 8.46-51)—belongs to the hopes of this new Israel. Yahweh's inexorable answer, on the contrary, belongs to Deuteronomistic theology's pronouncement of doom for not having kept the Law (1 Kgs 9.3-9). Within a coherent narrative of theological logic, Yahweh cannot be unfaithful to his own determination. If promise is conditioned, such conditions must be upheld. Otherwise, the promise will be without value. Within this perspective, the Deuteronomistic history functions as an example of how Yahweh's Law sets the agenda for Israel's fate: that is, Israel cannot keep the Law (Deut. 31.29; Josh. 24.19).[213] Contrary to the usual definition of tragedy—that it reasons about how fate is inevitable—it seems that the narratives about such inevitable fate are not accounts

212. Von Rad's problem with the supposed co-redaction of the book of Judges and the books of Kings must be taken into consideration here: 'Warum unterscheidet er in der Richterzeit zwischen den Richtern und der Einstellung des Volkes ('aber auch ihren Richtern gehorchten sie nicht, Ri. 2.17), während er in der Königzeit alles auf die Haltung der Könige abstellt, hinter denen das Volk als eine stumme massa perditionis oder salutis zurücktritt und dessen Schuld unbedenklich den Königen aufgebürdet wird? Es ist schwer vorstellbar, dass die dtr Redaktion der Königsbücher und die des Richterbuches in einem Arbeitsgang erfolgt sein sollte.' Cf. von Rad, *Theologie des Alten Testaments*, I, p. 344. In the Hezekiah narrative we have found that it exhibited the pattern of the book of Judges. The people were given an opportunity to choose their own way and, as we have seen, they chose to follow their king.

213. Noth, *Überlieferungsgeschichtliche Studien*, pp. 108-109. F.A.J. Nielsen, *The Tragedy in History*, p. 121: 'The Israelites are given a choice and they seal their own fate by choosing Yahweh, who is holy and jealous and whom they are not capable of serving'.

but creations. The inevitable fate is a fact, created in a self-fulfilling argument that it 'should not have been so'. This understanding demands a different orientation be given to Wolff's question to Noth:

> When, on the other hand, the author's goal was to demonstrate that Yahweh had fulfilled his old curse from the covenant of the time of Moses and that the history of Israel had rightfully terminated, one must ask—especially in light of the extensive exposition—why did this not happen much earlier? Why does the author entertain his audience with centuries of ups and downs?[214]

Wolff's question might also have been the author's problem. In composing a story from the implied narrative present of the author back to his narrative's beginning, whether we think in terms of 2 Kings–Genesis, 2 Kings–Exodus, 2 Kings–Deuteronomy, 2 Kings–Joshua or 2 Kings–Judges, he certainly had a great need of finding solutions to such a basic problem. This accounts well for the reiterative threat–salvation motif, which allows the Salvation Story to continue.[215] Wolff's own solution to the problem suggests that the final message of the DtrG is neither one of despair or hope, but rather a didactic voice's admonition for a return to piety, which interprets the rationale for the whole story. Placed in the exile without any immediate hope for a return or a renewal of temple and kingship, the admonition to turn (שׁוב) to Yahweh has the purpose of strengthening the patron–client relationship, so that 'Israel listens to nobody but God and expects all good from him'.[216] Included in the return is confession of guilt, prayer of salvation and submission to new obedience.[217] The guidance for the return is given by the Law of Moses and the sermons of the prophets (2 Kgs 23.25 and 17.13). Wolff's inclusion of Josiah as the last example of a king who returned to Yahweh is intriguing. While we can read this narrative as an example of what Israel should do in exile,[218] we have to question whether Wolff is right in assuming that DtrG's admonition to a return is a return to the Mosaic Law.[219] Does the hope for a new Israel lie in obedience or in

---

214. Wolff, 'Das Kerygma, pp. 174-75 (my translation).
215. Wolff, 'Das Kerygma', p. 176: 'Das Thema Umkehr finden wir aber nun an fast allen bedeutsamen Stellen, die uns den eigenen Aussagewillen des DtrG erkennen lassen, neben der Warnrede vor dem Abfall und der Androhung des Gerichts. Dagegen treffen wir nirgendwo eine Ermunterung zur Hoffnung [Judg. 2.11-21; 1 Sam. 7.3; 12.14-25; 1 Kgs 8.33, 35, 46-53; 2 Kgs 17.13; 23.25].'
216. Wolff, 'Das Kerygma', pp. 185-86: 'dass Israel mit ganzem Herzen auf die Stimme seines Gottes allein höre und von ihm allein alles Gute erwarte, damit es ganz Gottes Eigentum inmitten der Völkerwelt werde'.
217. Wolff, 'Das Kerygma', p. 183.
218. Wolff, 'Das Kerygma', pp. 178, 183.
219. Wolff, 'Das Kerygma', p. 184: 'Die Umkehr als Rückkehr in den Väterbund, den Jahwe noch nicht vergessen hat, ist das einzige, was Israel zu tun übriggeblieben ist'. So also Dietrich, *Prophetie und Geschichte*, pp. 147-48: 'Eben deshalb sind DtrG und DtrP noch keine Nomisten, so gewiss sie auf den anderen Seite dem Nomismus eines DtrN den Weg bereitet haben. Alle drei Redaktoren aber wollen dem Israel der Exilszeit zeigen, wie es zur der Katastrophe gekommen ist und wie es nun weitergehen kann und muss.' Hoffmann, *Reform und Reformen*, p. 269: 'Im Idealbild des Josia hält Dtr seinen Zeitgenossen des Exils und der frühnachexilischen Zeit das Modell vor Augen, dem es nachzueifern gilt. Dieses ist inhaltlich zusammengefasst in der

forgiveness? Josiah and his people's return to the Law did not turn away Yahweh's anger, and it was not the god whom Solomon asked to forgive him (1 Kgs 8.46-53) who answered Solomon (1 Kgs 9.3-9) or Josiah (22.15-20). It was the jealous god of the Shechem covenant (Josh. 24.19-24). Demonstrating that the *hubris* of the Israelites at Shechem can only lead to a fall, 'since there is no man, who does not sin' (not even the righteous kings: David, Hezekiah and Josiah), the hope for Israel lies in Yahweh's mercy that he will forgive. The theme of humility as part of royal ideology, so central in ancient Near Eastern literature,[220] might be the driving force for the narrative as a whole. Confronted with his human limits, will the king humble himself and ask for mercy? Or does he think himself capable of arguing with God about how conditions should be? It was not Hezekiah's righteousness, but his tears, which brought him salvation (2 Kgs 20.5). As David's sins did not define his fate, because of his repentance (2 Sam. 12.13; 24.10) and choice of Yahweh's mercy (24.14), so Saul's, Solomon's and Jeroboam's failure to repent led to their fall. The invocation of the memory of David in both the Jeroboam (Abijah) 'sickness' story (1 Kgs 14.8) and in the Hezekiah 'sickness' story (2 Kgs 20.6) contrasts the fates of the kings and their states. 'As Abijah's death was symbolic of the coming destruction of Jeroboams's house and the ultimate fall of Israel, so Hezekiah's recovery carries with it the salvation of Jerusalem from Assyrian hands.'[221] In wonder we ask: What if Jeroboam had repented?

The hope for Israel does not lie with the old past Israel, but with the faithful remnant, who, cleansed through trial, punishment and repentance, has accepted Yahweh as their God (Deut. 4.29-31; 13.2-5; 30.2-6; 1 Kgs 8.47-51). The understanding comes from experience and the outcome is the circumcision of the heart 'that you may love (אהב) Yahweh[222] with all your heart and all your soul, that you may live' (Deut. 30.6). The reasoning behind this experience does not belong to 'the fathomless mystery of the divine',[223] it belongs to the narrative's logic that warned against *hubris*, the Israelites nevertheless chose to serve the Yahweh of their fathers (Josh. 24.16-28).[224] The 'Deuteronomistic History's' implicit author belongs to the

Forderung der bedingungslosen Treue zum Gesetz, dem Dtn bzw. zur totalen Verwirklichung seiner Grundforderung, des ersten Gebotes.'

220. Thompson, 'Kingship and the Wrath of God', *passim*.

221. R.L. Cohn, 'Convention and Creativity in the Books of Kings: The Case of the Dying Monarch', *CBQ* 47 (1985), pp. 603-16 (613-14).

222. Although a rare expression in the books of Samuel and Kings, we find that not only did Solomon love Yahweh (1 Kgs 3.3), but Yahweh loved Solomon (2 Sam. 12.24). Solomon, however, later cleaved (דבק) to foreign women with love (1 Kgs 11.2), although he should have cleaved to Yahweh (as did Hezekiah, 2 Kgs 18.6) and loved him (Deut. 13.4-5; 30.20).

223. F.A.J. Nielsen, *Tragedy in History*, p. 123.

224. In such cases, Josh. 24 must be interpreted as a pro-oemium rather than the added conclusion of the Deuteronomistic History suggested by, among others, J. Van Seters, 'Joshua 24 & the Problem of Tradition in the Old Testament', in W.B. Barrick and J.R. Spencer (eds.), *In the Shelter of Elyon: Essays on Ancient Literature in Honor of G.W. Ahlström* (JSOTSup, 31; Sheffield: JSOT Press, 1984), pp. 139-58 (154), and T. Römer, *Israels Väter: Untersuchungen zur Väterthematik im Deuteronomium und in der Deuteronomistischen Tradition* (OBO, 99; Freiburg: Universitätsverlag; Göttingen: Vandenhoeck & Ruprecht, 1990), pp. 326-29. Van Seters's

experienced remnant. Using messages from the Law, he created a masterpiece of what unfaithfulness leads to. This places him within the guild of the prophets who, warning and admonishing the kings, throughout that story have 'proven' themselves to belong to that saved remnant, together with the faithful rulers from Enoch, Noah and the Patriarchs to Josiah (cf. Sir. 44–49). It is not their righteousness which is claimed, but their faithfulness, their serving Yahweh alone (1 Sam. 7.3; 2 Kgs 18.6; cf. the condemnation of the kings, who gave their power to others, Sir. 49.4-5). The Josiah story, although composed around the finding and the cutting of the covenant, in fact proves that the Law cannot bring salvation and that understanding comes with repentance (2 Kgs 23.19). Von Rad's thesis that the Deuteronomistic History is a 'history of Yahweh's word at work' based on prophetic influence,[225] needs to be analysed by the creative influence of the Law on the narrative's conclusions. As shown by Hoffmann, all the cult reforms, whether positive or negative, are stipulated by the Law.[226] Without the Law we would not have had Deuteronomistic History.[227] Keeping in mind Wolff's conclusion that guidance for the return is given by the Law of Moses and the sermons of the prophets (cf. 2 Kgs 23.25 and 17.13), we must now proceed to examine the theme of Jerusalem's rise to sovereignty in its prophetic setting. This examination must include considerations about the prophetic understanding of the Law. What was Jeremiah looking for when he searched in vain just a single righteous person to save the city? (Jer. 5.1).

---

argument might find support in a Samaritan version of the book of Joshua, which lacks the passages Josh. 24.2-13 ('replaced' by Deut. 4.34) and 17-21a; cf. E. Nodet, *A Search for the Origins of Judaism: From Joshua to the Mishnah* (JSOTSup, 248; Sheffield: Sheffield Academic Press, 1997), pp. 195-201 (197). The Samaritan chronicle referred to is, however, considered to be a late compilation and should be used with caution (see Chapter 4 below). Unfortunately Josh. 24 is not in Dead Sea Scrolls, which have other parts of Joshua that differ considerably from the MT and which support some of Josephus' readings as well as Samaritan versions; cf. M. Abegg, P. Flint and E. Ulrich, *The Dead Sea Scrolls Bible: The Oldest Known Bible. Translated For the First Time Into English* (San Francisco: HarperSanFrancisco, 1999), pp. 201-202. Van Seters' suggestion that Josh. 24 is from the hand of the Yahwist makes this author the primary theologian not only of the Yahwistic narratives, but of the tradition as a whole; cf. p. 155: 'It is the Yahwist as historian and theologian who through his work addresses the exilic crisis of faith and in the figure of Joshua calls out to the households of Israel—the children of Abraham—to join in the household of faith'. See also *idem*, *Life of Moses*, pp. 457-58, 464. The question will be taken up again in Chapter 4.

225.   Von Rad, *Deuteronomium-Studien*, p. 64.

226.   Hoffmann, *Reform und Reformen*, *passim* (especially pp. 341-66).

227.   Polzin, *Moses and the Deuteronomist*, p. 63: 'It is against the background of these two pericopes [Deut. 5.23-31 and 18.15-22] that the monumental historiographic work of Joshua–2 Kings is seen in the clearest light. It is the narrator's claim that his monumental work, by the very wealth and accuracy of its historical interpretation, is a true explanation of the various events that shaped Israel's life from their incursion into the land to their exile out of the land. If Moses is depicted in the law code as formulating the laws, statutes and commandments of the Lord in general terms (e.g. at the end of his first and second address), the narrator formulates the word of the Lord from another perspective: he puts the laws, statutes, and commandments of the Lord in the background of his own discourse by placing them in the mouth of Moses, and focuses his own discourse on establishing in great detail how the subsequent history of Israel is illuminated by such a background.'

Chapter 3

THE BOOK OF ISAIAH'S AHAZ AND HEZEKIAH
NARRATIVES AS FOUNDATION MYTHS

The closure of Chapter 2 left us with four major problems:
1. The provenance of the Hezekiah narrative.
2. The function of the Hezekiah narrative in the book of Isaiah.
3. The rise of Jerusalem's sovereignty in its prophetic setting.
4. The prophetic understanding of the status and the function of the Law:
   the question of the Israel of the fathers.

Of these problems, numbers 1 and 2 will be dealt with explicitly in this chapter. The question of Jerusalem's status in a prophetic setting is the underlying interpretative force of the analysis and cannot be separated from any of the problems listed above. However, the question also needs an explicit clarification and an examination in relation to other biblical books. This clarification will be the content of Chapter 5, in which also the status and the function of the Law in relation to a distinctive David covenant will be examined.

1. *Preliminary Remarks on the Composition of the Book of Isaiah*

Before examining the first question, some preliminary remarks must be given on the composition of the book of Isaiah. The standard division of the book into three main parts (chs. 1–39; 40–55; 56–66), assigning each of these parts to various prophets working in either Palestine (Proto- and Trito-Isaiah) or Babylonia (Deutero-Isaiah), is usually credited to the work of B. Duhm from 1892.[1] It was not Duhm, however, who first made this proposal. The mediaeval commentator Ibn Ezra and the seventeenth-century Dutch philosopher Baruch Spinoza both inferred that chs. 40–55 of the book derived from a sixth-century BCE Babylonian prophet. This reading of Isaiah was further argued in 1788 by the German scholar J.C. Doederlin.[2] The impact of Duhm's work has been immense. One just needs to think of the many commentaries referring to Proto-, Deutero- and Trito-Isaiah, whether they are commentaries on the Pentateuch, the Historical Books, Psalms or Prophetic literature. Although Duhm never assumed, but, in fact, argued against a Babylonian setting for Deutero-Isaiah, the idea of such a *Sitz im Leben* for the origin of the work is

---

1. B. Duhm, *Das Buch Jesaia* (HKAT, 3.1; Göttingen: Vandenhoeck & Ruprecht, 1892).
2. Cf. R.E. Clements, 'Beyond Tradition-History: Deutero-Isaianic Development of First Isaiah's Themes', *JSOT* 31 (1985), pp. 95-113 (95).

often viewed as the standard opinion in several recent works.[3] The argument's reliance on narrative chronology is most clearly demonstrated in J.L. McKenzie's commentary from 1968: 'the exiled community in Babylon fits the audience that can be discerned; a Palestinian community of this period or any other period, earlier or later, does not fit it'.[4] Contrary to this view, C.C. Torrey and S. Mowinckel had already argued against a Babylonian provenance because the author addresses the exiles from a non-Babylonian perspective.[5] Neither, however, questioned the appropriateness of historical criticism's division of the book or took into consideration that Duhm's theory was basically tied to a separation of chs. 40–66 from the preceding chs. 1–39, which secondarily focused attention on chs. 40–55, because of their placement in the middle of the work.[6] Based on terse form-critical investigations, which did not raise the later, so-important questions about the relationship between form and theme, the division well served the broader interest of historical-critical scholarship's antiquarian need for evolutionary explanation.

More recent changes in the theory as a whole have followed nicely the 'deconstruction' movement that rose to prominence in the 1970s, a movement which sought to investigate the Bible's status as a historical book. These changes have fostered quite a number of works that have investigated the editorial material in the book on a source-critical basis, including, as well, an analysis of its literary character and its hermeneutical perspective.[7] In Sweeney's characterization of these investigations, the shift of interest away 'from reconstructing the events and historical personages mentioned in the biblical tradition to identifying the literary work and theological perspectives of the anonymous tradents and redactors who shaped the tradition', is regarded as being in opposition to historical-critical scholarship. It should, however, rather be considered as representing what historical-critical scholarship should have been based on—namely, a thorough source-criticism—

---

3.   Cf. the discussion in C.R. Seitz, *Zion's Final Destiny: The Development of the Book of Isaiah: A Reassessment of Isaiah 36–39* (Minneapolis: Fortress Press, 1991), pp. 8-12, 205-207, who himself argues against a Babylonian provenance on the basis that 'Second Isaiah chapters operate from the same working perspectives as chs. 1–39 and 56–66: that of Zion' (p. 206). See also R.J. Clifford, 'Isaiah, Book of (Second Isaiah)', in *ABD*, III, pp. 490-501 (492, 493), arguing for a Babylonian provenance without any specific reference to the discussion.

4.   J.L. McKenzie, *Second Isaiah: Introduction, Translation and Notes* (AB, 20; Garden City NY: Doubleday, 1968), p. xviii.

5.   C.C. Torrey, *The Second Isaiah: A New Interpretation* (New York: Charles Scribner's Sons, 1928); S. Mowinckel, 'Die Komposition des deuterojesajanischen Buches', *ZAW* 49 (1931), pp. 87-112, 242-60. Later also H. Barstad, 'Lebte Deuterojesaja in Judäa?', *NorTT* 83 (1982), pp. 77-87 (85): 'Den dass es die Einwohner Jerusalems sind, an die sich die Verkündigung des Propheten richtet, ergibt sich nicht allein aus ihrem Inhalt, sondern ist auch daran ersichtlich, dass der *Adressat* durchweg Jerusalem/Zion ist... Dass es Jerusalem ist, an das sich die Verkündigung Deuterojesajas richtet, geht u.a. klar aus Stellen, wie Jes 40.2, 9, 27; 41.8, 14; 52.9; 54. Sieht man diese Stellen vor dem Hintergrund eines Werkes wie die Klagelieder, ist es erstaunlich, dass man überhaupt auf den Gedanken kam, der Prophet sei in Babylon tätig gewesen.'

6.   Seitz, *Zion's Final Destiny*, p. 12.

7.   M.A. Sweeney, 'The Book of Isaiah in Recent Research', *CR:BS* 1 (1993), pp. 141-62, and, *Isaiah 1–4 and the Post-Exilic Understanding of the Isaianic Tradition* (BZAW, 171; Berlin: W. de Gruyter, 1988), pp. 1-25.

before using the sources for historical reconstruction. This criticism should not be limited to form and redaction criticism, but should imply attention to 'the literary character and setting of biblical texts, including their structure and thematic development, their editorial formation and intent, and their social and institutional matrices',[8] which are now claimed to provide a new departure for critical research. In Isaiah studies, this new departure led to an increasing interest in the final form of the book of Isaiah as a whole.[9]

Most works, however, still maintain that editorial stages had taken place and that especially a post-exilic Trito-Isaiah has been influential in the final form of Proto-Isaiah, which is considered to have originated in the eighth century BCE. Whether Trito-Isaiah was understood to be an independent part of the book,[10] or to represent an editorial continuation of an earlier Isaianic corpus,[11] the correspondences between chs. 56–66 and the rest of the book begged for a further examination of its assumed redaction history.[12] The outcome resulted mainly in a reconsideration of the structuring of the book, of which chs. 32–33, 34–35[13] and 36–39[14] gained attention as

8.   Sweeney, 'The Book of Isaiah in Recent Research', p. 141.

9.   Initiated by the highly influential works of J. Vermeylen, *Du prophète Isaïe à l'apocalyptique* (EBib; 2 vols.; Paris: J. Gabalda, 1977–78); P.R. Ackroyd, 'Isaiah I–XII: Presentation of a Prophet', in J.A. Emerton *et al.* (eds.), *Congress Volume: Göttingen 1977* (VTSup, 29; Leiden: E.J. Brill, 1978), pp. 16-48; B.S. Childs, *Introduction to the Old Testament as Scripture* (Philadelphia: Fortress Press, 1979); R.E. Clements, *Isaiah 1–39* (NCB; Grand Rapids: Eerdmans; London: Marshall, Morgan & Scott, 1980).

10.   B.S. Childs, *Introduction to the Old Testament as Scripture* (Philadelphia: Fortress Press, 1979), pp. 325-31; W.A.M. Beuken, 'Isa. 56.9–57.13—An Example of the Isaianic Legacy of Trito-Isaiah', in J.W. Henten *et al.* (eds.), *Tradition and Reinterpretation in Jewish and Early Christian Literature* (Festschrift J.C.H. Lebram; Leiden: E.J. Brill, 1986), pp. 48-64; *idem*, 'The Main Theme of Trito-Isaiah "The Servants of YHWH"', *JSOT* 47 (1990), pp. 67-87.

11.   J. Vermeylen, 'L'Unité du livre d'Isaïe', in *idem* (ed.), *The Book of Isaiah*, pp. 11-53 (42-44), and, in the same volume, O.H. Steck, 'Tritojesaja im Jesajabuch', pp. 361-406.

12.   For a summery of the various works on compositional, linguistic, thematic and plot-driven correspondences, see Sweeney, *Isaiah 1–39*, pp. 41-42; R. Rendtorff, 'The Book of Isaiah: A Complex Unity. Synchronic and Diachronic Reading', in Melugin and Sweeney (eds.), *New Visions of Isaiah*, pp. 32-49 (45) (an updated and revised version of *idem*, 'The Book of Isaiah: A Complex Unity—Synchronic and Diachronic Reading', in E.H. Lovering, Jr [ed.], *Society of Biblical Literature Seminar Papers 1991* [Atlanta: Scholars Press, 1991], pp. 8-20).

13.   O.H. Steck, *Bereitete Heimkehr: Jesaja 35 als redaktionelle Brücke zwischen dem Ersten und dem Zweiten Jesaja* (SBS, 121; Stuttgart: Katholisches Bibelwerk, 1985); Sweeney, *Isaiah 1–39*, pp. 42-44: 'Thus the structure of the book of Isaiah comprises two major subunits. Chs. 1–33 focus on the projection of YHWH's plan to establish worldwide sovereignty at Zion, and chs. 34–66 focus on the realization of YHWH's plans for the establishment of worldwide sovereignty at Zion. Whereas chs. 1–33 are wholly anticipatory, chs. 34–66 present the process as a current event. The downfall of Edom, the Assyrian monarch, and Babylon, on the one hand, and the rise of Cyrus, on the other, partially fulfil the promises found in chs. 1–33 and support the contention of chs. 34–66 that YHWH's worldwide sovereignty is about to be manifested. In this context, chs. 1–33 thereby legitimise expectations for the final realization of YHWH's full sovereignty at Zion. The reader simply has to read the first part of the book to know that the prophecies in the second part will indeed be realised (34.16-17).' See also M.A. Sweeney, 'The Book of Isaiah as Prophetic Torah', in Melugin and Sweeney (eds.), *New Visions of Isaiah*, pp. 50-67 (54-56).

14.   P.R. Ackroyd, 'Isaiah 36–39: Structure and Function', in W.C. Delsman *et al.* (eds.), *Von*

possible transition chapters between the various parts, which they conclude and anticipate. The difficulties in assigning various text segments to one redactor or another, however, proved quite as impossible in regard to the book of Isaiah as it has been in regard to the Deuteronomistic History. As Laato has noted:

> Recent research vividly demonstrates that the search for unity in the book of Isaiah is a puzzling game where a collage of different texts and their literary layers must be combined into a large, coherent ideology. Every scholar can construct his own mosaic by arguing how the pieces should be arranged and how they should be interpreted against the synchronic whole of the Book of Isaiah.[15]

Assuming various redactions, whether they be pre-exilic and Josianic or post-exilic and 'fall of Jerusalem' redactions,[16] Isaiah studies have depended on the paradigmatic use of history as a chronological parameter for the literary creation that 'describes' that history as much as have Deuteronomistic History studies.[17] It is astonishing that neither scholars dealing with the Deuteronomistic History nor those working with the book of Isaiah have questioned linguistic assumptions about so-called Late and Early Biblical Hebrew. Even more astonishing is it to find linguists working intensively with comparative studies of the Masoretic texts and Dead Sea Scrolls who never speak of the redaction history of their text, as if somehow they were dealing with the same composition in all parts of the text. How do we explain that, for example, Kutscher, in his discussion of the Isaiah Scroll, mentions Chronicles, Ezekiel and Jeremiah when he speaks about Aramaic influence in Late Biblical Hebrew, but does not mention Trito-Isaiah, the text, he is analysing?[18] Even worse, Kutscher does not seem to be aware of the discussion about Second Isaiah's assumed provenance in Babylon, the geographic centre for Aramaic, a

---

Kanaan bis Kerala (Festschrift J.P.M. Van der Ploeg; AOAT, 211; Neukirchen–Vluyn: Neukirchener Verlag, 1982), pp. 3-21 (repr. in *idem, Studies in the Religious Tradition of the Old Testament* [London: SCM Press, 1987], pp. 105-20); R.E. Clements, 'The Unity of the Book of Isaiah', *Int* 36 (1982), pp. 117-29; Smelik, 'Distortion of Old Testament Prophecy', pp. 70-93; E.W. Conrad, 'The Royal Narratives and the Structure of the Book of Isaiah', *JSOT* 41 (1988), pp. 67-81; Seitz, *Zion's Final Destiny*; Laato, *About Zion I Will Not Be Silent*, pp. 45-46.

15. Laato, *About Zion I Will Not Be Silent*, p. 2.

16. H. Barth, *Die Jesaja-Worte in der Josiazeit: Israel und Assur als Thema einer produktiven Neuinterpretation der Jesajaüberlieferung* (WMANT, 48; Neukirchen–Vluyn: Neukirchener Verlag, 1977); Clements, *Isaiah and the Deliverance*; *idem*, 'The Prophecies of Isaiah and the Fall of Jerusalem in 587 BC', *VT* 30 (1980), pp. 421-36.

17. E.g. Sweeney, *Isaiah 1–39*, p. 51: 'The present commentary identifies four major stages in the composition of the book of Isaiah: (1) the final form of the book in Isaiah 1–66, which was produced in relation to the reforms of Ezra and Nehemiah in the mid- to late 5th century BCE; (2) a late-6th-century edition of the book on chs. 2–32*; 35–55; and 60–62, which was produced in conjunction with the return of the Babylonian exiles to Jerusalem and the building of the Second temple; (3) a late-7th-century edition comprising chs. 5–23*; 27–32; and 36–37, which was written to support King Josiah's program of national and religious reform; and (4) various texts found throughout 1–32* that stem from the 8th-century prophet, Isaiah ben Amoz'.

18. E.Y. Kutscher, *The Language and Linguistic Background of the Isaiah Scroll (1QIsaᵃ)* (Leiden: E.J. Brill, 1974), p. 25; *idem, A History of the Hebrew Language* (Jerusalem: Magnes Press, 1982), pp. 73, 94-105.

lingua franca since the Assyrio-Babylonian hegemony and the language later adopted by the Persian Empire.[19] Can the consequences of Kutscher's lack of 'detecting' clear linguistic differentiation in a work which is assumed to have had more than 400 year's development[20] and whose final stages are considered to have developed at a time when other works are said to be highly influenced by Aramaic, go unnoticed?[21] The implications do not only affect redaction criticism, but also the history of the Hebrew language.

The complex unity of the book of Isaiah does not give clear evidence of successive redaction, however much it encourages scholarly assumptions that it should not be united. Isaiah 1–12's presentation of the prophet's status as a messenger of doom and salvation[22] similarly testifies only to Isaiah's status as the *prophet par excellence* in the later period[23] if one presumes its chronological setting in the eighth century BCE. Without such assumption, Ackroyd's question, 'Why, alone among the eighth century prophets, has Isaiah acquired so enormous a prophetic collection now associated with his name and "somehow" linked to him?',[24] will be meaningless. The presentation of the prophet might not have created the book by such conscious application, as that suggested by Ackroyd:

> When the ultimate compiler of Isa. i–xii invites his readers or hearers to look back to the prophet, it is not with the aim of providing them with some kind of picture of the prophet's activity—for which indeed only minimal information is to be found here—but to show the basis for the acceptance of the present application of what is associated with the prophet to lie in a view of his authoritative status, tied on the one hand to the record of a particular commissioning and on the other hand to the authenticating of the prophet's word in the sequel—that is, in the fulfilment of his words in events, in the continued vitality of that word in new situations.[25]

If the book is not redacted, but written at a certain time in history—and the fact that we have not penetrated its self-presentation only gives evidence that it was written by a skilled author—then the presentation of the prophet did not attract further

---

19. Kutscher, *The Language and Linguistic Background of the Isaiah Scroll*, p. 9. In his quite extensive bibliography, one looks in vain for just a single reference to a work discussing the editorial character of the MT.

20. The latest redactions might have taken place in the third–second century BCE; cf. O. Kaiser, *Das Buch des Propheten Jesaja: Kapitel 1–12: Übersetzt und erklärt* (Göttingen: Vandenhoeck & Ruprecht, 5th rev. edn. 1981), pp. 19-27; Steck, *Bereitete Heimkehr*, p. 102; P. Hanson, *The Dawn of Apocalyptic: The Historical and Sociological Roots of Jewish Apocalyptic Eschatology* (Philadelphia: Fortress Press, 1989). For further references see, Laato, *About Zion I Will Not Be Silent*, pp. 55-56.

21. The placement of Isa. 55–66 among post-exilic literature, together with Ezekiel, Haggai, Zechariah and Malachi in A. Sáenz-Badillos, *A History of the Hebrew Language* (trans. J. Elwolde; Cambridge: Cambridge University Press, 1997), pp. 114-25, seems to be due to convention rather than language.

22. Ackroyd, 'Isaiah I–XII: Presentation', pp. 45-46.

23. G. Fohrer, *Einleitung in das Alte Testament* (Heidelberg: Quelle, 1965), p. 411.

24. Ackroyd, 'Isaiah I–XII: Presentation', p. 22.

25. Ackroyd, 'Isaiah I–XII: Presentation', p. 46.

applications, but belongs to the narrative structure of the book as a whole. The problem raised here is not a simple one. It affects our reading of the book, and we are only half way better off if we follow Rendtorff's proposal to dispense with redaction-critical considerations, because of their highly hypothetical character:

> The result [of diachronic analysis] is, on the one hand an extremely complicated hypothetical editorial history, from the prophet Isaiah in the eighth century through to the Hellenistic era. On the other hand, it is no longer possible to read the book of Isaiah in its continuity at any point before the final ("canonical") shape of the text. The other position [a synchronic reading] reads the book of Isaiah mainly in its given "canonical" shape, though in full awareness of its ("diachronic") complexity. In my view, it is the great advantage of such a sophisticated synchronic reading that the interpreter is able to read the text in its given continuity.[26]

Dispensing with, yet being fully aware of its (diachronic) complexity, makes the book homeless and timeless. I can fully appreciate such an enterprise. It gives wonderful new readings, as demonstrated by the recent works of Anderson,[27] Conrad,[28] Seitz,[29] Carr[30] and Laato.[31] The immediate profit in such readings is a certain dissolution of the assumed disunity and complexity and, in fact, a clearer authorial profile. On the other hand such gains are endangered by creating new disjunctures through a much too rigid understanding of the dynamics of the text and an assertion of its literary 'coherence' with modern scholarly principles. Carr's reading of Isa. 1.29-30 as a secondary insertion[32] exactly fails to see that its link is not so much with Isaiah 65–66, but with 1.1-3's call to a return to the nursing God, since the cult they now attend will do them no good (cf. the way of the godless in Ps. 1). The shift in person is part of the text's dramatic form, addressed to its ancient listener, who, I believe, clearly understood the cohesiveness of the given message. Carr's conclusion, that 'a construal' of Isaiah 1 and 65–66, 'as parts of an overarching literary whole, does not represent any reconstructable intent of the editors',[33] belongs to his paradigmatic assumption that 'ancient readers' were less preoccupied 'with literary coherence' than 'modern readers often are'.[34] The danger of creating

26. Rendtorff, 'The Book of Isaiah: A Complex Unity' p. 45.

27. B.W. Anderson, 'The Apocalyptic Rendering of the Isaiah Tradition', in J. Neusner *et al.* (eds.), *The Social World of Formative Christianity and Judaism: Essays in Tribute to Howard Clark Kee* (Philadelphia: Fortress Press, 1988), pp. 17-38.

28. Conrad, 'Royal Narratives & Structure of Isaiah', *JSOT* 41 (1988), pp. 67-81.

29. C.R. Seitz, 'Isaiah 1–66: Making Sense of the Whole', in *idem* (ed.), *Reading and Preaching the Book of Isaiah* (Philadelphia: Fortress Press, 1988), pp. 105-26.

30. D.M. Carr, 'Reading Isaiah from Beginning (Isaiah 1) to End (Isaiah 65–66): Multiple Modern Possibilities', in Melugin and Sweeney (eds.), *New Visions of*, pp. 188-218.

31. Laato, *About Zion I Will Not Be Silent*.

32. Carr, 'Reading Isaiah from Beginning to End', pp. 215-16.

33. Carr, 'Reading Isaiah from Beginning to End', p. 217.

34. Carr, 'Reading Isaiah from Beginning to End', p. 216. I fully agree with Laato's critique of Carr (Laato, *About Zion I Will Not Be Silent*, p. 4): 'that the ideological coherence of the Book of Isaiah is too deep to be penetrated by a simple search for parallel linguistic expressions (despite their importance). It is more important to consider the content and function of each textual unit in the overall composition of the Book of Isaiah.'

a new form and redaction criticism based on intertextually driven interpretations lies right at the centre of such an assumption. Carr's distinction between a modern reading of the text as apparently coherent and his interpretation of the text's purported incoherence is tied firmly to redaction criticism's need for chronology. It might appear to be reading the book 'as a whole', but, in fact, it demonstrates a reading that is conditional and circular.[35] Contrary also to Sweeney's argument, advocating a compositional chronology, that 'genres do not always define texts; they function within them as compositional tools',[36] I find Muilenburg's conclusion that 'generic distinctions within a prophetic text may well represent a rhetorical device within a larger text that an author employs to create an impression or to make a particular point to his or her audience',[37] far more convincing.

The unsolved problem still relates to the copyright of the material. Whether we think in terms of authorial or editorial enterprises, the book was written with purpose.[38] If there were redaction, why should the redactors have followed the currents of history? That the prophet Isaiah presented in the book of Isaiah is anchored chronologically in the eighth–seventh century BCE is explicit in the author's presentation of the prophet, but how does that relate to the appearance of a book that carries his name? If so-called later redactors of Isaiah took his visions as historical events, would they have changed the work of such a famous master, once they had seen that his visions had turned out wrong or that he had not 'seen' enough to comprehend fully history's course up to their own time? What would be the significance of such a redacted work for a later audience? How do such scholarly assumptions about a growing Isaiah tradition fit its 'canonical' status in Dead Sea Scrolls material? Why did this assumed process of redaction stop as late (or should we say early?) as the third or second century BCE and develop into the wider spectrum of *pesharim*, of which the Gospels became its ultimate independent result? What, moreover, does the Hebrew word חזון ('vision') signify? Is it to be understood as some sort of marvellous revelation, or should we think rather of its

---

35. Cf. also Melugin's conclusion with regard to both synchronic and diachronic interpretations: 'the meaning which we see in texts is always in large measure the result of what interpreters do' (R.F. Melugin, 'The Book of Isaiah and the Construction of Meaning', in Broyles and Evans [eds.], *Writing and Reading the Scroll of Isaiah*, pp. 39-56 [50]). G.T. Sheppard, 'The Book of Isaiah: Competing Structures According to a Late Modern Description of Its Shape and Scope', in E.H. Lovering (ed.), *Society of Biblical Literature Seminar Papers 1992* (Atlanta: Scholars Press, 1992), pp. 549-82 (553) states: 'a structural analysis, based on one historical and literary preunderstanding, will betray the tyranny and temporality of its own choice. It may be done with a full awareness of these limitations. The reward is a relative rather than an absolute objectivity, an objectivity peculiar to this particular relationship between reader and text, and the prospect of new discoveries within the possibilities intrinsic to this pragmatically chosen hermeneutical system.'

36. Sweeney, *Isaiah 1–39*, p. 14.

37. J. Muilenburg, 'Form Criticism and Beyond', *JBL* 88 (1969), pp. 1-18; cf. Sweeney, *Isaiah 1–39*, p. 14.

38. Laato, *About Zion I Will Not Be Silent*, pp. 5-6: 'Nevertheless, it is possible to regard the Book of Isaiah as one literary unit and envisage a relevant context or contexts against which its ideology could be interpreted'.

interpretative function as insight?[39] The author of the book of Isaiah presents the prophet as prophesying 'history's course'. The prophet's 'voice', however, is rather a philosopher or priest's didactic sermon offering 'interpretations'. If one dispenses with the book's explicit narrative chronology in headlines and in the Ahaz and Hezekiah stories, Isaiah could have 'prophesied' at any time between the first return from exile until the book's physical appearance among the Dead Sea Scrolls. We should not too quickly forget that Isaiah is a character in a book, which bears his name, someone who pronounces salvation for Israel's remnant.

2. *The Provenance of the Hezekiah Narrative:*
The Form- and Redaction-Critical Discussion

In Chapter 2, I assumed that the provenance of the Hezekiah narrative belongs to the book of Isaiah. The impact of such an assumption (not originally mine) has not quite made its way into Deuteronomistic History studies, which present the narrative as one small part of the Deuteronomistic History's discourse on *the Children of Israel's* history from creation to exile, without regarding the Hezekiah narrative's s possible intrusion into that story. The consequence of the lack of clear authorial identification has led to a diminished interest in the narrative, especially within Isaiah studies, where several scholars omit it entirely or handle it only sketchily,[40] but also in studies of Kings.[41] In neither area of study has the narrative's function within its larger context attracted much interest. It has only recently been more widely accepted that the narrative might belong to the book of Isaiah, where it plays a central role in the structuring of the book as a whole.[42]

It was Melugin's conclusion that Isaiah 40–55 was never meant to stand alone and that 'the closest thing to a setting for chs. 40ff. is the prophecy of Isaiah to Hezekiah in ch. 39 concerning the exile to Babylon',[43] which brought Ackroyd to reconsider the significance and the function of Isaiah 36–39. In his small essay from 1982,[44] he did not explicitly claim an Isaianic provenance for the material, but rather gave some suggestions about the linkage between Isa. 6.1–9.6 and 36–39 and especially the portraits of Ahaz and Hezekiah, which, he argued, formed a contrasting pair, although not as strongly as in their presentation in Kings. The linkage between these royal portraits are further underscored by both sections' concern 'with portraying the nature and function of Isaiah in relation to a particular series of

---

39.   R.P. Carroll, 'Blindsight and the Vision Thing: Blindness and Insight in the Book of Isaiah', in Broyles and Evans (eds.), *Writing and Reading the Scroll of Isaiah*, pp. 79-93; A.G. Auld, 'Prophets Through the Looking Glass: Between Writings and Moses', *JSOT* 27 (1983), pp. 3-23.

40.   Ackroyd, 'Isaiah 36–39', p. 115.

41.   Ackroyd, 'Isaiah 36–39', p. 114; Seitz, *Zion's Final Destiny*, offers a chapter-length discussion of the problem of provenance.

42.   Cf. some of the discussions of the 'Formation of the Book of Isaiah Seminar' at the SBL National Meetings, currently published in SBL Seminar Papers.

43.   Melugin, *The Formation of Isaiah 40–55*, p. 177; cf. Ackroyd, 'Isaiah 36–39', p. 106.

44.   Ackroyd, 'Isaiah 36–39'.

narrative as a presentation of the prophet'.[45] In Chapter 2, I have made the opposite claim that it is Kings which offers a contrasting presentation, while Isaiah's portraits mainly demonstrate their similarities. (I will discuss this aspect further below.) Ackroyd's work was taken further by Conrad, who demonstrated that:

> The close relationship between the two narratives extends to the larger contexts in which they occur, for each royal narrative is followed by a 'fear not' oracle addressed to the community: the Ahaz narrative (Isaiah 7) is followed by the community War Oracle of 10.24-27, and the Hezekiah narrative (Isaiah 36–39) is followed by the War Oracles in 41.8-13; 41.14-16; 43.1-4; 43.5-6; 44.1-5. Furthermore, when these two narratives are read in light of one another, a certain movement or progression can be detected in the book; the Hezekiah narrative is not simply a structural clone of the Ahaz narrative. The community War Oracle in 10.24-27 helps explain the movement or development between the Ahaz and Hezekiah narratives, just as the community War Oracles in 41.8-13; 41.14-16; 43.1-4; 43.5-6; 44.1-5 help explain the development beyond the Hezekiah narrative.[46]

Both the works of Ackroyd and Conrad discuss the structural aspects of the Hezekiah narrative related to the book of Isaiah as a whole, which, at least regarding Ackroyd, seems to imply an editorial movement from the Hezekiah narrative to a formation of chs. 6–9, based on this narrative.[47] Smelik, however, invited a reconsideration of the issue of provenance of Isaiah 36–39.[48] Taking up the claim of Gesenius that '2 Kings 18.13, 17–20.19 are an integral part of the book [of 2 Kings], whereas Isaiah 36–39 appear to be an appendage',[49] Smelik noted a series of compositional incompatibilities with Gesenius' claim, which was based primarily on form critical grounds:[50]

1. Gesenius' textual argument that the text of Kings was to be preferred above the text of Isaiah has no conclusive force. Sometimes Kings has the preferred reading, while at other times it is Isaiah.[51]
2. The occurrence of a prophet whose sayings have been recorded in the books of the Latter Prophets, within a larger narrative, is exceptional. Not even in 2 Kgs 25.22-26 does Jeremiah figure, although this passage

---

45. Ackroyd, 'Isaiah 36–39', p. 116.

46. Conrad, 'Royal Narratives & Structure of Isaiah', p. 68.

47. Ackroyd, 'Isaiah 36–39'. So also Gonçalves, '2 Rois 18.13–20.19 par. Isaïe 36–39', p. 49: 'À ma connaissance, Is 7.1–9.6 est le seul texte du livre d'Isaïe qui dépende probablement d'Is 36–39'.

48. Smelik, 'Distortion of Old Testament Prophecy'. Earlier arguments for an Isaianic provenance include Jepsen, *Die Quellen des Königsbuches*, p. 77; S.I.L. Norin, 'An Important Kennicott Reading in 2 Kings xviii 13', *VT* 32 (1982), pp. 337-38.

49. W. Gesenius, *Der Prophet Jesaja* (3 vols.; Leipzig: F.C.W. Vogel, 1821), II, pp. 932-36.

50. Smelik, 'Distortion of Old Testament Prophecy', pp. 70-74.

51. Argued also by H. Wildberger, *Jesaja 28–39* (BKAT, 10/3; Neukirchen–Vluyn: Neukirchener Verlag, 1982), pp. 1370-74. Wildberger's unconvincing arguments sought to mediate form-critical arguments related to *lectior difficilior* and *brevior* by claiming an independent Hezekiah narrative, which is inserted secondarily first in Kings and from there brought into Isaiah.

is clearly a summary of Jeremiah 40–43. Isaiah's occurrence in other narratives of the book of Isaiah, but not in Kings, further stresses the exceptionality of 2 Kgs 18.17–20.19.

3. The poetic portions of 2 Kgs 18.17–20.19 are exceptional in the context of the book as a whole.

4. Hezekiah's illness story is better understood as composed in Isaiah than in Kings. Furthermore, in Kings, this story and the Babylonian envoys narrative would naturally have preceded the story of Jerusalem's deliverance, while, in Isaiah, such more logical arrangement would destroy the connection between the account of the Babylonian embassy and Isaiah 40.

5. Isaiah 36–39 functions as an editorial bridge between First and Second Isaiah, the themes of which are introduced from Isaiah 35 onwards. The linkage between earlier parts of First Isaiah and these chapters involve the remnant motif, the role of Assyria, the rejection of Egypt as an ally and, finally and most importantly, parallels to Isaiah 7. Since Isaiah 7 is only to be found in the book of Isaiah, it is evident that its counterpart, Isaiah 36–39, must also have been intended for Isaiah and not for Kings.

These observations led Smelik to the very important conclusion:

> The general opinion that Isaiah 36–39 are borrowed from Kings has to be reconsidered. In my view, these narratives were intended to be inserted between the two parts of Isaiah. Words and themes from the preceding and following chapters have been introduced because of the function of these narratives as an editorial bridge. Only some time afterwards, they were added to the book of Kings because of the prominent part played by King Hezekiah in these narratives.[52]

The second part of Smelik's article deals with Stade's influential division of the Hezekiah narrative (2 Kgs 18.17–19.37) into two complete, separate accounts (B[1] and B[2], with 2 Kgs 19.9 as an editorial seam, and 19.36-37 belonging to the first account, while 19.35 belongs to the second one), which with few exceptions has become the standard opinion.[53] We do not need to dwell with this discussion long, as it demonstrates perfectly that every reading is conditional and that Stade's approach is conditioned by his opinion of how a coherent story should be written.[54] While Stade considered the repetition of oracles concerning the fate of the Assyrian king to be superfluous and a sign of editorial activity,[55] Smelik argued the opposite: that 'the repetition of the oracles has the function of intensifying the suspense'.[56] Based on a literary reading of the narrative, and assuming that repetition in biblical

52. Smelik, 'Distortion of Old Testament Prophecy', p. 74.

53. B. Stade, 'Miscellen', *ZAW* 6 (1886), pp. 122-88 (173-82). For further references to this discussion see Childs, *Isaiah and the Assyrian Crisis*, pp. 73-76; Gonçalves, *L'expédition de Sennachérib*, pp. 351-54; Seitz, *Zion's Final Destiny*, Chapter 3 *passim*; Laato, *About Zion I Will Not Be Silent*, p. 67.

54. Smelik, 'Distortion of Old Testament Prophecy', p. 74.

55. Stade, 'Miscellen', pp. 174-75.

56. Smelik, 'Distortion of Old Testament Prophecy', p. 84.

material is to be interpreted as a literary device rather than as an invitation to source analysis, Smelik's analysis showed that it was not merely Sennacherib's messages and Hezekiah's reactions which served the author's rhetorical intentions. Also Isaiah's oracles (2 Kgs 19.6-7 and 21-34, with a division of vv. 22-29 and 32-33 into two oracles) function in this way. The conclusion of the narrative in 2 Kgs 19.35-37 'alludes to the three oracles together. Therefore it is impossible to divide these verses into two strands without serious exegetical loss.'[57]

The historical implications of Smelik's conclusions are far-reaching, not so much because he opts for a Persian period setting after the completion of Second Isaiah and the end of the Davidic kingship, nor because he concludes that the Isaianic version of the narrative 'has almost no bearing on the historical reconstruction of the events in 701 BCE' and that 'this reconstruction must be based on 2 Kgs 18.13-16 and Assyrian sources'.[58]

There is no real challenge in such conclusions anymore. Smelik's further consideration, however, based on De Jong's work on the similarity between Isaiah 36–37 and Jeremiah 37,[59] is intriguing. If one concludes with De Jong that the Hezekiah account is based on Jeremiah's story of Zedekiah and not the other way around, as is usually assumed, the significance of the Hezekiah narrative is overwhelming.[60] If

---

57. Smelik, 'Distortion of Old Testament Prophecy', pp. 84-85. N. Na'aman's recent conclusion, that the author of B[1] selected his examples of cities from Sargon II's campaigns, whereas the author of B[1] selected his examples from the Babylonian campaigns of the late seventh century BCE, might be seen to support standard source-critical views (cf. N. Na'aman, 'New Light on Hezekiah's Second Prophetic Story [2 Kings 19,9b-35]', *Bib* 81 [2000], pp. 393-402). However, the increasing plotline expressed hereby and a possible implicit inclusion of the Babylonian period, which is lacking in the book of Isaiah, can as well be argued to have motivated the author. Na'aman is not correct in his statement that 'the list of cities in 2 Kgs 19.12-13 is almost entirely different from the list in 2 Kgs 18.33-34' (p. 396). 2 Kgs 18.34 shares all the names with 19.12-13, which has also several other names. These additional names also occur in Assyrian lists of conquests from the time of Ashurnasirpal II (883–859) and Shalmaneser III (858–824) before Sennacherib's invasion. Considering the names to refer to Babylonian rather than Assyrian conquests is a matter of conviction, since both possibilities can equally be argued. C. Hardmeier, *Prophetie im Streit vor dem Untergang Judas: Erzählkommunikative Studien zur Entstehungssituation der Jesaja- und Jeremiaerzählungen in II Reg 18–20 und Jer 37–40* (BZAW, 187; Berlin: W. de Gruyter, 1990), pp. 399-406, argues for an allusion to the fight at Carchemish (605 BCE) behind the reference to Hamath and Arpad and for the syncretistic peoples of the Assyrian province *Samerina* behind Sephar-vaim, Hena and Ivvah in 2 Kgs 18.34; 19.13: 'Was die Erfahrungsperspektive aus dem Jahre 588 betrifft, so ist davon auszugehen, dass die unter Joschija befreiten Teile des ehemaligen Nordreichs bsw. der assyrischen Provinz Samaria spätestens in der ersten Belagerungsphase Jerusalems um 588, wenn nicht schon nach 597 unter babylonische Kontrolle gerieten' (p. 406).

58. Smelik, 'Distortion of Old Testament Prophecy', p. 85.

59. S. De Jong, 'Hizkia en Zedekia: Over de verhouding van 2 Kon. 18.17–19.37/Jes. 36–37 tot Jer. 37.1-10', *ACEBT* 5 (1984), pp. 135-46.

60. Later argued independently of De Jong and Smelik by A. Laato, 'Hezekiah and the Assyrian Crisis in 701 B.C.', *SJOT* 2 (1987), pp. 49-68, and Hardmeier, *Prophetie im Streit vor dem Untergang Judas*. Of these, only Laato argues for an Isaianic provenance of the Hezekiah narratives, which is further supported in his meticulous study on the Hezekiah narrative's linguistic and thematic coherence with the rest of the book of Isaiah; cf. *idem*, *About Zion I Will Not Be Silent*. Hardmeier's arguments for a provenance in Kings relates to elements he himself judges as

Smelik is right in his proposal, that 'Hezekiah is not only a counterpart of his father Ahaz, but also of Judah's last king Zedekiah, who failed to listen and instead relied on Egypt',[61] the Hezekiah narrative must be seen in a totally different light. Laato's argument, based on a separation of narrative B[1] and B[2], in fact, makes the Egyptian 'alliance' a positive one, while it is Zedekiah's non-righteousness, contrasted to Hezekiah's righteousness, that makes it possible for the Babylonians to conquer Jerusalem.[62] These observations must include a consideration of Conrad's argument that 'the Hezekiah narrative is not simply a clone of the Ahaz story'.[63]

In line with my proposal (made at the end of Chapter 2) that the Hezekiah story did not belong to, but intrudes on, and even distorts, the narrative discourse in Kings,[64] our consideration that the hope for post-exilic Israel lies with Jerusalem's faithful remnant of the Hezekiah narrative, must be scrutinized. The potential impact of Smelik's proposal seems not to have been fully perceived in his further conclusion that the contrasting fates of Jerusalem in Hezekiah and Zedekiah's days 'clarified to the readers as to why they had to experience exile whereas their ancestors have been spared after Hezekiah's rebellion'.[65] Belonging to, but not identical

superfluous—'Nebenzügen und Details, die am Gesamtduktus der Erzählung und ihrer Hauptthematik gemessen, funktionslos erscheinen' (p. 125)—and therefore deleted in Isaiah's version.

61. Smelik, 'Distortion of Old Testament Prophecy', p. 86.

62. Laato, *About Zion I Will Not Be Silent*, p. 122: 'The "Assyria and Egypt"-confrontation in Isaiah 36–37 corresponds to the "Babylonia and Egypt"-confrontation during the reign of Zedekiah. Like Babylonia, Assyria also attempted to conquer Jerusalem, but was forced to leave it in peace in order to confront the Egyptian army. However, when the Babylonians returned and conquered Jerusalem during the reign of Zedekiah, Assyria did not suffer the same fate. Because of the righteous king, Hezekiah, Assyria could not conquer Jerusalem and its troops were decimated. From these considerations, we can conclude that Hezekiah simultaneously served as an anti-typos of Zedekiah and a typos of the Messiah.' Hardmeier, *Prophetie im Streit vor dem Untergang Judas*, pp. 418, 450-64, argues for the historical situation of 588 BCE (such as reflected in Jeremiah and the Deuteronomistic History) as a paradigm for the Hezekiah narrative (pp. 287-306), which, written in 588 BCE by high priestly family/party of Hilkiah, were meant to oppose a policy of submission to the Babylonians, as advised by Jeremiah and the Shaphanides (Jer. 37–40; written after 587 BCE and based on the Hezekiah narrative; cf. p. 449, and pp. 465-66: 'Ja, eine Reihe auffälliger Berührungspunkte zwischen der wenig jüngeren GBJ-Erzählung [Jeremiah] und der ABBJ-Erzählung [Hezekiah] von 588 lassen erkennen, dass sich die GBJ-Erzählung sogar direkt auf die ABBJ-Erzählung bezogen hat'). Although Hardmeier's socio-political context, established from the material he examines, is extremely problematic, based as it is on notably uncertain sources which either underwent later redactions before their present form (the Hezekiah narrative), or were written on the background of the discussion purported (Jer. 37–40), his intertextual readings of Isaiah (Kings), Jeremiah and Ezekiel is most welcome and will continue to challenge redaction historians (cf. the reviews of Hardmeier's book by C.R. Seitz in *JBL* 110 [1991], pp. 511-12, and R.D. Nelson in *CBQ* 55 [1993], pp. 337-38).

63. Conrad, 'Royal Narratives & Structure of Isaiah', p. 68.

64. So also Clements, 'Prophecies of Isaiah to Hezekiah Concerning Sennacherib', p. 69: 'A number of scholars have therefore argued that it is an expansion of the original DtrG and the question of the extent to which it can be called "Deuteronomistic" is questionable'.

65. Smelik, 'Distortion of Old Testament Prophecy', p. 86: 'Where Zedekiah failed to listen to Jeremiah and relied on Egypt, Hezekiah put his trust in the Lord alone and takes heed to Isaiah's words'.

with Hezekiah's faithful remnant, they can only hope to be found worthy of that qualification in their present lives modelled after what the book of Isaiah preaches as faithfulness.[66] As we shall see, were it not for that faithful remnant, there would be no ancestors to become compared with. This also lies implicit in Clements' post-587 redaction of the Hezekiah narrative: 'We may venture to draw the conclusion therefore that the "anti-Assyrian" saying of Isa. 14.24f. owes its origin, along with the comparable saying of Isa. 31.8 and the B[2] narrative now combined in 2 Kgs 18.17–19.37 to the desire to re-establish a rationale for restoring the Davidic kingship and for rebuilding the Jerusalem temple in the wake of what happened to both institutions in 587 BCE'.[67] We will have to discuss later whether Isaiah's concern is that of a restoration of past institutions, or whether his preaching aims at the faithful community as Yahweh's universal kingdom.[68] The few occurrences of explicit David ideology (Isa. 7.2, 13; 9.6; 16.5; 22.22; 29.1; 37.35; 38.5; 55.3) must lead to a reconsideration of the role of these institutions in Isaiah's writings.

Seitz, on the other hand, understood well the implicit danger of Smelik's observations for redaction-criticism's need for an early dating of Isaiah 36–37:

> If one posits a readership at a sufficiently late period, then all problems of a distinctly diachronic nature begin to merge indiscriminately. Moreover, while a degree of speculation always marked the traditional historical approach, at least it had in its favor the commendation of the narrative world, which situated the material in relatively perspicuous historical settings—at least when measured against putative settings in the postexilic period.[69]

Based on a late dating for the A account (which only occurs in 2 Kgs 18.13-16), after the formation of the Josiah narrative,[70] Seitz took on the task of demonstrating that Smelik's literary observations were right, though his historical and tradition-historical conclusions were wrong.[71] Seitz' analysis of account B[1-2] 'confirmed the view of Smelik that Isaiah 36–38 is essentially a unified narrative' and that the composite character of the two parts is of such artistry that it 'is impossible' to determine whether there once had been a briefer narrative.[72] Seitz' objection, however,

---

66. Laato, *About Zion I Will Not Be Silent*, p. 160: 'Therefore the loyal servant in Isaiah 40–55 is he who follows the steps of the Master Isaiah. His eyes and ears are opened to see and hear the programme of salvation which YHWH has revealed to Isaiah *long ago* and which will *now* be realized.'

67. Clements, 'Isaiah 14.22-27', pp. 253-62. Clements' reasons for the dating are not in contrast to Smelik's, as Seitz argues (*Zion's Final Destiny*, p. 129), since both agree that the Davidic kingship has come to and end. See also Clements, 'Prophecies of Isaiah to Hezekiah Concerning Sennacherib', pp. 68, 73-74.

68. Laato, *About Zion I Will Not Be Silent*, *passim* (pp. 156-69, 173-74).

69. Seitz, *Zion's Final Destiny*, p. 140.

70. Seitz, *Zion's Final Destiny*, pp. 61, 66, 71.

71. Seitz, *Zion's Final Destiny*, pp. 66-118

72. Seitz, *Zion's Final Destiny*, pp. 81, 95 and 117: 'The composite quality of the narrative, long-recognised by form-critics, is not to be denied, especially at certain junctures in Isa. 37.21-38. Nevertheless, these several formally distinct units (37.21-29, 30-32, 33-35, 36-38) function in such an integral way in the final form of the material that it is difficult to conceive of a narrative capable

does not really regard the composite character of the text, but rather the late dating of account B[2], based on its linguistic and thematic relationship to Second Isaiah.[73] Reversing the standard opinion that Second Isaiah had given voice to the Hezekiah narrative, Seitz argued for a continuous growth of the book of Isaiah following closely its own explicit chronology.[74] The wider purpose of Seitz' reconstruction was to find an historical setting for the Hezekiah narrative (chs. 36–38) within this growing Isaiah tradition's *Sitz im Leben* in the royal court of delivered Jerusalem of the eighth–seventh century BCE. More specifically, Seitz suggested this setting to imply an admonition to Manasseh, unfaithful son of Hezekiah, to follow in the steps of his faithful father.[75]

Separating the deliverance narrative and the story of Hezekiah's illness from the story about the Babylonian envoys, Seitz placed the latter within the authorship of his DtrH, within whose logic and structure he claimed it fully belonged, because of its 'considerable' editorial congruity with the final narratives in the DtrH:[76]

> In contrast to the Hezekiah–Isaiah narratives (Isa. 36–38), whose primary location was the Book of Isaiah, the Babylonian envoy episode (Isa. 39) has its primary home in the DtrH. Yet, because of its suitability for prefacing the 'Babylonian' material in Isa. 40–55 and because of the connection that was made in Kings with the other Hezekiah–Isaiah traditions (2 Kgs 18.13–19.37, 20.1-11), 2 Kgs 20.12-19 also found its way into the Book of Isaiah as the final episode in a trilogy whose main subject was Hezekiah and as a preface to the following Second Isaiah material. As such it would not be incorrect to say that it was composed for both contexts about a century later than the composition of 36–38.[77]

3. *The Linguistic Evidence for an Isaianic Provenance*

While form-critical analysis has the potential of establishing a provenance for the Hezekiah narratives within the authorship of the books of Kings, no 'evidence' for that hypothesis can be established on linguistic grounds. A comparative analysis of shared thematic elements will reveal that the language of the Hezekiah narratives has closer affinities with Isaiah than with the books of Kings. The examination (paragraphs a-c) deals with the narratives about the Babylonian envoys, Hezekiah's sickness and his reform, in this compositionally reversed order.

---

of making its point effectively lacking even one of them. Undoubtedly the tradition process behind Isa. 36–37 was a gradual one.'

73. Seitz, *Zion's Final Destiny*, pp. 67, 71.

74. Seitz, *Zion's Final Destiny*, pp. 196-206.

75. Seitz, *Zion's Final Destiny*, pp. 100-102, 185-91, 194, 196. For rejections of the Isaianic provenance and a discussion of both Smelik and Seitz, see D.M. Carr, 'What Can We Say about the Tradition History of Isaiah? A Response to Christopher Seitz's *Zion's Final Destiny*', in E.H. Lovering (ed.), *Society of Biblical Literature Seminar Papers 1991*, pp. 583-97; Gonçalves, '2 Rois 18.13–20.19 par. Isaïe 36–39'.

76. Seitz, *Zion's Final Destiny*, p. 159.

77. Seitz, *Zion's Final Destiny*, pp. 187-88.

a. *Isaiah's Pronouncement of Exile and its Fulfilment in 2 Kings 24–25*

Seitz's thematically driven division might solve the problems with 2 Kgs 20.12-19's correlation with the rest of the book of Kings', such as the transfer of royal treasures, and so on, to Babylon (2 Kgs 20.16-18; 24.12-16; 25.7, 27-30), when placed within the authorship of DtrH.[78] An examination of the language of the transfer, however, does not confirm that the author of 2 Kings 24–25 used this narrative as his linguistic or thematic source. In Isaiah's judgment we find that the items, which he pronounced should be transferred to Babylon are:

> everything in your house (כל אשר בביתך) that which your forefathers have collected (ואשר אצרו אבתיך), your sons, born to you (מבניך אשר יצאו ממך אשר תוליד), they shall become servants in the palace of the king of Babel (והיו סריסים מלך בבל בהיכל). (2 Kgs 20.17-18; cf. Isa. 39.6-7)

Of these only the first was shown to the envoys by Hezekiah:

> the house of treasures (את־כל־בית נכתה), the silver, the gold, the spices, the precious oil (את־הכסף ואת־הזהב ואת־הבשמים ואת־שמן הטוב), the house of his vessels (את־בית כליו),[79] all that was found in his treasures (את כל־אשר נמצא באוצרתיו). (2 Kgs 20.13; cf. Isa. 39.2)

While this language, of course, could be understood to anticipate everything that happens later, it does not bear significant linguistic correspondence so as to give evidence for a Deuteronomistic origin of the Hezekiah passage.[80] Of the few corresponding words, we find בבלה ('to Babylon', 20.17; 24.15), אוצרת ('treasures', 20.13; 24.13) and סריס ('servant', 20.18; 24.15). Of these only בבלה corresponds entirely.

אוצרת in 2 Kgs 24.13 occurs in a construct form אוצרות בית יהוה and אוצרות בית המלך similar to all the occurrences of the word in Kings.[81] Given the widespread use of this form in Kings and Chronicles, but never in Isaiah, we observe that in the Hezekiah story, the form occurs in the passage (2 Kgs 18.14-16), which is not in Isaiah. In the common passages (2 Kgs 20.13 and 15 par. Isa. 39.2 and 4), we find the only form of אוצרות with a pronominal suffix אוצרתיו in the entire Deuteronomistic History.[82] One must therefore conclude that this form is not Deuteronomistic. In Isaiah, Hezekiah's treasures are comparable to the treasures belonging to the house of Jacob (Isa. 2.7), belonging to the beasts of the Negeb (Isa. 30.6) and the treasure of fear of the Lord (Isa. 33.6); in all instances plural or singular with pronominal suffix. The verb form of the word (אצרו, 2 Kgs 20.17 par.

---

78.   Seitz, *Zion's Final Destiny*, p. 159; Carr, 'What Can We Say about the Tradition History of Isaiah?', p. 593.

79.   כלי can be vessels or armour; LXX: τῶν σκευῶν, Isa. 39.2 reads כל־בית כליו and LXX Isa. 39.2: πάντας τοὺς τῶν σκευῶν τῆς γάζης.

80.   Cf. also the discussion in Gonçalves, '2 Rois 18.13–20.19 par. Isaïe 36–39', pp. 47-48; M. Brettler, '2 Kings 24.13-14 as History', *CBQ* 53 (1991), pp. 541-52 (544-45).

81.   1 Kgs 7.51; 14.26; 15.18; 2 Kgs 12.19; 14.14; 16.8; 18.15.

82.   The two occurrences in Deut. 28.12 (singular) and 32.34 (plural) relate to Yahweh's transcendent treasures and should not be taken into consideration here.

Isa. 39.6) is moreover a *hapax legomenon* in the books of Kings, while it appears also in Isa. 23.18.[83]

The second corresponding word, סריס, functions antithetically in the stories involved. While Isaiah is promising Hezekiah's sons honorary positions at the Babylonian court (2 Kgs 20.18 par. Isa. 39.7),[84] we are not told that this happened, but only that the Judaean king Jehoiachin was taken to Babylon together with his officers (סריסיו, 2 Kgs 24.12, 15). The release of Jehoiachin (2 Kgs 25.27-30) hardly reflects an honorary position,[85] but rather fulfils Solomon's prayer for mercy (1 Kgs 8.50) and Jeremiah's prophecy of future greatness for Israel (Jer. 50.28-40). The words בית נכתה and בית כליו are *hapax legomena* in 2 Kgs 20.13 (par. Isa. 39.2).

Finally, we find that among the objects involved in the Hezekiah narrative, spices and oil are never mentioned in the later stories of Kings. The conclusion must be that the narrative belongs to the Isaianic material,[86] with which it shares significant linguistic traits.

b. *The Hezekiah Sickness Narrative*

This conclusion inevitably leads to an examination of the linguistic aspects in the Hezekiah sickness narrative and its correspondences with the sickness story of Jeroboam's son in 1 Kings 14. Thematically, both narratives are designed to give instruction about the fate of the kingship, in some way related to the Davidic promise (1 Kgs 14.8 and 2 Kgs 20.6, missing in Isa. 38.5). The specific linguistic correspondence relates to the introductory בעת ההיא (1 Kgs 14.1), בימים ההם (2 Kgs 20.1 par. Isa. 38.1) and the terms הלה, מות, בעיני, טוב. The introductory terms occur too frequently in both prophetic books (especially Jeremiah) and historical books (especially Judges) to carry any decisive significance. The same must be said about מות and הלה.

The theme, 'in the eyes of Yahweh', which, as we saw in Chapter 2, has become the standard expression in the books of Kings' divine judgment of the king as doing הרע or הישר בעיני יהוה also occurs in 1 Kgs 14.8 as a standard expression of how to behave like David. In the Hezekiah sickness narrative we do not find linguistic correspondence with the judgment formula in 2 Kgs 18.3. Hezekiah claims to have walked before Yahweh in faithfulness (באמת), with a whole heart (בלבב שלם) and to have done what is good in the eyes of Yahweh (הטוב בעיניך עשיתי, 2 Kgs 20.3). While Hezekiah walked before Yahweh in faithfulness (באמת), as also Solomon was admonished to do regarding his sons (1 Kgs 2.4), the linguistic terms for the rest of the admonition to Solomon (בכל־לבבם ובכל־נפשם) is not found in the Hezekiah narrative. Similarly, David's behaviour in 1 Kgs 3.6 is characterized by כאשר הלך לפניך באמת ובצדקה ובישרת לבב עמך. We here notice the favourite term

---

83. Other occurrences are in Amos 3.10 and Neh. 13.13.

84. Cf. 1 Kgs 22.9; 2 Kgs 8.6; 9.32; 23.11; Est. 1; 2; 4; 6 *passim*.

85. Murray, 'Of All the Years the Hopes—or Fears?', p. 259: 'a modestly pensioned, detention'.

86. Smelik, 'Distortion of Old Testament Prophecy'.

ישׁר, which in fact never occurs in this form in Isaiah, except when combined with some term for 'way' (Isa. 26.7; 40.3; 45.2, 13).

The combination עשׂה טוב וישׁר is found in Deut. 6.18; 12.28; 2 Chron. 14.1 and 31.20.[87] Although טוב בעיני (in various suffixed forms) occurs frequently in all literature including the books of Kings (1 Kgs 21.2; 2 Kgs 10.5), we find that 2 Kgs 20.3 (par. Isa. 38.3) is the only text in which Yahweh is the indirect object of doing good in the books of Kings. In the form in which the term occurs in the Hezekiah narrative, it does not belong to 'distinctively Deuteronomistic language'.[88] One might, in fact, say that it is Deuteronomic and Chronistic. The intertextual play with these terms links the sickness narrative with the Babylonian envoy narrative. In reverse order we find that Hezekiah's prayer functions linguistically (2 Kgs 20.19 par. Isa. 39.8) as an anticipation of Yahweh's word, which is good (טוב) and secures peace (שׁלם) and faithfulness (אמת) in 'my days' (בימי), precisely in the manner the Chronicler interpreted the two narratives. As no significant linguistic parallel can be found between 1 Kings 14 and 2 Kgs 20.1-11,[89] we must also conclude that the thematic parallels are restricted to the sickness motif, but lack the elements of repentance, forgiveness and sign.

The addition of the reference to the Davidic promise in 2 Kings' Hezekiah narrative (20.6) further confirms the origin of these narratives in the book of Isaiah. The triple reason for saving the city in Kings' version of the sickness narrative diminishes the point that the city (and Hezekiah) is saved because of Hezekiah's prayer and tears (v. 5). The author's attempt to harmonize his material has led to his reuse of 2 Kgs 19.34b, which fits well in that narrative's focus on God's plans (2 Kgs 19.25-31), but which is superfluous here.[90] We notice Isaiah's choice of the verb גנן, occurring four times in Isaiah (31.5 [twice]; 36.35; 38.6), twice in Zechariah (9.15; 12.8), but only here in Kings (19.34; 20.6). In all of these instances, the text plays with the motif of Yahweh's protection of Jerusalem within the larger theme of the Zion ideology. Admitting that the David motif lies well within the authorship of the books of Kings[91] (and within the book of Isaiah as well: Isa. 7.2, 13; 9.6; 16.5; 22.22; 29.1; 37.35; 38.5; 55.3), we must be aware that the first reason for saving the city, 'for my sake' (למעני), is a specifically Isaianic theme which does not occur in other texts in Kings. Other occurrences in Isaiah (43.25; 48.11; and in 49.7 and 55.5 as למען יהוה) all deal with Yahweh's plans for the restoration of his

87.   2 Chron. 14.1: ויעשׂ הטוב והישׁר בעיני יהוה אלהיו (Asa); 31.20: ויעשׂ הטוב והישׁר והאמת לפני יהוה אלהיו (Hezekiah).

88.   Against Carr, 'What Can We Say about the Tradition History of Isaiah?', p. 594. Weinfeld, *Deuteronomy and the Deuteronomic School*, p. 335, who, however, does not distinguish between doing good (טוב) and doing right (ישׁר).

89.   Contrary to the opinion of Carr, 'What Can We Say about the Tradition History of Isaiah?', p. 594.

90.   For further references to the harmonizing tendency by the author of 2 Kings' Hezekiah narrative, see Laato, 'Hezekiah and the Assyrian Crisis', pp. 53-54.

91.   Carr, 'What Can We Say about the Tradition History of Isaiah?', p. 594; Gonçalves, '2 Rois 18.13–20.19 par. Isaïe 36–39', p. 55: 'La seconde raison que Yahvé donne pour son intervention en 2 R 19.34b par. Is 37.35b ("à cause de David, mon serviteur") est propre aux livres des Rois'.

people. Especially Isaiah 48 has close parallels to Isaiah's song in Isa. 37.22-35 (par. 2 Kgs 19.21-34).

Regarding the compositional structure of the sickness narratives, I do not agree with Smelik and Seitz that Isaiah's version is the more logical.[92] 2 Kings' attempt to solve Hezekiah's affirmative exclamation[93] at the end of Isaiah's narrative (Isa. 38.22) and to place it as a request for a sign following the promise of healing (2 Kgs 20.8), holds Isaiah's discussion with Ahaz (Isa. 7.11-13) implicit. In Kings' version, Hezekiah is piously asking for a sign at the appropriate time and actively participates in that sign. It might be that the story stresses the role of the prophet in Kings, but this is not done at the expense of Hezekiah's role.[94] In fact, it is not Isaiah's words nor his healing act which demonstrate divine power. It is Yahweh's reversal of time at the request of Hezekiah. The harmonization of the temple motif with the salvation motif by the addition of the third day (2 Kgs 20.5 and 8)—taken from Isaiah's song (2 Kgs 19.29 par. Isa. 37.30)—solves the problem in 2 Kings that had been created by the exclusion of Hezekiah's song (Isa. 38.9-20), which, in Isaiah, is linked with the temple motif (38.20). Linguistically, we notice that Kings' familiarity with אות for sign is restricted to the Hezekiah narratives, while, in Isaiah, it plays a central role as a designation of Yahweh's acts (Isa. 7.11-14; 8.18; 19.20; 55.13; 66.19).[95]

It furthermore seems arbitrary to separate the Babylonian envoy episode from that of Hezekiah's illness, with which it so clearly belongs,[96] and to argue for a modification of Isaiah's idealization of Hezekiah in Kings in order to fit it in with the subsequent history of the monarchy, as well as with 2 Kgs 18.14-16.[97] Seitz' argument for a similar modification in Sirach[98] is not convincing. Even if Hezekiah must share the stage with Isaiah (Sir. 48.20-25) and the people (48.19-20), Hezekiah is still portrayed as a righteous king, together with David and Josiah, who did not give their power to others (49.4-5). Sirach's implicit reference to the Babylonian envoy narrative in Sir. 48.24-25 explicitly avoids any negative perception of Hezekiah and focuses on Isaiah's prophecy of 'the last things' and his comforting of those who mourned in Zion. Furthermore, Seitz' allegation of a negative portrait of Hezekiah in Chronicles[99] does not relate to the Babylonian envoy story (2 Chron.

---

92. Smelik, 'Distortion of Old Testament Prophecy'; Seitz, *Zion's Final Destiny*, pp. 162-66.

93. Following Kaiser's translation: 'Was für ein Zeichen, dass ich (wieder) zum Hause Jahwes hinaufgehen kann!' (O. Kaiser, *Der Prophet Jesaja: Kapitel 13–39: Übersetzt und erklärt* [Göttingen: Vandenhoeck & Ruprecht, 1973], p. 317).

94. As argued by Seitz, *Zion's Final Destiny*, pp. 155-56.

95. Laato, 'Hezekiah and the Assyrian Crisis', p. 63.

96. P.R. Ackroyd, 'An Interpretation of the Babylonian Exile: A Study of II Kings 20 and Isaiah 38–39', in *idem, Studies in the Religious Tradition of the Old Testament*, pp. 152-71 (155); Clements, 'The Prophecies of Isaiah to Hezekiah', pp. 67-68.

97. Seitz, *Zion's Final Destiny*, p. 161. Seitz' conclusion that account A's negative portrait of Hezekiah produces tension with account B's positive portrait and Assyrian sources and therefore must be a late insertion (based on 2 Kgs 16.5, 7-9) fails to notice the pattern of threat–tribute–salvation in Kings (cf. Chapter 2 above).

98. Seitz, *Zion's Final Destiny*, p. 160 n. 28.

99. Seitz, *Zion's Final Destiny*, p. 158.

32.31) in which the negative characterization is rather reversed by its implicit reference to 2 Chron. 32.26—namely, that Hezekiah had humbled himself (יכנע), together with the citizen of Jerusalem,[100] and thus fulfilled the royal obligation. This theme occurs frequently in Chronicles as a way of turning Yahweh's wrath (Rehoboam, 2 Chron. 12.6-7, 12; Manasseh, 2 Chron. 33.12, 19; Josiah, 2 Chron. 34.27), or of causing Yahweh's punishment when the king does not humble himself (Amon, 2 Chron. 33.23; Zedekiah, 2 Chron. 36.12). The program for Chronicles' theology is set with Solomon's prayer and Yahweh's answer in the inauguration narrative (2 Chron. 6.14-42; 7.12-22). In contrast to 1 Kgs 9.1-9, the repentance and forgiveness theme is made primary in 2 Chron. 7.14: ויכנעו עמי אשר נקרא־שמי עליהם ויתפללו ויבקשו פני וישבו מדרכיהם הרעים ('When my people, who are called by my name humble themselves, pray and seek my face and turn from their evil ways'). The climax of the theme is given in Chronicles' anticipation of the Babylonian exile in Manasseh's exile, repentance and return (2 Chron. 33.10-13), which function paradigmatically as an advice for the whole community to listen to Yahweh.[101] We must note that, in Chronicles, Manasseh is not made responsible for the exile; quite the contrary. The books of Kings' tripartite use of the humility theme is combined with a delay, not a removal of Yahweh's wrath (Ahab, 1 Kgs 22.27-29; Hezekiah, 2 Kgs 20; Josiah, 2 Kgs 22.19-20).[102] How does this aspect fit the closure of the Hezekiah narrative that Hezekiah thought the word from Isaiah to be good, since it would secure peace during his own reign?

The various possibilities of interpreting the utterance positively or negatively are dealt with in Ackroyd's study. I fully agree with Ackroyd that the utterance should be interpreted positively in line with 2 Kings' use of the same theme in the Josiah narrative (2 Kgs 22.15-20),[103] a narrative which, however, does not give explicit reference to the exile. In a wider perspective, Isaiah's foretelling of the Babylonian exile supports hope, a hope that there will be an exile and that at its end there will be a new creation. This is the central solution of the book of Isaiah, and we might interpret the compositional inclusion of the exile in the material that precedes the Hezekiah narrative (especially chs. 27–29) as a way of handling the ideological problem, that it was the Assyrian threat, which could have eliminated the Judaean kingdom in a manner similar to what had happened to the Israelite. In this light, Isaiah's utterance functions as a promise of survival and the introductory emphatic כי (Isa. 39.8)—'there certainly will be peace', and so forth—must be read just so.[104] 2 Kings doubting הלוא אם (2 Kgs 20.19) does not point to such future promise, but functions rather as a fulfilment of the Hezekiah narrative's presentation of Hezekiah as a king, who succeeded in everything (2 Kgs 18.7).[105]

---

100. Ackroyd, 'An Interpretation of the Babylonian Exile', p. 159.
101. Ackroyd, 'An Interpretation of the Babylonian Exile', pp. 163-64.
102. Thompson, 'Kingship and the Wrath of God'.
103. Ackroyd, 'An Interpretation of the Babylonian Exile', pp. 158-60.
104. Sweeney, *Isaiah 1–39*, p. 510.
105. Josephus, who is highly favourable to Hezekiah, tells that Hezekiah was 'grieved at his [Isaiah's] words' and 'said that he would be unwilling to have his nation meet with such misfortunes'. He further interprets Hezekiah's utterance as a sign of piety that he 'prayed that there

In 2 Chronicles' Manasseh story, the promise is extended to all of repentant old Israel. While the result of the Assyrian deportation was complete annihilation according to Kings, the Babylonian exile, as devastating as it was, included salvation for the remnant, which had survived the Assyrian destruction. In the Deuteronomistic History there is little room for this remnant other than in the Hezekiah narrative's Isaianic praise of Yahweh's wonder (2 Kgs 19.31). Sharing the fate of the Northern Kingdom in the Manasseh story, the remnant is abandoned and given into the hand of its enemies (ונתתים ביד איביהם ונטשתי את שארית נחלתי), 'And I will cast off the remnant of my heritage and give them into the hand of their enemies', 2 Kgs 21.14). Chronicles' saving of this remnant, which had escaped the sword (ויגל השארית מן־החרב) to become servants (עבדים) of the Babylonian kings until the reign of the kingdom of Persia (עד־מלך מלכות פרס[106], 2 Chron. 36.20), carries this hope out in Cyrus' call for anyone who is of Yahweh's people to go to Jerusalem and rebuild it (2 Chron. 36.23; cf. Isa. 44.1-7; 45.4-9).

c. *Hezekiah's Reform*
The third significant parallel which needs to be dealt with since it has attracted quite a lot of attention in relation to the question of authorship, is found in the verses related to Hezekiah's reforms (2 Kgs 18.4, 22). We must separate v. 4 from v. 22 as v. 4 belongs to Kings' material and does not occur in Isaiah. The question is whether the *Rabshaqeh*'s reference to high places and altars bears any meaning apart from 2 Kgs 18.4.[107] We notice that in 2 Kgs 18.4 Hezekiah destroyed the high places (הבמות), broke the pillars (המצבת), cut down the *Asherah* (האשרה) and crushed the bronze serpent. Of these acts, we notice that in the *Rabshaqeh*'s speech Hezekiah is said to have destroyed *his* high places (במתיו)[108] and *his* altars (מזבחתיו), and has demanded that Judah and Jerusalem worship at this altar (המזבח הזה) in Jerusalem[109] (2 Kgs 18.22 par. Isa. 36.7). The theme of centralization in the *Rabshaqeh*'s speech does not explicitly belong to what 2 Kgs 18.4 says. We know, however, that, within the authorship of Kings, this is held implicit in the *bamot* theme (cf. the analysis in Chapter 2) and we understand that the Chronicler made this the primary theme in his Hezekiah narrative (2 Chron. 29–31). The question remains, therefore, whether the *Rabshaqeh*'s language has any parallel in the book of Isaiah?

should be peace during his own lifetime', since 'it was not possible to alter God's decrees' (*Ant.* 10.34). This further establishes Isaiah as a true prophet, foretelling this and other matters as did other prophets (*Ant.* 10.35). It also exposes the standard position of the all-knowing prophet and his ignorant audience.

106.   LXX: Μήδων.

107.   Carr, 'What Can We Say about the Tradition History of Isaiah?', pp. 594-95: 'Such characteristics are hardly enough to establish Deuteronomistic authorship of the passage as a whole. Nevertheless, they do suggest Deuteronomistic redaction of these stories, an editing most likely to have taken place in adapting the material to its context in Kings'. Note also Gonçalves, '2 Rois 18.13–20.19 par. Isaïe 36–39', p. 55: 'La notice de l'æuvre culturelle d'Ézéchias (2 R 18.22b par. Is 36.7b) dépend de 2 R 18.4, texte qui fait partie d'une trame commencée en 1 R 15.14'.

108.   The only occurrence of במה with a pronominal suffix in Kings.

109.   'In Jerusalem' is missing in Isaiah, and in 2 Chron. 32.12, which adds אחד.

In Isa. 17.8 and 27.9, we find significant parallels to the destruction of useless (stone) altars (כל־אבני מזבח/המזבחות), *Asherim* and incense altars (החמנים)[110] made by (men's) hands (מעשי ידיו).[111] Both chapters deal paradigmatically with the same themes: threat against Jerusalem, destruction of the enemy (Damascus or Ephraim and Assyria or Babylonia) and submission to Yahweh. In Isa. 27.13, this submission finds its linguistic expression (והשתחוו ליהוה בהר הקדש בירושלם, 'And they shall worship Yahweh on his holy mountain in Jerusalem)' in a form similar to what we find in Isa. 36.7 and 2 Kgs 18.22. Since we know well that cult centralization is a primary theme in the book of Isaiah, it is not surprising that, at the establishment of Zion, offerings and worship are to be brought to Yahweh's altar in Jerusalem (Isa. 56.7; 60.7; 66.18-23). Nor should we be surprised to find that, within the theme of monotheism, Hezekiah's thematic discussion about 'gods made by men's hands' as 'idle gods', occurs so frequently in the book that citations could be made from almost every chapter. The goal of Isaiah's theology is not only a rejection of these gods (e.g. Isa. 37.18-19 par. 2 Kgs 19.17-18; Isa. 2.20; 30.22; 31.7; 44.9-20; 45.15; 46.1-7), but also their adherents' submission to Yahweh in Jerusalem (e.g. Isa. 45.14, 22; 56.7; 60.7, 14; 66.23).

d. *Conclusions about the Linguistic Evidence*
On the basis of the linguistic arguments from the tripartite story, the assertion has been confirmed that the Hezekiah narrative had its origin within the authorship of Isaiah and that the stories are so interwoven that they cannot be separated. They function within a triadic presentation of the acts of Yahweh through Isaiah and Hezekiah. The way we read these narratives depends on whether we make the presentation of the *prophet* the primary theme with the book of Isaiah, or whether we make the presentation of *Hezekiah* our theme with the book of Kings. We might, however, decide to dispense with both readings and read the narratives as different ways of presenting Yahweh's rise as the superior God, with Jerusalem as his universal abode.[112]

---

110.   Cf. Lev. 26.30; Ezek. 6.3-4; 2 Chron. 14.4; 34.4, 7.

111.   The occurrence of the phrase in Deut. 4.28 as מעשה ידי אדם עץ ואבן does not make it Deuteronomistic (as claimed by Carr, 'What Can We Say about the Tradition History of Isaiah?', p. 594), since even more numerous variations of this phrase occur in the Prophets and Psalms (Isa. 2.8; Jer. 1.16; 25.6, 7; 32.30; 44.8; Hos. 14.4; Mic. 5.12; Pss. 115.4; 135.15).

112.   2 Chronicles' reference to the 'the acts of Hezekiah 'as written in the vision of the prophet Isaiah son of Amos in the books of the kings of Judah and Israel' (הנם כתובים בחזון ישעיהו בן־אמוץ הנביא על־ספר מלכי־יהודה וישראל, 2 Chron. 32.32; cf. also 1 Chron. 29.29, referring to Samuel, Nathan and Gad; 2 Chron. 9.29, referring to Iddo; 26.22, referring to Isaiah's writing about Uzziah) seems to imply that Chronicles' author considered the Hezekiah narrative to have been inserted from Isaiah. Note Smelik, 'Distortion of Old Testament Prophecy', p. 86 n. 1, and Seitz, *Zion's Final Destiny*, p. 5 n. 11, and p. 157 n. 21, with the modification that 'while the Chronicler's reference to the vision of the prophet Isaiah might well refer to the Book of Isaiah and the narratives concerning Hezekiah found therein (36–39), the reference is finally predicated on there being a "Book of the Kings of Judah and Israel", which contains Hezekiah–Isaiah narratives, in which Isaiah has a "vision" of the exile'.

Before we leave the question, some comments need to be given to Kaiser's argument that the Hezekiah narratives were transferred from Kings to Isaiah. Kaiser's conclusion is partly based on eight examples of similar readings between the Masoretic Kings' version and 1QIsa of the Dead Sea Scrolls.[113] Of Kaiser's list, 1QIsa 36.12bβ and 37.9aα can be ruled out as resulting from Qumran spelling, which does not distinguish clearly between laryngeals and pharyngeals and which tends to delete them when not clearly pronounced.[114] 1QIsa 36.5aα seems to be due to the Qumran scribe's confusion of masculine singular and feminine singular, which made him read אמרתי as feminine singular[115] and not second person masculine singular with a pronominal suffix in first person singular. Thus, he corrected the form to second person masculine singular אמרת, without the suffix. 1QIsa 36.7aα תאמרון for MT תאמר, similar to 2 Kings, is not due to the number of emissaries in 36.3, but to the first person plural in v. 7 and therefore is a harmonization of the forms, lacking in MT Isaiah. 1QIsa 36.7bγ can be ruled out as uncertain due to corruption of the scroll. 1QIsa 36.15bα carries no proof, since 1QIsa has a 'markedly greater tendency towards "syndetic constructions" than the MT'.[116] Altogether, 130 more *waw*s are found in 1QIsa than in the MT (there are 200 insertions and 70 deletions).[117]

The lack of the preposition את in both 1QIsa and MT Isa. 36.15 bα, but its appearance in 2 Kgs 18.30bα, does not support Kaiser's case either. 1QIsa 37.6 and 7's use of the preposition ל for אל implies more problems than Kaiser is aware of. Both instances occur in a passage which is very dense and it remains possible that the scribe 'forgot' to write vv. 5-7, had a corrupt text before him or 'invented' the passage,[118] wherefore the verses were inserted in a smaller script between vv. 4 and 8 afterwards.[119] Whether Kings' version had been of any use to the scribe we cannot know—we do not have that part of Kings in the Dead Sea Scrolls material.[120] Text-critically, we are faced with the utterly complex problem that the manuscripts of the

113. O. Kaiser, 'Die Verkündigung des Propheten Jesaja im Jahre 701', *ZAW* 81 (1969), pp. 305-15. Kaiser's form-critical arguments will not be taken into consideration here, since they do not add to the discussion raised in other literature.

114. Kutscher, *The Language and Linguistic Background of the Isaiah Scroll (1QIsa^a)*, pp. 56-58, 410. P. Joüon, SJ, and T. Muraoka, *A Grammar of Biblical Hebrew* (2 vols.; Rome: Editrice Pontificio Istituto Biblica, 1991), II, p. 485.

115. Kutscher, *The Language and Linguistic Background of the Isaiah Scroll (1QIsa^a)*, pp. 188-90.

116. Kutscher, *The Language and Linguistic Background of the Isaiah Scroll (1QIsa^a)*, p. 422.

117. Kutscher, *The Language and Linguistic Background of the Isaiah Scroll (1QIsa^a)*, pp. 414-29.

118. E. Tov, 'Scribal Practices Reflected in the Texts From the Judaean Desert', in P.W. Flint and J.C. VanderKam (eds.), *The Dead Sea Scrolls After Fifty Years: A Comprehensive Assessment* (2 vols.; Leiden: E.J. Brill, 1998–99), pp. 403-29 (424).

119. D.W. Parry and E. Qimron, *The Great Isaiah Scroll (1QIsa^a): A New Edition* (Leiden: E.J. Brill, 1999), pp. 60-61.

120. Abegg, Flint and Ulrich, *The Dead Sea Scrolls Bible*, p. 260: 'Despite the limited scope of text on most fragments, however, there are enough indications of text significantly divergent from the traditional Masoretic Text to suggest that the text of Kings was pluriform in antiquity, just as the text of Samuel has been demonstrated to be'.

MT are younger than the Dead Sea Scrolls. Any adequate comparison, in fact, must be done on manuscripts that belong to the same 'corpus'.

The similarities are not as conclusive as Kaiser argues,[121] but rather inform us that 1QIsa and 2 Kings both represent variants of the narratives, of which 1QIsa shares more features with the MT Isaianic version of the Hezekiah narrative than with the version in 2 Kings. Of the similarities with Kings, at least half of these are due to Qumranic scribal practices and the rest cannot carry any significant proof bearing on issues of provenance.

Finally, regarding the spelling of Hezekiah's name, 2 Kings' consistently long spelling חזקיהו in 18.17–20.21[122] (par. Isa. 36–39) is not attested in 1QIsa, which demonstrates four different spellings with corrections, as is well known.[123] MT Isaiah never uses the short form but only the 'older' חזקיהו, as in Isa. 1.1. The occurrence of the short form חזקיה in 2 Kgs 18.1, 10, 13-15, but of the long form in 18.9 and in a variant reading of 18.13,[124] might support Hardmeier's suggestion that v. 9 should be read together with v. 13,[125] but not with vv. 14-16.[126]

4. *The Function of the Hezekiah Narrative within the Book of Isaiah: Ahaz and Hezekiah: Competing Characters?*

The formal parallels between the Ahaz narratives in 2 Kings and Isaiah are restricted to the introductory verse, regarding the Syro-Ephraimite attack on Jerusalem (Isa. 7.1 par. 2 Kgs 16.5). In this introduction, we notice that while, in Isaiah, the attack is aimed at Jerusalem (cf. the double occurrence of עליה as object for the aggression), 2 Kings' interest concentrates on Ahaz, who is put under siege (ויצרו על־אחז). Although linguistically this is a minor difference, it reflects much more thorough-going differences in the text corpora: a concern for Jerusalem's fate or the king's fate. In Isaiah's Hezekiah narrative, even Hezekiah's recovery from sickness is linked to the salvation of the city (Isa. 38.6).[127]

Such different perspectives are further demonstrated in the Ahaz narrative of 2 Chronicles, which does not mention Jerusalem, but rather states that Ahaz and his people are given into the hands of their enemies because of their idolatrous practices (2 Chron. 28.2-6). In this narrative, the main tension lies between Israel and

---

121. Kaiser, 'Die Verkündigung des Propheten Jesaja', p. 314, and *Der Prophet Jesaja: Kapitel 13–39*, p. 291.

122. Kaiser, 'Die Verkündigung des Propheten Jesaja', p. 307.

123. Kutscher, *The Language and Linguistic Background of the Isaiah Scroll (1QIsaᵃ)*, pp. 103-106. Abegg, Flint and Ulrich, *The Dead Sea Scrolls Bible*, p. 326: '1QIsaᵃ usually uses the shorter forms *Hizqiyah* [*Yhizkiyah, Huzkiyah, Yhuzkiyah*] and *Yesha'yah* throughout these chapters, whereas 4QIsaᵇ and MT use the longer *Hizkiyahu* and *Yesha'yahu*'.

124. Norin, 'An Important Kennicott Reading in 2 Kings xviii 13', pp. 337-38.

125. Hardmeier, *Prophetie im Streit vor dem Untergang Judas*, pp. 106-21.

126. The difference in spellings of names in biblical material cannot be used for chronological statements, because of the alleged archaizing tendencies in supposedly later material, for example, the book of Chronicles, and similarly purported 'modernizing' tendencies in other material.

127. Laato, *About Zion I Will Not Be Silent*, p. 64: 'the fate of Jerusalem is an important theme throughout the Book [of Isaiah]'.

Judah. While both Isaiah and Kings purport that 'they [Aram and Israel-Ephraim] could not conquer', 2 Chronicles argues that Israel defeated Judah (28.5b-15), that Aram's gods helped Aram (28.23) and that Tiglath-pileser did Ahaz no good, but, in fact, harmed him (28.20-21). The reversal of Ahaz' acts by Hezekiah in 2 Chron. 29.3-10 hits right at the centre of what is implied: Judah's patronage relationship with Yahweh, whom their fathers had forsaken (root עזב, 29.6; cf. 28.6), to whom their fathers had been unfaithful (root מעל, 29.6; cf. 28.19, 22), from whose dwelling they had turned away their face (ויסבו פניהם ממשכן יהוה) and with whom Hezekiah intends to make a covenant (28.10).

The Chronicler's interpretation of Ahaz' idolatrous acts helps shed light on his replacement of Yahweh's altar in Jerusalem's temple with the altar of Damascus' gods (2 Kgs 16.14-15). Since these helped the kings of Aram, they might also be able to help Judah's king (cf. 2 Chron. 28.23), as Yahweh had not.[128] Although Ahaz met Tiglath-pileser in Damascus (2 Kgs 16.10), the altar seems to be of Aramaic rather than Assyrian style.[129] The elements of idol worship ascribed to Ahaz (2 Kgs 16.14-18) are shown to resemble Aramaic traits merged with local Palestinian pagan traditions.[130] 2 Kings' conclusion about Ahaz' changes—'because of the king of Ashur' (מפני מלך אשור, 2 Kgs 16.18)—might refer to his removal of valuable items from the temple rather than to his Damascene altar. As the changes are linked to Ahaz' meeting with Tiglath-pileser and involve a replacement of gold and bronze with stone (2 Kgs 16.17), 2 Kings might imply that Tiglath-pileser had raised the tribute Ahaz had to pay (2 Kgs 16.8; cf. 2 Chron. 28.21). Implicitly, 2 Kings' author exposes what it costs to be an Assyrian vassal and alludes to the opinion made explicit in 2 Chron. 28.21—namely, that it is not worth the price:

כי הלק[131] אחז את־בית יהוה ואת־בית המלך והשרים ויתן למלך אשור ולא לעזרה לו

And Ahaz plundered the temple of Yahweh and the palace of the king and the officers and he paid tribute to the king of Ashur, but it did not help him.

Whether historical or not, Ahaz' much-too-ready 'submission to Ashur' might reflect nothing more than Assyrian veneration for 'Hittite' fashion,[132] which Ahaz

---

128. J.W. McKay, *Religion in Judah under the Assyrians, 732–609 B.C.* (SBT, 2.26; London: SCM Press, 1973), p. 11.

129. McKay, *Religion in Judah under the Assyrians*, pp. 6-7; S.A. Irvine, *Isaiah, Ahaz, and the Syro-Ephraimitic Crisis* (SBLDS, 123; Atlanta: Scholars Press, 1990), p. 82; Ahlström, *History of Palestine*, p. 686.

130. McKay, *Religion in Judah under the Assyrians*, pp. 45-59; M. Cogan, *Imperialism and Religion: Assyria, Judah and Israel in the Eight and Seventh Centuries BCE* (SBLMS, 19; Missoula, MT: Scholars Press, 1974), pp. 72-88. Both McKay (*Religion in Judah under the Assyrians*, pp. 5-12, 60-66) and Cogan (*Imperialism and Religion*, pp. 42-61) rejected earlier scholarly assumptions that Ahaz' reforms reflected Assyrian practice of imposing their religion on subject peoples. For a critique of McKay and Cogan, see H. Spieckermann, *Juda unter Assur in der Sargonidenzeit* (FRLANT, 129; Göttingen: Vandenhoeck & Ruprecht, 1982), pp. 320-72 (362-72).

131. הלק might be an error for חלץ; cf. Ps. 7.5.

132. For example, the 'Hittite' styled portico (*bīt hil āni tam šīl ekal Hatti*) in palaces of Tiglath-pileser III, Sargon, Sennacherib and Ashurbanipal, cf. CAD, *hilānu*, pp. 184-85; H.W.F. Saggs,

imitated. At stake for the biblical authors, however, is Ahaz' violation of his patronage relationship with Yahweh, which also implies a violation of Judah's relationship with Israel, since they share the same patron (2 Chron. 28.9-15 [v. 11 has אחרים[133], 'brothers'). 2 Chronicles 28 does not state that Israel worked in coalition with Aram or the Philistines. This information we find in Isaiah 7 and 2 Kings 16.

While in Kings' version, Ahaz' shift of allegiance might be in favour of Ashur, in Chronicles it is in favour of Aram. The text does not mention any favourable relationship with the Assyrian king; instead, we find the contrary (2 Chron. 28.16, 20-21). 2 Chronicles' narrative is thus more in line with Isaiah's warning against Assyrian reliance than is 2 Kings' assertion of Assyrian support. Historiographically, the stories in Isiah and Chronicles might be closer to the events of 734–732 BCE than is Kings.[134] The Chronicler knows that Ahaz' game is a hazardous one (2 Chron. 28.23c), however, without informing his audience that Aram could not stand (cf. Isa. 7.16; 8.4; 17.1-3).[135] While Ahaz' act credits him with the blame for the fall of *all* Israel (כל־ישראל, 2 Chron. 28.23), Hezekiah's covenant with Yahweh, God of Israel (יהוה אלהי ישראל, 2 Chron. 29.10), prepares an inclusion of Israel/Ephraim in the atonement for *all* Israel (29.24) and the invitation to *all* Israel (Ephraim and Manasseh [30.1]; from Beersheba to Dan [30.5]) for the remnant's return to the ancestral God (אל־יהוה אלהי אברהם יצחק וישראל, 'to Yahweh God of Abraham, Isaac and Israel', 2 Chron. 30.6) in Jerusalem. The act is political, and Hezekiah's shift of allegiances expressed in the submission to the common God (יהוה אלהי ישראל, 'Yahweh God of Israel', 2 Chron. 32.17; 2 Kgs 18.5; 19.15, 20) implies an attempt to establish a common resistance against Assyrian hegemony. In light of 2 Chronicles' Amaziah narrative's thematic variant of 'worshipping the

---

The Encounter With the Divine in Mesopotamia and Israel (London: Athlone Pres, 1978), p. 87; K.L. Sparks, *Ethnicity and Identity in Ancient Israel: Prolegomena to the Study of Ethnic Sentiments and Their Expression in the Hebrew Bible* (Winona Lake, IN: Eisenbrauns, 1998), p. 34. Neo-Assyrian sources use of the term Hatti designates a geographical rather than political entity, since the Hittite Empire had ceased to exist in the thirteenth–twelfth century BCE; cf. Ahlström, *History of Palestine*, p. 275; N.P. Lemche, *Die Vorgeschichte Israels: Von den Anfängen bis zum Ausgang des 13. Jahrhunderts v. Chr.* (Biblische Enzyklopädie, 1; Stuttgart: W. Kohlhammer, 1996), p. 134.

133.   LXX: τῶν ἀδελφῶν ὑμῶν.

134.   McKay, *Religion in Judah under the Assyrians*, p. 6: 'However, Ahaz' dealings with Assyria are by no means as clear as the simple account in Kings suggest. The events leading to the fall of Damascus are related as if set in motion by the initiative of Ahaz himself, but Tiglath-pileser's own record makes no distinction between Ahaz and some eighteen other kings of the West who were forced to pay tribute. It is indeed likely that events would have taken a similar course whether Ahaz had appealed to Tiglath-pileser or not, for the activities of Samaria amounted to rebellion against Assyrian overlordship'.

135.   *ARAB*, I, § 777; *ANET*, p. 282a: 'I laid siege to and conquered the town Hadara, the inherited property of Rezin of Damascus (*Ša-merišu*)…592 towns…of the sixteen districts of the country of Damascus (*Ša-merišu*) I destroyed (making them look) like hills of (ruined cities over which) the flood (had swept'; *ARAB*, I, § 816: 'The land of Bît-Humria…all of its people together with their goods I carried off to Assyria. Pakaha, their king I deposed and I placed Ausi (Hosea) over them as king' (cf. also 2 Kgs 15.29-30).

enemy's gods'—the gods of Seir (אלהי בני שעיר), which Amaziah brought back (2 Chron. 25.14-16)—no foreign gods are appropriate for worship in Judah, whether conquered or conquering.

In Isaiah, there is no explicit reference to such a religio-political shift. The message is given implicitly only by the mention of the fear (וינע לבבו עמו כנוע עצי־יער מגני־רוח, 'and the hearts of the people trembled as trees of a forest sway before a wind/storm') that Aram's presence in Ephraim (נחה ארם על־אפרים)[136] created in the house of David (Isa. 7.2). The ambiguity of the terminology (נחה ארם על), that Aram's presence in Ephraim might not have been quite as planned as 2 Kings 16 wants us to believe,[137] is further indicated by Aram's leading role in the attack (יען כי־יעץ עליך ארם[138] רעה אפרים ובן־רמליהו), 'because Aram has plotted evil against you [together with] Ephraim and the son of Remaliah', Isa. 7.5).[139] Moreover, Isaiah's concern for Ephraim and his hope for a return of a remnant from the house of Israel (10.20-22; 17.4-7), indicate that, in his opinion, Ephraim 'departed from Judah' (סור־אפרים מעל יהודה, 7.17) and, together with Manasseh, attacked her (יחדו המה על־יהודה, 9.20). This disloyalty weakens Ephraim and Judah's possibility of fighting their neighbours (the Philistines, the People of the East [את־בני־קדם], Edom, Moab and Ammon's people, Isa. 11.13-14). In Isaiah's further elaboration, the Aramaean–Ephraimitic 'alliance' becomes a disaster for Israel (Isa. 7.7-9; 9.7-20; 17.1-3). In an ironic play on Israel's possibility of being head and not tail (ונתנך יהוה לראש ולא לזנב, Deut. 28.13), Ephraim forfeited its promise and became smoking fire-poking tails (זנבות האודים העשנים, Isa. 7.4) together with Aram. The fire they stirred up was the raging fire of the Assyrians, and what was expected to be an easy victory for Aram and Ephraim, became a total defeat (Isa. 8.3-4; 9.7-20; 17.1-3). The moral of the narrative belongs to the folklore motif of being hoisted with one's own petard.[140] Even more determinative of the narrative's course is the underlying Isaianic theology. Playing out 'the tail–head motif' to its extreme, we find a mortal human being at the heads of both Aram and Israel (vv. 8-9) at the expense of Yahweh (8.6; 9.12-15; cf. Deut. 28.13, 44). As human's time is limited, so is the time of Ephraim (Isa. 7.8), and Ashur (Isa. 10.5-19) and Babylon (Isa. 47.6-7), because they took pride in their own might.

---

136. The difficulty in translating the term is dealt with in several commentaries; cf. H. Wildberger, *Jesaja 1–12* (BKAT, 10/1; Neukirchen–Vluyn: Neukirchener Verlag, 2nd edn, 1980 [1972]) *ad loc*. Of the listed possibilities, we find a range of meaning from 'being allied to' (as in the LXX: συνεφώνεσεν) to 'having camped without consent'. Blenkinsopp's translation, 'that Syria had prevailed on Ephraim to join them', solves the ambiguities for the sake of precision; cf. J. Blenkinsopp, *Isaiah 1–39: A New Translation With Introduction and Commentary* (AB, 19; New York: Doubleday, 2000), pp. 16, 227-29.

137. Wildberger, *Jesaja 1–12*, pp. 266, 275.

138. Missing in the LXX, which hereby stresses Ephraim's role.

139. Irvine, *Isaiah, Ahaz, and the Syro-Ephraimitic Crisis*, p. 69; A. Laato, *Who Is Immanuel? The Rise and Foundering of Isaiah's Messianic Expectations* (Åbo: Åbo Academy Press, 1988), p. 129.

140. Following the logic of retribution, which is frequently voiced in Jewish and Samaritan narratives dealing with Samaritan–Judaean matters.

The often-purported claim that Aram and Ephraim went against Ahaz because he would not join the anti-Assyrian coalition[141] is nowhere stated in biblical material. This can only be deduced from the statements that he called on Assyria for help (2 Kgs 16.7-10; 2 Chron. 28.16, 20-21) and that Aram and Ephraim planned to replace Ahaz with the son of Tab'al[142] (Isa. 7.6).[143] Ahaz did not choose to call on Assyria for help among several possibilities. Most of Syria-Palestine's petty kingdoms had been Assyrian vassals for some years during the reign of Tiglath-pileser III (744–727 BCE).[144] Aram and Israel's (and Phoenicia's?)[145] coalition in 734 BCE was, in fact, a revolt in which Ahaz might not to have participated.[146] The biblical

141. E.g. Wildberger, *Jesaja 1–12*, p. 275; W. Dietrich, *Jesaja und die Politik* (Munich: Chr. Kaiser Verlag, 1976), p. 60; Y. Gitay, 'Isaiah and the Syro-Ephraimite War', in Vermeylen (ed.), *The Book of Isaiah*, pp. 216-30 (215); Laato, *A Star is Rising*, p. 101; Blenkinsopp, *Isaiah 1–39*, pp. 229-30

142. Tab'el in the LXX, Vulgate, Syriac and Ezra 4.7

143. The identity of this person is unknown. The name is Aramaic and might designate an area north of Gilead; cf. Wildberger, *Jesaja 1–12*, p. 266; Vermeylen, *Du prophète Isaïe à l'apocalyptique*, I, p. 205; Sweeney, *Isaiah 1–39*, p. 16. A. Vanel, 'Ṭâbe'él en Is. vii et le roi Tubail de Tyr', in G.W. Anderson (ed.), *Studies on Prophecy: A Collection of Twelve Papers* (VTSup, 26; Leiden: E.J. Brill, 1974), pp. 17-24, argues for an onomastic connection with the king Tubail/Tubalu of Tyre known from Assyria inscriptions related to Tiglath-pileser III (ND 4301, 4305; published by L.D. Levine, *Two Neo-Assyrian Stelae from Iran* [Toronto: Royal Orientario Museum, 1972], pp. 11-24) and Sennacherib (*ARAB*, II, §§ 239, 309); so also Irvine, *Isaiah, Ahaz, and the Syro-Ephraimitic Crisis*, p. 154.

144. Ahlström, *History of Palestine*, pp. 629-32; Luckenbill, *Ancient Records of Assyria and Babylonia*, I, § 770: '...I destroyed, I devastated with fire I burned...which had gone over to Azariah and had strengthened him' (cf. also 2 Chron. 26.6-15); I, § 772: 'The tribute of...Rasunnu (Rezin) of Aram, Menihimmu (Menahem) of Samerina (Samaria), Hirummu (Hiram) of Tyre, Sibitti-bi'li of Gubla (Gebail), Urikki of Kûe, Pisiris of Carchemish, Eni-ilu of Hamath'; I, § 801: 'The tribute of...Hamath...of Tabal...of Arvad...of Beth-Ammon, Salmanu of Moab...of Ashkelon...Iauhazi (Jehoahaz) of Judah...of Edom...of Gaza'; I, § 815: 'As for Menahem(?), terror overwhelmed him, like a bird, alone he fled and submitted to me...I received as his tribute' (cf. also 2 Kgs 15.19-20). For the chronological problems relating to the composition of *ARAB*, I, § 801 (the *Nimrûd Tablet*, K 3751, dating to 728 BCE), see Irvine, *Isaiah, Ahaz, and the Syro-Ephraimitic Crisis*, pp. 41-44. Irvine dates the entire list to 734/33, thus reflecting conditions 'immediately after Tiglath-pileser's campaign "against Philistea". These included: the continued submission of most of the states which had paid Assyrian tribute in 738; the forcible subjugation of Gaza and possibly also Arvad, and the voluntary submission to vassalage status by Ashkelon, Judah, and the Transjordan kingdoms.'

145. Vanel, 'Ṭâbe'él en Is. vii et le roi Tubail de Tyr', pp. 17-24; Cogan, *Imperialism and Religion*, p. 66; Irvine, *Isaiah, Ahaz, and the Syro-Ephraimitic Crisis*, p. 69: 'Participants in the anti-Assyrian movement included Rezin of Syria/Damascus, Hiram of Tyre, Pekah of Israel, Mitinti of Ashkelon, Samsi queen of the Arabs, and possibly Hanno of Gaza. The Meunites may also have joined the rebellion, but the Assyrian records (ND400.22-23) do not clearly document their involvement. The participation of Edom, Moab and Ammon is also uncertain'. Ahlström, *History of Palestine*, pp. 632-33, thinks it possible that Tyre, Ashkelon, Gaza, Edom, Moab and Ammon were 'part of this coalition, because they are listed as paying tribute to Tiglath-pileser at the same time as Ahaz of Judah (*ARAB*, I, § 801)'.

146. Cogan, *Imperialism and Religion*, pp. 65-66; Dietrich, *Jesaja und die Politik*, p. 60; Irvine *Isaiah, Ahaz, and the Syro-Ephraimitic Crisis*, p. 70; Ahlström, *History of Palestine*, pp. 630,

presentation, especially Chronicles' 'listing' of all Judah's neighbours as fighting against Judah, should not be taken at face value. Whether coloured by post-exilic events[147] or not, the listing serves to exaggerate the threat against Judah's king, who had 'no other way out than to request help from the Assyrian king'.[148] With this scenario, the road is prepared for the biblical presentation of Hezekiah's rebellion. Just as Ahaz almost lost his kingdom because he did not have the courage to separate himself from the powers of the world, so too his son Hezekiah almost lost his kingdom because he had that courage.[149]

5. Isaiah 7.9b

The closing of Isaiah's oracle (אם לא תאמינו כי לא תאמנו, Isa. 7.9b) has since Würthwein[150] usually been interpreted as an admonition to Ahaz to have confidence in Yahweh's promise to David (2 Sam. 7.16).[151] Its interpretation might, however, rather be made in light of the entire oracle against Aram and Ephraim (Isa. 7.7-9). The key term in the closing oracle, האמין, which Kaiser argued was part of Deuteronomistic theology,[152] is not less expressive of the language of the Tetrateuch, the

633-34. Ahlström's conclusion (based on biblical writings) that Judah did not join the coalition conflicts with his assumption of the participation of the remaining kingdoms mentioned in *ARAB*, I, § 801.

147. Ahlström, *History of Palestine*, p. 634.

148. Ahlström, *History of Palestine*, pp. 634, 684.

149. *ARAB*, II, § 347; *ANET*, p. 288b: 'I [Sennacherib] laid waste the large district of Judah and put the straps (abšāni) of my yoke upon Hezekiah, its king'. Ahlström, *History of Palestine*, p. 689: 'From a literary standpoint, Ahaz is painted as the opposite of his son and successor, Hezekiah, the king who takes Judah to the brink of disaster, but who scores the highest mark next to David. Ahaz, who saves the kingdom, is denounced, but his son, who almost destroys it, is extolled.' P. Machinist, 'The Crisis of History in the Study of Jewish Origins' (unpublished paper delivered at the closing session of the congress, 'The Origins of the Jewish People and Contemporary Biblical Scholarship', held in Chicago, 18 October 1999), made the same conclusion regarding the biblical presentation of Manasseh son of Hezekiah, who, according to Assyrian inscriptions, was regarded as a vassal of Assyria and had to participate in the building of Esarhaddon's capital Nineveh. Finkelstein and Silberman, *The Bible Unearthed* (appendix E), pp. 345-46: 'Since Manasseh was a loyal vassal of Assyria there were no wars in his time; no great destructions took place. His days were peaceful times for Judah… [T]he reign of Manasseh comes right after Sennacherib's campaign and represents a significant period of economic recovery'.

150. E. Würthwein, 'Jesaja 7,1-9', in *Theologie als Glaubenswagnis: Festschrift K. Heim zum 80. Geburtstag* (Hamburg: Furche-Verlag, 1954), pp. 47-63 (repr. as 'Jesaja 7,1-9: Ein Beitrag zu dem Thema: Prophetie und Politik', in *idem, Wort und Existens: Studien zum Alten Testament* [Göttingen: Vandenhoeck & Rupecht, 1970], pp. 127-43).

151. Wildberger, *Jesaja*, I, pp. 283-85; Vermeylen, *Du prophète Isaïe à l'apocalyptique*, I, p. 207; Kaiser, *Jesaja: Kapitel 1–12*, pp. 118-19, 142-47; M.E.W. Thompson, *Situation and Theology: Old Testament Interpretations of the Syro-Ephraimite War* (Prophets and Historians Series, 1; Sheffield: Almond Press, 1982), pp. 27-28. Gitay, 'Syro-Ephraimite War', pp. 216-30, interprets the oracle and 7.13 as addressed to the royal court, which is understood to be pro-Assyrian. See also Sweeney, *Isaiah 1–39*, p. 161. For further references to the discussion, see S.A. Irvine, *Isaiah, Ahaz, and the Syro-Ephraimitic Crisis*, pp. 8-10, 156-58.

152. Kaiser, *Jesaja: Kapitel 1–12*, pp. 142-43.

Prophets and the Psalms.[153] Within Isaiah a fourfold use of the verb in the hiphil form expresses the rejection of Ephraim for not having believed (Isa. 7.9), the safety in Zion for those who believe (28.16)[154] and future hope for Yahweh's redeemed remnant to become witnesses of the true God (43.10), as those who believed, what they had heard (53.1). In composition and narrative chronology, Isaiah's remnant functions chiastically as those who reverse the fate of the Israelites, who caused Moses to worry if they would believe either words or signs (Exod. 4.1-9), but ended up believing because of words and signs (Exod. 4.31; 14.31; 19.9). When this belief did not stand the test of wilderness' hardship in spite of these and further signs and wonders (Num. 14.11; Deut. 1.32; 9.23), rejection is the outcome for both people and leaders (Num. 14.22-23; 20.12).[155] Psalm 78 offers a condensed version of this *leitmotif* of narrative discourse, when the desert generation is slain because of dis-belief (דור סורר ומרה...ולא־נאמנה, 78.8, 22, 37) and Ephraim is rejected (78.67)— before the election of Judah and David (78.68-72)—because they had provoked (כעס) the supreme God (אלוהים עליון) with their high places and idols (בבמות ובפסילהם, 78.58).

It is 2 Chron. 20.20 which offers the closest Hebrew parallel to Isa. 7.9 (and chs. 36–37). In a similar narrative setting, Judah's king Jehoshaphat is threatened by the armies of Moab and Ammon and those from the mountains of Seir (בני־עמון ומואב[156] והר־שעיר, 2 Chron. 20.10). When Jehoshaphat is told that a great army is on its way from Aram,[157] he becomes afraid (ירא) and seeks (דרש) Yahweh (20.3). Coached in the ideology of the temple inauguration narrative (20.9; cf. 6.19-42; 7.13-16), he reminds Yahweh of his everlasting promise to Abraham (20.7). Yahweh's answer is given in the mouth of the levite Jehaziel who, with a word of Yahweh, exhorts the king and the people to have no fear (אל־תיראו ואל־תחתו) because Yahweh will fight for them (vv. 15-17). Awaiting Yahweh's salvation, Jehoshaphat entreats his people to trust Yahweh and his prophets: האמינו ביהוה אלהיכם ותאמנו האמינו בנביאיו והצליחו (2 Chron. 20.20). In the LXX, the hiphil and niphal forms of אמן (2 Chron. 20.20) are translated by the verb εμπιστεύω in both cases: 'Believe in the lord your God and you will be "established" (literally "be entrusted with")'. Regarding Isa. 7.9, both the Hebrew and the Greek texts are prob-lematic. While the Masoretic version has the hiphil–niphal pattern, 1QIsaᵃ has hiphil twice and the LXX has a different wording, πιστέω and σύνίημι, meaning 'if you do not believe, you will not understand or have insight'. So what did Isaiah intend to say?

153. C. Brekelmans, 'Deuteronomic Influence in Isaiah 1–12', in Vermeylen (ed.), *The Book of Isaiah*, pp. 167-76 (175); A. Jepsen, 'אמן', in G.J. Botterweck and H. Ringgren (eds.), *Theologisches Wörterbuch zum Alten Testament* (Stuttgart: W. Kohlhammer, 1973), I, pp. 314-47 (322).

154. In Isa. 26.2, the righteous people, keepers of fidelity (שמר אמנים), shall seek refuge in the city of strength.

155. In all references, hiphil forms of אמן.

156. 2 Chron. 20.1: מהעמונים; apparatus מהמעונים; LXX: ἐκ τῶν Μιναίων. For an identification of the people, see E.A. Knauf, 'Meunim', in *ABD*, IV, pp. 801-802.

157. In Latin editions: Edom.

Wildberger's translation, 'Glaubt ihr nicht, so[158] bleibt ihr nicht' ('if you do not believe, you will not remain'),[159] which is expressive of standard meanings of both forms, seems to be the most suitable translation.[160] While this, of course, implicitly functions as a warning to Ahaz, its literal sense functions to explain the cessation of Ephraim,[161] as does 2 Kgs 17.14 (לא אשר אבותם כעוף ערפם את ויקשו שמעו ולא האמינוביהוה אלהיהם, 'But they would not listen and they stiffened their necks in the manner of their fathers, who did not believe in Yahweh their God'). In an inter-related play on ephemeral limitation in contrast to divine eternity, Ephraim and Aram's glorious days will be as short as the days of a nursing child (Isa. 8.3-4). The cue name of Isaiah's child, בז חש שלל מהר ('quick spoil, hasty prey') leads us right back to 2 Chronicles' Judaeans, who, after their enemies slaughter each other (שעיר ביושבי ובכלותם להחרים הר־שעיר על־יושבי ומואב עמון בני ויעמדו עזרו[162] איש־ברעהו למשחית, 'For the men of Ammon and Moab rose against the inhabitants of the mountain of Seir to utterly destroy them, and when they had made an end of the inhabitants of Seir, each helped destroy his fellow', 2 Chron. 20.23), walk out to pick up the spoils (את־שללם לבז ועמו יהושפט ויבא, 'And Jeho-shaphat and his people came to confiscate their spoils', 20.25). Isaiah's Judaeans do not have such an immediate and absolute 'victory'. As in 2 Chron. 28.5-8's Ahaz narrative, the riches and the spoil have been brought to Damascus and Samaria (Isa. 8.4). It is Assyria, in the role of Yahweh's servant (Isa. 8.7; 10.5-6), who conquers the two enemies. In addition, the motif of the coalition's devastating internal wars (2 Chron. 20.23) also forms part of Isaiah's 'history' of Israel's fate (Isa. 9.10-20).

The *leitmotif* of 2 Chronicles' Jehoshaphat narrative and Isaiah's Ahaz narrative is expressed in Isaiah's warning to let human understanding and fear design resolu-tions (Isa. 8.12; cf. 2 Chron. 20.15-17). In both narratives, the message is: Do nothing, this is Yahweh's war (Isa. 7.4; 9.10-11; 10.13, 25; 2 Chron. 20.15-16, 22-23, 29); 'be quiet' (השקט, Isa. 7.4; 30.15; 37.57.20); 'wait' (חכה) for Yahweh, as does the prophet (Isa. 8.17) and Yahweh (Isa. 18.4; 30.18), and 'be blessed' (אשרי) as those waiting on Zion (Isa. 30.18; cf. also Dan. 12.12), or condemned as those who did not wait (Isa. 30.16-17; cf. also Ps. 106.13). The outcome of Yahweh's Holy War is peace and quietness (Isa. 14.7; 32.17; 2 Chron. 13.23; 14.4-5; 20.30). The admonition of quietness/silence (cf. also Isa. 30.15; 36.21) forms a striking contrast to the Psalmist's plea for Yahweh to end *his* silence[163] and save his peo-ple.[164] In Isaiah, the plea for Yahweh to 'make himself known' (e.g. 63.19–64.1) is

---

158. In the emphatic sense of the word, cf. also Joüon and Muraoka, *A Grammar of Biblical Hebrew*, II, pp. 617, 633.

159. Wildberger, *Jesaja*, I, p. 264; Kaiser, *Jesaja 1–12*, p. 137: 'Wenn ihr nicht vertraut, so werdet ihr nicht bleiben'.

160. For other possibilities, see Wildberger, *Jesaja*, I, pp. 283-85; Jepsen, 'אמן', pp. 314-33.

161. Vermeylen, *Du prophète Isaïe à l'apocalyptique*, I, p. 207.

162. *BHS* suggests the verb ערר in polal. LXX reads ανέστησαν. The narrative's play with the irony that they *helped* each other become obliterated, while the Judaeans were busy rejoicing Yahweh's faithfulness (חסד), fits the narrative well.

163. E.g. Pss. 28.1; 35.22; 39.13; 55.3; 83.2; 109.1.

164. E.g. Pss. 29.3-9; 35.1-8; 46.9-10; 58.7; 68 *passim*; 78.65-66; 83.10-12.

'answered' in the affirmative, that Yahweh will perform his salvation through acts, which, by implication, cannot be without noise.[165] Why this difference?

Because the city and the remnant are Yahweh's. As David could not build a house for Yahweh (2 Sam. 7.6, 11, 27), and Solomon certainly took care not to express such *hubris* (1 Kgs 8.26-27), so only Yahweh could defend his chosen place and secure his remnant.[166] If the prophet could not give witness to Yahweh's absolute performance of such salvation, how would he then be able to argue that 'this is the chosen place and the chosen people'?[167] Further, if Yahweh had given up Jerusalem and its remnant's prerogative as Yahweh's people, what would become of Yahweh? What were Yahweh's options when the whole world had been 'swallowed' by the Assyrians? Take the easy road, and become just one among other gods in Assyria's pantheon, as Ahaz might have arranged it (2 Kgs 16.10-18; 2 Chron. 28.22-25)? Well, these gods did not stand reality's test to become eternal. With the fall of Assur its gods also fell (Isa. 31.7-9), as did the Babylonian gods with the fall of Babylon (Isa. 21.9; 46.1-2). Isaiah's Yahweh had no plans of participating in that game. He put his stakes in the unpromising—a risky way, if seen from a 'contemporary' perspective (8.21-22). From a 'later' perspective, however, it is quite a clever step (7.7; 8.23–9.6; 10.20-21; chs. 11–12). Even the faithless remnant of Jacob will return to Yahweh (שאר ישוב יעקב אל־אל גבור, 10.20-22; 17.4-7)[168] and accept the teaching from his holy place (29.22-24). Isaiah's invocation of

165.   E.g. Isa. 7.18-25; 8.7-8; 10.25-33; 11.15; 18.3-6; 19.16-18; 30.27-28, 30-33; 42.13-16.

166.   The motif belongs to the 'Holy War' theme common to the Iron Age Near Eastern war ideology; cf. M. Weippert, '"Heiliger Krieg" in Israel und Assyrien', in *idem*, *Jahwe und die anderen Götter: Studien zur Religionsgeschichte des antiken Israel in ihrem syrisch-palästinischen Kontext* (FAT, 18; Tübingen: J.C.B. Mohr [Paul Siebeck], 1997), pp. 71-97 (90-95); Saggs, *Encounter With the Divine*, pp. 44-50, 84-85; T.L. Thompson, 'Holy War at the Center of Biblical Theology: *Shalom* and the Cleansing of Jerusalem', in *idem* (ed.), *Jerusalem in Ancient History and Tradition*, pp. 223-57 (first published as 'La Guerra santa al centro della teologia Biblica. "Shalom" e la purificazione di Gerusalemme', in M. Liverani [ed.], *Guerra santa e guerra giusta dal mondo antico alla prima età moderna* [Studi Storici, 43/3; Rome: Carocci editore, 2002], pp. 661-92).

167.   This specific theme of election seems to imply that only the god fights, while the king is either patiently awaiting the outcome or greatly inferior to his enemy. See, for example, Esarhaddon's 'fight' for the throne (K2401 II: 10-25; cf. Weippert, '"Heiliger Krieg" in Israel und Assyrien', p. 88; *ARAB*, II, § 504). The passivity forms a striking contrast to so-called Deuteronomistic battle-scenes, in which the orations serve to 'fortify the spirit of the people and eradicate their fear of waging war against the outnumbering enemy'; cf. Weinfeld, *Deuteronomy and the Deuteronomic School*, pp. 45-51 (47): 'The deuteronomic oration has accordingly shifted the focal point from the warring Deity to the warring Israelites'. Without going into discussion about the chronology involved in Weinfeld's analysis, I simply state here that the Hezekiah narrative, most of the prophetic literature and part of Chronicles agree with parts of the Tetrateuch and Joshua (see p. 50 of Weinfeld) on the deity's role as warrior for his people 'passively' awaiting the outcome, while Deuteronomy and Judges–2 Kings in general advocate active warfare as the only solution to threats of any sort.

168.   Sweeney, *Isaiah 1–39*, p. 207: 'Isa. 10.20-23 [Josianic redaction; cf. pp. 209-10] refers to the return of the northern kingdom to YHWH and the Davidic dynasty. The passage alludes to the northern kingdom as the "house of Jacob" and "remnant of Israel", and it refers to the promise of descendants "like the sand of the sea", all of which are linked to the traditions of the northern

those who have gone astray (וידעו תעי־רוח בינה, 'those who err in spirit shall understand', 29.24a) and of the murmuring desert generation (ורוגנים ילמדו־לקח, 'and those who murmur shall accept instruction', Isa. 29.24b; cf. Deut. 1.27; Ps. 106.25) implicitly clarifies the religio-political implications of Yahweh's contest to the implied reader.[169]

The various narrative characters (historical as they may be) act as puppets in the prophet's tale of Yahweh's acts.[170] This tale is not about a Judaean state with its kings and inhabitants, but about a city under threat of being swallowed up (Isa. 8.8), a mountain 'viewing' advancing Assyrian troops (10.28-32)[171] and a cornerstone for Jerusalem's trustful remnant to 'stand on' (28.16). In spite of such dreadful threat, the city was not swallowed or destroyed. Nor were its inhabitants scattered, as had been the inhabitants of Samaria and Damascus. The often-argued disaster for Judah (8.5-8)[172] does not take into consideration that Isaiah's interests do not lie with Judah's fate but with the fate of Jerusalem's remnant, and that the text plays with the theme of the nearly total disaster that befell that remnant. The waters even touched the neck (עד־צואר יגיע, 8.8; 30.28), yet left Zion-Jerusalem intact.[173] In contrast, when Isaiah speaks of the fate of Ephraim and of the faithless inhabitants of Judah, the water flows over them (8.7; 28.2, 15-19). Compositionally, in 28.15-19, the author's concentric play with themes of covenant, death, alliance and flood (vv. 15, 18) places Zion right in the middle as refuge for those who believe (המאמין). In Isaiah's interpretation, the cornerstone has proven its divine prerogative in a contest with other places.[174] The nearly overwhelmed Jerusalem, speaking from the soil (מעפר) as one who is dead (כאוב מארץ קולך), will experience the annihilation of its oppressors: themselves turned into dust (והיה כאבק דק המון זריך)

kingdom. Furthermore, v. 21 calls for their return to "*ēl gibbôr*", which appears in 9.5 as a name for the Davidic monarch.'

169. Sweeney, *Isaiah 1–39*, pp. 209-10.

170. H. Wildberger, 'Jesajas Verständnis der Geschichte', in *idem*, *Jahwe und sein Volk: Gesammelte Aufsätze zum Alten Testament* (TBAT, 66; Munich: Chr. Kaiser Verlag, 1979), pp. 75-109 (77-81).

171. For the improbability of seeing a reference to Aram-Ephraim in vv. 28-32, such as is argued by H. Donner, *Israel unter den Völkern* (VTSup, 11; Leiden: E.J. Brill, 1964), pp. 30-38, see Wildberger, *Jesaja 1–12*, p. 427, who dates the text to the Ashdodite revolution in 714–711 BCE. For a recent summary of the various scholarly positions and a discussion of the geographic improbabilities in ascribing the verses to Sennacherib's campaign in 701, see Blenkinsopp, *Isaiah 1–39*, pp. 260, who, following Sweeney, *Isaiah 1–39*, pp. 205-208, argues that Sargon II's first western campaign in 720 BCE is the most fitting date. For an interpretation of the passage as a projected prophetic vision of enemy invasion, not an actual event, see Laato, *Who is Immanuel?*, pp. 206-209.

172. E.g. Sweeney, *Isaiah 1–39*, pp. 167, 174.

173. Wildberger, *Jesaja 1–12*, pp. 326-27; Laato, *Who is Immanuel?*, pp. 168-72; P.D. Miscall, *Isaiah* (Sheffield: JSOT Press), p. 39.

174. Wildberger, 'Jesajas Verständnis', pp. 92-93; Ollenburger, *Zion the City of the Great King*, pp. 115-19. For a thematic and ideological connection with the traditions about Moses' fall at Meriba (Num. 20.2-13), see further below, pp. 126-30. In Jer. 51.26, Babylon's cornerstone (אבן לפנה) and foundation stone shall (אבן למוסדות) become a desert, a place where nobody lives (cf. Jer. 50.39; 51.37) and its fate shall be told in Zion (Jer. 50.28; 51.10).

and passed away like chaff (וכמץ עבר, 29.4-5).[175] In spite of what follows—the tribulations, the destruction, the scattered remnant—this was never meant to be the end, although it looks as if it were (63.7–65.10). The pronouncement of salvation is evoked in the symbolic meaning of the name of Isaiah's first child—'a remnant will return' (שאר ישוב)[176]—who, together with the cue-names of Isaiah ('Yahweh is salvation') and Isaiah's second son—'quick spoil, hasty prey' (מהר שלל חש בז)— are given as signs and omens (לאתות ולמופתים) for Israel 'from Yahweh of armies (*Yahweh Zebaoth*),[177] who dwells on mount Zion' (8.18).

In contrast to the ephemeral limitations of human plans, Yahweh's plans are from the beginning (37.26; 40.21; 41.3-4; 46.9-10; 48.3-6). The true God both plans and gives knowledge of his plans to those witnesses who have ears to listen (41.22; 43.8-10; 44.7-8; 48.12-16). In the role of Isaiah's audience, these witnesses are given the task of carrying out Yahweh's competition with the gods of the people through their testimony of Yahweh's pronouncement of the fate of both (43.9-10, 12, 21; 44.8; 45.21). In this manner, Second Isaiah's discussion about the true God finds its testimony in First Isaiah's narratives about Yahweh's redeeming acts with his people—'the former things' (הראשנות, 41.22; 42.9; 46.9; 48.3)—and in Trito-Isaiah's promise of future glory—'the new things' and 'the coming things' predicted long ago (החדשה, האתיות, הבאות, 41.23; 42.9; 43.19; 48.6).[178]

While the return from exile is already included in 'the former things' (46.10-11), as was Jerusalem's deliverance in Hezekiah's time (37.26), 'the new things' extend far beyond this return and find preliminary closure in Isaiah's vision of Jerusalem's rise to absolute sovereignty (2.1-5; 60.14-22). This however, is only the mediating function of the tradition, as is Hezekiah's messianic role as mediating God's presence—namely. 'God is with us' (עמנו אל).[179] Jerusalem is not an object of worship,

---

175. Cf. also Isa. 17.13; Pss. 1.4; 35.5; Hos. 13.3; Zeph. 2.2.

176. This implies the meaning of repentance as well, as in Isa. 6.10, which stands as a programmatic declaration of the purpose of the coming disaster (cf. also 9.12; 19.22; 30.15).

177. Isaiah's favourite epithet of Yahweh. The term occurs most frequently in Jeremiah, Amos, Haggai, Zechariah and Malachi, sporadically in Samuel, Kings, Chronicles, Hosea, Micah, Nahum, Habakkuk, Zephaniah and Psalms, but not in the Pentateuch, Joshua, Judges, Lamentations, Ezekiel, Daniel, Joel, Obadiah, Jonah and Trito-Isaiah. The name might belong to the 'Holy War' theme, rather than to any religious-historical development (cf. Wildberger, 'Jesajas Verstandnis', pp. 83-85). I will deal with that below in 'Excursus: Yahweh Zebaoth'.

178. B. Albrektson, *History and the Gods: An Essay on the Idea of Historical Events as Divine Manifestations in the Ancient Near East and in Israel* (Lund: C.W.K. Gleerup, 1967), pp. 85-87, who speaks of 'Yahweh's purposeful acts in history' rather than 'a plan in any strict sense of the word'; Laato, *About Zion I Will Not Be Silent*, pp. 141-52, stresses First and Second Isaiah's paradigmatic parallels between Yahweh's destruction of the Assyrian army and his destruction of Babylonia: 'The fate of Assyria in Isaiah 1–39 is a typos for the destruction of Babylon predicted in Isaiah 13–14 and fulfilled in Isaiah 47' (p. 147).

179. It is only in rabbinic literature that an historicizing interpretation of Isaiah explicitly equates 'Immanuel' of Isa. 7.14 and 2 Chron. 32.8 with Hezekiah as Messiah; cf. the discussion in Laato, *About Zion I Will Not Be Silent*, pp. 30-44, 65. Laato's own argument for such an implicit interpretation in MT 2 Chron. 32.7-8, LXX and 1QIsa[a] (pp. 30-31) is not convincing, especially as 2 Chronicles equates 'Immanuel' with Yahweh as warrior.

neither is the authorized teaching emanating from it. The transcendent god remains transcendent (66.1), as does the transcendent world of true worshippers (65.17-25). Enclosing the interpretation of 'history's course' in the framework of 'non-seeing and non-knowing' (6.9-10) and 'seeing and knowing' (40.5–42.1 [21]), this interpretation is the tradition's substance, which should open the eyes and ears of the audience. Compare and see, did it not happen as it was foretold? 'Did Yahweh not make rulers come to nought and the judges of the earth to nothingness?' (הנותן רוזנים לאין שפטי ארץ כתהו עשה, 40.23; 41.2). Tied to humanity's limitation as are those gods, who neither see, nor understand, nor tell what will come (41.22-24, 28-29; 44.9-11), Isaiah's audience is invited to transcend human understanding into a witness to Yahweh's acts in the past (45.19-21).[180]

6. *The Sign Motif, or Will they Stand the Water Test?*

We now have to analyse more specifically the function of the Ahaz and Hezekiah narratives in Isaiah. While their attitude towards worldly powers is basically in opposition to each other, the outcome, however, almost identical from a historical perspective. The judgment of each poses a riddle to the audience: What is the difference? One comes to think of the Danish philosopher S.A. Kierkegaard's statement: 'Whether you marry or not, you will regret it'.

The sign motif, so commonly interpreted as Ahaz' disobedience in contrast to Hezekiah's obedience,[181] might shed light on the question. The clue does not lie in Ahaz' refusal to accept a sign, but in Isaiah's offensive suggestion that Ahaz should seek an answer from Yahweh his god either in 'the valley'[182] or on 'the mountain' (Isa. 7.11). The usual, neutral translation of העמק שאלה או הגבה למעלה ('in the depth or in the height above')[183] obscures Isaiah's inter-textual play with the accusations of idol worship and removes the reason for Ahaz' double answer that he will not ask (לא אשאל) and he will not tempt Yahweh (ולא אנסה יהוה). With the implied accusation of not seeking Yahweh, but of offering at the high places, on the hills and under every green tree (ויזבח ויקטר בבמות ועל־הגבעות ותחת כל־עץ רענן,

---

180. Seitz, *Zion's Final Destiny*, pp. 199-202; Laato, *About Zion I Will Not Be Silent*, p. 149.

181. E.g. Ackroyd, 'Isaiah 36–39', p. 18; Blenkinsopp, *History of Prophecy in Israel*, pp. 109-10; Conrad, 'Royal Narratives & Structure of Isaiah', p. 73.

182. The vocalization gives a hiphil form of עמק—'make deep'—which might well be, but since Isaiah's text was unpunctuated until Masoretic time (as was its earliest witness: 1QIsa), the LXX translation βάθος might as well be the correct one, implicitly taking העמק שאלה ('the Valley of Sheol') as a construct referring to the underworld. The LXX does not read שאלה as a verb 'bitte doch' such as Wildberger suggests (Wildberger, *Isaiah 1–12*, p. 267), since the text only has that verb once. The early Greek translations Aq., Sym., and Theo. supports the LXX reading: εἰς ᾅδην.

183. KJV; NRSV: 'let it be deep as Sheol or high as Heaven'; The Authorised Danish translation of 1992, following the LXX, reads: 'nede fra dødsriget eller oppe fra det høje'. For Assyrian invocation of 'all the gods residing in heaven and in the nether world', see *ANET*, p. 289a (Esarhaddon). Invocation of Nergal, god of the underworld, occurs frequently in Neo-Assyrian texts; cf. R. Labat, *Le caractère religieux de la royauté assyro-babylonienne* (Paris: Librairie d'amérique et d'orient Adrien-Maisonneuve, 1929), pp. 251-74 (*passim*); Spieckermann, *Juda unter Assur in der Sargonidenzeit*, pp. 255-56.

2 Kgs 16.4 par. 2 Chron. 28.4), of burning incense (to Moloch) in the valley of the son of Hinnom and burning his children in fire (והוא הקטיר בגיא בן־הנם ויבער את־בניו באש, 2 Chron. 28.3; cf. 2 Kgs 23.10), of placing altars on the roof of the temple in Jerusalem (ואת־המזבחות אשר על־הגג עלית אחז, 2 Kgs 23.12), Isaiah is referring to circumstances well known from tradition, as Isa. 57.5-7, 9; Jer. 2.20, 23; 3.6; 17.2; 19.5-6, 11; 32.35; Ezek. 16.24-25; 20.29-31; 23.37-38 abundantly testify.[184] Of these references, Ezek. 20.31 and 23.39 help interpret Ahaz' answer that he will not tempt Yahweh. In both texts, Israel and Judah are accused of religious syncretism, that 'they let their children pass through the fire' (העביר בניהם באש, 20.31) or 'slaughter their sons to the idols' (שחט, 23.39; cf. Isa. 57.5), and, thus defiled (טמא), go to Yahweh's temple on the same day. In Ezek. 20.31, this behaviour leads to Yahweh's refusal to counsel Israel's house (ואני אדרש[185] לכם בית ישראל חי אני נאם אדני יהוה אם־אדרש[186] לכם, Ezek. 20.31). To infer that Ahaz' refraining from asking for a sign testifies to non-belief, or that his purported inspection of the water system implies that he did not trust Yahweh, are lively interpretations of Isaiah's rebuke, based on eisegesis from Kings and Chronicles. Were it not for Isaiah's answer, the reader would immediately recognize Ahaz as a pious Jew 'quoting' from the Pentateuch (לא תנסה את־יהוה אלהיכם, 'you shall not tempt Yahweh your God', Deut. 6.16) and showing that he observed the Law, which the Israelites did not. So why the rebuke?

The text does not only play with Ahaz' lingering faithfulness, it also plays with the murmuring Israelites, who tempted (נסה) their god in the desert (Exod. 17.2, 7; Num. 14.22; Deut. 6.16; Pss. 78.18, 41, 56; 95.9; 106.15). Exodus, Deuteronomy, Psalms 78 and 95 all refer to Meriba and Massah's water. Isaiah's encounter with Ahaz—at the end of the conduit at the upper pool (קצה תעלת הברכה העליונה אל־ מסלת שדה כובס, Isa. 7.3)—gives us the thematic key for interpreting the Syro-Ephraimite–Phoenician threat as Yahweh's testing of his people: 'will they stand the water test?' In Exod. 17.7, the Israelites' demand for water (17.2) is interpreted as an implicit demand for a reassurance of Yahweh's presence: 'Is Yahweh with us (בקרבנו) or is he not?' (17.7). The name of the place came to follow the 'crime': 'Massah' (מסה) noun of נסה ('tempt, test') and Meriba (מריבה) noun of ריב ('conflict, quarrel'). In Exodus, Moses is the narrative's hero, who rebukes the people for their behaviour, as did Isaiah rebuke Ahaz. In Numbers, however, Moses' (and Aaron's) mockery—'listen now you rebels, shall we bring water for you out of this rock?'—is turned back on themselves as disbelief and disloyalty, and is the cause for their non-entrance into the Promised Land.

It is within this motif that Isaiah is playing with water imagery as a metaphor of what awaits Jerusalem if its inhabitants will not put its trust in Yahweh: you will get more water than you ever wanted to think of; you will return to the chaos waters

---

184. Cf. also 1 Kgs 14.23 and 2 Kgs 17.10.

185. Niphal.

186. Niphal; KJV reads 'shall I be enquired of by you, O house of Israel? As I live, saith the Lord GOD, I will not be enquired of by you'. NRSV translates: 'And shall I be consulted by you, O house of Israel? As I live, says the Lord GOD, I will not be consulted by you.'

covering the earth![187] With the king of Assur and his presence (כבוד), pictured as waters flooding not only the neighbouring enemies but also Judah itself (Isa. 8.5-8; 28.17-19), Isaiah's prophecy of a devastating future awaiting Jerusalem's unfaithful people echoes Jer. 4.23-27's *tohu wa-bohu*[188] prophecy of deserted Jerusalem's exilic desert, as does Isa. 6.11-13. Both set the stage for Jerusalem's 're-creation', evoked in Isaiah 11–12; 27; 35; Jeremiah 30–31, and 'temporarily' fulfilled in Isa. 37.30-32.

In Isaiah's 'creation narrative', Ahaz' presence at the 'conduit of the upper pool' is contrasted to Hezekiah's absence from this place (Isa. 36.3). In both narratives, a threat of doom is uttered against those who might not trust. In Isa. 7.9 and 9.7-8 it is uttered against Ephraim and in 36.12, 18-20, against Jerusalem. In the Ahaz narrative the prediction of doom was fulfilled (10.5-6), while in the Hezekiah narrative the prediction is voided (37.6-7, 28-38). Isaiah's metaphorical portrayal of Judah's fate (8.5-8) finds its climax in 36.1's conquered Judaean cities[189] and its fulfilment in 37.31's surviving remnant. The prophet's ambiguity in explicitly ascribing Judaea's disaster to Ahaz, but rather conferring the guilt on his people (העם הזה, 8.6) and the Assyrian king (10.7-11), leaves open the possibility of condemning Judah, while retaining goodwill for the royal house,[190] the city and its saved remnant. In contrast, no such favour befalls Ephraim. Ahaz might not have been Isaiah's favourite king, but condemning him, as Kings and Chronicles do, would have led to insurmountable inconsistencies regarding Isaiah's theological agenda as set out in Isa. 7.9.

In a consistent play with Pentateuchal creation motifs, Isaiah's remnant survives the waters of Assyria by Yahweh raising his staff over the sea as in Egypt (Isa. 10.26). Invoking both the Exodus narrative's salvation of Israel from the Egyptians and the Gideon narrative's slaughter of the Midianites at the Rock of Oreb (Isa. 10.26; cf. Judg. 7.25; Ps. 83.10-12), Isaiah establishes Yahweh's people for whom Yahweh fights as his saved remnant (cf. Judg. 6.14, 16, 36; 7.2, 10, 14-15). Judges' anticipation of the north–south conflict (Judg. 8.1-3, 31) further aggravated by Gideon–Jerubbaal's Ephraimite son Abimelech's deceitful institution of the kingship at Shechem at the expense of his seventy brothers (Judg. 9), opens up a Pandora's box of interrelated biblical texts' struggling with that theme.[191] While the Benjaminite Gideon refused the offer to become king, because 'Yahweh shall reign' (לא־אמשל אני בכם ולא־ימשל בני בכם יהוה ימשל בכם, Judg. 8.22-23), his Ephraimite son achieved a kingdom in the north (Shechem), 'supported' by money from

---

187. A similar motif occurs in the Israelites' demand for meat instead of the manna they had tired of: they will get more meat than they ever wanted to have and were able to consume; it will make them sick and it will come out their noses (Num. 11.20).

188. Chaos and emptiness, as in Gen. 1.2

189. Conrad, 'Royal Narratives & Structure of Isaiah', p. 72.

190. See Y. Gitay, *Isaiah and his Audience: The Structure and Meaning of Isaiah 1–12* (Assen: Van Gorcum, 1991), pp. 132, 154, and 159: 'Isaiah blames the people for Ahaz' pro-Assyrian policy—they force him to call for Assyrian aid due to their rebellion against him'.

191. Hjelm, *Samaritans and Early Judaism*, pp. 146-52, 218-22, 247-48.

Ba'al-berith's temple (9.4). We cannot go into a detailed study of the book of Judges' narratives about Ephraim, Dan and Benjamin's deceitful acts and struggles with the remaining tribes. It should, however, be noticed that in the Former Prophets, Saul is a Benjaminite and Jeroboam an Ephraimite and that the tribe of Judah is never involved in any dishonourable act before the division of the kingdom and Rehoboam's civil war with Jeroboam's kingdom.

Raising his staff over the waters, Yahweh will not only remove the Assyrians (Isa. 10.27),[192] but also create a road (מסלה) for the remnant of his people (לשאר עמו) in Assur. As he did for Israel on the day they went out of Egypt (11.16), so he shall do again for the return of his people from far away (e.g. 42.15-16; 43.5-6, 16-20; 49.11-12). While Isaiah's 'Midian's day' is a day of joy for Jerusalem, Ephraim (and Judah) are left devastated (Isa. 10.17-23; 17.4-6). What was left after the Assyrian conquest—a desert-like country, covered with briers and thorns (7.23-25)—Yahweh will burn (9.17; 10.17-19). Enveloping Ephraim's fate within the fate of Judah–Jerusalem, Isaiah's vineyard, covered with briers and thorns (5.6; 27.4; 32.13), becomes the new creation after Yahweh's killing of Leviathan (לויתן), the fleeing (נחש ברח) and twisting snake (נחש עקלתון), and the dragon (תנין) in the sea (27.1).[193] This passage's inter-textual play with the Hezekiah narrative that Yahweh's sword is strong חזק (as is Hezekiah; cf. the reiterated motif in 45.1) makes it clear that the text is not dealing with any 'eschatological defeat'[194] but with creation mythology, creating Zion out of chaos, as Ps. 89.10-11 does:

> You rule the raging of the sea;
>   when its waves rise, you still them.
> You crushed Rahab like a carcass;
>   you scattered your enemies with your mighty arm.[195]

The imagery expressed in these verses—the raging sea (בגאות הים), the stilling of its rising waves (בשוא גליו) and the crushing of Rahab like a carcass (כחלל רהב)—all belong to creation mythology's establishment of Yahweh's universe. Set within the theme of Yahweh's election (and rejection?[196]) of David, it both contrasts with and follows Ps. 74.12-17's similar usage set within the theme of deserted Zion's endless ruins (משאות נצח, 74.3). In Isa. 51.9-10, the water imagery combines these metaphors of universal and particular creation's coming out of water (cf. Exod.

---

192.   With 1QIsa, v. 27 should be read as it stands in the Masoretic version. The suggested reconstruction in *BHS*, followed by some commentators (cf. Wildberger, *Isaiah 1–12*, pp. 423-24), has no witnesses and must be dismissed, as must also the NRSV translation. The Authorised Danish translation of 1992 reads the text of v. 27b correctly: 'the yoke shall become destroyed because of fatness', which refers to the euphemistic characterization of the Assyrian king's greedy conquests of countries he was not sent out to conquer; cf. Isa. 10.7-16 (also Isa. 17.4; Hab. 1.16).

193.   Cf. also Isa. 65.25.

194.   J. Day, 'Leviathan', in *ABD*, IV, pp. 295-96.

195.   Here following NRSV.

196.   For the possibility that the motif belongs to ritual and not to history, see G.W. Ahlström, *Psalm 89: Eine Liturgie aus dem Ritual des leidenden Königs* (Lund: Håkan Ohlssons Boktryckeri, 1959), pp. 131-53 (141-42).

15.7-8) in the arm of Yahweh's (זרוע יהוה) defeat of Rahab and Tannin (תנין, the dragon), as euphemisms for Egypt and Assur (cf. Isa. 30.7 and 27.1).[197]

7. Isaiah's Preaching in the Light of Assyrian Royal Ideology

In Assyrian royal propaganda, Shalmaneser III's self-description as UŠUM.GAL, 'the Great Dragon', builds on similar clusters of metaphors, as does Isaiah. This self-description is 'attested already in the Prologue of the code of Hammurabi, then taken up by the Assyrian kings'.[198] It seems not to appear in Assyrian texts after Shalmaneser III.[199] While it is widely assumed that the dragon and sea motif has roots in Ugaritic and Babylonian mythology,[200] its occurrence in Assyrian royal

197. M.S. Smith, 'Myth and Mythmaking in Canaan and Ancient Israel', in *CANE*, III, pp. 2031-41 (2038), declares Tannin to be a euphemism for Babylon (cf. Jer. 51.34). For תנין as a euphemism for Pharaoh in Ezek. 29.3-5 and 32.2-8 (reading *tannîn* 'dragon' for MT *tannîm* 'jackals'), see J. Day, 'Dragon and Sea, God's Conflict With', in *ABD*, II, pp. 228-31. Day's historicization of these metaphors, chronologically separating their application on the Egyptians from their application on the Assyrians makes no sense, especially not when he combines the Ezekiel passages with the Exodus 'event', without noticing that these passages speak of Egypt as a 'broken reed' as does the *Rabshaqeh* in the Hezekiah narrative. For Hezekiah's removal of the serpent, see Chapter 2 above. S.I.L. Norin, *Er spaltete das Meer: die Auszugsüberlieferung in Psalmen und Kult des alten Israel* (CBOTS, 9; Lund: C.W.K. Gleerup, 1977), argues for religious-historical developments of the biblical exodus myth from Egyptian and Canaanite Late Bronze Age material. His form- and tradition-critical examination of the biblical material does not include a consideration of a possible metaphorical use of the imageries. Day's favouring of a Canaanite origin (J. Day, *God's Conflict With the Dragon and the Sea: Echoes of a Canaanite Myth in the Old Testament* [Cambridge: Cambridge University Press, 1985], pp. 1-7) and Norin's preference of an Egyptian source both miss the point that the Hebrew Bible is playing with metaphors rather than 'presenting' ancient myths.

198. *ANET*, p. 276. See also Thompson, 'Kingship and the Wrath of God', p. 168. In Assyrian iconography, we find the horned snake (*bašmu/ušumgallu*, 'poisonous snake'), the snake-dragon (*mušḫuššu*, 'furious snake') and the scorpion-man (*girtablullû*). The *mušḫuššu*, the furious snake (can be seven-headed), remained fairly unchanged as a representative of the underworld at least from the Old Babylonian period. After Sennacherib's conquest of Babylon in 689 BCE, it is found in Assyrian art, usually as a symbol of the national god Ashur, whose cult assimilated much of the mythology and festivals associated with Marduk; cf. A. Green, 'Ancient Mesopotamian Religious Iconography', in *CANE*, pp. 1837-55 (1838, 1841, 1848).

199. However, references to deluge monsters in, for example, Sennacherib's self-presentation: 'I raged like a deluge-(*a-bu-bi-iš*) monster', and to weapons being (deluge) snakes in, for example, the epic of *Angim dimma* (CAD, III, pp. 35, l. 37): 'the *šibbu*-snake which attacks man, my deluge-bow' and '[my weapon with fifty heads] before which, as if it were a dragon from the sea, the enemy cannot stand still' (*CAD, abūbu*, pp. 77, 79) imply an identification with dragon and sea motifs.

200. Less well known are the Egyptian parallels presented by Norin, *Er spaltete das Meer*, pp. 42-76. See, however, the criticism of a too simplistic understanding of the Mesopotamian material, such as presented in especially H. Gunkel (with a contribution from H. Zimmern), *Schöpfung und Chaos in Urzeit und Endzeit: Eine religionsgeschichtliche Untersuchung über Gen 1 und Ap Joh 12* (Göttingen: Vandenhoeck & Ruprecht, 1895), and M.K. Wakeman, *God's Battle With the Monster: A Study in Biblical Imagery* (Leiden: E.J. Brill, 1973), cited by Saggs, *Encounter With the Divine*, pp. 54-63.

inscriptions has gone rather unnoticed. From at least Tiglath-pileser I to Esarhaddon, we find a widespread use of weather metaphors for warfare: thunder, storm, rain, flood and deluge.[201] Assyrian veneration of the rain god Adad (Hadad) as a warrior god[202] determines the language employed. A curse from the time of Adadnirari I (c. 1300 BCE) illustrates this language well: 'may Adad overwhelm him with an evil downpour, may flood and storm, confusion and tumult, tempest, want and famine, drought and hunger continue in his land; may he (Adad) come upon his land like a flood and turn it to tells and ruins'.[203] This imagery of a flood leaving the land in ruins occurs frequently in Neo-Assyrian warfare texts. Tukulti-ninurta and Tiglath-pileser are portrayed as bringing a 'deluge of battle' (*abūbu tamhāri*).[204] The epithet 'the Mighty Flood' (*abūbu izzu*) occurs in texts from the reigns of Assurnâsir-pal II and Shalmaneser III.[205] In these texts, the king 'thundered against them like Adad, (the god) of the storm, and [I] rained down flame upon them. With courage and might my warriors flew against them like Zû (the Storm-bird).'[206] '[L]ike Adad I rained down destruction upon them.'[207] Overthrowing the lands of the Upper Sea, Shalmaneser made them 'like the ruins (left by) a deluge'.[208] In another version of the event, Shalmaneser 'overwhelmed the Hittiteland to its farthest border (so that it was) like a mound (left by) the flood...the splendour of my sovereignty I poured out over the Hittiteland'[209]—an act commemorated by his grandson Adad-nirâri III[210] and by Tiglath-pileser III and Sargon II. While none of these kings are presented with the self-description 'Mighty Flood', nevertheless they 'made the sixteen districts of the country of Damascus (*Šaimerišu*) look like hills of (ruined cities over which) the flood (had swept)'[211] and 'smashed like a floodstorm the country of Hamath'.[212] Sargon II 'passed along destructively like Adad with chariotry and cavalry'.[213] Sennacherib 'rushed in like the onslaught of a storm and like a fog [he] overwhelmed him'.[214] 'He brought his enemy a destruction more severe than the destruction caused by the deluge.'[215] A close parallel to Isa. 8.7-8's

---

201. Wildberger, *Jesaja 1–2*, p. 326; Weippert, '"Heiliger Krieg" in Israel und Assyrien', pp. 86-87; Liverani (ed.), *Guerra santa e guerra giusta dal mondo antico alla prima età moderna*.

202. Cf. the name's numerous occurrences in the index of Luckenbill, *ARAB*, II, p. 444. In most of these instances it is linked with 'foes'; e.g. Adad as a Lord of the Deluge (*Adad bel abu-bi*); cf. *AHW*, I, p. 8.

203. *ARAB*, I, § 76.

204. *RIMA* 1, p. 275.9; *AKA*, p. 73.43; cf. B. Oded, *War, Peace and Empire: Justifications for War in Assyrian Royal Inscriptions* (Wiesbaden: Reichert, 1992), p. 154.

205. *ARAB*, I, §§ 486, 497, 515, 616.

206. Assur-nâsir-pal II, cf. *ARAB*, I, §§ 463, 482, 499. Esarhaddon 'spread [his] wings like the (swift)flying storm(bird) to overwhelm [his] enemies' (*ANET*, p. 289b).

207. Shalmaneser III; cf. *ARAB*, I, §§ 605, 611.

208. Shalmaneser III; cf. *ARAB*, I, § 600.

209. *ARAB*, I, § 617; *ANET*, p. 277a: 'I spread the terror-inspiring glare of my rule over Hatti'.

210. *ARAB*, I, § 743.

211. *ANET*, p. 283a; *ARAB*, I, § 777.

212. *ANET*, p. 284a, *ARAB*, II, § 183; see also *ARAB*, II, §§ 32, 158.

213. Cf. Oded, *War Peace and Empire*, p. 155.

214. *OIP*², p. 84, l. 44; cf. Oded, *War, Peace and Empire*, p. 154.

215. *OIP*², p. 84, l. 53; cf. Oded, *War, Peace and Empire*, p. 154.

description of the Assyrian advance is found in a description of Esarhaddon's attack against Egypt: 'Like a raging eagle [*arī nadri*] with wings outspread,[216] in front of (my troops) like a flood [*abūbiš*] I advanced'.[217] Both Sennacherib and Esarhaddon are said to have broken their enemies 'like a reed'.[218]

Not only did Assyrian kings use water imagery in descriptions of their warfare, they also fought the waters, especially the Upper Sea, the Mediterranean. These 'conquests' are expressed in well-known mythological language from the second and first millennium BCE. Tiglath-pileser I, the first Assyrian king to reach the 'Upper Sea', boasts of having killed a 'narwhale' (*naḫiru*), which the locals call a 'sea horse'.[219] Succeeding kings boast of having cleansed their weapons in the deep sea [of Amurru], performed sheep-offerings there and received tribute from the inhabitants of the seacoast.[220] Yet succeeding kings also boast of having 'embarked upon boats and of having made a journey into the high sea'.[221] With Sargon II, the sea has become so tamed that he can boast of having 'crossed many time the depths of the sea'.[222] He 'caught the Greeks who (live on Islands) in the sea like fish'. He furthermore 'subdued the seven kings of the country Ia', a district on Cyprus (*Ia-ad-na-na*), (who) dwell (on an island) in the sea, at (a distance of) a seven-day journey'.[223] Sennacherib boasts of having made Luli, king of Sidon so afraid that

---

216. For the eagle-headed staff in Neo-Assyrian military standards and winged anthropomorphic gods, see Green, 'Ancient Mesopotamian Religious Iconography'; H. Gressmann, *Altorientalische Texte und Bilder zum Alten Testament* (2 vols.; Berlin: W. de Gruyter, 1926–27), I, pp. 378-80. Labat, *caractère religieux de la royauté assyro-babylonienne* (Paris: Librairie d'amérique et d'orient Adrien-Maisonneuve, 1929), pp. 260-62.

217. S.-M. Kang, *Divine War in the Old Testament and in the Ancient Near East* (Berlin: W. de Gruyter, 1989), p. 41.

218. Oded, *War, Peace and Empire*, p. 154.

219. *ANET*, p. 275a; *ARAB*, I, § 302.

220. For example *ANET*, p. 276b: 'Tyre, Sidon, Byblos, Mahallata, Maiza, Kaiza, Amurru, and Arvad which is (an island) in the sea'; see also *ANET*, p. 277a; Assur-nâsir-pal receives a *nâḫiru* as tribute (*ARAB*, I, § 518).

221. *ANET*, p. 279b. Similar mythological crossings of rivers (mountains, deserts, marshes and woodlands) and setting up stelae on the opposite bank are also found in Egyptian and Assyrian Late Bronze Age inscriptions. The extreme border is not only reached, but also passed over; cf. M. Liverani, *Prestige and Interest: International Relations in the Near East ca. 1600–1100 B.C.* (HANE/S, 1; Padova: Sargon, 1990), pp. 60-64.

222. D.G. Lyon, *Keilschrifttext Sargon's, Königs von Assyrien (722–705 v.Chr.)* (Leipzig, 1883), p. 2, l. 11; *CAD*: *ebēru*, p. 11a. Cyprus Stele, H. Winckler, *Die Keilschrifttexte Sargons* (Leipzig: Eduard Pfeiffer, 1889), p. 180, ll. 28-35; cf. Oded, *War, Peace and Empire*, p. 156.

223. *ANET*, p. 284a and b. For the number seven applied to demons, see Saggs, *The Encounter With the Divine*, pp. 98-102. In Ugaritic mythology the well-known parallel is Anat's claim to have killed the seven-headed serpent. In H.L. Ginsberg's 'Shakespearian' translation of the Baal Myth, Anat asks: 'Crushed I not El's belov'd Yamm [*mdd.ilym.*]? Destroyed I not El's Flood Rabbim [*nhr.il.rbm.*]? Did I not, pry/muzzle the Dragon [*tnn.*]? I did crush the crooked serpent [*bṭn'.qltn.*], Shalyat [*šlyt.*],* the seven headed [*d. šb't.rašm.*]' (*ANET*, p. 137a); *'tyrant', see J.C. de Moor, *An Anthology of Religious Texts From Ugarit* (Leiden: E.J. Brill, 1987), pp. 11, 69; T. Binger, 'Fighting the Dragon: Another Look at the Theme in the Ugaritic Texts', *SJOT* 6 (1992), pp. 139-49. O. Loretz, *Ugarit und die Bibel: Kanaanäische Götter und Religion im Alten Testament* (Darmstadt: Wissenschaftliche Buchgesellschaft, 1990), p. 92: 'den Mächtigen mit sieben Köpfen'.

'he fled far overseas' to seek refuge in Cyprus in the midst of the sea, there however to meet an infamous death by the 'Weapon' of Ashur.[224] Esarhaddon, 'the conqueror of Sidon, which lies (on an island) amidst the sea', becomes even more courageous: 'I even tore up and cast into the sea its [Sidon's] wall and its foundation, destroying (thus) completely the (very) place it was built (upon). I caught out of the open sea, like a fish, Abdimilkutte, its king, who had fled before my attack into the high sea, and I cut off his head.'[225] Finally, we find that Ashurbanipal 'has laid the yoke (*nîru*) of his overlordship (upon them) from Tyre which is (an island) in the Upper Sea and (read: as far as) Tilmun which is (an island) in the Lower Sea'.[226] The old border designation 'from the Upper Sea to the Lower Sea', used already in middle Assyrian inscriptions, has thus been transformed from the supposed end of the habitable world[227] to the new habitats in the sea as the new border.

This narrative progression builds on two themes: (1) the prevailing of cosmos over the surrounding chaos, which leads to the imperialistic expansion of the central kingdom,[228] and (2) the theme of 'heroic priority', that is, the king is the first to do something that his predecessors have not done, whether it be related to warfare, penetration of unknown areas, building activities, technology, cult, art, and so on.[229] The mountain (and desert) areas thus play a considerable role in Neo-Assyrian texts as places where 'there is no path', their tops being inaccessible to human passage... 'wherein none of the kings, his fathers have ever set foot'. While Ashurnasirpal II and Shalmaneser III are the kings, 'who march over the highest mountain regions', Sargon II both traversed the mountains and the sea. Sennacherib pursued his enemies 'like a mountain god (*armu*) in mountainous terrain' and Ashurbanipal traversed 'a desert in which no bird flies'.[230] Tiglath-pileser III built a palace 'which was to be greater than that of earlier palaces of my fathers'.[231] Sargon II built Dur-Sharrukin through his keen understanding, which the gods had made to exceed that of all his royal ancestors.[232] Sennacherib brought water to the fields of Assyria 'that from days of old no one had seen, no one had known canals and (mechanical) irrigation'.[233] The *Bavian* inscription 'records' Sennacherib's various water projects, whether they be for irrigation and fruitfulness or for devastation.[234]

224. *ANET*, pp. 287a, 288b.

225. *ANET*, p. 290b. In another variant, Abdimilkutte is said to have cast off 'the yoke of the god Ashur, trusting the heaving sea (to protect him)'; *ANET*, p. 291a.

226. *ANET*, p. 297b.

227. Liverani, *Prestige and Interest*, p. 53.

228. See M. Liverani, 'The Ideology of the Assyrian Empire', in M.T. Larsen (ed.), *Power and Propaganda: A Symposium on Ancient Empires* (Mesopotamia, Copenhagen Studies in Assyriology, 7; Copenhagen: Akademisk Forlag, 1979), pp. 297-317 (307); *idem, Prestige and Interest*, pp. 135-43 for similar ideological motivation for Late Bronze Egyptian, Hittite and Assyrian policy.

229. Liverani, 'Ideology of the Assyrian Empire', pp. 308-309; Oded, *War, Peace and Empire*, pp. 155-57.

230. Oded, *War, Peace and Empire*, p. 156.

231. *ARAB*, I, § 804.

232. Winckler, *Die Keilschrifttexte Sargons*, p. 165, ll. 13-14.

233. *OIP*², p. 136.

234. *ARAB*, II, §§ 331-43.

In Isaiah's description of the Assyrian advance in Syria-Palestine, he speaks of 'the mighty and great waters of the river, the king of Assur and his splendour' (את־מי הנהר העצומים והרבים את־מלך אשור ואת־כל־כבודו). In biblical interpretation this phrase is most often associated with the assumed biblical designation 'flood' (הנהר) for the Euphrates, and Ashur's placement between the Euphrates and the Tigris.[235] Although the Euphrates (or any other river) never has divine status in biblical writings,[236] it nevertheless has a mythological significance as a branch of the Primeval River (Gen. 2.14).[237] Its mythological function as a border between Yahweh's cosmos and the world's chaos, which threatens to destroy Yahweh's kingdom, is well attested in biblical (e.g. Isa. 27.8-13; Jon. 2.4-8) as well as extra-biblical literature.[238] Zechariah's Yahweh, conquering 'the whole world' and reigning from 'sea to sea and from the river to the ends of the world',[239] brings his people home through the streams of Ashur and Egypt (Zech. 9–10 [especially 9.10; 10.11]). Through the conquest he brings peace (9.10), freedom (9.11-12; 10.8), fertility (9.17–10.1) and life (10.9).[240] While in Assyrian royal inscriptions the land to the west of the river represents chaos until it has become part of Great Assyria,[241] in biblical literature that same area represents chaos as soon as it is not reigned by Yahweh's Davidic king. In both, the water is representative of chaos, after which comes new creation.

In the Old Testament, the Flood story, of course, is the story *par excellence* of the Chaos mythology. In Isaiah, that narrative is invoked in Yahweh's new creation

235.   Wildberger, *Jesaja 1–12*, p. 325. The context must of course determine the interpretation, since the term is applied on a variety of floods as well as used for different metaphors. In Gen. 15.18, Deut. 1.7-8 and Josh. 1.4 Israel's inheritance should extend to the 'great river, the river Euphrates'. In Josh. 24.2, 3, 14, 15, it is the eastern frontier between two distinct cultures. In 2 Sam. 8 (par. 1 Chron. 18), David's reign extends to the River Euphrates, as does also Solomon's (1 Kgs 5.4). In 2 Kgs 24.7, the land from Egypt's river (brook?) to the Euphrates is taken over by the Babylonians (cf. the promise to Abraham in Gen. 15.18).

236.   As in second millennium Mari and Old Babylonian texts

237.   K. van der Toorn, 'Euphrates', in *DDD*[1], pp. 594-99.

238.   Van der Toorn, 'Euphrates', p. 598. In Rev. 9.14, the river is the boundary between the world of the living and the realm of the death. In 2 Esd. 13.39-45, the Israelites taken captive by Shalmaneser were taken to an unknown region, the netherworld, from which the Israelites would return at the end of time. The deportation of Samaria's population *to Habor, river of Gozan* (2 Kgs 17.6; 18.11; 1 Chron. 5.26) might bear an allusion *to Hubur,* the 'river of the netherworld' in Meso-potamian tradition, although this geographical name is never written with a divine determinative. See H.D. Galter, 'Hubur', in *DDD*[1], pp. 816-17.

239.   As does the righteous king in Ps. 72.8 and the Assyrian king Tiglath-pileser I: 'from the Great Sea, which is in the country Amurru as far as the Great Sea, which is in the Nairi country' (*ANET*, p. 275b); Shalmaneser III: 'a conqueror from the Upper Sea to the Lower Sea...who has visited the sources of both the Tigris and the Euphrates...and received tribute from all the kings of Chaldea' (*ANET*, pp. 276b-77); and Adad-nirari III: 'as far a the Great Sea of the Rising Sun, from the banks of the Euphrates...as far as the shore of the Great Sea of the Setting Sun' (*ANET*, p. 281b).

240.   For an elaboration of peace (שלום) as always being holy war's goal, see Thompson, 'Holy War at the Center of Biblical Theology', *passim*; Hjelm and Thompson, 'Merneptah', pp. 9-12.

241.   See further below, pp. 137-41.

after his overflowing wrath (Isa. 54.8) had left his dominion infertile. Even more expressive is Psalm 65's new creation after Yahweh's stilling of the noisy waters and its waves and the tumult of the peoples. The uncontrolled water is contrasted with Yahweh's controlled water, which makes the land fertile, dripping with fatness even from its poorest soil (Ps. 65.5-14).[242] While its inter-textual play on war metaphors makes the implied war recognizable in this poetry, Genesis' flood story demands greater efforts of the reader. In the closure of that story, Noah is told to become fruitful and prosperous (פרו ורבו) and to eat of all living creatures and plants. Because of that, fear (מורא) and dread (חת) of man shall be 'upon all beasts of the earth, all birds in the sky, all that moves on the ground and all fish in the sea'(Gen. 9.1-3). In this world governed by men, war has no place: 'only flesh, which has its life in the blood you cannot eat' (אך בשר בנפשו דמה לא תאכלו, v. 4). However, if man does eat, God will require his life of him (v. 5), as man shall require the life of any beast[243] which kills a man or a woman (Exod. 21.28). Breaking the pattern of endless revenge, in this new world man shall not seek revenge, but pay for his violence with his own life (שפך דם האדם באדם דמו ישפך, Gen 9.6; Num. 34.33). While this does not mean forgiveness, except in the case that the violence is unintended (Exod. 21.12-14; Lev. 24.17; Deut. 19.1-13), it means that the violator gains nothing from his violation.[244]

The chaos of uncontrolled blood revenge, the shedding of innocent blood (דם נקי, e.g. Deut. 19.10; 21.8; Jer. 7.6; 22.3, 17; Jon. 1.14) shall be as controlled as Yahweh's uncontrolled tribulation, which overwhelms even Yahweh himself (Gen. 9.15-16; Isa. 10.6-11, 25; 54.7-8; Nah. 1.12).[245] Paralleling Abraham's question, 'will you destroy the righteous with the wicked?' (Gen. 18.23), the 'great waters' of prophets and psalmists have become a figure of that tribulation of the righteous from which only God can save (e.g. Isa. 26.20-21; 43.2; 54.8-9; Pss. 18.5-7, 17-20; 46.2-4; 69.1-3, 15-16; 89.9-11; 93.3-4; 144.7).[246] In the role of just judge, Yahweh brings his people into security until he has avenged the blood of man (Isa. 26.20-21).

The adjective עצום ('mighty' or 'plentiful') used in biblical description of people(s), whether in a description of Israel[247] or the nations,[248] most often implies a

---

242. Cf. also the streams (of life), which gladden God's city (נהר פלגיו ישמחן עיר־אלהים, Ps. 46.5) and the heart and secures fertility (Ps. 65.10; Isa. 32.2; 41.18). A similar antagonism is played out in the Gilgamesh hero Utnapistim's tears, which predict the end of the flood (*ANET*, p. 94) as does Gen. 9's 'bow in the sky'; cf. Thompson, 'Holy War at the Center of Biblical Theology'.

243. SP: שור או כל בבמה; the MT: שור.

244. Implicitly commenting on this rule, Reuben declares: 'You must not shed blood' (אל־תשפכו־דם, Gen. 37.22) and Judah asks 'What is the profit of killing him [Joseph] and hiding his blood' (Gen. 37.26; cf. Isa. 26.21).

245. As the deluge of the Gilgamesh Epic left the gods themselves terror-stricken (*ilūiplahu a-bu-bu-am-ma*), cf. *CAD*: *abūbu*, p. 77.

246. J.P. Lewis, 'Flood', in *ABD*, II, pp. 798-803; Ahlström, *Psalm 89*, pp. 142-43.

247. E.g. Num. 14.12; Isa. 60.22.

248. E.g. Num. 22.6; Deut. 4.38; 7.1; 9.1; 11.23; Josh. 23.9; Isa. 53.12; Joel 1.6; 2.2, 5; Mic. 4.3; Zech. 8.22; Ps. 135.10.

warlike situation, since the 'mighty nations' are enemies of Israel.[249] In Isaiah's fourfold use of the term, its application describes a similar progressive transformation, as did his use of the term עמן. In Isa. 8.7 and 31.1 עצום[250] characterize the enemy (Assur and Egypt), in Isa. 53.12 Yahweh's servant shares the booty (שלל) with the mighty, while in Isa. 60.22 Yahweh's people themselves become mighty. As in Assyrian texts where the 'deluge' is an answer to 'rebellion',[251] so Isaiah's 'deluge' will be an answer to 'that people's' rebellion, that they have left the 'gently flowing waters of Shiloah', to please[252] Rezin and Remaliah's son (Isa. 8.6).[253] What made them shift allegiance was fear and dread (Isa. 8.12) of the Assyrian king's splendour, of his כבוד. What should have been their fear and dread, however, was Yahweh (והוא מוראכם והוא מערצכם, Isa. 8.13; cf. also Isa. 2.19, 21; 29.23; Ps. 89.8). Echoing Sennacherib's water building projects (Isa. 37.25), the *Rabshaqeh*'s deceptive offer to Jerusalem's remnant to drink water from his own cistern (36.16) is cast into its opposite in Isaiah's judgment of Assyrian war ideology. Neither the flood (8.7-8) nor the drought (37.26-27) caused by devastating wars are controlled by Ashur's king. Sennacherib's (and Judah's)[254] cistern projects might look trustworthy, but Yahweh (Isa. 24) and Hezekiah (2 Chron. 32.4) control the water.

The Akkadian equivalents of metaphors such as Isaiah's כבוד, מערץ and מורא are *melammu*, *puluḫtu*, *rašubbatu* and *namurrati*, meaning 'radiance, terror, terrifying splendour and supernatural awe-inspiring sheen', which commonly designate the 'presence' of Neo-Assyrian kings and the supreme god Ashur.[255] The result of being overwhelmed with that splendour or terror is flight or submission and taxa-

249.   Wildberger, *Jesaja 1–12*, p. 326. Of Wildberger's references only Dan. 11.25 uses the term in a description of an army (חיל גדול ועצום).

250.   The verb form is qal third person plural.

251.   Assyrian rhetoric does not distinguish between rebellion from a previous submission and rebellion from the Assyrian idea that all penetrated and explored areas should be integrated in the Assyrian Empire. See Oded, *War, Peace and Empire*, p. 175.

252.   The difficult application of the word משוש to Shiloah's waters suggests that Isaiah is in fact playing with ambiguities: the waters can be a joy/joyous, as can Yahweh's city (Isa. 32.13; 60.15; 65.18), or people can 'be joyous' with Rezin and Remaliah's son, as can those who mourned for Jerusalem rejoice (שישו אתה משוש) with her (Isa. 66.10). See also H. Klein, 'Freude an Rezin: Ein Versuch, mit dem Text Jes. viii 6 ohne Konjektur auszukommen', *VT* 30 (1980), pp. 229-33 (231): 'Wenn nämlich das Volk den König von Juda verworfen hat, kann es sich nur Rezin und dem Remalja-Sohn zugewandt haben. Wir würden heute sagen: es hat ihm zugejubelt. Und genau dass ist im jetzigen Text zu lesen: *mśwś 't-rṣyn*... Es hat also Freude an Rezin gefunden, wie N.H. Tur-Sinai (Torczyner) korrekt übersetzt'.

253.   Cf. also Ps. 73.10. Jer. 2.13-18 accuses Jerusalem of having left the living waters of Yahweh (מקור מים חיים), of having cut untenable cisterns, and gone to Egypt and Assur to drink water from the Nile and the Euphrates.

254.   Cf. Isa. 22.9-11; 2 Chron. 26.9-10; 32.2-4; 2 Kgs 20.20.

255.   *CAD*, *ad loc*.; K. Lawson Younger, Jr, *Ancient Conquest Accounts: A Study in Near Eastern and Biblical History Writing* (JSOTSup, 98; Sheffield: JSOT Press, 1990), pp. 73-74. For Egyptian parallels from the Amarna period, see C. Zaccagnini, 'Breath of Life and Water to Drink', in L. Milano (ed.), *Drinking in Ancient Societies, History and Culture of Drinks in the Ancient Near East: Papers of a Symposium Held in Rome, May 17-19, 1990* (History of Ancient Near East/ Studies, 6; Padova: Sargon, 1994), pp. 347-60 (359-60).

tion. In most texts it stands in opposition to being utterly 'destroyed, devastated and burned' or otherwise conquered.[256] 'The terrifying splendor (*melammu, puluḫtu, rašubbatu*) of the Assyrian king is such that the enemy even from afar is afraid (*adāru*; cf. *ḫattu, ḫurbašu*, etc.) and runs away. If there is a clash (*taḫāzu, tamḫāru*, etc.), it is a one-sided massacre (*abiktu*), not a clash between two armies.'[257] The most common literary expression for submission (*kanāšu*) is 'embraced' or 'kissed my feet' (*šēpē našāqu*) in an acceptance of the 'Assyrian Yoke' (*nīru, nēru*),[258] whether forced by conquest or out of fear.[259] Diplomacy and psychological warfare was far preferred to the more resource-demanding physical war.[260]

From an Assyrian perspective, the incorporation and assimilation of foreigners into the Assyrian Empire was seen as a creation of order out of chaos, a rebirth after the deluge. Whether destroyed by conquest or not, the non-Assyrian periphery was by definition unfruitful, disorderly and chaotic.[261] Thus, 'Assyrian imperialist expansion is presented in a favourable light and interpreted as a means of safeguarding universal order by eliminating constantly the monstrous forces of chaos represented by the enemy'.[262] As 'the periphery is a failed cosmos, or one not yet realised, but which should be eventually realised',[263] it was the task of the Assyrian king to set up stelae at the remotest boundaries and, thereby, bring under control what was not controlled:[264]

> The antithesis is between order and chaos, not between war and peace. Chaos is the opposite of order and peace. The enemy belongs to the chaotic forces. He is wicked by nature, he has sinned against the land of Assyria, against the gods, and against his own people and mankind. As such he has endangered the welfare of mankind and threatened to overwhelm the natural order. He must be either subjugated or eliminated; this can be achieved only by war.[265]

Couched in the language of myth and religion, the kings of Assur fought their enemies as Marduk had fought Tiamat, the primeval monster.[266] As the victory of Marduk gave rest to the gods, so the victory of the earthly king gives rest to the entire population. The inscription of Sennacherib on the bronze doors of Bit-Akitu

---

256. E.g. *ANET*, p. 282a (Adad-nirari III); pp. 285a, 286b (Sargon II), p. 288a (Sennacherib), p. 292a (Esarhaddon); *ARAB*, I, §§ 598-99 (Shalmaneser III).

257. Liverani, 'The Ideology of the Assyrian Empire', pp. 297-317 (311).

258. For the numerous occurrences of this term, see, *CAD, nīru*, pp. 260-63.

259. E.g. *ANET*, pp. 275b, 276b, 281b, 282a, 287b, 291b, 292a, 294b, 296a; *ARAB*, I, § 477. Liverani, 'Ideology of Assyrian Empire', p. 311; A.K. Grayson, 'Assyrian Rule of Conquered Territory in Ancient Western Asia', in *CANE*, II, pp. 959-68.

260. Grayson, 'Assyrian Rule', pp. 959-68.

261. Liverani, ' Ideology of Assyrian Empire', p. 306.

262. Oded, *War, Peace and Empire*, especially pp. 101-20 (111).

263. Liverani, ' Ideology of Assyrian Empire', p. 306.

264. Younger, *Ancient Conquest Accounts*, p. 123: 'The real sense of a campaign is to be found in its desire for the restoration of order. The enemy has brought about disorder and chaos, and the Assyrian king must reinstate order, righteousness and life.'

265. Oded, *War, Peace and Empire*, p. 186.

266. T. Fish, 'War and Religion in Ancient Mesopotamia', *BJRL* 23 (1937), pp. 387-402 (400-401); Oded, *War, Peace and Empire*, pp. 111-13; Kang, *Divine War*, pp. 37-42.

in the city of Assur says, 'Image of Ashur going to battle with Tiamat; image of Sennacherib, king of Assyria...the victorious prince, standing in Ashur's chariots; Tiamat and the creatures of her inside'.[267] This, however, is a never-ending battle, since 'according to the ancient cosmological view, the world is situated precariously between order and chaos'.[268] Furthermore, as soon as the periphery has become incorporated in the Assyrian cosmos, by implication it is no longer the periphery. There is always another, yet more inaccessible periphery, which calls for penetration, investigation and assimilation.[269] The goal of Assyrian expansion was nothing less than worldwide dominion of the imperial god Ashur and his servant, the Assyrian 'king of the world'.[270]

Following conquest and submission, the 'strangeness' of the foreigners had to be transformed and acculturated.[271] The Assyrian idea of cultural assimilation probably reached its climax in the reign of Sargon II.[272] The reason is simple: in the peripheries of the empire 'conquered' by former Assyrian kings, constant sedition, withholding of tributes and attempts at forming anti-Assyrian coalitions, 'forced' central Assyria to replace local royal administrations with Assyrian governors (*bēl pīḫati, pāḫīti, šaknu*).[273] Mass deportations became standard practice for subduing rebellion.[274] Having been declared 'citizens of Assur', local peoples (whether indigenous or imported) were bereaved of their own identity and had to live by Assyrian law and custom, such as expressed in this text from Sargon's Dûr-Sharrukîn cylinder:

> Peoples of the four regions of the world, of foreign tongue and divergent speech,
> dwellers of mountain and lowland, all that were ruled by the light of the gods, the
> lord of all, I carried off at Ashur, my lord's command, by the might of my sceptre,

---

267. *OIP*², pp. 141-42: 10-15, 1-2; cf. Oded, *War, Peace and Empire*, p. 112; Green, 'Ancient Mesopotamian Religious Iconography', p. 1853; Thompson, 'Kingship and the Wrath of God', pp. 6-8.

268. Oded, *War, Peace and Empire*, p. 111.

269. Liverani, 'Ideology of the Assyrian Empire', pp. 306-308.

270. E.g. *ANET*, pp. 274b, 276b, 289a, 297b. For the huge variety of such terminology, for example, *šar kiššat kibrate, šar (kullat) matate, šar gimri*, see Oded, *War, Peace and Empire*, pp. 163-64, 169-75; Saggs, *Encounter with the Divine*, pp. 83-85. In Middle Assyrian texts from Ashur-uballit I to Tiglath-pileser I: king of totality, *šar kiššati*; cf. Liverani, *Prestige and Interest*, p. 44. From Tukulti-Ninurta I, 'roi de quatre régions (du monde)', cf. Labat, *Caractère religieux*, p. 20.

271. Liverani, 'Ideology of the Assyrian Empire', p. 312.

272. Sparks, *Ethnicity and Identity*, pp. 30-36.

273. E.g. Shalmaneser III: *ANET*, p. 283a, b; *ARAB*, I, §§ 770, 777-79; Sargon II: *ANET*, p. 284b; *ARAB*, II, §§ 4, 183; *ANET*, p. 285a, *ARAB*, II, § 55; *ANET*, p. 286a, *ARAB*, II, § 30. Sennacherib: *ARAB*, II, § 237. For a distinction in Assyrian practice between vassal states and provinces, see B. Meissner, *Babylonien und Assyrien* (2 vols.; Heidelberg: C. Winters/Universitätsbuchhandlung, 1920–25), I, pp. 138-42; M. Cogan, *Imperialism and Religion: Assyria, Judah and Israel in the Eight and Seventh Centuries BCE* (SBLMS, 19; Missoula, MT: Scholars Press, 1974), pp. 42-61.

274. H.W.F. Saggs, *The Might that Was Assyria* (London: Sidgwick & Jackson, 1984), p. 128; B. Oded, *Mass Deportations and Deportees in the Neo-Assyrian Empire* (Wiesbaden: Reichert, 1979); Ahlström, *History of Palestine*, pp. 637-38.

> I unified them (made them of one mouth) and settled them therein. Assyrians, fully competent to teach them how to fear god and the king, I dispatched to them as scribes and sheriffs (superintendents).[275]

By means of language,[276] administration and religion,[277] the periphery is subjected to the will of the centre. However, practice did not follow ideology and subjects did not become free citizens, however much they were called people of Assur (*nišê*/^{māt} *Aššur*).[278] Assyria's interest was exploitation: the exchange of goods for order, justice and protection,

> which only the Assyrian king was able to provide, as an intermediary between men and gods. To the centralization of the productive labour (deportations: *nasāḫu>> wašābu Š* corresponds a spreading of the service labour (administrators, priests, guards, etc.) of Assyrian origin. Even in a less clear fashion than in other imperial ideologies of the Ancient Orient (particularly the Egyptian one), it is possible to notice how, in a way, some of the services provided (life, protection) are the ideological translation of those very concrete goods which are in fact taken from the periphery.[279]

The burden of subservience was clearly felt by Assur's subdued neighbours as several texts indicate. Conspiracy and sedition were the weapons they used to throw off that yoke. Several Neo-Assyrian texts, referring to 'wicked' and 'evil Hittites', 'plotters of iniquity',[280] also count Syria and Palestine (including Judaea) with those rebel vassals who were under revenue obligations.[281] Rebellion (*nabalkutu*), judged against the ideology of a dualistic system of order and chaos, normal and strange, 'is truly a sin (*ḫiṭṭu, arnu, gillatu*). It is a symptom of madness (cf. *maḫḫūtiš, alāku, milik ṭēmi šanû*, etc.), a typical symptom of that strangeness which

---

275. *ARAB*, II, § 122. 2 Kgs 17.24-41 offers an ironic play on such tendencies of Assyrian dominion, when Samaria's replaced population worships Yahweh rather than Ashur. See further, Cogan, *Imperialism and Religion*, pp. 49-50, 105-10, 113. However, caution must be advised regarding Cogan's reconstruction of Palestine's history, based as it is on biblical material's supersessionist interests in entirely removing Israel from the scene and replacing its population with the later 'Samaritans' (e.g. Ezra 4.2).

276. Liverani, 'Ideology of Assyrian Empire', p. 312: 'a transformation of the foreigners, who become homogenous with the Assyrians, unified in language and purpose (*pêištēn šakānu Š*) and by the Assyrian presence in the new lands annexed to the cosmos'.

277. Cogan, *Imperialism and Religion*, argues that Assyrian practice of cultic administration 'distinguished between territories annexed as provinces directly under her control and vassal lands under native rule. The latter were free of any cultic obligations toward their master' (pp. 60, 112). This, however, did not prevent vassal states from becoming influenced by the cultural patterns dominant in the Assyrian empire (pp. 88-96). Oded, *War, Peace and Empire*, p. 187: 'To bring the world under the sway of the god Ashur did not require enforcement of the cult of Ashur, but submission to sovereignty of Ashur's representative and being aware of Ashur'.

278. Oded, *War, Peace and Empire*, pp. 118-20.

279. Liverani, 'Ideology of the Assyrian Empire', p. 313; Fish, 'War and Religion in Ancient Mesopotamia', p. 390; Oded, *War, Peace and Empire*, pp. 2-3,

280. E.g. *ARAB*, II, §§ 30, 62 (Sargon II); *ANET*, p. 286a: 'always planning treachery'; p. 286b: 'evil deeds'.

281. Sparks, *Ethnicity and Identity*, pp. 31-34.

in fact constitutes the very nature of the foreign enemy.'[282] An increasing use of 'anti-rebellion' language, manifested in epithets applied to the national god Ashur, expresses well the problems faced by the Assyrian monarch. He 'overthrows all the disobedient', 'scatters the wicked' and 'acts against him who does not fear his word'. He is the one 'from whose net the evil-doers cannot flee'; the one who 'does not fear his word', who 'trusts in his own strength'[283] and, 'forgetting the might of his divinity, speaks arrogance, rushes against him furiously in the clash of battle and shatters his weapons'.[284]

> The Assyrian king, trusting in Ashur (and other Assyrian deities also), will surely prevail; the enemies who foolishly trust either themselves (*ana emūqi ramāni*) or each other or the multitude of their troops or the inaccessibility of their positions, cannot rely on any valid support and run toward certain defeat. Analogously, the 'fear' of the deity (*palāḫu, adāru*), aptly felt by the Assyrian king, becomes in the case of the enemies a shameful feeling because their fear is of other men.[285]

We should, however, take care not to be deceived by the propagandistic justification for waging war. The intention of the scribe was to give a legal and religious justification for wars. 'The Assyrian king did not wage war out of selfish ambition, love of battle, avarice and rapacity, and his military actions were not violent brigandage. On the contrary, he fulfilled an important function: he annihilated the evil embodied in the enemy. It was a defensive measure, an act of retribution. In this respect, Isaiah said the exact opposite of what the king of Assyria wanted to hear (Isa. 10.7-18 [especially vv. 13-14]; 14.4-23). The image that emerged from Isaiah's description of the Assyrian king was a ruler who acted 'out of mere lust for dominion and rapine'.[286] In the light of Assyrian justification for war, as carrying out the 'divine mission and fighting whenever and wherever the god command him',[287] Isaiah's judgment ridicules the basic ideology of Assyrian warfare as 'holy war'. Echoing the idealization of the combatant king as religiously motivated acting solely as his god's agent,[288] the *Rabshaqeh*'s question about Yahweh's sanction of the Assyrian attack (Isa. 36.10) functions antithetically to expose the *hubris* of the Assyrian king and identify Yahweh's true servant,[289] the one awaiting Yahweh's

282. Liverani, 'Ideology of the Assyrian Empire', p. 311. For Egyptian parallels to that ideology, see Younger, *Ancient Conquest Accounts*, pp. 177-94.

283. Liverani, 'Ideology of the Assyrian Empire', p. 311.

284. Saggs, *Encounter With the Divine*, p. 84.

285. Liverani, 'Ideology of the Assyrian Empire', p. 311; Younger, *Ancient Conquest Accounts*, pp. 79-124.

286. Oded, *War, Peace and Empire*, p. 180.

287. Oded, *War, Peace and Empire*, pp. 13-27 (27); Labat, *Caractère Religieux*, pp. 253-74; Kang, *Divine War*, pp. 40-48.

288. Oded, *War, Peace and Empire*, p. 27: 'The Assyrian Royal Inscriptions propagate the idea that the king can and does accomplish the god's will. Absolute royal authority is delimited by the will of the gods, who are recognised by the king and his subjects as the font of authority and as the cause behind events.'

289. For the servant ideology in Assyrian, Babylonian and Persian royal inscriptions, see A. Laato, *The Servant of Yahweh and Cyrus: A Reinterpretation of the Exilic Messianic Programme in Isaiah 40–55* (CBOTS, 35; Stockholm: Almqvist & Wiksell, 1992), pp. 47-68.

actions. The might of Ashur's servant might appear overwhelming, but Yahweh's punishment is already determined (10.12, 15-19; 37.28-29). Raging against Yahweh (יען התרגזך אלי ושאננך עלה באזני, 37.29) and trusting his own strength (vv. 24-25), Sennacherib's 'retreat' to where he came from (v. 29b) is pictured as the taming of a bull.[290] Isaiah's imagery hits ironically at Sennacherib's boastful leading of 'his troops over difficult terrain (*ašru šupšuqu*), like a fierce wild bull (*rēmi ekdi*)'.[291] A hook (חח) Yahweh places in his nose and a bridle (מתג)[292] on his lips (v. 29).

Isaiah's ironic play with Assyrian ideology is brilliant, however much it echoes traditional imagery found in, for example, Sargon II's eighth campaign as fulfilling 'his solemn promise "that the lips of the proud should be bridled, and the feet of the wicked hobbled"',[293] or Esarhaddon, who, in his celebration of the victory over Phoenicia and Egypt, is pictured holding Baal of Tyre and Tirhakah of Egypt with ropes that are pierced through their lips.[294] In Ashurbanipal's victory over the rebellious Uate son of Bir-dadda, he 'pierced his jaw [and put a rope through his] jawbone'.[295] A similar fate befell Manasseh (2 Chron. 33.11), who is caught with hooks and taken to Babylon, because of his arrogance against Yahweh (33.10). Also Ezekiel 19's lamentation of the deportation of the young lions of Israel has them taken to Egypt and Babylon with hooks (19.4, 9). Marking their actions with retribution, Ezekiel later portrays Pharaoh as a dragon (תנים), which will be tamed (Ezek. 29.3-4), while Ezek. 38.4's variant of Isaiah's threat of doom over Assur (Isa. 37.29) confers on Gog the fate of becoming hooked in the jaw and dragged away with his armies, horses and charioteers to be slain on the mountains of Israel (Ezek. 39.2).[296] His defeat ends in Yahweh's great meal, the consumption of heroes

290. The imagery occurs frequently as a metaphor for the enemy as do also lions and dogs (e.g. Pss. 22.13-14, 17, 21-22; 35.17); cf. Ahlström, *Psalm 89*, p. 143.

291. Sennacherib's fifth campaign: *OIP*², p. 36, l. 2; cf. Oded, *War, Peace and Empire*, p. 154. Second Campaign: 'Like a wild bull I crashed through (*ri-ma-niš at-tag-giš*)'; cf. Younger, *Ancient Conquest Accounts*, pp. 111-12. Spieckermann, *Juda unter Assur in der Sargonidenzeit*, p. 256: 'Die herkömmliche Verbindung Adads mit den Standarten durch das emblem des Wildstiers ist schon bekannt. Doch auch ihre Verbindung mit Nergal ist alt; beide können mit demselben Ideogramm dÙRI.GAL geschrieben werden.' Weippert, '"Heiliger Krieg" in Israel und Assyrien', p. 87: 'Mulissu, die Wildkuh, die höchste Göttin, die angriffsbereiteste unter den Göttinnen, die bei Anu und Ellil majestätisch (ihren) Standort hat, stiess meine Feinde mit ihren starken Hörnen nieder (Assurbanipal, Prism A IX 75-89)'. In Assyrian art, the bull, the lion and the dragon-snake are the most common sculptures 'guarding' the gates of the palaces of Sargon, Sennacherib and Esarhaddon. One account of Sennacherib's campaign against Judah and Hezekiah was written on such a great bull statue placed at the entrance to his temple in Nineveh. For further references, see *CAD*, *rīmu*, pp. 361-63.

292. Cf. also Ps. 32.6-9's taming of the ignorant in Yahweh's salvation of his pious (חסיד), whom the great waters shall not touch (לא יגיעו).

293. Oded, *War, Peace and Empire*, pp. 41-42.

294. Meissner, *Babylonien und Assyrien I*, p. 328; Taf.-Abb. 38.

295. Kujundjik Collection, British Museum: 3405, reverse l. 10; cf. Cogan, *Imperialism and Religion*, p. 19.

296. A similar motif is found in Yahweh's great speech responding to Job's challenge of Yahweh's justice, which is tested against man's ability to tame and pierce Behemoth and Leviathan (creatures of Yahweh, Job 40.15) through either nose or jaw (40.24-26).

and princes as if they were 'rams, lambs, goats and bulls, all of them fatlings of Bashan' (Ezek. 39.18).[297] In Isa. 34.6-7, Yahweh's offering of Edom in Bosra also includes wild oxen (רמאים), young steer (פרים) and mighty bulls (אבירים)[298] with lambs, goats and rams.

Most explicit in terms of the taming of 'wild nature' is Isa. 11.6-8's vision of the young boy who will lead the fiercest animals (the wolf, the leopard, the bull, the bear and the lion) lying and grazing with the weakest animals (the lamb, the kid, the calf and their young), while the nursing child plays over the poisonous snake's 'hole and an infant passes his hand over an adder's den' (חר פתן). Similar is Psalm 91's vision of treading on the lion and the poisonous snake (על־שחל ופתן תדרך), of trampling down the young lion and the dragon (תרמס כפיר ותנין, Ps. 91.13). Isaiah's visionary salvation through war asserts the protective might of Yahweh and his abode's orderly cosmic centre ([299]לא־ירעו ולא־ישחיתו בכל־הר־קדשי, Isa. 11.9) against the surrounding chaos (Isa. 11.10–12.6; cf. Ps. 91.1-8; Isa. 16.4-5; 26.1-6).[300] With Hos. 5.14 and 13.7-8's Yahweh in the role of a lion (כשחל), a young lion (ככפיר), a leopard (כנמר) and a bear (כדב) devouring Ephraim and Judah, Isaiah's taming of the 'wild nature' implies a taming of Yahweh as well.

8. *Isaiah 37.3-4: Yahweh's Day of Wrath—The Birth Motif*

'And they [Eliakim, Shebna and the elders of the priests] said to him [Isaiah]: "Thus says Hezekiah, 'This is the day of distress (יום־צרה), of rebuke (ותוכחה) and of disgrace (ונאצה), for children have come to the cervical opening (כי באו בנים עד־משבר) and there is no strength to deliver them'"' (Isa. 37.3).

With the continuation of Hezekiah's speech addressing the issue of the king of Assur's mockery of 'the living God', as well as the need of salvation for the remnant that is left (37.4), we are able to decide for whom the 'day' is and who the children stuck in the birth passage are. In the scholarly debate, Isa. 37.3's disgraceful day is usually understood to be referring to the calamitous day of Jerusalem's remnant, whether punished by Yahweh or the Assyrian king.[301] However, the interpretation by Watts and Beuken, that the 'chastisement' (i.e. the rebuke and the

---

297.   The 'event' has the purpose of demonstrating Yahweh's sovereignty, making himself known to the nations (Ezek. 38.16, 23) and to Israel (39.7).

298.   Similar euphemisms for the 'mighty' occur in Ps. 68.31; Job 24.22; 34.20. In Isa. 10.13, the Assyrian king calls himself 'mighty/bull' (אביר).

299.   Usually designating Jerusalem; e.g. Pss. 2.6; 3.5; 48.2; 99.9; Jer. 31.23.

300.   For other references (including the so-called Zion psalms and the *Völkerkampf* motif) and a comparison with Ugaritic material, see Clifford, *Cosmic Mountain*, pp. 141-60: 'These passages cannot be directly related to the holy mountain of El and Baal from the Ugaritic myths, yet they do fit into the general picture of the holy mountain as a source of rain and fertility and even of order in the universe.'

301.   G. Fohrer, *Das Buch Jesaja*. II. *Kapitel 24–39* (Züricher Bibelkommentare; Zürich: Zwingli Verlag, 1960), p. 173; Wildberger; *Jesaja 28–39*, p. 1408; Kaiser, *Jesaja: Kapitel 13–39*, p. 309; Miscall, *Isaiah*, p. 90; Sweeney, *Isaiah 1–39*, p. 474; Blenkinsopp, *Isaiah 1–39*, p. 474. For further references to works not employed in this study, see W.A.M. Beuken, *Isaiah*. II. *Isaiah 28–39* (Leuven: Peeters, 2000), p. 357.

disgrace) refers to the actions Yahweh will take against Assyria because it has treated God with 'rejection and blasphemy', is far more convincing,[302] as also Hos. 5.9's day of rebuke as a day on which Ephraim shall become a desert (אפרים לשמה תהיה ביום תוכחה) testifies. The day of distress and the lacking of strength for delivering the babies call for Yahweh's actions to intervene to save his remnant, those addressed by the Assyrian commander (Isa. 36.13-22). Turning the Assyrian king's mockery against himself, he is the one who will be rebuked and disgraced, however, not in open fight, but by the weapons he used to instil fear in the mind of Jerusalem's remnant: rumours of danger, a game of words.[303] Affirming the *Rabshaqeh*'s question: 'can words alone be strategy (עצה) and power (וגבורה) in war?' (36.5), Isaiah's answer hits right at the centre of Assyrian psychological war strategy, expressed in the *Rabshaqeh*'s speech and known from Assyrian inscriptions. Furthermore, having tried to deceive Jerusalem's remnant to betray their king (37.14-20), Sennacherib is later betrayed by his own sons (37.38). In the view of the Babylonian scribe, the assassination was well deserved as divine punishment for Sennacherib's destruction of Babylon, its cult places and idols, part of which he transferred to Assur:

> [Against Akkad], he (i.e. Sennacherib) had evil intentions, he thought out crimes [agai]nst the country (Babylon), [he had] no mercy for the inhabitants of the co[untry]. With evil intentions against Babylon he let its sanctuaries fall in disrepair, disturbed [literally 'blotted out'] the(ir) foundation outlines and let the cultic rites fall into oblivion. He (even) led the princely Marduk away and brought (him) into Ashur. (But) he acted (thus against the country only) according to the wrath(ful will) of the gods.[304] The princely Marduk did not appease his anger, for 21 years he established his seat in Ashur. (But eventually) the time became full, the (predetermined) moment arrived, and the wrath of the king of the gods, the lord of lords calmed down; he remembered (again) Esagila and Babylon, his princely residence. (Therefore) he made his own son murder the king of Subartu (Assyria), he who (once) upon the wrath(ful command) of Marduk (himself) had brought about the downfall of the country. (The Nabonidus Stela; cf. *ANET*, p. 309a)[305]

'The destruction of Babylon [in 689 BCE[306]] was construed as a terrible sacrilege by both Babylonians and Assyrians. It mattered little that the Babylonians had misbehaved and had brought the wrath of Sennacherib upon themselves. Babylon was not just the seat of Mesopotamian religion and culture, but a privileged city under

---

302. Watts, *Isaiah 34–36*, p. 34; Beuken, *Isaiah*, II, p. 357.

303. Watts, *Isaiah 34–36*, p. 34.

304. For the widespread use of this motif in ancient literature, see, e.g., Albrektson, *History and the Gods*, pp. 24-41 (31-32); Oded, *War, Peace and Empire*, pp. 18-20.

305. Babylonian Chronicle; cf. *ANET*, p. 302a: 'In the month of Tebitu, the 20th day, his son killed Sennacherib, king of Assyria, during a rebellion'. For legendary development of the event, see A. Harrak, 'Tales About Sennacherib: The Contribution of the Syriac Sources', in P.M.M. Daviau, J.W. Wevers and M. Weigl (eds.), *The World of the Aramaeans*. III. *Studies in Language and Literature in Honour of Paul-Eugène Dion* (JSOTSup, 326; Sheffield: Sheffield Academic Press, 2001), pp. 168-89.

306. *ARAB*, II, § 341.

protection of the gods; it was an unforgivable sin to destroy it.'[307] If the book of Isaiah implicitly shares in expressing revenge for that sacrilege, it may be found in the opposition that is set between Jerusalem's temple, in which Hezekiah finds salvation (Isa. 38.20-22), and the assassination of Sennacherib while praying in the temple of his god Nisroch in Nineveh.[308]

Such logic of retribution, so common in biblical literature,[309] is most expressively argued in Ezekiel's Yahweh's laying Edom waste: 'Because I have heard all the abusive speech (את־כל־נאצותיך) that you uttered against the mountains of Israel,[310] saying, "They are laid desolate (שממה), they are given us to devour (לאכלה)".[311] And you magnified yourselves against me with your mouth (ותגדילו עלי בפיכם) and multiplied your words (והעתרתם עלי דבריכם)[312] against me; I heard it' (35.12-13 [NRSV]). As Yahweh's doom over Assur is made justifiable by the retributive character of his actions (as is Assyrian warfare), he similarly punishes Edom according to its actions: 'As you rejoiced over the inheritance of the house of Israel, because it was desolate (שממה), so I will deal with you (כן אעשה־לך); you shall be desolate (שממה), Mt Seir, and all Edom, all of it. Then they shall know that I am Yahweh' (35.15 [NRSV]). In Ezekiel's Job-like tale of an Israel laid waste and suffering scorn and contempt (36.2-5), a reversal of fortune changes Israel into a utopia of fruitfulness likened to the Garden of Eden (כגן־עדן, 36.35), of children born, of dead made alive, and of an Israel reunited in the land given to Jacob and, forever (לעולם) ruled by Yahweh's servant David (דוד עבדי נשיא, chs. 36 and 37). Swearing by his life (לכן חי־אני, 35.6, 11), Yahweh will punish the Edomites according to their crimes: the killing of the Israelites and the destruction of their land. Proverbially fashioned, Yahweh's conviction is a transparent illustration of Gen. 9.6's law against endless blood revenge. As man must pay for his violence with his own life (שפך דם האדם באדם דמו ישפך, Gen. 9.6; cf. Num. 34.33; Ezek. 35.6), he gains nothing from his violation.[313] Playing out this life–death contrast, the Edomites pay with their lives in the deserts of the mountains of Seir for the lives they have taken (Ezek. 35.7-8). Their contempt for the realm of the living god brings them into the realm of death, as did the contempt of Yahweh's might, his viability, expressed by Moses' Israelites'[314] and Ashur's kings and armies.

---

307. E. Leichty, 'Esarhaddon, King of Assyria', in *CANE*, II, pp. 949-58 (951).

308. For a discussion of the identity of this deity, see C. Uehlinger, 'Nisroch, נסרך', in *DDD*[1], pp. 1186-90.

309. Thompson, 'Holy War at the Center of Biblical Theology', pp. 223-57 (244): 'This principle of retribution—that God will deal with Israel as they themselves deal—sets the logic which the story requires to hold. It is a message to the reader: "Punishment fits the crime" or "evil turns back upon itself".'

310. אל־הרי ישראל, missing in the LXX*.

311. In Exod. 32.10 and 33.5, Yahweh threatens to devour/annihilate Israel.

312. Missing in the LXX*.

313. Variants of the theme of retributive judgment against Edom (and the nations) are found in Isa. 34.5–35.10; Jer. 49.7-22; Ezek. 25.12, 14 and Obadiah, all of which celebrate the return of Yahweh's people (Isa. 35.10), Israel and Judah (Jer. 50.4-5, 19; Ezek. 28.25-26; 39.25-29; Obad. 20-21 [Israel and Jerusalem]).

314. Num. 14; see above Chapter 2.

As Ezekiel's vision ends in creation, so Isaiah's stressful day promises creation: children are to be born. Isaiah's choice of מַשְׁבֵּר (root שׁבר, 'break through, destroy') allows at least two interpretations based on intertextuality. The most obvious is the water imagery, the birth water and the breaking of waves in Jon. 2.4 and Pss. 42.8; 88.8 and 93.4, all of which speak of the threatening waters and Yahweh's salvation as the only possible salvation. Psalms 48 and 88 both belong to the Korah Psalms, of which we also find the so-called Zion Psalms (46, 48, 84, and 87).[315] A common feature in these psalms is a reiterative pattern of movements between despair and hope, lament and trust mounting to joy, either within a single psalm or within the two corpora and the corpus as a whole. In this wave-like rhetoric, the temple as object of despair and yearning (Pss. 42.3, 5; 43.3-4; 84.2-3), confidence (46.5-6; 84.5, 11; 87.1-3, 5-7) and joy ([47.6-10;] 48.2-4, 9-15), is a symbol of order in a world of chaos: the world governed by the ungodly. Thematically the psalms reflect Hezekiah's sickbed prayer: standing in the gates of the underworld (בְּשַׁעֲרֵי שְׁאוֹל) will he ever see God in the land of the living? (אָמַרְתִּי לֹא־אֶרְאֶה יָהּ יָהּ[316] בְּאֶרֶץ הַחַיִּים, Isa. 38.10-11; cf. Pss. 42.2-3; 84.3; 88.1-9, 14). Crying for redemption all night (Isa. 38.13; cf. Pss. 42.4, 9-10; 88.2, 14), will God end his sufferings (Isa. 38.13-16; cf. Ps. 85.5-6) and redeem him from the realm of death, where no one praises God? (Isa. 38.18; cf. Ps. 88.11-13). As Hezekiah's lament closes in praise of Yahweh in his temple 'all his days of life' (Isa. 38.19-20), the Psalmist, 'redeemed from the hands of Sheol' (Ps. 49.16), shall witness his God's actions of salvation (Pss. 46–48, 85–87) in the temple (Ps. 48.10).

Compositionally, Psalm 48's great witness of Yahweh's protection of Zion forms the numeric[317] as well as the thematic centre of the eleven Korah psalms, which begin and end in lament (Pss. 42–43 and 88). Whether intended by composition[318] or by authorship, one cannot avoid the impression that the psalms form a coherent whole, which centres on Yahweh's election of Jerusalem as his abode. Although often considered to be 'independent' psalms, Psalms 45 and 49 share linguistic and thematic features with the remainder of the Korah Psalms, with which their linguistic parallels are such that one has to consider a common authorship. Assuming this to be the case, the narrative progression becomes evident, as does also the psalmist's use of the term 'Zion'. While such progression can be seen as representing a

315.   Wanke, *Die Zionstheologie der Korachiten*, also reckons Ps. 42/43 as a Zion Psalm, although the name is not used in this psalm.

316.   יָהּ is missing in 1QIsa; 2 Mss ό, Syr. יהוה; LXX: τὸ σωτήριον τοῦ θεοῦ.

317.   If one counts Pss. 42 and 43 as one psalm, justified by the lack of heading for Ps. 43 and a reiteration of the refrain of 42.6 and 12 in 43.5. So also Wanke, *Die Zionstheologie der Korachiten*, pp. 4-9.

318.   Most commentators would see these psalms as a composite product containing original as well as foreign material, for example, Wanke, *Die Zionstheologie der Korachiten*, p. 5: 'Man gewinnt nach diesen Überlegungen den Eindruck, dass die Korachitenpsalmen eine Sammlung von Liedern darstellen, die, nach formalen Geschichtspunkten angeordnet und durch ein zweifaches sachliches Interesse bestimmt, ein Liederbuch bilden, das einerseits Lieder fremder Herkunft und andererseits wahrscheinlich auch Lieder aus dem eigenen Kreis der Sammler enthält'. Of the last mentioned, Wanke considers the Zion Psalms to be from the hand of the Korahites (cf. pp. 38, 113).

religio-historical development,[319] it forces us to ask whether it is possible at all to separate a narrative progression from its purported chronological *Sitzen im Leben*. While Wanke's statement about motif is obvious and well known, although not always respected,[320] his statement about traditions reflects a confidence in our ability to write tradition history which has been undermined in scholarship of recent years.

It might not be accidental that the term 'Zion' does not occur before Ps. 48.3 in the composition of the Korah Psalms. In the light of Isaiah's water imagery, we have to consider the etymological meaning of the root צִיָּה as the 'dry place'[321] (e.g. Isa. 35.1; 41.18; Jer. 2.6; 50.12; 51.13; Ezek. 19.13; Hos. 2.5; Ps. 63.2). Likened with Isaiah 28's cornerstone, which in that author's concentric play with themes of covenant, death, alliance and flood (vv. 15 and 18) places Zion in the middle as refuge for those who believe (הַמַּאֲמִין), Psalm 48 places Zion in chaos' centre as a world of order, with Yahweh as king. Implicitly, Zion is also a place of protection—a citadel[322]—such as we find it in its explicit appearance in Ps. 48.13-14's description of Mt Zion (cf. Ps. 48.3-4) and in Isa. 28.16's allusion to both meanings. With Isaiah's criticism about relying on ephemeral protection, such as water supply systems and protective walls (Isa. 22.8-11), Isaiah's 'citadel' is metaphorically understood to be Yahweh's protective presence on his holy mountain, without any concomitant rationalistic explanation, such as Ps. 48.4's presence of Yahweh in the citadels (בְּאַרְמְנוֹתֶיהָ) of Zion. Isaiah's fourfold use of this term refers to the uselessness of such installations. Whether these are the citadels of the Chaldaeans (Isa. 23.13), foreigners (25.2), Jerusalem (32.14) or Edom (34.13), they have become subject to destruction, as have the citadels of Damascus, Gaza, Tyre, Bosra, Rabba, Kerijjot, Jerusalem and Samaria.[323] The frailty of these man-made fortifications is made explicit in Mic. 5.4 and Jer. 17.27's threats against Jerusalem's citadels. Psalm 48's conditional confidence in Jerusalem's walls finds its closest parallel in 2 Chron. 32.5-8's ephemeral measures, which Hezekiah made against the Assyrian threat. The walls give protection only when Yahweh fights with his people (32.7-8).

The lack of fortifications in the psalmodic literature, which is otherwise filled with language about war, but which mostly knows of only a single type of defence —namely, Yahweh's presence on his mountain and in his temple—must lead to a reconsideration of the presentation of Zion's walls and citadels in Ps. 48.13-14. It

---

319. Wanke, *Die Zionstheologie der Korachiten*, pp. 34-39, 100-13, who, arguing for a separation of motif and tradition (pp. 39-40) bases himself on a literary tradition, which, he believes, he can anchor in history: 'Während Traditionen immer einem bestimmten Haftpunkt, sei es geographischer und kultureller oder soziologischer und religiöser Natur, aufweisen, kann ein Motiv in seinen verschiedenen Interpretationsformen völlig losgelöst von irgendwelchen Lokalisierungen in literarisch ganz verschiedenen Zusammenhängen auftauschen'.

320. Wanke, *Die Zionstheologie der Korachiten*, pp. 109-12.

321. E. Otto, 'El und Jhwh in Jerusalem', *VT* 30 (1980), pp. 316-29 (321).

322. A. Robinson, 'Zion and Ṣāphôn in Psalm XLVIII 3', *VT* 24 (1974), pp. 118-23 (122).

323. Amos 1.4–2.5; 3.9-11; cf. also Jer. 6.5; 9.20; 30.18; 49.27; Hos. 8.14; Lam. 2.5-7; 2 Chron. 36.19.

does not seem to be their qualities as fortifications that the author wants to present, but their inviolability. They are untouched, as is the city of the 'Yahweh of armies' (עיר־יהוה צבאות), the city of our God (Ps. 48.9; cf. 46.6). This epithet, so frequently found in Isaiah, is strikingly absent from the Psalms,[324] although 'war imagery' plays such a considerable role throughout that entire book. Its occurrences in the Korahite Zion Psalms numbers six times in three psalms, while the remaining eleven occurrences in the Psalms are found in psalms referring to Jacob's God (Pss. 24 and 59; as do also the Korah Psalms, Pss. 46 and 84) or to Yahweh Israel's God (Pss. 69, 80 and 89) as 'Israel's Shepherd' (80.2) and 'Israel's Holy One' (89.19). None of the psalms mentions Jerusalem. Psalms 48 and 84 address Zion, Psalm 69 addresses Zion and Judah, Psalm 80 addresses Joseph, Ephraim, Benjamin and Manasseh. Psalm 89 mentions David. A shared motif in the psalms relates to Yahweh's presence (Pss. 24, 46 and 48) or absence (Pss. 59, 69, 80 and 89), which either leads to victory or to catastrophe, or to the threats thereof. In Psalm 84, it is the psalmist who is absent from Yahweh's dwelling place. Although six psalms refer to dwelling places and fortifications, either Yahweh's, the king's or the people's, none of these are described as being used as fortification systems. The metaphorical language thus parallels a similar use of the Zebaoth title in Psalms and the Prophets: 'The use of the term as a designation of God is clearly adversatively correlated to its employment in the literal sense... In most of the books, where the word is used in its ordinary sense, it is never a designation of God.'[325] It is, however, a 'designation' of Yahweh's people and it is rarely used in any ordinary sense in the Pentateuch, Joshua and Judges (see below).

9. *Excursus: Yahweh Zebaoth*

In the scholarly debate, the occurrence of the Zebaoth title in 1 Sam. 4.4 and 2 Sam. 6.2's ark narratives is usually taken together with Psalm 80's appeal to Israel's Shepherd and Psalm 99's Yahweh in Zion 'sitting on the cherubs' (ישבי הכרובים, Pss. 80.2; 99.1), as well as 1 Kgs 6.25-28's cherubs in Jerusalem's temple, to establish Yahweh Zebaoth's presence there with the transfer of the ark from Shiloh to Jerusalem.[326] The infrequent use of the epithet in the historical books, however, seems not to support such a religio-historical development. Even the books of Samuel know the title only second-hand as 2 Sam. 6.2's explicative reiteration of 1 Sam. 4.4 testifies. Its

324.   15 times in eight psalms (Pss. 24, 46, 48, 59, 69, 80, 84 and 89), of which three are David Psalms, three are Korah Psalms, one is an Asaph Psalm, and the remainder a Psalm assigned to Ethan the Ezrahite; see Wanke, *Die Zionstheologie der Korachiten*, p. 41. With some uncertainty, the epithet numbers 279-287 times in the Hebrew Bible. It occurs most frequently in Jeremiah, Amos, Haggai, Zechariah and Malachi, sporadically in Samuel, Kings, Chronicles, Hosea, Micah, Nahum, Habakkuk, Zephaniah and Psalms, but not in the Pentateuch, Joshua, Judges, Lamentations, Ezekiel, Daniel, Joel, Obadiah, Jonah and Trito-Isaiah.

325.   S. Olofsson, *God Is My Rock: A Study of Translation Technique and Theological Exegesis in the Septuagint* (CBOTS, 31; Stockholm: Almqvist & Wiksell, 1990), p. 120.

326.   For references to the discussion, see Wanke, *Die Zionstheologie der Korachiten*, pp. 41-44; H.-J. Kraus, *Theologie der Psalmen* (BKAT, 15.3; Neukirchen–Vluyn: Neukircherner Verlag, 1979), pp. 18-20; H.-J. Zobel, 'צבאות', in *ThWAT*, VI, pp. 876-91; T.N.D. Mettinger, 'Yahweh Zebaoth', in *DDD²*, pp. 920-24.

148   *Jerusalem's Rise to Sovereignty*

other occurrences in Samuel are related to Elkanah and Hannah's prayer to Yahweh Zebaoth in Shiloh (1 Sam. 1.3, 11) with its reiteration in David's prayer to 'Yahweh Zebaoth, God of Israel' in Jerusalem (יהוה צבאות אלהי ישראל, 2 Sam. 7.26, 27), which implicitly transfers the name 'Yahweh Zebaoth of Shiloh' to 'Yahweh Zebaoth of Israel and the house of David'. Rather than confirming that this actually happened, the books of Samuel testify to the lack of what is understood as an Iron Age epithet for Yahweh, when no occurrence of the name appears after David's prayer.[327] For the epithet's appearance in the books of Kings, four of five are in the Elijah–Elisha cycle (1 Kgs 18.15; 19.10, 14; 2 Kgs 3.14). The remaining one can be disregarded, since it occurs in the *qere* form of the Hezekiah narrative (2 Kgs 19.31), which belongs to Isaianic terminology.[328] Its three occurrences in Chronicles are related' to David's conquest of Zion (1 Chron. 11.4-9) and to Nathan's prophecy to David (1 Chron. 17.7, 24), all having their parallels in 2 Sam. 5.10; 7.8, 24.

While the transference, of course, *can* be seen as a religio-historical development, such as O. Eissfeldt,[329] Wanke[330] and others[331] have seen it, we are probably far better off by dispensing with biblical chronology and regarding the epithet's 'later' occurrences in the prophets as the starting point for its literary use. Mettinger's conclusion that the absence of the royal epithet in texts 'relating' the 'history' of the monarchies is due to convenience[332] is not convincing. The epithet's absence from Ezra (and Nehemiah), which refer to 'the prophets Haggai and Zechariah', who prophesy in the 'name of the God of Israel' (Ezra 5.1), without mentioning that name, which occurs so frequently in the books carrying their names, does not support Mettinger's conclusion. The fact that the epithet, which Mettinger believes 'is an Israelite creation originating from Shiloh, where the El qualities of Yahweh played an important part',[333] does not occur in the literature relating the period after its transference or its 'reinstitution', poses a literary rather than a religio-historical problem.

The 'evidence' of Yahweh Zebaoth as stemming from Shiloh comes from the very literature, which relates the transference. No other reference to Shiloh has the term (not even Josh. 18.10;

327.   The remaining occurrences appear in 1 Sam. 15.2 (David's war with the Amalekites) and 17.45 (David's fight with Goliath), which has close parallels to Isaianic discussions about the living God.

328.   In Isaiah's Hezekiah narrative we find the epithet in Isa. 37.16, 32, and 39.5.

329.   O. Eissfeldt, 'Jahwe Zebaoth', in R. Sellheim and F. Maass (eds.), *Otto Eissfeldt, Kleine Schriften* (6 vols.; Tübingen: J.C.B. Mohr [Paul Siebeck], 1962–79), III, pp. 103-23 (first published in *Miscellanea Academica Berolinensia* II.2 [1950], pp. 128-50).

330.   Wanke, *Die Zionstheologie der Korachiten*, pp. 44, 103, who argues for a religio-historical development based on biblical chronology with the conclusion that after the transference of the ark to Jerusalem the original epithet lost its cultic adherence to the ark and only retained its literary meaning—'Mächtiger, Mächtigkeit'—in which form it occurs in the Prophets and the Psalms.

331.   For example, Mettinger, *The Dethronement of Sabaoth*, pp. 15, 37, 114-15, 133-34, who understands the distribution to reflect a twofold development from the Jerusalem cult, indicated by the epithet's occurrence in the 'older literature' of the Deuteronomistic History, its disappearance in exilic time, indicated by its absence in exilic literature ([DtrH] Ezekiel), but gaining importance in post-exilic time such as reflected in Haggai, Zechariah and Malachi. In the exilic situation the 'glory' and the 'name' were better suited to a description of the presence of Yahweh. See Mettinger, 'Yahweh Zebaoth', pp. 923-24 and 920: 'Serving as an important divine epithet in the Zion-Zebaoth theology of the Jerusalemite temple, it is attested from the pre-monarchic period to postexilic times. The Zebaoth designation is an important signpost in the religious history of ancient Israel'. See also H.-J. Zobel, 'צבאות', p. 885: 'JHWH ṣebāôt war der Kultname des Gottes Israel in Schilo geworden, und JHWH ṣebāôt lautete nun auch die Titulatur dieses Gottes in Jerusalem. Das Epitheton ṣebāôt war kultisch und blieb kultisch.'

332.   Mettinger, *The Dethronement of Sabaoth*, pp. 14-16, 78-79, 115, 132-34; cf. Olofsson, *God Is My Rock*, p. 119.

333.   Cf. Olofsson, *God Is My Rock*, p. 119; Mettinger, 'Yahweh Zebaoth', p. 921.

19.51), the Israelites' appearance before Yahweh in Shiloh, or the allusions to Shiloh as the cultic and administrative centre in pre-monarchic time.[334] No extra-biblical material supports the assumption, although the title and the ark, as well as the Zion ideology as such, may have some similarities with so-called Syro-Canaanite tradition.[335] It seems reasonable, therefore, to conclude that not only did the term have its *Sitz im Leben* in the cult of Jerusalem,[336] its relation to Shiloh is projected back from the very temple ideology which created the tradition.[337] While Mettinger and Albertz assume a religio-historical as well as a literary development, we here emphasize the literary qualities of the biblical argument: the projection creates a relationship to pre-monarchic biblical Israel, which would otherwise be difficult to argue.[338] David's Yahweh does not belong to some unknown newcomer. He is the Yahweh of Jerusalem, the Yahweh Zebaoth, who furthermore is identical with the Yahweh, God of Israel, who speaks to Moses from the seat of the ark between the cherubs (הכרבים שני מבין העדה על־ארן אשר הכפרת מעל אליו מדבר הקול[339] וישמע, Num. 7.89; cf. Exod. 25.22). As he formerly spoke to Moses, he now speaks to David (לדוד לעבדי תאמר כה ועתה, 2 Sam. 7.5-17 [8]),[340] who replies at the very same place (לפני וישב המלך ויבא 2 ,בה אמר יהוה צבאות Sam. 7.18; cf. 6.2, 16, 21). The supersessionist function of the transference is transparent, as is the mutual promise: an eternal House for David in exchange for the universal elevation of Yahweh Zebaoth as God for Israel (7.25-26).

We here notice that the combination of יהוה צבאות with אלהי ישראל, which appears some 34 times in the MT, occurs only in Isaiah, Jeremiah and Psalms as well as in 1 Sam. 17.45 and 2 Sam. 7.26-27 (par. 1 Chron. 17.24), explaining who Yahweh Zebaoth is. The combination never occurs in the LXX, which, however, always has the equivalent of יהוה אלהי ישראל, when צבאות is lacking from the MT (14 times).[341] It is hardly accidental that Isaiah's first usage of Yahweh Zebaoth in formulaic language is linked with another term, אביר ישראל (Isa. 1.24), which is likewise believed to derive from the Shiloh cult and connected with the Zion tradition.[342] Intertextually linked with Gen. 49.24's blessing of Joseph, that term's few other occurrences in the Old Testament (Isa. 49.26; 60.16; Ps. 132.2, 5) combine it with the Zion ideology's supersessionist election of David and Jerusalem (e.g. Pss. 76[343] and 78[344]). The term is 'in itself a variant of the title אל־יעקב/

334. E.g. Josh. 18.1; 21.2; 22.12; Judg. 18.31; 21.19; 1 Sam. 3.14; 14.3; 1 Kgs 2.27; Jer. 7.12, 14.

335. Kraus, *Theologie der Psalmen*, pp. 94-101; Mettinger, 'Yahweh Zebaoth', p. 921.

336. Mettinger, *The Dethronement of Sabaoth*, pp. 19-24.

337. R. Albertz, *Religionsgeschichte Israels*, pp. 51-54.

338. J. Maier, *Das altisraelitische Ladeheiligtum* (BZAW, 93; Berlin: Alfred Töpelmann, 1965), pp. 69-73: 'So verfasste in nachsalomonischer Zeit der "Lade-Erzähler" sein Werk, dessen Ziel es war, die "Stadt Davids" als den legitimen und endgültigen Ort der kultischen Präsenz des Gottes Gesamtisrahels, wie er sich als Jahwe (Gott der) Zebaoth offenbart hatte, zu erweisen'. Kraus, *Theologie der Psalmen*, pp. 90-91: 'Der *hieros logos* der Lade-Erzählung will denn auch deutlich bekunden, dass die Geschichte des Kultus in Jerusalem an die letzte Station der Lade, an Silo, anknüpft. Ohne Zweifel besass die Lade-Erzählung als *Grunddokument der Erwählung Jerusalems* eine grosse Bedeutung.'

339. LXX: τὴν φωνὴν κυρίου.

340. Notice, the formulaic form, known mostly from Jeremiah, Haggai and Zechariah.

341. Olofsson, *God Is My Rock*, p. 123.

342. Olofsson, *God Is My Rock*, p. 90.

343. Lutz, *Jahwe, Jerusalem und die Völker*, p. 168: 'Israel, Juda und Jerusalem stehen als selbständige politische Einheiten nebeneinander, wobei Jerusalem als dem kultischen Zentrum der Vorrang eingeräumt wird'.

344. R.J. Clifford, 'In Zion and David a New Beginning: An Interpretation of Psalm 78', in Halpern and Levenson (eds.), *Traditions in* Transformation, pp. 121-41, argues against this generally accepted interpretation of the psalm as rejecting Ephraim in favour of Judah (cf. the

אלהי־יעקב "the God of Jacob",[345] one of the ancient Israelite divine names, which is probably a designation from northern Israel'.[346] Of the term's few occurrences,[347] Psalms 20, 46, 75–76, 84 and 146 link Zion with Jacob's God as does Isa. 2.2-4's equation of Yahweh's Temple Mount in Jerusalem with Zion and the temple of Jacob's God.

Whether the term has lost its traditional meaning,[348] or whether it became a designation of the whole of an often-idealized Israel from the exile onwards,[349] is a question belonging to religious history. In literature, the transference creates the past as well as the idealized Israel of which Jacob-Israel is the eponym. This is most clearly expressed in Isaiah's word of Yahweh against Jacob, which has fallen in Israel because of the *hubris* of Ephraim and Samaria (Isa. 9.7-11); in the return of the survivors of the house of Jacob to יהוה קדוש ישראל[350] and Jacob's remnant to אל גבור (10.20-21; cf. 17.3-7); in the redemption of the house of Abraham and the house of Jacob's sanctification of קדוש יעקב,[351] following which they shall fear Yahweh as אלהי ישראל (29.22-23). Linked to the rise of the Davidic kingdom (Isa. 9.5-6; 1 Sam. 16.13-14; 2 Sam. 7.15-16; 22.44–23.7), we are not surprised to find that David is called Jacob's God's Messiah (משיח אלהי יעקב) to whom Yahweh, Israel's God (אלהי ישראל)[352] has spoken (2 Sam. 23.1-3). Seeking recognition in 'all Israel',[353] Jacob's God called David to speak the words of יהוה (2 Sam. 23.2), אלהי ישראל (2 Sam. 23.3), as Abraham, Isaac and Jacob's God called Moses to speak on his behalf (Exod. 3.6, 15, 16; 4.5, 12, 15). This deity Moses and Aaron call יהוה אלהי ישראל (Exod. 5.1).

Since the Yahweh Zebaoth title is so closely connected with the salvation of Jerusalem's remnant in a 'liberation' and 'resurrection' of Jerusalem-Zion,[354] we should not fail to notice its inter-textual linkage with Yahweh's salvation of the Israelites in the Mosaic tradition: 'And Yahweh said to Aaron and Moses: 'lead the Israelites out of Egypt, according to their armies' (הוציאו את־בני ישראל מארץ מצרים על־צבאותם, Exod. 6.26). Accordingly, 'all Yahweh's armies' went out of Egypt (יצאו כל־צבאות יהוה מארץ מצרים), Exod. 12.41, 51; Num. 33.1). Consistent with this characterization of the Israelites, their organization and their function are like that of an army (צבא, e.g., Num. 1–2; 10; 26; 31; Josh. 4). However, with the exception of Numbers 31 and Josh. 4.13-14, it is not Israel's צבא that fights in Joshua and Judges' conquest narratives. Transcending the ephemeral, the first conquest within Canaan (that of Jericho, Josh. 6) is designed as 'Yahweh's Holy war', sanctified by the presence of שר־צבא־יהוה (Josh. 5.13-15) and the ark (Josh. 6.6-14), however with no mention of any צבא in the battle narrative. Although 'war' is the most common behaviour in Joshua and Judges, צבא is not used to describe Israel's armies, but Israel as a people. This is most

---

works of B. Duhm, H.-J. Kraus, J. Hofbauer and R.P. Carroll). In Clifford's opinion, the rejection of Ephraim includes all of ancient Israel (which came to an end with the Assyrian destruction, cf. pp. 132, 138-41), worshipping at Shiloh, and an election of Zion as a sign of God's mercy that he is ready to begin again (p. 138).

345.   Wildberger, 'Gottesnahmen und Gottesepitheta bei Jesaja', in *idem*, *Jahwe und sein Volk*, pp. 219-48 (224).

346.   Wildberger, 'Gottesnahmen und Gottesepitheta bei Jesaja', p. 222; Olofsson, *God Is My Rock*, p. 90.

347.   2 Sam. 23.1; Isa. 2.3; Mic. 4.2; Pss. 20.2; 46.8, 12; 75.10; 76.7; 81.2, 5; 84.9; 94.7; 114.7; 146.5.

348.   Wildberger, 'Gottesnahmen und Gottesepitheta bei Jesaja', p. 224; Wanke, *Zionstheologie*, p. 58.

349.   Olofsson, *God Is My Rock*, p. 90.

350.   קדוש ישראל is an Isaianic term (25 times); Jeremiah (twice, chs. 50–51); Psalms (three times, 71.22; 78.41; 89.19); cf. Wildberger, 'Gottesnahmen und Gottesepitheta bei Jesaja', p. 241. See also, however, 2 Kgs 19.22 par. Isa. 37.23; 1 Sam. 6.20; Ezek. 39.7.

351.   Isa. 8.13: Yahweh Zebaoth.

352.   LXX[L] and Vetus Latina[93-94] read 'Jacob's God'.

353.   Wildberger, 'Gottesnahmen und Gottesepitheta bei Jesaja', p. 223.

354.   Wildberger, 'Jesajas Geschichtsverständnis', pp. 84-86, 102-104.

explicitly expressed in Yahweh's promise to Moses and Aaron to lead his armies, his people, the Israelites out of Egypt (והוצאתי את־צבאתי את־עמי בני־ישראל מארץ מצרים, Exod. 7.4; 12.17). The explicative parallelism expresses the meaning of the term as does 1 Sam. 17.45.

When the army is a faction of the people, the term is [355]עם המלחמה or in a more individual form, warriors: [356]אנשי המלחמה and [357]גבורי החיל. Deuteronomy 20.9 and 24.5's regulations for warfare use the term צבא, however, without making any distinction between the people and the army. Similarly, Josh. 22.12 and 33 imply all Israel in Shiloh, although the war they plan is against the Transjordanian tribes (וישמעי בני ישראל ויקהלו כל־עדת בני־ישראל שלה לעלות עליהם לצבא, Josh. 22.12). With this we must conclude that the term is not used less metaphorically in the Pentateuch, Joshua and Judges than in the Prophets and the Psalms.[358] Samuel and Kings do not deviate from that usage. As in Joshua (5.14-15) and Judges (4.2, 7), the term mainly occurs in the titular form שׂר־צבא,[359] used for Israelites as well as non-Israelites. Nowhere does צבא refer to a functioning army. In several instances it occurs as צבא־השמים.[360] In the books of Chronicles we mostly find צבא as it is used in variant texts of the Pentateuch and the Former Prophets without exhibiting any specific theological pattern.[361] In general, more literal forms are found in Chronicles than in other books.[362] Olofsson's further conclusion—'the authors or editors of Old Testament books did not want associations from the literal sense to intrude into the meaning of the expression as a divine title'[363]—fits better, when 'divine title' is exchanged with 'metaphorical use', since this is the most consistent form in which the word occurs in the Hebrew Bible.

While the Masoretic book of Jeremiah presents the most widespread use of the צבאות epithet in the Hebrew Bible (82 times), this usage conflicts with the LXX version of Jeremiah, which only uses the term ten times.[364] In as many as 74 (70) instances in the MT Jeremiah, it is used as formulaic language.[365] The absence of the epithet in the LXX, which mostly renders the term παντοκράτωρ, which is also the dominant form in the Minor Prophets, apocryphal and Pseudepigraphic literature,[366] seems to be due to the *Vorlage* rather than any translation technique.[367] One might

355. Josh. 8.1, 3, 11; 10.7; 11.7

356. Num. 31.28, 49; Josh. 6.3; 10.24; Judg. 20.17. Deut. 2.14, 16 and Josh. 5.4 and 6 also uses this form, although the implicit reference is to all Israel (cf. Num. 14.28-35). However a remnant (women and children, distinguished from the army) is implied in both Deuteronomy and Joshua.

357. Josh. 1.14; 6.2; 8.3; 10.7.

358. Against Olofsson, *God Is My Rock*, pp. 120-21: 'In most of the books where the word is used in its ordinary sense, it is never a designation of God, e.g. the Pentateuch (90×), Josh (5×), Judg. (4×), 2 Chron. (12×), Neh. (2×), Job (3×) and Dan. (6×). If the literal sense of the word is employed in books where the term also appears as a divine title; e.g. 1–2 Samuel, 1–2 Kings, 1 Chronicles, Isaiah, Jeremiah, the occurrences are sporadical where the title is common and vice versa. The Book of Psalms is, apart from perhaps 1–2 Samuel, the only book, where the term often occurs in the literal sense and in a divine title, although never in one and the same psalm.'

359. 1 Sam. 12.9; 14.50; 17.55; 26.5; 2 Sam. 2.8; 10.16, 18; 19.14 (8.16; 17.25; 20.23); 1 Kgs 1.19, 25; 2.5, 32; 11.15, 21; 16.16 (2.35; 4.4); 2 Kgs 4.13; 5.1; 25.19.

360. 2 Kgs 17.16; 21.3, 5; 23.4 as well as Deut. 4.19 and 17.3.

361. 1 Chron. 5.18; 7.4, 11, 40; 11.9; 17.7, 24; 18.15; 19.16, 18; 26.26; 27.3, 5, 34; 2 Chron. 18.18; 33.3, 5, 11.

362. E.g. 1 Chron. 12.9, 15, 22, 24; 20.1; 2 Chron. 17.18; 25.5, 7; 26.14; 28.9.

363. Olofsson, *God Is My Rock*, p. 121.

364. Mettinger, 'Yahweh Zebaoth', p. 12; Olofsson, *God Is My Rock*, p. 122, counts 82/9; Eissfeldt, 'Jahwe Zebaoth', p. 122, counts 62/7.

365. Olofsson, *God Is My Rock*, p. 122.

366. Olofsson, *God Is My Rock*, pp. 122, 124.

367. Olofsson, *God Is My Rock*, pp. 122-24. E. Tov, 'Exegetical Notes on the Hebrew Vorlage of the LXX of Jeremiah 27 (34)', *ZAW* 91 (1971), pp. 73-93 (82): 'צבאות was thus often added in

suspect that its absence from LXX Jeremiah is due to the formulaic form in which it primarily occurs in MT Jeremiah.[368] Isaiah and 1 Samuel are the only books of the LXX which transcribe צבאות by Σαβαωθ, where it mainly occurs in non-formulaic language.[369] However, the 'additions' of Zebaoth in LXX Isaiah conflict with such suspicion, since two of five 'additions' occur in formulaic language. Also, its frequent use in Haggai and Zechariah occurs mainly in formulaic language, and here we find no great deviation in the LXX.[370] Apart from Jeremiah, the distribution of the epithet in the LXX as a whole correlates fairly consistently with the Masoretic text. Except in LXX Josh. 6.17, no other book of the LXX disagrees with the MT on the scriptural dispersion of the title.[371] For Jeremiah as well as other texts, some variants in the texts of the Dead Sea Scrolls correspond with the LXX variants against the MT and *vice versa*. Of the available texts, no single text corresponds completely with any assumed *Vorlage* and the possible variations are multiple. With these insecurities, it seems reasonable to accept, as a principle, Olofsson's conclusion that *Vorlage* and not translation determines the epithet's occurrence in the LXX.[372]

For the Greek rendering of the Hebrew term, its equivalents are the transcription Σαβαωθ, as in Josh. 6.17, and those in LXX Isaiah and 1 Samuel (1.3, 11; 15.2; 17.45). In the Psalms, it is always translated κύριος τῶν δυνάμεων (15 times), while in the remaining books, it is παντοκράτωρ (127 times) and κύριος τῶν δυνάμεων (7 times).[373] Παντοκράτωρ is not restricted to a 'translation of Zebaoth', but is also used for the term שׁדי in the book of Job, however, not in other books of the Greek Old Testament, which translate שׁדי with a variety of terms.[374] With distributive variants as well as different 'translations'—although a certain consistency appears in single units—the LXX can be used cautiously as a witness to the distribution of divine epithets in the pre-Masoretic texts of the Hebrew Bible.[375] With such caution, we notice that in the David narrative Σαβαωθ or its equivalents are missing in 1 Sam. 4.4,[376] that Σαβαωθ occurs four times (1 Sam. 1.3, 11; 15.2; 17.45), but is replaced after its 'translation' in 17.45 by παντοκράτωρ (2 Sam. 5.10; 7.8, 25, 26)[377]

ed. II [of the Hebrew text]'. For a more recent discussion and a confirmation of the statement based on Dead Sea Scrolls evidence, see E. Tov, *Textual Criticism of the Hebrew Bible* (Minneapolis: Fortress Press, 1992), pp. 319-27.

368.   Olofsson, *God Is My Rock*, pp. 121, 123: 'The cases where צבאות are not rendered in LXX often occur in these two formulas'. Wildberger, 'Gottesnahmen und Gottesepitheta bei Jesaja', p. 226: For the entire Hebrew Bible 85, of 285 occurrences are in formulaic language.

369.   C.H. Dodd, *The Bible and the Greeks* (London: Hodder & Stoughton, 1935), p. 19; Wildberger, 'Gottesnahmen und Gottesepitheta bei Jesaja', p. 226; Olofsson, *God Is My Rock*, p. 121. Furthermore, in the LXX, it occurs without counterpart in the MT in Josh. 6.17; 1 Sam. 1.20; Isa. 5.25 (also 4QIsaᵇ); 7.7; 22.17; 23.11; 45.14.

370.   MT Haggai 13 times; LXX Haggai 9 times, of which one is not in the MT; MT Zechariah 52 times; LXX Zechariah 58 times, of which 8 times is not in the MT; cf. Olofsson, *God Is My Rock*, p. 122.

371.   Olofsson, *God Is My Rock*, p. 121. This is generally seen also to be true of the Dead Sea Scrolls, of which only few occurrences are found in non-biblical books: 1QSb = 1Q 28b frg.4.25; 4Q385 frg.2.18; 4Q503, frg.65, 1.2; 4QpIsᶜ = 4Q163, frg.6, 2.19; 4pNah = 4Q169, frg.3, 2.20; cf. J.H. Charlesworth, *Graphic Concordance to the Dead Sea Scrolls* (Tübingen: J.C.B. Mohr [Paul Siebeck], 1991).

372.   Olofsson, *God Is My Rock*, p. 126.

373.   Κύριος τῶν δυνάμεων might be secondary, stemming from Origen's *Hexapla* where it is inserted from Theodotion's translation; cf. Eissfeldt, 'Jahwe Zebaoth', p. 105 n. 1.

374.   Olofsson, *God Is My Rock*, pp. 155-63. For example, Joel 1.15, which capturing the meaning of the term, translates it with ταλαίπωρια ('scarcity, need') which Isa. 13.6 in a similar passage translates with θεος.

375.   Olofsson, *God Is My Rock*, p. 126.

376.   LXXᵒ, LXXᴸ, LXXᴹˢˢ, LXXᴬ: κύριος τῶν δυνάμεων.

377.   Also in 1 Chronicles' parallels.

and κύριος τῶν δυνάμεων (2 Sam. 6.2, 18).[378] The title is missing in 4QSamᵃ and 2 Sam. 6.2, and is added in the reconstruction of the text in 6.18.[379] If the LXX 'evidence' regarding 1 Sam. 4.4[380] and the Dead Sea Scrolls 'evidence' regarding 2 Sam. 6.2 can be taken as witness to earlier strata of the Masoretic text, we must conclude that the 'Yahweh צבאות, enthroned on the cherubim' in fact has no firm witness in any text, since even Isa. 37.16's יהוה צבאות אלהי ישראל ישב הכרבים lacks צבאות in 2 Kgs 19.15 MT and LXX. Since no Hebrew, Greek or Latin text gives witness to any variants of MT Isa. 37.16, the phrase seems best established as Isaianic rather than Deuteronomistic.[381]

With this, we have come far from where we began. The epithet, which is mainly Isaianic and expresses Isaianic theology, whose relationship with any cultic *Sitz im Leben* is obscure, but whose literary relationships within a Jerusalem-Zion theology is obvious, though not as literally equivalent as we might think,[382] is nevertheless believed to have its origin in an Israel, which we only know from literature. Attempts to adapt that literature to religio-historical questions have never been able to break the circularity of the argumentation implied in the biblical literature.[383] However, as we have seen, the relationship of צבאות to the 'primary history' is more thorough than any religio-historical transference from Shiloh to Jerusalem. The forms in which we find it are literary and their function theological. Claiming that Yahweh is Israel's god, this deity, known under various other names, plays the role of signifying coherence and continuity for all of biblical Israel's traditions, from the first election in the Abraham tradition, through the renewed elections in the Moses and David traditions, and to the people's renewal of the covenant in the return tradition of Nehemiah, in which narrative the deity's name appears as Yahweh.[384] Although literary, the case is also political as are all supersessionist movements in history. The step between 'Yahweh's armies' coming out of Egypt and 'Yahweh of the armies' leading his remnant to their new abode in

378. In the Elijah–Elisha cycle: 1 Kgs 18.15 (par. 2 Kgs 3.14): κύριος τῶν δυνάμεων; 1 Kgs 19.10, 14: παντοκράτωρ.

379. Abegg, Flint and Ulrich, *The Dead Sea Scrolls Bible*, pp. 241-42

380. No Dead Sea Scrolls material is available.

381. Against Eissfeldt, 'Jahwe Zebaoth', p. 116: 'Aber wenn auch in 2. Reg. 19.15, in Ps. 80.2 und in Ps. 99.1 wohl "der Keruben-Throner", aber nicht "Zebaoth" als Gottesbezeichnung gebraucht wird, so lassen doch die anderen Stellen, vor allem 2 Sam. 6.2 mit ihrer feierlichen Benennung der Lade als der "über der der Name Jahwe Zebaoths, des Keruben-Throners, genannt ist", keinen Zweifel daran aufkommen, dass "Keruben-Throner" von Haus aus an "Zebaoth" haftet und erst in einem späteren Entwicklungsstadium "Jahwe" oder anderen Benennungen des alttestamentlichen Gottes als Attribut beigegeben wird'.

382. Cf. Chart 2 (next page): the distribution of Zebaoth and Zion in biblical books. From the list, seven books stand out as problematic because they either contain the term Zion but not Zebaoth (Joel and Obadiah), or the term Zebaoth but not Zion (Hosea, Nahum, Habakkuk, Haggai and Malachi). Of these, Joel's close thematic relationship with Isaiah and Jeremiah, but without the Zebaoth title, is striking. So also Micah's single employment of Zebaoth (Mic. 4.4), occurring in a passage with close affinities to Isaiah. Haggai and Malachi, which, respectively, have Zebaoth 13 and 24 times, but lack the term Zion, are no less striking.

383. E.g. Wildberger, 'Gottesnahmen und Gottesepitheta bei Jesaja', pp. 245-48 (especially p. 247): 'Insofern vertritt Jesaja trotz seiner starken Verwurzelung in seiner Heimatstadt nicht eine exklusiv jerusalemische Ausprägung des Glaubens Israel; er ist exponent einer breiteren Entwicklung, die bereits in der "Richterzeit" begonnen haben muss. Aber er hat Tendenzen zum Durchbruch verholfen, die in manchen Kreisen gerade auch in Jerusalem—auf Widerstand gestossen sind. Es bestanden offensichtlich starke Hemmungen, JHWH צבאות aber auch zu nennen, und selbst die Bezeichnung war keineswegs allgemeint anerkannt, ja in gewissen Kreisen offensichtlich geradezu verfemt.'

384. Neh. 9.5-6, 10; cf. Josh. 24. For a correlation of Josh. 24 with Neh. 9, see Römer, *Israels Väter*, pp. 323-29, 539-43.

Jerusalem must be found in the formation of literature. Here, we face a considerable problem, since we do not know whether Isaianic theology's use of the Zebaoth title is based on Exodus' 'armies' or vice versa,[385] or, furthermore, whether such a polemic mode has influenced either use.

Chart 2. *Distribution of Zion and Yahweh Zebaoth in Old Testament Books*

	+ Zion	+ Zebaoth	- Zion	- Zebaoth
Pentateuch			-	-
Joshua			-	-
Judges			-	-
Samuel	+	+		
Kings	+	+		
Chronicles	+	+		
Ezra			-	-
Nehemiah			-	-
Isaiah	+	+		
Jeremiah	+	+		
Ezekiel			-	-
Daniel			-	-
Hosea		+	-	
Joel	+			-
Amos	+	+		
Obadiah	+			-
Jonah			-	-
Micah	+	+		
Nahum		+	-	
Habakkuk		+	-	
Zephaniah	+	+		
Haggai		+	-	
Zechariah	+	+		
Malachi		+	-	
Psalms	+	+		
Lamentations	+			-
Job			-	-
Esther			-	-
Ruth			-	-
Proverbs			-	-

Wanke's attempt to separate motif and tradition lacks evidence of the anchor he uses for a chronological basis for his history of religion as well as for his tradition history. I do not argue here against Wanke's late dating of the biblical Zion tradition, which he rightly assumes cannot be earlier than the Assyrian occupation of Northern Israel,[386] nor against its theological rather than cultic *Sitz im Leben*.[387] What I argue against is the paradigm he uses for his examination, his belief

385. In Van Seters, *Life of Moses*, pp. 97, 109, 118, 123, 160, these Exodus passages are assigned to P, while Num. 33.1 might be either P or J.

386. Wanke, *Die Zionstheologie der Korachiten*, pp. 94-98, who regard the Assyrian conquest of 701 BCE as the most possible *a quo* dating of a tradition, which did not become fully developed until post-exilic times.

387. Wanke, *Die Zionstheologie der Korachiten*, pp. 74, 112-13.

that he has a tradition history in which 'die eschatologischen Prophetie' represents the latest narrative as well as theological stratum. Wanke's *a quo* dating, whether regarding the Korah Psalms, the book of Isaiah or any biblical book, allows for all kinds of geographical, cultural, sociological and religious contexts for our texts, until at least the second century BCE.

If Van Seters is right about the Yahwist as complementing and modifying the Deuteronomistic History,[388] my assertion that Isaiah reinterprets Pentateuch traditions to serve his presentation of the 'true Israel' must take into consideration that the written traditions we have may have gone through several stages of religious-political modification, whether contemporaneous or not.[389] While redaction critics believe they can detect such modifications from the surface of the texts we have, I do not. While they believe that plot-driven text examination can be separated from the characteristics of the language of a text, I do not. That texts reflect texts[390] only gives evidence that their authors used the same theological or literary language, but, as we have seen, regarding the terms צבא, צבאות and ציון, their dispersion in the biblical books gives no *a priori* information about the theology or the chronology of the texts in which they are found.[391] Detecting reciprocity, demands a *tertium comparationis*, a chronologically anchored text tradition and an independent history of Palestine's religion, none of which we possess.

What we learn from Van Seters' examination is that Isaiah knows an exodus tradition, which, combined with creation mythology, 'is then associated in the closest way with the return to Zion and the blissful reign of Yahweh there. Isaiah 44.26-28 clearly shows that the myth of Yahweh's victory over the primeval waters—"who says to the deep, 'Be dry, I will dry up your rivers'" (v. 27)—is connected with the founding of Jerusalem and the temple'.[392] This narrative progression, however, does not need any reciprocal redaction, only a skilled author, who is able to create a comprehensive work on the basis of different sources. What Van Seters forgets is that Second

388.   Van Seters, *Life of Moses*, p. 464.

389.   Van Seters, *Life of Moses*, pp. 143-46, with reference to Isa. 43.16-17; 51.9-11 and 52.12 concerning the Crossing of the Sea, which Isa. 43 ('the first, within the prophetic books, to make any reference to the crossing of the sea') got from J, took it a step further and combined it with creation mythology (Isa. 51 and 52), which P interprets 'to refer to a specific act of splitting the sea and therefore uses the divine rod of the plague narrative to accomplish his purpose. He also extended the same motif to the Jordan crossing. This would suggest that Second Isaiah stands between J and P in the development of the exodus tradition'. See also p. 468 n. 28: 'Since I believe they were contemporaries, the relationship of J and Second Isaiah may have been reciprocal'. See also K. Kiesow, *Exodustexte im Jesajabuch: Literarkritische und motivgeschichtliche Analysen* (OBO, 24; Göttingen: Vandenhoeck & Ruprecht, 1979), pp. 168-75.

390.   Wanke, *Die Zionstheologie der Korachiten*, p. 115: 'Die hier an kurzen Beispielen gezeigte gegenseitige literarische Beeinflussung der eschatologischen Texte und der korachitischen Zionspsalmen ist ebenfalls ein Beweis dafür, dass beide Textgruppen der gleichen Zeit angehören'.

391.   Wanke, *Die Zionstheologie der Korachiten*, p. 46: 'Das umso mehr, als dem häufigen Gebrauch dieses Epithetons [Zebaoth] bei den nachexilischen Propheten Haggai, Sacharja und Maleachi ein völliges Fehlen desselben bei dem Propheten Joel gegenübersteht, obwohl alle vier Prophetenbücher ein auffallendes Interesse an Zion-Jerusalem und seinem Tempel zeigen'. Olofsson, *God Is My Rock*, p. 119: 'This designation [Zebaoth] was thus especially common during and just after the exile, but it was less frequent before the exile and in the later books of the Old Testament, although in some books from the same period it occurs seldom or not at all. The reason for these anomalies in the distribution of the title is obscure'. Mettinger, 'Yahweh Zebaoth', p. 921: 'the relatively low number of attestations of the formula [Zebaoth] in the Psalms is still a problem'.

392.   Van Seters, *Life of Moses*, p. 146. Kiesow, *Exodustexte im Jesajabuch*, pp. 109-10: 'Diese eigentümliche Ausprägung der Exodustradition erinnert wiederum an Ex. 15, wo der Auszug vom Schilfmeer in V. 13, 17 auch geradewegs zum Zion führt. Möglicherweise nimmt der Verfasser von Jesaja 51 eine Jerusalemer Exodustradition auf.'

Isaiah is a scholarly construction, which has never been verified. Therefore, what he says about Second Isaiah might be right or wrong for Isaiah as a whole. Without knowing what modifying redaction our texts might have undergone, we can know that Isaiah's exodus narrative, whether built on J, P or another version,[393] serves its own religio-political interests within biblical Zion ideology. With these problems in mind, we must now continue our examination of the distress and birth motifs.

10. *Isaiah 37.3-4: The Day of Distress,* עת צרה, יום צרה

All occurrences of the day of distress theme are linked with Yahweh's competition with other gods. This is so whether they be (1) the gods Jacob removes after his flight from Esau in Gen. 35.1-7's origin narrative of the Bethel/Luz cult,[394] (2) the god who helps Israel against the nations in Judg. 10.10-16's anticipation of Jephtah's fight with external (Ammonites, 11.1-33) and internal (the Ephraimites, 12.1-6) enemies, (3) the god who survives the 'fire test' in Isaiah 36–37's narrative about potent and impotent gods, (4) the worship of the empty gods of the fathers, which leads to Israel's rejection in Jeremiah 16's prophecy of a replacement of the exodus generation with the exile generation, brought home from the countries to which they have been driven (cf. Jer. 16.14-15, 19-21; 30.2-7; 46.27-28), (5) Yahweh's removal of the distress (Nah. 1.9) on the day of curse for Nineveh and its gods (Nah. 1.14), (6) the day of curse for the tyrants (Hab. 3.16), or, finally, (7) the submission of all nations on the day when Yahweh will shrivel all the gods of the earth (כי רזה את־כל אלהי הארץ) because their people scoffed and boasted against Yahweh Zebaoth's people (כי חרפו ויגדלו על־עם יהוה צבאות, Zeph. 2.10-11).[395]

The rarity with which the specific terms (עת צרה, יום צרה) occur in the books of Psalms,[396] although laments are common in Books I–III of the Psalter,[397] gives a clue to its theological bearing. While the Asaph Psalm 77's day of distress awaits Yahweh's salvation in the future, recalling Yahweh's deeds in the past: his saving of Jacob and Joseph's children (77.12-21), the David Psalms 20 and 86's day of distress finds its immediate abolition in an anticipation of Yahweh's salvation (Pss. 20.7; 86.7, 12-13). Similar to the Hezekiah narrative, the day of distress implies a hope for the singer: trust God, do well and he will save you, so the psalmist teaches his listeners (Ps. 37). This confidence contrasts sharply with the general lament in

---

393.   F.A.J. Nielsen, 'The Exodus Story According to Ezekiel the Tragedian and the Exodus Manuscripts from Qumran: A Study of the Early History of the Book of Exodus' (unpublished PhD dissertation, University of Copenhagen, 2000), p. 124: 'Though the overall structure of the exodus account found in the first fifteen chapters of our present Book of Exodus is firm, the additions identified indicate that during the last two centuries before the Common Era, the story was still being improved upon as part of an ongoing debate as to the proper understanding of the origin myth of the biblical Israel'.

394.   For a conflation of Bethel/Luz/Gerizim in biblical tradition, see A.D. Crown, 'Redating the Schism', p. 32; Nodet, *Origins of Judaism*, pp. 174-76; Hjelm, *Samaritans and Early Judaism*, p. 56.

395.   As he shrivels the Assyrian king (Isa. 10.16) for the same reasons (37.23-25).

396.   Pss. 20.2; 37.39; 50.15; 77.3; 86.7.

397.   J. Limburg, 'Psalms, Book of', in *ABD*, V, pp. 523-36 (532).

the Asaph Psalms. Although salvation is set within Zion ideology's veneration of David (Ps. 78.65-72), it is only temporarily, as the lament in Psalms 74, 79–80 and 83 indicate. Addressing their unfaithfulness (דור לא־הכין לבו ולא נאמנה את־אל רוחו, Ps. 78.8-11 [8b], 57), the psalmist's reiteration of 'past' accusations against Ephraim (cf. Judg. 12.1-3; Isa. 7.9) justifies Yahweh's rejection of Israel with its cultic centre in Shiloh (Ps. 78.59-60; cf. Jer. 7.12-15) and his election of Judah (Ps. 78.67-68). While Yahweh's rejection of Ephraim found its solution in the election of Judah,[398] his rejection of Judah (Pss. 74.1-2; 77.8-11) leaves the singer empty-handed: Will there ever be a future? The question lingers in the background. Will God again show himself mighty as in days of old? 'Which god is great like god (מי־אל גדולכאלהים[399])? You are the god who makes wonders, who showed the nations your strength' (Ps. 77.14b-15; cf. 71.19; 86.8-11; 135.5). The outlook, utterly distressed as in the Korah Psalms 42–44 and 88, is most dramatically expressed in the doubting [400]למה, [401]עד־מתי, [402]עד־מה, which also closes the third book of the Psalter (Ps. 89.47).[403]

As the singer's confidence finds its grounds in God's deeds of old, before the Davidic covenant, so the Psalter's answer to the lament is given transitionally as an answer to Moses' prayer in Psalm 90. Not only does the mood change, but also the psalm's orientation.[404] The psalmist who laments the loss of the temple, trampled down by the enemies (Pss. 74.3-8; 79.1), is cast right into the protecting shelter of the Supreme God (בסתר עליון), the Almighty (מצל שדי, 91.1), as his true 'dwelling' (מעון, 90.1; 91.9). Playing with the motif of time, with eternity against ephemerality—if God waits, man will die; man is like grass, in the evening it is withered and dry (90.4-5)—the psalmist asks for salvation in his time, as did Hezekiah (Isa. 38.15-16). The answer (put in the mouth of David, in the LXX) does not praise a rebuilding of the temple, but of the heart:

> When/If he loves me (כי בי חשק), I will save him (ואפלטהו),
> I will protect him (אשגבהו), because he knows my name;
> when he cries to me will I answer him (יקראני ואענהו),
> I will be with him in distress (עמו אנכי בצרה),
> I will save him (אחלצהו) and make him great/honoured (ואכבדהו);
> I will satisfy him with a long life,
> and he shall see my salvation. (Ps. 91.14-16)

In this Job-like tale of paradise lost, everything will be given back to those who have emerged purified out of the suffering: 'Blessed is the man you punish, Yahweh' (אשרי הגבר אשר תיסרנו יה, Ps. 94.12a; cf. Job 5.17-18). The basic meaning of

398. R.P. Carroll, 'Psalm LXXVIII: Vestiges of a Tribal Polemic', *VT* 21 (1971), pp. 133-50 (135-36).

399. LXX, Syriac + first person plural suffix.

400. Pss. 74.1; 79.10; 80.13; cf. 42.10; 43.2; 44.25; 88.15.

401. Ps. 80.5.

402. Ps. 79.5.

403. D.M. Howard, Jr, 'A Contextual Reading of Psalms 90–94', in J.C. McCann (ed.), *The Shape and Shaping of the Psalter* (JSOTSup, 159; Sheffield: JSOT Press, 1993), pp. 108-23 (110).

404. Howard, Jr, 'A Contextual Reading', p. 110.

the root יסר, 'discipline, warn, instruct, train', is apparent in the continuation of the verse: 'the one you teach your law or instructions' (ומתורתך תלמדנו, Ps. 94.12b).

Within the logic of retribution, evil shall come upon the evildoers, whether it is the foreigners or the unfaithful of Israel (94.2, 9, 23). 'Give us joy for as long as you have afflicted us, for the years we have experienced evil' (90.15). The unspoken question, which closed the third book of the Psalter, is answered in the affirmative: 'Sing a new song for Yahweh for he has performed wonders' (98.1). The wonder he has performed, however, is not a reinstitution of David's ephemeral kingship, but of Yahweh's divine kingship on Zion. Invoking Moses, Aaron and Samuel as those, who cried to Yahweh, and whom he answered, forgave, avenged and restored (99.6-9), the psalmist pronounces Yahweh as king, priest and prophet. It is not Moses, Aaron or David who is shepherd, it is Yahweh (100.3). While the old song had Yahweh leading his people as a flock by the hand of Moses and Aaron (77.21), or by the hand of David (78.72), the new song declares Yahweh to be the true shepherd (95.7; 100.3).

Now we begin to understand the day of distress in Psalm 50, the day when it is not possible to bring animal offerings. Thank offerings are what God wants (זבח לאלהים תודה),[405] the keeping of vows is what the Supreme God asks for (ושלם לעליון נדריך, 50.14).[406] 'Cry to me on the day of distress, I will save you and you shall honour me' (50.15). This is exactly what the psalmist asks his audience to do: 'go through his gates with thanks, his courts with praise; thank him, bless his name' (באו שעריו בתודה חצרתיו בתהלה הודו־לו ברכו שמו, 100.4). Not a single hymn that declare Yahweh's divine kingship[407] celebrates Yahweh with animal offerings on his mountain. The psalmist's complaint of the loss of temple and dwellings (74.7) is a false one. It is not the maintenance of the old cult, but Yahweh's presence on his mountain that brings salvation. This god hears prayers from far away, as David and Jonah experience on their day of distress (2 Sam. 22.7 par. Ps. 18.7; Jon. 2.3-10). This is Deuteronomy 30's 'God' in the heart, whom the prophet and the psalmist remember at the end of their lives (Jon. 2.8; Ps. 18.5-7). In the psalmist's vision, it is not the old mourned Jerusalem that will be rebuilt. It is not Jeremiah's, Ezekiel's or Ezra's new temple with its old cult that the psalmist presents. It is Isaiah's vision of Yahweh's cosmic temple, heaven and earth as Yahweh's abode, the place where offerings are in contrast to Yahweh's peaceful reign (Isa. 65.17–66.4).[408] Offerings do not bring salvation, so the authors argue. What brings salvation is crying, wisdom and praise (Pss. 119.164-76; 141.2).

In Isaiah, the *Rabshaqeh* asks: 'And did he [Hezekiah] not say to Judah and Jerusalem: "At this altar you must worship"' (לפני המזבח הזה תשתחוו, Isa. 36.7). The Chronicler was well aware of the theology behind Isaiah's utterance, so he added 'and bring offerings' (ועליה תקטירו, 2 Chron. 32.12) and narrated in detail

---

405. Cf. Ps. 69.31-32.
406. Cf. Deut. 23.23; Judg. 11.39; Isa. 19.21; Jon. 2.10; Pss. 22.26; 56.13; 61.9; 65.2; 116.17-19.
407. E.g. Pss. 24, 29, 93, 95–99, 145, 149.
408. Cf. Isa. 1.11-14.

Hezekiah's reforms, which reinstated the offer cult (2 Chron. 29–31). As mentioned earlier, invoking the time of Solomon in Hezekiah's passover celebration (2 Chron. 30.26), the Chronicler reinstates the time of the undivided monarchy as the true beginning. While Isaiah's Hezekiah narrative belongs to the Psalter's 'new song' theology of Yahweh as king (Isa. 37.13, 16, 20),[409] the Chronicler's Hezekiah portrait places him within the paradigm of the 'old song' tradition, a tradition doomed to fail. Upholding the logical coherence of his narrative's discourse, the Chronicler implicitly argues 'One swallow does not make a summer'. If the template is the same, the final result will not change.

In Isaiah, this old template is voiced in the *Rabshaqeh*'s question about the fate of the kings of Hamath, Arpad, Sephar-vaim, Hena and Ivvah (Isa. 37.13). Hezekiah's answer is an elevation of Yahweh as god for all the kingdoms of the earth (37.16).[410] The salvation is not temporary. It institutes a new song, an eternity that stands in contrast to the way of men (40.6-8; 51.12), a highway to Mt Zion (40.3-5, 9) for Yahweh as shepherd for his people (40.9-11).[411] This is the victorious king, as in Isaiah 51–52 and Jeremiah 46–51's contrast between the divine king, 'whose name is Yahweh Zebaoth',[412] and the worldly kings, whose kingdoms do not last, whether these be the kings of the nations or of Israel and Judah (Jer. 52.3). While it is a new song, it is also a new birth and a new creation.[413]

11. *Isaiah 37.3-4: Children Have Come to the Cervical Opening and there is No Strength to Deliver Them*

As we have seen, biblical tradition offers several new beginnings or creations. While it is only the first creation that does not leave suffering behind it, all succeeding creations arise from destruction and death, a day of distress, a day of wrath: ashes, from which the bird Phoenix can rise. As we also saw, to become a new creation requires a relationship with the Living God, to a God that cannot be thrown away like the foreign gods in Genesis 35's 'creation' of Luz/Bethel, Israel's false god in Exodus 32's 'creation' of Mosaic authority,[414] the gods of the fathers in

---

409. Cf. also Isa. 6.5; 33.22; 41.21; 52.7.

410. Cf. also Zech. 9.1-10; 14.9, 16-17.

411. Cf. Jer. 31.10-12

412. Isa. 52.7; 54.5; Jer. 51.57. For the refrain's close relationship to motives of idolatry, judgment, creation and oath (used 17 times in the Old Testament), see J.L. Crenshaw, '*YHWH Ṣebāôt Šemô*: A Form-Critical Analysis', *ZAW* 81 (1969), pp. 156-75: 'it is an expression of profound faith in Yahweh as creator and judge, the only sovereign, in whose name all oaths must be sworn, a confession added to the texts [by the exilic community] that reflect the fourfold themes of ancient days of penitence'. Crenshaw distinguishes the refrain from the *Zebaoth* epithet, which he dates to the period of the judges.

413. For the underlying mythopoetic pattern: battle-kingship and palace in Isa. 40–55, see T.N.D. Mettinger, 'In Search of the Hidden Structure: YHWH as King in Isaiah 40–55', in Broyles and Evans (eds.), *Writing & Reading the Scroll of Isaiah*, I, pp. 143-54. From our examination of Assyrian Royal Inscriptions (above), we know that this 'mythology' was as much part of a political programme as of any primordial victory over chaos.

414. Hjelm, *Samaritans and Early Judaism*, p. 153.

Jerusalem's Rise to Sovereignty

Joshua 24's 'creation' of Yahweh's people, the gods whom the righteous kings and prophets of Israel's and Judah's past tore into pieces and burned over and over again and, finally, the foreign gods Yahweh Zebaoth removed in his 'creation' of a righteous remnant.

The birth water, so promising for the accomplishment of the birth, also signifies danger, threat of drowning, as the psalmist cries repeatedly, when the waters cover his head (Ps. 18.5). It is, however, only David's song of 2 Samuel 22's breaking waves of death (כי אפפני משברי־מות, v. 5a), which parallels Isaiah's breaking waves of birth. As a testimony of David's reign, the song celebrates 'the day when Yahweh has saved him from the hand of all his enemies and the hand of Saul' (ביום הציל יהוה אתו מכף כל־איביו ומכף שאול, 2 Sam. 22.1). Psalm 18's ומיד שאול as also some manuscripts have for 2 Samuel's מכף reveals the double meaning of the word Shaul, which unvocalized is not distinguishable from 'Sheol' and 'the hand of death' (Hos. 13.14; Pss. 49.16; 89.49). Bound by the ropes of death (חבלי שאול סבני, 2 Sam. 22.6a), David is as endangered as are the children stuck in the birth passage or Hezekiah standing in the gates of Sheol (Isa. 38.10). With David's celebration of the birth of his kingdom and his everlasting kingship (2 Sam. 22.51), we read Isaiah's birth metaphor as a battle from which a new kingdom emerges.

In ancient Near Eastern incantation texts, childbirth is often likened with a siege situation. As an army or a city hemmed in and unable to escape, so is a baby trapped in the birth canal.[415] As the midwives cried to their god on behalf of the baby—'Now is the battle on, I am surrounded! Reach me!'[416]—so Hezekiah asked Isaiah to cry for him (Isa. 37.4). While Darr interprets the cry as a cry of repentance because of failed politics,[417] the text does not offer such an interpretation. Neither David nor Hezekiah's deathbed prayer speaks of repentance, but of confidence (2 Sam. 22.4, 7, 22; Isa. 38.13-16) and justification (2 Sam. 22.21-25; Isa. 38.3). This is Job's lamentation, not that of his three friends; nor is it the book of Judges' request for penitence. The watchword is Elihu's request for humility in front of God's justice (Job 36.5-15): God is God, he does what he sees as right (Job 36.22-23; Isa. 38.15-16).[418] Insight and fear of God is tribulation's goal, as the books of Job and Isaiah univocally argue (Job 34.35-37; 42.1-6; Isa. 11.1).

With the term כה we are once again led to 2 Chronicles 20's Jehoshaphat narrative about his war with the remaining enemies of Judah, the Moabites, the Ammonites and those from Seir. In Jehoshaphat's prayer, he addresses Yahweh with the words 'Lord, God of our fathers, are you not the God of heaven and ruler of all kingdoms on earth, in whose hand is strength and power so that no one can oppose you?' (2 Chron. 20.6). In contrast to this confidence in Yahweh's might, Jehoshaphat and his people declare themselves to be powerless and helpless (כי אין בנו כח,

---

415. K.F. Darr, 'No Strength to Deliver: A Contextual Analysis of Hezekiah's Proverb in Isaiah 37.3b', in Melugin and Sweeney (eds.), *New Visions of Isaiah*, pp. 219-56 (230).

416. Darr, 'No Strength to Deliver, p. 229.

417. Darr, 'No Strength to Deliver, pp. 242-46.

418. T.L. Thompson, 'From the Mouth of Babes, Strength: Psalm 8 and the Book of Isaiah', *SJOT* 16 (2002), pp. 226-45.

2 Chron. 20.12-13), knowing of nothing else to do but lift their eyes to their god. Just as Yahweh's salvation of David from all his enemies ends in rejoicing, so the salvation of Jehoshaphat and his people also ends in rejoicing in Yahweh's temple in Jerusalem; Hezekiah's salvation is marked by similar scenes (Isa. 38.20). For the nations, dread of god (פחד אלהים, 2 Chron. 20.29) came over them, as it came over Jacob (Gen. 35.5), Moses (Deut. 2.25) and Judah's enemies (Isa. 19.16-17). This is the dread which leaves men powerless as if they were women in labour (e.g. Isa. 13.8; 19.16; 21.3; Jer. 6.24; 30.6-7; 49.24, 50.43; Ps. 48.7). In all these instances, the reason is a threat of war, a day of wrath and destruction.

Hezekiah and his people's lack of strength is comparable to the strength of men, which disappears when they do not eat (Isa. 44.12; 1 Sam. 28.20). In 1 Samuel the event introduces the death of Saul and the birth of the Davidic kingship with echoes of the exodus narrative's birth of Israel. While Saul died because Yahweh had left him and no longer answered him (ואלהים סר מעלי ולא ענני עוד, 1 Sam. 28.15b), Hezekiah lived because Yahweh, his father David's God, heard his prayer and saw his tears (Isa. 38.5). The affirmation of David's kingship, threatened to disappear, is intentional, as the very rare use of the term David's God signifies. Except from the book of Chronicles, it is found only here, paralleled in 2 Kgs 20.5.[419]

If children have come to birth, but cannot be delivered, they will die, as will a people when no children are born. This is Ephraim's fate in Hosea 13's devastating judgment, because of Ephraim's ignorance—'he is a child without knowledge' (הוא בן לא חכם)[420]—when pangs of birth come to him, it is not time for children to have come to the opening of the cervix (חבלי יולדה יבאו לו הוא בן לא חכם כי עת־לא יעמד במשבר בנים, Hos. 13.13). The reason for the lack of children is Yahweh's curse that Ephraim be doomed to extinction: 'When their glory flutters away (יתעופף כבודם), there will be no birth, no pregnancy and no conception, and even if they raise their children, will I make them childless among men' (Hos. 9.11-12; cf. also 14.1). This is Leviticus 26's curse of what happens to a people that forsakes its god, Deuteronomy 32's prophecy of what happens to a people without knowledge, a people who would have understood if they were wise (ואין בהם תבונה לו חכמה ישכילו זות, Deut. 32.28b-29a), and 1 Samuel 2–4's pronouncement of the extinction of Israel, symbolized in the loss of the ark, the glory from Israel (גלה כבוד מישראל כי נלקח ארון האלהים, 1 Sam. 4.22).[421]

And what should they have understood? Hosea 14.2-4's answer parallels Isaiah 36–37's illustration of what the righteous king and people do and what Ps. 33.16-19 teaches its audience. Of Hezekiah's choices—horses from Egypt, the kings of

---

419.   In Chronicles, one occurrence is in Elijah's 'word from Yahweh, your father David's God' against Jehoram's failure to follow in the paths of Jehoshaphat and Asa (2 Chron. 21.12). Another is in the Josiah narrative, stating that 'he began to seek his father David's God' (2 Chron. 34.3).

420.   Some translators understand this to be a characterization of the unborn child. This, however, does not fit the theological message of Hosea, that Israel/Ephraim, as a people without knowledge (Hos. 4.6, 14; 7.11; 11.3), can be saved if they will accept suffering's wisdom that only Yahweh can give salvation (Hos. 6.1-3; 14.10).

421.   Cf. Pss. 78.61; 132.8.

Assur and foreign gods—the prophet chose implicitly to declare that 'Assur does not bring salvation; we will not ride on horses and we will not call "Our God" what is made by our hands' (cf. Hos. 14.4). What should they to do then? Bring the fruits of their lips to Yahweh as the prophet advised (שפתינו[422] פרים ונשלמה, Hos. 14.3b; cf. Isa. 37.16-20). While Hosea's Ephraim is advised to return and to repent (שובה ישראל עד יהוה אלהיך, Hos. 14.2-3), because they have trusted Assur's kings, Egypt's horses and gods made by men's hands (e.g. Hos. 4.17; 5.13; 12.2; 14.9), Hezekiah might have done so—but neither Isaiah nor 2 Kings argue that. Hezekiah's remnant is not a repentant remnant, but a righteous one which survives tribulation, as we have already demonstrated. If it were not for that remnant, Israel would have been utterly destroyed. The people, which began so promisingly, fruitful son of reeds ([423]יפריא אחים בן, Hos. 13.15) and leader of Israel (הוא נשא בישראל, Hos. 13.1), have been found guilty and died (Hos. 13.1). The ambiguity of the text, which arises from the fact that אחים can mean either 'brothers' or 'reeds', brings into mind both Joseph's dream of having his brothers bowing down for him (Gen. 37.6-8), and Moses' salvation of Israel through the reeds (Exod. 15.4), which is foreshadowed by the infant Moses' own reedbed protection and salvation.[424] It also brings us to Bildad's first speech to Job, which urges him to take notice of the experience of the fathers: as 'reeds without water', so are those who forget God (Job 8.8-19). Both wither and die (Job 8.11-13),[425] as does Ephraim when the east wind comes. Yahweh's storm rises from the desert (יבאו קדים רוח יהוה ממדבר עלה) and dries up his fountains and his springs (Hos. 13.15). 'Out of sight, out of mind' the philosopher claims, 'others will sprout from the dust' (Job 8.18-19).

While in Hosea the scenario serves as a call to return, it also stands within remnant theology's didactic explanation of why Ephraim disappeared at the same time that Judah with its purified remnant continued and took over Joseph and Ephraim's role as leader of Israel.[426] Retributive as the curse is, Ephraim's herding the wind and pursuing the east wind (רעה רוח ורדף קדים כל־היום), that is, his covenant with Ashur (Hos. 12.2), fall back on him. The wind, a symbol of emptiness and destruction (cf. Hos. 8.7-8a),[427] is the wind which ties (צרר) Ephraim up in its wings (Hos. 4.19). As Ahab died because he listened to the lying spirit (רוח שקר) in the mouth of his prophets (2 Chron. 18.22), Ephraim (and Judah) will be devoured (אכל, Hos. 5.7) because a spirit of harlotry is in their midst; they do not know

422.   LXX: καπρον.

423.   Suggested translations 'fruitful among brothers'; LXX: ἀνὰ μέσον ἀδελφῶν δαστελεῖ = בין אחים יפריד ('separated/removed from').

424.   The Hebrew term here is סוף.

425.   Here, of course, Ps. 1 springs into mind.

426.   Scholars have argued that this perspective forms the Book of the Twelve into a coherent theological statement laid out in Hos. 1 and reiterated as a chronological closure in Zech. 1 and 7; cf. J. Högenhaven, 'Historien om profeterne: nogle bemærkninger om de gammeltestamentlige profetbøger som historieskrivning', in G. Hallbäck and J. Strange (eds.), *Bibel og historieskrivning* (FBE, 10; Copenhagen: Museum Tusculanums Forlag, 1999), pp. 103-15 (112-13).

427.   G. Eidevall, *Grapes in the Desert: Metaphors, Models, and Themes in Hosea 4–14* (CBOTS, 43; Stockholm: Almqvist & Wiksell, 1996), p. 188; Thompson, 'Historiography in the Pentateuch', pp. 258-60.

Yahweh (בי רוח זנונים סבקרבם ואת־יהוה לא ידעו, Hos. 5.4; 4.12).[428] Wobbling as drunkards, they walk around and stumble, as do Isaiah's Egyptians, because Yahweh has infused them with a giddy spirit, which leads them astray (Isa. 19.14-15).[429] The opposite to Hosea's unfaithful Ephraim, who, full of lies, even betrays Ashur by nursing relationships with Egypt (כזב ושד ירבה וברית עם־אשור יכרתו ושמן למצרים יובל, Hos. 12.2),[430] is Judah, who 'still walks with God and is faithful to the Holy One' (ויהודה עד רד עם־אל ועם־קדושים נאמן, 12.1b).[431] In the continuation (vv. 3-7), Jacob's example serves to remind Hosea's audience of what it must do, but what Ephraim has not done, although they had the tradition.[432] Macintosh's translation of 12.1b—'(and Judah) still seeks to gain the mastery with God and with the Most Holy remains immovable'[433]—allows him to interpret the verse together with vv. 3-5 as an utterance about 'the nation, which still seeks to dominate, to prevail in its dealings with God himself; it persists in its implacable striving with the Holy One and thus shares the thrusting ambition of Jacob who wrestled with God at the Jabbok'.[434] Macintosh's interpretation is based on a translation of Hosea which makes Jacob and not the angel the subject of בכה ויתחנן־לו (Hos. 12.5a).[435] Although common in translations, the poetic ambiguities of Hosea's text do not give clear evidence that the author is in conflict with Genesis about who begs whom (cf. Gen. 32.27). It might be that Jacob is rebuked for his insistence and advised to give up the struggle, but the narrative might as well be used as an illustration of what the gifts of faithfulness are.[436] In the Genesis tradition, although wounded,

428.   Notice the Immanuel allusion here.

429.   Laato's reference to Isa. 29.11-12 (*About Zion I Will Not Be Silent*, pp. 97, 117) does not fit the context. The spirit of lethargy (cf. also Gen. 2.21; 15.12; 1 Sam. 26.12; Job 4.13; 33.15), which makes the people look drunk, does not belong to the hardening motif, but to the salvation motif: hidden behind prophets and seers as those hidden in chambers (Isa. 26.20), Yahweh's day of wrath shall pass over those who in the future shall see and hear what is written in the book (Isa. 29.17-24 [especially v. 18]). Isa. 28.7-13's priests and prophets are exactly not in 'deep *tardema*', they *are* drunk because of beer and wine! The closest parallel to Isa. 29.9-10 is Daniel's deep sleep, when he receives messages he could not otherwise understand; cf. Dan. 8.18; 10.9.

430.   A.A. Macintosh, *A Critical and Exegetical Commentary on Hosea* (Edinburgh: T. & T. Clark, 1997), p. 478.

431.   English translation following the NRSV. The text is problematic, as commentators notice, and the utterance could be understood negatively as a criticism of following idols (אלים) and cult prostitutes (קדושים). Hosea's terminology and thematic in general, however, suggests that the utterance should be understood positively; cf. H.W. Wolff, *Dodekapropheton 1: Hosea* (BKAT, 14/1; Neukirchen–Vluyn: Neukirchener Verlag, 1961), pp. 271-73.

432.   The scholarly debates of whether Jacob is presented positively or negatively must be sought in relevant literature. Here I am aware that Hosea's text offers both possibilities, which might mean that the ambiguity is intentional.

433.   Macintosh, *Hosea*, p. 473.

434.   Macintosh, *Hosea*, p. 475.

435.   Macintosh, *Hosea*, pp. 483, 485; so also E.K. Holt, *Prophesying the Past: The Use of Israel's History in the Book of Hosea* (JSOTSup, 194; Sheffield: Sheffield Academic Press, 1995), pp. 35-36.

436.   The translation of Hos. 12.4 depends on whether one regards the term עקב to have negative connotations or to be neutral. The Greek form ἐπτέρνισεν of the nomen πτέρνα ('heel') is

Jacob is blessed (Gen. 32.30). Although having seen God face to face, he saved his life (כי־ראיתי אלהים פנים אל־פנים ותנצל נפשי, Gen. 32.31), as did Job after his struggle with the Almighty (ועתה עיני ראתך, Job 42.5). Tradition is invoked to remind the audience from where it came,[437] namely, that Yahweh found Israel in Bethel and spoke with us there. The uncertain plural עמנו has the possibility of constituting Hosea's audience as Jacob, who should turn to the god whom Hosea calls יהוה אלהי הצבאות ('Yahweh God of the armies', Hos. 12.6).[438]

This single appearance of the Zebaoth title in Hosea has made commentators suggest that it was a late insertion.[439] It is, however, more likely that Hosea gives the name to Israel's unnamed god (Gen. 32.30), whom he identifies with Jerusalem's god in a passage addressing Judah. Hosea's lack of clear subjects also makes this passage problematic to interpret.[440] That Beth-el, which Hosea elsewhere calls Beth-Aven (Hos. 4.15; 10.5),[441] cannot be the place to seek God,[442] suggests that Hos. 12.5b-6a (with Gen. 35.7; Jer. 48.13; Amos 3.14) plays with the ambiguity that Beth-el can be the name of a place and of a god.[443] If Bethel is a late Aramaean god,[444] invoked also by an Assyrian king as a supreme god of the region with his sanctuary in Bethel (Beitin),[445] his linguistic connection with the biblical house of

---

of no help as also this term can have ambiguous meanings (cf. LXX Gen. 27.36 and Ps. 40.10). Hosea's reference to Jacob's fight (Gen. 33.26-33), which in Genesis is placed between Jacob's fear of meeting Esau and his and Esau's encounter, which ends peacefully, might suggest that Hosea argues for a peaceful solution to Judah's prevailing over Ephraim.

437. Holt, *Prophesying the Past*, p. 43.

438. Macintosh, *Hosea*, pp. 487, 489-91; Holt, *Prophesying the Past*, p. 45.

439. E.g. Wolff, *Dodekapropheton 1*. However, if one posits an eight-century dating of Hosea, most of the book is a late insertion!

440. For various possibilities, see Holt, *Prophesying the Past*, p. 38.

441. Translated as 'house of deception/nothingness/iniquity'; LXX: οἶκος ὠν.

442. 'Do not go up to the house of iniquity' (Hos. 4.15 which adds Gilgal); 'Shout at the house of iniquity' (Hos. 5.8 which adds Gibeah and Ramah); Amos 1.5; 5.5-6; 8.14.

443. S. Ribichini, 'Baetyl βαίτυλος', in *DDD²*, pp. 157-59. Although believed to be an old Semitic deity, it is not firmly attested in script before the seventh century BCE, where it appears in an Akkadian tablet embodying the text of a treaty consummated between Esarhaddon of Assyria and Baal, king of Tyre, c. 675 BCE (*ANET*, p. 534a). To preserve inviolate this compact, the great gods of heaven and earth, the gods of Assyria, the gods of Akkad and the gods of Eber-nari (= Syria) are enjoined. One of the great gods of Eber-nari so implicated was the god Bethel (Akkad). dBa-a-a-ti-DINGER.MEŠ= *Bayt-'il* = Bethel. The relevant imprecation reads: 'May Bethel and 'Anath-Bethel deliver you to a man-eating lion'; cf. E.R. Dalglish, 'Bethel (Deity)', in *ABD*, I, pp. 706-10. In the Elephantine papyri, we find references to the gods Bethel, Eshembethel, Herem-bethel and the goddess 'Anath-Bethel (*CAP* 22.1, 123–25), as well as theophoric elements in personal names (cf. also Zech. 7.2). In the third century CE, the deity is attested in Greek inscriptions from Syria.

444. K. van der Toorn, 'Anat-Yahu, Some Other Deities, and the Jews of Elephantine', *Numen* 39 (1992), pp. 80-101 (85); cf. Ribichini, 'Baetyl Βαίτυλος', p. 158

445. The importance of this border city (10.5 miles north of Jerusalem), which, after its assumed destruction in the late eigth century, was rebuilt in late Assyrian times as a major cult site, experiencing an almost continuous prosperity to well into the Roman period—with no destruction during the Babylonian conquest and only a minor decline in the Persian period—should not be ignored.

Jacob at Bethel might imply a polemic against Northern Israelite suzerainty in Assyrian, Babylonian, Persian and perhaps also Hellenistic times down to the partly independent Judaean state of the second century BCE. While this interpretation is quite possible regarding Hosea, Genesis 32–35's Bethel is exactly not Beitin, but Bethel/Luz,[446] which is always on Mt Gerizim in Samaritan traditions.[447] A possible conflation of Gerizim and Bethel as well as intertextual plays on Heliopolis traditions[448] must be kept in mind.

In such cases, Beth-el, or the god in Bethel, tells Jacob (and 'us') to seek the god, whom they shall address: 'Yahweh, God of the Armies, known as Yahweh' (יהוה אלהי הצבאות יהוה זכרו).[449] Just as Micah's single reference to Yahweh Zebaoth occurs in a passage 'quoting' Isaiah, so is Hos. 12.5-6's single occurrence of the term found in a passage having close affinities with Amos 3.13-14's אדני יהוה אלהי התבאות, which warns Jacob's House that 'on the day of my punishment (ביום פקדי),[450] [because of] Israel's sins against me, I will punish the altars of Bethel (ופקדתי על־מזבחות בית־אל)'.[451] Hosea 10.15's בשחר plays intertextually with the Jacob narrative's theme of the rising sun (Gen. 32.24, 26) as a sign of destruction or blessing; with Gen. 19.15's sunrise destruction of Sodom and Gomorra, which spares Lot's family; with Josh. 6.15's destruction of Jericho at sunrise, which spares Rahab; with Jonah 4's unjust prophet, who wants to die because the Ninevites believed the oracle and were spared (Jon. 3.5-10), which the Sodomites (Gen. 19.14, 26) and the Israelites (Amos 9.10) did not. The dawn, a sign of blessing, as is also the morning dew and the silent rain for those who repent (Hos. 6.1-3), turns into its opposite and pronounces destruction and extinction for the unfaithful of Ephraim and Judah (Hos. 6.4-6; 7.13).[452] This is the book of Joel's Valley of Jehoshaphat, a day of judgment and destruction for the enemies of Yahweh's people (Joel 4); a day when, like twilight (כשחר), the mighty armies (עם רב ועצום, 2.2) signify the presence of Yahweh's day (יום יהוה) as a day of destruction from the Almighty (כשד משדי, 1.15).[453] For repentant Judah and Jerusalem with its Israelites (4.16), the day is offered as a day of salvation and a day of blessing (2.13-14).[454]

As Hos. 12.6 is the only case of Zebaoth in Hosea and, because its appearance is presented in a way similar to Amos' determined form of Zebaoth with prefixed

---

446. Against A. de Pury, *Promesse divine et légende cultuelle dans le cycle de Jacob: Genèse 28 et les traditions patriarchales* (2 vols.; Paris: J. Gabalda, 1975), II, pp. 564, 580-81.

447. See further Chapter 4 below.

448. Hjelm, *Samaritans and Early Judaism*, pp. 56, 228-32, 240-42, and 'Cult Centralization as a Device of Cult Control', *SJOT* 13/2 (1999), pp. 298-309.

449. Hos. 12.6; Exod. 3.15 (זה שמי לעולם וזה זכרי לדר דר), and Isa. 26.8; זכר about God without שם: Pss. 6.6; 102.13; 135.13.

450. Same verb as in Hos. 12.3b.

451. Cf. Hos. 10.15 (LXX οἶκος τοῦ Ισραηλ); Exod. 32.34.

452. Cf. also Amos 5.8-9.

453. Cf. Isa. 13.6 against Babylon.

454. The theme is well known from Egyptian texts. Both Thutmosis III and Merneptah gain their decisive victories at sunrise. In Akhenaton's hymn for Aten, the Pharaoh is the rising sun, who tames the lions of chaos prowling at night. The day of destruction as a day of shalom; cf. Hjelm and Thompson, 'Merneptah', pp. 10-11.

–ה,[455] which we find in no other book of the Hebrew Bible, we might be justified in thinking that the Hosea passage relies on Amos and not the opposite. The phrase mentioning Yahweh, whose name is Yahweh Zebaoth (יהוה אלהי־צבאות שמו, Amos 4.13; 5.27) is found also in Isaiah and Jeremiah.[456] In all those texts, Yahweh's qualities as warrior for Israel and Judah, in his role of creator and destroyer, elector and rejecter, liberator and re-creator, are thematized. As it was Yahweh Zebaoth, creator of space and time (Isa. 51.15-16; Jer. 31.35), who elected Jacob-Israel (Isa. 48.1-2, 12; Jer. 10.16 par. 51.19), it is Yahweh Zebaoth who creates Zion as 'my people' (Isa. 51.16) when he destroys the nations of Egypt (Jer. 46.18), Moab (48.15) and Babylon (50.34; 51.47) in his redemption of Israel, Judah and Jerusalem. Isaiah 54's vision of redeemed Jerusalem as Yahweh Zebaoth's wife (Isa. 54.5-6), rejected and taken back, is a vision of recreation after the flood, of children taught by Yahweh and having 'great peace'[457] (וכל־בניך למודייהוה ורב שלום בניך) or 'great prosperity'[458] (Isa. 54.13). The NRSV translation bears clearer allusions to the closure of the book of Job than does the KJV translation.

The remnant, the prophets argue, is the continuation—the pregnant woman waiting for Yahweh to wake up, to give strength to those without strength (Isa. 40.28-31), to be with his people as Immanuel (Isa. 7.14; 8.8)—the opposite of the devouring destructive god with whom Abraham quarrelled about Sodom and Gomorra, and with whom Moses argued about the Exodus generation.[459] The children born will be those experiencing another tribulation, that of the exile (Mic. 4.10), from which comes a new creation and a people redeemed by Yahweh, the Holy One of Israel, whose name is Yahweh Zebaoth (Isa. 47.4; 54.5). With that creation comes the birth that finally answers Hezekiah's cry. Yahweh's answer comes from the temple: 'Should I bring to the cervical opening and not bring forth? (האני אשביר ולא אוליד) or 'should I who cause to bring forth, shut the womb?' (אם־אני המוליד ועצרתי, Isa. 66.9). And we could here continue with Yahweh's question about Hos. 13.14's unwise children: 'should I ransom them from the realm of Sheol, redeem them from death?' Isaiah's children born are those 'conceived' by

---

455. Also MT Amos 6.14 (> LXX*) and 9.5; LXX: κύριος ὁ θεὸς ὁ παντοκράτωρ; also LXX Amos 3.13; 4.13; 5.8, 14, 15, 16, 27; 9.5, 15; (Nah. 2.14; 3.5;) Zech. 10.3; Mal. 2.16.

456. Isa. 47.4; 48.2; 51.15; 54.5; Jer. 10.16; 31.35; 32.18; 46.18; 48.15; 50.34; 51.19, 57 (most of these phrases are missing in the LXX Jeremiah: 10.16; 26.18; 28.19; 31.15). It occurs in LXX Jer. 27.34 and 38.36 = MT Jer. 50.34 and 31.35 formalistically paralleling Amos 4.13 and 5.27, which do not have determinative ὁ). Of the listed occurrences, MT Isa. 51.15; Jer. 31.35; 48.15 par. Amos 4.13 and 5.27 form a refrain.

457. So KJV; LXX: πολλῇ εἰρήνῃ; Vulgate: *multitudinem pacis*.

458. So NRSV.

459. Gitay, *Isaiah and his Audience*, p. 143, interprets the Immanuel prophecy to be a 'word of destruction rather than salvation', because of the oracles of destruction joined to it and the mention of curds and honey, interpreted as a threat rather than a blessing. In the Hezekiah narrative, however, the sparseness of the country (Isa. 37.30) is given as a sign of salvation for the remnant that survives, and it seems to me that the Immanuel prophecy of a child living on food provided by Yahweh (Isa. 7.15; cf. Isa. 7.21-22; Deut. 32.13) exactly pronounces salvation for those who are left in the midst of the country (כל־הנותר בקרב הארץ, Isa. 7.22).

Yahweh Zebaoth, when he takes Daughter Zion as his wife (Isa. 54.1-7; 62.4-5).[460] For the children lost (51.18), new children will be born as Yahweh's children (65.23). Eschatological as this consolation is, the author wants his reader to face imminent threat in the confidence that Yahweh brings salvation. He also wants his reader to identify this consolation as stemming from Jerusalem (66.13, 20), as it did in former times when the present remnant was 'born'.[461] The text plays magnificently with narrative patterns of divine intervention in the birth of a legitimate successor, such as found in, for example, Sarah's conception of Isaac after her captivity in Abimelech's house (Gen. 20.17–21.2) or Bathsheba's conception of Solomon after the death of the son (1 Sam. 24–25), about whose Davidic paternity no-one could be certain.

The closing of Isaiah parallels its opening, as several scholars have pointed out.[462] In the imagery of Genesis 19's destruction of Sodom and Gomorra, Jerusalem, Zion's daughter, likened with a shelter in the vineyard (כסכה בכרם), a lodging for the night during difficulties ([463]כמלונה במקשה) and a city under siege (כעיר נצורה), is spared because of its remnant (Isa. 1.8-9). The book of Isaiah's inter-textual play with the Hezekiah narrative's king of Ashur, who has come to the most distant quarters for the night ([464]ואבוא מרום קצו, Isa. 37.24) might not be intentional. מלון as a night shelter for soldiers, however, suggests that the author consciously contrasted Zion's life-giving shelter function with the Assyrian camp, in which the angel of death brought destruction (Isa. 37.36). However glorious the salvation in the book of Isaiah is, its temporary function[465] parallels 'historiographical' discourse of a second tribulation, which only finds its closure in the return, geographically, theologically and metaphorically, to a certain place, a certain god and a certain teaching (Isa. 2.1-5; 4.1-6; 35.8-10; 62.10-12). Paralleling the Exodus tradition, Isaiah's remnant, brought out of Ashur, experiences the purifying function of the desert before the new entrance in the Promised Land by the hand of Yahweh *Zebaoth*.

In Hosea, these children of the living god (בני אל־חי), Judah and Israel together (Hos. 2.1-3), are the fruits of supersessionism's rejected mother as unfaithful wife. As in Jer. 3.14-20, this new relationship creates a possibility of commonness, a healing of the breach created by the removal of the ark (3.16). In the role of a father for Israel (31.9), Yahweh Zebaoth turns Israel's fate (בשובי את־שבותם, 31.23). In this utopian turning and return, all Israel's past is reversed in an allusive removal of Jacob and Esau's conflict, and of Abel and Cain's, to a situation when farmers and

---

460. Cf. Hos. 2.16-25.

461. Laato, *About Zion I Will Not Be Silent*, p. 113.

462. W.A.M. Beuken, 'Isaiah Chapter LXV–LXVI: Trito-Isaiah and the Closure of the Book of Isaiah', in J.A. Emerton (ed.), *Congress Volume: Leuven 1989* (VTSup, 43; Leiden: E.J. Brill, 1991), pp. 204-21; R.F. Melugin, 'Figurative Speech and the Reading of Isaiah 1 as Scripture', in Melugin and Sweeney (eds.), *New Visions of Isaiah*, pp. 282-305.

463. It is possible that this is a reference to a cucumber field. Intertextually, however, it is more probable that מקשה refers to the difficult birth, as in Gen. 35.16-17: ויהי בהקשתה בלדתה.

464. 2 Kgs 19.23: מלון.

465. Laato, *About Zion I Will Not Be Silent*, pp. 76, 88.

shepherds live together, Yahweh satisfies the weary soul and replenishes every languishing soul (הרויתי נפש עיפה וכל־נפש דאבה מלאתי, Jer. 31.24-25). In Isa. 51.2, it is Abraham and Sarah's singular beginning which is invoked as an example of how Yahweh blessed and increased him. As Abraham and Jacob received the blessing of becoming a great people (Gen. 12.1; 35.11), and Moses was told to tell 'the house of Jacob and the Israelites' that they could become a kingdom of priests and a holy people' (ממלכת בהנים וגוי קדוש, Exod. 19.6),[466] so Yahweh pronounces to Zion: 'You are my people' (Isa. 51.16).[467] With Isa. 61.6 and 62.12, this people shall be called 'Yahweh's priests, servants for our God' (כהני יהוה...משרת[468] אלהינו) and 'a holy people, the redeemed of Yahweh' (עמ־הקדש[469] גאולי יהוה). In Numbers' competition between Korah, Dathan and Abiram and between Moses and Aaron, the question of holiness is a question of election: יהוה האיש אשר־יבחר יהוה הוא הקדוש ('and the man Yahweh chooses, he is the holy one', Num. 16.7).

While Isaiah's eschatological children of Zion as Yahweh's people includes the foreigners (Isa. 56.3-8; 66.18-23), Jeremiah and Ezekiel's people are the families and kingdoms of Israel and Judah (e.g. Jer. 30.20; 31.1, 10-11, 17; 33.7-8; Ezek. 37.21-22). While Isaiah's people will become a holy people with Yahweh as king, Jeremiah, Ezekiel and Hosea's people will return to past traditions with king, priests and levites, temple and offerings (Jer. 33; Ezek. 37; Hos. 3). The beginning is not absolute, but offers a new fate for the Davidic kingdom, this time in undisputed and united Jerusalem. This Jerusalem has been affirmed as the place for Yahweh's dwelling, the place he has chosen, as he chose Moses in the book of Numbers' competition about the true priest and prophet. It is Yahweh, the temple and the priests, which shall be holy[470] not the people.

With this, we are able to continue in our next chapters the examination of questions of the Law, questions which had been raised at the end of Chapter 2. Since the Law is the foundation of the Mosaic covenant, a possible Davidic covenant, a ניר דוד, must be considered as a replacement of the Mosaic covenant. Does Isaiah 55's closure in an eschatological 'new Jerusalem'[471] belong to the old template, or is the Davidic covenant distinct from the Sinaitic?[472] To these questions must be linked another question—namely, that of the communities which shaped, collected and authorized our texts. Is it possible to see the same community behind the Pentateuch, the Former Prophets, Isaiah, Jeremiah and Ezekiel? If or if not, where must we look for the social identity of our authors?

---

466.   Cf. Lev. 11.44-45; 19.2; 20.7, 26; Num. 15.40; 16.3, 7; Jer. 2.3
467.   Cf. Jer. 24.7; 30.22; Ezek. 11.20; 14.11; 34.30; 36.28; 37.23, 27.
468.   Cf. Joel 1.9, 13; 2.17.
469.   Deut. 7.6; 14.2, 21; 26.19; 28.9;
470.   Cf. Jer. 31.23, 40; Ezek. 20.40-41; 28.25; 36.25; 37.28; 40–48.
471.   H.C. Spykerboer, 'Isaiah 55.1-5: The Climax of Deutero-Isaiah: An Invitation to Come to the New Jerusalem', in Vermeylen (ed.), *The Book of Isaiah*, pp. 357-59.
472.   Levenson, *Sinai and Zion*, p. 100.

Chapter 4

DEUTERONOMIST VS. YAHWIST: AGREEMENT AND CONFLICT IN JEWISH AND SAMARITAN TEXT TRADITIONS

1. *Tradition History According to Van Seters: Some Considerations*

In his *Life of Moses*, J. van Seters, following H.H. Schmid,[1] argues that

> the Yahwist has attempted to counter the whole thrust of Dtn/Dtr emphasis on the law and divine judgment as a consequence of disobedience by his preoccupation with divine promise and favour to the fathers and mercy as a mitigation of judgment. The promise supersedes the law as the basis of the covenant, and in the face of covenant annulment through violation of the first and second Commandments it is renewed through God's forgiveness (Exod. 34.9-10). For J the role of Moses is less that of admonishing and instructing the people in the law and more that of divine grace and mercy.[2]

In this characterization of the law lies an implied assertion of a contrast between the Shechem covenant as conditional and the Abraham and David covenants as unconditional.[3] Using Abraham as an example of what righteousness means (Gen. 26.5; cf. 22.18), J's keeping of God's 'commandments, statutes and laws' has become a matter of righteous behaviour rather than a commitment to keep certain laws laid down in the Deuteronomic law code.[4] In Van Seters' view, J's theology 'has had a major impact on Second Isaiah', which expresses the same universalistic—and less cultic—Judaism than the 'restrictive nationalism' of the Deuteronomistic Historian.[5]

While, the classic documentary hypothesis operated with a twofold movement —first, a movement from an unconditional covenant in the JE stratum to a conditional one in the D stratum and then a revival, a recalling of the unconditional promise in exilic and post-exilic literature[6]—Van Seters' tradition-historical conclusion

---

1. H.H. Schmid, 'Vers une théologie du Pentateuque', in A. de Pury (ed.), *Le Pentateuque en question* (Geneva: Labor et Fides, 1989), pp. 361-86.
2. Van Seters, *Life of Moses*, pp. 465-66. Van Seters (p. 468), says of the J source: 'The Yahwist's history, which includes the primeval history, the patriarchs and the life of Moses, was the work of an ancient Israelite (or more specifically, Judaean) scholar living among the exiles in Babylonia'.
3. Van Seters, *Life of Moses*, p. 467; cf. also *idem, Prologue to History*, p. 242.
4. Van Seters, *Life of Moses*, p. 467.
5. Van Seters, *Life of Moses*, p. 468.
6. Cf. the surveys in, among others, J. Högenhaven, *Den gamle pagt: en introduktion til den nyere debat om pagten i det Gamle Testamente* (Tekst og Tolkning, 8; Copenhagen: Akademisk

removes the first development and operates with a single movement in late pre-exilic and exilic times.[7] Needless to say, the documentary hypothesis secured an early dating for the patriarchal traditions, although at the same time it condemned them to an inexplicable 'oblivion' for some 200–300 years.[8] For tradition history, similar problems of 'oblivion' have arisen. Although the existence of oral traditions predating the written material has been one of tradition history's main assumptions, no studies have been able to establish the character of such assumed traditions.[9] Taken together, the inevitable conclusion must be that neither documentary nor tradition history have accounted for the lack of interest in the patriarchs in the Deuteronomistic History and the so-called pre-exilic Prophets. While Noth assumed that the Deuteronomistic History did not form part of a common work (Genesis–2 Kings) because there was 'no sign of Deuteronomistic editing in Genesis–Numbers',[10] scholars like Schmid[11] and Rendtorff[12] argued for the opposite: that Genesis–Numbers were markedly Deuteronomistic.[13]

Forlag, 1989); E.W. Nicholson, *God and His People: Covenant and Theology in the Old Testament* (Oxford: Clarendon Press, 1986); Van Seters, *Prologue to History*, pp. 215-26. The complex history of Pentateuch research must be consulted in recent publications; for example, C. Houtman, *Inleiding in de Pentateuch* (Kampen: Kok, 1980 [German translation: *Der Pentateuch: Die Geschichte seiner Erforschung neben einer Auswertung* (Kampen: Kok, 1994)]); R.N. Whybray, *The Making of the Pentateuch: A Methodological Study* (JSOTSup, 53; Sheffield: JSOT Press, 1987); E.W. Nicholson, *The Pentateuch in the Twentieth Century: The Legacy of Julius Wellhausen* (Oxford: Clarendon Press, 1998).

    7.   Van Seters, *Prologue to History*, p. 222, and *idem*, *Life of Moses*, pp. 286-89; so also to some extent L. Perlitt, *Bundestheologie im Alten Testament* (WMANT, 36; Neukirchen–Vluyn: Neukirchener Verlag, 1969); Högenhaven, *Den gamle pagt*.

    8.   Högenhaven, *Den gamle pagt*, pp. 69-75; Perlitt, *Bundestheologie im Alten Testament*, pp. 55-77, 152-55; Nicholson, *God and His People* (*passim*); Römer, *Israels Väter*, pp. 1-8.

    9.   Cf. Whybray, *Making of the Pentateuch*, pp. 133-219, 235-36.

    10.   Noth, *Überlieferungsgeschichtliche Studien*, p. 13; cf. Whybray, *Making of the Pentateuch*, p. 223. Davies, *Scribes and Schools*, p. 95: 'Noth's reconstruction is seriously wrong in its dating of the process, but may well be correct in determining that Deuteronomy is not the core of the Mosaic canon's evolution. For while some traces of Deuteronomic language are found here and there in Exodus, there is little evidence of Exodus–Numbers having been influenced by Deuteronomy—or by each other.'

    11.   H.H. Schmid, *Sogenannte Jahwist*, pp. 166-67.

    12.   R. Rendtorff, *Das überlieferungsgeschichtliche Problem des Pentateuchs* (BZAW, 147; Berlin: W. de Gruyter, 1977), p. 170, and *idem*, *Theologie des Alten Testaments: Ein kanonischer Entwurf* (Neukirchen–Vluyn: Neukirchener Verlag, 1998), p. 11.

    13.   Cf. Whybray, *Making of the Pentateuch*, pp. 223-24. We must add Perlitt, *Bundestheologie im Alten Testament*; M. Rose, *Deuteronomist und Jahwist: Untersuchungen zu den Berührungspunkten beider Literaturwerke* (ATANT, 67; Zürich: Theologischer Verlag, 1981); E. Blum, *Studien zur Komposition des Pentateuch* (BZAW, 189; Berlin: W. de Gruyter, 1990), pp. 101, 165-66; J. Blenkinsopp, *The Pentateuch: An Introduction to the First Five Books of the Bible* (Garden City, NY: Doubleday, 1992). Van Seters (*Prologue to History* and *Life of Moses*), however, stressed that Deuteronomistic influence was due to inspiration rather than redaction; cf. *idem*, 'Is There Evidence of a Dtr Redaction in the Sinai Pericope (Exodus 19–24, 32–34)', in Shearing and McKenzie (eds.), *Those Elusive Deuteronomists*, pp. 160-70: 'There is, therefore, no dtr redaction in the Tetrateuch'. For a critique of Van Seters, see J. Blenkinsopp, 'Deuteronomic Contribution to the Narrative in Genesis–Numbers: A Test Case', in Shearing and McKenzie (eds.), *Those*

Van Seters' argument about the relationship between J and 'Second Isaiah' is in itself interesting, since it implies the existence of an author one can call Second-Isaiah, who furthermore must be subordinate to J. Recent works on the composition of the book of Isaiah, however, has greatly challenged assumptions of a composite tri-partite Isaiah resulting from authorial and editorial activity.

Although Van Seters argues that the 'Yahwist's history from creation to the death of Moses was not intended to supersede the DtrH, but to provide it with a prologue that would give to it a new perspective and direction',[14] the hermeneutic implications of Van Seters' statement must be that J, in fact, supersedes D and that his Judges–2 Kings must be read forwards, while his Yahwist must be read backwards from Joshua 24.[15] That being the case, we cannot avoid the further conclusion that the closure of Genesis–Joshua, from the promise of the land to the entrance into that land, parallels a similar opening to an insecure future as found in the books of Ezra and Nehemiah.[16] Under the threat of reiterating the sins of their pre-exilic fathers,[17] post-exilic Jews must now reiterate the act of separating themselves from all their neighbours, the women they have intermarried and the children begotten by them. Sending away these wives and children, the narratives demonstrate the horrific result of simplistic obedience to the Law.

The reference to the Law of Moses[18] as constitutional for the demand to separate is as critical as it is positive. Wives and children, now transformed into widows and orphans, strangers to be taken care of, are as challenging to the just mind as are the foreign women. The prophecy of Moses 'that the mistreatment of foreigners, or of widows and orphans, will make widows and orphans of Israel's own wives and children,[19] finds its fulfilment in Ezra's story'.[20] Disillusionment with the reader's implicit expectations has changed the narrative into never-ending story.[21]

Elusive Deuteronomists, pp. 84-115 (112): the Sinai pericope is 'a Deuteronomic account of national origins'.

14. Van Seters, 'Joshua 24 & the Problem of Tradition', p. 154; so also Rose, *Deuteronomist und Jahwist*, p. 327; C. Levin, *Der Jahwist* (FRLANT, 157; Göttingen: Vandenhoeck & Ruprecht, 1993), pp. 430-35.

15. Van Seters, *Prologue to History*, p. 332: 'In ancient historiography, the "prologue" or *archaiologia* set forth the ancient background for the historical work, and, in doing so, often laid the principles by which the history was to be understood. By his presentation of the origins of humanity and that of the people's ancestry, the Yahwist has given a radical revision and reinterpretation of the national tradition.'

16. Cf. the parallelism between Josh. 24 and Neh. 9–10, mentioned above in Chapter 3.

17. Ezra 9.7; Neh. 13.26.

18. Neh. 13.1; cf. 10.29-30; Ezra 10.3.

19. Exod. 22.20-23.

20. Thompson, 'Holy War at the Center of Biblical Theology', p. 233. In contrast stands 1 Esdras' harmonious narrative in which 'the book comes to a full circle' in the great celebration that follows the reading of the Law; see K. de Troyer, 'A Lost Hebrew Vorlage? A Closer Look at the Temple Builder in 1 Esdras', in *idem, Rewriting the Sacred Text: What the Old Greek Texts Tell Us about the Literary Growth of the Bible* (Text Critical Studies, 4; Atlanta: Society of Biblical Literature, 2003), pp. 91-126 (120).

21. Thompson, 'Holy War at the Center of Biblical Theology', p. 234.

Asking for mercy on their own behalf (Neh. 13.14, 22, 31; Ezra 9.15; 10.3), the 'Moses' of this new Jerusalem show no mercy for the people they are in charge of, whether it is their wives, their children or the survivors given into their hands (Ezra 9.13). In contrast, the Moses of the wilderness stories offers his own life for the sake of the salvation of the people (Exod. 32.32) and asks for mercy on their behalf (Exod. 32.30-32; Num. 14.14-19). Demonstrating the futility of man-made interpretations, the Law they transgress is not the Mosaic law of the Pentateuch, but the epitome of the law to which they have just submitted themselves (Neh. 10.31-40)[22] and the interpretation given by Ezra and those who tremble before the Law (Ezra 10.3). The question implied might not be a choice between 'righteous behaviour and a commitment to keep certain laws laid down in the Deuteronomic law code', as suggested by Van Seters concerning the Yahwist and the Deuteronomistic History.[23] The question implied might rather be between one and another interpretation. Recalling Yahweh's promise (Neh. 9.8, 23, 32) and his mercy (Neh. 9.17, 19, 27, 28, 31) as a foundation for the new covenant, the author of the book of Nehemiah provocatively challenges his implied audience with the question of whether the Law is given as a curse or a blessing. Does man live by the observances (Neh. 9.29), or are they a threat to life? Euphemistically transforming the Torah's commandment of not worshipping other gods into a question of marriage with foreign women (Neh. 9.17, 19, 27, 28, 31), the shortcomings of both language and theology have forced Ezra and Nehemiah's observant Jew to cut himself off from Yahweh's mercy and blessing. Having 'married foreign women' for generations (Ezra 9.1-2, 13-14),[24] there will be no one left to stay. The narrative solution is intentionally false, creating a separation that is not possible. Genesis' placement of people in each their own regions,[25] is something to begin with not to reiterate.

Here, we are well into questions about the formation of the existent canon. This formation, we can assume, served the interest of a single group; but what about the individual books? Why do we assume that the authors of the so-called Yahwistic and Deuteronomistic Histories shared common interests or came from related circles—separated *only* chronologically—even though their theology differed? Whether Van Seters' Yahwist 'gave a new orientation and perspective' to the Deuteronomistic History, thereby stressing the unconditional promise given to the fathers, or whether Weinfeld's Deuteronomist 'made both the grant of the Land and the promise of a dynasty conditional on observance of the Law',[26] both scholars base their conclusions on an existent canon, without considering whether these two groups of texts, in fact, came originally from the same religious community.[27] The

---

22. This epitome thematizes the transgressions mentioned in Neh. 13.
23. Van Seters, *Life of Moses*, p. 467.
24. Cf. Thompson, 'Holy War at the Center of Biblical Theology', p. 250.
25. Hjelm, 'Brothers Fighting Brothers'.
26. Weinfeld, *Deuteronomy and the Deuteronomic School*, p. 81.
27. Even Van Seters' argument for a single author rather than a school assumes that this author is to be found among those exiled from Jerusalem, who had suffered the fate presented in the DtrH. So also von Rad, *Theologie des Alten Testament*; H. Vorländer, *Die Entstehungszeit des jehowistischen Geschichtswerkes* (Europäische Hochschulschriften, Series 23, 109; Frankfurt: Peter

differences might not belong so much to chronology as to different religious communities,[28] for instance Samaritans and Jews, Sadducees, Pharisees, Essenes, Hasidim, Babylonian or Alexandrian Jews. Such differences certainly do play a role regarding the 'Deuteronomistic' and 'Chronistic Histories', which in Samaritan variants are quite different from the Masoretic text in *BHS*, though at the same time reflecting knowledge of traditions found therein. Of these differences, we find that some agree with Dead Sea Scroll biblical texts, some with Old Greek variants, some with Eupolemus as well as other 'Jewish' Pseudepigrapha and some with Josephus, to mention only the most widely known variants.

Given the discussions of the status of various scriptures between, for example, Samaritans and Jews and Sadducees and Pharisees in the centuries around the turn of the era, we should be cautious in assuming that the collection that was shared by all these groups as canonical—namely, the Pentateuch—originated with the group which wrote the books of the the the canon. The differences between the so-called Deuteronomistic History (with or without Deuteronomy) and the Pentateuch (with or without an additional book of Joshua) might be a difference between Jerusalem and Samaria. While one can easily perceive a Genesis–Deuteronomy, a Genesis–Joshua[29] or a Genesis–Numbers and Joshua[30] as comprehensive literary units, a Deuteronomy–2 Kings does not make much sense as an independent narrative unit without a prologue of some sort.[31] Where does Deuteronomy begin? Or does it begin?

As I have previously argued, the issue might, after all, not be *when* did Samaritans form their own version of the Pentateuch, but *why* and *when* did Jerusalem 'adopt' a 'Samaritan' Pentateuch'.[32] If it did, the question would then be: Did Samaritans and Jews agree to 'write' a common work based on the theology of returned 'Nehemiah Jews', with Deuteronomy as its latest addition, as has been

Lang, 1978); Rose, *Deuteronomist und Jahwist*; Levin, *Jahwist*. In fact, the same is also claimed by E.T. Mullen, *Ethnic Myths and Pentateuchal Foundations: A New Approach to the Formation of the Pentateuch* (Atlanta, GA: Scholars Press, 1997), though he maintains that the identity is ideologically rather than genealogically based (pp. 71-86).

28. Lemche, *Early Israel*, pp. 375-77 (376): 'It would be much more natural to assume that a number of different theological movements were active in this period [the Exile] which must have existed independently of each other to the extent that each group appears to have had its own special interests'.

29. S. Tengström, *Die Hexateucherzählung: eine literaturgeschichtliche Studie* (CBOTS, 7; Lund, C.W.K. Gleerup, 1976), argued for a coherence of these traditions based on a promise–fulfilment scheme, running from Gen. 12 to Josh. 24.

30. Found for instance in the Samaritan book of Joshua published by Juynboll (see below, pp. 186-87), which connects Numbers with Joshua, passing quickly over Moses' instructions.

31. K. Schmid, *Erzväter und Exodus: Untersuchungen zur doppelten Begründung der Ursprünge Israels innerhalb der Geschichtsbücher des Alten Testaments* (WMANT, 81; Neukirchen–Vluyn: Neukirchener Verlag, 1999), pp. 36-39, reasserting the hypothesis of an Exodus tradition vs. a Patriarch tradition, which has been quite influential in German scholarship since it was first suggested by J. Wellhausen, *Prolegomena zur Geschichte Israels* (Berlin: W. de Gruyter, 1885), and K. Galling, *Die Erwählungstraditionen Israels* (Giessen: Alfred Töpelmann, 1928). Cf. also Römer, *Israels Väter*.

32. Hjelm, *Samaritans and Early Judaism*, pp. 282-84.

suggested by E. Nodet?[33] These matters are not as idle as some scholars might assume. The composite character of the Pentateuch[34] and its assumed origin in the non-monarchic milieu of Persian-Hellenistic times, rather than the Israelite kingdoms of the Iron II,[35] requires a consideration of new paradigms for its development.[36] That neither Van Seters' Yahwist nor the Former Prophets and some of the Latter Prophets 'know' each other is hardly a question to be answered solely by theories of composition history. Wellhausen's purported chronological development from prophecy to law,[37] established on an examination of the present canon, leaves no room for considering the existence of different religious societies. It rather assumes an all-Israelite state religion from the tenth century BCE!

We must keep in mind that the Pentateuch 'exists' in a more fixed form centuries before Joshua–2 Kings, also with a lower dating of both these text units. When Noth and Jepsen assumed that the author of the Deuteronomistic History was not a member of the clergy or the official intelligentsia, but someone living in Palestine who privately wrote up an assessment of the situation after 587 BCE,[38] they held the existence of 'a Tetrateuch' implicit. They also held implicit selective use of texts, non-knowledge of texts and non-access to texts. The ancient writer did not have the JB, the *BHS* or the like in front of him. It was exceedingly difficult for him to check the accuracy of a story, a passage, a phrase, or a word in a scrolled text which was not divided into chapters or verses.[39] The priority of the Exodus theme against the Patriarch theme might result from cultic influence rather than literary dependency. We shall see later (Chapter 5) that the books of Samuel are, in fact, quite autochthonous.

Suggestions of independent origin have also been made regarding JE, because of its purported 'lack of literary influence' on the Deuteronomistic History and

33. Nodet, *A Search for the Origins of Judaism*, pp. 92, 191-95, 281-89, 381.

34. K. Schmid, *Erzväter und Exodus*, p. 300: 'Der Pentateuch als Tora ist ein Kompromisswerk, das sowohl in priesterlicher als auch in deuteronomistisch-"eschatologischer" Perspektive gestaltet und lesbar ist'; Blum, *Studien zur Komposition des Pentateuchs*, pp. 356-60.

35. Blum, *Studien zur Komposition des Pentateuchs*, pp. 345-60; Blenkinsopp, *The Pentateuch*, pp. 239-43; K. Schmid, *Erzväter und Exodus*, p. 276.

36. Mullen, *Ethnic Myths and Pentateuchal Foundations*, p. 196; Davies, *Scribes and Schools*, pp. 97-99, 106.

37. Wellhausen, *Prolegomena*, pp. 3-4; cf. Nicholson, *Pentateuch*, pp. 4-6, with reference to earlier works. K. Zobel, *Prophetie und Deuteronomium: Die Rezeption prophetischer Theologie durch das Deuteronomium* (Berlin: W. de Gruyter, 1992).

38. Cf. T. Römer and A. de Pury, 'Deuteronomistic Historiography (DH): History of Research and Debated Issues', in A. de Pury, T. Römer and J.-D. Macchi (eds.), *Israel Constructs its History: Deuteronomistic Historiography in Recent Research* (JSOTSup, 306; Sheffield: Sheffield Academic Press, 2000), pp. 24-143 (52, 54) (first published as *Israël construit son histoire. L'historiographie deutéronomiste à la lumière des recherches récentes* [Le Monde de la Bible, 34; Geneva: Labor et Fides, 1996]).

39. A. Spiro, *Samaritans, Tobiads, and Judahites in Pseudo-Philo: Use and Abuse of the Bible by Polemicists and Doctrinaires* (New York: The American Academy for Jewish Research, 1951), pp. 5-13 (Spiro's book was first published as an article bearing the same title in *Proceedings of the American Academy for Jewish Research* 20 [1951], pp. 279-355).

so-called pre-exilic Prophets.[40] This purported 'ignorance' of Tetrateuch themes in so-called pre-exilic prophetic literature is, however, not as thorough as Vorländer's work concludes, since this conclusion rests on assumptions of 'post-exilic additions' in both pre-exilic and exilic Prophets.[41] Without such assumptions—which appeared to have greater validity in 1978, though they inevitably lead to circular arguments[42]—Vorländer's examination betrays no difference between so-called earlier and later Prophets. Of 47 'post-exilic additions' to the Prophets, 42 are found in pre- and exilic Prophets (Amos 9, Hos. 10, Proto-Isa. 9, Mic. 7, Ezek. 1, Jer. 6), while the remaining five are in Zechariah, Zephaniah, Malachi and Haggai. Only one reference—namely, Amos 7.16's mention of Isaac—is listed as belonging to Amos, while Amos 7.9 (which mentions the house of Isaac) is not listed at all.[43] 'Genuine' exilic and post-exilic references' to Tetrateuch themes and names count 31 (in Deutero-Isa. 16, Ezek. 11, Jer. 1 and Trito-Isa. 3).[44] If we give credit to the inconsequence of dating Jeremiah and Ezekiel together with the alleged pre-exilic Prophets Amos, Hosea, Proto-Isaiah and Micah, the lack of difference is even more striking, with 35 'pre-exilic' and 43 'exilic' and 'post-exilic' references. What we learn from Vorländer's work is that Amos, Hosea, Micah, Isaiah, Jeremiah and Ezekiel 'use' themes and names known from the Tetrateuch, while Daniel and post-exilic Minor Prophets rarely have such references![45] From distribution alone, it is still the Deuteronomistic History, without Deuteronomy–Joshua, which is most

40. Cf. Vorländer, *Entstehungszeit des jehowistischen Geschichtswerkes*, pp. 281-82; Römer, *Israels Väter*, p. 394: the Patriarch tradition reflects an 'autochthonous' theology promoted by those who stayed in the land, while Deuteronomy–2 Kings (in its first redaction) represents an 'exodus' theology originating with the exiled in Babylon. The complexities of assumptions of a once (semi-) independent Genesis, an Exodus–Numbers, a Tetrateuch, a Pentateuch, a Hexateuch, a Deuteronomistic History, an Exodus–2 Kings, a Genesis–2 Kings, must be sought in relevant literature. However useful and interesting they are, the discussions mainly demonstrate the lack of clear methodological principles for source analysis, when reconstruction of ancient texts are based mainly on form- and redaction-critical evaluation of mediaeval to modern texts. Schmid's analysis of the early reception history of Patriarch and Exodus traditions is a most needed *addendum* to the discussion (K. Schmid, *Erzväter und Exodus*, pp. 316-57), as are the numerous studies on Dead Sea Scrolls and non-Masoretic texts, especially the Old Greek variants.

41. Vorländer, *Entstehungszeit des jehowistischen Geschichtswerkes*, pp. 27-283 (especially pp. 261-83).

42. Vorländer, *Entstehungszeit des jehowistischen Geschichtswerkes*, p. 282: 'Eine ganze Reihe von Bezugnahmen auf Pentateuchstoffe in der vorexilischen Literatur wurden als sekundär erkannt, zumeist in Übereinstimmung mit der Mehrzahl der Forscher. Die Tatsache [*sic*], dass spätere Redaktoren diese Bezugnahmen eingefügt haben, beweist [*sic*] dass nach ihrer Meinung in der Botschaft der Propheten "etwas fehlte".'

43. Vorländer, *Entstehungszeit des jehowistischen Geschichtswerkes*, pp. 261-65; however, mentioned in the examination, p. 68.

44. Vorländer, *Entstehungszeit des jehowistischen Geschichtswerkes*, pp. 261-65, 283.

45. Unfortunately, we also learn that Vorländer's counting is incorrect (Tabelle A and B) and cannot be used as proof of distribution; for instance, the distribution of the eponym Jacob, who according to Vorländer's list is found in 1 Kgs 18.31; Mal. 1.2-3 and Hos. 12.4-6, 13—missing are references in Josh. 24.4, 32; 1 Sam. 12.8; 2 Kgs 17.34, just to mention the most obvious but leaving out the numerous references to Jacob as Israel not counted by Vorländer.

negligent of most of the Primary History. That Chronicles and Nehemiah 9 seem to be primary 'evidence' of the existence of Vorländer's JE[46] should not surprise us, given the chronology implied in these works as epitomes of 'history from creation to exile'.[47] In fact, according to Vorländer's list, his DtrG (without Deuteronomy) 'knows' the 'Patriarchs', the 'Exodus', the 'Sea of Reeds', the 'Golden Calf' and 'Moses', while Chronicles 'knows' the 'Patriarchs', the 'Exodus', 'Moses' and 'Aaron'. When we count references in Joshua, Judges, Samuel and Kings from Vorländer's list,[48] we still have 25 references in these books,[49] while we have only 21 in Chronicles. If there should be any *argumentum ex silentio* to be used as a method in establishing a composition history, the questions must be more sophisticated, as has been argued also by A.H.J. Gunneweg,[50] with reference to similar 'ignorance' among and of the Prophets in most of the Hebrew Bible.[51] Vorländer's conclusion that 'the earlier one moves in exilic and pre-exilic times, the less is the evidence of a knowledge of elements in the Yahwistic History',[52] in fact contradicts a late dating of Chronicles, Daniel and the Minor Prophets (apart from Amos, Hosea and Micah), none of which betray great 'knowledge' of JE themes. Vorländer's *late* dated prophetic passages, which reflect JE themes and narratives, but which employ somewhat different terminology, are considered to be late *only* because they cannot be dated earlier than JE on the basis of terminology, some of which reflects D[53] and some P, or appear as totally independent of any of these categories.[54] But if they are later than JE, why do they differ so much in style from JE as Vorländer argues? And how is JE's relationship to Deutero-Isaiah different from its relationship to these other works, since Deutero-Isaiah, according to Vorländer's analysis, shows no literary dependency on JE?[55] That some 'Tetrateuch'-passages are 'late' in

46. Vorländer, *Entstehungszeit des jehowistischen Geschichtswerkes*, p. 280.

47. K. Schmid, *Erzväter und Exodus*, pp. 302-306. Neh. 9, however, does not end in exile, but in occupation ('today we are slaves; we are slaves in the land which you gave to our fathers to eat its fruit and its riches', Neh. 9.36; Lev. 26.16-31; Deut. 28.48-57). That Neh. 9.26-31 knows 'die Richter-und Königzeit' is unquestionable, but that vv. 30-31 should refer to the Exile, so that vv. 32-37 face 'die Gegenwartige [post exilic] Untertanensituation Israels im eigenen Land' (see pp. 302-303 of Schmid's study), is less certain.

48. Simply counting, without playing redaction criticism's game, which can make everything fit.

49. There are 15 occurrences in Joshua, one in Judges and and nine in 2 Kings.

50. A.H.J. Gunneweg, 'Anmerkungen und Anfragen zur neueren Pentateuchforschung', *ThR* 50 (1985), pp. 107-31 (112-13).

51. See also, Nicholson, *Pentateuch*, pp. 158-59.

52. Vorländer, *Entstehungszeit des jehowistischen Geschichtswerkes*, p. 280: 'Je früher man zurück geht in die exilisch-vorexilische Zeit, desto spärlicher werden die Belege für eine Kenntnis der Elemente des jehowistischen Geschichtsaufrisses'.

53. For a recent discussion of earlier assumptions of Deuteronomic influence in the Prophets, see R.A. Kugler, 'The Deuteronomists and the Latter Prophets', in Shearing and McKenzie (eds.), *Those Elusive Deuteronomists*, pp. 127-44.

54. Vorländer, *Entstehungszeit des jehowistischen Geschichtswerkes*, pp. 27-260 (*passim*).

55. Vorländer, *Entstehungszeit des jehowistischen Geschichtswerkes*, pp. 33-34, 53-55, 73-74, 76, 94-97, 141, 149-51, 269, and p. 283: 'Überlegungen haben die vorangehenden Analysen das

Amos, Hosea and Micah might well be. However, it seems that chronological distinctions regarding Deuteronomic influence have been made because of theme and conviction, rather than on the basis of proper linguistic considerations.[56] A consequence of Vorländer's conclusion—that 'if JE were pre-exilic, one should expect the prophets to betray explicit literary dependency'[57]—must be that, apart from the passages mentioned in Vorländer,[58] JE is the youngest 'book' in the *entire* Bible.[59] That P presupposed JE[60] is an argument as valid as the purported non-existence of JE because of lack of explicit dependency in works prior to D. However few these direct dependencies are, the conclusion is made that JE is based on the Deuteronomistic History and that especially Deuteronomy 1–11 betrays close formalistic and thematic ties with JE.

In contrast to Vorländer, Van Seters' argument is based on the opposite premise —namely, a literary development from so-called proto-D 'Tetrateuch'-traditions in the pre-exilic Prophets', which are further elaborated in the exilic Prophets: Deutero-Isaiah, Jeremiah and Ezekiel as well as Deuteronomy (which betrays no knowledge of JE[61]), and which come into full existence in the Yahwistic material.[62] Paying little attention to several passages in Amos, Hosea, Proto-Isaiah[63] and Micah, Van Seters, in fact, avoids the problems of dating these passages, which, if dated early, would conflict with Vorländer's conclusion. In this scholarly *argumentum ex*

Ergebnis gebracht, dass nur in folgenden Texten mit Sicherheit nachzuweisen ist, dass JE als literarische Grundlage benutzt wurde: Dtn 1.9ff; 9.7ff; 11.3ff; Ri 11.9ff; Neh 9; Ps 78 and Jer 48.45f. Nahe verwandt sind Jos 24.2ff und Ps 105. In allen übrigen Fällen handelt es sich um die selbstständige Wiedergabe von Stoffen, die auch im jehowistischen Werk aufgenommen wurden… Die oben aufgeführten Texte, die eine literarische Abhängigkeit von JE erkennen lassen, stammen sämtlich aus exilisch-nachexilischer Zeit. Erst damals hat also das jehowistischen Werk in der heutigen Form mit Sicherheit schriftlich vorgelegen. Dass es bereits früher existiert hat, ist nach den Ergebnissen dieser Analyse unwahrscheinlich bzw. unbeweisbar. Bei einer vorexilischen Entstehungszeit wäre zu erwarten, dass die Propheten direkte literarische Anleihen bei J oder E machten. Dies ist jedoch nicht der Fall.'

56. Kugler, 'Deuteronomists and the Latter Prophets', pp. 137-40. From Kugler's examination, Amos 3.7; 5.4-5 and 14-15, appear as the only passages which 'indicate a deuteronomic redaction of this book, light though it may be' (p. 138) on linguistic criteria, while in Hosea and Micah such linguistic differences cannot be maintained. Kugler rejected entirely that a 'Deuteronomistic school' ever took on such redactions of the Latter Prophets (p. 144).

57. Vorländer, *Entstehungszeit des jehowistischen Geschichtswerkes*, p. 283.

58. Vorländer lists the passages as Deut. 1.9ff; 8.7ff; 11.3ff; Judg. 11.9ff; Neh. 9; Ps. 78; Jer. 48.45ff (Josh. 24.2ff and Ps. 105); cf. Vorländer, *Entstehungszeit des jehowistischen Geschichtswerkes*, pp. 283, 367.

59. Vorländer, *Entstehungszeit des jehowistischen Geschichtswerkes*, p. 368: 'Der überwiegende Teil der aussertetrateuchischen Belege für Erzväter, Exodus, Wüstenaufenthalt und Sinai stammet aus dem dtr. Bereich'.

60. Vorländer, *Entstehungszeit des jehowistischen Geschichtswerkes*, p. 367.

61. Van Seters, *Life of Moses*, pp. 458-61.

62. Van Seters, *Prologue to History*, and *idem*, *Life of Moses*, *passim*.

63. Notable is Isa. 19.19-25's 'midrashic reformulations' of Exod. 1–12 at the conclusion of the oracles against Egypt; cf. M. Fishbane, 'Torah and Tradition', in D.A. Knight (ed.), *Tradition and Theology in the Old Testament* (London: SPCK, 1977), pp. 275-300.

silentio, Van Seters implicitly follows Vorländer, nevertheless arguing for an earlier dating when suitable.[64]

The documentary hypothesis' effort to account for varying opinions stemming from either northern or southern sources, which, synthesized by D and P redactors,[65] kept their differences and became transformed around new solutions, still lacks the answers of why these redactors retained the differences.[66] What was it their audience should learn? Is the antiquarian interest of modern scholarship to view the Bible as an aperture to its implied past an interest that is shared by the Bible's authors? Does the Moses–Aaron competition in Exodus 19–34 reflect a question of Mosaic (E) *contra* Aaronide (J/P) authority? Or does the tri-partite narrative cycle state that priestly authority rests on the written Law of Moses, and that the people's request (32.1, 23) for a transgression of the first and second commandment (20.2-4) is an illegal request?[67] In narrative composition, Aaron has not yet become high priest and the Law is given before the priesthood is established (Exod. 39–40; Lev. 8). Both before and after his consecration, Aaron acts only when commissioned by Moses.[68] His acts in the Golden Calf episode, based on his own and the people's authority, specifically stresses this fact. Numerous are the instances in Leviticus where 'Yahweh spoke to Moses': 'Tell Aaron...', 'Tell Aaron and his sons...', 'Tell the priests, the sons of Aaron...'.[69] What Moses is to tell is what 'becomes' written in the text authorized as the 'laws and statutes given by Yahweh through Moses'.[70] Implicitly, the author argues that whenever the priests have some questions of priestly concern they have to consult that book. He also argues that the proper priesthood is the Aaronide priesthood, since they are those explicitly addressed. The narrative about the Korahite rebellion stresses that fact. Hecataeus of Abdera, who wrote around 300 BCE, made explicit note of Moses' status as 'law-giver': 'And at the end of their laws, there is an appended statement: 'These are the words that Moses heard from God and declared unto the Jews'.[71]

---

64. E.g. Van Seters, *Prologue to History*, pp. 231-32, and *idem*, *Life of Moses*, pp. 82, 174-75.

65. Or P and D redactors; cf. R.E. Friedman, 'Torah (Pentateuch)', in *ABD*, VI, pp. 605-21 (616-17); Weinfeld, *Deuteronomy and the Deuteronomic School*, pp. 180-89.

66. Nicholson, *Pentateuch*, p. 234, raises a similar criticism, however, in support of the documentary hypothesis.

67. Hjelm, *Samaritans and Early Judaism*, p. 153.

68. E.g. Exod. 7.1-2; 16.9; Lev. 8.36.

69. E.g. Lev. 6.1, 18; 8.31; 9.1, 7; 10.6; 21.1; 22.1, 18.

70. The terminology varies, but the implication that the law just consulted is divinely sanctioned is the *leitmotif*; e.g. Lev. 7.37-38; 23.44; 26.46; 27.34; Num. 36.13.

71. Hecataeus of Abdera; cf. Diodorus Siculus, *Bibliotheca Historica* 40.3.6; cf. M. Stern, *Greek and Latin Authors on Jews and Judaism* (3 vols.; Jerusalem: Israel Academy of Sciences and Humanities, 1974–84), I, pp. 26-35 (28). Hecataeus' work has been transmitted through Diodorus Siculus, *Bibliotheca Historica* (around 100 BCE) and Josephus. The former is considered the most genuine, while Josephus seems to have overlaid Hecataeus' text with his own ideologies;cf. M. Stern, 'The Jews in Greek and Latin Literature', in S. Safrai *et al.* (eds.), *The Jewish People in the First Century* (CRINT, II; Assen: Van Gorcum, 1976), pp. 1101-59. The uncertainty about the transmission of Hecataeus makes it difficult to use him as a witness of a fourth–third century dating of the Law. Our concern here is only with his 'interpretation' of Moses' role.

In a similar manner, the people, the Israelites, who, standing together with Aaron at Moses' third descent from Mt Sinai (Exod. 34.30), fearing to come near to him, are instructed to listen to Moses: 'Yahweh told Moses...': 'Tell the Israelites...'.[72] Again, this implicitly argues that what is written in the book they are listening to is the authority they have to obey. Hecataeus of Abdera also made note of the fearfulness of the people in his statement that 'the Jews are so docile in such matters that straightway they fall to the ground and do reverence to the high priest when he expounds the commandments to them'.[73]

When we consider the sociological circumstances implied within the narrative plot of the Pentateuch, our first scenes (Exodus–Numbers) have Moses speak to the priests and the people, instructing them about matters each is obliged to obey. Setting up statutes for their duties and rights, each is put in his proper relationship according to the Laws promulgated. Our next scene (Deuteronomy), has Moses preparing his (and Aaron's) departure by adding teachers to the priests and leaders appointed already. We should notice that the Levites are not appointed before Aaron's death (Deut. 10.6-9). One of the main duties of the Levites is to promulgate the written Law (ויכתב משה את־התורה הזות ויתנה אל־הכהנים בני לוי, 31.9) by reading it for all Israel, so that 'their sons, who do not yet know this law might hear it and learn to fear Yahweh' (ובניהם אשר לא־ידעו שמעו ולמדו ליראאו־יהוה, 31.9-13 [13]). While the narrator of Exodus-Numbers plays a considerable role, reporting what Moses did and said in the past, Deuteronomy's author 'remains mostly in the background of his narrative',[74] presenting Moses as 'speaking' (1.5; 4.1; 31.1), which, however, has the form of a written testimony in the present (31.9, 24). It is this testimony with which the Levites are to read and teach the Law (31.11-12), just as Moses teaches[75] the people the laws, statutes and rules (4.1). Not only the priests, in Deuteronomy called Levitical priests, but also Moses have taken on the roles of teachers and instructors, rather than leaders and spokesmen of God.[76] The question remains: Does that teaching include the preceding books of the Pentateuch? Following Van Seters, one must answer in the negative, since these books were not yet written at the time Deuteronomy instituted the teaching function of the Levites. Deuteronomy, however, constantly interprets past experiences as examples of what happened to those not obeying the words Yahweh spoke in the desert.[77] Since these

---

72. E.g. Lev. 1.2; 4.2; 7.23; 23.2; 24.2; 25.1.

73. Hecataeus of Abdera; cf. Diodorus Siculus, *Bibliotheca Historica* 40.3.6; cf. M. Stern, *Greek and Latin Authors*, p. 28. Hecataeus' portrait of the Jewish nation as a theocracy both reflects the Pentateuch and the books of Ezra and Nehemiah, however not Samuel–2 Kings.

74. Polzin, *Moses and the Deuteronomist*, pp. 9-10.

75. Of the root למד, occurring 17 times in Deuteronomy, but never in the Tetrateuch; see further Weinfeld *Deuteronomy and the Deuteronomic School*, pp. 189, 298-306.

76. Polzin, *Moses and the Deuteronomist*, pp. 205-208: 'Moses is portrayed by the implied author of Deuteronomy as interpreting God's word *and* applying it to Israel's present and future situation'. S. Tengström, 'Moses and the Prophets in the Deuteronomistic History', *SJOT* 8 (1994), pp. 257-66 (260).

77. This is especially true of Deut. 4–10, while the closing chs. 28–32 anticipate what will be the fate of those who transgress the law just given.

experiences do not form part of Deuteronomy 1–3's recalling of the wandering in
the desert after the departure from Horeb (Deut. 1.6; cf. Num. 10.11 [Sinai]), it
seems to me that at least Deuteronomy's implied audience should be familiar with
some more fully developed versions of such stories.[78] Whether these are those written in Exodus–Numbers or in some unknown pre-Yahwistic[79] or pre-Deuteronomistic[80] source, we certainly cannot know. What I think we can know, is that some
'source', apart from the memory appealed to, precedes these interpretations in the
present book of Deuteronomy. As these 'events' are presented in linear chronology
in Exodus–Numbers, they have become past events in Deuteronomy. The impera-
tive, 'remember',[81] followed by a reference to past events,[82] is the introduction to
these interpretations.[83]

Exodus 12–13 presents a condensed example of that literary technique, when in
Exod. 12.14 'this day' is instituted (in the present) as a memorial (זכרון), before the
realization of the Exodus event, and Exod. 13.3 appeals to 'remember' that day
when Yahweh brought you out of Egypt, out of the house of slaves 'with a strong
hand', which has now become an event of the past. Following Van Seters' logic,
the summaries of the Exodus event in Exod. 13.3-16 (especially vv. 3, 9, 15) should
precede the narrative of the event. Lacking details of the event in Exod. 11.1-8 and
12.29-39's (J),[84] they should be ascribed to D,[85] characteristic of exactly such lack
of detail (e.g. Deut. 4.34; 5.15; 6.21-22; 7.8; 8.14; 9.26; 11.2-4; 16.3, 6; 26.5-8).[86]
Of the mentioned passages, Deut. 11.2-4 and 26.5-8 are the most elaborate, as is
also Exod. 13.15. Deuteronomy 11.2-4 knows of the drowning of Egypt's armies,

---

78. E. Otto, 'Stehen wir vor einem Umbruch in der Pentateuchkritik?', *Verkündigung und
Forschung* 22/2 (1977), pp. 82-98; Nicholson, *Pentateuch*, p. 157.

79. Levin, *Jahwist, passim* (especially pp. 389-98). Van Seters, *Prologue to History*, established
this 'source' behind the patriarchal narratives mainly in parallels from Israel's environment. In *Life
of Moses*, he argues that DtrH, Isaiah, Ezekiel and Jeremiah are the main sources behind Exodus–
Numbers, supplying the Yahwistic author with a template for his construction of narratives and
plots. A.G. Auld, 'Samuel and Genesis: Some Questions of Van Seters's "Yahwist"', in McKenzie
and T. Römer (eds.), *Rethinking the Foundations*, pp. 23-32, does not follow Van Seters'
distinction, but argues that relations between the Yahwist and the Former Prophets also relate to
Genesis' 'midrashic' variants on Samuel–Kings narratives.

80. Blum, *Studien zur Komposition des Pentateuch*.

81. Of the root זכר.

82. E.g. the exodus event: Deut. 5.15; 7.18; 8.2; 9.26; 15.15; 16.3; 24.18; the wandering in the
desert: Deut. 8.2; 24.9; the golden calf episode: Deut. 9.7; Tabera and Massah: Deut. 9.22;
Abraham, Isaac and Jacob: Deut. 9.27; Miriam: Deut. 24.9; the Amalekites: 25.17.

83. Cf. also Ps. 105.5-45.

84. Van Seters, *Life of Moses*, p. 120.

85. As most scholars actually do; cf. S. Boorer, *The Promise of the Land as Oath: A Key to the
Formation of the Pentateuch* (BZAW, 205; Berlin: W. de Gruyter, 1992), p. 144; Römer, *Israels
Väter*, pp. 556-57, who assigns Exod. 13.3-16 to a Dtr2.

86. Van Seters, 'Joshua 24 & the Problem of Tradition', pp. 148-49; *idem, Life of Moses*,
pp. 119-20, 127: 'All the pre-exilic prophets give only meager information about the exodus. The
Dtn/Dtr tradition merely affirms that Yahweh brought Israel out of Egypt "with a strong hand and
with signs and wonders", but with no details as to how it happened. The imaginative reconstruction
of events is entirely the work of the Yahwist.'

while 26.2-5 knows of 'the wandering Aramaean', the settlement in Egypt, slavery, oppression and deliverance 'with a strong hand and an outstretched arm (בְּיָד חֲזָקָה וּבִזְרוֹעַ נְטוּיָה) and with sign and wonders'. The expression occurs in this 'presumably later stage of development' in several passages in Deuteronomy, however never in the MT of Joshua and the Tetrateuch.[87] In the SP, Exod. 6.1 and 32.11 agree with the LXX and Syriac on the long form 'with a strong hand and an outstretched arm', while the MT has 'with a strong hand' (6.1) and 'with great might and a strong hand' (בְּכֹחַ גָּדוֹל וּבְיָד חֲזָקָה, 32.11).[88] In 13.3, 9, 14 and 16, we find the short form, 'with a strong hand',[89] which also occurs in numerous passages of Deuteronomy.[90] Exodus 13.15 knows of the killing of Egypt's firstborn, a theme not mentioned in Deuteronomy.[91] Since the text in 13.3-16 summarizes ritual matters—mentioning *maṣṣôt*, phylacteries and dedication of firstlings—following the order of Exod. 12.14-27—unleavened bread, signs on the lintel and the two door posts (forehead and hand), and the sparing of Israel as firstborn (12.27; cf. 4.22-23)—one might as well regard 13.3-6 as belonging to P, as do 12.1-28, 43-50; 13.1-2, according to Van Seters.[92] Van Seters' conclusion, however, is that 13.3-16 belongs to J, because of its transformation of child sacrifice, practised 'in the late monarchy', into the law of redemption, linked with the Passover sacrifice. The prooftext of this transformation is Deut. 15.19-23, which only includes the firstborn of herd or flock and does not mention the Passover.[93] Numbers 3.13 and 8.16-17's (P) dedication of firstborn as Levites, and relating the argument to the killing of Egypt's firstborn, are not dealt with by Van Seters. They would have made a useful comparison, especially since Exod. 13.1-2 (P) anticipates 13.3-16 'by a divine speech'.[94] A comparison would have revealed that, although dealing with similar matters, linguistically Numbers differs considerably from Exod. 13.3-16. One might question the validity of Van Seters' religio-historical argument, based as it is on an interpretation of purported prophetic polemic against child sacrifice (especially Ezekiel, Jeremiah and Micah) and a late dating of 22.29b-30 (P). Other problems, however, are more pertinent to our examination.

---

87. Deut. 4.34; 5.15; 7.19; 11.2; 26.8; 1 Kgs 8.42; 2 Chron. 6.32; Ps. 136.12; Jer. 21.5; 32.21; Ezek. 20.33, 34; cf. K. Martens, 'With a Strong Hand and an Outstretched Arm', *SJOT* 15/1 (2001), pp. 123-41 (124, 129).

88. 4QpaleoExod[m] 32.11: '[with great power and] with a mighty arm'. Exod. 6.1 is missing in DSS. Other biblical occurrences are 2 Kgs 17.36; Neh. 1.10; Jer. 27.5; 32.17; cf. Martens, 'With a Strong Hand and an Outstretched Arm', p. 138.

89. בְּיָד הֲזָקָה or בְּחֹזֶק יָד.

90. Deut. 3.24; 6.21; 7.8; 9.26; 34.12; Dan. 9.15; cf. Martens, 'With a Strong Hand and an Outstretched Arm', p. 124.

91. Van Seters, *Life of Moses*, pp. 124-25.

92. Van Seters, *Life of Moses*, pp. 114-23.

93. Van Seters, *Life of Moses*, pp. 122-25. Neither does Neh. 9.9-11 mention Passover or killing of Egypt's firstborn and, although Neh. 10.36-37's mention of the law of firstborn is clearly reminiscent of Deut. 12.6; 14.23; 15.19, men are included. The passages are not dealt with by Van Seters.

94. Van Seters, *Life of Moses*, pp. 122-23.

If we accept Van Seters' conclusion that 13.3-16 belongs to J, we must ask: Did the Yahwist then write the summary before he wrote the narrative?[95] If so, did he write it on the basis of Deuteronomic summaries, of which Deut. 16.1-8 is exceptional for its detailed knowledge of matters related by P—the slaughter at sunset[96] and the haste[97]—details not related in Exod. 13.3-16?[98] Or did he write it on the basis of the Deuteronomic summaries in chs. 11 and 26, none of which mention the 'house of slavery' (בית־עבדים), an expression occurring as a gloss in non-elaborated Deuteronomic passages similar to 13.3-16 (especially vv. 3, 14).[99] The term is missing in Exod. 34.18-20, which, furthermore, does not mention the killing of the Egyptians, but nevertheless is ascribed to J by Van Seters?[100] The gloss also occurs in Exod. 20.2, a passage Van Seters ascribes to P.[101] None of the plague narratives ascribed to J in Exodus 7–12[102] contain the gloss. In three instances, a plural form of the Hebrew term בית־עבד is used as a designation of the house(s) of Pharaoh's servants (7.28; 8.20; 10.6), which will become affected by the plagues as will Pharaoh's own house (or chamber) and all of Egypt. Outside Deuteronomy, we find references to Israel's release from the 'house of slaves' in such 'Deuteronomistic passages' as Josh. 24.17; Judg. 6.8,[103] Jer. 34.13[104] and Mic. 6.4. Summing up: the gloss, which seems to be Deuteronomistic, in two instances is ascribed to either J or P. Back to our question: Did J make his summary in Exod. 13.3-16 on the basis of D or J? If it is affirmed that J made his summary on the basis of D, how is the relationship to be understood between J's use of the term בית־עבד in Exodus 7–12 as a designation of servant houses in Pharaoh's court and his use of the same term

95. Boorer, *Promise of the Land*, pp. 152: 'In short, Exod. 12.29-39 forms the basis and the rationale of Exod. 13.3-16 [D]; and Exod. 13.3-16 immortalizes the narrated events of Exod. 12.29-39 for succeeding generations as part of the ongoing experience for the people over time'.

96. Deut. 16.6; cf. Exod. 12.6

97. בחפזון; Deut. 16.3; cf. Exod. 12.11 and reflected in Isa. 52.12, whose people 'shall not go out in haste and not go out in flight'.

98. Boorer, *Promise of the Land*, p. 185 'it can be concluded that Exod. 13.3-16 is earlier than Deut. 16.1-8'. Blenkinsopp, *The Pentateuch*, p. 157: 'The additional instructions about the consecration of the firstborn (13.1-2, 11-16) and Unleavened Bread (13.3-10) were added for good measure and are clearly Deuteronomic in character (cf. Deut. 15.19–16.8). The description of the land and its inhabitants, the ancestral promise of land, emphasis on family instruction (Exod. 13.8, 14-15) and allusion to frontlet bands of phylacteries (13.9; cf. Deut. 6.8; 11.18) provide further confirmation. With this supplement, the Egypt narrative is brought to a close and a new phase of the story can begin.'

99. Deut. 5.6; 6.12; 7.8; 8.14 (which, however, relates about the wanderings in the desert); 13.6, 11.

100. Van Seters, *Life of Moses*, p. 120: 'Yet in Exod. 34.18-20, the same juxtaposition of *maṣṣôt* and the law of first born occurs, but in abbreviated form. The author of the unit in Exod. 13.3-16 as well as in 34.18-20 can be none other than the Yahwist.' Boorer, *Promise of the Land*, p. 184: 'The framing verses in Exod. 13.3-16, not found in Exod. 34.18-20, and which consists of language that approximates more closely to Deuteronomy, speak against seeing Exod. 13.3-16 and Exod. 34.18-20 as belonging to precisely the same literary level'.

101. Van Seters, *Life of Moses*, p. 251.

102. Van Seters, *Life of Moses*, pp. 78-112.

103. Van Seters, 'Joshua 24', pp. 147-48.

104. Van Seters, *Life of Moses*, p. 288.

as a gloss in Exodus 13? If, on the contrary, he made his summary on the basis of his J narratives in Exodus 7–12, how is 13.3-16's summary different from Deuteronomistic summaries, based on narratives yet to be written?

Leaving these questions aside, I will return to my examination of diachronically based sociological setting in the Pentateuch and ask if the change of scenes, from that of Exodus–Numbers to that of Deuteronomy, indicates an existence of different sources, which we can label JEPD? With the implication that neither Moses and Aaron, nor the people that came out of Egypt and received the Law on Sinai are to enter the Promised Land, the author needs to create a coherence, which includes his own generation.[105] With these deceased ancestors, who will be left to remind the people of past experiences, if not those capable of reading the testimony just written? Furthermore, moving from a situation of unity to dispersion, how should the Aaronide priests, whose duties are tied to the centralized sanctuary of the camp, maintain the education of the people who will soon be dispersed throughout the country? Whether we think that Levitical priests were meant to replace the Aaronides, whether there was a competition between these groups or whether the sociological situation reflects that of the 'diaspora' or 'dispersion', the narrative plot demands that either a new group is introduced or that the Aaronide priests take on new roles. Biblical controversies over the roles of the Levites are not related to their synagogue functions, but to temple functions. The question is: How near can they come to Yahweh?[106]

Implying the literary sociological changes in our examination, we must ask: How do we distinguish between narrative progression and sources? Is a text levitical because it favours the role of the Levites, or is it Priestly because it favours priestly duties? Does P and E's preference of Aaron and Moses in their competition with levitical (Korah) and non-priestly (Dathan and Abiram) authority point to the existence of stories 'which are intertwined' from two different sources,[107] or does the double narrative serve the function of giving answers to various problems at the same time?[108] Does the establishment of genealogies and hierarchies, so pervasive in the Pentateuchal narratives, point to some religio-political conflicts over law and

---

105.   The reference to the covenant of the fathers—which is not the covenant made with the survivors (Deut. 5.3)—reflecting the Sinai covenant, but conflating its tradition with Horeb, rather points to the author's use of both traditions, than to a later development of Exodus' Sinai tradition on the basis of Deuteronomy. That Horeb is the place for the new covenant made after Israel's wandering in the desert and before their entrance into the Promised Land (Deut. 1.6-8) is a logical consequence of narrative progression.

106.   Hjelm, *Samaritans and Early Judaism*, pp. 155-58.

107.   Friedman, 'Torah', p. 612, and *idem*, *The Exile and Biblical Narrative: The Formation of the Deuteronomistic and Priestly Works* (HMS, 22; Chico, CA: Scholars Press, 1981), p. 109; Cross, *Canaanite Myth*, p. 315 n. 77; Van Seters, *Life of Moses*, p. 240.

108.   R. Alter, *The Art of Biblical Narrative* (London: George Allen & Unwin, 1981), pp. 133-37 (136): 'Perhaps all these considerations of narrative coherence seemed less important to the writer than the need to assert thematically that the two separate events—the attempt to seize political power and the usurpation of the sacerdotal function—comprised one archetypal rebellion against divine authority and so must be told as one tale'.

cult, involving perhaps some of the formerly mentioned groups? Or does the Pentateuch use narratives as illustrations of its religiously based discourse on ideal social structures? Having assigned the Levites with the task of teaching and instructing, they are also given a method with which to interpret the Law, namely as Moses did in Deuteronomy, combining Law and experience. As such, 'memory' becomes a major factor in interpretation—as illustration, however, not as a replacement of the Law.[109]

What we might learn from these considerations is that law came first and narratives came afterwards. The competition involved in the composition of the Former Prophets and the narratives of the Pentateuch is not as innocent as Van Seters assumes. What is problematic in Van Seters' scenario that Deuteronomy comes first and is followed by the Deuteronomistic History and the Yahwist-Elohist, is Moses' relationship to David. Why should the author of Deuteronomy 'create' a Moses and a Mosaic Law if he already has a David who institutes justice and order (2 Sam. 8.15)?[110] That Moses is not brought into connection with David until David —on his deathbed—transfers the Law of Moses to his son (1 Kgs 2.3), begs for an explanation beyond tradition-historical considerations.[111] The assignment of laws to the Patriarchs, rather than to Moses, in the book of *Jubilees* shows that literary competition could take place. The Patriarchs might be later than Moses, but are they also later than David? The relationship between the biblical Prophets, the Deuteronomistic prophets and the Law poses another problem. Before handling these questions, we must make a digression and look at other Jewish and Samaritan traditions about text composition.

2. Deuteronomist and Yahwist: Jewish and Samaritan Traditions of Text Composition—The Pre-Exilic Period

a. Introduction to Samaritan Chronicles
There are three main obstacles for comparative studies of Samaritan traditions.[112] The first is the late dating of Samaritan non-Pentateuchal manuscripts, most of

---

109. Blum, *Studien zur Komposition des Pentateuch*, pp. 197-207.

110. Mullen, *Ethnic Myths and Pentateuchal Foundations*, p. 323: 'In terms of their material culture, kingship and national identity had been [consciously] replaced by hierocratic home-rule and a new concept of ethnic identity...' p. 324: 'no longer did the monarchy represent the ideal'.

111. See below, Chapter 5.

112. For general introductions to the Samaritan literature, see, e.g., J.A. Montgomery, *The Samaritans: The Earliest Jewish Sect: Their History, Theology and Literature* (Philadelphia: The John C. Winston Co., 1907 [repr. New York: Ktav, 1968]); M. Gaster, *The Samaritans, Their History, Doctrines and Literature* (London: Oxford University Press, 1925 [repr. in 1976 and 1980]; J. Macdonald, *Samaritan Chronicle No. II (or: Sepher Ha-Yamim) From Joshua to Nebuchadnezzar* (Berlin: W. de Gruyter, 1969), pp. 3-14; A.D. Crown, 'New Light on the Inter-Relationships of Samaritan Chronicles from Some Manuscripts in The John Rylands Library', *BJRL* 54 (1972), pp. 282-313; *BJRL* 55 (1973), pp. 86-111; *idem, Samaritan Scribes and Manuscripts* (Texts and Studies in Ancient Judaism, 80; Tübingen: J.C.B. Mohr [Paul Siebeck], 2001), pp. 1-39; R.J. Coggins, *Samaritans and Jews: The Origins of Samaritanism Reconsidered* (Oxford: Basil

which cannot be dated earlier than the tenth–fourteenth century CE, at which time, 'Arabic replaced Aramaic in all aspects of community's life, with the exception of religious activity. For liturgical purposes a new language arose, which consisted of amalgamated Hebrew and Aramaic.'[113] From the thirteenth century, Arabic also became introduced in translations of the Pentateuch[114] and translations of non-Pentateuchal texts. Arabic, however,

> never entered their liturgy which is either Hebrew or Aramaic, the former language being holy, the latter hallowed by the Targum and the liturgical hymns, the most ancient of which were written in the fourth century and the latest are still attributed to the greatest Samaritan Arabic writer, Abū l-Ḥasan al-Ṣūrī, in the eleventh century.[115]

The influence of Arabic begins from then on to appear in Hebrew writings also, which 'in spite of its Hebrew basis is thoroughly saturated by Aramaic and occasionally also Arabic elements or neologisms formed from both mentioned languages; its syntax is entirely influenced by Arabic'.[116] The 'flourishing' of this 'Late Samaritan Neo-Hebrew', seems to have been in the early twentieth century.[117] Needless to say, this time span of about 500 years creates great insecurity in dating Samaritan manuscripts on linguistic criteria alone, although earlier forms, called Samaritan Neo-Hebrew or *Shomronit* can be discerned by its greater content of Aramaic.[118] This form was mainly used by poets, while late Samaritan Neo-Hebrew was used for prose writings, such as Samaritan correspondence with European

Blackwell, 1975); J. Bowman, *Samaritan Documents Relating to their History, Religion and Life* (Pittsburgh: Pickwick Press, 1977); P. Stenhouse, 'Samaritan Chronicles', in Crown (ed.), *The Samaritans*, pp. 218-65; J.-D. Macchi, *Les Samaritains: Histoire d'une légende: Israël et la province de Samarie* (Le Monde de la Bible, 30; Geneva: Labor et Fides, 1994); Hjelm, *Samaritans and Early Judaism*, pp. 94-103; F. Niessen, *Eine Samaritanische Version des Buches Yehošuaʿ und die Šobaḵ Erzählung: Die Samaritanische Chronik Nr. II, Handschrift 2: JR(G) 1168 = Ryl. Sam. MS 259, Folio 8b-53a* (Texte und Studien zur Orientalistik, 12; Hildesheim: Georg Olms, 2000), pp. 4-18; For earlier literature and references to text editions, see bibliographies in the works mentioned and in A.D. Crown, *A Bibliography of the Samaritans* (London: Scarecrow Press, 2nd edn, 1993 [1984]).

113.   Z. Ben Ḥayyim, 'The Language of Tibåt Mårqe and Its Time', in A. Tal and M. Florentin (eds.), *Proceedings of the First International Congress of the Société d'Études Samaritaines Tel-Aviv, April 11-13, 1988* (Tel Aviv: Chaim Rosenberg School of Jewish Studies, Tel Aviv University, 1991), pp. 331-45 (332-33), who called this language 'Samaritan Aramaic'.

114.   H. Shehadeh, 'The Groups of the Samaritan Manuscripts of the Arabic Translation of the Pentateuch', in J.P. Rothschild and G.D. Sixdenier (eds.), *Études samaritaines Pentateuque et Targum exégèse et philology, chroniques: Communication présentées à la table ronde internationale 'Les Manuscrits samaritains. Problèmes et méthodes' (Paris 7–9 octobre 1985)* (Leuven: Peeters, 1988), pp. 205-17; Niessen, *Buches Yehošuaʿ*, p. 19.

115.   R. Macuch, 'Samaritan Languages: Samaritan Hebrew, Samaritan Aramaic', in Crown (ed.), *The Samaritans*, pp. 531-84 (534).

116.   Macuch, 'Samaritan Languages', p. 533.

117.   Macuch, 'Samaritan Languages', p. 534; Niessen, *Buches Yehošuaʿ*, p. 37.

118.   M. Florentin, '"Shomronit": A Grammatical Description and Lexical Characterisation' (unpublished PhD dissertation, Tel Aviv University, 1989 [Hebrew]).

scholars, Samaritan Chronicles and late nineteenth–early twentieth century Hebrew translations of Samaritan Arabic works.[119]

The second obstacle is a lack of comparable material in the oldest sources, which cover chronologically the biblical period between the division of the Davidic kingdom until the exile.[120] It is only in later Samaritan Neo-Hebrew compilations, allegedly from the nineteenth–twentieth century, such as those presented in *Chronicle Adler* (= *Chronicle VII*)[121] and Macdonald, *Samaritan Chronicle No. II* that synthesized(?) narratives appear as closer parallels to the biblical tradition. These should be used with great caution.[122] The matter is, however, far from settled and especially the Samaritan Joshua traditions seem to be of high antiquity.[123]

119. H. Shehadeh, 'The Arabic of the Samaritans and its Importance', in A.D. Crown and L. Davey (eds.), *New Samaritan Studies of the Société d'Études Samaritaines: Essays in Honour of G.D. Sixdenier, III-IV* (Studies in Judaica, 5; Sydney: Mandelbaum Publishing), pp. 551-75.

120. See, P. Stenhouse, *The Kitāb al Tarīkh of Abu 'l-Fath: Translated into English with Notes* (Sydney: The Mandelbaum Trust, University of Sydney, 1985; Arabic editions: Stenhouse, 'The Kitāb al Tarīkh of Abu 'l-Fath: New Edition' [unpublished PhD dissertation, University of Sydney, 1980]; E. Vilmar, *Abulfathi Annales Samaritani* [Gothae: F.A. Perthes, 1865]). T.W.J. Juynboll, *Chronicon samaritanum, arabice conscriptum, cui titulus est Liber Josuae* (Leiden: S. & J. Luchtmans, 1848; Eng. trans. O.T. Crane, *The Samaritan Chronicle, or the Book of Joshua the Son of Nun* [New York: John B. Alden, 1890]); J. Bowman, *Transcript of the Original Text of the Samaritan Chronicle Tolidah* (Leeds: University of Leeds Press, 1954); M. Florentin, *The Tulida, A Samaritan Chronicle* (Jerusalem: Yad Izhak Ben-Zvi, 1999), offering alternative readings to those in Bowman's version.

121. E.N. Adler and M. Séligsohn, 'Une nouvelle chronique samaritaine', *REJ* 44 (1902), pp. 188-222; *REJ* 45 (1902), pp. 70-98, 223-54; *REJ* 46 (1903), pp. 123-46, and, *Une nouvelle chronique samaritaine/Texte samaritaine transcrit et édité pour le première fois avec une traduction française par Elkan-Nathan Adler et M. Séligsohn* (Paris: Librairie Durlacher, 1903).

122. Z. Ben Ḥayyim, 'A Samaritan Text of the Former Prophets?', *Lešonénu* 35 (1970), pp. 293-302; M. Baillet, 'Review of Macdonald, *Samaritan Chronicle No. II*', *RB* 7 (1970), pp. 592-602; R. Pummer, 'Einführung in den stand der Samaritanerforschung', in F. Dexinger and R. Pummer (eds.), *Die Samaritaner* (Wege der Forschung, 604; Darmstadt: Wissenschaftliche Buchgesellschaft, 1992), pp. 1-66 (22-29); P. Stenhouse, 'Chronicles of the Samaritans', in A.D. Crown, R. Pummer and A. Tal (eds.), *A Companion to Samaritan Studies* (Tübingen: J.C.B. Mohr, 1993), pp. 50-53; Hjelm, *Samaritans and Early Judaism*, pp. 98-101; Niessen, *Buches Yehošua'*, pp. 8-9.

123. See further, the discussion in my 'What Do Samaritans and Jews Have in Common? Recent Trends in Samaritan Studies', *CBR* 3.1 (2004), pp. 9-62; M. Gaster, 'Das Buch Josua in hebräisch-samaritanischer Rezension. Entdeckt und sum ersten Male herausgegeben', *ZDMG* 62/2/3 (1908), pp. 209-79, 475-549; *idem*, 'On the Newly Discovered Samaritan Book of Joshua', *JRAS* (1908), pp. 795-809; *idem*, 'Das Buch Josua' ('Nachtrag'), pp. 533-49; *idem*, *The Samaritans*, pp. 135-40. Macdonald, *Samaritan Chronicle No. II*, pp. 5-10; A.D. Crown, 'The Date and Authenticity of the Samaritan Hebrew Book of Joshua as Seen in Its Territorial Allotments', *PEQ* 96 (1974), pp. 79-100 (repr. with 'Addendum 1986', in Dexinger and Pummer [eds.], *Die Samaritaner*, pp. 281-311); Cohen, *A Samaritan Chronicle*, pp. 174-92, 212-13; Nodet, *Origins of Judaism*, pp. 195-201. For a critique of Gaster's dating, see P. Kahle, 'Zum hebräischen Buch Josua der Samaritaner', *ZDMG* 62/3 (1908), pp. 550-51; A.S. Yahuda, 'Über die Unechtheit des Samaritanischen Josuabuches', *Sitzungsberichte der Berliner Akademie des Wissenschaftes* 39 (1908), pp. 887-914; *idem*, 'Zum Samaritanischen Josua: eine Erklärung', *ZDMG* 62/4 (1908), p. 754; D. Yellin, 'A Book of Joshua or a Sepher Hayamim', *Jerusalem Yearbook* 7.7 (1908). Yellin had

The third obstacle is a continuous chronicle tradition resulting in a variety of manuscripts reflecting linguistic and cultural tastes of their own time. This makes it extremely difficult to separate earlier traditions from later development.[124] Attempts based on linguistic criteria,[125] about which there is no absolute consensus, leave aside the methodological problem that manuscript and text are not identical entities.[126] For the sake of clarity, the following analyses are based on translations of the hitherto agreed oldest manuscripts written in Arabic[127] with reference to allegedly later compilations written in Hebrew and Samaritan Neo-Hebrew[128] in footnotes.

himself published another Samaritan Manuscript (Macdonald's J4) some years earlier: D. Yellin, 'Das Buch Josua der Samaritaner in hebräisch', *Jerusalem Yearbook* 6.2 (ed. A.M. Luncz) (1902), pp. 138-55; 6.3 (1903), pp. 203-205 (Hebrew).

124. Pummer, 'Einführung in den stand der Samaritanerforschung', p. 27: 'schwer zu bestimmen, wenn überhaupt'.

125. E.g. Z. Ben Ḥayyim, *The Literary and Oral Tradition of Hebrew and Aramaic amongst the Samaritans* (5 vols.; Jerusalem: The Academy of the Hebrew Language, 1957–77 [Hebrew]); and Florentin, *The Tulida*. J.M. Cohen, *A Samaritan Chronicle: A Source-Critical Analysis of the Life and Time of the Great Samaritan Reformer, Baba Rabbah* (Leiden: E.J. Brill, 1981), and Niessen, *Buches Yehošuaʿ*, both date the same manuscript (JR[G] 1168 = Ryl. Sam. MS 259) to either the fourteenth century, because of its 'evenly balanced synthesis of Hebrew and Aramaic (Cohen, *A Samaritan Chronicle*, p. 176) or much later 'als die Arabisierung der Samaritaner abgeschlossen war' (Niessen, *Buches Yehošuaʿ*, p. 37). See further, Hjelm, 'What Do Samaritans and Jews Have in Common?', pp. 219-21.

126. Gaster, 'Das Buch Josua', p. 534; *idem*, *The Asatir, The Samaritan Book of the 'Secrets of Moses' Together with the Pitron or Samaritan Commentary and the Samaritan story of the Death of Moses* (Oriental Translation Fund, NS 26; London: The Royal Asiatic Society, 1927), p. 180; Niessen, *Buches Yehošuaʿ*, p. 16; G. Wedel, 'Abūl-Ḥasan aṣ-Ṣuri's *Kitāb aṭ-Ṭabbaḫ*. Results of the Edition, Translation and Commentary of Half of the Book', in Tal and Florentin (eds.), *Proceedings of the First International Congress of the Société d'Études Samaritaines Tel-Aviv, April 11-13, 1988*, pp. 305-12 (310), regarding Arabic copies of *Kitāb aṭ-Ṭabbaḫ*.

127. Juynboll, *Liber Josuae* (= *Chronicle IV*). Parts of the chronicle, covering the period until the arrival of Alexander the Great, date to the fourteenth century CE (1362), while matters regarding the later period until the seventh century CE were added in 1513 CE. Juynboll's edition is based on Or. 249, a manuscript acquired by J.J. Scaliger in 1584 and now in the University of Leiden Library. The book is written in Arabic with Samaritan characters, which Juynboll transcribed into Arabic on the basis of other manuscripts written in Arabic characters (close variants are: MSS JR[G] 1167 and 1168). Crown, *Samaritan Scribes and Manuscripts*, p. 29, notes: 'The compiler claims that he used a Hebrew source for the first part and behind the Arabic text one can find sources in Greek, Aramaic and Hebrew'. Stenhouse, *The The Kitāb al Tarīkh of Abu 'l-Fath* (= *Chronicle VI*). The manuscripts of this chronicle can safely be dated from the seventeenth century CE, but the writing of the chronicle (based on earlier sources) dates to the fourteenth century CE (1355); cf. Stenhouse, *Kitāb al-Tarīkh* (1985), pp. xxiv-xxix, 3; Crown, *Samaritan Scribes and Manuscripts*, pp. 28-29. B. Tsedaka, 'Special Samaritan Traditions in non-Samaritan Sources', in Tal and Florentin (eds.), *Proceedings of the First International Congress of the Société d'Études Samaritaines Tel-Aviv, April 11-13, 1988*, pp. 189-201 (193): '[AF] is the most important historical work of the Samaritans, inter alia because the author took pains to name the sources on which he based his outstanding work'; *idem* (private conversation): the oldest manuscript is Paris 10 (1523); see, however, Stenhouse (*Kitāb al-Tarīkh* [1985], p. xxi), who lists Sassoon MS Sam. 36 (+ 1502) among the manuscripts used for his edition.

128. Gaster, 'Das buch Josua' (based on Text A, cod. Gaster 864, 4° [1905] = JR[G] 864 with additional use of Text B, cod. Gaster 863, 8° = JR[G] 863, and Text C, cod. Gaster 874 = JR[G]

Crown's anticipation of the 'Hebrew Book of Joshua' (JR[G] 864) as authentically a third–fourth century CE[129] work and antedating *Liber Josuae* (Or. 249), *AF*[130] and *Chronicle II* (JR[G] 1142),[131] will be considered, but not dealt with systematically. If, in fact, a Samaritan Hebrew book of Joshua, not the existent compilations, ante-dates the Arabic versions by more than a millennium, and the indications are strongly in favor of that,[132] we must think of the Arabic versions as secondary.[133] As the Arabic *AF* claims[134] and the Hebrew *Chronicle II* exposes,[135] both are compilations which include a Samaritan book of Joshua.[136] If, moreover, the text of JR(G) 1142 = Ryl. Sam. MS 375[137] (written in Classical Hebrew) and JR(G) 1168 = Ryl. Sam. MS 259 (written in Hebrew with Aramaisms and Arabisms) can be dated much earlier than the twentieth century, this will call for a revision of our scholarly traditions about Samaritan languages and historiography, as these two manuscripts contain the most detailed parallels to the MT. This discussion, however, falls on the fringe of the present study. Our interest in Samaritan traditions is thematic rather than linguistic, and redaction-critical questions are raised in regard to comparative analyses of Samaritan, Jewish and Greek text traditions.

---

874. Gaster did not conflate his text [Crown, 'Samaritan Hebrew Book', p. 284], only his translation); Macdonald, *Samaritan Chronicle No. II* (based on JR[G] 1142 = Ryl. Sam. MS 375 [1908?/1616?] with additional use of Yellin's text [J4], which he considered to represent an earlier stage than those of Gaster; cf. Macdonald, *Samaritan Chronicle No. II*, p. 71); Niessen, *Buches Yehošua'* (based on Macdonald's H2 [JR(G) 1168 = Ryl. Sam. MS 259 (twentieth century?/fourteenth century?)], which Macdonald considered to be 'a later version of H1' [H = *Sepher ha-Yamin*]; cf. Macdonald, *Samaritan Chronicle No. II*, pp. 10-11). Other parts of H2, which consists of 264 folios, have been published by Gaster, *Asatir* (JR[G] 1168, fol. 1b-8b), pp. 55-59 (text) and 303-21 (translation), and Cohen, *A Samaritan Chronicle* (H2 fol. 174a, l. 4–195b, l. 13), pp. 6-57 (text) and 58-109 (translation), who considered (pp. 174-92 [176], 212-13) Macdonald's H1 to depend on H2 and not *vice versa*. Yellin's text is not used.

　　129. Gaster, 'Das Buch Josua', p. 235: 'lange vor Josephus liegt'.
　　130. Gaster, 'Das Buch Josua', p. 543: 'Jedenfalls existierte ein Buch Josua vor Abu'l-Fath und dieses Buch Josua ist aus dem Hebräischen übersetzt'.
　　131. Crown, 'Samaritan Hebrew Book of Joshua' (*Addendum 1986*), pp. 309-11. See, however, Crown, *Samaritan Scribes and Manuscripts* p. 29.
　　132. Gaster, 'Das Buch Josua', pp. 544-46; Crown, 'Samaritan Hebrew Book of Joshua', *passim* (especially p. 310); see, however, Crown, *Samaritan Scribes and Manuscripts* p. 29; Nodet, *Origins of Judaism*, pp. 198-200; Zsengellér, *Gerizim as Israel*, pp. 28-33.
　　133. Crown, 'New Light on The Inter-relationships of Samaritan Chronicles', p. 105.
　　134. *AF*, Introduction, pp. 3-4; Crown, 'Samaritan Hebrew Book of Joshua', p. 310.
　　135. Macdonald, *Samaritan Chronicle No. II*, pp. 9-10, 70-72.
　　136. Juynboll 'deduced [*Chronicon*, pp. 77ff.] that the Book of Joshua represented only chapters 9–25 of the Scaliger MS. The introductory chapters (i.e. 1–8) and the concluding chapters (i.e. 26–50) he considered to have been drawn from various sources'; cf. P. Stenhouse, 'The Reliability of the Chronicle of Abū 'l-Fath, with Special reference to the Dating of Baba Rabba', in Rothschild and Sixdenier (eds.), *Études samaritaines Pentateuque*, pp. 233-57 (251).
　　137. Niessen, *Buches Yehošua'*, p. 14, applies Ryl. Sam. MS 257 to both JR(G) 863 and 1142. The confusion is due to the re-cataloguing of the Gaster Manuscripts in the John Rylands Library. The correct number of JR(G) 1142 seems to be Ryl. Sam. MS 375. The new numbers are the following: JR(G) 863 = Ryl. Sam. MS 257; JR(G) 864 = Ryl. Sam. MS 268; JR(G) 1142 = Ryl. Sam. MS 375; JR(G) 1167 = Ryl. Sam. MS 374; JR(G) 1168 = Ryl. Sam. MS 259.

b. *Samaritan 'Variants' to the Deuteronomistic History*

Regarding Samaritan 'variants' to the Deuteronomistic History, we learn that in older Samaritan compilations there is a gap in the history from the period of Eli and Samuel's heresy, and of the Philistines' capture of the ark, until the arrival of Nebuchadnezzar and the exile.[138] *Liber Josuae* names only three 'biblical judges' (called 'kings'),[139] but reveals knowledge of twelve kings of which Joshua is the first and Samson the last. 'Solomon son of David' is mentioned as constructor of buildings and monuments destroyed by Nebuchadnezzar.[140] In *AF*, the gap is from the reign of Jeroboam—at which time Samaritans, belonging to the houses of Phinehas and Joseph, separated from the rest of Israel (*AF*, ch. XIV, p. 56)[141]—until the reign of Yuma'qīm (Jehoiachin), who, appointed by Nebuchadnezzar to gather the tribute, is said to rule over all the tribes of Israel (*AF*, ch. XVI, p. 60).[142] This period is in *AF* (ch. XV, pp. 59-60) presented chronistically as a 'recollection of the Great High Priests' and some of the chiefs of the families.[143]

In *AF*, we learn that it was Solomon, who had dug water tunnels under Jerusalem, 'reaching as far as Jericho and Lydda' and 'from Bethlehem to Jerusalem' (*AF*, ch. XVI, p. 61). We also learn that Yuma'qīm, after his refusal to send tribute to Nebuchadnezzar, was first confronted with 'messengers from Iraq', and later, after persistent refusal, defeated the force that Nebuchadnezzar had sent with a

138.   Juynboll, *Liber Josuae*, chs. xliv-xlv. Interesting to note that Book 5 of Josephus' *Antiquities* closes with the capture of the ark, the death of Eli, the birth of Ichabod and the genealogy of Eli as the first high priest from the house of Ithamar, which held the office 'down to the times of the reign of Solomon. Then the descendants of Eleazar once more recovered it' (*Ant.* 5.362).

139.   Juynboll, *Liber Josuae*, ch. xxxix: 'Abīl, filius patris Calabi ex Tribu Judaïcâ' (might be Othniel), 'Tarfi'a ex Tribu Afrīmi' (could be Jephtah, although the tribe should be Gilead), and 'Šamšan'. Rofé's argument that 'once Othniel is excluded [from MT Judges] there is not even one saviour-judge from Judah', does not apply to this Samaritan Chronicle. Given that Judah is only one, while Israel is twelve, the dispersion of tribes in the Masoretic calculation is not so entirely northern oriented as Rofé claims. One might even argue that from a Masoretic perspective, chaos applies to the northern tribes, while order applies to the southern tribe(s).

140.   Juynboll, *Liber Josuae*, ch. xlv.

141.   Macdonald, *Samaritan Chronicle No. II*, p. 65: 'The H1 material from here to the end is sparsely represented in the other chrons., only the description of the downfall of Samaria & Judah being recorded in any detail'. Macdonald's apparatus only lists variants in other Samaritan chronicles for the book of Joshua part of his manuscript.

142.   It is a strange coincidence that references to the Chronicle (דברי־הימים [mentioned only in Kings, Neh. 12.23; Est. 2.23; 6.1; 10.2; 1 Chron. 27.24]) of the Kings of Israel [1 Kgs 14.19; 15.31; 16.5, 14, 20, 27; 22.39; 2 Kgs 1.18; 10.34; 13.8, 12; 14.15, 28; 15.11, 15, 21, 26, 31] and Judah [1 Kgs 14.29; 15.7, 23; 22.46; 2 Kgs 8.23; 12.20; 14.18; 15.6, 36; 16.19; 20.20; 21.17, 25; 23.28; 24.5]) begin with the conclusion of the narratives about Jeroboam (1 Kgs 14.19) and Rehoboam (1 Kgs 14.29) and ends with the conclusion of the Jehoiakim narrative (2 Kgs 24.5) and the introduction of Jehoiachin. For similar gaps in *Eupolemus* and *Pseudo-Philo*, see B.Z. Wacholder, *Eupolemus: A Study of Judeo-Greek Literature* (Cincinnati: Hebrew Union College Press, 1974), and Spiro, *Samaritans, Tobiads, and Judahites in Pseudo-Philo*.

143.   Stenhouse, *Kitāb al-Tarīkh* (1985), n. 273, counts 580 years from the beginning of the Fanūta (the disappearance of the tabernacle; cf. *AF*, ch. XIII, p. 55) to the coming of Nebuchadnezzar.

'high-ranking official'. We learn that the Samaritans inform Nebuchadnezzar about Yuma'qīm's rebellion and that Nebuchadnezzar himself went up to lay siege to Jerusalem for some years. He decided, however, to withdraw from the city, because he thought it was divinely protected, when, in spite of the siege, its inhabitants 'went on showing off roasted meat, fresh fish and ripe fruit' (*AF*, ch. XVI, p. 61).

When God, however, sent an earthquake to destroy the city,[144] because of 'their rebellion and their continuing villainy, and their abandonment of the worship of the Lord, and of their indifference to what he had done for them' (*AF*, ch. XVI, p. 62), Nebuchadnezzar held back, destroyed the city wall, entered the city and destroyed the temple that Solomon had built. Those who survived the conquest, he brought into captivity (*AF*, ch. XVI, pp. 62-63). The Samaritans at Shechem are also brought into exile to al-Rha' and Ḥarān, while the Judaeans are brought to Babylon and the remaining Israelites to Egypt (*AF*, ch. XVI, pp. 63-64).[145] The Samaritan temple on Gerizim, rebuilt after Saul's men had demolished it,[146] was deserted, its doors left open, when the remnant of 'the tribe of Ephraim and the halves of them from the tribe of Manasseh' also went into exile (*AF*, ch. XVI, pp. 63-64). Thus, 'the Holy Land was emptied of the sons of Israel and men came from foreign nations[147] and dwelt in the land of Canaan instead of the sons of Israel' (*AF*, ch. XVI, p. 64). Similar to the books of Chronicles, *AF* has no Assyrian conquest or deportation narrative. The conquest of Samaria (Sebaste) follows the conquest of Jerusalem. An exile is also related to Saul's attack on the Samaritans (*AF*, chs. X–XI, pp. 47-48).

Whether or not we have here a distorted version of biblical traditions, it is worth noticing that *AF*'s lengthy 'summary' of several biblical narratives, incorporated in a single event and figure,[148] to some extent matches what scholars such as de Jong, Smelik, Hardmeier and Laato have argued about late seventh–early sixth century BCE events as an origin for the Hezekiah narrative.[149] *AF*'s 'reuse' of such traditions,

---

144. Not mentioned in any biblical text, which only dates one earthquake, namely that from the time of Uzziah (Amos 1.1; Zech. 14.5; cf. Josephus, *Ant.* 9.225). Earthquakes as metaphors for Yahweh's appearance and his devastating wrath against Israel or its enemies are numerous; see, for instance, 2 Sam. 22.8; Isa. 13.13; 24.18; 29.6; Jer. 4.29; Ezek. 38.19-20; Pss. 46.3-4; 77.19; see further B.S. Childs, 'The Enemy from the North and the Chaos Tradition', *JBL* 78 (1955), pp. 187-98.

145. *AF*, ch. XVI, pp. 64-65 is basically a midrashic narration of the exile based on Lev. 26 and Deut. 28.

146. Cf. *AF*, ch. X, pp. 46-47. The destruction was a result of the cult centralization instituted under Saul's reign, at which time quarrels about cult places broke out between the Israelites, some opting for Shiloh, others for Mt Gerizim and others for neither of these places, but 'agreed upon the Beit Maktesh Kifna, which is al-Quds (Jerusalem)'. The narrative resembles similar narratives about second-century BCE cult place destructions. See further below.

147. Juynboll, *Liber Joshua*, ch. xlv: 'ex Persià'; cf. Neh. 9.32-37, in which 'The land of the fathers given to (foreign) kings' (v. 36), and the distress 'from the kings of Assur until today' (v. 32).

148. Macchi, *Les Samaritains*, p. 27. A similar phenomenon is found in Eupolemus' story about Jewish kings, whose spelling of Jehoiachin's name (Greek: ʼΙωναχέμ) has puzzled scholars; Wacholder, *Eupolemus*, pp. 227-28.

149. See above, Chapter 3. Macchi, *Les Samaritains*, p. 27: 'Ce livre semble connaître l'histoire de la résistance de Jérusalem et sa délivrance miraculeuse; cependant, il ne la situe pas durant

which might not have been based on Hebrew Old Testament manuscripts,[150] is combined with similarly 'reused' traditions in, for example, the books of Maccabees.[151] *AF* thus brings Yuma'qīm's men to Antioch (*AF*, ch. XVI, p. 62) instead of Ribla,[152] and has his '*two* sons' slaughtered in his presence (*AF*, ch. XVI, p. 62) instead of 'sons' (2 Kgs 25.7; Jer. 39.6). The story bears allusions to 1 Macc. 12.48– 13.24's Jonathan, who is taken captive to Ptolemais/Antioch and whose *two* sons offered as ransom, though in vain. *Liber Josuae*, which does not have such close parallels to elements found in the Hezekiah narrative, nevertheless places the attack in the fourteenth year.[153]

While knowledge of biblical historical traditions about Judaean kings[154] and prophets (Hanani, Elijah, Eli son of Abikush; Abdil son of Hananīa, Ṣadaqīa and Alyishm, 'Ailūsūs [Elisha] and others; cf. *AF*, ch. XV, p. 58) is reflected in these late mediaeval Samaritan manuscripts, they expose no interest in that history as such. While the Jewish 'Deuteronomistic History' is mainly a tradition about kings and prophets,[155] Samaritan tradition is mainly a tradition about high priests, whose chronology forms the skeleton of the narratives attached to some of them. It is only in supposedly late compilations, such as Macdonald's *Samaritan Chronicle II*, that we find synchronized narratives about the kingdoms of Israel and Judah.[156] Whether this difference in interest reflects an early rejection of the Jewish historical tradition or gives evidence that this tradition is, in fact, later than any alleged split between Jews and Samaritans,[157] is difficult to say. According to biblical tradition, Israelites and Judaeans did not form a coherent state or community after the division of the Davidic–Solomonic kingdom. This makes it extremely difficult to 'create' a

le règne d'Ezékias lors de l'attaque assyrienne de Sennachérib en 701, mais à l'époque de l'attaque babylonienne de Nabuchodnosor'.

150. Macchi, *Les Samaritains*, p. 28.

151. See further Chapter 6.

152. Cf. the fate of Zedekiah in 2 Kgs 25.6; Jer. 39.5.

153. Juynboll, *Liber Joshua*, ch. xlv, relating its much shorter story to 'the Chronicles of Nebuchadnezzar', tells that they were submissive for twelve years, that they revolted in the thirteenth year and that the king marched against them in the fourteenth year; cf. SP Gen. 14.4-5, which reads: 'they served Chedorlaomer for twelve years, in the thirteenth year they revolted and in the fourteenth year came Chedorlaomer'; see also Isa. 36.1 and 2 Kgs 18.13, which refer to the fourteenth year of Hezekiah.

154. Cf. *AF*, ch. XV, p. 57: 'Among the kings of Judah there were some who worshipped [idols, probably] and some of them who did not worship. Those who did not worship called the Beit Miktesh [Jerusalem] "Holy"'. Of the Northern kings there is no mention except for Jeroboam.

155. Tengström, 'Moses and the Prophets', p. 258: 'essentially a history of kings, wars and prophets'.

156. Hjelm, *Samaritans and Early Judaism*, pp. 98-99; Crown, *Samaritan Scribes and Manuscripts*, pp. 31-32.

157. A. Mikoláŝek, 'Les Samaritains Gardiens de la Loi contre les Prophètes', *Communio Viatorum* 12 (1969), pp. 139-48, made the observation that all Jewish Sects (ancient and mediaeval) include the Former and Latter Prophets as part of their theology, while the Samaritans and the Dositheans consciously refused the Prophets and never made them part of their theology. His conclusion was that the Samaritans, in fact, were guardians of the Law against the Prophets. Cf. also S. Lowy, *The Principles of Samaritan Bible Exegesis* (Leiden: E.J. Brill, 1977), p. 86.

historical *Sitz im Leben* for a shared Samaritan and Jewish interest in the 'Jewish Bible', whether prior to or during the Hasmonaean uprising, which might be the only period when Jews and Samaritans politically formed a 'unified' group in Palestine.[158] From a historiographical perspective, it is clear that, apart from the Pentateuch (Hexateuch),[159] the Masoretic Bible serves the interest of a Jerusalem-oriented community.[160] This community is portrayed with royal and nationalistic frames of reference, while Samaritan tradition,[161] apart from traditions paralleling the biblical Judges, projects a tribal system and theocracy as its sociological setting.[162]

It might be telling that Jewish and Samaritan traditions deviate most significantly in narrative material dealing with transitions from tribal to royal government. The characterization of the time of the judges as chaotic in Jewish biblical tradition is not shared by Samaritan writers. Kings succeed kings, as high priests succeed high priests. *AF* (ch. VIII, p. 36) does not have narrative material similar to the Masoretic book of Judges. A list of 13 kings (including Joshua) reigning for 260 years[163] and a list of six high priests in office for 260 years (ch. IX, p. 39),[164] covers the period from the entrance into the land until the death of Samson, after which chaos and apostasy become the norm, because 'there was no king to lead the people' (ch. IX, p. 40). This situation causes a civil war to break out between the followers of Eli son of Yafnī, of the line of Ithamar, and those of the sons of Phinehas (ch. IX, pp. 40-45).

---

158.   Josephus' Alexander legend (*Ant.* 11.297-347) cannot serve as evidence of Samaritan origin from Jerusalem's priesthood at the advent of Alexander the Great; cf. Hjelm, *Samaritans and Early Judaism*, pp. 41-45, 200-207. Nodet, *Origins of Judaism*, pp. 277, 335, has argued for a common Jewish–Samaritan editing of the Pentateuch in the time of Antiochus III (223–187 BCE), however, not for political unity or lasting co-operation.

159.   Tengström, *Die Hexateucherzählung*, p. 44: 'Zusammenfassend wäre zu sagen, dass in der Hexateucherzählung jegliche spur einer Verknüpfung mit Jerusalem fehlt, dass ihre Perspektive mit grösster Sicherheit nicht judäisch, ja nicht einmal südpalästinisch ist. Die lokale Verknüpfung mit *Sichem* und die Hervorhebung der Gestalt Josephs gehören dagegen zu den wichtigsten verbindenden Elementen der literarischen Komposition.'

160.   Nodet, *Origins of Judaism*, p. 163.

161.   In the Pentateuch and Samaritan Chronicles.

162.   A. Rofé, 'Ephraimite versus Deuteronomistic History', in G.N. Knoppers and J.G. McConville (eds.), *Reconsidering Israel and Judah: Recent Studies on the Deuteronomistic History* (Winona Lake, IN: Eisenbrauns, 2000), pp. 462-74, argues that this perspective pervades MT Josh. 24–1 Sam. 12, which he takes as an independent unit, labelling it 'Ephraimite history'. Its different perspective on kingship and war justifies, for Rofé, a separation of the unit from the rest of Samuel–Kings. The thesis needs more investigation as Rofé's historicist reading of ideological discourses imbedded in narrative chronology stands in the way of what he attempts to prove.

163.   Joshua, Nathaniel son of Kaleb's brother, Yāwat (Ehud), Shmr (who might be Shamgar), Farak, Gideon, Abimelech, Tola, Jair, Jephtah, Nathaniel from Ephraim, Antiel from Judah and Samson. Of the MT judges, Debora, Ibson, Elon and Abdon are missing.

164.   Eleazar, Phinehas, 'Abisha, Shisi, Bohki (Beki), Ozzi ('Azzi). Cf. also MT 1 Chron. 5.35-36 and Josephus *Ant.* 5.362, neither of which mention Shisi, who was in office for 50 years; For the Samaritan spelling (עזי ,בחקי ,שישי ,אבישע ,פינחס ,אלעזר), see B. Tsedaka, *A Summary of the History of the Israelite-Samaritans* (Holon: A.B. Institute of Samaritan Studies Press, 2000 [Hebrew]), p. 12.

If textual chronology can be made on an existence of references to persons and events in other books of the Hebrew Bible, one must assert that the Masoretic book of Judges is a late product. Apart from genealogies, the Chronicler does not deal with the period at all[165] and names of judges and events occur very rarely in other books of the Hebrew Bible: Sisera (1 Sam. 13.9), together with Jabin (Ps. 83.9), Zeba and Zalmunnah (Ps. 83.11; cf. 'day of Midian' in Isa. 9.4 and 'defeat of Midian at Oreb' in Isa. 8.1-3) and Abimelech (2 Sam. 11.21).[166] These references correspond fairly well with events connected with the kings mentioned in *AF*.[167]

The Deuteronomistic categories of 'sin, cry, return and deliver, as well as the return to bad behavior whenever the judge died', paradigmatic for the Masoretic book of Judges, are nearly absent from the Samaritan Chronicles.[168] It is only in the judgment of the evil deeds of Eli that the formula is given that 'the people of Israel again did at that time, what was evil in the sight of Yahweh' (*Chron. II*. Judg. §K xiii 1).[169] Wellhausen's judgment of MT Judg. 2.6–3.6; 10.6-16; 17–21 to be either Deuteronomistic or post-Deuteronomistic[170] agrees to some extent with the Samaritan *Chronicle II*, which begins according to MT Judg. 3.9 and has no parallel to Judges 17–21.[171]

---

165.   Spiro, *Samaritans, Tobiads, and Judahites*, p. 21. Spiro's own solution to this problem was to suggest that the book of Judges was not widely used, not that it did not exist.

166.   R.G. Boling, 'Judges, Book of', in *ABD*, III, pp. 1107-17.

167.   *AF*, ch. VIII, p. 36: '…Yāwat (Ehud), from the tribe of Ephraim, 18 years: it was he who fought against Jil'ūn (Eglon) king of Moab and killed him…Farak (Barak) from Naphtali, 30 years: it was he who fought against Sisera, commander of the army of Sūsī and struck him with an iron knife which went into the ground—a much wondered-at happening in Israel; Gideon, 7 years: it was he who fought Zaib (Zeeb) and Raib (Oreb) the two kings of Midian of whose followers he killed twelve groups of 300 men'. Against Spiro, *Samaritans, Tobiads, and Judahites*, p. 28, and p. 34: 'Chr. is the book they [the Samaritans] imitated'.

168.   Hjelm, *Samaritans and Early Judaism*, p. 242.

169.   Considered by Macdonald, *Samaritan Chronicle No. II*, p. 110, to be 'clearly a late addition with strong polemical bias'. This judgment finds support in *AF* (ch. IX, pp. 40-41) and in Juynboll, *Liber Josuae*, ch. xli, both of which do not combine the utterance with Eli, but with another faction of the Israelites, which at that time broke off and formed their own cult in Pirathon (cf. MT Judg. 12.15).

170.   J. Wellhausen, *Die Composition des Hexateuchs und der historischen Bücher des Alten Testaments* (Berlin: Georg Reimer, 1899), p. 214. J.A. Soggin, *Judges: A Commentary* (London: SCM Press, 1981), p. 37, called Judg. 2.6–3.6 'the Deuteronomistic Introduction'; A. Rofé, 'The End of the Book of Joshua According to the Septuagint', *Henoch* 4 (1982), pp. 17-36, 'asserted that the entire section comprising Judg. 1.1–3.11 in all witnesses appear to be secondary', cf. Tov, *Textual Criticism*, pp. 331-32. A.G. Auld, 'What Makes Judges Deuteronomistic', in *idem, Joshua Retold: Synoptic Perspectives* (Edinburgh: T. & T. Clark, 1998), pp. 120-26, asks (p. 125) 'whether these passages were not late additions to an already complex book, rather than constitutive elements of its substratum', such as has been suggested by Noth and his followers.

171.   Rofé, 'Ephraimite versus Deuteronomistic History', p. 465: 'From this work [Josh. 24– 1 Sam. 12] one should subtract the stories extraneous to the theme, in the first place Judges 17–21, chapters that do not mention either judge or saviour. These chapters were appended to the present Book of Judges, because they tell about the times when "no king was in Israel". Another subtraction is less obvious, but not less certain; Judg. 1.1–3.11. These seventy verses were not extant in the Vorlage of the Septuagint to Joshua 24.' Josephus (*Ant.* 5.132-78), who generally deviates

In the small fragments of the book of Judges found among Dead Sea Scrolls, 4QJudg[a] does not contain Judg. 6.7-10, but continues from 6.6 directly to 6.11.[172] The division is also argued by Wellhausen[173] and indicated in the layout of the text in Codices Aleppo and Leningrad.[174] Wellhausen's further conclusion:

> Sin as a reason for bad fortune is not present in the earlier version of the book of Judges. This aspect is added by the Deuteronomists in a stereotypical accusation of apostasy and worship of the *Baalim* and *Astaroth*,[175]

fits the lack of so-called Deuteronomistic[176] theology in Samaritan material.

Judges 9—considered by Wellhausen to belong to the oldest narratives of the Old Testament, but written during the monarchy, because of its preference of kingship in Judg. 9.2[177]—is missing in the Samaritan Chronicles.[178] In two chronicles, it is mentioned that Abimelech became king after Gideon. He reigned for either 30[179] or 13 years, died and was buried in Shechem, the city of his rule.[180] 1QJudges 9, although heavily damaged, seems to resemble the Masoretic version fairly well. In the LXX, both version A and B present lengthy narratives similar to the MT. In the Samaritan book of Joshua, *AF* and *Chronicle II*, there are no judges: only kings stemming from various tribes and elected by the people in Shechem under the conduct of the high priest. The tradition of kingship in Samaritan traditions resembles the political reality of Late Bronze–Iron I Palestine,[181] while judges as

greatly from the Masoretic book of Judges, places his version of Judg. 17–21 between the capture of Bethel, Judg. 1.22 and the attack by 'Chusarsathus, the king of the Assyrians' (Judg. 3.8) as an example of how bad the people behaved when prosperity led them to neglect the divinity.

172.   Abegg, Flint and Ulrich, *The Dead Sea Scrolls Bible*, pp. 208-209: 'The Masoretic Text and all other traditions insert a theological paragraph here (Judg. 7–10), reciting the Deuteronomistic pattern: Israel cried to the Lord, the Lord sent a prophet, and the prophet charged the people with disobedience. 4QJudg[a] retains the original, unembellished narrative.' Ulrich, *Dead Sea Scrolls and the Origins of the Bible*, p. 105: 4QJudg[a], to my knowledge the oldest manuscript of the Book of Judges, dating from about 50–25 BCE'.

173.   Wellhausen, *Composition des Hexateuchs*, p. 214.

174.   W.T. Koopmans, *Joshua 24 as Poetic Narrative* (JSOTSup, 93; Sheffield: JSOT Press, 1990), pp. 363-79; Tov, *Textual Criticism*, pp. 344-45.

175.   Wellhausen, *Composition des Hexateuchs*, p. 214 (my translation); Soggin, *Judges*, p. 43: 'One characteristic of the book of Judges is the fact that from 3.7ff. onwards it [sin, judgment, penitence, salvation] precedes every narrative episode, the substance of which is usually much earlier'.

176.   Auld, 'What Makes Judges Deuteronomistic', p. 125: 'just how far is Deuteronomistic an appropriate description of such passages?'

177.   Wellhausen, *Composition des Hexateuchs*, p. 223. Josephus (*Ant.* 5.233-53) gives a full elaborated version of Abimelech's kingship in Shechem.

178.   Soggin, *Judges*, p. 4: 'two figures, Shamgar (3.31; cf. 5.6) and Abimelech (ch. 9) do not have anything to do with the judges, but have been inserted into the text for reasons we can no longer establish'.

179.   *AF*, ch. VIII, p. 36: 'Abimelech his son 30 years: though the true figure is 3 years'. The passage is not in Juynboll, *Liber Josuae*.

180.   *Chron. II*, Judges § E Q*.

181.   T. Ishida, *The Royal Dynasties in Ancient Israel: A Study on the Formation and Development of Royal-Dynastic Ideology* (Berlin: W. de Gruyter, 1977), pp. 18-25; Ahlström, *History of*

'governors' in the Masoretic tradition,[182] in fact, resembles the function of the governors of the Persian-Hellenistic period. I do not intend a historicist reading of the narrative as a reflection of Shechem's position as 'the largest city-state in the whole of the highlands' in the Amarna period.[183] In my opinion, the polemics of the MT Judges refer to conflicts in the post-exilic period and might belong to what John Strange has termed a 'Hasmonaean redaction of the Deuteronomistic History'.[184] The Masoretic calculation of about 400 years for the period of judges similarly resembles fairly closely the 400 years from the end of the exile in 539 BCE until the first Maccabaean king in 141 BCE. Another 400-year period correlates year 562 BCE for Jehoiachin's release with Jonathan's 'appointment' as leader of the Jewish nation in 161/160 BCE. The problem with the statement 'that there was no king' in Masoretic and Samaritan material is, of course, that the kingship instituted by Samuel does not solve the problem of chaos purportedly created by the lack of a king. In Masoretic tradition, there has in fact only been one, namely Abimelech (Judg. 9), who is given the role of 'a false king'. One must state that for the Masoretic material, the statement is out of place, whatever its referential meaning might be. In Samaritan tradition, the statement refers to the situation after the death of Samson, who is 'the last king of the Raḍwān'.[185] In Masoretic tradition, the title of 'judge', given to the so-called pre-monarchic leaders, creates the literary possibility of assigning Saul and David—the kings that Samuel anointed—the roles of being the first *kings* for *all* Israel. In the succession of judges, 'the narrator also "created" the nation Israel long before it existed'.[186]

3. *Shiloh between Shechem and Jerusalem?*

The provisional character of the time of the judges in Masoretic tradition also includes the status of Shiloh as a cult place for all Israel[187] from the division of the land (Josh. 18.1) until the capture of the ark during Eli's reign (1 Sam. 1–4). Under the priestly leadership of Eli as a judge in Shiloh,[188] Israel is no better off than during the tribal leadership of the judges. Biblical ambivalence towards Shiloh might be the reason that the covenant making in Joshua 24 takes place in Shechem and not in Shiloh. The narrative about the covenant, considered by Wellhausen to

---

Ancient Palestine, p. 372: 'the judges (rulers) of the Old Testament have to be seen in the same light as all other Canaanite princes and petty kings. They were princes, rulers, chieftains over certain territories and clans, societies, that were more or less well organized.

182.   Whitelam, *The Just King*, pp. 51-59; A. Alt, *Kleine Schriften* (3 vols.; Munich: Beck, 1953), II, p. 333.

183.   Soggin, *Judges*, p. 182.

184.   J. Strange, 'The Book of Joshua: A Hasmonaean Manifesto?', in A. Lemaire and B. Otzen (eds.), *History and Traditions of Early Israel* (VTSup, 50; Leiden: E.J. Brill, 1993), pp. 136-41; *idem*, 'The Book of Joshua: Origin and Dating', *SJOT* 16/1 (2002), pp. 44-51.

185.   Juynboll, *Liber Josuae*, ch. xxxix; *AF*, ch. IX, p. 39.

186.   Ahlström, *History of Ancient Palestine*, pp. 370-73 (373).

187.   Cf. Josh. 18–19; 1 Sam. 3.20–4.1

188.   1 Sam. 4.18.

be Yahwistic (E) with few additions,[189] is found in both Samaritan tradition and Josephus, however, in a significantly shorter version in Josephus, lacking any direct reference to the past and with no renewal of the covenant and no sacrifice (*Ant.* 5.115-19). In the Samaritan *Chronicle II*, Jos. 24.2-5, 6b-10, 11b-12, 14bβ and 19-21a of the Masoretic version are lacking, all of which are passages that caused Wellhausen, Noth and quite a number of scholars trouble assigning their provenance.[190] At the opening, reference is given to the exodus event:

> You know all that Yahweh did to you; how he brought your fathers out from Egypt with sign, with wonders and with a strong hand and an outstretched arm and with great miracles (באתות ובמופתים וביד חזקה ובזרוע נטויה ובמראים גדלים; how you crossed the Sea of Reeds on dry land (ותעברו את ים סוף ביבשה) and everything he did for you in the wilderness (ואת כל אשר עשה לכם במדבר); how you also went over the Jordan on dry land (ותעברו גם את הירדן ביבשה). (*Chron. II*, Jos. UB*)[191]

Reference to MT Josh. 24.14-15's 'the Gods your fathers worshipped' is missing in all Samaritan chronicles. In most texts it is 'replaced' by 'foreign Gods' without a father reference.[192] Gaster, 'Das Buch Josua', xxii.13, implicitly argues against MT's negative characterization of the fathers in the people's declaration that 'Yahweh our God will we serve, for he is our God and our father's God'.[193]

AF brings a version, which in length, though not in content, comes closest to Josephus' version. Without any reference to the past, Joshua, after having summoned the assembly of Israel to the plain of Nablus, said to them:

> Do not swerve from the service of the Lord, neither to the right nor to the left [cf. Josh. 23.6]; do not serve foreign gods; accept no Qibla[194] other than the illustrious Mountain which God made known to you in his unchangeable Law, lest the disasters written down on the scroll of the Law fall upon you'. They replied and said, 'Far be it from us to do such a thing, or to follow anybody but our Lord. We will swerve neither to right nor to left: we will serve our Lord on this mountain forever.'[195] So Joshua then took a young lamb and sacrificed it on the Mountain,

189. Wellhausen, *Composition des Hexateuchs*, pp. 133-34. So also Van Seters, 'Joshua 24 & the Problem of Tradition'.

190. Cf. Perlitt, *Bundestheologie im Alten Testament*, pp. 239-84; Van Seters, 'Joshua 24 & the Problem of Tradition', pp. 141-46; Koopmans, *Joshua 24 as Poetic Narrative*, pp. 7-95; Römer, *Israel's Väter*, pp. 320-30; K. Schmid, *Erzväter und Exodus*, pp. 212-24.

191. Macdonald, *Samaritan Chronicle No. II*, p. 98; Hebrew text, p. 30 (my translation). Niessen, *Buches Yehošua'*, fol. 47b-49b, which gives the most detailed account of the exodus, has no parallels to MT Josh. 24.2b-5, 14-15, 23-24, while 16-21 is only alluded to.

192. Cf. LXX: αλλοτρίους + father reference.

193. Consult Gaster's text, not his list of references to MT (pp. 216-18), which is misleading. The phrase appears also in Ryl. Sam. MS 269 and 257 (Gaster's text B); cf. Macdonald, *Samaritan Chronicle No. II*, apparatus *ad loc*. It is not found in *Liber Josuae*, *AF* or Macdonald's and Niessen's texts.

194. An Arabic term referring to the direction towards which one should pray. For the Samaritans, Mt Gerizim is the Qibla, the 'Chosen Place'; cf. Stenhouse, *Kitāb al-Tarīkh* (1985), p. i n. 3.

195. Niessen, *Buches Yehošua'*, fol. 48b-49a, in particular stresses the election of Gerizim and warning against following prophets, 'die Jahve nicht erwählt und beauftragt hat'.

because of the covenant they had made with him on behalf of themselves and their children. (*AF*, ch. VIII, p. 37; underlined text is not in MT Josh. 24)[196]

The LXX stands out as the only text, which names the place as Shiloh. Except for a harmonizing tendency with Josh. 18.1; 19.51; 21.2; 22.9, 12; Judg. 18.31 and 21.12-24, there is no obvious reason for this variant and it may well belong to a different *Vorlage*.[197] The possibility that the reason is theological, as has been argued by some scholars,[198] has serious implications, given the ambiguous attitude towards Shechem and Shiloh in Masoretic tradition.[199] Josephus' silence about the covenant or any cultic ceremonies, as found in biblical and non-biblical traditions, might be his solution to a diminishing of Samaritan claims of importance—a tendency noticed also with regards to Abraham and Jacob's altars at Shechem,[200] the burial of Joseph's bones at Shechem[201] and the 'transformation' of the El-Berith

---

196.   The sacrifice appears in all editions. In Gaster, 'Das Buch Josua', Macdonald, *Samaritan Chronicle No. II*, and Niessen, *Buches Yehošua'*, Joshua builds an altar at the foot of Mount Gerizim, next to the stone of witness. In Sam. Ryl. MSS 257, 268 and 269, Shechem is called holy; cf. also the Epic of Theodotius quoted by Eusebius, *Praep. Ev.* 9.22 (see *OTP*; Hjelm, *Samaritans and Early Judaism*, pp. 138-46).

197.   Tov, *Textual Criticism*, pp. 327-30; Koopmans, *Joshua 24 as Poetic Narrative*, p. 94, with bibliographic references. Old Greek variants to the book of Joshua represent a much shorter text than that of the MT. 4QJosh shares some readings with the Old Greek, some with the MT. See further A.G. Auld, 'Joshua: The Hebrew and Greek Texts', in *idem, Joshua Retold*, pp. 7-18; revised version of a paper given at the SOTS Cambridge Summer Meeting (1977), published in J.A. Emerton (ed.), *Studies in the Historical Books of the Old Testament* (VTSup, 30; Leiden: E.J. Brill, 1979), pp. 1-14; *idem*, 'Textual and Literary Studies in the Book of Joshua', in *idem, Joshua Retold*, pp. 19-24; first published in *ZAW* 90 (1978), pp. 412-17; L.J. Greenspoon, 'The Qumran Fragments of Joshua: Which Puzzle are they Part of and Where do they Fit', in G.J. Brooke and B. Lindars (eds.), *Septuagint, Scrolls and Cognate Writings* (SCS, 33; Atlanta, GA: Scholars Press, 1992), pp. 159-94.

198.   E. Nielsen, *Shechem: A Traditio-Historical Investigation* (Copenhagen: G.E.C. Gad, 1955), p. 86: 'the ancient translator felt there was a problem in the prominence held by Shechem in this tradition'; H.G. Kippenberg, *Garizim und Synagoge: Traditionsgeschichtliche Untersuchungen zur samaritanischen Religion der aramäischen Periode* (Berlin: W. de Gruyter, 1971), p. 91: 'Wir erkennen in dieser neuen Lokalisierung [LXX: Shiloh] ein Stück von jenen Diskussionen wieder, die in Ägypten—dem Heimatland der LXX—zwischen Juden und Samar. geführt wurden'; Crown, 'Redating the Schism', p. 32: 'The Septuagint reading of Shiloh instead of Shechem (Joshua 24) and the statement in the Testament of Joseph (2.6) that Joseph was buried in Hebron rather than near Shechem suggests that the Jewish authorities were already troubled by Samaritan interpretations of the sacred writ in favour of Shechem and Mt Gerizim'; K. Schmid, *Erzväter und Exodus*, p. 212: 'Der Szene 1 Kön 12 steht Jos 24 als positiv gezeichnete gegenüber: König über "alle Stamme Israels ist" und soll Jhwh sein'.

199.   Hjelm, *Samaritans and Early Judaism*, pp. 146-49.

200.   Shechem is not mentioned in Josephus, *Ant.* 1.157; cf. Gen. 12.6-7; the verses are missing in Josephus, *Ant.* 1.337; cf. Gen. 33.18-20.

201.   Shechem is not mentioned: Josephus, *Ant.* 2.200; 5.117-19; cf. Gen. 50.25; Exod. 13.19; Josh. 24.29-33. The burial is not mentioned in *Liber Josuae* and *AF*. In Gaster ('Das Buch Josua', ix.31), Macdonald (*Samaritan Chronicle No. II*, Jos. § MH*) and Niessen (*Buches Yehošua'*, fol. 25a), the burial takes place after the blessing and cursing event on Gerizim-Ebal; the *Testamemt of Joseph* 2.6 states that Joseph was buried in Hebron, while Acts 7.16 states that 'they' (Jacob and our fathers) were buried in Shechem.

temple at Shechem[202] into a rocky place.[203] From Josephus' denigration of Shechem to his favouring of Shiloh, most explicitly expressed in Joshua's relocation of the camp from Gilgal:

> A fifth year had now passed away and there was no longer any Canaanite left, save for such as had escaped through the solidity of their walls. So Joshua moved his camp up from Galgala into the hill country and set up the holy tabernacle at the city of Shiloh, since that spot seemed suitable on an account of its beauty until circumstances should permit them to build a temple,[204]

it becomes clear that the LXX has not merely changed a name, but reflects a tradition that purports a continuity from the Shiloh tabernacle in the time of Joshua to Solomon's temple in Jerusalem. In Josephus, the problem of competing traditions is solved by his addition:

> Proceeding thence to Shechem,[205] with all the people, he erected an altar at the spot foreordained by Moses,[206] and divided his army, posted one half of it on mount Garizin and the other half on Ebal ('Ηβήλω),[207] whereon also stood the altar, along with the Levites and the Priests. After sacrificing (θύσαντες) and pronouncing imprecations (δὲ καὶ ἀρὰς ποιησάμενοι), which they also left graven upon the altar, they returned to Shiloh.[208]

Combining traditions of Joshua 8 and 18, Josephus has 'solved' the difficult placement of the blessing and cursing event (Josh. 8.30-35) after the conquest of Ai in the Masoretic tradition (8.1-29). We here notice Josephus' 'change' of the Deuteronomistic Law that the event should take place after 'the crossing of the Jordan' (והיה ביום אשר תעברו את־הירדן, Deut. 27.2, 4, 12) or the more imprecise 'when Yahweh your God has brought you into the land' (והיה כי יביאך יהוה אלהיך אל־הארץ, Deut. 11.29) to 'when they had utterly vanquished the land of Canaan and destroyed its whole population' (Josephus, *Ant.* 4.305).

---

202. Josephus, *Ant.* 5.248; cf. Judg. 9.46.

203. T. Thornton, 'Anti-Samaritan Exegesis Reflected in Josephus' Retelling of Deuteronomy, Joshua and Judges', *JTS* 47 (1996), pp. 125-30. For similar tendencies in Pseudo-Philo, see Spiro, *Samaritans, Tobiads, and Judahites*, pp. 43-50.

204. Josephus, *Ant.* 5.68; cf. Josh. 8.30-35; 18.1. For other references to Josephus' preference of Shiloh for other cult places, such as Mizpah, Gilgal and Nob, see Thornton, 'Anti-Samaritan Exegesis', pp. 127-29.

205. Not mentioned in the biblical account, but SP Deut. 11.30 states that the place should be 'facing Shechem' (מול שכם), which also the Mishnah confirms: 'When Israel crossed the Jordan and came upon Mt Gerizim and unto Mt Ebal in Samaria, near by Shechem, beside the oaks of Moreh, as it is written, *Are they not beyond Jordan* (there it is written, *And Abraham passed through the land unto the place of Shechem unto the oak of Moreh*); as there the oak of Moreh that is spoken of is at Shechem, so here the oak of Moreh that is spoken of is at Shechem' (*m. Soṭ.* 7.5).

206. Deut. 11.29-30; 27.4; Josephus, *Ant.* 4.305: 'when they had utterly vanquished the land of Canaan and destroyed its whole population, as was met, they were to erect the altar pointing towards the rising sun, not far from the city of Shechem (οὐ πόρρω τῆς Ζικίμων πολεώς) between the two mountains, the Garizaean on the right and that called "Counsel" (Βουλὴ) on the left'.

207. LXX: Γαιβάλ.

208. Josephus, *Ant.* 5.69-70; cf. Josh. 8.30-31.

In 4QJosh[a], this same problem is 'solved' by placing MT Josh. 8.30-35 between the crossing of the Jordan in Joshua 4 and the beginning of Joshua 5. The variant appears similar to Josephus' description of 'Joshua's building of an altar immediately after the crossing of the Jordan,[209] while not mentioning either the journey to Mt Ebal or an altar at the point where the Masoretic text places it.[210] Though he eventually describes an altar at Shechem, it is not until noticeably later in the narrative,[211] and certainly the tradition of Joshua's covenant at Shechem after the conquest would have been widely known'.[212] To this we must add Thornton's observation that 'Josephus' version emphasizes, in a passage unparalleled in Deuteronomy that the sacrifices in the Ebal-Gerizim area are to be a strictly singular affair, never to be repeated'.[213] In *Ant.* 5.20, Josephus does not mention Gilgal, but settles the camp 'at a distance of ten stades from Jericho'.[214] He mentions sacrifices, the Passover, but no circumcision and no blessings or curses.[215] In the LXX, a parallel to MT Josh. 8.30-35 is placed after Josh. 9.2.

AF (ch. II, pp. 10-11) reflects both biblical (Josh. 5.10-12) and Josephus' (*Ant.* 5.16-21) variants by referring to the camping in Gilgal on the first night and on the plain of Jericho on the fourteenth day of the first month, the eating of unleavened bread, the produce of the land and the cessation of eating manna.[216] The altar, sacrifice and circumcision[217] are not mentioned.

Paralleling Masoretic tradition (Josh. 8.30–9.2), Joshua builds an altar on Gerizim after the conquest of Ai and before the forming of the coalition of the nations. Compared to the repetitive MT, *AF* (ch. IV, p. 14) offers rather a paraphrase(?) of MT Josh. 8.30-35:

> It was at that time that Joshua built an altar of stones on Mount Gerizim,[218] as the Almighty had told him (to do) and offered sacrifices upon it. *Half the people stood facing* Mount Gerizim, while *the other half faced* Mount Ebal. *Joshua read out the*

209. Josephus, *Ant.* 5.16-21.

210. Josephus, *Ant.* 5.45-48, 49-57; cf. Josh. 8.1-29 (missing 30-35); 9.3-27.

211. Josephus, *Ant.* 5.68-69.

212. Josephus, *Ant.* 5.68-69; cf. Abegg, Flint and Ulrich (eds.), *Dead Sea Scrolls Bible*, pp. 201-202.

213. Josephus, *Ant.* 4.308; Thornton, 'Anti-Samaritan Exegesis', p. 127; Spiro, *Samaritans, Tobiads, and Judahites*, p. 60; *AF*, ch. XIX, p. 72: 'The Text (Deut. 27.4-8] involves the building of (such) a place and continuing to offer sacrifice in it'.

214. However, Josephus, *Ant.* 5.34: 'The place where Joshua had established his camp was called Galgala (Γάλγαλα)'; cf. Josh. 5.9, which in Josephus appears interceded between Josh. 7.1 and 2; cf. also Josephus, *Ant.* 5.48, 62, Joshua's camp in Galgala, which he moves to Shiloh after the conquest of the land (5.68).

215. Josephus' text is thus not quite as similar to 4QJosh[a] as the authors of *Dead Sea Scrolls Bible*, assert.

216. Cf. MT. Josh. 5.10-12; Josephus, *Ant.* 5.16-21; Juynboll, *Liber Josuae*, ch. xvi-xvii; Gaster, 'Das Buch Josua', vi.3-6; Macdonald, *Samaritan Chronicle No. II*, Jos. § GA*; Niessen, *Buches Yehošua'*, fol. 18b.

217. No Samaritan tradition mentions the circumcision in Gilgal (MT Josh. 5.2-8).

218. MT: בהר עיבל; LXX: ἐν ὄρει Γαιβαλ.

Torah in its entirety in the hearing of all Israel, *men, women and children and the stranger who was in their midst.*[219]

The 'paraphrase', however, might be that of 4QJosh[a] (or a similar text), about which we cannot know whether the entire passage of MT Josh. 8.30-35 was intended, as only the last word of v. 34 and the entire v. 35 are present in a slightly varied form followed by an editorial transition to Josh. 5.2.[220] Ulrich, however, assumes that although there is no textual certainty of the building of the altar,[221] scripture links the building of the altar with the reading of the Torah. Thus the first altar was in Gilgal. The names Gerizim and Ebal were added secondarily to Deut. 27.4 and linked with Deut. 27.9-26, while 'Deut. 27.12-13 appears to be redactionally connected with Deut. 11.29-30'.[222] Although a neat solution to a difficult problem, Ulrich's assertion 'that 4QJosh[a] and Josephus preserve the earlier and/or preferable form'[223] is far from being proven.[224] It might as well be that Josh. 8.30-35 has been 'inserted' in 4QJosh[a] at the junction of chs. 4 and 5, in order to show the expediency with which Joshua carried out the Deuteronomistic Law, such as has been suggested by A. Rofé.[225] His interpretation finds support in rabbinic tradition:

everything, the ceremonies near Shechem and the journey from Gilgal and back, took place on the very day of the crossing into Canaan (*t. Soṭ.* 8.7; cf. *m. Soṭ.* 7.5); Rabbi Eliezer (ben Hyrcanus, second half of the first century CE) 'transferred' Gerizim and Ebal to two artificial mounds which had allegedly been heaped up by the Israelites near Gilgal (*y. Soṭ.* 7.3).[226] A divergent opinion, however, also appears from the 2nd century CE, Rabbi Ishmael, who 'ruled that all the laws that had to be performed upon entering the land were really enforced after the fourteen years of conquest and distribution of tribal inheritances (*y. Soṭ.* 7.3). Thus, in his

---

219. Italics indidicate parallels to MT Josh. 8.30-35 which are not in Deut. 11.29 and 27.2-8. Gaster, 'Das Buch Josua', ix.31; Macdonald, *Samaritan Chronicle No. II*, Jos. § MH*; Niessen, *Buches Yehošua'*, fol. 24a-25a, also follows the composition of the MT, but have Joshua 'conquer' Luzah on Mt Gerizim before the blessing and cursing event (9.11; Jos. § KB*-C*; fol. 23.a); cf. MT Josh. 8.17, 'and Bethel' (missing in the LXX), and 8.12, 'between Bethel and Ai' (also missing in the LXX).

220. E. Ulrich, '4QJosh[a] and Joshua's First Altar in the Promised Land', in G.J. Brooke (ed.), *New Qumran Texts and Studies: Proceedings of the First Meeting of the International Organization for Qumran Studies, Paris 1992* (Leiden: E.J. Brill, 1994), pp. 89-104.

221. Ulrich, '4QJosh[a]', p. 91: 'Though the first two lines of frg. 1 correspond with Josh. 34–35 (the reading of the Torah), it is not certain that 8.30-31 (the building of the altar) preceded, since that would occur at the unpreserved bottom of the preceding column'.

222. Ulrich, '4QJosh[a]', p. 96; *idem*, '4QJosh[a] (Pls. XXXII-XXXIV)', in E. Ulrich and F.M Cross (eds.), *DJD* XIV (1995), pp. 143-52.

223. Ulrich, '4QJosh[a]', p. 96.

224. See, however, A.G. Auld, 'Reading Joshua After Kings', in *idem, Joshua Retold*, pp. 102-12 (111), for a different opinion based on the LXX's 'clumsily' reuse of elements of Josh. 5.1 in 9.1-2.

225. A. Rofé, 'The Editing of the Book of Joshua in the Light of 4QJosh[a]', in Brooke (ed.), *New Qumran Texts and Studies*, pp. 73-80.

226. Rofé, 'Editing of the Book of Joshua', p. 79.

view, the right chronological position of Josh. 8.30-35 would be after 19.31 or 21.42 (LXX).[227]

Rofé is well aware of Josephus' second narrative at exactly this point, but he seems not to have noticed that, similar to Josephus' proceeding from Gilgal to Shiloh, passing quickly over Shechem, also Rabbi Ishmael's mention of the fourteen years of conquest implies the transference of the tabernacle from Gilgal directly to Shiloh.[228] Here mention shall be made of a Samaritan variant.

Paralleling Josephus (*Ant.* 5.68-69), a third narrative appears (*AF*, ch. VII, p. 28) after the conquests of the land (in traditions, which vary greatly from MT and LXX Josh. 9–17). On Gerizim, they set up the stones (from the Jordan).[229] Joshua built the temple on Mt Gerizim in the second year, put the tabernacle in it and constructed an altar of stones (*AF*, ch. VII, p. 28).[230] After the sacrifice, the tribes uttered the blessings from Mt Gerizim and the curses from Mt Ebal. Compositionally placed after the conquests, the text, however, recalls the entrance situation and claims that, according to 'tradition', the event took place 'in the first month'[231] of the second year[232] after the entrance into the land of Canaan. This, of course, marks the conquest narratives as *inclusio* and lends priority to Gerizim as the first 'settlement' of the Tabernacle, which had 'stood in the Plain for the space of a year: from Passover to Passover'.

It seems that it is not literary chronology, as asserted by Rofé,[233] but location which is the driving force behind the existence of variant traditions. The agreement between MT and Samaritan traditions that the reading of the law took place on Gerizim and Ebal necessarily separates this event from the entrance event. While

227. Rofé, 'Editing of the Book of Joshua', pp. 79-80.

228. Cf. the 14 years of the sanctuary at Gilgal (*b. Zeb.* 118b).

229. The parentheses belong to Stenhouse's translation. No Samaritan tradition relates that the stones from the Jordan were transported to Gerizim. Juynboll, *Liber Josuae*, ch. xvi: 'Deinde Jūsa.a, Nūni filius, 12 lapides pavimenti, quod in Al-Ordonnis alveo depositum fuerat, erexit [cf. Josh. 4.9], et (alios ejusmodi) 12 lapides Principes erexerunt in loco, cui nomen est Galil' (cf. Josh. 4.20, 24); Niessen, *Buches Yehošua'*, fol. 23b-24a: the Torah is written on 'zwölf grosse Steine, nachdem man sie mit reinen Kalk überzogen hatte. Er richtete sie auf Gerizim auf' (cf. Deut. 27.2, 4).

230. Cf. Macdonald, *Samaritan Chronicle No. II*, Jos. § QG*.

231. Reflective of MT Josh. 4.19-20's erection of the 12 stones in Gilgal.

232. Cf. also Juynboll, *Liber Josuae*, ch. xxi; Josephus, *Ant.* 5.68: the sixth year, which appears also in a nineteenth–twentieth century Sam. manuscript composed by Ab-Sikkuwa b. Saed the Danfi (1856–1912) or the priest Jacob b. Ezzi (1899–1987). The manuscript is based on the writings of Pinhas b. Yitzhak (Samaritan: Phinas ban Yessak) (1841–98); cf. B. Tsedaka, 'The Origin of the Samaritans From the Children of Israel: The Quarrel Between the High Priest 'Azzi and the Priest 'Eli', *A.B.- The Samaritan News* 801-803 (2001), pp. 23-33 (32) (Hebrew). For Samaritan spelling of names based on pronunciation, I am guided by a private conversation with B. Tsedaka.

233. Rofé, 'Editing of the Book of Joshua', p. 80: 'the same problems which troubled scribes of the Second Commonwealth kept bothering later Tannaim and Amoraim: what is the proper time of the execution of the ceremonies enjoined in Deut. 27? Or in other words, how does Joshua carry out what is commanded in the Torah.'

MT presents this as a single event including the blessings and the curses, ST separates the two. Similar to Josephus, the blessing and the cursing are placed at the end of the conquests, before the land distribution, which in *AF* (ch. VII, p. 29) takes place on Gerizim, but in Josephus in Shiloh (*Ant.* 5.72, 79). Hence, the quick return to Shiloh (εἰς τὴν Σιλῖυν ἀνέξευξαν) in Josephus (*Ant.* 5.70), where the tabernacle has already been set up (*Ant.* 5.68). In MT Josh. 18.1: 'Then the whole congregation of the Israelites assembled at Shiloh, and they set up the tabernacle there; the whole land lay subdued before them'. Why did Josephus harmonize the Shiloh with the Shechem event? The answer probably lies in the troublesome passage of 8.30-35, which gives priority to Shechem against Gilgal and Shiloh. Hence, the compositional separation of the Shechem event with the Gilgal event is prior to their combination in 4QJosh^a. It is not that 4QJosh^a and Josephus present an earlier form, which did not specify the place where the altar was to be built, prior to a possible Samaritan claim that the first altar should be 'on Mount Gerizim', as suggested by Ulrich.[234] Josephus' denigration of Shechem has this claim as its background. It rather seems that variant traditions existed contemporaneously.[235] Josephus' choice had its own reason: a support of Jewish claims for cultic sovereignty, and hence a denial of any Samaritan claim to such sovereignty, were the driving forces behind Josephus' attitude towards 'the Samaritans' in his *Antiquities*.[236]

With this examination, it has become clear that in the LXX, Joshua 24 underscores a text tradition which points forward to the Deuteronomistic History's replacement of the cult in Shiloh with that in Jerusalem,[237] while the MT creates a continuum in its thematic reference to the Patriarchs of the past.[238] As Joshua's removal of

234. Ulrich, '4QJosh^a (Pls. XXXII-XXXIV)', p. 146: 'Thus it may be conjectured that the witnesses display three stages in the history of the text. First, 4QJosh^a and Josephus present an early form of the narrative which places the building of the altar at Gilgal at the end of ch. 4, in accord with the command as read in Deut. 27.2-3 and Deut. 27.4 without the insertion of a place-name. Secondly, the Samaritan tradition includes בהר גריזין [גריזים; *Vetus Latina*: Garzin] at Deut. 27.4, constituting a Samaritan claim. A tertiary sequence is preserved in MT and LXX, with בהר עיבל in MT at Deut. 27.4 as a Judaean counterclaim to בהר גריזין. According to this hypothesis then, the narrative about the building of the altar, which originally followed the crossing of the Jordan and preceded the circumcision account, was subsequently transposed in accordance with Moses' revised command in MT to its present, curious position at Josh. 8.30-35.'

235. Auld, 'Reading Joshua after Kings', suggests, however, opting for a priority of the beginning of ch. 5 before its move to ch. 8 (p. 111), that the passage 'is, in fact, not original at all, but a latecomer looking for a suitable home' (p. 110).

236. Hjelm, *Samaritans and Early Judaism*, pp. 222-38.

237. In the Hebrew Bible, most explicitly argued in Ps. 78 and Jer. 7; cf. D.G. Schley, *Shiloh: A Biblical City in Tradition and History* (JSOTSup, 63; Sheffield: JSOT Press, 1989), pp. 167-81. Kippenberg, *Garizim und Synagoge*, p. 91: 'Dass LXX in Jos 24 Sichem streicht und Silo einsetzt passt überraschend genau zur samar. Hohenpriesterliste, die in der Errichtung des Silo-Heiligtums die Gründung einer illegitimen Hohenpreisersukzession erblickt'. K. Schmid, *Erzväter und Exodus*, p. 218: 'Jos 24 und 1 Sam 12 rahmen so die Epoche der Richter', which seems to support the LXX's Shiloh against MT's Shechem.

238. Tengström, *Hexateucherzählung*, pp. 118-19, 153-54; K. Schmid, *Erzväter und Exodus*, p. 224: 'Was es also literarhistorisch vermutlich nie gegeben hat will Jos 24.26 von Josua niedergeschrieben wissen; nämlich einen literarischen Hexateuch [ספר־תורת־אלהים]'. All Samaritan

foreign gods imitates Jacob's act of removal of foreign gods, which he buries under the oak at Shechem (Gen. 35.4)[239] before he leaves to go to Bethel, so also Joshua's people are sent to their inheritance (Josh. 24.28). In both narratives, the act is initiated by land 'acquisition',[240] as is also Abraham, Jacob[241] and Joshua's[242] building of an altar in Shechem.

Diachronically, in biblical tradition, whether Hebrew or Greek, and in Samaritan writings, Shiloh stands between the Shechem of the Patriarchs and the Jerusalem of the Davidides. While in biblical traditions, its connotations are ambiguous, in Samaritan tradition, it is presented entirely negatively, as a competing cult place from the time of the interim between the kings of the *Raḍwān* (MT: 'judges') and the kings of the Israelite monarchies. In Samaritan tradition, Shiloh owes its origin to the priest Eli's departure from Gerizim. The narrative occurs in all Samaritan traditions with slight variations.[243] According to Macdonald, *Chron. II*, Sam. § JI*; KS* and *AF* (ch. IX, p. 41), the young Eli son of Jefunneh of the lineage of Ithamar, is given the honorary office of being the chancellor of the temple treasures[244] under the leadership of the high priest Uzzi (עֻזִּי), whose authority he challenges. The quarrel results in Eli's departure from Gerizim and his erection of a temple and cult in Shiloh. A variant tradition involves exclusion. In a paradigmatic use of Genesis 4, it gives the role of Cain to Eli, as the unsuccessful priest, whose offering God rejects because it has not been properly salted (*Chron. II*, § LK*, U*; *AF*, ch. IX, p. 41).[245] Eli's departure turns the fate of all Israel, which looses its coherence and becomes split into three separate groups (*Chron. II*, Judg. § LO*-T*; 1 Sam. § BA*-F*; *AF*, ch. IX, p. 42): 'A faction on Mount Gerizim; a heretical faction that followed false gods; and the faction that followed Eli son of Yafnī in Shiloh'. Later, in the beginning of Saul's reign, another quarrel broke out, with some opting for Shiloh and others for Mt Gerizim, while still others said 'Neither here nor there' (*AF*, ch. X, p. 46). Abandoning Shiloh, they chose Jerusalem at the initiative of David, who went to Saul to counsel him to

traditions close the Joshua-Phinehas narratives with reference to the 'Holy Book' written by 'Abisha son of Phinehas son of Eleazar son of Aaron, in the thirteenth year of the dominion of the sons of Israel over the land of Canaan'. Although this is a reference to the Torah, the Joshua and Phinehas traditions might be implied.

239. Van Seters, *Prologue to History*, p. 293.

240. Gen. 33.18-20; (34.1–35.5;) Josh. 24.13

241. Gen. 12.7-8; 33.19-20. While the MT and SP do not have a narrative about Abraham's removal of foreign gods, *Jubilees* presents an Abraham, who burns the house of idols in Ur before he leaves to go to Haran (*Jub.* 12.12).

242. Josephus, *Ant.* 5.68-70; Gaster, 'Das Buch Josua', xxii.20; Macdonald, *Samaritan Chronicle No. II*, Jos. § UD*, and Niessen, *Buches Yehošua'*, fol. 49b. In *AF* (ch. VII, p. 28) the altar is built on Gerizim.

243. Tsedaka, 'Special Samaritan Traditions', p. 191.

244. Cf. Lev. 38.21.

245. Cf. Lev. 2.13, for salt as a sign of eternal covenant is mentioned twice in the Old Testament; Num. 18.19, regarding the Aaronide priests; and 2 Chron. 13.5, regarding the everlasting kingship over Israel, which 'Yahweh, Israel's God gave to David and his sons by a covenant of salt' (ברית מלח).

make war on the sons of Israel who were still living in the Beautiful Plain[246] because they had not abandoned the illustrious mountain nor followed their (i.e. Jesse and Saul's) whims, nor were they sacrificing wherever they sacrificed; and because they (the Samaritans) had the remnants of the Philistines fighting on their side. For when the sons of Israel had become weak and fewer in number, they had entered into a treaty with the nations and sued for peace. Consequently the hatred between them and the erroneous children of Israel intensified and hardened. (*AF*, ch. X, p. 47)

The attack, 'on the Feast of Tabernacles', results in a killing of 'Shīshī the Great High Priest in Greater Salem'[247] and a great number of the people, women and children being taken captive, the destruction of the stone altar on the top of the mountain and a demolishing of Luzah, the city on the top of the mountain.[248] A possible variant is found in 1 Samuel 22's narration about Saul's killing of Ahimelech son of Ahitub, and the priests in Nob (בנ).[249] Josephus implicitly bears witness to the Samaritan variant in his statement that Saul 'not only slaughtered a whole family of priestly rank, but furthermore demolished the city (Ναβα),[250] which the Deity himself had chosen as the home and nurse of priests and prophets',[251] and furthermore 'strove to leave what was virtually their temple destitute of priests and prophets, by first slaying so many of them and not suffering even their native place to remain, that others might come after them'.[252] This last non-scriptural sentence resembles the destruction of the soil by planting 'salt', as did Abimelech in Shechem (Judg. 9.45; Josephus, *Ant.* 5.248) or 'an undesirable plant', as did Simon on Gerizim (*Megillat Taanit*).[253] In *AF* (ch. XI, p. 48), 'they (Saul and his men) sowed it, like (all other) fields', and the sons of Israel were abandoned from

---

246. Synonym for the Plain of Nablus.

247. According to Macdonald, *Samaritan Chronicle II*, p. 125, this is Salem Rabhta, southeast of Sychar and northeast of Sam. Gilgal. R. Abel, *La Géographie de Palestine* (2 vols.; Paris: J. Gabalda, 1933–38), II, p. 442: 'Les Samaritains la nomment Salem la Grande dont le nom est conservé par le village de *Salīm*, à 5 kilomètres à l'est de Balāṭa. Mais le site ancien, d'après Alt, serait *Šeih Naṣrallah* éminence isolée à l'ouest de ce village. Sa prospérité aurait commencé avec la déchéance de Sichem, c'est-à-dire aux temps hellénistiques.' The location finds support in Epiphanius, *Panarion Haeresium* 60.22, Eusebius, *Onomasticon* 160.13 and Jdt. 4.4. For a discussion of Alt and Abel, see L. Wächter, 'Salem bei Sichem', *ZDPV* 84 (1968), pp. 63-72, who equates Shalem with Sālim. For identifycations of biblical Shalem, see L. Koehler and W. Baumgartner (subsequently revised by W. Baumgartner and J.J. Stamm with assistance from B. Hartmann *et al.*), *The Hebrew and Aramaic Lexicon of the Old Testament* (5 vols.; Leiden : E.J. Brill, 1994–2000), *ad. loc.* See also n. 281 below.

248. The narrative is missing in Juynboll, *Liber Josuae*, and far more elaborated in Macdonald, *Samaritan Chronicle No. II*.

249. Hjelm, *Samaritans and Early Judaism*, pp. 246-49.

250. An act not mentioned in scripture.

251. Josephus, *Ant.* 6.262. Scripture does not mention prophets.

252. Josephus, *Ant.* 6.268.

253. Lichtenstein, 'Die Fastenrolle', pp. 288, 339-40; *b. Yom.* 69a; cf. Hjelm, *Samaritans and Early Judaism*, pp. 128-29. The act belongs to the curse for not keeping the Law (Deut. 29.22), illustrated in the Sodom and Gomorrah narrative and invoked as the ultimate curse in, for instance, Amos 4.11; Hos. 11.8; Jer. 23.14-15; 49.18; 50.40; Zeph. 2.9; Ps. 107.34; Sir. 39.23.

the mountain for 22 years. The Samaritan narrative shares a good many features with variants related to second century BCE 'events', known from the books of Maccabees and Josephus.

The biblical narrative of the extermination of the priesthood in Nob is yet another variant of the supersessionist theme, which allows a continuation in the single remnant, Ahimelech's son Abiathar, who escapes the slaughter (1 Sam. 22.20) to become a chief priest in David's court together with Zadok,[254] until his degradation by Solomon (1 Kgs 2.26-27)[255] for the elevation of Zadok (1 Kgs 2.35), who sided with Solomon.[256] Combining the narratives of the rejection of the Elides[257] with those of Shiloh and Nob, the biblical authors have succeeded in claiming a continuation in spite of the split. As the Yahweh *Zebaoth* is not presented as a new invention in Jerusalem's court,[258] so its cult does not belong to some unknown tradition, but is a direct continuation of the old tribal cult, albeit its priesthood is replaced with that of the Zadokites. This priesthood, albeit its origin is unknown, is claimed to belong to the Eleazarites,[259] the pre-Shilonite priesthood. Josephus is the only writer who confirms the Samaritan tradition that Eli, being of the Ithamar line, usurped the high priesthood and, accordingly, broke the Eleazar line until the reign of Solomon. Indirectly, however, the rejection of the house of Eli (1 Kgs 2.27, 35) is given reference in the various lists of high priests in the Hebrew Bible, all of which leave out Eli[260] and form a continuation from Aaron to Seraiah, using the names of the Eleazar family members, *Meraioth, Amariah* and *Ahitub*, who, according to Josephus (*Ant.* 8.11-12), lived as private persons during the interim. Josephus' various references to high priests 'confirm' the split, which is furthermore testified in his enumeration of high priests in *Ant.* 20.229, that the first thirteen high priests until Solomon were descendants of Aaron's two sons.[261]

Whatever historical realities lie behind these traditions—and they probably belong to Persian-Hellenistic times[262] rather than to the Iron Age—they reveal that two issues are at stake: continuity and sovereignty. While Samaritan tradition claims that sovereignty shifted from Gerizim-Shechem to Zion-Jerusalem by way of Shiloh, Deuteronomistic tradition agrees that Jerusalem replaced Shiloh, however

---

254. 2 Sam. 15.24-29, 35-36; 17.15; 19.12; 20.25.

255. As a result of his support of Adonijah's struggle for the throne against Solomon (1 Kgs 1.7, 19; 2.22).

256. 1 Kgs 1.8, 32-40, 44.

257. 1 Kgs 2.27; cf. 1 Sam. 2.31-36.

258. Cf. *AF*, ch. X, p. 46: 'He [Samuel] changed the name of God'.

259. Ezra 7.1-5; Neh. 10.11-12; 1 Chron. 9.10-13; 1 Esd. 8.1; Josephus, *Ant.* 5.361-62; 8.11-12.

260. Tsedaka, 'Special Samaritan Traditions', p. 191: 'the continuation of the passage [1 Chron. 5.30-31] from verse 32 onward shows that it is no longer similar to the continuation which is cited in the chronicles of the Samaritans. In both traditions, the turning point occurred after Izzi'.

261. Hjelm, *Samaritans and Early Judaism*, p. 243.

262. Kippenberg, *Garizim und Synagoge*, p. 68: 'Formuliert wurde die Liste [the Samaritan list of High Priests], als im 2. Jh. v. Chr. die zadokitische Sukzession in Jerusalem zerbrach und die samar. Gemeinde sich als Erbin der alten Priesterfolge verstand.'

not that Shechem (and other cult places)[263] should become compared to either Shiloh or Jerusalem.[264]

The, since Ewald,[265] often-purported interpretation that pre-monarchic Shiloh was destroyed,[266] finds no explicit support in biblical tradition or in Josephus.[267] Re-evaluation of the early archaeological excavations[268] seriously challenged the validity of such a conclusion, which, according to Buhl and Holm-Nielsen[269] rested on Ewald, Wellhausen[270] and other scholars' misreading of biblical texts, especially Judg. 18.30-31; 2 Samuel 7; Jer. 7.14 and Amos 5.5.[271] Finkelstein's refutation of Buhl and Holm-Nielsen, based mainly on disagreements about the dating of the

263. Gilgal, Bethel, Mizpah, Nob, Hebron.

264. H. Ewald, *Geschichte des Volkes Israel* (8 vols.; Göttingen: Dietrichsche Buchhandlung, 3rd edn, 1864–66), II, p. 392; cf. Schley, *Shiloh*, p. 71.

265. Ewald, *Geschichte des Volkes Israel*, II, pp. 584-85; reassessed by J. Wellhausen, *Israelitische und jüdische Geschichte* (Berlin: Georg Reimer, 4th edn, 1901 [1887]), who seemingly unaware of Samaritan tradition, concluded (p. 54): 'the power of Joseph was broken. The Philistines knew how to exploit their victory; they subjugated not only the plain of Jezreel and the abutting hills to the south but also the stronghold itself, the mountains of Ephraim. They destroyed the ancient sanctuary at Shiloh, its priesthood fled southwards and settled in Nob, in the territory of Benjamin. The Philistine sovereignty extended as far as Benjamin, their governor being settled in Gibea.' Cf. Schley, *Shiloh*, p. 46.

266. So also W.F. Albright, 'New Israelite and Pre-Israelite Sites: The Spring Trip of 1929', *BASOR* 35 (1929), pp. 1-14; and H. Kjaer, 'The Excavations of Shiloh 1929', *JPOS* 10 (1930), pp. 87-104.

267. In the Babylonian Talmud, 'it is taught: when Eli died, Shiloh was destroyed and they went to Nob; and when Samuel from Rama died, Nob was destroyed and they went to Gibeon' (*b. Zeb.* 118b [my translation]). The duration of each place is Gilgal: 14 years; Nob and Gibeon: 57 years; and Shiloh: 369 years (a total of 430 years!).

268. Carried out by the Danish excavators H. Kjaer, A. Schmidt *et al.*, and supervised by W.F. Albright; cf. H. Kjaer, 'The Danish Excavation of Shiloh', *PEFQS* (1929), pp. 202-13; *idem*, 'Excavations of Shiloh 1929'; *idem*, 'Shiloh: A Summary Report of the Second Danish Excavation, 1929', *PEFQS* (1931), pp. 71-88.

269. M.-L. Buhl and S. Holm-Nielsen, *Shiloh—The Danish Excavations at Tall Sailun, Palestine, in 1926, 1929, 1932 and 1963: The Pre-Hellenistic Remains* (Copenhagen: The National Museum of Denmark, 1969). For reactions to Buhl and Holm-Nielsen, see Schley, *Shiloh*, pp. 72-80, and Ahlström, *History of Ancient Palestine*, pp. 367-70, 428. Notable is the critique by the Israeli archaeologists Yigael Shiloh, 'Review of Marie-Louise Buhl and Svend Holm-Nielsen, *Shiloh—The Danish Excavations at Tall Sailun, Palestine, in 1926, 1929, 1932 and 1963: The Pre-Hellenistic Remains* (Copenhagen: The National Museum of Denmark, 1969), in *IEJ* 21 (1971), pp. 67-69 and Israel Finkelstein, 'Shiloh, 1981', *IEJ* 32 (1982), pp. 148-50; *idem*, 'Shiloh 1982', *IEJ* 33 (1983), pp. 123-26; *idem, The Archaeology of the Israelite Settlement* (Jerusalem: Israel Exploration Society, 1988), who, in broad terms, confirmed the biblical tradition of Shiloh as a sort of amphictyonic centre in Iron I, destroyed around 1050 BCE. While Schley refuted Shiloh's and Finkelstein's conclusion about the destruction of Shiloh in the eleventh century BCE, Ahlström disputed only Finkelstein's assumption that Shiloh was a cult centre for all Israel or that anything could be known about the tabernacle, but agreed that some destruction had taken place in the eleventh century.

270. Wellhausen, *Composition des Hexateuchs*, p. 240.

271. Buhl and Holm-Nielsen, *Shiloh*, pp. 56-62; cf. Schley, *Shiloh*, p. 72.

pottery,[272] supported the conclusion that 'the flourishing Iron Age I Shiloh was destroyed in a great conflagration',[273] that 'the site was not occupied in the early phases of Iron II' and that 'in the late-Iron Age II it was a tiny, insignificant settlement.[274] This late-Iron II site was not destroyed by fire but was apparently gradually abandoned.'[275] At the beginning of the Hellenistic period Shiloh resumed full-scale occupation.[276] Finkelstein's restriction of the collared rim jars to the Iron I and Israelite settlement has not won common acceptance, since other works have shown that this type of pottery has been in existence from Late Bronze until late in Iron II and is found in indeed very different places.[277] According to Buhl, Holm-Nielsen and Schley, the destruction, mentioned in Jer. 7.12-15 and 26.6-9, might relate to the fall of the Northern Kingdom in the eighth century, rather than any eleventh-century BCE destruction,[278] although no temple structures have ever been found.[279] The obvious implication of Schley's conclusion would be that Jerusalem supplanted Shiloh at a very late time. This, however, is refuted in his argument that Jer. 7.12-15 'has nothing to do with the order of events by which Jerusalem supplanted Shiloh', but only with Shiloh's glory and demise as a literary paradigm for what might happen to Jerusalem, 'the other place where Yahweh has caused his name to dwell'.[280]

While Lemche's tradition-historical conclusion implies the supersessionist mode of the biblical authors, though no historical reality about biblical Shiloh, Schley's

272.   Especially, the collared rim jars, which S. Bunimowitz and I. Finkelstein ('Pottery', in I. Finkelstein, S. Bunimowitz and Z. Lederman [eds.], *Shiloh: The Archaeology of a Biblical Site* [Tel Aviv: Institute of Archaeology of Tel Aviv University, 1993], pp. 81-196 [162]), date exclusively to the Iron I period.

273.   I. Finkelstein, *The Archaeology of the Israelite Settlement* (Jerusalem: Israel Exploration Society, 1988), pp. 178-82; *idem*, 'The History and Archaeology of Shiloh from the Middle Bronze Age II to Iron Age II', in Finkelstein, Bunimowitz and Lederman (eds.), *Shiloh*, pp. 371-93 (386): 'Shiloh itself undoubtedly played an important role in fostering settlement; more than half the sites in the vicinity were apparently founded in an advanced phase of Iron I Age when Shiloh was at the height of its prosperity'. For a critique of Finkelstein's settlement theories, see Thompson, *Early History*, pp. 223-27.

274.   Against Buhl and Holm-Nielsen's flourishing Iron II Shiloh; cf. Buhl and Holm-Nielsen, *Shiloh*, pp. 60-62.

275.   Finkelstein, 'History and Archaeology of Shiloh', p. 389.

276.   A. Kempinski, 'Shiloh', in E. Stern (ed.), *The New Encyclopedia of Archaeological Excavations in the Holy Land* (4 vols.; New York: Shimon & Schuster, 1993), IV, pp. 1364-66 (1365); Finkelstein, 'History and Archaeology of Shiloh', p. 389.

277.   J. Strange, 'Arkaeologisk syntese og historieskrivning', in Hallbäck and Strange (eds.), *Bibel og historieskrivning*, pp. 43-57 (53); Schley, *Shiloh*, pp. 75-78.

278.   Buhl and Holm-Nielsen, *Shiloh*, pp. 58-59, 62; Schley, *Shiloh*, pp. 179-80. See also S. Holm-Nielsen, 'Silo—endnu engang', *SEÅ* 54 (1989), pp. 80-89.

279.   Cf. the critique of a historicist reading of Jer. 7.12-14 in N.P. Lemche, 'Mysteriet om det forsvundne tempel: Overleveringen om Shilos ødelæggelse i Jer. 7.12-14', *SEÅ* 54 (1989), pp. 118-26.

280.   Schley, *Shiloh*, pp. 180-82. So also, R.P. Carroll, *Jeremiah: A Commentary* (London: SCM Press, 1986), pp. 210-11, and Lemche, 'Mysteriet om det forsvundne tempel', p. 125, arguing for 1 Sam. 1–4 and the work of the Deuteronomists as a precondition for Jeremiah's comparison of Jerusalem with Shiloh.

historically based (however, not verified) conclusion asserts the possibility that Shiloh and Jerusalem were in existence at the same time, as were the Northern and Southern Kingdoms. In this perspective, Shiloh partakes in the fate of Samaria and Shechem as those rejected by Yahweh, as well as those supplanted by Jerusalem, to which place 'eighty men from Shechem, Shiloh[281] and Samaria' went to bring offerings (Jer. 41.5). The *crux interpretum* of Jer. 7.12-14 is therefore not that Yahweh rejected Shiloh, but that he rejected Jerusalem's brothers, 'the whole seed of Ephraim' (את כל־זרע אפתים, Jer. 7.15),[282] his firstborn (Jer. 31.8).[283] As Shiloh and Shechem were interchangeable in Joshua 24 traditions, the implication of Jeremiah's text (and Schley's conclusion) is that Jeremiah could as well have said: 'Look to Shechem, the place where I set my name at the first' (אשר שכנתי שמי שם בראשונה, cf. Jer. 7.12).[284] Jeremiah, however, who 'knows' nothing about a Shechem sanctuary,[285] asserts that the temple in Shiloh—and not in Shechem, as Hos. 6.9-10 seems to imply—had been the central sanctuary for the Ephraimites, similar to what Jerusalem's temple was for the Judahites (cf. Jer. 7.30). This is the more striking, since Jeremiah is unique among biblical authors for making such a distinction regarding a cult place, which in other biblical traditions connotes unity rather than the divisiveness that marks the role of Shechem.

In the Mishnah, the tabernacle's stay in Gilgal, Nob and Gibeon are characterized as the periods in which 'the high places were again permitted, while during its

---

281. LXX*, Jer. 48.5: καὶ ἀπο Σαλημ; LXX^A α´ σ´: Σαλωμ. The order of names has puzzled scholars, as one should expect Shiloh to be the last mentioned. E. Nielsen, *Shechem*, pp. 291-92, suggests that the order accords with the chronological succession of these cult places. The LXX reading might, however, rightly refer to the Shalem, known also from Samaritan tradition, cf. n. 247 above. LXX Gen. 33.18: 'and Jacob came to Shalem, a town in Shechem' (καὶ ἦλθεν Ιακωβ εἰς Σαλημ πόλιν Σικιμων); MT: שבם; ויבא יעקב שלם עיר שכם; SP: שלום. The bilingual JB follows the LXX reading): 'And Ya'aqov came to Shalem, a city of Shekhem' (so also Vulgate, Peshitta and *Jub.* 34.1) while the Authorised Danish translation of 1992 and the RSV follows the SP: 'And Jacob came safely to the city of Shechem'. Cf. Ps. 76.3, ויהי בשלם סכו ומעונתי בצון, which JB translates: 'In Shalem also is his tabernacle, and his dwelling place is in Zion'. In the LXX, Ps. 75.3 appears without any parallelism by translating Shalem 'in peace': καὶ ἐγενήθη ἐν εἰρήνη ὁ τόπος αὐτοῦ. Since this is clearly a linguistic solution to a theological problem, we must ask why the translator did not exchange Shalem with Shiloh? For the possibility that the Shalem of Gen. 14.17 refers to an older name for Shechem, see S. Landersdorfer, 'Das Priesterkönigtum von Salem', *JSOR* 9 (1925), pp. 203-16 (cf. E. Nielsen, *Shechem*, p. 343, for a dismissal of Landersdorfer); Spiro, *Samaritans, Tobiads and Judahites*, p. 40: 'the Samaritans rightly argued that Salem is a locality near Shechem (cf. *Jub.* 30.1; Judt. 4.4)'; R.H. Smith, 'Abram and Melchizedek (Gen 14.18-20)', *ZAW* 77 (1965), pp. 129-53 (150-52); B.Z. Wacholder, 'Pseudo-Eupolemus' Two Greek Fragments on the Life of Abraham', *HUCA* 34 (1963), pp. 83-113 (107). That the identification of Shalem with Jerusalem was a case of polemic is clearly demonstrated in, for example, *Gen. Ap.* 22.13; *Targ. Gen.* 14.18; Josephus, *Ant.* 1.181; 7.7.67; *Apion* 1.175, and early Christian and Rabbinic writings.

282. Schley, *Shiloh*, pp. 179-80. So also Ps. 78.67; cf. Carroll, 'Psalm LXXVIII', pp. 135-36.

283. Cf. also Jer. 31.18-20.

284. A. Mikolášek, 'Silo et Salem à Sichem', in Tal and Florentin (eds.), *Proceedings of the First International Congress of the Société d'Études Samaritaines Tel-Aviv, April 11-13, 1988*, pp. 79-80.

285. He only mentions Shechem once: Jer. 41.5.

stay in Shiloh (after Gilgal) and Jerusalem, 'the high places were forbidden'. About Shiloh, it is said that 'there was no roof-beam there, but below was a house of stone and above were hangings and this was the "resting place" '.[286] About Jerusalem it is said that 'after they came to Jerusalem, the high places were never again permitted'.[287] The Babylonian Talmud's discussion about Psalm 78's reference to Shiloh raises the question whether the temple was in Benjamin and the Sanhedrin in Joseph, as might the temple have been in Benjamin and the Sanhedrin in Judah. A conclusion is made (R. Ḥanina) that 'A strip of the region of Judah, in which the altar was, protruded into the region of Benjamin, and the pious Benjamin sought to occupy it. A strip of the region of Joseph also protruded into the region of Benjamin' (*b. Zeb.* 118b). Thus neither Benjamin, nor Joseph was the 'home' for the Shilonite temple.

A similar literary 'development' can be detected regarding Gilgal as symbol of the unification of tribes, however also anticipating their division (see further below). In the Prophets, Gilgal is rejected as a symbol of the apostate Northern Kingdom,[288] which Judah should be cautious not to imitate. Elisha's presence there (2 Kgs 4.38) rather underscores that depravity, as does his presence in Jericho and Bethel (2.19-23). His 'removal' of pestilence, hunger, 'mockery' and the like, marks these places as godless. A variant of the motif is found in 2 Kings 17's heathen foreigners, whose rescue from attacking lions is mediated by the teaching Israelite priest sent back to Bethel from captivity.

The book of Jeremiah's pronounced fate of Jerusalem, that, as Shiloh, it shall be desolated (חרב, Jer. 26.9), resembles the destruction of Bethel's altars (Amos 3.14) and the desolation of Isaac's high places and Israel's sanctuaries (נשמו במות יצחק ומקדשי ישראל יחרבו) in Amos 7.9b's pronouncement of Yahweh's sword 'against the house of Jeroboam' (וקמתי על־בית ירבעם בחרב). Jeremiah's Shiloh might be as theological as is Joshua 24's Shiloh in the LXX. Shiloh became desolate, but Ephraim can find a future in a rebuilt Jerusalem (Jer. 31.6), to which place all the tribes of Israel shall gather (31.1). From this examination, it has become clear that Jeremiah's destroyed Shiloh should not be sought in the Iron I period. Neither should it, perhaps, be sought in Iron II. It may belong to the author of Jeremiah's 'imagination' of pre-exilic Israel's institutions or it may bear a metaphorical notion as the Northern Kingdom.

While diachrony, as expressed in rabbinic tradition, and supersessionism, as expressed in MT and ST traditions, are paradigmatic for the literary traditions of 'Israel's' past, synchrony and co-existence were the norm for Palestine's regional cult centres. From history, we know of only one period, that of the Hasmonaeans, when cult centralization was effected and regional borders removed. In all other periods of the first millennium BCE, 'the cult of Yahweh was disseminated from a

---

286. A nice way of solving the ambiguity in biblical tradition that the sanctuary at Shiloh might refer to a tent rather than a temple; cf. Laato, *A Star is Rising*, pp. 76-77; Schley, *Shiloh*, pp. 140-42.

287. *M. Zeb.* 14.5-6; *Meg.* 1.11; see also *Lam. R.* 2.17; *Gen. R.* 95: Shiloh is temporary and Jerusalem is eternal, as Saul is temporary and David is eternal.

288. Hos. 4.15; 9.15; 12.12; Amos 4.4; 5.5.

number of centres known to us—Haran, Elephantine, Babylonia, Lachish, Samaria, Gerizim, Tabor, Carmel, Hebron, Mamre, Deir 'Alla, Tell es-Sa'idiyeh, Araq el-Emir, Leontopolis—and probably from others of which we have no record'.[289] What the Bible exposes, and Samaritan tradition and Josephus confirm, is that north–south competition does not belong to the Iron Age kingdoms of Israel and Judah, but to a later period, whether initiated in Persian time,[290] as some traditions maintain, or in Hellenistic time, in which period Ptolemies and Seleucids 'sought to make "central sanctuaries" in their sphere of rule, independent of "apostate" Jerusalem, for the use of the Jews'.[291]

4. Samaritan–Jewish Discussions over Cult Place and Tradition— The Post-Exilic Period

Competition over cult places is a recurrent theme in several post-exilic biblical and non-biblical Samaritan and Jewish narratives. In these narratives, Gerizim-Shechem and Jerusalem occupy the scene. Rebuilding and destruction events, related to both temples, supported by Persian, Greek, Ptolemaic and Seleucid rulers, are the main issues.[292] While narratives about the Jewish temple deal with opposition to its rebuilding, its political role and its devastation,[293] narratives about the Samaritan temple deal with its (re)building and destruction.[294] No narratives tell about any open resistance to temple building activities on Gerizim. According to *AF*, the destructions led to increased hostilities on both sides. These might be illustrations of the never-ending story. It might, however, also be a single story spelled out in many variations, to give credence to its antiquity and subsequent historicity. No Samaritan stories tell about any attempts at co-operation between Samaritans and Jews apart from the return narrative, presented below. The cessation of mutual hostility is always due to the interference of foreign rulers, as expressed also in the biblical books of Ezra and Nehemiah.

289.   M. Smith, *Palestinian Parties and Politics that Shaped the Old Testament* (London: SCM Press, 2nd corrected edn, 1987), pp. 82-98 (93).

290.   Carroll, 'Psalm LXXVIII', pp. 147-50: 'Psalm lxxviii may be regarded as the charter myth explaining how Judah was the rightful heir to the exodus movement and therefore could claim leadership of the people of Israel... Such a polemic became increasingly important after the exile when the Samaritan claim confronted that of Judaism'.

291.   M. Hengel, *Judaism and Hellenism* (repr., London: Xpress Reprints, 1996 [1981]), p. 274.

292.   Gaster, *Samaritans*, pp. 34-39, B. Hall, 'From John Hyrcanus to Baba Rabbah', in Crown (ed.), *The Samaritans*, pp. 32-54; J. Zangenberg, *ΣAMAPEIA: Antike Quellen zur Geschichte und Kultur der Samaritaner in deutscher Übersetzung* (TANZ, 15; Tübingen: Francke Verlag, 1994), pp. 159-62, 191-94; Hjelm, *Samaritans and Early Judaism*, pp. 195-216, 226-38, 258-66.

293.   E.g. 1 Esdras; Ezra; 1 and 2 Maccabees; Josephus, *War* and *Ant.* 11.1-119; *AF*, ch. XX, p. 81, ch. XXIV, p. 89.

294.   For example, narratives related to Gen. 34 (cf. Hjelm, *Samaritans and Early Judaism*, pp. 138-46); Josephus, *Ant.* 11.297-347; 13.254-56; the rabbinic tractate *Megillat Taanit* (cf. H. Lichtenstein, 'Die Fastenrolle, eine Untersuchung zur jüdisch-hellenistischen Geschichte', *HUCA* 8-9 [1931–32], pp. 257-52); *Liber Josuae*, ch. xlv; *AF*, ch. XX, p. 79, ch. XXIII, p. 87 (chs. X–XI, pp. 47-48).

If Van Seters' hypothesis about the tradition history of the Pentateuch is correct, can we then assume that the authors of J and P succeeded in persuading some of the 'nationalistic' Jews behind the Deuteronomistic History to return to the traditions of the Patriarchs?[295] According to Samaritan traditions,[296] this forms part of a discussion which Samaritans and Jews had with each other before their return from exile. The reason for their return resembles the complaint brought in 2 Kings 17. Mirroring this narrative, 'those who dwelt in the land of Canaan wrote letters to king Sūrdī, king of Harān',[297] complaining that drought and destruction of crops had caused severe privation.[298] They therefore want to know from those who used to live there what they used to do to make the land fertile. Summoned by the king, the leaders of the Israelites convince the king that it is the cessation of the worship of God on 'Mt Gerizim, Beth El',[299] which has caused the infertility. When Sūrdī commands the Samaritan Israelites to go home, rebuild Beth El and worship their God, they want to bring home all their brothers. The Great High Priest 'Abdāl and his assembly send letters to everyone to come to Harān for a united return. Not everyone accepted this letter, and a great number remained in exile and never returned. When the Jews arrive at Harān, the disagreement about where to go to worship begins. The request brought by the Jewish representative Zerubbabel is not unimportant: 'You and your assembly must do as we tell you: that is, we must go up to Jerusalem, and be all of us one nation' (*AF*, ch. XVIII, p. 70).[300] The Samaritan answer expresses the hope that if the people return to the chosen place of the forefathers, then God might 'be content and take pity on us, and ratify for us the covenant of our fathers' (*AF*, ch. XVIII, p. 71).[301] The discussion clearly places itself in an

---

295.   Van Seters, *Prologue to History, passim* (especially pp. 241-42, 328-33); Galling, *Erwählungstraditionen*, p. 75; Römer, *Israels Väter, passim* (especially pp. 392-94, 568-75); Mullen, *Ethnic Myths and Pentateuchal Foundations*, pp. 319-30; K. Schmid, *Erzväter und Exodus*, pp. 158-65, 287-90.

296.   *Liber Josuae*, ch. xlv; *AF*, ch. XVII-XX, pp. 65-79.

297.   Usually identified with Darius I (522–486), whose length of reign is said to be 36 years (*AF*, ch. XX, p. 80). The name probably is spelled backwards; cf. Stenhouse, *Kitāb al-Tarīkh* (1985), nn. 306 and 375a.

298.   Cf. Lev. 26.32; 2 Kgs 17.26: 'Yahweh sent lions'; Josephus, *Ant.* 9.288-90: 'pestilence'.

299.   *Liber Josuae* does not mention Gerizim or Beth El, but the 'Holy Mountain'.

300.   For the centralization and one nation theme as main issues in 'Jewish' literature from at least the second century BCE onwards, see Mendels, *Land of Israel as a Political Concept*; *idem, Rise and Fall of Jewish Nationalism*; Hjelm, *Samaritans and Early Judaism*, pp. 59-60, 277-78.

301.   It is worth noticing that scholarship has been aware that such discussions form part of the Old Testament; for instance, Römer, *Israels Väter*, pp. 536-38: 'Es ist oft bemerkt worden, dass "Tritojesaja" die Probleme und Diskussionen der nachexilischen Gemeinde widerspiegelt (vgl. z. B. K. Pauritsch, *Die neue Gemeinde: Gott sammelt Ausgestossene und Arme (Jesaja 56–66)*, AnBib 47, Rome [1971], *passim*). Zu diesen Diskussionen gehörte wohl auch die frage nach dem Stellenwert der Abraham- und Jacobtraditionen bzw. nach der Möglichkeit, die Patriarchen als Väter zu bezeichnen. Insofern könnte Jes 63.16 nicht nur 51.2, sondern auch 58.14 kritisieren. Deutlich ist, dass im jesajanischen Milieu (das sowohl sprachlich als auch theologisch seine Eigenständigkeit gegenüber dem dtr Milieu besitzt) die Patriarchen Abraham und Jacob seit der exilischen Zeit eine theologischer Relevanz erhalten (wiewohl bei Deuterojesaja deutlich eine

implicitly much broader discussion about the new and the old Israel, with the Samaritans opting for a return to pre-monarchic traditions and the Jews for a continuation of traditions related to the Davidic kingship. Between these two traditions are the Laws of Moses, accepted by both groups. The court hearing in front of King Sūrdī falls within that discussion. By reference to the Torah scroll, which had been kept in custody in Nineveh, during the exile, the Samaritans 'read out the verses, which show that Mt Gerizim is the Qibla. Zerubbabel then produced a scroll, which he maintained was the scroll of David,[302] and which (he claimed) showed that David said that the threshing floor in Jerusalem was the Qibla' (*AF*, ch. XIX, p. 71). A theological reflection answers the question of why the chosen place has to be Gerizim and why Joshua had erected the altar on Gerizim and not on Ebal (cf. MT Josh. 8.30), which would have conflicted with the tradition of curses from Mt Ebal (Deut. 11.29; 27.12; cf. *AF*, ch. XIX, pp. 71-76). When Zerubbabel and his companions are given permission to reply, they do not refer to the Law of Moses, but rather to their tradition, which says that 'David and Solomon both said that the Qibla is Jerusalem'.[303] Thereupon, Sanballat, 'the levite', accuses the Jews of accepting only parts of the Law and, with reference to Deut. 15.19-20, of ignoring the question of where the priests should bring their offerings before the temple was built in the time of David and Solomon. When Zerubbabel, in response to this accusation, refers to his writings which 'prophesy that sacrifices will (only) be offered in Jerusalem' (p. 76), Sanballat claims that the Jewish books are forgeries, deceits and lies, and he asks permission to throw them into the fire. The ordeal by fire reveals the truth. The Books of David burn immediately, while the Book of the Torah is thrown into the fire three times from whence it returns undamaged each time. Before this, Zerubbabel had tried hard to escape the test. He took the Book of the Torah 'opened it, looked in it and then said, "I cannot throw it. For my Book was mine alone; but this Book is mine and his, because the one who wrote it is the lord, the Messenger (of God) Moses, upon whom be perfect peace"' (*AF*, ch. XIX, p. 77). This wonderful play on a well-known literary motif reorients the attention towards the behaviour of the combatants rather than on the outcome of the test.

The explicit reference to the common tradition, which should be given priority over the particular tradition, implicitly reverses Jewish accusations against the Samaritans for having forged the Pentateuch. King Sūrdī's anger leads to the execution of 36 of the Jewish chiefs and wise men and an order to Sanballat to 'stop the rebuilding of Jerusalem'.[304] Sanballat is not only honoured by the king with gifts, garments, and so on, but also by the tribes. After having paid the ransom for the Torah scroll and sacred vestments, 'they all set out in joy and good spirits and with them went people from the sons of Benjamin, and the sons of Kohath

---

"exodische" Orientation vorherrscht [cf. Kiesow, *Exodustexte*, *passim*]) und so der Weg zu einer symbiose zwischen Patriarchentheologie und dtr Vätertheologie vorbereitet wird.'

302.   Cf. also 2 Macc. 2.13.

303.   *Jubilees* and *2 Maccabees* both invoke Moses in their argumentation for Jerusalem as the chosen place, see further Chapter 6 below.

304.   Juynboll, *Liber Josuae*, does not mention any such order.

[Kehath] and Gershon and Merari, who had been with Eli in Shiloh' (*AF*, ch. XX, p. 78). Note the return of the 'apostates' both to their tradition and to their home.[305] Of the peoples settled in the land, the king 'sent and withdrew'[306] those few left who had survived the famine. On Gerizim, they constructed the altar, '10 cubits long, 10 cubits wide and 5 cubits high. The temple building was 35 cubits square. They made a candlestick of one gold quintar, and made a table and put the shewbread upon it; and they sacrificed 100 head of cattle to God, wine and oil, as is laid down in the illustrious book' (*AF*, ch. XX, p. 79).[307]

As can be seen from this paraphrase, several issues are at stake for the author of the story, of which one is the question of origin and a counter to the claim of the Old Testament and Josephus that the northern tribes disappeared, never to return again. While 2 Kings 17 states that the people deported to the land remained, their absence from other biblical texts makes the statement suspicious. *AF*'s narrative states that the foreigners were removed from the country to be replaced by the returning Israelites. While the book of Ezra rejects the offer of cooperation with the 'enemies of Judah and Benjamin', whom Josephus calls Cuthaeans or Samaritans, *AF*'s narrative invites cooperation, however, at Gerizim alone and not in Jerusalem.[308]

Another troubling question is the Law, which, *AF* claims, the Israelites brought back from exile, thus surpassing Jewish traditions in which Ezra brought the Law from Babylon during the reign of some Artaxerxes (I, 465–424; II, 404–359; III 359–338), as late as a hundred years or more after the first return from exile during Cyrus I (539–529) and fifty years or more after the alleged building of Jerusalem's temple during the reign of Darius (I, 522–486).

The third problem relates to the Samaritan temple on Gerizim, which Josephus claimed did not exist before Alexander the Great gave Sanballat permission to build it (Josephus *Ant.* 11.322-24). In *AF*, it is built in the time of Darius (I, 522–486), Sanballat and the High Priest 'Abdāl, while in Josephus (*Ant.* 11.302), 'Darius, the last king' seems to refer to Darius III (336–331), who gave his consent to the building (11.311). Since Darius was so quickly conquered by Alexander, Sanballat brought his request to Alexander, who gave his consent to the building of the temple (11.324). Suspicion about Josephus' chronology, however, appears when he has 'the Samaritans—whose chief city at that time was Shechem,[309] which lay

---

305. *AF*, ch. X, p. 45, states that Samuel was son of Kohath…son of Korah—the one who rebelled against Moses.

306. Juynboll, *Liber Josuae*, ch. xlv: 'And the king sent unto all the Persians who had taken up residence in their assigned land, and removed them from it to their own country' (Crane's translation).

307. *Liber Josuae*, ch. xlv: 'and the people [of Israel] entered into their assigned land, which is their holy place. And they made the sacred apparatus similar unto that which was in the [former] temple, and they offered up a multitude of offerings' (Crane's translation).

308. Cf. also Josephus, *Ant.* 11.87's invitation to the Samaritans to come to Jerusalem to worship there.

309. For the destruction of Samaria by Alexander in 331 BCE and Shechem's role as the main city for the survivors of the indigenous population, to which belonged also the Samaritans, see

beside Mt Gerizim'—less than a year later (cf. 11.325, 342), invite Alexander to come and revere 'their city and honour the temple as well' (11.342).[310] In *AF* (ch. XXVI, pp. 92-96), Alexander visits the Samaritans in Shechem and on Gerizim in a narrative mirroring Josephus' narrative about Alexander's visit to Jerusalem (*Ant* 11.325-39). Temples, Sanballat or Manasseh go unmentioned in that narrative and Alexander's wish to erect statues of himself and build a 'place of worship for himself' on the mountain (*AF*, ch. XXVI, pp. 93-95) is kindly refused. One should pay attention to the character of Alexander's building projects that it was for veneration of himself and not of God, which is *AF*'s main point. In place of the requested images and monuments 'that cannot speak or move', the Samaritans decided to call all new-born children after Alexander's name as 'images of you that have minds and can speak' (*AF*, ch. XXVI, p. 94; cf. *Liber Josuae*, ch. lxvi).

a. *Samaritan Temple: Fiction or Fact?*
It has been a moot point whether there ever has been a temple on Mt Gerizim or just an altar.[311] Inscriptions from Delos 'make it clear that Samaritans from the diaspora sent offerings εἰς Αργαριζειν sometime between the third to first century BCE.[312] It is, however, 'not certain whether these inscriptions speak of a "temple" or only of the "holy Argarizin"'.[313] Recent excavations on Gerizim have shown that the stone podium underneath the Roman temple dates to the Roman, rather than to the Hellenistic period,[314] as was asserted by earlier excavators. The Hellenistic structures, on the contrary, are located beneath and on the slopes near the Byzantine Mary Theotokos church.[315] Findings of more than 60 dedicatory inscriptions in paleo-Hebrew, Aramaic (lapidary and early Jewish) and Greek scripts, dating from the fifth century BCE to the fourth century CE, and in Samaritan script from the

G.E. Wright, 'The Samaritans at Shechem', *HTR* 55 (1962), pp. 357-66; *idem*, *Shechem: The Biography of a Biblical City* (New York: McGraw–Hill, 1965). For a critique of Wright's chronology regarding Shechem, see Ahlström, *History of Palestine*, pp. 901-902; I. Magen, 'Gerizim Mount', in Stern (ed.), *The New Encyclopedia of Archaeological Excavations*, II, pp. 484-92, as well as, in the same work (IV, pp. 1345-54), E.F. Campbell, 'Shechem'.

310.   A.D. Crown, 'Another Look at Samaritan Origins', in Crown and Davey (eds.), *New Samaritan* Studies, pp. 133-55, arguing for the building of the Samaritan temple during the reign of Artaxerxes III, rather than Alexander the Great.

311.   R. Pummer, 'Samaritan Material Remains', in Crown (ed.), *The Samaritans*, pp. 135-77.

312.   Pummer, 'Samaritan Material Remains', pp. 150-50; the inscriptions have been been published by P. Brunneau, 'Les Israélites de Délos et la juiverie délienne', *Bulletin de Correspondance Hellénique* 106 (1982), pp. 465-504.

313.   Pummer, 'Samaritan Material Remains', pp. 172-73; Rappaport, 'Reflections of the Origins of the Samaritans', pp. 10-19; cf. also Pseudo-Eupolemus in Eusebius, *Praep. Ev.* 9.17.1-9; 1 Macc. 11.34 and 2 Macc. 6.2.

314.   Magen, 'Gerizim Mount', pp. 484-92; Magen, 'Mount Gerizim and the Samaritans', in F. Manns, *et al.* (eds.), *Early Christianity in Context: Monuments and Documents* (Jerusalem: The Franciscan Printing Press, 1993), 91-147.

315.   I. Magen, 'A Fortified Town of the Hellenistic Period on Mount Gerizim', *Qadmoniot* 19 (1986), pp. 91-101; *idem*, 'Excavations at Mt-Gerizim—A Temple City', *Qadmoniot* 23 (1989), pp. 70-96; Zsengellér, *Gerizim as Israel*, p. 162.

Middle Ages,[316] as well as burned bones of year-old cattle, sheep, goats and pigeons[317] underneath the Byzantine Mary Theotokos church, suggested that, if not a temple, at least a cult place of the Samaritans had been located in this place in the Hellenistic period.[318]

Further excavations have revealed at least two building stages of the ancient precinct:[319] one 'in the time of Nehemiah' and the other in the reign of Antiochus III. The finds include great quantities of coins (c. 13,000), pottery and metalware, dating from the Persian period to the time of John Hyrcanus and Alexander Jannaeus, and again from the Byzantine (fourth century CE) to the Umayyad period.[320] In addition, 480 marble inscriptions have been uncovered, 90 per cent of which are dedicatory inscriptions in Aramaic. The totality of the inscriptions indicates the existence of an Israelite holy centre to which people brought tithes and donations from as early as the beginning of the Persian period.[321] The temple, which Magen assumes had stood in the western part of the sacred precinct, 'was modelled after the temple at Jerusalem', as stated by Josephus (*Ant.* 11.310-11) and 'corroborated by the finds'. The construction, however, does not date to the reign of Alexander the Great as Josephus claimed, since 'we now know that it was built in the time of Nehemiah'.[322] The structures of the Samaritan cult place fit the description of the temple in Ezechiel's vision, measurements of which, however, cannot be associated to the temple in Jerusalem earlier than the Hellenistic or Roman periods.[323] As Josephus got it wrong regarding the building of the Samaritan temple, he furthermore neglected its enlargement and Gerizim's change from cult place to temple city (about 10,000 inhabitants) in the time of Antiochus III.[324] The destruction of the temple, Josephus argues, had taken place at the beginning of the reign of John

316.   L. Di Segni, 'The Church of Mary Theotokos on Mount Gerizim: The Inscriptions', in G.C. Bottini *et al.* (eds.), *Christian Archaeology in the Holy Land: New Discoveries: Archaeological Essays in Honor of Vigilio C. Corbo* (Collectio Maior, 36; Jerusalem: Franciscan Printing Press, 1990), pp. 343-50; J. Naveh and I. Magen, 'Aramaic and Hebrew Inscriptions of the Second Century BCE at Mount Gerizim', *Atiqot* 32 (1997), pp. 9-17.

317.   Naveh and Magen, 'Aramaic and Hebrew Inscriptions'.

318.   Magen, 'Mount Gerizim and the Samaritans', p. 139; J. Zangenberg, *Frühes Christentum in Samarien: Topographische und traditionsgeschichtliche Studien zu den Samarientexten im Johannesevangelium* (Texte und Arbeiten zum Neutestamentlichen Zeitalter, 27; Tübingen: A. Francke Verlag, 1998), p. 44.

319.   I. Magen, 'Mt. Gerizim—A Temple City', *Qadmoniot* 33/2 (120) (2000), pp. 74-118 (97) (Hebrew).

320.   Naveh and Magen, 'Aramaic and Hebrew Inscriptions', p. 9.

321.   B. Tsedaka, '480 Stone Inscriptions and 13,000 Coins Ranging from the Persian to the Roman Period Were discovered in Ancient Luza on Mount Gerizim', *A.B.- The Samaritan News* 845-47 (2003), pp. 136-37 (English translation by L. Bernstein); *The Samaritan Update* (visit <http.//www.the-samaritans.com>).

322.   Naveh and Magen, 'Aramaic and Hebrew Inscriptions', p. 10; Magen, 'Mt. Gerizim—A Temple City', p. 117: 'in the first half of the fifth century BCE, in the time of Nehemiah and Sanballat the first [*sic*], the Horonite'.

323.   Magen, 'Mt. Gerizim—A Temple City', p. 109.

324.   Magen, 'Mt. Gerizim—A Temple City', pp. 117-18; Hjelm, 'What Do Samaritans and Jews Have in Common?', p. 208.

Hyrcanus (135–104 BCE), rather than at the end of his reign. From the coinage, a dating later than 111 BCE is the more probable.[325] The duration of the Samaritan temple to '*Yahweh-el-'Eljon*'[326] was thus not the 200 years stated by Josephus (*Ant.* 13.256), but closer and probably far beyond the 343 years, he ascribes to the existence of the temple in Heliopolis/Leontopolis (*War* 7.436), stories of which Josephus mingles with stories about Gerizim.[327]

Rowley's statement that 'if there had been a temple, we have no means of knowing when it was built',[328] still bears some validity, but the means for our knowledge have expanded considerably. We still have to wait for the final reports and the publication of the inscriptions[329] in order to take the discussion much further. The conclusions not only affect questions of the existence of a Samaritan temple, but of its religio-political role in Persian-Hellenistic times, which is the formative periods of most of biblical literature.

The only Samaritan high priest named Manasseh son of Eleazar, officiating for 36 years, appears 201 years after the High Priest Hezekiah had officiated for 21 years at the time of the advent of Alexander the Great. This would date Manasseh to the time of John Hyrcanus and Alexander Jannai.[330]

b. *Which Law?*

However legendary *AF*'s Sanballat narrative is, as is also Josephus' narrative about a similar discussion held in front of Ptolemy (IV Philometor [181–146 BCE]),[331] both these narratives implicitly inform us that the Torah does not explicitly state where the chosen place should be. Although the SP contains explicit statements on the matter in 'additions' to the Decalogue (SP Exod. 20.17b and Deut. 5.18b),[332] the argumentation is based on exegesis of the Law, which points out the illogic of having a law of offerings 'year after year…in the place which the Lord will choose' without having such a place before the building of the Solomonic temple.[333] The Jewish argument is a reference to additional traditions, called the Books of David.[334]

325. Magen, 'Mt. Gerizim—A Temple City', p. 118.

326. Magen, 'Mt. Gerizim—A Temple City', pp. 108, 113.

327. Hjelm, 'Cult Centralization', and *Samaritans and Early Judaism*, pp. 227-32.

328. H.H. Rowley, 'Sanballat and the Samaritan Temple', in *idem, Men of God: Studies in Old Testament History and Prophecy* (London: Thomas Nelson, 1963), pp. 246-76 (266) (article first published in *BJRL* 38 [1955–56], pp. 166-98).

329. Y. Magen, H. Misgav and L. Tsefania, *Mount Gerizim Excavations*. I. *The Aramaic, Hebrew and Samaritan Inscriptions* (English translations by E. Levin and M. Guggenheimer; Judea and Samaria Publications, 2; Jerusalem: Staff Officer of Archaeology, Civil Administration of Judea and Samaria, 2004 [Hebrew and English]) (vols. II-V forthcoming).

330. Tsedaka, *A Summary*, p. 23; *AF*, ch. LV, p. 189 (205 years); Josephus (*Ant.* 12.157) mentions an Oniad high priest Manasseh officiating in the third century BCE.

331. Josephus, *Ant.* 13.74-79, in which discussion the Jewish representatives win the case. Josephus does not offer any theological discussion or explicit proofs from the Law, and the Samaritans are silenced. See further, Hjelm, *Samaritans and Early Judaism*, pp. 213-15.

332. Cf. *AF*, ch. XXVIII, pp. 104-105.

333. *AF*, ch. XIX, p. 76; cf. also p. 105.

334. Macchi, *Les Samaritains*, p. 29.

The implied difference between Jewish and Samaritan argumentation, based on claims of historical truth or exegesis, reveals that the traditions about the Patriarchs and the 'fathers'[335] are subordinate to the implications of the Law based on exegesis. From the discussion, it becomes clear that the narrative material of the Pentateuch (Hexateuch) and the Books of David are considered by the Samaritan scribe to be interpretations: merely illustrations of the Law. As such, Joshua's sacrifice on Gerizim (*AF*, ch. IV, p. 14) has gained considerable importance as a fulfilment of the Law (Deut. 11.29 and 27.4-8) and as signifying what place Yahweh has chosen (*AF*, ch. XIX, pp. 71-76, ch. XXVIII, p. 105).

Although the narrative seeks to give the impression that Jews and Samaritans shared the same text of the Pentateuch, the apology for the Samaritan version implies that the author wrote from a situation in which Jewish and Samaritan versions were at variance with each other. According to Samaritan tradition, this situation arose when Ezra and Zerubbabel changed the alphabet, 'cut out many passages of the Holy Law because of the fourth of the ten commandments, and the reference to Mt Gerizim and its boundaries. They added to it, cut things from it, changed it and misconstrued it.' Afterwards, Ezra declared that God had given him the book and said: 'this is the Book of God, the authentic truth. Put your faith in it and make copies of this alone' (*AF*, ch. XX, p. 81).[336] In narrative chronology, this took place at the time when 'Anūsharwān succeeding Sūrdī gave permission to Zerubbabel and Ezra ('leaders of the Jews') to rebuild Jerusalem (*AF*, ch. XX, pp. 80-81). Based on biblical chronology, Stenhouse[337] regarded the king to be Cyrus (538/7–529 BCE). A reference to 'Anūsharwān's wars with the Hellenes, however, suggests that he should rather be identified with Xerxes (486–465 BCE) or Artaxerxes I (465–424). This further supports the usual dating of Ezra's mission to the time of Artaxerxes I around 458 BCE.[338] The chronology in *AF*, however, is as

335. I here apply Römer's distinction (Römer, *Israels Väter*, pp. 538-43) between the 'Fathers' from the desert generation to the exile, who are not identical with the Patriarchs.

336. Cf. also the Pitron (commentary) to the *Asatir* 9 in Gaster, *The Asatir*, p. 285. For Jewish refutation to these and other charges in *Sepher Taggin*, see Spiro, *Samaritans, Tobiads, and Judahites*, pp. 20-21.

337. Stenhouse, *Kitāb al-Tarīkh* (1985), n. 376,

338. Cf. M. Smith, *Palestinian Parties*, pp. 122-23; Grabbe, *Judaism from Cyrus to Hadrian*, I, pp. 88-93, who (pp. 128-32) warns against a historicist reading of the Ezra narratives; Cohen, *A Samaritan Chronicle*, p. 75. Rowley, Emerton and Ackroyd opt for Ezra's mission as taking place from the seventh year of Artaxerxes II (i.e. 398 BCE); cf. H.H. Rowley, 'The Chronological Order of Ezra and Nehemiah', in *idem, The Servant of the Lord and Other Essays on the Old Testament* [London: Lutterworth Press, 1952]), pp. 129-60; J.A. Emerton, 'Did Ezra Go to Jerusalem in 428 B.C.?', *JTS* 17 (1966), pp. 1-19; P.R. Ackroyd, *Israel under Babylon and Persia* (The New Clarendon Bible: Old Testament, 4; Oxford: Clarendon Press, 1970), pp. 191-96. Nodet, *Origins of Judaism*, pp. 225, 386, placed the reform activities in the time of Antiochus III (223–187), the Great Synagogue and Simon the Just, and Garbini, *History and Ideology*, pp. 165-69, considered the biblical figure of Ezra to be pseudonymous for the reforms of the Jewish high priest Alcimus (around 159 BCE). Both these scholars date the first appearance of the Pentateuch as an authoritative compilation liable to be called the 'Law of Moses', around 250–200 BCE. Davies, *Scribes and Schools*, pp. 99-106, argues for a sort of a Tetrateuch (Exodus–Deuteronomy) at the end of the

garbled as the chronology in Ezra–Nehemiah, for 'Anūsharwān is followed by 'Ahshīrūs, in whose days Jerusalem was rebuilt (ch. XXI, p. 82). This king is followed by Artaxerxes, whose reign lasted 43 years (*AF*, ch. XXI, p. 83). During his reign lived Hippocrates (born in the eighty-fourth Olympiad, i.e. 460 BCE[339]). Artaxerxes is followed by Darius, 'who helped the sect of the Jews to build Aelia' (*AF*, ch. XXIII, p. 85). The next king mentioned is Alexander the Great (*AF*, ch. XXV, p. 91).[340]

Ezra's function as innovator and competitor to Moses is known also from rabbinic literature (cf. *b. Suk.* 20a: 'He restored and re-established the Torah that had been almost forgotten;[341] *b. Sanh.* 21b: 'He also had the Bible rewritten in "Assyrian" characters, leaving the old Hebrew characters to the Samaritans'; and *t. Sanh.* 4.7: 'If Moses had not anticipated him, Ezra would have received the Torah').[342] The 'ignorance' of such activities in Josephus and sources pre-dating him, none of which 'knows' anything about Ezra not related in the biblical book carrying his name,[343] still puzzles scholars. In fact, Josephus mentions that the proper succession of prophets had come to an end in the time of Artaxerxes, whence the tradition was closed (*Apion* 1.40-42), without any reference to Ezra, whom it might have been relevant to mention.

Discussion of these variants of the Pentateuch is given in yet another narrative about Samaritan-Jewish controversies over traditions held in the court of Ptolemy during the pontificate of Dalīa son of Hezekīah (*AF*, ch. XVIII, pp. 103-11). Since the narrative deals with the Greek translation of the Pentateuch, Ptolemy Soter

---

fourth century and a later incorporation of Genesis and Joshua traditions by scribes, who in the figures of Ezra and Nehemiah create the origin of Judaism around the second century BCE.

339.   Stenhouse, *Kitāb al-Tarīkh* (1985), n. 394.

340.   The number and succession of Persian kings bears some structural resemblance of Josephus' six Persian kings: Cyrus, Cambyses, Darius, Xerxes, Artaxerxes and Darius, followed by Alexander (Josephus, *Ant.* 11.1-305).

341.   Mentioned also in the second-century CE writings of Irenaeus (*Adversus haereses* 3.21) and in the late first century CE *4 Ezra* 14.37-48, both of which place Ezra's activities during the reign of Artaxerxes (465–424 BCE); cf. M. Müller, *The First Bible of the Church: A Plea for the Septuagint* (CIS, 1; JSOTSup, 206; Sheffield: Sheffield Academic Press, 1996), p. 74. *4 Ezra* even states, that 'the Law has been burned, and therefore no one knows the deeds that have been done and are to be done by you' (14.21); cf. Davies, *Scribes and Schools*, p. 178.

342.   E. Davis, 'Ezra', in *EncJud*, VI, p. 1106; *Meg.* 31b; *y. Meg.* 4.1.75a: 'He ordained that public readings from the Torah take place not only on Sabbaths, but also on Mondays and Thursdays'; *B. Bat.* 21b-22a: 'He established schools everywhere to fill the existing needs and in the hope that the rivalry between the institutions would redound to the benefit of the pupils'; *B. Qam.* 82a-b, *y. Meg.* 4.1.75a: 'He also enacted the ordinances known as 'the ten regulations of Ezra' and together with five of his companions, compiled the Mishnah (tractate *Kelim*, in A. Jellinek, *Beit ha Midrash. Sammlungen kleiner Midrashim und Vermischter Abhandlungen aus der ältern jüdischen Literatur* [6 vols.; Jerusalem: Bamberger & Wahrmann, 3rd rev. edn, 1967 (1853)], p. 88). Aside from the book which bears his name, Ezra wrote the genealogies of the book of Chronicles up to his own time (*B. Bat.* 15a) and had a hand in writing the book of Psalms (*Song R.* 4.19). The rabbis identify him with the prophet Malachi (*Meg.* 15a). He is one of the wise men whose piety is especially extolled by the rabbis (*Midr. Ps.* to 105.2).

343.   Garbini, *History & Ideology*, pp. 151-54.

(323–283 BCE) or Ptolemy Philadelphus (283–246 BCE) are considered.[344] The Samaritan deputation ('a number of elders') is led by Aaron and the Jewish 'group' by Eleazar. Jews and Samaritans produce each their own version and the argument seeks to convince the king that the Jewish version, which is without any clear reference to *the* cult place (*AF*, ch. XXVIII, p. 105), is illogical, since the Israelites could not have been left without such a decision for so many years after the exodus. Furthermore, it is 'inconceivable that Moses, the Giver of the Law, should have died without saying something about this; without specifying its direction for the people' (p. 104). Although this written tradition is, in fact, a much later text, it reflects similar Jewish argumentation found in the second century BCE book of *Jubilees*, which refers to the acts of the patriarchs[345] and the crossing of the sea[346] in its promotion of Jerusalem. While in *Jubilees*, 'they will set up the tabernacle of the Lord in the midst of the land, in one of their tribes, until the sanctuary of the Lord is built upon the land' (*Jub.* 49.18), *AF* asserts this to have been the place to which Abraham took Isaac, the place mentioned in 'the Hymn of the Sea' and the place given to Joseph as heritage from his father (*AF*, ch. XXVIII, p. 106).

Questioned by the king about 'those whom the Jews call prophets', the Samaritans refused to recognize the validity of their 'prophethood and their books', because they are in conflict with the Mosaic Law that 'forbids the coming of any prophet after Moses the prophet, as in the passage, "No prophet arose like Moses, in Israel"' (*AF*, ch. XXVIII, p. 108; cf. Deut. 34.10).

In the *Letter of Aristeas* (§§ 46-51, 306-11) and Josephus (*Ant.* 12.11-118), the Greek translation is done by representatives of the twelve tribes of Israel, called 'Jews'. Neither work implies a division of the tribes or brings a discussion similar to that of *AF*. The approval of the translation in *Letter of Aristeas* (§§ 306-311) implicitly reflects discussions of the validity of the Greek translation. These discussions might not be related to Samaritan-Jewish controversies, rather than Jewish discussions about former translations of the Law, as might be indicated in *Aristeas* (§§ 30-31) and Josephus (*Ant.* 12.36). However, the mention of damaged books (*Aristeas* § 30) and of the Jewish High Priest Eliezer's sending from Jerusalem 'a magnificent edition of the Law', at least imply disagreements about the validity of

---

344. Stenhouse, *Kitāb al-Tarīkh* (1985), n. 485: Dalīa took office around 323 BCE; Josephus, *Ant.* 12.6-12, mentions that the descendants of those taken captive ('from the hill country of Judaea and the district around Jerusalem and from Samaria and those on Mt Garizein') to Egypt by Ptolemy Soter had such quarrels, Samaritans opting for Gerizim and Jews for Jerusalem. N. Collins, '281 BCE: The Year of the Translation of the Pentateuch into Greek under Ptolemy II', in Brooke and Lindars (eds.), *Septuagint, Scrolls and Cognate Writings*, pp. 403-503, bases her dating 'on sources which are independent of Aristeas and have confirmed the essence of his basic report' (p. 477). Müller, *First Bible of the Church*, and R. Hanhart, *Studien zur Septuaginta und zum hellenistischen Judentum* (Tübingen: J.C.B. Mohr [Paul Siebeck], 1999), do not give exact dates of the translation, but rather imply a third-century origin. For a rejection of a third-century origin and an argument for a dating after 150 BCE, see F. Clancy, 'The Date of LXX', *SJOT* 16/2 (2002), pp. 207-25.

345. *Jub.* 18.13; 32.16-24; cf. *AF*, ch. XXVIII, pp. 105-106.

346. *Jub.* 8.19; cf. *AF*, ch. XXVIII, p. 105.

the Hebrew texts.[347] Josephus' mention of later quarrels among Samaritans and Jews in Egypt,[348] just before his paraphrase of the *Letter of Aristeas*, might imply the existence of variant traditions about the translation, similar to that presented in *AF*. The anticipation of these quarrels has no function in Josephus' narrative apart from implicitly 'testifying' that since these controversies took place at a later time, the Pentateuch translated in Egypt is unrelated to later discussions about the validity of the text in regards to Jewish-Samaritan disagreements. In *AF*, it was the 'dispute between Samaritans and Jews over the Torah, and the fact that the Samaritans refused to accept any books claimed to be by the hand of a prophet, other than the Torah', that necessitated a translation be made for the king's investigation of the matter (*AF*, ch. XXVIII, p. 103). Josephus somewhat accords with the Samaritan tradition in his remark, that 'they [the Samaritans] were determined to keep alive their fathers' way of life and customs' and so they fought with each other, those from Jerusalem saying that their temple was the holy one, and requiring that the sacrifices be sent there, while the Shechemites wanted these to go to Mount Garizein' (Josephus, *Ant.* 12.10). Josephus' mention of 70 (*Ant.* 12.57) against *Aristeas*' 72 elders (§ 51) accord with *AF* (ch. XXVIII, p. 110): the 70 elders of the Samaritan deputation. The 70 occurs frequently in patristic writings.[349]

In *AF*, the outcome of the hearing is an order to make pilgrimage to 'the Place' and a curse on everyone who does not submit to this, followed by the clarifying remark that the 'Jews had forbidden pilgrimage to the Mount of Blessing' (*AF*, ch. XXVIII, p. 111; cf. pp. 87-88[350]). Probably as a result of this prohibition, the Jews split into three groups: the Pharisees, Sadducees and Ḥasidīm.[351] According to ch. XXIX, p. 111, not only Samaritans, but also Sadducees and Ḥasidīm agreed on

---

347.   Müller, *First Bible of the Church*, p. 52: 'The text undoubtedly refers to manuscripts which have been carelessly copied out, not carelessly translated, which means that Aristeas 3 does not refer to Greek translations, but to Hebrew manuscripts in general, and perhaps in particular to those available in Alexandria'.

348.   Josephus, *Ant.* 12.10. The discussion Josephus relates was among the descendants of those living in Egypt, which might be his reason for placing it in the second century BCE, as held in front of Ptolemy [IV Philometor [181–146 BCE]; *Ant.* 13.74-79).

349.   Müller, *First Bible of the Church*, pp. 68-78.

350.   The attack on the Samaritans during the time of the Jewish king Simon followed by Hyrcanus is placed before the advent of Alexander the Great. The 'event' might be related to Jewish–Samaritan animosities in the latter part of the fourth century, at which time the Jews enjoyed Persian support; cf. Gaster, *The Samaritans*, pp. 33-34. A Jewish high priest named Simon and the tax-collector Hyrcanus son of Joseph, whose mother was a sister of the high priest of Jerusalem and whose father was a descendant of Tobias the Ammonite are both related to the period of Antiochus III (223–187) in Josephus (*Ant.* 12.154-236; cf. M. Smith, *Palestinian Parties*, pp. 185-86). A third possibility is to correct the chronology and place the event in the time of the Maccabaeans; cf. Stenhouse, *Kitāb al-Tarīkh* (1985), n. 407; Hjelm, *Samaritans and Early Judaism*, pp. 260-61.

351.   In *AF*, ch. XXIX, p. 111, the Ḥasidīm 'rallied around the Samaritans all without exception, and followed their school of thought, dwelling in the villages near to the Mount of Blessings, with the intention of devoting themselves to worship'. *Chronicle Adler* states that the Ḥasidīm consisted of the community of the Samaritans, the sons of Joseph and Phinehas, and members of other tribes, who adhered to them (cf. Zangenberg, *Samareia*, p. 217).

the authority of the Torah against the other books promoted by the Pharisees ('which means the Separatists'). Josephus (*Ant.* 18.16-17; 13.297-98) relates that 'the Pharisees had passed on to the people certain regulations handed down by former generations and not recorded in the Laws of Moses, for which reason they are rejected by the Sadducaean group, who hold that only those regulations should be considered valid which were written down, and that those which had been handed down by former generations (by the fathers) need not be observed'. Josephus does not give any date to the split, but records that the 'Jews since most ancient times had three philosophies pertaining to their traditions'.[352] As characters in his narratives, however, they do not occur before the Hasmonaean uprising, the first mention being from the time of John Hyrcanus' quarrel with the Pharisees.[353] The same chronological feature is found in *AF* (ch. XXIX, pp. 112-13), which resembles Josephus' narrative. That narrative is extremely anti-Pharisaic and favours Sadducees *and* Samaritans: 'After John had gone over to the Sadducees and had done what he did to the Separatists—burnt their books and forbidden the young to receive instruction from them—he restored the practice of going on pilgrimage to Nablus, to the Mount of Blessing, and firmly held that it was the house of God'.[354]

While the Samaritan Chronicle seems to imply that the books referred to are the 'Books of David' and 'the biblical Prophets' (cf. *AF*, ch. XXVIII, p. 108), Josephus' statement does not clarify whether the Sadducaean rejection of regulations not written down in the Laws of Moses also includes a rejection of historical traditions that became part of the Canon. 'The regulations of the fathers', promoted by the Pharisees and rejected by the Sadducees (τὰ δ' ἐκ παραδόσεως τῶν πατέρων μὴ τηρεῖν, Josephus, *Ant.* 13.297), might relate to the Oral Torah and legal matters proper.[355] Keeping in mind the existence of literature (and sects) from at least the second century BCE, dealing with (re)interpretations of patriarchal and Mosaic laws, and early rabbinic discussions, such as those reflected in, for example, the New Testament, and systematically written down in the Mishnah, a range of possibilities are at hand. Second–first century BCE 'Jewish' literature's seeming reuse of biblical traditions for its own (hi)story writing[356] raises questions about historical validity

---

352. Josephus, *Ant.* 18.11. Josephus does not mention Ḥasidīm, but names the third school 'the Essenes'.

353. Josephus, *Ant.* 13.288-300; which, of course, have led most scholars to assert that they emerged in the second century BCE.

354. It is uncertain whether the text implies that he had once made the pilgrimage or whether he restored the practice; Stenhouse, *Kitāb al-Tarīkh* (1985), n. 572.

355. S.J. Isser, *The Dositheans: A Samaritan Sect in Late Antiquity* (Leiden: E.J. Brill, 1976), p. 36: 'The Sadducees did not accept resurrection, as we know from Josephus and the rabbinic literature, but nothing is said in those sources about their non-acceptance of the Prophets'. L.H. Schiffman, *Reclaiming the Dead Sea Scrolls: The History of Judaism, the Background of Christianity, the Lost Library of Qumran* (Philadelphia: Jewish Publication Society of America, 1994), p. 74: 'later rabbinic sources picture them as rejecting the Oral Law...the notion promulgated by some church fathers that the Sadducees accepted only the Torah as authoritative, rejecting the Prophets and the emerging corpus of Writings, is unsubstantiated by any earlier sources'.

356. See below Chapter 6.

as well as polemic interest for both types of literature. The Books of David and of the biblical Prophets might not have been quite as ancient to these interpreters as modern scholars assume. What can be deduced from *AF*, Josephus and the New Testament is that Sadducees regarded the written 'Laws of Moses' to be the authorised law code. However, the words of the Law as well as its interpretation are open to dispute. This brings us back to questions about the relationship between law, prophet and king. With whom does Yahweh speak?

Chapter 5

PROPHETIC UNDERSTANDING OF THE STATUS AND THE FUNCTION
OF THE LAW: DAVID AND MOSES IN COMPETITION

1. *From Priesthood to Kingship*

Although both Eli and Samuel, priest and prophet, are evaluated positively, the unjust conduct of their sons leads to a rejection of both houses as leaders. The first is rejected by Yahweh by the word of a messenger (איש אלהים, 1 Sam. 2.27-36); the second by the people (1 Sam. 8.3-5). Their 'choice' for kingship similarly proves false, although the king had been elected by Yahweh (1 Sam. 9.15-17; 15.1, 11). In successive steps of abandonment—from judge to priest to prophet to king— the road has been prepared for the institution of the hereditary Davidic kingship from the tribe of Judah.[1] The authority of that king is based on the authorization of the prophet as mediator between the king and his god. In this role, the prophet retains supreme authority, untouchable by king, people and priest. Any challenge to the trustworthiness of the word of the runs the risk of taking away Yahweh's favour.[2] Saul did not fall from grace because he had failed to listen to Yahweh, but because he did not obey the words Samuel gave him 'from Yahweh Zebaoth' (1 Sam. 15.2-23). With this authorization of the prophet, any deviation from the Law has the potential of being judged as a deviation from the 'words', the 'teaching' of the prophets, such as is characteristic of Samuel–Kings.

Although Shiloh connotes ambiguity in Masoretic tradition, the negative connotation of its priesthood found in Samaritan tradition is one that is shared by both. In both, disobedience and revolt lead to rejection. While in Samaritan tradition Eli challenges the authority of the high priest 'Azzi/Ozzi, in Masoretic tradition his sons challenge the authority of Yahweh. The text even states that 'his sons cursed' (מקללים) God[3] (1 Sam. 3.13). While in Samaritan tradition Eli's relocation of the cult to Shiloh caused an enduring split among the tribes of Israel, Masoretic tradition implicitly removes that competition by rejecting the Elide priesthood and

---

1.   1 Sam. 15.28; 28.17; cf. the similar 'double witness' formulation in 1 Kgs 11.31 and 14.8's transference of part of the kingdom to Jeroboam. The concentric pattern highlights David as Yahweh's true king, further indicated in the judgment of Abijam of Judah (1 Kgs 15.4-5), who reigned while Jeroboam was king in Israel.

2.   D.F. Murray, *Divine Prerogative and Royal Pretension: Pragmatics, Poetics and Polemics in a Narrative Sequence about David (2 Samuel 5.17–7.29)* (JSOTSup, 264; Sheffield: Sheffield Academic Press, 1998), pp. 315-16.

3.   There are some text-critical problems: להם; *Tiqqun sopherim* אלהים; LXX θεòν.

neglecting the Shilonite temple. The removal of the house of Eli does not imply a return to any past situation or to an immediate institution of another priestly house. It institutes the prophets as mediators between God and men. As such, 1 Samuel 1–4's double narrative of the Elide priesthood and the prophet Samuel presents the latter as the opposite of the Elides. Intertextually, the narrative points in two directions: namely, to the traditions about the Levitical priesthood and Samuel's role as successor to Moses and Aaron.

In a variant of Lev. 10.12-20's narrative about the 'remaining sons of Aaron',[4] Eleazar and Ithamar's critical non-eating of the goat of the sin offering (הַחַטָּאת) at the altar,[5] 1 Samuel narrates that Eli's sons, Hophni and Phinehas, blasphemed (piel of [6]נעץ) Yahweh's offering (זבח) by demanding some uncooked meat for themselves (1 Sam. 2.15-16), with the further implication that they ate the fat, which was reserved for Yahweh (2.16, 29).[7] Additionally, they broke the bond with the community by not participating in the offering.[8] While in Leviticus Aaron defends his sons against Moses' anger, in 1 Samuel Eli rebukes his sons (2.22-24), but doubts that man can intercede (התפלל) for man against Yahweh (2.25): 'If man sins against man, God (אלהים) can mediate, but if man sins against Yahweh, who can intercede for him?'[9] It cannot, of course, be proven that Leviticus is polemical against Eli's question, but one must not fail to notice that Aaron's defensive question—'Had I eaten the sin offering today, would it have been good in the eyes of Yahweh?'—is accepted by Moses on Yahweh's behalf (Lev. 10.19-20).[10] The various problems of interpreting the incident[11] shall not concern us here. For the present study, it is Aaron's role as intercessor and Moses' role as mediator that are important.[12] While in Leviticus Aaron's defence saves his sons' lives, in 1 Samuel Eli's failure not to 'restrain' his sons[13] leads to their death and Yahweh's eternal

---

4.   Aaron's eldest sons, Nadab and Abihu, have just been struck down by Yahweh's devouring fire because they had 'offered unauthorized coals, which he had not commanded them' (Lev. 10.1-2).

5.   Cf. Lev. 6.18-23 (19): the people's purification offering (cf. also 2 Chron. 29.23-24), which must be eaten by the officiating priest, namely Aaron, and what he cannot finish, must be eaten by the rest of the priestly cadre. The offering referred to is that brought (Lev. 9.3, 15), which has not yet been eaten; cf. J. Milgrom, *Leviticus 1–16: A New Translation with Introduction and Commentary* (AB, 3; New York: Doubleday, 1991), pp. 596, 622.

6.   The term implies a sin, which deserves rejection and death (e.g. Num. 14.11, 23; 16.30; 2 Kgs 19.3; Isa. 1.4; 5.24; 37.3; Ps. 10.3, 13; Jer. 23.17); cf. Chapters 2 and 3 above.

7.   Cf. Lev. 3.16-17; 7.31. The custom (משפט) of plunging a fork into the pot to take whatever is brought up is at variance with Lev. 7.31-34, 'the right thigh and the breast', and Deut. 18.3, 'the foreleg, the cheeks and the stomach', which should be given to the priest.

8.   H.J. Stoebe, *Das Erste Buch Samuelis* (Kommentar zum Alten Testament, 8.1; Gütersloh: Gütersloher Verlagshaus/Gerd Mohn, 1993), p. 112.

9.   Cf. also Eli's resignation after Samuel's report of Yahweh's message (1 Sam. 3.18): 'and Eli said, "He is Yahweh, let him do what is good in his eyes"'.

10.   Milgrom, *Leviticus 1–16*, p. 627.

11.   For this, see Milgrom, *Leviticus 1–16*, pp. 595-640.

12.   Milgrom, *Leviticus 1–16*, p. 627.

13.   Piel of כהה; cf. the translation suggested by P. Kyle McCarter, Jr, *I Samuel: A New Translation with Introduction, Notes and Commentary* (AB, 8; New York: Doubleday, 1980), p. 98.

rejection of 'the house of Eli' (1 Sam. 3.12-14), which, in Egypt, he had elected as priests from all the tribes of Israel (2.27-28):

> And a man of God came to Eli, and said to him, 'Thus Yahweh has said', I revealed myself to the house of your father when they were in Egypt subject to the house of Pharaoh. And I chose him out of all the tribes of Israel to be my priest (וּבָחֹר אֹתוֹ מִכָּל־שִׁבְטֵי יִשְׂרָאֵל לִי לְכֹהֵן), to go up to my altar, to burn incense, to wear an *ephod* before me; and I gave to the house of your father all my fire offerings (אֶת־כָּל־אִשֵּׁי) from the people of Israel.

Thus Eli's eligibility as father and priest has failed.[14]

While 1 Samuel does not give further information about the house of Eli's relationship, one might suggest that a complete break with past relations to the priesthood of the desert generation is intended.[15] Thus, the second sin mentioned, Hophni and Phinehas' fornication with 'the women who served at the entrance to the tent of meeting' (וְאֵת אֲשֶׁר־יִשְׁכְּבוּן אֶת־הַנָּשִׁים הַצֹּבְאוֹת פֶּתַח אֹהֶל מוֹעֵד, 1 Sam. 2.22b),[16] finds another parallel in Numbers 25's narrative about Phinehas son of Eleazar son of Aaron. The variability of the occurrence of 1 Sam. 2.22b might depend on whether a clear distinction is sought between the houses of Eleazar and Ithamar, as in Josephus (*Ant.* 5.350). In this text, as a result of the death of Eli's sons, 'the priesthood shall be transferred into the family of Eleazar'. Thus the house of Eleazar remains pure during the Ithamar interim, a period, which the Old Testament does not specify, but Josephus claims the existence of in his closing genealogy to the Eli narratives (5.361-62). That being the case, the zealous act of Phinehas son of Eleazar, who kills the Israelite and his Midianite woman, whom he brought with him to 'the entrance of the tent of meeting' (Num. 25.6), functions as a contrast to the impious acts of Eli's sons (of the family of Ithamar). With Eli's 'successor' Zadok placed literally and traditionally in the genealogy of Eleazar,[17] a clear distinction seems to have become necessary.

While Eli's house forfeits Yahweh's promise of eternal priesthood (1 Sam. 3.30), Yahweh rewards Phinehas son of Eleazar son of Aaron, with the eternal priesthood (בְּרִית כְּהֻנַּת עוֹלָם), because he 'turned back my wrath from the Israelites in his jealousy of my jealousy [i.e. "in his passion for me"] among them (הֵשִׁיב אֶת־חֲמָתִי מֵעַל בְּנֵי־יִשְׂרָאֵל בְּקַנְאוֹ אֶת־קִנְאָתִי בְּתוֹכָם) so that I did not consume (וְלֹא־כִלִּיתִי)[18] the Israelites in my jealousy [passion]' (בְּקִנְאָתִי, Num. 25.11). Phinehas's absorption of Yahweh's jealousy is compatible with the officiating priest's absorption of the

---

14. Against Stoebe, *Erste Buch Saumelis*, p. 114: 'Ist Gott aber selbst der Betroffene, so ist eine Milderung der Strafe durch fürbittendes Einstehen nicht möglich. In diesen Worten ist also unüberhörbar die Katastrophe der Eliden vorhergesagt, zugleich in folgerichtiger Strenge V. 25b vorbereitet.' Samuel's intercession (1 Sam. 12.19-23; cf. 8.7) exactly proves the opposite.

15. Otto, *Massotfest*, pp. 170-71.

16. The passage is missing in some Qumran manuscripts and LXX[Mss], but occurs in an elaborated version in Josephus (*Ant.* 5.339) and in Origen; also *AF*, ch. IX, pp. 41-42.

17. Ezra 7.1-5; Neh. 10.11-12; 1 Chron. 9.10-13.

18. Cf. Jer. 4.27; 5.18; 30.11, and its protagonist in 1 Sam. 3.13: 'from beginning to end', that is destruction.

people's iniquity,[19] wherefore we also find that his act is termed in cultic language as 'atonement' (ויכפר, 25.13b).[20] Implicitly offering a possibility of averting Yahweh's swearing 'to the house of Eli (ולכן נשבעתי לבית עלי) that the iniquity of Eli's house (עון בית־עלי) shall not be expiated (אם־יתכפר) by sacrifice (בזבח)[21] or offering forever (ובמנחת עד־עולם)' (1 Sam. 3.14), Numbers' solution to that iniquity would have been Eli's slaying his sons. However, Eli loves his sons more than he loves Yahweh (ותכבד את־בניך ממני, 1 Sam. 2.29) and has thus disapproved himself.

As Yahweh's favour has left Eli's house, it is no wonder that Yahweh's Ark has lost its power, so that Israel not only is defeated by the Philistines (1 Sam. 4.10-11), but also turns to foreign gods (7.3). Although the Ark has returned to Israel (1 Sam. 6), it is the removal (hiphil of סור) of foreign gods, the *Baalim* and *Ashtorot*, confession and intercession, which finally turn the former catastrophe into a victory, a defeat of the Philistines and a regaining of the lost areas (1 Sam. 7). As Samuel is absent from the narrative during the 20 years of Philistine occupation and idol worship, his entry is compatible with the saving entry of the judges,[22] who, similarly, are attributed the hero's role, without in any way being responsible for or 'defiled' by the sin they remove.[23] The motif is paradigmatically described in Judg. 2.11-19, incorporating several elements found in 1 Sam. 7.2-13. The removal of foreign gods in 1 Sam. 7.3-4 has no parallel in Judg. 2.11-19. The closest parallel to that element is found in Judg. 10.6-16 (anticipating the Jephthah narratives) and Josh. 24.14-24. Judges 6.25-32 (the Gideon–Jerubbaal narrative) offers a variant of the theme. It is therefore no coincidence that the judge Samuel compares himself with these two leaders from the past: 'Jerubbaal, Bedan, and Jephthah and Samuel'[24] (1 Sam. 12.11). Jephthah ruled from Mizpah (Judg. 11.34), to which place Israel gathered before the war with the Ammonites,[25] Benjaminites (Judg. 20.1, 3) and

---

19. Milgrom, *Leviticus 1–16*, p. 624.

20. Cf. also Sir. 45.23-25, which does not mention Eli, but sets Phinehas ('third in honour') on a par with David's eternal priesthood and kingship.

21. Note the irony of using this term, which is 'limited to slain offering which meat is eaten by the worshiper' (Milgrom, *Leviticus 1–16*, p. 218).

22. M. Garsiel, *The First Book of Samuel: A Literary Study of Comparative Structures, Analogies and Parallels* (Jerusalem: Revivim Publishing House, 1985 [Hebrew original: Jerusalem: Revivim Publishing House, 1983]), p. 55.

23. Whether this belongs to editorial activity based on the existence of some ancient (from 'late ninth century' onwards) Prophetic Record(s), which influenced successive redaction of the DtrH (cf. O'Brien, *Deuteronomistic History Hypothesis*, pp. 101-109), shall not concern us here; especially so, as the highly speculative hypothesis has remained unfounded. In the present texts, it is integral to the presentation of the prophet.

24. Bedan occurs only here and in Manasseh's genealogy in 1 Chron. 7.17. LXX: Jerubaal (Jeroboam), Barak, Jephthah (LXX^MS: + Simson), Samuel; Syriac: Debora, Barak, Gideon, Simson; Targum: Gideon, Simson (Targ.f: Bedan), Jephthah, Samuel. Heb. 11.32: Gideon, Barak, Samson, Jephthah, David and Samuel and the prophets.

25. Judg. 10.17. Although the Mizpah mentioned in the Jephthah narrative might lie in Gilead and not in Benjamin, the similarity of names bears allusions to each other. The possibility that two 'Mizpahs' are involved in the story cannot be excluded and the site of the cultic Israelite assembly (10.17; 11.11) might be none other than Mizpah of Benjamin (Judg. 20; 1 Sam. 7); cf. P.M. Arnold, 'Mizpah', in *ABD*, IV, pp. 879-81.

Philistines (1 Sam. 7.6, 7, 11), to inquire (Judg. 11.11), cry (Judg. 21.2) or pray
(1 Sam. 7.5-6) before Yahweh. Once a year Samuel went from his residence in
Ramah to 'judge' Israel in Bethel, Gilgal and Mizpah (1 Sam. 7.16).

Although implicitly claimed to designate all Israel, 'these cities were thus the
centers of Samuel's administration, indicating that his leadership was limited to a
small part of the hills'.[26] This conclusion is important, as Mizpah's status as a
regional administrative centre is resumed in narrative chronology after the destruction of Jerusalem in the books of Kings. Thus 'replacing' Jerusalem, the c. 400
years of governorship in Judah begins and ends in Mizpah,[27] which similarly 'disappears' from the scene after the Maccabaean conquest of Jerusalem.[28] These and
other 'coincidences' suggest that the pre-monarchical narratives are mainly a product of post-exilic time and projected back in order to create a framework for the
monarchies of Iron II Palestine.[29] It is significant that Josephus does not mention
Mizpah or Michmas in other contexts than those known from the Old Testament
and 1 Maccabees.

1 Samuel 12's comparison of Samuel with Jerubbaal and Jephthah places him
among those judges whose reigns are characterized by great victories leading to
disagreement (Judg. 8.1-3) and to a civil war (Judg. 12.1-6) with the Ephraimites
(Judg. 8.1-3; 12.1-6). Again, the Jephthah narratives offer the closest parallel. As
Jephthah's victory over the Ammonites (Judg. 11.32-33) causes envy among the
Ephraimites, so Samuel's appointment of Saul (1 Sam. 10.17-27) is met with resistance by 'the sons of Belial' (בני בליעל, 1 Sam. 10.27), which we might translate
'worthless fellows' (NRSV) or 'wicked men', but which bear allusions to 'the sons
of Eli' (1 Sam. 2.12)[30] and the Benjaminites (Judg. 19.22; 20.13). In Samaritan

---

26. Ahlström, *History of Palestine*, p. 427. Scholarly consensus maintains that Mizpah is to be
identified with Tell en-Nasbeh, located 12 km north of Jerusalem and serving as a border fortress in
Iron I-II, Babylonian, Persian and Hellenistic times.

27. 2 Kgs 25.22-26; Jer. 40.5–41.18: Nebuchadnezzar's appointment of Gedaliah as governor
over Judah. 1 Macc. 3.46: the people gather in Mizpah (Μασσηφα), opposite Jerusalem, because
Mizpah has in earlier times been the place to which Israel came to pray. The gathering anticipates
Judah's defeat of the Seleucid governor Lysias and his men, the deliverance of Jerusalem and the
temple inauguration in 165/164 BCE.

28. In the Bible it is mentioned once in the time of the monarchies as a Judaean border fortress
(1 Kgs 15.22); Josephus, in his *Antiquities*, knows only the biblical Mizpah and does not mention
Judas Maccabaeus' gathering of men in Mizpah; cf. *Ant.* 12.300.

29. Arnold, 'Mizpah', p. 880: 'It is likely that Mizpah retained its status as capital of Judah and
primary temple for many decades, until the reestablishment of Jerusalem late in the 6th century
B.C.E. It is also possible that postexilic literary circles were active in the city during this period,
which may account for its inclusion and legitimation in premonarchical stories such as Judges 20,
1 Samuel 7, and possibly Judges 11.' A similar literary distribution occurs for the Benjaminite town
Mikmas, the place where the Philistines gathered, whom Saul and his son Jonathan defeated
(1 Sam. 13.2–14.31), 'invoked' in Isaiah's vision of the enemy's advance (Isa. 10.27-32), and the
residence of Jonathan Maccabaeus, 'who settled in Mikmas (Μαχμας) and began to judge the
people and made the ungodly disappear (ἠφάνισεν) from Israel' (1 Macc. 9.73); cf. also Josephus,
Ant. 6.98, 103; 13.34.

30. McCarter, *I Samuel*, p. 194: the disloyal בני בליעל in contrast to the loyal (בני) החיל
(1 Sam. 10.26-27).

tradition, the opponents of Saul's election are 'the tribe of Phinehas and the tribe of Joseph, who, with a few others from the remaining tribes, remained on the Holy Mountain' (Gerizim; *AF*, ch. X, pp. 46-47). In Josephus (*Ant.* 6.82), Saul calls his opponents 'kinsfolk' (ὁμοφύλων) and 'of their own race' (ἐκ τούτου γένους αὐτοῖς). As Saul's request to all Israel for support of his and Samuel's war with the Ammonites is associative[31] with the Ephraimite Levite's message about the evil deed (נבלה)[32] of the בני בליעל in Benjamin (Judg. 19.22-23),[33] the MT opens up the possibility that both the Ephraimites and the Benjaminites are intended. That being the case, Saul's[34] sparing of the lives of those, who had despised him ([35]יבזהו, 1 Sam. 11.12), implicitly removes all former controversies alluded to in the narrative. In contrast, Jephthah's controversy with the Ephraimites caused the death of 42,000 Ephraimites (Judg. 12.6). Having thus 'restored' Israel, the renewal (piel of חדש) of the kingship with the participation of 'all Israel's men' takes place in Gilgal (1 Sam. 11.15), indicating a mental return to the entrance into the Promised Land (Josh. 4.19) and to Joshua's camp in Gilgal (Josh. 10.6-7, 15, 43;[36] 14.6). As Joshua conquered the whole country from Gilgal (Josh. 10.40-43), so Saul (and Samuel) conquer(s) the whole country and fight(s) against his (their) neighbours from Gilgal (1 Sam. 13–15 [13.4; 15.12]).

The confusion that has arisen among scholars concerning the location of biblical Gilgal, as well as the possibility that in some instances the place might be closer to Shechem than to Jericho (Josh. 4.19),[37] are not considered here, as the name's associative function is phonetic and literary rather than related to geography and the history of religion.[38] It should, however, be noted that as the name's etymological

31. Garsiel, *First Book of Samuel*, p. 83.

32. Although נבל is found mostly in texts dealing with sexual transgression, its deeper meaning is rooted in questions of sacrilege and disobedience; cf. A. Philips, 'Nebalah—A Term for Serious Disorderly and Unruly Conduct, *VT* 25 (1975), pp. 237-41; Hjelm, *Samaritans and Early Judaism*, pp. 141-42.

33. They both send pieces of oxen to the other tribes (Judg. 19.29-30; 1 Sam. 11.7), Saul declaring that 'whoever do not come out after Saul and Samuel, so shall be done to his oxen'.

34. LXX[MSS] reads Samuel.

35. 1 Sam. 10.27; this term also appears in 1 Sam. 2.30's doom against Eli's house (those who despise Yahweh shall be treated with contempt); cf. Isa. 37.22 par. 2 Kgs 19.21.

36. For a discussion of LXX's 'omission' of 'Joshua and all Israel's return to Gilgal' in MT Josh. 10.15 and 43, based on *Vorlage* rather than redaction, see K. de Troyer, 'A Pre-Masoretic Biblical Text: The Final Touches to an Old Joshua', in *idem, Rewriting the Sacred Text*, pp. 29-58. In light of de Troyer's argument it must be noted that *AF* (ch. IV, p. 16) agrees with the LXX on this issue, while Niessen, *Buches Yehošua'*, fol. 28a, agrees with the MT.

37. Scholarly consensus suggests that Khirbet el-Mefjir, which is 1–2 miles Northeast of Tell es-Sultan (Jericho), is identifiable with biblical Gilgal of the Joshua, Judges and Samuel narratives; Jiljulieh, which is some 7 miles to the north of Beitīn, has been considered regarding the Elijah–Elisha narratives and some of the Prophets' polemic against Gilgal; cf. J. Muilenburg, 'The Site of Ancient Gilgal', *BASOR* 140 (1955), pp. 11-27 (18).

38. For a quick overview of possibilities, see David J.A. Clines (ed.), *The Dictionary of Classical Hebrew* (Sheffield: Sheffield Academic Press, 1995–), *ad loc.* For discussions of historical-critical issues, see, among others, D.E. Sellin, *Gilgal: Ein Beitrag zur Geschichte der*

meaning is 'a circle (of stones)',[39] which in all instances but two (Josh. 5.9; 12.23) appears in a determined form in the Old Testament,[40] scholars' inability to find its location might rest on false assumptions about Gilgal's role as a pre-Davidic pan-Israelite cult place[41] from at least the time of Saul.[42] The ambiguities in biblical material might deliberately be aimed at implying both the Benjaminite and the Ephraimite traditions in order to polemicize against the Samaritan claim that the first camp was in Gilgal,[43] in which also the stones were placed.[44] That Jerusalem of the Iron I-II transition supersedes Gilgal and Shiloh[45] is something we know from tradition, not from history. Josephus' unwillingness to acknowledge the Gilgal of biblical Saul narratives (MT and LXX) as a sanctuary or a cult place[46] and rabbinic tradition's 'neglect' of such a place leave the impression that the referential meaning of the name 'Gilgal' was open to discussion.

Ambiguous as are also Gilgal's connotations, David's renewal of his kingship after Absalom's death (2 Sam. 19.10-44) anticipates the later division of the Davidic kingdom, when only his kinsmen, the tribe of Judah, are invited to accompany him across the Jordan. In Gilgal, they meet all the Israelites (כל־איש ישראל), who claim to have ten shares (עשר־ידות)[47] in the king and to having been the first to suggest bringing the king back (19.42-44). Similarly, as Gilgal was the place for David's renewal of his kingship, it also partakes in Shiloh's role of being the place where

---

Einwanderung Israels in Palästina (Leipzig: Deichert, 1917); E. Nielsen, *Shechem*; E. Otto, *Das Mazzotfest in Gilgal* (BWANT, 107; Stuttgart: W. Kohlhammer, 1975).

39. However, Josephus, *Ant.* 5.34: 'Galgala. This name signifies "freedom" (ἐλευθερία); for having crossed the river, they felt themselves henceforth free both from the Egyptians and from their miseries in the desert.' Theodoret made a similar translation (cf. LCL, *ad. loc.*). Note Josh. 5.9: 'Today I have rolled away (גלותי) from you the disgrace of Egypt (את־חרפת מצרים). And so the place is called Gilgal to this day.'

40. W.R. Kotter, 'Gilgal', in *ABD*, II, pp. 1022-24.

41. Lemche, *Early Israel*, p. 292: 'scholars have attempted in desperation to manoeuvre the pan-Israelite ideas into a hypothetical hiatus between the period of the judges and the sources of the beginnings of the monarchy; to this end they have claimed that, for example, Gilgal was the central sanctuary at this time'. See also, Soggin, *An Introduction to the History of Israel of Judah*, pp. 155-56, 182-90.

42. Otto, *Mazzotfest* (following H.-J. Kraus [Alt, Noth, von Rad and F. Langlamet, regarding the amphictyony thesis]), pp. 167-98: 'Die Analyse von Jos. 1; 3–6 hat also gezeigt, dass das Gilgalfest aus zwei grossen kultischen Festakten bestand, nähmlich einer Ladeprocession von Šittim nach Gilgal, in deren Mittelpunkt der Durchzug durch den Jordan stand, und der Feier der Beschneidung und des Mazzotfestes am Heiligtum von Gilgal. Im Rahmen dieses sieben Tage dauernden Festes wurden an jedem Tag die Ruinen von Jericho in einer Ladeprocession umzogen [*sic*]'.

43. *AF*, ch. II, p. 10: 'The name of the place where they camped for the night across the Jordan was called Jalīla and that is the name to our day'.

44. Niessen, *Buches Yehošua'*, especially stresses Gilgal's closeness to Gerizim; cf. fol. 28a and 32a: 'nach ihrer Errichtung für ein ganzes Jahr in Gilgal, das gegenüber dem heiligen Berg liegt'.

45. Otto, *Mazzotfest*, pp. 351-54, 365: Shiloh and Gilgal.

46. Thornton, 'Anti-Samaritan Exegesis', pp. 127-29; Josephus, *Ant.* 6.83 (cf. 1 Sam. 11.14-15); *Ant.* 6.147, 155 (cf. 1 Sam. 15.21, 33).

47. 2 Sam. 19.44; cf. 1 Kgs 11.29-39.

Yahweh rejects the king he has elected first (1 Sam. 13.13-14; 15.21-29). In yet other variants of the offering motif, Saul forfeits his possibility of an everlasting kingdom (אֶת־מַמְלַכְתְּךָ אֶל־יִשְׂרָאֵל עַד־עוֹלָם, 13.13) because he did not observe (כִּי לֹא שָׁמַרְתָּ) what Yahweh had commanded him (אֲשֶׁר צִוְּךָ יְהוָה, 13.14).[48] Echoing the retribution theme of 1 Sam. 2.30—'those who honour me, I will honour, and those who despise me, shall be despised' (כִּי־מְכַבְּדַי אֲכַבֵּד וּבֹזַי יֵקָלּוּ)—Samuel twice pronounces the doom over Saul's kingship: 'because you have rejected Yahweh's word, has he rejected you from being king' (יַעַן[50] מָאַסְתָּ אֶת־דְּבַר יְהוָה וַיִּמְאָסְךָ[49] מִמֶּלֶךְ, 15.23, 26). Because of his fear of man (כִּי יָרֵאתִי אֶת־הָעָם וָאֶשְׁמַע בְּקוֹלָם) rather than fear of God (15.24) and lying about his own role in the transgression,[51] Saul's confession is as dethroning for him as was Aaron's in the golden calf episode (Exod. 32.22-24) and the Elides' non-confession, none of whom feared God or men. On the road to perfection, Yahweh's pronouncement that 'I will raise up for myself (וַהֲקִימֹתִי לִי) a faithful priest (כֹּהֵן נֶאֱמָן[52]), who will do according to my heart and my soul (כַּאֲשֶׁר בִּלְבָבִי וּבְנַפְשִׁי יַעֲשֶׂה[53]); and I will build for him a sure house (וּבָנִיתִי לוֹ[55] בַּיִת נֶאֱמָן[54]) and he shall go in and out before my anointed all his days (וְהִתְהַלֵּךְ לִפְנֵי מְשִׁיחִי[56] כָּל־הַיָּמִים)' (1 Sam. 2.35), has come closer to its fulfilment in the elimination of 'competing' candidates (13.14; 15.28).

2. *David and Moses: Prophet vs. Prophet?*

As noted above, the immediate substitute for the removal of the Elides is not Zadok (and the Eleazarites), but Samuel. Although the name Zadok bears allusions to the כֹּהֵן נֶאֱמָן ('a faithful priest'), Zadok's role is quite limited in the Deuteronomistic History. Together with Abiathar, he serves as priest under David's rule (cf. 2 Sam. 8.17; 20.25; 1 Kgs 2.4; 1 Chron. 18.16). He supports David during his fight with Absalom (2 Sam. 15.24-37; 17.15-16) and he supports Solomon during his fight with Adonijah (1 Kgs 1.8, 26). He anoints Solomon for kingship (1 Kgs 1.38-40). 1 Chronicles 29.22 relates that Zadok was anointed for the priesthood at this event. Thus Zadok's faithfulness is basically restricted to remaining faithful to the Davidic house during David and Solomon's struggles for the kingship, and is contrasted to Abiathar's unfaithfulness, whom he replaces (1 Kgs 2.35). Except from the 'basically fictive and schematic' genealogies in the books of Chronicles, Ezra and Nehemiah,[57] he is mentioned in 2 Chron. 31.10 (Hezekiah's temple reform) in his

---

48. Cf. 1 Sam. 10.8; 15.1-3.

49. 1 Sam. 15.26 adds יְהוָה מִהְיוֹת מֶלֶךְ עַל־יִשְׂרָאֵל.

50. 1 Sam. 15.26 reads כִּי.

51. 1 Sam. 15.9 ('Saul and the people') vs. 15.21 ('the people').

52. LXX: ἱερέα πιστόν.

53. Some Targum Syriac, and Vulgate MSS read אֲשֶׁר כָּל...וּכְנ'.

54. LXX: οἶκον πιστόν.

55. 2-3 Hebrew MSS and LXX^Ms read לִי; the Dead Sea Scrolls text is corrupt here.

56. LXX: Χριστοῦ μου.

57. Blenkinsopp, *Sage, Priest, Prophet: Religious and Intellectual Leadership in Ancient Israel* (Louisville, KY: Westminster/John Knox Press, 1995), p. 84; Nodet, *Origins of Judaism*, p. 163; Hjelm, *Samaritans and Early Judaism*, pp. 158-59.

capacity as member of the house of Zadok, from which came the high priest. Ezekiel is exceptional for his praise of the faithfulness of the sons of Zadok, who did not go astray (אשר לא תעו) at a time when Israel and the Levites went astray (בתעות בני ישראל כאשר תעו הלוים, Ezek. 48.11).[58] Literarily, Ezekiel's subordination of the Levites under the authority of the Zadokites parallels the doom pronounced over the house of Eli in 1 Sam. 2.36, followed by the establishment of a new priestly house, the Davidic kingship[59] and the building of another temple.[60] As no narratives support Ezekiel's accusation, one can speculate on numerous scenarios from a narrative eleventh century Israelite–Judaean controversy based on narratives such as an eighth–second century BCE priestly collaboration with various foreign occupation powers;[61] an internal conflict in Jerusalem's temple in the fourth–second century BCE, as related, for example, in Josephus, the books of Maccabees and alluded to in Sirach.[62] 'Evaporating' historically and literarily, the unknown 'sons of Zadok' left their imprints on significant writings among the Dead Sea Scrolls, in which they claim to be the true Israel.[63] These, however, are not necessarily identical with any biblical priestly house of Zadok.[64] The absence of the Zadokite priesthood outside the David–Solomon narratives is a tradition-historical problem rather than a historical one.[65]

---

58.   Cf. Ezek. 14.11; 44.10-15. Blenkinsopp, *Sage, Priest, Prophet*, p. 89, speaks of 'Zadokite additions to Ezekiel 40–48'; cf. W. Zimmerli, *Ezekiel 2* (Philadelphia: Fortress Press, 1983), pp. 456-59.

59.   Cf. Sir. 45.23-25.

60.   McCarter, *I Samuel*, p. 93: 'The Books of Samuel and Kings display a relentless march of history toward not only David, the chosen king, but also Jerusalem, the chosen city and, along with the latter, Zadok of Jerusalem, the chosen priest'.

61.   Blenkinsopp, *Sage, Priest, Prophet*, pp. 77-89. Most scholars take the utterance as related to the Josianic reform, at which time 'the non-Zadokites from outside Jerusalem were reduced in status to minor cultic functionaries'; cf. McCarter, *I Samuel*, pp. 92-93. Accusations against leading the people astray (hiphil of תעה) appear in 2 Kgs 21.9's condemnation of Manasseh and Jer. 23.13's judgment of Samaria's prophets.

62.   Hjelm, *Samaritans and Early Judaism*, pp. 163-70.

63.   B.Z. Wacholder, 'Historiography of Qumran: The Sons of Zadok and their Enemies', in F.H. Cryer and T.L Thompson (eds.), *Qumran between the Old and New Testaments* (CIS, 6; JSOTSup, 290; Sheffield: Sheffield Academic Press, 1998), pp. 347-77.

64.   D. Dimant, 'Qumran Sectarian Literature', in M.E. Stone (ed.), *Jewish Writings of the Second Temple Period: Apocrypha, Pseudepigrapha, Qumran Sectarian Writings, Philo, Josephus* (CRINT, 2, II; Van Gorcum: Fortress Press, 1984), pp. 483-550 (545-46). For the opposite opinion that the Sadducees of Jerusalem's temple and the Dead Sea Scrolls are related to the biblical house of Zadok, see Schiffman, *Reclaiming the Dead Sea Scrolls*, pp. 71-76, 113-17.

65.   Blenkinsopp, *Sage, Priest, Prophet*, p. 84: 'While there is nothing inherently improbable about a Zadokite dynasty of priests in control of the temple under the monarchy, it is poorly supported and may be another example of the tendency to construct the past in the light of contemporary realities'. See also Nodet, *Origins of Judaism*, pp. 269-71; Davies, *Scribes and Schools*, p. 56: 'a canonised priesthood represented by a tribe (Levi) or, more strictly, descendants of Aaron, or even more strictly descendants of Zadok... To an appreciable extent, Jewish literary canons can readily be associated with the canonization of such institutions, linking the canonical books with real or ideal political institutions.'

Because Samuel is the immediate substitute for the Elides and 1 Sam. 2.35 is unclear about which faithful priest is intended to officiate before the king,[66] we must consider whether the rhetorical ambiguity is deliberately aimed at conveying more than one message. The easiest solution to the problem is of course to see 1 Sam. 2.35-36 as a late addition,[67] but that does not account for any compositional problems created thereby. It neither accounts for the incorporation of several official roles in the figure of Samuel, nor for possible implied questions about hierarchic structures between priest and prophet.

In the role of a 'new' Moses, the acts and roles of Samuel parallel those of Moses. Analogously built up,

> the figure of Samuel is strengthened and elucidated from the force of the positive contrast between him and the great leaders of the past and of the contrast between him and the house of Eli. The story of the capture of the Ark, the plagues in Philistea and the Ark's departure and return to Israelite territory, recall to us the tradition of the Exodus, the plagues in Egypt and the return of Israel to the Promised Land.[68]

Intertwined in contrasting portraits,[69] the young Samuel appears as the ideal 'priest' ('clad in a linen ephod') against the corruption of the Elides. While 'the lad Samuel ministered before Yahweh' (והנער היה משרת את־יהוה, 1 Sam. 2.11, 18 and 3.1), and was in favour of both God and men (וגדל וטוב גם עם־יהוה וגם עם־אנשים, 2.26), Eli's sons' estrangement from Yahweh (ובני עלי בני בליעל לא ידעו את־יהוה, 2.12) brought 'the lads' in conflict with both God and men (2.15-17, 25).[70] While Samuel did *not yet know* Yahweh since the word of Yahweh had *not yet been revealed* to him (ושמואל טרם ידע את־יהוה וטרם יגלה אליו דבר־יהוה, 1 Sam. 3.7), Eli's knowledge about his sons' iniquity, his failure to restrain them and his pronounced rejection (3.12-14) is the revelation which establishes Samuel as 'prophet'.[71] Because none of Yahweh's words fell to the ground (ולא־הפיל מכל־דבריו ארצה),[72] 'all Israel, from Dan to Beersheba, *knew* that Samuel had been established (literally: trusted with [נאמן]) as a prophet (לנביא) for Yahweh' (3.19-20).[73] Although the Elides are rejected, Shiloh regains prominence as the place from where Samuel's words came out to all Israel (4.1), because 'Yahweh, *continued* (ויסף) to appear in

66. McCarter, *I Samuel*, p. 92: 'Samuel emerges incontestably as the successor to the prerogatives of the house of Eli. But the author of the present passage, which interrupts the story of Samuel, had something else in mind.'

67. O'Brien, *Deuteronomic History Hypothesis*, pp. 88, 107; R.W. Klein, *I Samuel* (WBC, 10: Waco: Word Books, 1983), p. 28; Stoebe, *Das Erste Buch Samuelis*, p. 120.

68. Garsiel, *First Book of Samuel*, p. 34.

69. Garsiel, *First Book of Samuel*, pp. 37-44.

70. Garsiel, *First Book of Samuel*.

71. Josephus, *Ant.* 5.348: 'Now when Samuel was twelve years old, he began to prophesy'.

72. Cf. 'not one of the good words has fallen to the ground' in Josh. 21.45; 23.14. 1 Kgs 8.56 adds 'which were spoken by his servant Moses'.

73. In Sir. 46.13-29 (15) Samuel's faithfulness proves his trustworthiness as a prophet: ἐν πίστει αὐτοῦ ἐκριβάσθη προφήτης καὶ ἐγνώσθη ἐν ῥήμασιν αὐτοῦ πιστὸς ὁράσεως.

Shiloh, for Yahweh revealed (נגלה) himself to Samuel *in Shiloh through his word*[74] (3.21).[75] The return of Yahweh's word is set in contrast to the complaint: 'In those days, Yahweh's word was rare (יקר) and there was no frequent (נפרץ) vision' (1 Sam. 3.1).

The phrase 'through his word' is ambiguous. One must ask whether Israel did not have a divine word already, that is, whether they did not have the word from Yahweh given through Moses? Or does the addition mean that in Samuel an interpreter of that word has been established. In other words, does the author replace Moses with Samuel as a competitor, a successor or neither? Is there a mosaic tradition with which to compete or succeed, and what 'word of Yahweh' is at work in the narratives?

As Yahweh's word was rare (1 Sam. 3.1), so is Moses appearance throughout Judges–2 Kings.[76] The references to the 'Torah'[77]—or more specifically 'Yahweh's Torah'[78] and 'Moses' Torah'[79]—in Judges–2 Kings are notable enough to raise suspicion about its status as authoritative judicial code. Although Samuel functions as a judge (1 Sam. 7.15-16), judging the people twice (1 Sam. 7.6 and 12.6-25) and calling to obedience, the words of Yahweh are exactly that, words to be listened to (ושמעתם בקלו ולא תמרו את־פי יהוה, cf. 12.14-15), mediated by the prophet (12.23).[80] It is not the law-giver, but the leader Moses, whom Samuel refers to in his testimony (12.6-8)—the only occurrence of that name in the books of Samuel. Integrating several traits of his predecessors, Samuel is described as a prophet (1 Sam. 3.7, 20-21),[81] a judge (7.6, 15-17), a ritual celebrant (7.9; 9.12-13; 10.8; 13.8-14), a religious leader (7.3-7; 12.23) and a national and military leader (ch. 7 and 11.7; 12.11).[82] The complete silence about the Mosaic Law code in the Samuel–Saul–David narratives, and its introduction into the Solomon narrative as the foundation for Solomon's success (1 Kgs 2.3) is indeed very strange.[83] Coming from the mouth of David as paternal royal advice—'And you must keep the charge

74. The words between asterisks are missing in LXX and *Vetus Latina* 115; some manuscripts read כדבר.
75. In some manuscripts of the LXX the anti-Elide polemic is underscored by a summaric addition: 'And Samuel was trusted as a prophet to the Lord by all Israel from one end of the country to the other; and Eli was very old and his sons went astray and perverted their way before God' (LXX 1 Kgdms 3.21); cf. Garsiel, *First Book of Samuel*, p. 145 n. 22.
76. Judg. 1.16, 20; 3.4; 4.11; 1 Sam. 12.6, 8; 1 Kgs 2.3; 8.9, 53, 56; 2 Kgs 14.6; 18.4, 6; 21.8; 23.25.
77. 2 Kgs 17.13, 34, 37; 22.8, 11; 23.24.
78. 2 Kgs 10.31.
79. 1 Kgs 2.3; 2 Kgs 14.6; 21.8; 23.25.
80. Sir. 46.14: 'he judged the congregation according to the law of the Lord (ἐν νόμῳ κυρίου ἔκρινεν συναγωγήν)'.
81. 1 Sam. 9.9, 11, 19; 1 Chron. 9.22; 26.28; 29.29 calls him הראה; the title is not found in the Pentateuch. Neither is the variant החזה (חזה and חזיון) frequently found in the Prophets as a designation of their 'office'.
82. Garsiel, *First Book of Samuel*, p. 45.
83. If the 'absence of the key notion of '*Moses' tôrâ*' [in Jeremiah] seems to indicate that the redaction of the book of Jeremiah is not essentially deuteronomistic' (Tengström, 'Moses and the Prophets', p. 260), this would apply even more to 1–2 Samuel.

of Yahweh your God, walking in his ways (ושמרת את־משמרת יהוה אלהיך ללכת בדרכיו) and keeping his statutes, his commandments, his ordinances and his testimonies (לשמר חקתיו מצותיו ומשפטיו ועדותיו) as written in the Law of Moses (ככתוב בתורת משה)'—the Law is as complete as ever before—namely, when Moses instructed his people to 'love Yahweh, walking in his ways (לאהבה את־יהוה אלהיך ללכת בדרכיו), keeping his commandments, his statutes and his ordinances' (ולשמר מצותיו וחקתיו ומשפטיו, Deut. 30.16).[84] With Deut. 31.24-26, we know that these are the laws Moses wrote in the Law Book (בספר התורה),[85] which only hereafter is called 'Law of Moses' (תורת משה, Josh. 8.31-32; 23.6).[86]

The 'transference' of the Mosaic Law from David to Solomon carries with it another 'transference'—namely, that of the behaviour of David. Consequently, Solomon's first act as a king and Yahweh's address to him, does not mention Moses' statutes, but David's, which Solomon walks in (ויאהב שלמה את־יהוה ללכת בחקות דוד אביו, 1 Kgs 3.3) and whose example he is instructed to follow (ואם תלך בדרכי לשמר חקי ומצותי כאשר הלך דוד אביך, 3.14). As we saw in Chapter 2, this is the standard for the judgment of the Judaean kings. While David 'transfers' the 'Law of Moses' to his son, his own testimony does not mention Moses, but states that 'I have kept the ways of Yahweh (שמרתי דרכי יהוה) and not wickedly departed from my God (לא רשעתי מאלהי);[87] I have had all his ordinances before me (משפטיו לנגדי) and not turned aside from his statutes' (חקתיו לא־אסיר, 2 Sam. 22.22-23).[88] The form in which David had Yahweh's ordinances and statutes is not specified. No law books are mentioned, apart from the book in which Samuel wrote the 'non-Deuteronomic statute'[89] about the kingship (משפט המלכה, 1 Sam. 10.25).[90] From

---

84. Cf. also Deut. 4.2, 40; 5.29; 10.12; 11.1, 22; 19.9. The language of 1 Kgs 2.3-4 is considered to be entirely Deuteronomic; cf. Jones, *I and II Kings*, I, p. 107; M.J. Mulder, *1 Kings 1–11* (Leuven: Peeters, 1998), p. 89; Weinfeld, *Deuteronomy and the Deuteronomic School*, p. 11: 'The deuteronomic editor, however, interrupted the testament in the middle and inserted a didactic speech (vv. 3-4), which completely altered the original import of the speech'.

85. Cf. also Deut. 28.58, 61; 29.20; 30.10.

86. Apart from its few occurrences in the Deuteronomistic History, the term appears in Mal. 3.22; Dan. 9.11, 13; Ezra 3.2; 7.6; Neh. 8.1; 2 Chron. 23.18; 30.16; 2 Chron. 8.13 reads מצות משה; Neh. 13.1; 2 Chron. 25.4 (= 2 Kgs 14.6, תורת משה); 35.12 reads ספר משה.

87. 'Godlessly' is a better translation; cf. LXX 2 Kgdms 22.22 and Ps. 17.22: ἠσέβησα; cf. also Ps. 1.1. The expression is not Deuteronomistic. Similar to צדק, the root רשע is a favourite term in Psalms, Wisdom Literature and the Prophets. In the Pentateuch, its use is legalistic to mean 'guilty' (Exod. 22.8; Deut. 25.1 [1 Kgs 8.32]); see H. Ringgren, 'רשע', in *ThWAT*, VII, pp. 675-83.

88. 2 Sam. 21–24 is usually taken to be a post-Deuteronomistic transitional addition similar to Josh. 24.1–Judg. 2.5 and Judg. 17–21; cf. Veijola, *Ewige Dynastie*, pp. 126-27, 141; Römer and de Pury, 'Deuteronomistic Historiography', pp. 43, 122, 139; P. Kyle McCarter, *II Samuel: A New Translation with Introduction, Notes and Commentary* (AB, 9; New York: Doubleday, 1984), pp. 18-19. This view is rejected by R. Alter, *The David Story: A Translation with Commentary of 1 and 2 Samuel* (New York: W.W. Norton, 1999), p. 339.

89. Weinfeld, *Deuteronomy and the Deuteronomic School*, p. 169.

90. W. Dietrich, 'History and Law: Deuteronomistic Historiography and Deuteronomic Law Exemplified in the Passage from the Period of the Judges to the Monarchical Period', in de Pury, Römer and Macchi (eds.), *Israel Constructs its History*, pp. 315-42 (325), refers to 'a pre-Deuteronomistic satirical tract'. Although this is not part of the ongoing discussion, a word must be said

this act, we are implicitly informed that the 'ordinances and statutes' David followed must have been in written form. However, no information about who wrote them is provided. In 2 Sam. 8.15, we are told that David 'established justice and righteousness for all his people' (ויהי דוד עשה משפט וצדקה לכל־עמו). Although the language is reminiscent of ancient Near Eastern royal ideology known from at least the third millennium BCE,[91] David's act must be seen also in the light of Gen. 18.19's children of Abraham who shall 'keep the way of Yahweh by doing what is right and just' (שמרו דרך יהוה לעשת צדקה ומשפט),[92] Lev. 19.15's Israelite who shall judge his kinsman justly (בצדק תשפט עמיתך) and Deut. 1.16 and 16.18's judges who shall 'judge with righteousness' (ושפטתם צדק). The phrase עשה משפט וצדקה ('established justice and righteousness') might be Deuteronomistic,[93] however, not Deuteronomic and only indirectly applied to Moses: צדקת יהוה עשה ומשפטיו עם־ישראל (Deut. 33.21). It occurs frequently in the Prophets, Psalms and Wisdom Literature[94] as a characterization of 'the ideal (Davidic) king',[95] a sign of divine order,[96] and a sign of Yahweh's sovereignty.[97] Quite astonishingly, apart from two exceptions (Deborah's song in Judg. 5.11 and Jehu's speech in 2 Kgs 10.9), the distribution of צדק (excluding names) in Samuel–Kings is restricted to the David–Solomon narratives. Its first appearance is found in Saul's words to David—צדיק אתה ממני כי אתה גמלתני הטובה ואני גמלתיך הרעה, 'You are more righteous than I, for you have been gracious to me when I treated you with evil' (1 Sam. 24.18)—at his transference of the kingship to David (24.21). The background is David's surprise sparing of his enemy Saul's life, which made him worthy

---

against Dietrich's handling of the Samuel narrative's explicit discussion about kingship as belonging to a variant redaction. The discussions are exactly that, literature and discourse, but certainly not redaction, reflecting the works of a pre-exilic pro-royalist, a post-exilic anti-royalist with some less anti-royalist in between (cf. pp. 331-32). The prophet's fight for his own status (1 Sam. 8.5-6), taken to a higher level as a fight for or against Yahweh (1 Sam. 8.7-8; 12.12) does not reflect editorial activity, rather than theological argumentation for keeping the prophet blameless (and in office), although kingship is an unavoidable fact. As the discussion opens with a rejection of the prophet (and Yahweh), it ends in a reassurance of both. In this discourse different voices are presented, as they are in all discussions. The 'satirical tract' in 1 Sam. 8 does not belong to a 'movement opposed to the monarchy' (Dietrich, 'History and Law', p. 325), it belongs to a literary trope paralleled in, for example, Josh. 24's warning against choosing Yahweh as god.

91.   Weinfeld, *Deuteronomy and the Deuteronomic School*, pp. 150-56; H. Niehr, 'The Constitutive Principles for Establishing Justice and Order in Northwest Semitic Societies with Special Reference to Ancient Israel and Judah', *Zeitschrift für Altorientalische und biblische Rechtsgeschichte* 3 (1977), pp. 112-30.

92.   Van Seters, *Abraham*, pp. 273-74.

93.   Niehr, 'Constitutive Principles', p. 121.

94.   There are around 520 occurrences of the various forms of the root צדק in the Hebrew Bible (excluding names). Most of the occurrences are found in the Prophets, Psalms and Wisdom Literature. In the Pentateuch (especially Genesis and Deuteronomy) there are around 40 occurrences; in Joshua–2 Kings around 20 occurrences; in Chronicles 6 occurrences; in Ezra 1 occurrence; in Nehemiah 3 occurrences.

95.   E.g. Isa. 9.6; 16.5; Jer. 22.3, 15 (Josiah); 23.5; 32.2; 33.15; Ezek. 45.9.

96.   E.g. Jer. 9.23.

97.   Ps. 99.4; Isa. 60.17-21.

of obtaining the kingship over Israel. Its last appearance is found in the queen of Sheba's word to Solomon: וישימך למלך לעשות משפט וצדקה ('And he established you as king to administer justice and righteousness', 1 Kgs 10.9). A variant form, שים לו חק ומשפט ('made for them statute and ordinance'), is ascribed to Yahweh or Moses (Exod. 15.25),[98] Joshua (Josh. 24.25) and David (1 Sam. 30.25).

According to Weinfeld, the institution of justice and righteousness signifies a change in social circumstances as a result of the sovereign's seizing of power.[99] Whether one reads this historically or thematically, the introduction of Zadok son of Ahitub, together with Ahimelech son of Abiathar (2 Sam. 8.17), at exactly this point in the narrative, underscores David's role as innovator. As ties are kept with the past, he also appears as unifier of different priestly houses in his newly established capital. Although the unification theme is not made explicit in the books of Samuel (this was the interest of the Chronicler—e.g. 1 Chron. 24), it is nevertheless the basic interest of the author's presentation of David as king for all Israel. Solomon's rejection of Abiathar at the beginning of his reign[100] underscores the portrayal of David in the books of Samuel as absolute sovereign in whose kingdom ultimate peace has been established.

In contrast to the almost total silence about written laws in the books of Samuel, we are frequently informed that the Mosaic Law is a written document.[101] Without any mention of a consultation of this Law,[102] both Samuel and David are informed about the will of Yahweh by 'hearing' Yahweh's voice or word,[103] as was Moses. Being part of narratives and transmitted in writings, these words are as legal,[104] as are his words to Abraham[105] and Moses in the Law, which stipulates the conditions of these promises. Compositionally, both Abraham and David receive unconditioned promises,[106] which only become conditioned after the institution of the Law. Whether this relates to a redaction carried out by the Deuteronomists,[107] based

---

98. The text allows for both interpretations, but intertextually it refers to Moses' handling of the threatening division of the people in the conflict with the Transjordanian tribes (Num. 32). Solidarity and unification are the themes of all three narratives (Num. 32; Josh. 24; 1 Sam. 30).

99. Weinfeld, *Deuteronomy and the Deuteronomic School*, pp. 152-53 + addenda cc (p. 385): 'The verse [2 Sam. 8.15] should be translated: "And David was enthroned over all Israel and David became the establisher of justice for all his people". ויהי with the participle expresses at once origination and continuance.'

100. 1 Kgs 2.26-27. Chronicles has no parallel to that, as it has no parallel to the Shiloh and Samuel narratives.

101. Usual phrases are בספר or בכתוב ב...; see, e.g., Deut. 17.18; 27.3, 8; 28.61; 29.20; 30.10; 31.26; Josh. 1.8; 8.34; 23.6; 24.26; 1 Kgs 2.3; 2 Kgs 14.6; 22.8, 11; Hos. 8.12; Dan. 9.11, 13; Neh. 8.1, 3, 8, 14; 9.3; 10.35; 1 Chron. 16.40; 2 Chron. 17.9; 23.18; 25.4; 30.16; 31.3; 34.14, 15; 35.26.

102. As in, e.g., 2 Kgs 14.6; 23.3, 24.

103. Samuel: 1 Sam. 3.10, 21; 7.9; 8.7, 22; 9.15-17; 16.1-13; David: 1 Sam. 23.1-13; 2 Sam. 2.1; 5.19; 7.18-29; 24.1.

104. Yahweh's promise to David; e.g. 2 Sam. 7.16; 1 Kgs 2.4; 8.25; 11.12-13, 36; 15.4; 2 Kgs 8.19; 20.6; 23.27; Isa. 9.6; 37.35; 55.3.

105. Yahweh's promise to Abraham (Isaac and Jacob); e.g. Gen. 17.7-8; 26.3-5; 50.24; Exod. 6.2-4, 8; 33.1; Lev. 26.42; Deut. 1.8; 2 Kgs 13.23; Isa. 41.8-9; 51.2; Ps. 105.8-11, 42.

106. Weinfeld, *Deuteronomy and Deuteronomic School*, p. 75.

107. Weinfeld, *Deuteronomy and Deuteronomic School*, p. 79.

on the occurrence of or adherence to the Mosaic Law, rather than literary technique and purpose, is a moot point. David's 'transference' of the Mosaic Law to Solomon and the implementation of the Law in the judgment of the 'history' of the monarchies repeat the pattern found in Deuteronomy–Judges: Moses' 'transference' of the Law to Joshua and the apostasy and tribal divisiveness following the conquest of the land.[108]

Regarding literary purpose, the implied theological problem might be related to questions about intentional and inadvertent sin.[109] As this problem was a matter of discussion in Jewish writings known from the second century BCE—*Jubilees, Damascus Covenant, Rule of the Community*, and so on—and alluded to in Deut. 29.28 and 30.2, it might also have been pertinent to the author of the David narrative. If the Law is given and accepted (as in Exod. 24.3 and Josh. 24.25), it is binding and any sin against the Law can be classified as intentional, done in stubbornness and disobedience.[110] In canonical narrative chronology, David should be considered to be under the obligations of the Law. The *Damascus Covenant* clearly demonstrates this, when David is excused from not obliging the Law, because the Law was hidden in the ark and hence unknown to him (CD 5.2-3). Sin against such hidden laws is of an inadvertent nature and leads not to death but result merely to a fine.[111] In the books of Samuel, David might be presented in canonical chronology, but regarding the Law he is rather portrayed in the image of the pre-Mosaic fathers to whom the Law has not yet been completely revealed.

While Samuel is informed directly by Yahweh, David both speaks with Yahweh, as well as listens to instructions mediated by the prophets Nathan (2 Sam. 7 and 12) and Gad (2 Sam. 24). Samuel, in fact, never speaks to David, whom he meets only twice: at his anointing (1 Sam. 16.12-13) and in his flight from Saul (19.18-24).[112] Thus Samuel's role in the David narratives is restricted to his replacement of Saul with David.[113] Minor as this role may seem, it nevertheless provides a witness to

---

108. A.G. Auld, 'The Deuteronomists and the Former Prophets', in Shearing and McKenzie (eds.), *Those Elusive Deuteronomists*, pp. 116-26 (125), who, however, claims that 'the earlier story was built by redeveloping the classic [*sic*] story of Jerusalem's kings'.

109. G.A. Anderson, 'Intentional and Unintentional Sin in the Dead Sea Scrolls', in D.P. Wright, D.N. Freedman and A. Hurvitz (eds.), *Pomegranates and Golden Bells: Studies in Biblical, Jewish, and Near Eastern Ritual, Law, and Literature in Honor of Jacob Milgrom* (Winona Lake, IN: Eisenbrauns, 1995), pp. 49-64.

110. G.A. Anderson, 'Intentional and Unintentional Sin', p. 58.

111. G.A. Anderson, 'Intentional and Unintentional Sin', pp. 59-62.

112. These narratives are not in Chronicles. Here in Chronicles Samuel's mediating role in the election of David takes the form of law rather than narrative (כדבר יהוה ביד־שמואל, 1 Chron. 11.3; cf. 2 Sam. 5.3). Similarly, Samuel and David's organization of the temple administration (1 Chron. 9.22; 26.28) and Josiah's Passover celebration (2 Chron. 35.18). References are made to Samuel's writings about David (1 Chron. 29.29) and he occurs in genealogies (1 Chron. 6.13, 18).

113. Murray, *Divine Prerogative and Royal Pretension*, p. 25: 'Samuel holds the centre stage in the inauguration of Saul as king of Israel, and continues to figure prominently in the account of Saul's rejection by Yahweh. But from his first foreshadowing as Yahweh's replacement for the flawed Saul, David quickly comes to dominate the narrative of Saul's ill-starred reign, replacing Samuel as the focal point for religious sympathy in the story.'

divine sanction of the Davidic kingship. In Nathan's affirmation of that kingship,[114] another promise is cast in the future for Gad to confirm—namely, that of Yahweh's temple in Jebusite Jerusalem.[115] It is therefore no surprise that the Chronicler refers to the writings of exactly these three prophets in his closure of the David narratives (על־דברי שמואל הראה ועל־דברי נתן הנביא ועל־דברי גד החזה, 1 Chron. 29.29-30 [29]) and that Hezekiah's inauguration of 'Yahweh's temple' follows instructions given through David, Gad and Nathan (2 Chron. 29.25).

It is apparent that circular legitimation or a double witness system lies behind the role of the prophets in the Deuteronomistic History. The king did not remove the Elide priests; they were removed by Yahweh, as the prophet witnesses. David did not usurp the kingship; it was given to him, as the prophet witnesses. Jerusalem was not chosen as yet another cult place; it was dramatically pointed out by Yahweh, as the prophet witnesses.[116] Jeroboam did not usurp the kingship of Israel; it was given to him by Yahweh, as the prophet witnesses. Jehu did not usurp the kingship of Israel from the house of Omri; it was given to him by Yahweh, as the prophet witnesses from his cave on Mt Horeb ([*sic*] 1 Kgs 19.8).[117] The purported worsening of Yahweh's relationship to David after the Bathsheba episode,[118] his living at the perimeter of events and his impotence regarding the intrigues carried out around him,[119] in fact, protect David from becoming defiled by these all too mundane affairs.[120] Furthermore, it protects him from openly being blamed for having established Jerusalem as *the* cult place (2 Sam. 24), for having deprived his sons of their birthright for the sake of Solomon and for having removed entirely the Elide priesthood. The supremacy of Jerusalem, of Solomon and of the Zadokite priesthood is presented as less planned by its beneficiaries, as was David's own supremacy.

3. Law and Prophecy: Davidic Institutions vs. Mosaic Law

Could the Law have legitimized these actions? At first glance the answer is 'no', as some of these 'institutions' seem to be in conflict with the Law. However, priestly competition and the favouring of the Eleazarites (into which house David's chief priest Zadok becomes integrated) is part of the Law (Num. 25.11-13).

114.   2 Sam. 7.5-17; cf. 1 Chron. 17.4-15.

115.   2 Sam. 24.18; cf. 1 Chron. 21.18; 22.1.

116.   The Chronicler furthermore set David's offering at Arunah in contrast to Gibeon, at which place was 'Yahweh's tabernacle made by Moses in the wilderness and the altar of burnt offering. But David could not go there to inquire of God, because he feared the sword of Yahweh's angel' (1 Chron. 21.29-30).

117.   Apart from Deuteronomy (1.2, 6, 19; 4.10, 15; 5.2; 9.8; 18.16; 28.69) and 1 Kings (8.9; cf. Deut. 5.2), Mt Horeb appears only here in the Deuteronomistic History. The form הר האלהים חרב is reminiscent of Moses' first 'encounter' with Yahweh (Exod. 3.1) and Yahweh's voice from the fire (Deut. 18.15-22 [16]) in the legitimation of the prophet.

118.   R.A. Carlson, *David, the Chosen King: A Traditio-Historical Approach to the Second Book of Samuel* (Stockholm: Almqvist & Wiksell, 1964).

119.   F.A.J. Nielsen, *Tragedy in History*, pp. 138-39.

120.   O'Brien, *Deuteronomistic History Hypothesis*, pp. 139-41, who (following A.F. Campbell, *Of Prophets and Kings*) does not consider 2 Sam. 9–20 to be part of 'his' Prophetic Record.

a. *Kingship vs. Priestly Leadership*

Kingship against priestly leadership is part of the Law, which states that the king's authority rests on the Levitical priests' communication of the Law (Deut. 17.8-20). However, the king should have the copy of the Law for study,[121] not for acting as a worldly king, searching his strength in horses, riches and women.[122] No king lived up to that requirement, except maybe the David of the Psalms. The David of the narratives appears as worldly as any king.[123] His capability of confessing his sin against Yahweh (ויאמר דוד...חטאתי ליהוה, 2 Sam. 12.13; 24.10), however, saves him and even leaves him blessed with what he had not asked for: an heir and a place for Yahweh's house. As such, David's example illustrates well the conversion theology expressed in Ezek. 18.21-32 and 33.10-20's interpretation of what righteous behaviour implies—namely, to turn away from sin and do right and justice.[124] It also implicitly answers Eli's question: 'f man sins against God, who can intercede?' Left blameless, although being deeply implicated in mundane affairs, the portrayal of David in the Court narrative is not so conflicting with Deuteronomistic perspective of David as 'ideal monarch', as Van Seters' argues.[125]

b. *Jerusalem as the Chosen Place*

Jerusalem as a chosen place for Yahweh's dwelling(s) is as possible as any other place (Deut. 12.8-14).[126] The confirmation of that place—in narratives that underscore its inviolability and its protective force (2 Sam. 24 and the Hezekiah narrative)—does not belong to the Law and is therefore open to discussion, as we have seen. The author of 2 Samuel 24 has revealed his dependency on the inviolability theme, when Yahweh sends pestilence against Israel (ויתן יהוה דבר בישראל, 24.15) and the angel stretches out his hand to destroy Jerusalem.[127] Intertextually, the location's saving force is echoed in Solomon's prayer, listing not only the hunger, pestilence and enemies of 24.12-13,[128] but many other 'plagues'.[129] Reminiscent

121. G.A. Cooke, *The Book of Ezekiel* (ICC; repr., Edinburgh: T. & T. Clark, 1970 [1936]), pp. 402-403, speaks of Ezekiel's visionary Davidic king, who 'will have a pastoral charge, to watch over the morals and religion of his people'.

122. Davies, *Scribes and Schools*, pp. 97-98; Dietrich, 'History and Law', p. 341. For the David narrative as polemical against ancient Near Eastern royal ideology, see Murray, *Divine Prerogative and Royal Pretension*, pp. 247-80.

123. This might be the reason Dietrich, 'History and Law', p. 341, does not mention the books of Samuel in his references to David as ideal king. Van Seters, *In Search of History*, pp. 287-91, considered these narratives (2 Sam. 2–4; 9–20; 1 Kgs 1–2) to be post-Dtr fabrications added to counter the 'strong messianic overtones' developing on the basis of the divine promise to David in 2 Sam. 7; on p. 290 Van Seters states: 'There is scarcely anything exemplary in David's actions in the whole of the court story'.

124. Ezek. 18.21; 33.14, 19; cf. Lev. 26.39-42; Deut. 30.2.

125. Van Seters, *In Search of History*, p. 290.

126. B. Halpern, 'The Centralisation Formula in Deuteronomy', *VT* 31 (1981), pp. 20-38; I.R.M. Bóid, *Principles of Samaritan Halachah* (Leiden: E.J. Brill, 1989), p. 340; Hjelm, 'Cult Centralisation'.

127. לשחת + feminine singular suffix in 2 Sam. 24.16; cf. 2 Kgs 18.25; 19.12.

128. Cf. 1 Kgs 8.37; 2 Chron. 6.28; 20.9 (Jehoshaphat's prayer).

129. The triad 'sword, famine and pestilence' (חרב, רעב, דבר) is a favourite gloss in

of Yahweh's angel stretching out his hand (וישלח ידו המלאך) against Jerusalem (2 Sam. 24.16), each man, all of Israel, shall spread out his hands towards this house (ופרש כפיו אל־הבית הזה, 1 Kgs 8.38) in prayer for forgiveness and retribution, every man according to his behaviour (בדרכו, 1 Kgs 8.39). Although the closest parallel to 1 Kgs 8.37-39 is Moses' spreading out his hands towards Yahweh in the plague narrative (Exod. 9.29, 33), we shall not overlook the fact that this is the only place in Solomon's prayer where the phrase is used in connection with 'this house'. The single other use of the phrase is Solomon's spreading out his hands towards the heaven before he begins his prayer (1 Kgs 8.22; cf. 8.54).[130] In the Hezekiah narrative, it is not his hands, but the letter Hezekiah has received from the messengers (מיד המלאכים) that he spreads out before Yahweh (2 Kgs 19.14 par. Isa. 37.14).

The salvation of the city and the marking of Arunah's threshing floor are combined with the 'sparing' of the Davidic House (2 Sam. 24.17). That sparing echoes the sparing of Moses in other rebellion narratives, where Yahweh threatens to destroy the entire population (Exod. 32.10; Num. 14.12: בדבר), while promising to make Moses into a great people (ועאה הניחה לי ויחר אפי בהם ואכלם ואעשה אותך לגוי גדול, 'Now, leave me alone, let my anger burn against them that I may devour them; but of you I'll make a great nation', Exod. 32.10).[131] A similar opposition is found in the Abraham narratives, when the destruction (hiphil of שחת, Gen. 18.28, 31) of Sodom and Gomorrah is contrasted against Yahweh's promise to Abraham to make him a great people (לגוי גדול ועצום, Gen. 18.18). As this narrative follows immediately after the promise of an heir to Abraham's house, in spite of Sarah's barrenness (18.9-15), her unexpected fertility forms the strongest contrast to the future infertility of Sodom and Gomorrah. While David willingly takes responsibility for his own sin—'I alone have sinned and I have done wickedly (אנוכי חטאתי ואנוכי העויתי[132]), but these sheep, what have they done?' (2 Sam. 24.17)[133]—Moses' redemptive intercession is on behalf of the people's sin (Exod. 32.32),[134] as is also Abraham's courageous intercession, appealing to Yahweh's justice—'should he

Jeremiah's threats against the inhabitants in Judah and Jerusalem (e.g. Jer. 14.12; 21.7, 9; 24.10; 29.17; 32.36; 34.17; 38.2; 42.17; 44.13; the order might vary, but the dense form is closer to 1 Chron. 21.12 than to 2 Sam. 24.12-13). Jeremiah is notable for presenting the plagues as a result of non-surrender to the Babylonians or of seeking refuge in Egypt; cf., however, 2 Chron. 24.12-13, Zedekiah's rebellion against Jeremiah and Nebuchadnezzar, both of whom represent Yahweh. In other instances, especially Ezekiel, the maledictions are related to transgression of the Law and idolatry as in Lev. 26 and Deut. 28.

130. Cf. 2 Chron. 6.12, 13, 29; Ezra 9.5 (Ezra's prayer).

131. Cf. Joab's words to David: 'May Yahweh your God increase the number of the people a hundredfold, while the eyes of my lord the king can still see it' (2 Sam. 24.3).

132. 1 Chron. 21.17: הרע הרעותי. The LXX reads '[It is] I the shepherd (ὁ ποιμήν), who did evil', alluding to the flock motif in the following, but probably also to the motif of David as shepherd in, for example, 1 Sam. 16.11; 17.15; 2 Sam. 5.2; Jer. 23.4-5; Ezek. 34.23; Ps. 78.72; 1 Chron. 11.2; 17.6-7.

133. Cf. 2 Sam. 7.14; 1 Kgs 8.47 par. 2 Chron. 6.37; so also the confession of Shimei from the house of Joseph and David's sparing his life at the closure of the Absalom conflict (2 Sam. 19.20-24 [21]).

134. Van Seters, *Life of Moses*, pp. 169-75, 466.

who judges the whole earth not do justice?' (השפט כל־הארץ לא יעשה משפט, Gen. 18.25)—on behalf of a righteous (צדיקים) minority (Gen. 18.22-33).

Just as Yahweh is testing Abraham's justice (Gen. 18.19), albeit the narrative is not explicitly presented as a test case, so is Yahweh's anger against Israel (ויסף אף־יהוה לחרות בישראל, 'And again Yahweh's anger flared up against Israel', 2 Sam. 24.1) a similar test case on David's justice. Thus, we need not look into ancient Near Eastern fear or prohibition of census or taxation prescriptions,[135] however useful that might be, to understand the narrative's implications. The census is for a purpose—namely, to measure the relative strengths between the Israelites and the Judahites (2 Sam. 24.1-2, 9), as expressed in Yahweh's seduction of David to put himself in opposition to them (ויסת[136] את־דוד בהם, 24.1). The disturbance it is about to create relates to the hitherto unsettled tribal divisiveness expressed in Israel's support of Saul[137] and Absalom[138] and the lingering faithfulness of David's nephew[139] and chief commander, Joab, towards his king.[140] Thus, the closure of the books of Samuel, in a narrative which could have ended in a civil war between the Israelites and the Judahites, reminiscent also of David's fight with Absalom,[141] is significant for the composition as a whole. It should therefore not be treated as a hardly noticed appendix,[142] which has been a widespread custom, since Wellhausen declared 2 Samuel 21–24 to be different from 2 Samuel 9–20 and more in line with the Yahwist and the book of Judges.[143] That the narrative forms a thematic unit with 2 Samuel 21,[144] using hunger and sword to anticipate the plague and rival themes in ch. 24, does not mean that the section is not integrated with the rest of the David–Solomon narratives as many scholars argue.[145]

---

135. Cf. Exod. 30.12 and Josephus, *Ant.* 7.316, who seems to be giving an interpretation of the narratives, including features, which are not in the biblical material. Some are found in the LXX, Targum and Dead Sea Scrolls. Most commentaries give lengthy comments on the matter, without actually getting any closer to the dynamics of the narrative.

136. Hiphil of סות; cf. 1 Sam. 26.19; 2 Kgs 18.32 par. Isa. 36.18; 2 Chron. 32.11, 15; Jer. 38.19-23 (22); 43.3. In 2 Chron. 18.2, 31, the term appears in a narrative about Ahab and Jehoshaphat's war with the Aramaeans, in which situation Israel's king gets killed, while Judah's Jehoshaphat is spared because of Yahweh's intervention.

137. Cf. the intertextual links to David's question to Saul in 1 Sam. 26.17-20 (18-19): 'what have I done and what evil is in my hand? [Saul's sword!]. Listen to your servant's word my lord king: "If Yahweh has set you up against me [הסיתך בי] may he accept...an offering, but if it is man, then let them be cursed by Yahweh"'.

138. 2 Sam. 15–19.

139. Son of David's sister Zeruiah and brother to Abishai and Asahel; cf. 1 Chron. 2.17.

140. D.G. Schley, 'Joab', in *ABD*, III, pp. 852-54; S.W. Holloway, 'Distaff, Crutch or Chain Gang: The Curse of the House of Joab in 2 Sam. 3.29', *VT* 37 (1987), pp. 370-75.

141. Cf. Hushai's advice to Absalom to gather all the Israelites from Dan to Beersheba, so that they can be as many as the sand at the sea (2 Sam. 17.11), to pursue David, and entirely destroy the city where David might seek refuge (17.13).

142. Stoebe, *Zweite Buch Samuelis*, p. 513.

143. Wellhausen, *Composition des Hexateuchs*, p. 261.

144. Wellhausen, *Composition des Hexateuchs*, pp. 260-63; P. Dhorme, *Les Livres de Samuel* (Paris: J. Gabalda, 1910), p. 446; Veijola, *Ewige Dynastie*, pp. 106-26.

145. McCarter, *II Samuel*, p. 16: 'In the received text, II Samuel ends with a conglomeration

Since David regrets having called for the census (understandable, given the figures of 800,000 soldiers in Israel against 500,000 in Judah), he leaves it for Solomon to carry out the confrontations and remove what might have been left of former oppositions (1 Kgs 1–2). The Chronicler is more clear about David's motives, when he says that David was beguiled to make a census in Israel, and Joab avoids counting Levi and Benjamin, because the king's word is disgusting to him (כי־נתעב דבר־ המלך את־יואב). Even then, the Israelite soldiers number more than twice as many as the Judahites (1,100,000 against 470,000, 2 Chron. 21.1-6).

Following the logic of retribution, David's demand to Hushai to mislead Absalom by pretending to support him (2 Sam. 15.34; 17.6-14) now threatens to rebound on him. While Absalom was in favour of following Ahitophel's advice and sparing the army by catching David and killing him alone (2 Sam. 17.1-4), Hushai persuaded Absalom to intensify the hunt and make an end of David's men also (17.12), and even destroying completely the city where he might seek refuge (17.13). As David succeeded in fleeing from Absalom (17.16-22), he once again seeks to escape the logical consequence of his decision, namely to be in flight from his adversaries for three months, given him as the second choice of three: famine, flight or pestilence (24.13). Trapped by his 'pious' wish to let Yahweh decide (24.14), the 70,000 deaths from Dan to Beersheba on the first day of the pestilence that Yahweh sent (24.15), and the angel of Yahweh extending his hand against Jerusalem (24.16), which, however, Yahweh stops at Arunah's threshing floor, force David to take up responsibility for his own sin (24.17). The implied danger of ending David's reign as it began—namely, in tribal divisiveness and civil war—is averted as David offers himself and his father's house (to which also Joab belongs) in return for Yahweh's sparing of the population (2 Sam. 24.17). The tribal opposition parallels another tribal division, namely that of Levites against the rest of the people in the golden calf episode. In neither tradition is the offer explicitly accepted and, only in the David narrative, is the plague lifted from Israel (ותעצר המגפה מעל ישראל, 2 Sam. 24.25).[146] As David's impotence increases (1 Kgs 1.1-4) and as Joab is given the scapegoat's role of avenging also David's own sin (2.5),[147] the fulfilment of David's offer seems to have come to an end in Solomon's provision of eternal security for David's house by his removal of David's enemies (2.12-46 [24], 33, 45: וכסא דוד יהיה נכון לפני יהוה עד־עולם), 'and the throne of David shall be

of material (20.23–24.25) that is not in sequence with the narrative that precedes or follows it… neither part of the Deuteronomistic History nor related to the earlier literature it embraced'. W. Dietrich and T. Naumann, *Die Samuelbücher* (Darmstadt: Wissenschaftliche Buchgesellschaft, 1995), p. 157: 'Mit dieser Thematik der Thronnachvolge Davids—wenn sie denn die zweite Hälfte des 2. Samuel—und den Anfang des Königsbuches bestimmt—haben die II 21–24 zusammengestellte Textstücke nichts zu tun'. For an opposite opinion, see Veijola, *Ewige Dynastie*, p. 124: 'Die Einzelanalysen innerhalb von 2 Sam. 21–24 brachten in reichem Masse dtr Material zutage, welches das Vertrautsein der dtr Redaktion mit den hier gesammelten Stoffen zeigt und wertfolle Einblicke in die verschiedenen Davidbilder, die im Geschichtswerk einander ablösen, gewährt'.

146. Cf. Aaron and Phinehas' atonement (Num. 17.13-15; 24.9), which made the plague stop (cf. also Ps. 106.30).

147. Schley, 'Joab', p. 853; Holloway, 'Distaff, Crutch or Chain Gang'.

established before Yahweh forever'). Yahweh's mercy ('Yahweh was entreated for the land', וַיֵּעָתֵר יְהוָה לָאָרֶץ)[148] as a reply to David's offering on the altar built on Arunah's threshing floor rather underscores David's favourable relationship with his god.

As the narrative is testing the mind of a supposed righteous leader, it not only interrelates with Genesis' Sodom–Gomorrah narrative, in which Abraham seeks to rescue his nephew Lot. It also relates to Yahweh's testing of Abraham's faithfulness in Genesis 22's narrative about the non-sacrifice of Isaac. If it can be said about the god of 2 Samuel 24 that he is 'decidedly an interventionist god, pulling the human actors by strings' and 'he may well be capricious',[149] this is no less true of Abraham's god. One should, however, read the narratives before making the judgment and asking: Who is under ordeal and what matters is the narrative intended to settle? If we take a shortcut and turn to Josephus' narrative about David's census in *Ant.* 7.318-35 (333), the last question is easily answered:

> As it happened, it was to this very place that Abraham brought his son Isaac, to sacrifice him as a burnt offering, and as he was about to slaughter him, there suddenly appeared beside the altar a ram, which Abraham sacrificed in place of his son, as we have related earlier.

Josephus here refers to *Ant.* 1.226:

> For two days the servants accompanied him, but on the third, when the mountain was in view, he left his companions in the plain and proceeded with his son alone to that mount whereon King David afterwards erected the temple.

Although these are unscriptural notes belonging to interpretation, there is no reason to believe that 2 Samuel 24 and Genesis 22 are unrelated to discussions about the location of the proper cult place.[150] As the angel stretched out his hand (וַיִּשְׁלַח יָדוֹ הַמַּלְאָךְ) to destroy Jerusalem (2 Sam. 24.16), so Abraham stretched out his hand (וַיִּשְׁלַח אַבְרָהָם יָדוֹ) to take the knife for the slaughter of his son Isaac (Gen. 22.10). As Yahweh said to the angel of destruction (וַיֹּאמֶר לַמַּלְאָךְ הַמַּשְׁחִית, 2 Sam. 24.16), so Yahweh's angel cried to him from heaven and said (וַיִּקְרָא אֵלָיו מַלְאַךְ יְהוָה מִן־הַשָּׁמַיִם וַיֹּאמֶר, Gen. 22.11). As David saw the angel of Yahweh (2 Sam. 24.16), so Abraham saw the ram (Gen. 22.13) and praised Yahweh by naming the place 'Yahweh sees' (וַיִּקְרָא אַבְרָהָם שֵׁם־הַמָּקוֹם הַהוּא יְהוָה יִרְאֶה אֲשֶׁר יֵאָמֵר הַיּוֹם בְּהַר יְהוָה יֵרָאֶה, 22.14). 'In both cases there is a play on Moriah and the verb *rā'â* "to see" and its derivative nouns *mar'â* and *mar'ê* meaning "sight, spectacle, vision"'.[151] As David implicitly spared his heir by offering himself and his fathers house, so

---

148. Niphal; cf. 2 Sam. 21.14; Gen. 25.21-22 (Yahweh's blessing of Rebecca with fighting twins); 2 Chron. 33.13 (Yahweh is entreated by Manasseh's prayer and brings him back from Babylon); qal and hiphil forms of the verb are frequent in Exod. 8–10's plague narratives.

149. Alter, *David Story*, p. 353.

150. Cf. also Pseudepigraphic and Targumic interpretations of Gen. 22 in which the mountain is called 'Mt Zion or the Mount of the Holy Temple'; see J.A. Fitzmeyer, 'The Sacrifice of Isaac in Qumran Literature', *Bib* 83 (2002), pp. 211-29.

151. Levenson, *Sinai and Zion*, pp. 94-95. Cf. also *Jub.* 18.13's midrashic addition to the place Abraham called 'The Lord has seen': 'It is Mt Zion'.

Abraham saved his heir, whom he had been willing to offer. As David built there an altar for Yahweh (ויבן שם דוד מזבח ליהוה, 2 Sam. 24.25), so Abraham built there the altar (ויבן שם אברהם את־המזבח, Gen. 22.9). As the Jebusite Arunah offered David the oxen for the holocaust (ויאמר ארונה אל־דוד יקח ויעל אדני המלך הטוב בעיניו ראה הבקר לעלה, 2 Sam. 24.22), which he, however refused to accept, so God gave Abraham the ram for the holocaust which he gratefully accepted (וישא אברהם את־עיניו וירא והנה־איל...ויקח את־האיל ויעלהו לעלה, Gen. 22.13). As David had the possibility of becoming twice as many as he already was (ויוסף יהוה אלהיך אל־[152]העם כהם וכהם מאה פעמים, 2 Sam. 24.3), but ended up diminishing the number of his people, so Abraham began as a threatened minority,[153] but ended up receiving a further confirmation of the already pronounced promise of becoming a great people (ככוכבי השמים וכחול אשר על־שפת הים, 'as numerous as the stars of heaven and the sands on the seashore', Gen. 22.17), who 'shall posses the gate of your enemy' (v. 17b).[154] This first occurrence of the sand on the seashore theme,[155] related to the blessing of the nations, might hint at the diminishing of Abraham's seed in the Deuteronomistic History, in which composition, the enemies of Israel (e.g. Josh. 11.4; Judg. 7.12) and David (2 Sam. 17.11) and their belongings are as numerous as the sand on the seashore. In Solomon's great realm of peace (1 Kgs 4.20–5.5), the promise to Abraham has come to its climax, when 'Judah and Israel are as numerous as the sand at the sea' and 'Solomon reigns over all the kingdoms' (1 Kgs 4.20–5.1).[156]

Closing the books of Samuel with salvation of the people, the Davidic house and Jerusalem, a significant counterclaim is made against the books of Kings' and Chronicles' destruction and removal of king, people, city and temple, none of which is spared at the Babylonian conquest. A similar compositional 'climax' is found in Jeremiah 33's sermon of restored Jerusalem and Davidic dynasty (his offspring numbering as many as the armies of heaven and the sand of the sea; Jer. 33.22). Placed before the Babylonian destruction, it carries with it a hope for the future in spite of the impending disaster.[157] Invoking tradition, Yahweh will show mercy (ורחמתים) 'and reverse all the devastation of the past and revive the destroyed institutions in a new age when the seed of Abraham, Isaac and Jacob will enjoy all the expectations ever entertained for the nation'.[158] Given the ephemeral and local

---

152. 2 Mss: את; cf. Job 42.10.

153. Hjelm, 'Brothers Fighting Brothers', p. 200.

154. For a discussion and rejection of the often asserted secondary status of Gen. 22.15-18, see, for example, Van Seters, *Abraham*, pp. 229-40, and *Prologue*, pp. 261-64, who ascribes the whole narrative to J; G.J. Wenham, *Genesis 16–50* (WBC, 2; Waco, TX: Word Books, 1994), pp. 99-103, sees the narrative in itself and in relation to the preceding narratives about Abraham as a highly integrated piece of literature.

155. Cf. Gen. 32.13; Isa. 10.22.

156. The verses have some text-critical problems: Judah is omitted in some LXX manuscripts and LXX^{MN min} omit both verses. Josephus, *Ant.* 8.38 reads ὅ τε τῶν Εβραιων λαος καὶ ἡ Ἰουδα φυλή.

157. Carroll, *Jeremiah*, pp. 634-35.

158. Carroll, *Jeremiah*, p. 639.

nature of the Davidic kingship, any claim of future glory would have sounded hollow, without such invocation.

c. *'No Prophet Arose Again Like Moses'*

The legitimation of the prophets is as ambiguous (Deut. 13.2-6; 18.15-22; 29.28; 34.10) as is the statement about 'God's word's presence in the mouth and the heart' (30.14). Moses' supreme authority as the prophet, whom 'Yahweh knew face to face' (Deut. 34.10; cf. Exod. 33.11), is not challenged. It is confirmed, since no other prophet is characterized in that way.[159] Numbers 12's paradigmatic distinction between those prophets with whom Yahweh speaks 'in visions and dreams' (Num. 12.6), and Moses, with whom Yahweh speaks 'face to face' (Num. 12.7-8),[160] does not remove the legitimacy of prophecy *per se*, but rather states that prophecy cannot rule out the Mosaic Law.[161] Against this view, stands the opinion of Tengström that 'the idea of a subordination of the prophets to Moses reveals to some extent the communicative intentions of the Deuteronomistic history...the prophets were his living voice'.[162] Thus, the verification of the message given by the prophets is part of the narrative's goal as a witness to 'divine' providence.[163] Neat as it sounds, the fact, however, remains that in this 'subordination', the prophet is given control over the tradition he interprets.

Since both possibilities are inherent in Deuteronomy's statements, they might deliberately be formulated just so. If the law of the prophet in Deuteronomy 18, and the homage to Moses in Deut. 34.10-12 are Deuteronomistic additions—'intended to reconcile the Deuteronomic tradition about Moses with the prophetic tradition in the Deuteronomistic History'[164]—the ambiguity has to be intended.[165] The

159. Tengström, 'Moses and the Prophets', p. 264.

160. Cf. also Gen. 32.31 (Jacob's encounter with God [אלהים]); Judg. 6.22 (Gideon's encounter with Yahweh's messenger [מלאך יהוה]); Ezek. 20.35's answer to Yahweh's covenant with the people in Deut. 5.4.

161. H.M. Barstad, 'The Understanding of the Prophets in Deuteronomy', *SJOT* 8 (1994), pp. 236-51 (241): 'The fact that prophets are not discussed in a positive sense, but only negatively, thus implies a powerful demotion of the authority of prophecy to the status of a sort of second-rate revelation, subordinate to the "Law of Moses". It is Deuteronomy that is the actual expression of the will of YHWH.'

162. Tengström, 'Moses and the Prophets', p. 264; Van Seters, *Life of Moses*, p. 463.

163. Tengström, 'Moses and the Prophets', pp. 264-65: 'Although Moses' teaching represented the highest norm for moral and justice, the prophets revealed the true signification of concrete historical events'.

164. Tengström, 'Moses and the Prophets', p. 261. Van Seters, *Life of Moses*, p. 463: 'While Deuteronomy makes quite explicit its understanding of the role of Moses as the paradigm for prophecy, such that all prophets have the primary task of confirming the Deuteronomic understanding of law and covenant, this is hardly the case for J'. Van Seters continues (p. 466): '[In J] Moses is the prophet of judgement to Israel's enemies, spokesman of the one supreme deity whom even the non-Israelite must acknowledge. Moses is the prophet of salvation to his own people. Above all, Moses is intercessor, the one who suffers with them and for them, as in the case of Jeremiah and the suffering servant of Second Isaiah.'

165. For ambiguity as a governing principle behind the formation of the Torah, see Bóid, *Principles of Samaritan Halachah*, pp. 328-42 (340-42); Davies, *Scribes and Schools*, p. 173.

possibility of interpreting Deut. 18.18's 'prophet as you' as a projection of Joshua[166] —who 'never is called a prophet'[167]—or of those Old Testament prophets who lived up to the requirement of a fulfilment of their words,[168] might be a sign that the group which created the Torah successfully met the opinions of various groups.[169] Here, it is important to keep in mind that all ancient sects, except for Samaritans and Dositheans, accepted the Prophets and the Writings as 'all alike parts of Scripture'.[170] Both these groups shared 'Hasmonaic', 'Qumranic' and New Testament expectations of the coming of a prophet like Moses, while rabbinic tradition asserted that Jeremiah was the prophet spoken of in Deuteronomy.[171] While the Dositheans saw a fulfilment of their expectation in the figure of Dositheus, the Samaritans, who rejected entirely the idea that Moses and the Torah could be superseded, transformed their expectation of a prophet like Moses into an eschatological hope for a return of Moses as saviour (*Taheb*).[172]

If Bóid is right in his conclusion that 'there is a halachic tradition common to all Israel, both Jews and Samaritan', which thereby must be 'older than the division between Samaritans and Jews',[173] then one might assume that there is also a common literary tradition prior to all differences.[174] This, however, seems not to

---

166. Barstad, 'Understanding of the Prophets', p. 247: 'The prophet in question is to have the same function as Moses. But the only one who actually does this is Joshua.'

167. Tengström, 'Moses and the Prophets', p. 262: 'Rather there seems to be a special hint pointing to the prophet Jeremiah [cf. the formulation of Deut. 18.18bα found only in Jer. 1.9]'. Note, however, Sir. 46.1: 'Joshua, who followed Moses in prophet hood' (ἐν πτοφητείαις); Eupol. 30.1-2 has a succession of prophets, from Moses, Joshua to Samuel.

168. Blenkinsopp, *Sage, Priest, Prophet*, p. 122: 'a prophetic succession from Moses…to Jeremiah, last of 'his servants the prophets''; and later, p. 164: 'the reader is encouraged to view prophecy retrospectively, as essentially belonging to the past… The idea seems to be that the promulgation of a written law renders appeal to prophetic inspiration both unnecessary and undesirable.' For a survey of the scholarly opinion that the prophets intended were a succession of Mosaic prophets, see Barstad, 'Understanding of the Prophets, pp. 242-43; C.R. Seitz, 'Mose als Prophet: Redaktionsthemen und Gesamtstruktur des Jeremiasbuches', *BZ* 34 (1990), pp. 234-45.

169. Auld, 'Prophets through the Looking Glass', p. 20: 'The last words of the Torah knows the Prophets substantially as we know them—even the earlier Deuteronomy 13 and 18 would seem to know Jeremiah 1 and 23. Prophets then precede—but have no precedence over—Moses'. See also Mullen, *Ethnic Myths and Pentateuchal Foundations*, p. 324: 'While Moses has provided the model for prophecy in the deuteronomistic literature, the newly formed Pentateuch redirected the channels of authority, establishing Moses as the primary mediator of Yahweh's revelation of his will, but Aaron, the ancestor of the priesthood, as the functionary who would maintain those traditions'.

170. Lowy, *Principles*, p. 86.

171. Kippenberg, *Garizim und Synagoge*, pp. 306-13; P. Billerbeck, *Kommentar zum Neuen Testament aus Talmud und Midrasch* (4 vols.; Munich: Beck, 1922–28), II, pp. 626-27.

172. Kippenberg, *Garizim und Synagoge*, pp. 324-27; F. Dexinger, *Der Taheb: Ein 'messianischer' Heilsbringer der Samaritaner* (Salzburg: Otto Müller, 1986).

173. Bóid, *Principles of Samaritan Halachah*, p. 328.

174. Auld, 'Prophets through the Looking Glass', p. 20: 'Yet the argument between the Sadducee (Jewish or Samaritan) and Pharisee was not whether to add Prophets as a new scripture beside Torah, but whether to retain Prophets once it had been ensured that Moses had said enough'.

have been the case. If the Torah is a compromise between various opinions, it is a product of a later time—and here Nodet's thesis of a third–second-century BCE work springs into mind—not least because at that time we begin to sense the contours of an emergent Mosaic canon.[175]

The true competitor to the Masoretic 'no prophet arose again like Moses' (ולא‎ קם נביא עוד בישראל כמשה‎, Deut. 34.10)[176] might, however, not be any of the biblical prophets[177]—although Hosea speaks about the coming prophets,[178] Amos[179] and Zechariah,[180] about 'the former prophets', Samuel appears as a candidate and Jeremiah attempts to replace both Moses and Samuel[181]—but rather David as ideal king. As such, David's example and the Mosaic Law were the standards with which the author of Kings evaluated the behaviour of the Davidic kings. As no prophet arose like Moses, so no king like Hezekiah (לא־היה כמהו בכל מלכי יהודה‎, 2 Kgs 18.5) and Josiah (וכמהו לא־היה לפניו מלך...ואחריו לא־קם כמהו‎, 23.25) followed in the paths of both David and Moses. As Abraham was judged righteous because he believed Yahweh (והאמן ביהוה ויחשבה לו צדקה‎, Gen. 15.6), so David was judged righteous (יגמלני יהוה כצדקתי/וישב יהוה לי כצדקתי‎) because he, having Yahweh's ordinances before him, remained blameless (ואהיה תמים לו‎, 2 Sam. 22.21-25).[182] That righteousness is a variant of Deut. 6.25's righteousness: (וצדקה תהיה־לנו‎ כי־נשמר לעשות את־כל־המצות הזאת לפני יהוה אלהינו כאשר צונו‎[183] ('And it shall be righteousness for us, when we observe faithfully before Yahweh our God all the instructions he has commanded us') and Ezek. 18.5's definition of a righteous person. The psalmist's characterization of David's righteousness is not conversion theology's return to whole-hearted obedience or the rather innocent inadvertent sin described in interpretations. The characterization rather belongs to a Platonic world of ideals or to Aristotelian philosophy's hierarchic first mover, in which pattern David can be seen as just a little less than God (2 Sam. 7.25-27),[184] and so closely adherent to Yahweh that his will becomes David's will (15.25-26). As such,

---

175. Davies, *Scribes and Schools*, pp. 94, 102-106.

176. SP reads עוד נביא‎ as in the LXX reading καὶ οὐκ ἀνέστη ἔτι προφήτης. The ST renders this expression in the future sense: 'there never will arise (ולא יקום עורי‎)'. In *Memar Marqah*'s paraphrase we read 'there has not risen any like Moses, and there never will arise'; cf. Lowy, *Principles*, pp. 86-94, 381.

177. Davies, *Scribes and Schools*, p. 115: 'It remains possible that a "prophecy" canon originated as a counterweight to the Mosaic canon and that Deuteronomy's presentation of Moses as a prophet like no other and its concern to control prophecy is influenced by the existence of a prophetic canon'. So also Kippenberg, *Garizim und Synagoge*, pp. 312-13.

178. Hos. 12.11; K. Zobel, *Prophetie und Deuteronomium*, p. 213.

179. Amos 2.11; K. Zobel, *Prophetie und Deuteronomium*, pp. 207-208.

180. Zech. 1.4; 7.7, 8.

181. Jer. 15.1-2; LXX^A: καὶ Ααρων. The reference seems to have both 2 Chron. 35 and 2 Kgs 23 in mind (cf. Jer. 15.4). See further Blenkinsopp, *History of Prophecy*, pp. 158-60; Seitz, 'Mose als Prophet'; Van Seters, *Life of Moses*, pp. 171-75.

182. As did the righteous Noah (איש צדיק תמים‎, Gen. 6.9) and as should Abraham (Gen. 17.1) and the Israelites (Deut. 18.13; Josh. 24.14) do.

183. Cf. also Deut. 24.13.

184. Murray, *Divine Prerogative and Royal Pretension*, pp. 208-11, 312.

David's example as a paradigm for the behaviour of succeeding kings parallels Abraham's role as a model of tribal leadership and Moses' role as legislator, conferring divine law unto the people. In canonical chronology, David's role serves to illustrate the king's dependency on the Law and its interpreters, whether it be an implied written Mosaic Law or a message conveyed by prophets. In narrative chronology, however, the author has presented the king David as being separated from past institutions: temple, priesthood and Law. Compositionally, even David's transgressions (2 Sam. 9–24) appear after he has instituted 'law and justice' (8.15). In such composition, David's reign is best characterized as a creation of 'something new'. We must ask whether the author of 1–2 Samuel is, in fact, creating an autochthonous tradition, paralleling the Yahwist's Patriarchs, rather than being part of a Moses–Exodus tradition.[185]

4. *'Look, I Have Created Something New'*

Jeremiah 33.14-26[186] and Ezek. 37.16-28 ultimately bring these traditions together in their visions of a reunited Israel with 'David' as king. Although neither mentions Moses' Torah and mostly use the word *torah* in a negative sense, as the forsaken[187] or the mendacious law,[188] there can be no doubt that the law implied belongs to the Mosaic tradition.[189] As true interpreters of Yahweh's will against priests, scribes, prophets, leaders and people,[190] Jeremiah and Ezekiel's solution to the disaster, which have resulted from the neglect, is not a simple reinstitution of the Law, but a

185. The question has not been explicitly addressed by Römer (*Israel's Väter*) or by K. Schmid (*Erzväter und Exodus*) but their choice of parallels reveal that the books of Samuel seem not to fit the hypothesis of a Moses–Exodus narrative, which Schmid considers contain 'im wesentlichen das Textgut des klassischen "deuteronomistischen Geschichtswerks"' (*Erzväter und Exodus*, p. 163). Schmid, however, has some reservation regarding Judges.

186. These verses are not in the LXX, which is considered to have used an earlier *Vorlage* than the text of MT; cf. E. Tov, *The Septuagint Translation of Jeremiah and Baruch* (HSM, 8; Missoula, MT: Scholars Press, 1976); Carroll, *Jeremiah*, p. 637. In 4QJer^c there is a gap between 32.25 and 42.7, with 33.16-21 appearing in a heavily damaged form. The so-called restoration story, ch. 30–33 (= LXX Jer. 37–40) is generally considered to be a later interpolation; cf. A. Rofé, 'The Arrangement of the Book of Jeremiah', *ZAW* 101 (1989), pp. 390-98; Tov, *Textual Criticism*, p. 321.

187. E.g. Jer. 9.12; 16.11; 32.23; 44.10; Ezek. 22.26.

188. Jer. 8.8; the only occurrence of תורת יהוה in Jeremiah. Jeremiah is not arguing against the Law as R.A. Kugler maintains ('The Deuteronomists and Later Prophets', in Shearing and McKenzie [eds.], *Those Elusive Deuteronomists*, pp. 127-44 [128]), but against the tampering with the Law.

189. R.V. Bergren, *The Prophets and the Law* (Cincinnati: Hebrew Union College Press, 1974), pp. 204-207; H. Cazelles, 'Jeremiah and Deuteronomy', in L.G. Perdue and B.W. Kovacs (eds.), *A Prophet to the Nations: Essays in Jeremiah Studies* (Winona Lake, IN: Eisenbrauns, 1984), pp. 89-111; J.P. Hyatt, 'Jeremiah and Deuteronomy', in Perdue and Kovacs (eds.), *A Prophet to the Nations*, pp. 113-27; Blenkinsopp, *History of Prophecy*, pp. 160-62, 196-200; Zobel, *Prophetie und Deuteronomium*; Seitz, 'Mose als Prophet'; T. Römer, 'Is there a Deuteronomistic Redaction in the Book of Jeremiah?', in Pury, Römer and Macchi (eds.), *Israel Constructs its History*, pp. 399-421.

190. Blenkinsopp, *History of Prophecy*, pp. 166, 198-99; Carroll, *Jeremiah*, pp. 73-78.

new understanding (Jer. 3.15-17;[191] 31.33-34; Ezek. 36.26-27; cf. Isa. 59.20), and ultimately also a new law based on individualism (Jer. 31.29-30; Ezek. 18.1-4; Deut. 24.16), rather than the collective punishment leading to the exile of all Israel.[192] While projected into a utopian future,[193] its realization might not have been viewed as quite as unattainable by its contemporaries as modern scholars see it. The shift is most expressively voiced in Ezra and Nehemiah's lists of returnees and new covenanters, those responsible for the rebuilding of the city and its institutions. While everyone is expelled collectively from the country in Kings, Chronicles and Jeremiah's exile narratives,[194] individuals are held responsible for their own transgressions in Ezra and Nehemiah's purging of Jerusalem.[195] Favouring Babylon against Egypt and being 'markedly *gōlâ*-oriented',[196] Jeremiah might represent a view similar to that found in Ezra 4's rejection of those not having suffered the Babylonian exile. Having interiorized the covenant, that is, the Law,[197] it is not the words of the prophets these returnees transgress, but the Law made available for them. Does this interiorization account for Yahweh giving his law in their midst (נתתי את־תורתי בקרב) and writing it on their heart (ועל־לבם אכתבנה, Jer. 31.33; 32.40)?[198] Does Jeremiah consider teaching as unnecessary because everyone will know Yahweh (כי־כולם ידעו אותי, 31.34) naturally, or because the kingdom he pronounces for Israel is a Yahwistic kingdom in which 'he [I] will be their god and they shall be his [my] people (31.33)'? With Deut. 30.6, 14-16 and 32.46-47, we are taught that 'natural theology' does not rule out the word of the law. Quite the contrary—the law written in the heart (namely, the knowledge of Yahweh as God) is a precondition for following the Law, as Moses teaches his people in his warning of turning away the heart from Yahweh (ואם יפנה לבבך, Deut. 30.16-17 [17]).[199] While Jeremiah envisages that the people have learned their lesson and no longer need or should be reminded of the ark of Yahweh's covenant (ארון ברית־יהוה, Jer. 3.16), Moses' people are yet to challenge the teaching they have been given (Deut. 31.24-29), such as Deut. 30.1-10's 'fictive'[200] summaric paraphrase pronounces. As a guide and protector (Num. 10.33-36) and as a warning signal (Deut. 31.26), the

191. Jer. 3.14-18 are usually considered to stem from the same redaction as the restoration story; so Carroll, *Jeremiah*, p. 149; M.E. Biddle, *A Redaction History of Jeremiah 2.1–4.2* (ATANT, 77; Zürich: Theologischer Verlag, 1990), pp. 97-104; Römer, *Israels Väter*, pp. 470-75.

192. Cazelles, 'Jeremiah and Deuteronomy', p. 97; Fishbane, 'Torah and Tradition', p. 279; Biddle, *Redaction History*, p. 104.

193. Carroll, *Jeremiah*, p. 614.

194. Most expressively voiced in Lam. 5.7: 'Our fathers sinned, they are no more, we must carry their guilt'; cf. Neh. 9.16-37 (36); Exod. 20.5-6; 34.7; Num. 14.18; Deut. 5.9-10; Isa. 14.21: against Babylon; Jer. 32.18.

195. Ezra 10.18-44; Neh. 13.7-28, cf. also Lev. 26.40-41; Jer. 14.20.

196. L. Stulman, 'Insiders and Outsiders in the Book of Jeremiah: Shifts in Symbolic Arrangements', *JSOT* 66 (1995), pp. 65-85 (72).

197. Carroll, *Jeremiah*, p. 611.

198. Cf. Isa. 51.7.

199. Nicholson, *God and His People*, p. 212; Zobel, *Prophetie und Deuteronomium*, p. 63.

200. Zobel, *Prophetie und Deuteronomium*, p. 65.

ark of the Pentateuch signifies the dual function of the Law: as blessing and curse. It also signifies the bond between Yahweh and his people, the covenant given to the fathers at the exodus from Egypt (1 Kgs 8.21; 2 Chron. 5.10; 6.11: to the Israelites). In Jeremiah's preaching, that covenant has become a curse (אָרוּר הָאִישׁ אֲשֶׁר לֹא יִשְׁמַע אֶת־דִּבְרֵי הַבְּרִית הַזֹּאת, Jer. 11.3)[201] from which there is no escape (11.1-14; 32.27-36), such as also Joshua warned his people (Josh. 24.20). Not mentioning the Shechem covenant, but clearly alluding to its conditions, Jeremiah is not allowed to intercede for the people, who, following other gods, have returned to the sin of their fathers (Jer. 11.9-14 [14]; cf. Josh. 24.15). Ambiguous as the Masoretic Joshua covenant is, Shechem connotes positively the place where Yahweh chose Abraham and Jacob, but negatively the place where the people chose Yahweh (עֵדִים אַתֶּם בָּכֶם כִּי־אַתֶּם בְּחַרְתֶּם לָכֶם אֶת־יְהוָה, 'you are witnesses against yourselves that you have chosen Yahweh', Josh. 24.22); a choice, that, however pious it might look, has proven its invalidity. Here it might be useful to remember that the LXX places the act in Shiloh, Jerusalem's alter ego in Jeremiah's accusations against unforgivable apostasy (Jer. 7.12-20), which curse can only be removed by a return to Law obedience, mediated by prophetic initiative (Jer. 26.1-6 [5]). Historicizing Jeremiah's preaching as words belonging to a historical Jeremiah's support of a biblical seventh-century BCE Josianic reform[202] is as misleading as reading the *Rabshaqeh*'s speech to Jerusalem as an authentic voice from an eighth-century BCE's Assyrian siege of Jerusalem. Both voices belong to the literature in which they occur,[203] which, however, does not mean that authors wrote them without function. If it is stated that Jeremiah's promise of a 'new covenant'[204] belongs to editorial activity, it does not go without saying that his rejection of the 'old covenant'[205] is a necessary literary pre-condition for the supersessionism expressed thereby.[206]

Since Moses' people already carry the sign of circumcision, which will not protect them from breaking the covenant and receiving the punishment,[207] its renewal

201. Cf. Deut. 27.15-26; 28.15-19; Josh. 24.20; Jer. 17.5; Ps. 119.25.

202. Cazelles, 'Jeremiah and Deuteronomy', p. 108: 'If one admits that Jeremiah supported the reform, then everything falls into place. He left Anathoth in order to settle in Jerusalem, where, however, the reform of Josiah did not provide him with all the rights stipulated by Deuteronomy'; Hyatt, 'Jeremiah and Deuteronomy', p. 114: 'Jeremiah did not begin his career until about a decade after Josiah's reforms of 621 BCE. He was acquainted with the original edition of Deuteronomy, but never expressed approval either of the principles or the methods of the Deuteronomic reforms. Indeed his outlook was on many important questions diametrically opposed to that of the writers of Deuteronomy. The Book of Jeremiah as we have it, however, has received expansion and redaction at the hands of "Deuteronomic" editors, whose purpose in part was to claim for Deuteronomy the sanction of the great prophet.' So also Blenkinsopp, *History of Prophecy*, pp. 160-69.

203. Blenkinsopp, *History of Prophecy*, p. 160: 'What we see in the book, then is the Deuteronomic portrait of Jeremiah and—to pursue the metaphor—the recovery of the prophet's real likeness would call for a painstaking work of restoration', which, however, does not prevent Blenkinsopp from attempting the enterprise.

204. Jer. 3.16; 31.31-32; 32.40; 50.5.

205. Jer. 11.10; 22.9; 34.18.

206. Römer, 'Deuteronomistic Redaction in Jeremiah', pp. 409-10.

207. Cf. Jer. 9.25-26; Carroll, *Jeremiah*, pp. 250-52.

will be given invisibly as a circumcision of the heart (ומל יהוה אלהיך את־לבבך ואת
לבב זרעך, Deut. 30.6; cf. 10.16). That metaphor (not used in Jer. 30–33, but in
4.4[208] and 9.26), is yet another variant of inscribing the Law in the heart.[209] Having
finally come home, purified through the experience of curse and with foreskins
removed,[210] Jeremiah's returnees will not receive a covenant they can break.[211]
'"Only if these regulations [i.e. the order of creation] depart from before me
(אם ימשו החקים האלה מלפני)", says Yahweh, "will also the seed of Israel forever
cease to be my people" (גם זרע ישראל ישבתו מהיות גוי לפני כל־הימים, 31.35-36).[212]
The text is implicitly playing with 4.23-28's almost final return to chaos[213]—caused
by the people's disobedience (5.25)—from which Daughter Zion gives birth (4.31).

The people's return to Jerusalem-Zion is also Yahweh's return to a city which
shall become rebuilt for Yahweh (Jer. 31.38),[214] and be called 'the seat of Yahweh'
(ויקראו לירושלם כסא יהוה, 3.17). In Ezekiel's vision of rebuilt Jerusalem,
Yahweh's seat and footstool shall be placed in splendid isolation in the holiest part
of his holy temple (Ezek. 43.7),[215] and the city's name shall from that day be
'Yahweh is there' (ושם העיר מיום יהוה שמה, 48.35).[216] These spatial limitations
contrast sharply with Isa. 66.1's Yahweh, whose dimensions comprise both heaven
and earth as seat and footstool (השמים כסא וארץ הדם רגלי). This, however, does not
imply that Yahweh should not be addressed in the temple,[217] only that no building can contain Yahweh, as Solomon states (1 Kgs 8.27; 2 Chron. 6.18). In Chronicles, it is not Yahweh, but Solomon, who sits on Yahweh's throne (על־כסא יהוה,
1 Chron. 29.23; cf. 28.5: על־כסא מלכות יהוה).

---

208. Cf. Lev. 26.41.

209. Carroll, *Jeremiah*, p. 610.

210. Cf. Jer. 6.10; 9.26; Ezek. 44.7, 9; *Jub.* 1.23.

211. Carroll, *Jeremiah*, p. 611; Biddle, *Redaction History*, p. 104; Cooke, *Ezekiel*, p. 403:
'"And I will make a covenant of peace *for* them" (Ezek. 37.26). There is to be no covenant *with*
Israel'; cf. also Ezek. 34.25; Isa. 54.10.

212. Cf. Jer. 33.20-21: Yahweh's covenant with David.

213. Cf. also Isa. 51.15-16; 54.10.

214. Cf. 'the city of Yahweh' in Isa. 60.14; Ps. 101.8; (Jer. 25.29) and God's city in Pss. 46.5;
48.2, 9; 87.3.

215. Cooke, *Ezekiel*, p. 403: 'the territory of Israel is mapped out in such a way that the temple
occupies the centre of the land and thence radiates holiness throughout the nation'. Blenkinsopp,
Sage, Priest, Prophet, pp. 111-14, speaks of gradations of holiness along the spatial axis as in
Num. 2.1-34 and 10.13-28's description of the wilderness camp. Niessen, *Buches Yehošua'*, fol.
28a, exposes a similar disposition, which places Gerizim in the centre of the land.

216. Galambush, *Jerusalem in the Book of Ezekiel*, pp. 152-53: 'Because the life-powers are
so carefully controlled, and the pollutants without so thoroughly excluded, the new temple is a
suitable and acceptable dwelling for Yahweh. The new, ideal, and unpersonified city can now be
trusted not to defile Yahweh's name (through sancta trespass). Therefore that divine name which
the former Jerusalem so thoroughly defiled may safely be bestowed upon the new sanctuary.
Instead of "Jerusalem", the name of this city is "Yahweh Is There", a final reversal of the rejection
of the old city.'

217. Cf. Yahweh's residence in heaven and his presence in the temple: Pss. 11, 14, 18, 20, 76.
Van Seters, *Life of Moses*, p. 267.

The envisioned return is not a return to a restored pre-exilic Israel, fighting for independence or being under the vassalage of foreign rulers. The return is a recapture of a long-vanished past, a golden age of unity coming into being, as is Israel's people in Ezekiel's pesher-like closure in a prediction of everlasting unity under a Davidic 'prince': 'and never again shall they become two people and never again shall they be divided into two kingdoms' (Ezek. 37.22; cf. 34.23-24). Resembling the structures of the transition in Samuel–Kings and the instruction for the Solomonic temple in Chronicles, Ezekiel's vision of rebuilt Jerusalem, placed after the cleansing of the land (Ezek. 38–39), anticipates a glory whose literary qualities far surpass reality's limitations.[218] The same is true of Jeremiah's visionary opening scene, which brings the house of Judah to the house of Israel for a common return 'from the land of the north' (ויבאו יחדו מארץ צפון)[219] to the land Yahweh had given as heritage to their fathers (הנחלתי את־אבותיכם, Jer. 3.18; cf. Ezek. 28.25; 36.28; 37.25).[220] The 'replacement' of fathers with Jacob in Ezek. 28.25 and 37.25— אשר נתתי לעבדי ליעקב ('Which I gave to my servant Jacob')—underscores that unity, when it is not the conquered land with its tribal divisions to which Israel shall return, but an ancestral beginning cast in the future in the figure of the eponymous David ('my servant') as 'prince over them forever' (ודוד עבדי נשיא[221] להם לעולם, Ezek. 37.25).

While this land in which 'their fathers (Jacob's sons) lived', had, in fact and literature, several centres, temples, leaders and priestly houses, the new Israel of Isaiah, Jeremiah and Ezekiel has room only for Jerusalem, its temple, its priesthood and its Davidic king, to whose authority everyone shall be subjected. As such, Zion's predicted heritage as 'the legacy of Mount Sinai',[222] invites the reader to bring to realization 2 Sam. 5.1-12's unified monarchy with David as 'shepherd' and 'king' (5.2, 12) in the 'city of David', Zion-Jerusalem (5.6-7). Sanctifying that unity, Solomon gathers all Israel in Jerusalem (1 Kgs 8.1-3, 65) to bring the ark from the 'city of David, the same as Zion',[223] to Jerusalem's temple. Merely a mirror's reflection of Isaiah's preaching of restored Jerusalem-Zion, from whose Temple Mount teaching shall go forth to all peoples (Isa. 2.2-4), Solomon's inauguration prayer illustrates well the teaching intended in its ephemeral limitations. While Solomon's Jerusalem represents the controversial, the unsettled Israel, as might also Moses'

---

218.   Cooke, *Ezekiel*, p. 402.

219.   The direction from which catastrophe and the enemies come; e.g. Jer. 1.14; 5.6-7; 6.1-5, 22-23; 10.22; W.L. Holladay, *Jeremiah 1: A Commentary on the Book of the Prophet Jeremiah 1–25* (Philadelphia: Fortress Press, 1986), pp. 42-43; Childs, 'The Enemy from the North', pp. 151-61.

220.   Notice Jeremiah's thematic parallel with *AF*, ch. XIX, p. 70; Chapter 4 above.

221.   Ezek. 37.22, 24: מלך.

222.   Levenson, *Sinai and Zion*, p. 187. For different opinions, see Van Seters, *Life of Moses*, pp. 247-89 (Sinai is the heir of Zion); T.B. Dozeman, *God on the Mountain: A Study of Redaction, Theology and Canon in Exodus 19–24* (SBLMS, 37; Atlanta: Scholars Press, 1989) (Sinai provides a critique of Zion).

223.   We must remember that, apart from the Hezekiah narrative, these are the only occurrences of 'Zion' in the Deuteronomistic History.

Sinai,[224] Isaiah's (and David's) Zion is predicted as the place for 'God's continuing availability'.[225] While 'the canonical division of the Pentateuch from the rest of the Hebrew Bible, adumbrated in Deut. 34.10, ensures that the heir will be eternally subordinate to the testator, Zion to Sinai, David to Moses',[226] this, however, might not have been the intent of those biblical authors who advanced the Zion ideology. The authors of a narrative which favours those who adhere to the Davidic and Mosaic covenant against those who only submit to the Mosaic covenant, tied to 'the precariousness of life and a subsequent need for a continuously reinvigorated obedience',[227] bring heavy charge against those who do not submit to the Davidic covenant. The remaining chapters of this study will deal with Zion ideology's controversial realization.

224. Levenson, *Sinai and Zion*, p. 189.
225. Levenson, *Sinai and Zion*, p. 188.
226. Levenson, *Sinai and Zion*, p. 188: 'The presence is the presence of Zion, but the voice is the voice of Sinai'.
227. Levenson, *Sinai and Zion*, p. 101.

Chapter 6

MOUNTAIN VS. MOUNTAIN: THE PLACE YAHWEH HAS CHOSEN

1. *Mt Zion as the Mountain of the House of Yahweh*

While general definitions of Zion are made mainly on the basis of its qualities in comparison with similar themes in ancient Near Eastern holy mountain ideology,[1] its relationship to royal ideologies have been established intertextually as a reflection of a purported 'Zionistic' Davidic kingdom in the Iron Age. Seemingly unaware that 'Deuteronomistic' and 'Chronistic' authors of these narratives do not present any explicit Zion or mountain ideology, modern interpreters have linked the Zion ideology in the Prophets and the Psalms with the biblical David–Solomonic kingdom. 2 Kings 19.31's mention of the 'Mountain of Zion' (par. Isa. 37.32),[2] as the Chronicler's explicit reference to 'Mt Moriah' (2 Chron. 3.1) and the 'mountain of the house of Yahweh and Jerusalem' (בהר בית־יהוה ובירושלם, 2 Chron. 33.15), are exceptions that underscore the fact.

Interpreting their biblical colleagues' projection of ideal kingship in the Prophets and Psalms as descriptions of an ephemeral Davidic kingdom 'known' from prose literature, modern scholars have created historical scenarios of a tenth-century BCE golden age by synthesizing these forms. Biblical projections, however, which appear as paraphrastic forms of such prose descriptions, can hardly count as source material for historical reconstruction. Psalm 132, however fitting its thematic elements are to biblical as well as ancient Near Eastern ideology,[3] is nothing other than a confirmation of the Samuel–Kings' traditions about the Davidic kingship, now set within the terms of Zion as elected (Ps. 132.13). The occurrence of Zion in this context refers to its symbolic literary value rather than any historical pre-Davidic or Davidic Zion-Jerusalem ideology. Similarly, Psalm 78, which, linked with Psalms 2 and 110, is claimed to support tenth-century royal ideology, in fact, mirrors narratives whose provenance is conceivably datable to any period between the tenth and the second century BCE. Dating these and other (Zion) psalms to early

---

1. E.g. R.E. Clements, *God and Temple* (Philadelphia: Fortress Press, 1965), pp. 42-53; Clifford, *Cosmic Mountain*; R.L. Cohn, *The Shape of Sacred Space: Four Biblical Studies* (AAR Studies in Religion; Philadelphia: Scholars Press, 1981), pp. 66-74; Dozeman, *God on the Mountain*, pp. 29-35; Levenson, *Sinai and Zion*, pp. 111-37.

2. Further occurrences are found in Isa. 4.5; 8.18; 10.12; 24.23; 29.8; 31.4; Mic. 4.7; Joel 3.5; Obad. 17, 21; Pss. 48.3, 12; 74.2; 78.68; 125.1; 133.3; Lam. 5.18.

3. Laato, *A Star is Rising*, pp. 84-92.

Iron II, of course, removes the uneasiness created by the usually much later dating of the prose material to the late seventh century BCE and later.

Of the qualifications of Zion, we have hitherto dealt with its inviolability, election, rejection and predicted restoration. As we saw, the restoration of Zion is combined with a wish for a unification of Israel and a restoration of a Davidic kingship. In a move from periphery to center, the temple will be restored and teaching will go forth from it in a world governed by justice and peace.[4] In Isaiah's vision, 'the mountain of the House of Yahweh (הר בית־יהוה) shall be established as the highest of mountains (בראש ההרים) and raised above the hills (מגבעות)' (Isa. 2.2 par. Mic. 4.1).[5] The site is also called 'Yahweh's mountain' (הר־יהוה) and 'the House of the God of Jacob' (בית אלהי יעקב, v. 3aα), from which place, located as 'Zion' (v. 3bα) and 'Jerusalem' (v. 3bβ), the Law and the word of Yahweh shall go forth (מציון תצא תורה ודבר־יהוה מירושלם, v. 3b = Mic. 4.2).

Because 'the mountain of Yahweh' (הר־יהוה) does not occur often in Old Testament texts,[6] its significance in this text should not be underestimated. Intertextually, the term forms a continuum between the Israelites who leave Sinai, 'the mountain of Yahweh, walk for three days with the ark of the covenant...to seek a resting place' (מהר יהוה דרך שלשת ימים וארון ברית־יהוה נסע לפניהם...לתור להם מנוחה, Num. 10.33; cf. Deut. 1.33) on their way to 'the place about which Yahweh has said: "I will give it to you"' (אל־המקום אשר אמר יהוה אתו אתן לכם, Num. 10.29). This place, Isaiah implicitly claims, they found, when they urged each other to go up to 'the Mountain of Yahweh' (לכו ונעלה אל־הר־יהוה, Isa. 2.3).[7] Here they will listen to the Torah and the 'word of Yahweh'. Intertextually, the תורה is the Law[8] given on Mt Sinai, as Numbers 10 marks the narrative closure of the teaching from that mountain. Its last occurrence in the Pentateuch (Num. 28.3) evokes the past.[9] In Isaiah, the 'word of Yahweh' is always a word mediated by the prophet (Isa. 1.10; 2.1; 28.13, 14; 39.5, 8; 66.5), who fits the standard role of the biblical prophets.[10] Thus we might rightly understand Isaiah's דבר־יהוה and תורה as referring to the

4. N.W. Porteous, 'Jerusalem-Zion: "The Growth of a Symbol"', in A. Kuschke (ed.), *Verbannung und Heimkehr: Beiträge zur Geschichte und Theologie Israels im 6. und 5. Jahrhundert v. Chr.* (Tübingen: J.C.B. Mohr [Paul Siebeck], 1961), pp. 235-52.

5. Cf. Pss. 48.3; 68.16-19; 78.69; Ezek. 40.2; Zech. 14.10.

6. Num. 10.33; Isa. 2.3 par. Mic. 4.2; Isa. 30.29; Ps. 24.3.

7. Ps. 24.3: מי־יעלה בהר־יהוה ומי־יקום במקום קדשו; cf. Pss. 15.1; 68.17-18; 99.6-7; Isa. 33.14.

8. Against Wildberger, *Jesaja 1–12*, p. 85: 'Weisung'; Levenson, *Sinai and Zion*, p. 126: 'instruction'.

9. הר־סיני Exod. 19.11, 18, 20, 23; 24.16; 31.18; 34.2, 4, 29, 32; Lev. 7.38; 25.1; 26.46; 27.34; Num. 3.1; 28.6; Neh. 9.13. Against a pre-exilic provenance of the Sinai covenant, see Dozeman, *God on the Mountain*, pp. 120-26 (126): 'the transformation of Sinai as a specific mountain of revelation is best interpreted as an innovation by exilic/post-exilic Priestly tradents... Mount Sinai functions to qualify the pre-exilic temple theology of Mount Zion'. Van Seters, *Life of Moses*, *passim*, generally ascribes the texts in which Mt Sinai occurs to his late J; Blenkinsopp, 'Deuteronomic Contribution', p. 102, opts for 'a P or at least a non-Deuteronomic context'.

10. Wildberger, *Jesaja 1–12*, pp. 36-37; Carroll, *Jeremiah*, pp. 48-49; Holladay, *Jeremiah 1*, p. 14.

Law[11] *and* the interpretative instruction by the prophets.[12] As both have, in fact, been preserved through writing,[13] the hermeneutical key to interpreting Isaiah's utterance is the written word, which follows, for example, in Isa. 1.10 and 30.8-12.[14]

While in Numbers the resting place was temporary, threatened by enemy attacks along the road (Num. 33.35-36), Isaiah's mountain shall become a place of eternal peace,[15] with one sovereign, one 'law' and one mind, with swords transformed into ploughshares and spears into pruning hooks (Isa. 2.4). In the closure of Isaiah's 'summary' of Israel's 'journey' from grace to fall to grace (Isa. 2.6–4.6),[16] Yahweh will create (וברא יהוה[17]) over all the place of Mt Zion (על כל־מכון הר־ציון[18]) and its assembly (מקראה[19]) a cloud for daytime (עמן יומם) and smoke and the shining of a flaming fire for the night (ועשן ונגה אש להבה לילה, Isa. 4.5). As Yahweh's presence in Exodus and Numbers' daytime cloud (ענן יומם) and fire by night (אש לילה) stood over the Tabernacle and lead the Israelites through the wilderness,[20] so Isaiah's cloud and fire confirm that Mt Zion is Yahweh's abode, the dwelling of his splendour (כבוד). Because of the holiness of the people (4.3), it will also be their dwelling place; its temple (סכה) a shade against the heat (לצל־יומם מחרב),[21] a refuge and a shelter from storm and rain (ולמחסה ולמסתור מזרם וממטר, 4.6). While the text presents eschatological hope, its context is one of immediate disaster and threat: the heat, storm and rain symbolizing Yahweh's cleansing acts—as in Isa. 25.4; 28.2; 30.30; 32.2—from which Zion and the righteous king offer protection (Isa. 1.8, 27;

---

11. Clifford, *Cosmic Mountain*, p. 158: 'The logical outcome was to see Zion as the place from which the Law went forth'; Sweeney, *Isaiah 1–39*, p. 93: '[Isa] 51.4, "torah goes forth from me and my justice for a light to the peoples", serves as a model for the composition of 2.2-4 as indicated by its similar vocabulary and syntactical construction as well as its sending torah to the nations [cf. also Isa. 42.4]'; Laato, *About Zion I Will Not Be Silent*, pp. 119-20, 152.

12. In Sir. 24, Wisdom settled in Zion and beloved Jerusalem (v. 10), is identified with the Book of the Covenant, the Law given by Moses as heritage to the congregations of Jacob (v. 23), from which the 'I' person (the sage, Ben Sirach) will 'make instructions shine forth like dawn (v. 32), and 'pour out teaching like prophecy' (v. 33); see further, Hengel, *Judentum und Hellenismus*, p. 289; Nickelsburg, *Jewish Literature*, p. 60; Laato, *A Star is Rising*, p. 235

13. E.W. Conrad, 'Reading Isaiah and the Twelve as Prophetic Books', in Broyles and Evans (eds.), *Writing and Reading the Scroll of Isaiah*, pp. 3-17.

14. Cf. Ps. 78.1-5's double use of *torah* as instruction and Law.

15. Cf. also Isa. 66.20-22; *Jub.* 8.19; 1.28-29, in which similar connections are made between the Law from Sinai, and Zion envisioned as the location of the Lord's sanctuary in recreated peaceful Israel, with God as king. Compositionally, the written Law follows (*Jub.* 2–50) immediately after the utterance in *Jub.* 1.29.

16. For the thematic and linguistic unity of Isa. 2.1–4.6, see Sweeney, *Isaiah 1–4*, pp. 35-36, 134-84; *idem*, *Isaiah 1–39*, pp. 87-96: 'a programmatic introduction to chs. 5–27 and 28–35'.

17. LXX: καὶ ἔξει καὶ ἔσται.

18. For other references to Yahweh's place, see Exod. 15.17; 1 Kgs 8.13; 2 Chron. 6.2;.

19. LXX Neh. 8.8: πάντα τὰ περικύκλω. מקרא־קדש is found in Exod. 12.16; Lev. 23; Num. 28 and 29 (regulations for the feasts).

20. Exod. 13.21; 40.34-38; Num. 9.15-23; Deut. 1.33; Ps. 78.14; cf. Ps. 18.13 par. 2 Sam. 22.13; Ps. 97.2. Fire is not mentioned in Exod. 16.11; 19.9; Num. 10.33; 1 Kgs 8.10-11; 2 Chron. 5.13-14; cf. also 2 Chron. 6.41's variant of Num. 10.35.

21. Cf. Jon. 4.5-6.

16.1-5; 31.9–32.2).[22] The opposite of Yahweh's protective shade is Egypt (Isa. 30.2-3; Ezek. 31.12), Assur (Hos. 14.4-8; Ezek. 31.6), Babylon (Ezek. 17.22-24) and ephemeral Jerusalem's (Isa. 22.8-11; Jer. 33.4) illusory and limited shade in which the people should never have sought refuge.

Although Jerusalem and Zion occur with equal frequency in Isaiah,[23] their interchangeability relates only to their occurrence in synonymous parallelism.[24] While Israel, Judah, Jerusalem (Isa. 1.21; 3.8; 10.10-11; 40.1-2; 52.9)[25] and the daughters of Zion (3.16-17)[26] are accused of adulterous and sinful behaviour, this is never the case with victimized Zion (and daughter Zion [singular]),[27] which shall experience salvation.[28] While Jerusalem is the name of a mundane city, partaking in mundane affairs and therefore liable to judgment (5.3), Zion is an ideal, a divine abode, a holy mountain (4.5; 8.18; 12.6; 16.1),[29] which can be abandoned by its god (64.9-11),[30] but not accused.[31] Its symmetry with Jerusalem equalises an ideal Jerusalem: elected, victorious, exalted and infinite. As such, the Jerusalem of the narratives can be the rejected Jerusalem (which is never called Zion),[32] as could the house of David. The Jerusalem-Zion of poetry, on the contrary, plays a role similar to that of the suffering and victorious David in the Prophets and Psalms. It is their future status, which is our authors' concern.

As these visions of future glory might reflect a glorious return from the historical Babylonian exile, one is surprised to notice that this is not what we find in Ezra and Nehemiah's restoration narratives. Similar to biblical literature describing pre-exilic matters, the prophets mentioned (Jeremiah in Ezra 1.1; Haggai and Zechariah in Ezra 5.1) speak about Zion's future restoration (Jeremiah and Zechariah).[33] Their language, however, never found its way into the books of Ezra and Nehemiah, where terms like 'Zion', 'Holy Mountain',[34] 'Yahweh Zebaoth',[35] 'Yahweh as king'

---

22. Cf. Pss. 17.8; 57.2; 63.8; 121.5.

23. Zion occurs 47 times and Jerusalem 49 times; see Laato, *About Zion I Will Not Be Silent*, p. 64.

24. Isa. 2.3; 4.3, 4; 10.12; 24.23; 30.19; 31.9; 33.20; 37.22, 37; 40.9; 41.27; 52.1, 2; 62.1; 64.9; 66.8-9.

25. Cf. Jer. 4.14; 33.5; Lam. 1.8; Ezek. 16.1-52; Zech. 1.12.

26. Singular in Jer. 6.2; Lam. 5.22; Mic. 1.13; 4.10.

27. Isa. 3.26; 10.32; 37.22; 49.14; 51.1-3; 64.9; cf. Jer. 30.17; Lam. 1.4, 17; 2.1, 13, 18; 4.11; Mic. 4.11; Zech. 1.17; Pss. 102.14-15; 126.1-6.

28. Isa. 1.27; 12.6; 46.13; 51.3; 52.2; 59.20; 62.11.

29. Cf. Jer. 31.6; 50.5, 28; Zeph. 3.14-17; Zech. 1.14-16; 8.3; Pss. 2; 9; 48; 50; 74; 87; 99; 132.

30. Cf. Jer. 8.19; 14.19; 26.18; Lam. 5.18-20; Zech. 8.3; 9.9.

31. Against A. Labahn, 'Metaphor and Intertextuality: "Daughter of Zion" as a Test Case', *SJOT* 17/1 (2003), pp. 49-67, who fails to distinguish between daughter(s) of Zion and Zion.

32. This is most apparent in Isaiah and Jeremiah's prose narratives, which never use Zion in a negative way, although mentioning Zion 47 and 17 times respectively throughout their books.

33. 'Zion' is not found in Haggai.

34. The only references to 'mountain' is Neh. 8.15 (the mountains from where the people bring branches for the making of the booths) and 9.13 (Mt Sinai).

35. Which, as we saw in Chapter 3, occurs with great frequency in Jeremiah, Haggai and Zechariah.

and 'David as exalted (political) King'[36] do not occur.[37] Neither is royal ideology's goal of a unification of Israel's tribes and the submission of the nations to Yahweh in Jerusalem part of a restored Jerusalem and Judah. This restoration creates hostility rather than amicability, divisiveness rather than unification, with the result that, in Josephus, these narratives are interpreted as reflecting Jewish–Samaritan antagonism.[38] The sadness which closes the books of Ezra and Nehemiah, in which the temple offers no protection against the rain (Ezra 10.9) nor has room for any foreigner (Ezra 9–10; Neh. 13.1-3; 23–30), contrasts sharply with the optimistic recapture of a glorious Jerusalem-Zion expressed in Isaiah, Jeremiah (Ezekiel), Joel, Amos, Obadiah, Micah, Zephaniah (Haggai), Zechariah and the Psalms.[39] Some of these writings emphasize defeat and submission of the nations,[40] rather than any freewill wandering to Jerusalem-Zion. Since no biblical book narrates a fulfilment of these expectations, we will extend our examination of the visions of Zion to extra-biblical material.

2. Zion and David Traditions in Extra-Biblical Literature

Our examination centres on 1 Maccabees, which not only exposes knowledge of Mt Zion traditions but also of a fulfilment of its expectations in 1 Maccabees 5's stories about Judas and Simeon's return of the Jews from Gilead and the Galilee (cf. v. 54): 'So they went up to Mt Zion with gladness and joy, and offered burnt offerings, because not one of them had fallen before they returned in safety'. The Zion expectation is hereby given its first explicit fulfilment, and that in narratives which seemingly use the term in a dynamic way. As the book is considered to have been written sometime between the death of John Hyrcanus (104 BCE) and the Roman occupation (63 BCE),[41] it is safe to expect that its author is familiar with most aspects of biblical Zion ideology. However, before scrutinising that book, a few notes will be given on literature which is earlier or contemporary with 1 Maccabees or the events described therein.

36.   Mendels, *Land of Israel*, p. 5: 'the House of David should not become the central authority, but rather a spiritual leadership like that of Moses'.

37.   In contrast, mentions of Zion are found in 1 Esdras (probably first century BCE–first century CE; used by Josephus): 1 Esd. 8.81: 'and glorified the temple of our Lord, and raised Zion from desolation' (cf. Ezra 9.9); 2 Esdras (probably first–second century CE): 2 Esd. 2.40, 42: Ezra exhorts the nations to come to Zion (cf. 13.35); 3.2: 'I saw the desolation of Zion' (cf. 10.19, 23; 12.44, 48); 6.19: 'humiliation of Zion'; 3.28, 31: '[Roman] dominion over Zion'; 5.25; 6.4: Zion consecrated for God; 10.7: Mother Zion; 14.31: the land given as 'a possession in the land of Zion'.

38.   Hjelm, *Samaritans and Early Judaism*, pp. 195-207.

39.   Of the Prophets listed, Ezekiel and Haggai do not use 'Zion'.

40.   E.g. Isa. 60.14-16; 66.18-20, 23-24; Amos 9.11-12; Obad. 19-21; Mic. 7.11-13, 16-17; Zeph. 3.8-9; Zech. 14.16-19.

41.   J.A. Goldstein, *I Maccabees: A New Translation with Introduction and Commentary* (AB, 41; Garden City, NY: Doubleday, 1977), p. 62; G.W.E. Nickelsburg, *Jewish Literature Between the Bible and the Mishnah: A Historical and Literary Introduction* (London: SCM Press, 1981), p. 117.

a. *Baruch, Sirach, Judith and* Jubilees

Of the books usually considered to be earlier than 1 Maccabees, Baruch,[42] Sirach,[43] Judith[44] and *Jubilees*[45] contain few references to Zion and none of them treat the theme of a realization of its glory. In this context, it is interesting to note that in Sirach's 'interpretation of Isaiah',[46] the wandering to Zion-Jerusalem is in futuristic terms (Sir. 36.13-16). Similarly Bar. 4.5–5.9's victimized Mother Zion, who laments the exile of her children, whom she, comforting and appealing to conversion, is assured of their return. This section, which stands out separately from the remainder of Baruch,[47] is reminiscent of Isaianic phraseology.[48] In Sirach, no mention is made of Zion in references to David and Solomon's temple (Sir. 47.9-10, 13), but rather in references to Hezekiah, Isaiah and the Assyrian threat against Jerusalem (Sir. 48.18-24; cf. also Jdt. 9.13's single use of the term Mt Zion: κορυφῆς Σιων). Further references in Sirach 24 allude to Isaianic visions about teaching Moses' Torah from Zion-Jerusalem (Sir. 24.10-23; cf. Isa. 2.3).

Jubilees, a 'retelling' of Genesis through Exodus 24, does not deal with the periods after the entrance into the land. Its author, nevertheless, draws extensively on most of the biblical books as well as some non-biblical material.[49] The book's introduction recollects the apostasy, punishment and restoration that will take place in the future (ch. 1). Its concern is the 'rewritten' Law, which shall go forth from

---

42. The book's division into three parts requires that each part be dated separately. G.W.E. Nickelsburg, 'The Bible Rewritten and Expanded', in Stone (ed.), *Jewish Writings of the Second Temple Period*, pp. 89-156 (143-46): dated variously between the fourth century BCE and the second century CE; cf. R.H. Pfeiffer, *History of the New Testament Times with an Introduction to the Apocrypha* (New York: Harper & Brothers, 1949), pp. 415-23.

43. By most scholars dated to 190–175 BCE, cf. Nickelsburg, *Jewish Literature*, p. 64; Mendels, *Land of Israel*, pp. 9-12. The dating is based mainly on assumptions that the high priest Simeon (Sir. 50) is the legendary and otherwise unknown Simon (II) 'the Just', which would fit another assumption of a long time span between the 'grandfather's' original Hebrew manuscript and his 'grandson's' Greek 'translation', made after 132 BCE according to its Foreword. This, however, implies either a young age of the grandfather at the time he wrote the book, or an old age of the grandson at the time of its translation. Without such assumptions, the book can date at least as late as 132 BCE and we must speculate about other figures behind the Simeon son of John mentioned, as well as possible Jewish–Samaritan controversies behind ben Sira's praise of the Jerusalem cult. The attribution of a work to an ancestor or an older source is a common trope in ancient literature. See my discussion in *Samaritans and Early Judaism*, pp. 129-36.

44. A work which might date from the Persian period. However, its assumed redaction between 140 and 134/43 BCE places it within the mode of post-140 BCE enthusiasm; cf. Pfeiffer, *History*, pp. 294-95; Nickelsburg, *Jewish Literature*, pp. 108-109; Mendels, *Land of Israel*, pp. 51-56. A dating between 135 and 63 BCE has also been suggested.

45. Suggested datings of *Jubilees* range between 200–105 BCE, with mid-second century (170–140 BCE) as the favoured date; cf. Nickelsburg, 'The Bible Rewritten and Expanded', pp. 101-03; Mendels, *Land of Israel*, pp. 57-58, argues for a dating around 125 BCE.

46. Laato, *About Zion I Will Not Be Silent*, pp. 15-17.

47. E. Tov, *The Book of Baruch* (SBLTT; Missoula, MT: Scholars Press, 1975), pp. 13-27, and *Septuagint Translation of Jeremiah and Baruch*, p. 126.

48. Nickelsburg, 'The Bible Rewritten', pp. 142-43.

49. O.S. Wintermute, 'Jubilees: A New Translation and Introduction', in *OTP*, II, pp. 35-142 (48-49).

God's sanctuary in Jerusalem on Mt Zion (*Jub.* 1.28-29). This Zion is identified in *Jub.* 8.19 as 'the navel of the earth' (cf. Exod. 15.13; Judg. 9.37; Ezek. 38.12), and in *Jub.* 18.13 as the mountain which Abraham called 'The Lord has seen' (cf. Gen. 22.14). Since the temple is the 'focal point'[50] of the composition, the author makes sure to convey the message that although God had revealed himself to Jacob in Luz-Bethel, in which place Jacob had vowed to return to build 'the House of the Lord' (*Jub.* 27.19-27) and Levi served as priest (32.9), Jacob's plans of building a temple and a wall in Bethel and of making the place holy for himself and his children (32.16-24) is not approved by God: 'Do not build this place and do not make an eternal sanctuary and do not dwell here because this is not the place. Go to the house of Abraham, your father and dwell with Isaac your father' (32.23). That Jacob becomes Israel (32.18), which is not Bethel, and returns to his father's house in Beersheba (44.1) symbolizes a unification of the houses of Abraham, Isaac and Jacob, prior to their descent to Egypt (32.24). At their return, the Tabernacle shall be set up temporarily in the midst of the land until the building of the House of the Name of Yahweh (49.18). Although the passage does not mention Jerusalem, it explicitly answers Deuteronomy 12's implicit and the explicit question in *AF* (ch. XIX, p. 76) about where Yahweh had been worshipped before the building of the temple, namely, in the Tabernacle, which *Jubilees'* audience will know has been replaced by Jerusalem's temple (*Jub.* 49.21). Similar is Sir. 24.7-12's claim regarding Wisdom's unsuccessful search for a resting place for her tent, which made the 'Fashioner of all' (i.e. God) choose a place; namely the holy tent (i.e. the Tabernacle), given rest in Zion-Jerusalem.[51] Compare also Sir. 47.13-17 and Wis. 9.8, which mention no names, but which seem to imply biblical David–Solomon traditions. In *1 En.* 42.1-3, 'Wisdom remained in the heavens, because she could not find a dwelling place. However, iniquity could' (cf. also 2 Sam. 7.6-7).

b. *Eupolemus,* Pseudo-Eupolemus, 1 Enoch *and Tobit*
Of the second-century BCE authors and books which never use the term 'Zion' although they put emphasis on Jerusalem and its temple, we must comment briefly on *Eupolemus, Pseudo-Eupolemus,*[52] *1 Enoch*[53] and Tobit.[54] Eupolemus, who wrote

50. Mendels, *Jewish Nationalism*, p. 94.

51. P.W. Skehan and A.A. Di Lella, *The Wisdom of Ben Sira: A New Translation, with Notes, Introduction and Commentary* (AB, 39; Garden City, NY: Doubleday, 1987), p. 333.

52. By most scholars considered to be a second-century BCE Samaritan writer transmitted erroneously as 'Eupolemus' through Eusebius, *Praeparatio Evangelica*, quoting Alexander Polyhistor; see further Wacholder, 'Pseudo-Eupolemus'; Mendels, *Land of Israel*, p. 116; Gaster, *Samaritans*, pp. 140-42; *idem, The Asatir*, pp. 17-42, for *Pseudo-Eupolemus'* dependency on Samaritan tradition. For the opinion that the author is, in fact, Eupolemus the Jew, see R. Doran, 'Pseudo-Eupolemus: A New Translation and Introduction', in *OTP*, II, pp. 873-82.

53. Most scholars date the book, especially chs. 83–90, before 161 BCE, and chs. 72–82, before 110 BCE; cf. Wacholder, *Eupolemus*, p. 75, who dates the composition of 'the "Book on the Courses of Heavenly Luminaries", bearing Enoch's name' to 150 BCE. M. Rist, 'Enoch', in *IBD* (1962), II, p. 103b, dates the book to the Herodian period; Nickelsburg, 'The Bible Rewritten and Expanded', p. 90, considers it to have been 'composed during the last three centuries BCE and

a work, 'probably entitled *On the Kings in Judea*',[55] is believed to have been a Jewish writer living in Palestine in the second century BCE. Closely connected to the Hasmonaean court, he might have been the Eupolemus son of John, mentioned as one of the emissaries whom Judas Maccabaeus sent to Rome (1 Macc. 8.17; 2 Macc. 4.11).[56] His work has survived in fragments only, transmitted through Alexander Polyhistor, Clement of Alexandria and Eusebius of Caesarea. Of these, Eusebius is considered to be closest to the original.[57] Although Eupolemus wrote elaborate narratives about Saul, David and Solomon, which he set in the context of second-century BCE geopolitical and ethnographic circumstances,[58] focusing on the antiquity, exclusivity and superior legitimacy of Jerusalem's temple,[59] the term 'Zion' is not found in his writings. Not mentioning David's census, Eupolemus relates that David requested God to show him a place for the altar: 'Then an angel appeared to him standing above the place where the altar is set up in Jerusalem' (*Praep. Ev.* 9.30.5). In Eupolemus' description of the temple, he uses a mixture of elements, virtually creating a new temple, synthesizing 'the Tabernacle, the Solomonic temple and the Second temple', in order to create 'structural' continuity, however, surpassing the 'poor condition' of the temple of his own time.[60] An interesting detail is the implicit legitimizing of the temple in David's turning over the materials for the building of the temple 'in the presence of Eli and the leaders of the twelve tribes' (*Praep. Ev.* 9.30.8). Its parallel is the return to Gerizim of the sons of Benjamin, and the sons of Kohath and Gershon and Merari, who had been with Eli in Shiloh' (*AF*, ch. XX, p. 78).[61] Having built the temple, Solomon 'encircled Jerusalem as a city with walls and towers and trenches (περιβαλεῖν δὲ καὶ τὰ Ἱεροσό-λυμα τὴν πόλιν τείχεσι καὶ πύργοις καὶ τάφροις) and he built a palace for himself' (*Praep. Ev.* 9.34.10). The trenches are wholly unscriptural, and they reflect rather

accumulated in stages'; cf. *idem*, *Jewish Literature*, pp. 46-47, 150-51; M.E. Stone, 'Apocalyptic Literature', in *idem* (ed.) *Jewish Writings of the Second Temple Period*, pp. 383-441 (395-408).

54.   The dating is uncertain, though some time between 200 and 168 BCE has been favoured; cf. Nickelsburg, *Jewish Literature*, p. 35. The criticism of the Second Temple and future rebuilding of the third temple (Tob. 14.5) parallels similar visions in *1 En.* 85–90, *Testament of Levi*, *Testament of Moses* and *Jubilees* (see below). Fragments of the Aramaic original and an early Hebrew translation have been found among the Dead Sea Scrolls.

55.   The title appears in Clement of Alexandria, *Strom.* 1.153.4; cf. F. Fallon, 'Eupolemus', in *OTP*, II, pp. 861-72 (865).

56.   See Wacholder, *Eupolemus*, pp. 7-26; Mendels, *Land of Israel*, pp. 27-29; and Fallon, 'Eupolemus', for bibliographic references.

57.   Wacholder, *Eupolemus*, pp. 46-49; Fallon, 'Eupolemus', p. 861.

58.   Mendels, *Land of Israel*, pp. 35-40.

59.   Mendels, *Land of Israel*, p. 32, and *Jewish Nationalism*, p. 144.

60.   Mendels, *Land of Israel*, p. 44. For the opinion that Eupolemus was depicting an ideal 'future temple', see Wacholder, *Eupolemus*, p. 201.

61.   Wacholder, *Eupolemus*, pp. 151-53, 211: 'He [Eupolemus] seems to maintain that Shiloh remained the only shrine of Yahweh until, by God's command and the angel's guidance, the site of Solomon's temple was chosen. Just as Joshua, Moses' assistant in the desert, formed a link between the sanctuary of the desert and that of Shiloh, so Eli, the chief priest of Shiloh, according to Eupolemus, was present at Solomon's coronation.' Cf. also Jeremiah's replacement of Shiloh with Jerusalem and his narratives about Judah's last kings mirrored against David.

the 'elevated' temple of the Maccabaeans mentioned by Josephus (*War*. 4.139; *Ant*. 13.217). Implicitly confirming that Solomon actually built the temple, Eupolemus relates that 'the shrine was first called the "Temple of Solomon" (*hieron Solomōnos*)', which later gave name to the city (*hierusalēm*); and 'by the Greeks it is correspondingly called "Hierosolyma"'' (*Praep. Ev.* 9.34.11). Interestingly, in *War*, Josephus offers a variant of that tradition, arguing that the city's name, which at Abraham's time was *Salem*, was changed when Melchizedek 'the Righteous King', who, being 'the first priest of God', erected the first temple there (*War* 6.438). In *Antiquities*, he struggles to combine both traditions, stating that after David's conquest of the city, 'he named it after himself; for in the time of our forefather Abraham it was called Solyma, but afterwards[62] they named it Hierosolyma, calling the temple (*hieron*) Solyma, which in the Hebrew tongue means 'security' (ἀσφάλεια, *Ant*. 7.68). In *Pseudo-Eupolemus*, the city of Melchizedek ('ruler and priest of God')[63] is unnamed, however its temple is 'Argarizin, which means of the Most High' (*Praep. Ev.* 9.17.6). *Pseudo-Eupolemus*' favourable attitude towards Gerizim and Heliopolis (*Praep. Ev.* 9.17.8) might reflect a non-Judaean provenance, but not necessarily so, as none of these places are said to belong to the Israelites. They are places visited by Abraham, who was honoured there (Gerizim) and who taught 'Jewish' wisdom to the Egyptians (Heliopolis). Similarly, Eupolemus' favouring of Solomon's temple against Heliopolis, legitimated by a later Pharaoh,[64] helps to legitimize the antiquity of Solomon's temple at the expense of purported later temples, whether Egyptian, Phoenician[65] or Israelite. If *Pseudo-Eupolemus* is, in fact, a Samaritan,[66] we must ask why he (or his transmitters) link Gerizim with Heliopolis, as Josephus also did in his struggle to establish Jerusalem's sovereignty.[67]

Having completed the temple and the city walls, Solomon went to Shiloh to bring offerings and carry the tent, the altar of sacrifice and the vessels, which

---

62. μετὰ ταῦτα δὲ; the text is doubtful and the text might refer to a tradition which claims that 'afterwards Homer called it Jerusalem', cf. Josephus, *Apion* 1.172, where Josephus quotes from the Greek poet Choerilus (a contemporary of Herodotus), who took over 'Solymian hills' from Homer (*Odyssey* 5.283). Both Homer and Choerilus probably spoke about Ethiopians.

63. ἱρέως ὄντος τοῦ θεοῦ; Wacholder, 'Pseudo-Eupolemus', pp. 106-07: 'a literal rendering of the Hebrew וְהוּא כֹהֵן לְאֵל עֶלְיוֹן (Gen. 14.18) except for the last word' (עֶלְיוֹן), which *Pseudo-Eupolemus* 'evidently omitted because he had already given a technical meaning to the word: 'Argarizin, which may be translated as the Mount of the Most High (ὄρος ὑψίστου)'. Several Samaritan manuscripts, however, 'omit' עֶלְיוֹן, also in Gen. 14.19-20; cf. Gall, *Samaritan Pentateuch*. Josephus, *Ant*. 12.257-59 (257): 'But when the Samaritans (οἱ Σαμαρεῖται) saw the Jews suffering these misfortunes, they would no longer admit they were of their kin or that the temple on Garizein (ἐν Γαριζεὶν ναὸν) was that of the Most Great God (τοῦ μεγίστου θεοῦ). Cf. also 2 Macc. 6.2's additional explanation (καθὼς ἐτύγχανον οἱ τόν τόπον οἰκοῦντες, Διὸς Ξενίου) which fits the hospitable treatment of Abraham (Ξενισθῆναι; *Praep. Ev.* 9.17.5 [*Pseudo-Eupolemus*]), and Mendels, *Land of Israel*, p. 117.

64. Mendels, *Land of Israel*, pp. 29-46; D. Mendels, '"Creative History" in the Hellenistic Near East in the Third and Second Centuries BCE: The Jewish Case', *JSP* 2 (1988), pp. 13-20 (17).

65. For a possible anti-Phoenician bias in Eupolemus, see Mendels, *Land of Israel*, pp. 131-43.

66. Wacholder, *Eupolemus*, p. 206.

67. See my 'Cult Centralisation'.

Moses had made, to Jerusalem to be placed in the temple. Perhaps indicating a second move, Eupolemus continues to say that he also placed the ark there, the golden altar, the lamp stand, the table and the other vessels (*Praep. Ev.* 9.34.12-13). Eupolemus might, however, attempt to imply that the ark and the tablets were always in Jerusalem, as they also remained there in the care of Jeremiah during the exile (*Praep. Ev.* 9.39.5). This unscriptural tradition appears also in 2 Macc. 2.4-8.[68] Since no fragments of Eupolemus relating the history of Judaean kings between Solomon and Jonachim (Jehoiakim) have been preserved (if they existed), we are unable to know whether he would have mentioned Zion, as do Sirach and Judith in reference to Isaiah and Hezekiah. Although he exposes knowledge of Jeremiah traditions, the fall of Jerusalem and the captivity, he does not mention Zion. This, however, is no indication that he was not familiar with the term. Josephus, who must have known the term, never used it. And we should keep in mind that the term does not appear in the prose parts of Jeremiah.

1 Enoch's 'zoomorphic' retelling of Israelite history is of no help regarding Zion ideology since neither that name nor Jerusalem appears. It can, however, be inferred from other traditions that the author is speaking about Jerusalem's temple: its building (*1 En.* 89.50), its destruction (89.67), the exile, its rebuilding in spite of the opposition by 'the wild boars' (89.72-73),[69] a second tribulation (89.74–90.12),[70] the re-establishment of the Davidic kingship (90.19-20) and the transformation of the ancient house, to become 'greater and loftier than the first one' (90.28-29), which was 'great and spacious' (89.50). In the image of the righteous people as 'sheep', the elected king is a 'ram' (89.45-49; 90.13), the temple is 'the house of sheep' and God is 'the Lord of the sheep', *1 Enoch*'s allusion to the 'David as shepherd' motif is apparent. Its closest parallels are similar allegorical retellings in the books of Ezekiel and Daniel. Similar to Eupolemus and *Samaritan Chronicles IV* and *VI*, the author's interest is in the first and the last kings of Judah (89.56), completely 'ignoring' the reforms of Josiah and Hezekiah.[71] The repetition of history, connecting the first temple to the coming temple, is the narrative's central point. Both temples are viewed as places of purity in contrast to the Second Temple, in

---

68. Variations of the motif are applied to Samaritans: *AF*, ch. IX, pp. 42-43, 63; Macdonald, *Sam. Chr. II*, Sam. §LK*-N*I; Josephus, *Ant.* 18.85-86; to Jews: *2 Bar.* 6.7-9; *4 Bar.* 3.10-11; *m. Šeq.* 6.1-2; *b. Yom.* 53b-54a. See I. Kalimi and J.D. Purvis, 'The Hiding of the Temple Vessels in Jewish and Samaritan Literature', *CBQ* 56 (1994), pp. 679-85; Hjelm, *Samaritans and Early Judaism*, pp. 252-53. Wacholder, *Eupolemus*, p. 241, mentions mediaeval variants found in *Yosippon* and *Chronicles of Jerameel*, which may have been based on earlier documents than those found in present editions of the Apocrypha.

69. P.A. Tiller, *A Commentary on the Animal Apocalypse of 1 Enoch* (Early Judaism and Its Literature, 4; Atlanta: Scholars Press, 1993), pp. 331-32, 339, suggests that this is an allusion to Edom rather than the traditional interpretation that the 'boars' are the Samaritans. Tiller's interpretation finds support in *1 En.* 89.12, 43, 49, 66, and 1 Esd. 5.66, 57 (and 4.50), as well as the accusation of Edomite participation or rejoicing in the destruction of Jerusalem (1 Esd. 4.45; Ps. 137.7; Lam. 4.21-22; Obad. 10-16; Ezek. 25.12-14; 35).

70. Cf. Tob. 14.5, not noticed by Nickelsburg, *Jewish Literature*, pp. 33, 35, who mentions only one exile, though suggesting a Diaspora context for the book.

71. Tiller, *A Commentary on the Animal Apocalypse*, p. 318.

which impure food is served (89.73).[72] Because the people 'abandoned the House of the Lord and his tower' (89.54), 'he [the Lord of Sheep] left that house of theirs and that tower of theirs and cast them into the hand of the lions—into the hands of the wild beasts' (89.56). As the first temple was entirely destroyed—'they burned that tower and ploughed that house' (89.67; 90.29)[73]—so the building of the third temple on its foundations (90.29) will be initiated by a removal of the Second Temple, its pillars, columns and ornaments 'abandoned in a certain place in the south of the land' (90.28). It has been discussed whether the allusion is in fact to the temple, the city,[74] or 'an idealization of the desert camp' in which there is no temple, as in Rev. 21.22 and Jer. 3.16's 'new Jerusalem'.[75] Tiller's argument is contradicted by contemporary documents of the Dead Sea Scrolls (e.g. 4Q174 [= 4QFlor]; 5Q15 and *The Temple Scroll*), all of which envision a future temple.[76] The context for Revelation's eschatological temple, envisioned after the destruction of Jerusalem's temple, differs from *1 Enoch*'s second century BCE context of a defiled temple, as Tiller rightly notes. Jeremiah both speaks about Jerusalem as the throne of Yahweh (Jer. 3.17), the city as holy for Yahweh (31.40), and includes a future temple (בית יהוה, 33.11). It might thus be safer to interpret *1 Enoch*'s rebuilding in connection with his removal of the Second Temple—the one which had become defiled. As the defiled constructions of that temple should be removed to 'a certain place in the south of the land' (*Praep. Ev.* 90.28), so the restoration of Jerusalem's temple in the time of Judas Maccabaeus implies a removal of its defiled stones, which they brought to an unclean place (1 Macc. 4.43). In both texts, the allusion to the Kidron Valley (south of the Temple Mount), which Josiah made impure by throwing into it the rubble of constructions and altars made by the kings of Judah, Ahaz and Manasseh (2 Kgs 23.12; cf. Jer. 31.40), is apparent. Regarding the defiled altar of the Second Temple, second-century BCE Jews obviously faced a dilemma, since what was defiled by idol worship had to be destroyed (Deut. 12.2-3). As it was in fact a Yahwist altar, it should, however, not be destroyed (Deut. 11.4).[77] Hence 'they put the stones away on the temple hill in a suitable place until a prophet should come to give an oracle concerning them' (1 Macc. 4.46). It might be that *1 Enoch* is looking forward to the ideal city, and that the temple encompasses the city,[78] but *1 Enoch*'s future return of 'those, who have been destroyed and dispersed

---

72. Nickelsburg, *Jewish Literature*, p. 94; Tiller, *A Commentary on the Animal Apocalypse*, p. 47 n. 65: 'The negative evaluation of the Second Temple can be paralleled in a number of texts, e.g. *T. Mos.* 4.8; 5.3-4; *T. Levi* 14.7–16.5; *Jub.* 23.21'. See also Tob. 14.5. J.A. Goldstein, 'How the Authors of 1 and 2 Maccabees Treated the "Messianic Promises"', in J. Neusner, W.S. Green and E.S. Frerichs (eds.), *Judaism and Their Messiahs at the Turn of the Christian Era* (Cambridge: Cambridge University Press, 1987), pp. 69-96 (70).

73. Cf. Jer. 26.18; Mic. 3.12: 'because of you, Zion shall become ploughed as a field and Jerusalem a heap of ruins'.

74. Nickelsburg, *Jewish Literature*, p. 94: 'both city and temple'.

75. Tiller, *A Commentary on the Animal Apocalypse*, pp. 46-51, 376.

76. Tiller, *A Commentary on the Animal Apocalypse*, p. 48.

77. Goldstein, *I Maccabees*, p. 285.

78. Tiller, *A Commentary on the Animal Apocalypse*, pp. 48, 376.

to 'that house', in which 'the sword, which was given to the sheep' shall 'be sealed', has its closest parallel in Isaiah's visions of Jerusalem's Temple Mount, to which 'House of Jacob's God' (i.e. the temple) people shall walk (Isa. 2.1-5). *1 Enoch*'s limitation of 'that house', which 'was large, wide and exceedingly full', but could not contain them all (*1 En.* 90.34), reflects Isa. 49.19-21 and Zech. 10.10's overwhelming return.[79] Its contrast is Neh. 7.4 and 11.1-2's reluctant return to a Jerusalem, which likewise is said to be wide and large, but its inhabitants few (7.4).

A recapture of an ideal past is included in the reiteration of the first temple. That might refer to Davidic messianism, paralleling Ezekiel 34's vision of a David *redivivus* as Yahweh's shepherd.[80] Whether this implies that 'the fighting horned ram' (interpreted as Judas Maccabaeus; *1 En.* 90.9, 12) 'was not regarded as the fulfilment of eschatological hopes', and was seen as being in opposition to the 'snow-white cow' (= the Davidic Messiah),[81] rests on the dating of the book prior to the death of Judas Maccabaeus,[82] though implying the historicity of 1 and 2 Maccabees as a paradigm for its interpretation. Against this reading stands the readings of Milik, Tiller and Tronier:[83] 'the white bull' of 90.37 is obviously the new Adam (cf. 85.3), but more glorious than the first, for 'his horns are large'. Just as the descendants of Adam were 'white bulls' (85.8-10), so the contemporaries of the second Adam will become 'white bulls' (90.38).[84] In the figure of Jacob as the first of the sheep (89.12), a transition from individuals to the people of Israel is indicated. Its converse is the eschatological transformation of these sheep to non-nationalistic bulls (90.37-39).[85] This might be so. However, the notion that horns are not mentioned in the allusion to Jacob, because 'rams and only rams have conspicuous horns', might not be as lacking in significance as Tiller thinks.[86] The horn, as a royal (Davidic) symbol,[87] could well imply that in a double image of a snow-white bull with large horns (feared by 'all the beasts of the field and the birds in the sky'), and 'the first of those transformed into snow-white cows, who become a wild ox with huge black horns on its head' (90.37-38), *1 Enoch* has combined traditions

79. Tiller, *A Commentary on the Animal Apocalypse*, p. 382.

80. Laato, *A Star is Rising*, p. 262; cf. Goldstein, 'How the Authors of 1 and 2 Maccabees Treated the "Messianic Promises"', pp. 69-96. For a critique of Goldstein, see J.J. Collins, 'Messianism in the Maccabean Period', in Neusner, Green and Frerichs (eds.), *Judaism and Their Messiahs*, pp. 97-109.

81. Laato, *A Star is Rising*, p. 261.

82. Laato, *A Star is Rising*, p. 261: 'around 165–161 [BCE]'.

83. J.T. Milik (with the collaboration of M. Black), *The Books of Enoch: Aramaic Fragments of Qumran Cave 4* (Oxford: Clarendon Press, 1976); Tiller, *A Commentary on the Animal Apocalypse*; H. Tronier, 'Apokalyptikkens historiefilosofi: Erkendelse og historiekonstruktion i Dyreapokalypsen, Første Enoks Bog 85–89', in Hallbäck and Strange (eds.), *Bibel og historieskrivning*, pp. 140-61.

84. Milik, *Books of Enoch*, p. 45; cf. Tiller, *A Commentary on the Animal Apocalypse*, pp. 19, 384.

85. Tiller, *A Commentary on the Animal Apocalypse*, p. 19 n. 9; Tronier, 'Apokalyptikkens historiefilosofi', pp. 146-48

86. Tiller, *A Commentary on the Animal Apocalypse*, p. 385.

87. 1 Sam. 2.10; Ps. 132.17; cf. Ezek. 29.21; Pss. 89.25, 18-19; 92.11; 148.14.

of Adam and the Patriarchs with Davidic universalism. Milik's observation that the second creation represents an ascending development to perfection against the first creation's descending sequence—of bulls–calves–sheep, surrounded by injurious animals and birds[88]—would support such an interpretation. However, as Tiller rightly notes, avoiding a clear interpretation of the wild ox motif, 'it is not clear that the "wild ox with black horns" is a successor to the white bull, because black elsewhere in the *An. Apoc.* [*Animal Apocalypse*] has negative connotations'.[89] The closure of the vision, that Enoch 'wept greatly' (90.41), invites us to interpret the wild ox with black horns as the adversary of the white bull and the final battle still awaiting, as in Daniel 7 and 8's similar closure in dread and agony.

c. *1 Maccabees* as Apologia?

1 Maccabees, dated by most scholars to the last quarter of the second[90] or to the beginning of the first[91] century BCE, relates the story of the Hasmonaean[92] family from the outbreak of the revolt against the Seleucids (c. 167 BCE) until the end of the reign of Simon (141–134 BCE) and the ascension of his son John Hyrcanus I (134–104 BCE), whom the book does not deal with, but mentions in reference to another work: 'the Chronicles of his high priesthood, from the time he took that office after his father' (1 Macc. 16.24). This reference suggests that 1 Maccabees was written 'late in the reign of Hyrcanus or possibly shortly after his death' and before the Roman occupation in 63 BCE, because of its 'favourable attitude towards the Romans'.[93] This is, however, a slippery indicator, not least since the book, in fact, is ambiguous about the Romans. The author might have several reasons for his attitude towards the Romans, as had Josephus, when he blamed his fellow Jews rather than the Romans for the destruction of Jerusalem's temple in 70 CE.

The main heroes of the book are the three brothers, Judah, Jonathan and Simon, sons of Mattathias son of John and grandson of Simeon. He is a priest of the tribe of Joiarib, but living in Modeïn[94] (1 Macc. 2.1; 14.29). By this description, he is connected to the Aaron–Eleazar–Phinehas–Zadok genealogy of 1 Chron. 5.29-41; 9.11; 24.7 and Neh. 11.10-11. In the Old Testament, Joiarib (Jehoiarib) is usually mentioned together with Jedaiah as those priests who went to Babylon together with Jehoshua (Jeshua) son of Jozadak (Neh. 12.6, 19). In the organization of the priests in 1 Chronicles 24, the first lot fell to Joiarib and the second to Jedaiah.

---

88. Milik, *1 Enoch*, p. 45.

89. Tiller, *A Commentary on the Animal Apocalypse*, pp. 388-89.

90. H.W. Attridge, 'Historiography', in Stone (ed.), *Jewish Writings of the Second Temple Period*, pp. 157-84 (171).

91. Goldstein, *I Maccabees*, p. 63: in the reign of Alexander Jannaeus, but before 90 BCE; Laato, *A Star is Rising*, p. 278: 'from the reign of [Alexander] Jannaeus'.

92. The name, otherwise unknown, occurs for the first time in Josephus (*War* 1.36), who calls Matthatias 'son of Asamonaios'.

93. Attridge, 'Historiography', p. 171; J. Sievers, *The Hasmoneans and Their Supporters: From Mattathias to the Death of John Hyrcanus I* (Studies in the History of Judaism, 6; Atlanta: Scholars Press, 1990), p. 3.

94. Usually identified as the modern el-Medieh, 7 miles east of Lod and belonging to Samaria until the time of Jonathan; cf. Sievers, *Hasmoneans*, p. 27.

Regardless the uselessness of these genealogies for historical reconstruction, they give information that 1 Maccabees associates the Hasmonaean priesthood with a 'correct' genealogy.[95] This is given special weight in 1 Macc. 2.26's comparison of the zealousness of Mattathias with that of Phinehas (cf. Num. 25.6-13), whom Mattathias calls 'our father', receiving the covenant of everlasting priesthood, 'because of his zealousness' (ἐν τῷ ζηλῶσαι ζῆλον, 1 Macc. 2.54). In the closure of Mattathias' speech, he transfers that covenant to Simeon, whom he appoints to be leader and 'father' for his brothers (2.65), implicitly superior to Judas who is appointed leader for the battle (2.66). Since Simon does not 'take center stage in the account until 142 BCE', the title anticipates his role as dynastic ancestor,[96] his fathers' house and his sons, who succeed him (14.25-26, 49).[97]

Structurally, 1 Maccabees' story of three brothers resembles Eupolemus' story of Judaea's (three) kings. As in Eupolemus, where Saul, David and Solomon succeed each other without genealogical or ideological opposition between Saul and David,[98] 1 Maccabees' 'brothers' (1 Macc. 2.2) succeed each other, albeit Judas Maccabaeus might not have been originally from that family.[99] In successive waves of conquests, these brothers free Israel of its occupants, however at the expense of part of its population, who are accused of siding with the foreigners. They cleanse and rebuild the temple more than once, restore the cult and bring home scattered inhabitants. In their newly won independence they establish amicable contacts with mighty Rome: first by Judas (8.1-13)[100] and renewed under Jonathan (12.1-4) and Simon (14.16-19).[101] When they inform the Spartans of their Roman alliance (12.5-18), they remind them of their familial relationship, that through Abraham they are brothers and should treat each other accordingly (12.19-20). The language is reminiscent of Gen. 34.23, and one might suspect that the 'Spartans' are, in fact, a euphemism for pro-Hellenistic elements in Palestine. Whatever the intention is, the correspondence helps place the Oniads in a non-Jewish context; their replacement, from which the Hasmonaeans hold themselves aloof, being entirely justified.[102]

Acting in the roles of the 'expected' liberators of Israel, the role of the anointed (= messiah), who should restore Israel to its former greatness, the Hasmonaeans had problems of legitimacy regarding priesthood and kingship. The first was solved by genealogy, the second by agency (1 Macc. 5.62), which established the Has-

---

95. It is of course equally possible that 1 Chronicles underwent a 'pro-Hasmonaean revision'; cf. Nodet, *Origins of Judaism*, p. 240.

96. Sievers, *Hasmoneans*, p. 36.

97. Cf. the 'adoption' narratives in 1 Sam. 24 and 26, in which David calls Saul 'father' (24.12) and Saul calls David 'son' (24.17; 26.17, 21, 25). The narratives establish David and his sons as Saul's successor.

98. Eupolemus (*Praep. Ev.* 9.30.3). Attridge, 'Historiography', p. 164. For the quite ambiguous attitude towards Saul in biblical and extrabiblical literature, see Spiro, *Samaritans, Tobiads and Judahites*, p. 22 n. 47. The 'error' is not found in *Samaritan Chronicles*.

99. Nodet, *Origins of Judaism*, pp. 215-16, 237-48.

100. Cf. Josephus, *Ant.* 13.414.

101. Attridge, 'Historiography', p. 174.

102. Hjelm, *Samaritans and Early Judaism*, pp. 166-70, 274-76.

monaeans as temporary rulers until the coming of the true prophet (14.41).[103] The implicit critique of placing themselves in the role of a Davidic scion without being of the right genealogy is justified in their actions that they liberated Israel at a time when no Davidide fulfilled messianic expectations. According to Goldstein, the Hasmonaean propagandist had even hinted that God's election of David's dynasty (2.57) might not be permanent, but that the *eis aionas* of 1 Macc. 2.57 might mean 'for a long time'.[104] This interpretation has been challenged by Collins, who thinks it more likely that the author of 1 Maccabees regarded the Hasmonaean salvation of Israel as an interim, prior to the fulfilment of eschatological hopes. 'The Davidic Messiah need not be an agent of salvation in history, any more than the white bull in the Animal Apocalypse'.[105] The truth lies probably somewhere in between these positions and the author might have sought to mediate internal as well as external opinions. As we shall see, the author of 1 Maccabees placed his narrative both within the context of a recapture of a 'Deuteronomistic History's' golden age and a Zion ideology's expectations of sovereignty. He did, however not place his narrative in eschatology's ideal Davidic kingdom.

The author of 2 Maccabees[106] worked from a different perspective in his attempts at proving that the city, the temple and the Hasmonaean high priesthood had been firmly established through divine war as works of the 'Greatest God' (τοῦ μεγίστου θεοῦ),[107] fought by the Almighty (ὁ παντοκράτωρ,[108] i.e. the Yahweh Zebaoth), who furthermore is called 'the Highest' (ὁ ὕψιστος).[109] The term 'Zion' does not occur in 2 Maccabees.

3. *1 Maccabees: The Introduction*

In Mattathias' testimony to his sons (1 Macc. 2.49-68), he reminds them of their obligation to fight zealously for the Law and follow in the paths of biblical heroes

103.   J.J. Collins, 'Messianism in the Maccabean Period', pp. 103-104. For opinions on 1 Maccabees as a defence of Hasmonaean dynastic claims, see Goldstein, *I Maccabees*, p. 77; Sievers, *Hasmoneans*, pp. 2-3.

104.   Goldstein, *I Maccabees*, pp. 240-41, and 'Biblical Promises and 1 and 2 Maccabees', p. 75.

105.   Collins, 'Messiansim in the Maccabean Period', p. 104; Laato, *A Star is Rising*, pp. 277-78.

106.   The dating is difficult, as the author claims an underlying work by Jason of Cyrene, a writer otherwise unknown. Attridge, 'Historiography', suggests a dating of 2 Maccabees between 125–63 BCE; so also J.A Goldstein, *II Maccabees: A New Translation with Introduction and Commentary* (AB, 41A; Garden City, NY: Doubleday, 1983), p. 72.

107.   2 Macc. 3.36. The epithet appears in *3 Macc.* 1.9, 16; 3.11; 5.25; 7.2, 22; Josephus, *Ant.* 12.257.

108.   Cf. 2 Macc. 3.30; 5.20; 6.26; 7.35, 38; 8.11, 18, 24; 15.8, 32; Jdt. 15.10; Sir. 42.17; Wis. 7.25. The epithet is not found in 1 Maccabees, but in *3 Maccabees* (2.8; 5.7; 6.28), which has close parallels to 2 Maccabees; cf. H. Anderson, '3 Maccabees', in *OTP*, II, pp. 509-29 (515).

109.   2 Macc. 3.31; the name occurs about 70 times in the LXX, mostly as equivalent to the Hebrew עליון or אלהי־השמים: Gen. 14.18-22; Deut. 32.8; 2 Sam. 22.14; Isa. 14.14; 57.15; Est. 8.18; Job 31.28; frequently in Psalms; Dan. 2–7; 1 Esdras; Sirach.

such as Abraham, Joseph, Phinehas, Joshua, Caleb, David, Elijah, Hananiah, Azariah, Mishael and Daniel. As each is rewarded for his conduct, the implication is that by imitating and 'emulating'[110] those heroes, the sons will share similar rewards. Like Abraham, God will regard them as righteous; like Joseph (καὶ ἐγένετο κύριος Αἰγύπτου),[111] God will raise them to be masters over Egypt; like Phinehas, God will assign them an everlasting priesthood; like Joshua, they will become judges in Israel; like Caleb (ἔλαβεν γῆς κληρονομίαν), they will have the land as their inheritance; like David (εκληρονόμησεν θρόνον βασιλείας εἰς αἰῶνας), they will inherit an everlasting kingship; like Elijah, they will be taken up to heaven; like Hananiah, Azariah and Mishael, they will be rescued from the flames; like Daniel, they will be saved from the mouth of the lions. The list functions programmatically to create the image of the Hasmonaeans as righteous leaders, priests, judges, kings and prophets, whose reward is land and eternity. As heroes are invoked, so traditions are connected with them[112] in the author's search for 'asserting for the Hasmonaeans prerogatives reserved to David's line in earlier Jewish tradition'.[113] Compositionally, David, the only king mentioned, is placed in the centre of the list of eleven 'generations' (cf. 2.61), the future of which depends on the initiative and faithfulness of the twelfth generation—namely, the Hasmonaeans. The initial goal of their fight is the liberation of Jerusalem, the restoration of its temple and cult and a return of the people scattered.

The situation, which leads up to the Hasmonaean revolt, is a period of increasing disloyalty and apostasy. The Seleucid king Antioch IV Epiphanes' (175–164 BCE), presented as 'a sinful root' (ῥίζα ἁμαρτωλὸς)[114]and former hostage in Rome (1.10),[115] is used as a chronological marker for that development,[116] albeit all kings from Alexander the Great onwards are characterized as wicked (1.1-9). Allying themselves with 'the Gentiles round about', 'lawless men'[117] of Israel got the consent of Antiochus to introduce gentile customs (1.11-15). Seemingly unaware of their loyalty, after a victorious campaign in Egypt, Antiochus in 169 BCE went up against Israel (ἀνέβη ἐπὶ Ἰσραηλ) and came to Jerusalem with a mighty army. He contemptuously (ἐν ὑπερηφανίᾳ, 1.21) pillaged the temple of its valuables, which

110. Goldstein, 'Biblical Promises and 1 and 2 Maccabees', p. 79.

111. Goldstein, 'Biblical Promises and 1 and 2 Maccabees', p. 79: 'they will be raised to high office under kings'. The text does not mention kings.

112. Goldstein, *I Maccabees*, pp. 6-8.

113. Goldstein, 'Biblical Promises and 1 and 2 Maccabees', pp. 79-80.

114. Dan. 11.7; its contrast, the 'root of Jesse' (Isa. 11.10).

115. As is also Seleucus IV's son Demetrius, legal claimant to the throne, who does not return before 162 BCE.

116. Antiochus IV's brother Seleucus IV Philopator reigns over the Seleucid empire from 187–175 BCE; cf. 2 Macc. 3.3–4.7, in which Seleucus is praised for his favours to the Temple of Jerusalem. V. Tcherikover, *Hellenistic Civilization and the Jews* (New York: Atheneum, 1975), p. 88.

117. παρανόμοι; cf. 1.11, 34; 10.61; 11.21; another term is ἄνομοι, which is used, for example, in 2.44; 3.5, 6; 7.5; 9.23, 58, 69; 11.25; 14.14. Both are primarily used as a characterization of apostate Israelites/Jews; see F.-M. Abel, *Les Livres des Maccabeés* (Paris: J. Gabalda, 1949), p. 17; Goldstein, *I Maccabees*, p. 129; Sievers, *Hasmoneans*, p. 18.

he brought back to his own country after having committed deeds of murder and having spoken arrogantly (1.20-24).[118] Two years later the king sent a chief collector of tribute, Appolonius, who attacked the city, plundered it, burned it with fire, tore down its houses and its walls, took its women and children captive and seized its cattle (1.29-32).[119] He then 'fortified the city of David with a strong wall and strong towers and it became their citadel' (*Akra*), in which 'a sinful people' (ἔθνος ἁμαρτωλόν), 'lawless men' (ἄνδρας παρανόμους), were stationed and spoils of Jerusalem stored (1.34-35). Shedding innocent blood about the temple and polluting it, they caused the inhabitants of Jerusalem to abandon the city (1.37-38).

Later, the king wrote to 'his whole kingdom' that they should be one people and each give up his customs (εἰς λαὸν ἕνα καὶ ἐγκαταλειπεῖν ἕκαστον τὰ νόμινα αὐτοῦ, 1.41-42). All the Gentiles followed the kings command (κατὰ τὸν λόγον τοῦ βασιλέως). Many even from Israel were pleased with the king's religion (εὐδόκησαν τῇ λατρείᾳ) and offered to the idols and profaned the Sabbaths (1.43). The king also sent to Jerusalem and Judah letters by messenger, directing them to follow 'customs strange to the land' (νομίνων ἀλλοτρίων τῆς γῆς, 1.44): to forbid burnt offerings, sacrifices and drink offerings in the sanctuary, to profane Sabbaths and feasts, to defile the sanctuary and the priests, to build altars and sacred precincts and shrines for idols, to sacrifice swine and unclean animals, and to leave their sons uncircumcised (1.45-48). In addition, on the fifteenth day of Chislev, in the one hundred and forty-fifth year, 'they' erected a desolating sacrilege upon the altar of burnt offering. They also built altars in the surrounding cities of Judah and burned incense at the doors of the houses and in the streets. They tore to pieces and burned with fire the books of the Law (τὰ βιβλία τοῦ νόμου, 1.54-56) which the found. On the twenty-fifth day of 'the month' they offered sacrifice on the altar of burnt offering. Resistance against the decrees were met with the death penalty (1.50, 60, 61, 63). 'And a very great wrath (ὀργὴ μεγάλη) came upon Israel' (1.64). The closure of the introduction is set in ambiguity. Does the text speak of human wrath, created by the disaster[120] or of divine wrath created, by the people's apostasy as in 2 Macc. 5.20? As the author relates that 'many in Israel stood firm' and 'chose to die' rather than profane the 'holy covenant' (1.62-63), the ambiguity relates a theological interpretation of his narrative's events, his invocation of tradition: violation leading to divine wrath, rather than history proper (cf. also 2.49 and 3.8).

The structure of the introduction, an increasing threat conveyed by a decreasing presence of the Seleucid administration, resembles the structure of 2 Kings' Hezekiah narrative, in which first King Sennacherib went up against Judah and,

118.   Goldstein, *I Maccabees*, p. 210: the campaigns of Assyrian kings (e.g. Isa. 10.5-27; Dan. 11.10) are applied by the author of 1 Maccabees to the campaigns of Seleucid kings, called kings of Syria (i.e. Assyria) (cf. Bickerman, *Institutions*, pp. 4-5; Th. Nöldeke, 'Assyrios, Syrios, Syros', *Hermes* 5 [1871], pp. 443-68). In the Dead Sea Scrolls we find the term Ashur used as a characterization of Antiochus (1QM 1.2, 6; 2.12; 11.11; 18.2; 19.10).

119.   2 Macc. 5.24 names this person Apollonius, governor of Coele-Syria (cf. 3.5; 4.4), whom Judas defeats (1 Macc. 3.11-12).

120.   For example, Mattathias' 'zeal and anger' (1 Macc. 2.24) in his imitation of Phinehas' 'zeal', which Phinehas shows on behalf of Yahweh's anger in Num. 25.11.

stationed in Lachish, received Hezekiah's payment, the gold and silver, which he had stripped off the temple and palace. Then the king sent his commander, his *Rabshaqeh*, and finally he sent letters by his messengers. While the Assyrians never went into the city, the Seleucids conquered the city and made it their garrison, from which 'they' carried out the king's decree.[121]

Similar to the biblical theme of 'Israelite apostasy', which, according to the opinion of the Prophets, spreads to Judah and to Jerusalem, the disaster begins in 1 Maccabees, when 'lawless people' of Israel ally themselves with the Gentiles. In 1 Macc. 2.15-18, the reader gets the impression that only Mattathias and his sons have resisted falling into apostasy. In the seductive speech of the 'king's officers', they tell Mattathias, who is called 'leader, honoured and great in this city' (Modeïn), that all the Gentiles, the Judaeans and 'those left in Jerusalem' have followed the king (2.17-18). Echoing the *Rabshaqeh*'s 'loud voice' of the Hezekiah narrative (2 Kgs 18.28), Mattathias, 'in a loud voice', put himself and his sons in contrast to the obedience of 'all the nations' to rebel (ἀποστῆναι) against their ancestral religion and follow the king's commandments:[122] 'yet I and my sons and my brothers will live by the covenant of our fathers (ἐν διαθήκῃ πατέρων ἡμῶν). Far be it from us to desert law and ordinances (νόμον καὶ δικαιώματα). We will not obey the king's words by turning aside from our religion to the right hand or to the left' (1 Macc. 2.19-22).[123] As the *Rabshaqeh* had offered the inhabitants of Jerusalem a prosperous future if they would renounce Hezekiah and Yahweh, the 'king's officers' offer Mattathias and his sons a prosperous future as the kings 'friends'[124] if they will follow the example of the Gentiles, the Judaeans and those left in Jerusalem (2.18). While in the Hezekiah narrative Jerusalem was a place of refuge, in 1 Maccabees, Mattathias and his followers, who have fled to the mountains (2.28)[125] and the desert (2.29), are pursued by the king's officers and troops *from* Jerusalem, the 'city of David' (2.31).

The narrative opening is thus not a defence of Jerusalem but a liberation of the city, from where disaster spreads over the country (2.35-36). Presented as a fight against foreigners, the opposition is as internal[126] as it is external, and 'civil war' is

---

121. For the historical importance of this event, see Tcherikover, *Hellenistic Civilization*, pp. 189-90: 'the severest that could be imposed on civilians'.

122. For an implicit reference to LXX Num. 13–14's rebellion narrative, see Goldstein, *I Maccabees*, p. 7.

123. Cf. Deut. 5.32; 28.14; Josh. 1.7; 2 Kgs 22.2; Isa. 30.21; Prov. 4.27.

124. Cf. also 2 Macc. 7.24.

125. According to Goldstein, *I Maccabees*, p. 7, the story recalls the similar act of David's flight to the mountains (1 Sam. 22.1-2; 23.14) and the massacre of innocents. In 1 Sam. 22.7-19 it is the priests of Nob who had given David bread and Goliath's sword and in 1 Macc. 2.29-38 it is those, who refuse to take arms on the Sabbath who are massacred. 1 Maccabees uses the 'event' as an 'excuse' for Mattathias and his friends' decision to make defensive war on the Sabbath (1 Macc. 2.40-41), in which they are joined also by the Ḥasidim (1 Macc. 2.42; 2 Macc. 14.6). In contrast, the author of 2 Maccabees makes a point of presenting Judas as strictly observing the Sabbath (2 Macc. 5.25-27; 6.11; 12.28; 15.1-5).

126. 1 Macc. 2.44-48; 7.5-25; 9.23-27; cf. Dan. 11.31-35. E.J. Bickerman, *Der Gott der Makkabäer. Untersuchung über Sinn und Ursprung der makkabäischen Erhebung* (Berlin: Schocken

an equally appropriate term for the narrative reality, most of which resolves around the sons of Antiochus III (223–187 BCE): Seleucus and Antiochus and their descendants' struggle for the throne.[127] Navigating between demands of loyalty towards these kings and their governors in order to maintain their own interests, the second-century Jews of 1 Maccabees were as exposed to the wills and whims of the occupation powers as their biblical ancestors had been. In addition to the Seleucids, the Jews also had Egypt, Rome and Sparta as their playmates.

The remnant created by Antiochus' oppression is but a reflex of the thousands of Israelites, who crossed the Jordan to conquer the Promised Land. Similar to the David narratives (1 Sam. 22.1-2), 1 Maccabees begins in disunity. Warriors with small armies (1 Macc. 2.42-44) fight against the enemies' great armies,[128] and end up receiving the recognition of 'the whole people' at the electing of Simon as high priest, commander and ethnarch of Judah (1 Macc. 13.8; 14.25-46). Since the elevation of Simon also implies an elevation of the role of Jerusalem-Zion's temple, we will give specific attention to this motif.

4. *1 Maccabees: Jerusalem-Zion vs. Antioch: Fighting the Seven-Headed Monster*[129]

At the advent of Antiochus IV, the western capital of the Seleucid Empire was Antioch of the Orontes, which at that time had become the third greatest city after Rome and Alexandria. As there existed, in fact, several *Antioch*s (for instance the coastal city *Acco*, named *Ptolemais* by Ptolemy II Philadelphus and *Antioch* by Antiochus IV,[130] and Jason's *Antiochene Polis* in Jerusalem),[131] the name has the potential of functioning in the books of Maccabees on several levels as a designation of Seleucid or Hellenist imperialism. It occurs seven times in 1 Maccabees[132] and seven (plus two) times in 2 Maccabees,[133] but rarely if at all in the apocryphal

Books, 1937), pp. 168-69; Tcherikover, *Hellenistic Civilisation*, pp. 190-92; Sievers, *Hasmoneans*, pp. 15-16.

127.   Seleucus' line held power: Seleucus IV (187–175); Demetrius I (162–150); Demetrius II (145–140 + 129–126); Antiochus VII, brother to Demetrius II (138–129). Antiochus' line held power: Antiochus IV (175–164); Antiochus V (+ Lysias) (164–162); Alexander Balas (150–145). Alexander's son Antiochus VI (145–142) got killed by Trypho, who claims himself king of the Seleucid empire (142–138); source, L.L. Grabbe, *Judaism from Cyrus to Hadrian* (2 vols.; Minneapolis: Fortress Press, 1992), II, pp. 624-26.

128.   E.g. 1 Macc. 3.10, 15; 4.30; 5.6, 38; 6.6, 41; 7.10, 27; 9.43, 60; 10.69, 73; 11.63; 12.24; 13.1, 12; 16.5.

129.   For the number seven as characterization of chaos and evil, see above Chapter 3, p. 132 n. 223. See also Chapter 2, pp. 42-43: the seven 'attacks' on Jerusalem in books of Kings; 1QM 11.9: 'the seven nations of futility'.

130.   Tcherikover, *Hellenistic Civilization*, p. 92.

131.   2 Macc. 4.9, 19: τοὺς ἐν Ἱεροσολύμοις Ἀντιοχεῖς; Hengel, *Judentum und Hellenismus*, pp. 505-507. The interpretation is disputed, see Goldstein, *I Maccabees*, pp. 11-16, who suggests that its meaning is related to citizenship and not to location, as Jerusalem never was named *Antioch*.

132.   1 Macc. 3.37; 4.35; 6.63; 10.68; 11.13, 44, 56.

133.   2 Macc. 4.33; 5.21; 8.35; 11.36; 13.23, 26; 14.27; plus 4.9, 19: the 'Antiochenes of Jerusalem'.

literature. As a symbol of power, the city's impotence in these writings is significant.

In 1 Maccabees, the first mention of the city (1 Macc. 3.37) involves Antiochus
IV's departure from Antioch to Persia to collect money for his war against the
growing threat from Judas and his brothers (3.25-28), who had already defeated the
'great army' of Apollonius, his governor (3.10-12) and the 'huge army' of Seron,
commander of the Syrian army (3.13-24).[134] While Judas took Apollonius' sword,
which he afterwards used in the battle (3.12),[135] Antiochus obviously had spent the
money and valuables taken from Jerusalem, without managing to get his troops into
war against the Jews (3.28-30). Antiochus IV is first defeated in Elymais in Persia,
where he was about to plunder the temple. When, having retreated to Babylon, he
furthermore learned about Lysias' defeat (cf. 4.28-35), he became ill, recalled the
evil he had done in Jerusalem and Judaea and died (6.1-16).

The second mention of the city refers to the retreat to Antioch by Lysias (4.35),
whom Antiochus had placed in charge of his affairs and with whom he had left half
of his army to go up to erase entirely Judaea, Jerusalem and the power of Israel
(3.32-35). During his retreat, Judas and his brothers went into Jerusalem-Zion,
cleansed the temple, and so on (4.36-61).

The third reference (6.63) recounts Lysias' second retreat to Antioch. The
narrative, with implicit allusion to the Hezekiah narrative, has Lysias laying siege
to Jerusalem after his conquest of Beth-Zur. He is stopped by 'hearing' (6.55) that
Philip is on his way from Persia and Media to take over power. He therefore
decides to make a peace treaty with the Jews (6.58-61). However, on his way out,
he breaks down the wall around the city (6.62). In Antioch, he and Antiochus V are
killed by Demetrius I Soter, who had just arrived from Rome (7.1-4).

The fourth mention of the city (10.63) is Alexander Balas' retreat to Antioch at
the advent of Demetrius II son of Demetrius I. This Demetrius instates Apollonius
as governor of Coele-Syria and sends him with a huge army against Jonathan and
Simon and is defeated (10.69-87).

The fifth reference (11.13) is Ptolemy VI's usurpation of the kingdom and his
crowning in Antioch as king over Egypt and Asia. At Alexander's return from
Cilicia to regain power, he is defeated and flees to Arabia, where he is killed
(11.14-17). When Ptolemy dies on the third day, Demetrius II is back in office.

The sixth reference to Antioch (11.44) is Jonathan's support of Demetrius
against Tryphon.[136] Arriving with 3000 soldiers, Jonathan liberates the king, who
has fled to the castle. Of the city's 120,000 inhabitants, the Jews kill 100,000, burn
the city, save the king, have the population surrender and return to Jerusalem with
great booty (11.44-51).

---

134. Eupolemus, *Praep. Ev.* 30.4: Sourun, king of Tyre and Phoenicia, whom David defeats,
might refer to Seron; see Mendels, *Land of Israel*, p. 36. The defeat took place in the narrow pass at
Beth-Horon, a suitable ambush site.

135. Cf. David's use of Goliath's sword (1 Sam. 17.51; 21.10; 22.10). For a comparison
of 1 Maccabees' sword motif with *1 En.* 89–90 and Zech. 9–10, see Goldstein, *I Maccabees*,
pp. 40-42, 96.

136. A general of Alexander Balas, according to 1 Macc. 11.39.

Jerusalem's Rise to Sovereignty

The seventh reference to Antioch in 1 Maccabees has Tryphon returning with Alexander Balas' young son, Antiochus V, who takes Antioch (11.56) and the kingship, after Demetrius' betrayal of Jonathan (11.52-56). Antiochus assigns Jonathan the high priestly office with royal prerogatives, and Simon the role as *strategus* for the area from Tyre to the border of Egypt (11.57-59). Tryphon later kills Antiochus in order to take the kingship himself (13.31-32). The story of the decline of Jonathan's power (12.39–13.23) has Ptolemais as the enemy's power base.

The seven tales in 2 Maccabees expose a similar pattern: Onias seeks refuge in Daphne near Antioch,[137] but is killed (2 Macc. 4.33). Antiochus IV brings treasures from Jerusalem's temple to Antioch (5.21). Nicanor flees to Antioch (8.35), while Judas celebrates victory in Jerusalem (10.1-9). The Romans go to Antioch (11.36) to negotiate to the advantage of the Jews, to whom Lysias and Antiochus V have 'surrendered'. Philip creates an insurrection in Antioch (13.23), causing Lysias to lift his siege of Beth-Zur and retreat to Antioch (13.26). Alcimus, who wanted the high priestly office for himself (14.3-13), urges Demetrius to request that Nicanor, who had appointed Judas as high priest (14.26), send Judas to Antioch as prisoner (14.26-27). Obedient to the king's order, Nicanor fails Judas, attacks him on a Sabbath, but gets killed (15.27-28). Judas returns victoriously to the temple in a Jerusalem, which 'since then has been in the power of the "Hebrews"' (15.28-37; cf. 7.31; 11.13).

The opposite of the story of the decline of Antioch is the narrative of the elevation of victimized Jerusalem-Zion, in which story 1 Maccabees joins the biblical lament over Jerusalem as victim.[138] At the beginning of the book, we find Jerusalem's temple pillaged of its cultic vessels and its decorations (1 Macc. 1.21-23). Our author laments the situation in the following words:[139]

> Israel mourned deeply in every community,
>   rulers and elders groaned,[140]
> young women and young men became faint,
>   the beauty of the women faded.[141]
> Every bridegroom took up the lament;
>   she who sat in the bridal chamber was mourning.[142]
> Even the land trembled for its inhabitants,
>   and all the house of Jacob was clothed with shame. (1.25-28)[143]

137. Nodet, *Origins of Judaism*, p. 206 n. 8: 'About 5 miles from Antioch. Daphne was renowned for its temple of Apollo and Artemis, founded by Seleucus I, in which the right of asylum was recognised (Strabo, *Geography* 16.2, 6)'.

138. The chosen references to biblical texts are thematically rather than linguistically motivated.

139. The following biblical quotations follow the NRSV.

140. Cf. Lam. 2.10.

141. Cf. Amos 8.13;

142. Cf. Jer. 7.34; 16.9; 25.10; Joel 1.8; 2.16; Ps. 78.63; Bar. 2.23.

143. Cf. Isa. 28.22; Lam. 1.17; Joel 2.6; Job 8.22; Pss. 35.26; 44.16.

Our next step finds a plundered and burned city, citizens led into captivity, foreigners settled in their place and a temple polluted (1.31-38).[144] Our author thus laments:

> for the citadel became an ambush against the sanctuary,
> an evil adversary[145] of Israel at all times.[146]
> On every side of the sanctuary they shed innocent blood;
> they even defiled the sanctuary.[147]
> Because of them the residents of Jerusalem fled;
> she became a dwelling of strangers;[148]
> she became strange to her offspring,
> and her children forsook her.[149]
> Her sanctuary became desolate like a desert;
> her feasts were turned into mourning,[150]
> her Sabbaths into a reproach,[151]
> her honour into contempt.
> Her dishonour now grew as great as her glory;
> her exaltation was turned into mourning. (1.36-40)[152]

Our third step finds a dethroned city and temple, replaced by a decentralization of the cult: the erection of altars, sacred precincts and shrines for idols (1.47, 54-55) and a standing order to the towns of Judah to offer sacrifice, town-by-town (1.51). Our author has Mattathias lament:

> Alas! Why was I born to see this,[153]
> the ruin of my people, the ruin of the holy city,[154]
> and to live there when it was given over to the enemy,
> the sanctuary given over to aliens?[155]
> Her temple has become like a person without honour;
> her glorious vessels have been carried into exile.[156]
> Her infants have been killed in her streets,
> her youths by the sword of the foe.[157]
> What nation has not inherited her palaces
> and has not seized her spoils?

---

144.   Cf. 2 Macc. 5.12-16; 6.1-6.
145.   εἰς διαβολον; cf. LXX Num. 22.32; 1 Chron. 21.1; Job 2.1.
146.   Cf. 1 Macc. 4.41; 6.18.
147.   Cf. Lam. 4.13-14; Ezek. 9.7; 2 Macc. 1.8; 6.2-6.
148.   Cf. Isa. 1.7-8; 2 Macc. 6.4.
149.   Cf. Isa. 27.10; Lam. 5.2-3; Amos 8.10.
150.   Cf. Lam. 1.4; 2 Macc. 6.6.
151.   Cf. Jer. 17.19-27; Lam. 2.6.
152.   Cf. Lam. 2.15-16; 5.1; 1 Macc. 1.38.
153.   Jer. 20.14-18; Job 3.3.
154.   Cf. Isa. 24.12; 64.9; Jer. 9.10; 26.18 par. Mic. 3.12; Neh. 2.3, 17. For the holy city, see Isa. 48.2; 52.1; Dan. 9.24; Neh. 11.1, 18; 2 Macc. 1.12; 3.1; 15.14; LXX Isa. 66.20.
155.   Cf. Jer. 51.51; Lam. 1.10; Ps. 74.3-4.
156.   Cf. 2 Kgs 24.13; 25.14-15; Joel 4.5; 2 Chron. 36.7, 18; 2 Macc. 5.15-16.
157.   Cf. 2 Chron. 36.17; Lam. 2.21-22; 2 Macc. 5.13.

> All her adornment has been taken away;
>   no longer free, she has become a slave.[158]
> And see, our holy place, our beauty,
>   and our glory have been laid waste;
> the Gentiles have profaned them.[159]
>   Why should we live any longer? (2.7-13)

The way to restitution goes through a removal of the decentralized idolatrous cult (2.45; cf. 3.8) and a forced implementation of the Law (2.46-48). This causes Antiochus to send Lysias with an army 'against them to wipe out and destroy the strength of Israel and the remnant of Jerusalem. He was to banish the memory of them from the place, settle aliens in all their territory and distribute their land by lot' (3.35-36).[160] The threat causes our author to lament:

> Jerusalem was uninhabited like a wilderness;[161]
>   not one of her children went in or out.[162]
> The sanctuary was trampled down,[163]
>   and aliens held the citadel;
>   it was a lodging place for the Gentiles.[164]
> Joy was taken from Jacob;
>   the flute and the harp ceased to play. (3.45)[165]

From Mizpah Judas and his people cry to the Heaven:

> What shall we do with these?
>   Where shall we take them?[166]
> Your sanctuary is trampled down and profaned,
>   and your priests mourn in humiliation.[167]
> Here the Gentiles are assembled against us to destroy us;
>   you know what they plot against us.[168]
> How will we be able to withstand them,
>   if you do not help us? (3.50-53)

In succeeding battles with increasing threats, Judas' final 'David–Goliath battle' (4.28-35) causes Lysias to retreat to Antioch to hire mercenaries after the defeat of his army, while Judas and his brothers declare:

---

158.   Cf. Jer. 7.30; Lam. 1.3; 2 Macc. 5.14.

159.   Cf. Ps. 79.1, 7.

160.   Cf. 1 Macc. 3.58: 'these Gentiles, who have assembled against us to destroy us and our sanctuary'; Joel. 4.2.

161.   Cf. Isa. 27.10.

162.   Cf. Jer. 33.10, 12.

163.   Cf. Isa. 63.18; Ps. 79.1.

164.   Cf. Dan. 11.31; Isa. 25.2; Zech. 9.11-12.

165.   Cf. Isa. 24.11; Lam. 5.14-15.

166.   That is, the garments of the priesthood, the first fruits, the tithes, and the 'Nazirithes who had completed their days (1 Macc. 3.48; cf. Num. 6.1-21 [13-20]).

167.   Cf. Joel 1.9, 13.

168.   Cf. Ps. 83.3-5.

Behold, our enemies are crushed; let us go up to cleanse the sanctuary and dedicate it. (4.36)

So, all the army assembled and they went up to Mt Zion (εἰς ὄρος Ζιων). There they saw the sanctuary desolate, the altar profaned, and the gates burned.[169] In the courts they saw bushes sprung up as in a thicket, or as on one of the mountains.[170] They saw also the chambers of the priests in ruins (4.36-38).

Similar to the introduction of the name 'Zion' in Samuel and Chronicles' narrative about David's conquest of Jerusalem and its 'stronghold' (2 Sam. 5.7; 1 Chron. 11.5) which anticipate the building of the temple (2 Sam. 5.8), our author too has his first mention of Zion at the time that the temple is liberated (1 Macc. 4.41).[171] The citadel (ἄκρα), however, is still in the hands of enemies. The cleansing of the temple and its rededication have close parallels to Hezekiah's reform in 2 Chron. 28.22–30.27,[172] and is reminiscent only of Solomon's dedication of the first temple (2 Chron. 7.1-10).[173]

Following this event, Judas and his brothers, in yet another imitation of Hezekiah, fortify Mt Zion with high walls and strong towers (1 Macc. 4.60; cf. 2 Chron. 32.5). They furthermore fortify Beth-Zur (4.61) on the Idumaean border, a place which plays the role of Lachish in 1 Maccabees 6–7's second variant of the Hezekiah narrative.

Since the temple area is in the hands of the Jews, its role as protection is our author's next concern. First, Judas, Jonathan and Simon attack the 'sons of Esau in Idumaea of the Akrabattene'[174] (5.3), the Baianites[175] (5.4-5) and the Ammonites (6.6-8). Then they liberate their brothers from Galilaea and Gilead and bring them to Zion (5.9-54). Finally, they go against the 'sons of Esau' in the south, where they conquer Hebron and its small hamlets (5.65). The reason for the conquests and liberation campaigns is the Gentiles' attack on the people of Jacob (τὸ γένος Ιακωβ) living among them, whom they began to kill and uproot (ἐξαίρειν) when they heard that the altar had been rebuilt and the temple restored (5.1-2, 9-15, 25-27).[176] The

169. Cf. Ps. 74.7-8.
170. Cf. Ps. 74.5-8; Isa. 32.13-14.
171. Other occurrences of Zion are 1 Macc. 4.60; 5.54; 6.48, 62; 7.33; 10.11; 14.26.
172. Goldstein, *I Maccabees*, p. 278. Cf. also 2 Chron. 33.15-16: Manasseh's temple cleansing.
173. Against Sievers, *Hasmoneans*, p. 47, who says the parallels are 'indeed striking'.
174. Abel, *Maccabées*, p. 89, see this as the ascent of Akrabbim, southwest of the Dead Sea. Goldstein, *I Maccabees*, p. 294, thinks it is probable that the reference is to the toparchy north of Judaea (cf. Josephus, *War* 2.234-35, 568, 652; 3.48; 4.504, 511, 551; *Ant.* 12.328), which at Judas' time was part of 'Samareitis' (cf. Josephus, *War* 3.48; 1 Macc. 10.33; 11.34), and 'evidently' had a considerable settlement of Idumaeans. The main territory of Idumaea is described in 1 Macc. 5.65 as the fight against 'sons of Esau in the land, which lays to the south'.
175. Abel, *Maccabées*, p. 90, wonders whether this is a reference to a semi-nomadic tribe near Jericho?; Goldstein, *I Maccabees*, pp. 294-95, considers that the text bears reminiscences of 1 Sam. 15.2-3 and Exod. 17.14's passages on the Amalekites. Amalek was a descendant of Esau (Gen. 36.12), and the parallel account in 2 Macc. 10.15-23 calls the enemy besieged in the towers 'Idumaeans'. The text might be reflective of a 'fulfilment of the prophecy at Num. 24.18-19': first Israel crushes Edom and then Seir.
176. Cf. Ezra 4 and Neh. 4 for similar animosities and Jerusalem as a place of refuge.

success of the Hasmonaeans is contrasted to the failure of Joseph son of Zechariah,[177] and Azariah,[178] who, imitating 'the Israelites' of Num. 14.40-45,[179] suffer a heavy defeat (5.55-64), as Israel and the Elides of 1 Sam. 4.10, 17, also did, which language our author borrows.[180] When Judas and his brothers later break up to go to the land of the Philistines, they go through Marisa.[181] In those days, also some 'priests who wished to do a brave deed, fell in battle, for they went out to do battle unwisely' (5.67), our author states, without closer identification.[182] The Philistines, they conquer in Azotus.

The entire chapter is an elaborate 'fulfilment' of Obadiah's glorification of Mt Zion, at which time

> Those of the Negeb shall possess Mt Esau,
> > those in the Shephelah the land of the Philistines,
> they shall possess the land of Ephraim and the land of Samaria,
> > and Benjamin[183] (shall possess) Gilead.
> The exiles of the Israelites who are in Halah
> > shall possess Phoenicia as far as Zarephath;
> and the exiles of Jerusalem who are in Sepharad
> > shall possess the towns of Negeb.
> And the saviours[184] shall go up to[185] Mt Zion to judge Mt Esau;[186]
> > and the kingdom shall be Yahweh's. (Obad. 19-21)[187]

---

177. In 2 Macc. 8.22 he is a brother of Judas.

178. Might be the Eleazar mentioned in 1 Macc. 2.5 and 2 Macc. 8.23, identical with the Esdris mentioned in 12.36; cf. Goldstein, *I Maccabees*, p. 80.

179. Goldstein, *I Maccabees*, p. 304.

180. Goldstein, *I Maccabees*, p. 305.

181. Some manuscripts read Samaria. The placename occurs in Josephus (*Ant.* 13.353) as a city burned by Judas; as one of the Idumaean cities John Hyrcanus took (*Ant.* 13.257 and *War* 2.63); as one reason for John Hyrcanus' siege of Samaria that 'he was full of resentment against the Samaritans, because of all the harm they had done at the instigation of the kings of Syria to the people of Marisa, colonists stemming from the Jews and allied with them' (*Ant.* 13.275).

182. The verse is not in Josephus.

183. NRSV; it might be 'the land of Ammonites', or the area of Benjamin as in the LXX. Both verses have some text-critical difficulties and might have been redacted in order to fit other traditions.

184. Hiphil active participle, which the LXX translates as if it were a niphal or a passive form of the participle: 'those who have been saved'.

185. LXX ἐξ ὄρος.

186. In the MT, only in the book of Obadiah (vv. 8, 9, 19, 21); Mt Seir as the land of Esau is found in Gen. 36.8, 9; Deut. 1.2; 2.1, 5; Josh. 24.4; as part of the tribe of Simeon inhabits Mt Seir in 1 Chron. 4.42-43. Further references: Ezek. 35.2, 3, 7, 15; 2 Chron. 20.10, 22, 23; Sir. 50.26's 'Mt Seir' in some Greek manuscripts is called 'Mt Samaria'.

187. Cf. Ps. 60.8-10; Ezek. 25–28; 35. For the 'Deuteronomistic historian's' hostility against Edom as reflected in Gen. 25–33 and Num. 20, contrasting Deut. 2 and 23's 'deliberately' toning down this tradition, see J.R. Bartlett, 'Edom in the Nonprophetical Corpus', in D.V. Edelman (ed.), *You Shall Not Abhor an Edomite for He is Your Brother: Edom and Seir in History and Tradition* (Archaeology and Biblical Studies, 3; Atlanta: Scholars Press, 1995), pp. 13-21.

The regions are more or less identical with the regions from which Asa brings converts to Jerusalem—'Judah, Benjamin, Ephraim, Manasseh and Simeon' (2 Chron. 15.9-10)—and Josiah cleanses—'Judah and Jerusalem and 'also the towns of Manasseh, Ephraim, Simeon and Naphtali' (2 Chron. 34.5-6).[188] None of these kings conquered the areas. Framing the liberation narratives with attacks on 'sons of Esau' (1 Macc. 5.3, 65),[189] the author of 1 Maccabees has placed himself in the traditions of the books of Obadiah (16-17) and Isaiah (chs. 34 and 63), both of which view Edom's destruction 'as the indispensable prelude to Israel's restoration'.[190] Just as Edom functions antithetically as a symbol 'of the wider process of universal destruction' to apocalyptic 'Israel's triumphant return to Zion',[191] 1 Maccabees' 'creation' of a haven in Judaea and Zion to which Judas and his brothers can return (1 Macc. 5.8, 23, 53-54, 68)[192] anticipates the demonstration of sovereignty, which is our author's goal.

In the inviolability narratives of 1 Maccabees 6 and 7, Jerusalem's protective force is put to a test. Since Antiochus IV's deathbed repentance (1 Macc. 6.11-13) brings no change to the conditions of the Jews[193] and the men in the citadel are still harming them, Judas decides to besiege the citadel (6.19). This act causes King Antiochus V Eupator to assemble 'all his friends, the commanders over his forces and those over his reins (i.e. cavalry, elephant troops). In addition, mercenary forces came to him from other kingdoms and from the islands of the sea (i.e. the Mediterranean)' (6.28-29), so the number of his forces is 100,000 foot soldiers, 20,000 horsemen and 32 elephants. No wonder that the author of 2 Maccabees (almost doubling the number, 2 Macc. 13.2) has Judas and his men 'weeping, fasting and lying prostrate for three days' (13.12).[194] Taking the road through Idumea, Antiochus first lays siege to Beth-Zur, which is not able to withstand the siege, but surrenders, leaving the fortress in the hands of the Seleucids (1 Macc. 6.31-49). Thereafter, he goes up against Jerusalem, Judaea and Mt Zion (6.48). The siege is strong, the famine severe, 'because it was the sabbatical year when the land had been left fallow',[195] and people begin to leave the sanctuary (6.51-54). However, just as the *Rabshaqeh* of the Hezekiah narrative 'heard', so Lysias 'heard that Philip, whom king Antiochus [IV], while still living, had appointed to raise up

188. Cf. also Jer. 32.44; 33.13, which refer to the towns of the hill country, the towns of the Shephelah, the towns of the Negeb, the land of Benjamin, the surroundings of Jerusalem and the towns of Judah.

189. Cf. also 2 Macc. 10.14-18; Jdt. 7.8, 18, which have Idumaeans siding with the Seleucids/Assyrians against the Jews/Israel.

190. B. Glazier-McDonald, 'Edom in the Prophetical Corpus', in Edelman (ed.), *You Shall Not Abhor*, pp. 23-32 (31).

191. Glazier-McDonald, 'Edom in the Prophetical Corpus', p. 32.

192. Cf. also Amos 9.11-15, and note the similar role of Gilgal in Josh. 10.

193. Cf. the discrepancy between the authors of 1 and 2 Maccabees' description of Antiochus' promises and the letter he sends to the Jews in recommendation of his son Antiochus (V Eupator) as his successor (2 Macc. 9.19-27).

194. Cf. also Jdt. 4.9-15; 2 Chron. 20.3-13, 18.

195. Cf. Lev. 25.4-7, 20-21; Isa. 37.30.

Antiochus his son to be king, had returned from Persia and Media with the forces that had gone with the king (6.55-56).[196] The purpose of his return is not to aid Antiochus in the battle, but to take over the government himself. Lysias then gives orders to depart, advising 'the king, the commanders of the forces and the men' to 'make peace with them [the Jews] and with all their nation, and agree to let them live by their laws as they did before' (6.58-59). Having agreed to the peace offer, the Jews lift the siege of the citadel. Bittersweet as is also this 'victory', the king, entering Zion, gives 'orders to tear down the wall all around' (6.62; cf. 4.60).[197] Imitating the Hezekiah narrative's anticipation of the Babylonian conquest, our author, alluding to the tearing down of Jerusalem's walls by the Chaldaeans (2 Kgs 25.10; cf. 2 Chron. 36.19), anticipates the setback to Jewish fortunes (7.8-22) and the defeat of Judas (1 Macc. 9).

Returning to Antioch, the king fights against Philip and 'he took the city by force' (6.63). So much for the might of Antioch and the troops of Antiochus IV, which had once been mustered in order to sustain Jewish attacks when needed (3.27-28). As the real threat against Sennacherib was not the Egyptians, but his own sons, who 'struck him down by the sword' in his own temple in Niniveh (Isa. 37.37-38), so also our author has Antiochus V and Lysias killed in their castle in Antioch by the hand of the next claimant to the throne, Antiochus' cousin Demetrius (I Soter), who had been taken hostage to Rome at the death of his father Seleuchus IV (7.1-2).[198]

After the advent of Demetrius, 'all the lawless and ungodly men of Israel' came to him led by Alcimus, who wanted to be high priest' (7.5).[199] Their complaint over Judas and his brothers leads the king to send an army into the land of Judaea by the hand of Bacchides, governor of the province Beyond the River (7.6-10). While Judas and his brothers pay no attention to the 'peaceable and treacherous words' brought by messengers of Bacchides, who had come with 'a large force' (7.10-11), the Ḥasidim are easily persuaded to join a peace treaty when these same words are spoken by Alcimus, 'a priest of the line of Aaron',[200] who had come with the army (7.12-16). Treacherous as Alcimus' promises were—he had sixty men of the Ḥasidim slain 'in one day' (7.16)—Bacchides, camping in Beth-zaith,[201] has sup-

---

196.   Cf. 1 Macc. 3.37. 2 Macc. 13.23 has Philip 'left in charge of the government' revolt in Antioch.

197.   2 Macc. 13.23-24, which presents Judas in a more victorious role (2 Macc. 13.22; cf. 1 Macc. 6.47), offers an almost opposite picture: the king 'yielded and swore to observe all their [i.e. the Jews] rights, settled with them and offered sacrifice, honoured the sanctuary and showed generosity to the holy place. He received Maccabaeus.'

198.   1 Macc. 7.1: 151 Sel. year = 162/161 BCE. 2 Macc. 14.1 has 'three years later'.

199.   Cf. 2 Macc. 14.3: 'who had formerly been high priest, but had defiled himself'.

200.   No further details about his ancestry is given and the reference to the 'seed of Aaron', is intentionally bringing the qualification of the Hasmonaeans for the priesthood on a par with Alcimus, whose Oniad relationship might have been obscured (cf. Sievers, *Hasmoneans*, pp. 63-64). For a discussion of Josephus' conflicting explanations, see Hjelm, *Samaritans and Early Judaism*, pp. 169-70.

201.   Beth-zaith might have been situated 3 miles north of Beth-zur, or might have been Bezetha, north of the temple area in Jerusalem.

porters of the Hasmonaens killed and cast into the 'great cistern', while the land is given over to Alcimus, who is left with 'a force' to help him (7.20).

Here, the narrative plot resumes patterns of previous chapters: Judas, when seeing 'all the evil Alcimus and those with him had done', went out into all the surrounding parts of Judaea, and took vengeance on the men who had deserted (7.23-24; cf. 2.44; 3.5, 8). Alcimus, when seeing 'that Judas and those with him had grown strong', returned to blame the king (7.25). The king then sent Nicanor, 'one of his honoured princes, who hated and detested Israel and he commanded him to destroy the people' (7.25-26; cf. 3.32-34). When Nicanor, coming to Jerusalem with a great army, fails to capture Judas, he has 500 of his men slain by Judas in Caphar-salama, while the rest flee to 'the city of David' (7.27-31; cf. 4.34-35). Here, he goes up to Mt Zion, where he mocks, defiles and threatens the priests, swearing to burn down the temple when he returns, if they do not hand over 'Judas and his army' (7.33-35). Contrasting Alcimus' blaming of the king, the priests cry and pray to God in a prayer, which implies 2 Macc. 14.33's threat of replacing the temple with a temple for Dionysus: 'Thou didst choose this house to be called by thy name[202] and to be for thy people a house of prayer and supplication. Take vengeance on this man and on his army, and let them fall by the sword; remember their blasphemies and let them live no longer' (1 Macc. 7.37-38). Nicanor, camping in Beth-horon, is joined by an army from Syria, while Judas, camping in Adasa with his 3000 men, once again faces a David–Goliath dilemma, this time in the image of Hezekiah's blaspheming Assyrian king with his 185,000 men 'struck down' by the angel (7.39-41; cf. 4.29-33; 2 Macc. 15.22-24). As Nicanor had spoken wickedly against the sanctuary, he is the first to face a dishonourable death,[203] causing his entire army to fall 'by the sword (cf. 7.38); not even one of them was left' (7.43-47; cf. 2 Macc. 15.28-35). As Yahweh's destruction of the Assyrian army led to peace for a time, so the land of Judah now had peace for a 'few days' (7.59).

In a further reiteration of biblical narrative, our author has Rome take on Babylonia's role as supporter of the Jewish people (1 Macc. 8). As in the biblical narrative, in which Babylonia never directly supported Judah but got access to the king's treasures,[204] so, in 1 Maccabees, Rome's support of 'the Jewish people' is presented as indirect (8.27-32; 15.15-24), costly (1 Macc. 14.24; 15.18) and worthless (9.1ff.; 12.24ff.; 15.25ff.). Our author implicitly argues that it was not Rome that was the cause of the Hasmonaean victory. Neither was Rome able to prevent that Demetrius, when he had heard that Nicanor and his troops had fallen, again sent Bacchides (and Alcimus) to the land of Judaea (9.1).[205] Here, he defeats and kills Judas (9.2-17) in a war, which once again plays with the David–Goliath motif, but has

---

202. Cf. 1 Kgs 8.29, 43; 9.3; also 2 Macc. 6.2.
203. He has his head and right hand cut off and displayed outside of Jerusalem; cf. 2 Macc. 15.32-35; variants 1 Sam. 17.54; 31.8-10; Jdt. 14.11.
204. Isa. 39.1-2, 5; cf. also Ahaz' 'bad luck' with the Assyrians in 2 Chron. 28.16-21.
205. Sievers, *Hasmoneans*, p. 69: 'As is well known, however, the treaty had no immediate consequences. Demetrius' policy of aiming at full control of Judea did not change appreciably, except that perhaps he intensified his efforts.'

Judas, challenging his fate (9.10), presented in the image of a doubting Saul[206] rather than a victorious Joshua or David. As the deaths of Saul and his sons mark a setback to Israelite fortune with the Philistines returning to their areas (1 Sam. 31.7; 1 Chron. 10.7), so the death of Judas[207] leads to an increase in the power of his enemies and gives godless control of the land (9.23-27), while Jonathan, his brother Simon and their supporters flee to the desert. The situation makes our author state that 'a great distress (θλῖψις μεγάλη)[208] came upon Israel, as had not been seen since the time that prophets ceased to appear among them' (9.27).[209]

The scene leaves something for Jonathan and Simon to do, when, in yet another reiteration of previous themes, Bacchides attacks Jonathan and his people on the banks of the Jordan on a Sabbath day (9.34, 43; cf. 2.32-38). With Bacchides' army in front and the water of the Jordan behind, Jonathan's failed attempt to strike Bacchides forces him and his people to escape by crossing the Jordan, while the enemy gives up pursuing them (9.45-48). The situation for Judaea and Jerusalem reiterates the pre-Judas situation, this time with Bacchides and Alcimus as actors. Alcimus' attempt to tear down the wall of the inner court of the sanctuary, opening it to defilement, rewards him with a painful death (9.55-56), as also Antiochus IV (6.12-13; cf. 2 Macc. 9.7-23) and Nicanor's (1 Macc. 7.42-47) defilement of the temple had done to them.

Having no further interest in the affair, Bacchides returns to the king. The land has peace for two years (1 Macc. 9.57) until 'lawless men' persuade Bacchides to return with a great army (9.58), for the defeat of which they themselves are blamed (9.68-69). Jonathan makes a peace agreement with Bacchides, causing the sword to rest in Israel. Judging the people from Michmas, he makes the ungodly (ἀσεβεῖς)[210] disappear from Israel (9.70-73) as Judas also had done (3.8).

This peaceful interim is short. At the advent of Alexander Epiphanes (153/152 BCE) son of Antiochus IV,[211] as claimant to the throne (10.1), Demetrius seeks to make a treaty with Jonathan, who moves to Jerusalem, fortifies the city and the walls around Mt Zion (10.10-11). The foreigners leave the fortresses, which Bacchides had taken (cf. 9.50-52), but they continue to stay in Beth-zur, which had

---

206. 1 Macc. 9.2, 19-21; cf. 1 Sam. 13.8-12; 2 Sam. 1.4, 19; 1 Chron. 10.13-14. 1 Sam. 13.3-5 opens with the Philistines learning that Jonathan had slain the governor of the Philistines, Saul's muster of his armies in Gilgal and the Philistine attack.

207. Lamented in words imitating David's lament of Saul and Jonathan (1 Macc. 9.21; cf. 2 Sam. 1.19).

208. Cf. Neh. 9.37, the only appearance of this construction in the LXX; θλῖψις and its cognates appear 135 times in the LXX.

209. Cf. 1 Macc. 12.13; Isa. 30.20; Dan. 12.1. Josephus (*Ant.* 13.5) 'calls it the greatest calamity since the return from Babylon' (cf. Sievers, *Hasmoneans*, p. 73). 2 Macc. 2.1-8 seems to imply that Jeremiah is meant.

210. The term probably refers to the foreigners as in 3.15. When referring to the ungodly of Israel, the author makes specific note thereof (e.g. 6.21; 7.5, 9); 9.25's parallel to 3.8, however, is unclear.

211. Alexander I Epiphanes (= Alexander Balas), who posed as son of Antiochus and reigned by the recognition of the Roman senate.

become a refuge for those, 'who had forsaken the law and the commandments' (10.12-14). Outbidding Demetrius, Alexander offers Jonathan the high priesthood and royal privileges (10.15-21), which forces Demetrius to raise his stakes to utopian levels of reimbursement: tax exemption, land addition, control over the citadel, release of hostages, observation of appointed days, gifts for the temple and priests, use of the temple as asylum, repairs of the temple, of Jerusalem's walls and of the fortress walls in Judaea (10.22-45). The offer makes no impression on Jonathan and the people, who side with Alexander in his successful fight against Demetrius, who is killed (10.46-50). As in all good fairy tales, they lived happily ever after, even with Egypt's King Ptolemy, who gives (150 BCE) his daughter Cleopatra to Alexander in Ptolemais (10.51-58), at which event Jonathan receives great honour as the king's 'friend' and appointed general and governor of the province (10.59-65). The protest of the 'lawless' Israelites is overruled (10.61, 63-64).

Also this peace and happiness are short lived, as Demetrius' son appears on the scene three years later (148/147 BCE). Alexander flees to Antioch and Jonathan is left alone with Apollonius, whom Demetrius has appointed governor of Coele-Syria. Namesake of the Apollonius whom Judas had killed (3.10-12), he too suffers a great defeat at the hands of Simon and Jonathan, the latter receiving great honour from King Alexander (10.70-89). King Ptolemy, taking advantage of the situation, makes himself master of the coastal cities with the intention to take the kingdom from Alexander, his son-in law. As we saw above, both die one after the other and Demetrius II Nicator becomes king in 145 BCE (11.1-19). This Demetrius allies himself with Jonathan and makes effective several of the privileges to the Jewish people (11.26-37), which his father had previously offered to Jonathan. The protest of 'lawless' men of the Jewish people is overruled (11.25-26). In return, Jonathan supports Demetrius against Tryphon in Antioch. The Jews kill 100,000 of the 120,000 citizens,[212] who had gathered to kill the king. They burn the city, and receive great honour and spoil to bring back to Jerusalem (11.39-51). Deceitful as also his father had been, Demetrius afterwards fails Jonathan (11.52-53).

When Tryphon returns to put Antiochus VI son of Alexander, on the throne, Antiochus assigns Jonathan the high priestly office and royal prerogatives, and Simon the role as *strategus* for the area from Tyre to the border of Egypt (11.57-59). In return, Jonathan and Simon, supported by Syrian troops, fight against Demetrius II, who is not defeated (11.60-74). Neither was Demetrius I defeated in a similar narrative setting. Reiterating the course of events, our author has Jonathan renewing friendship with Rome (and Sparta; 12.1-23; cf. 8.1-32). Just as Demetrius I had heard and sent troops against Judaea (9.1), Jonathan hears that Demetrius II has returned with an even greater army (12.24). While Judas' battle with Demetrius I's general Bacchides had resulted in his (Judas) defeat and death (9.18), Jonathan and Simon's second fight with Demetrius II are victorious (12.25-38). Jonathan's real enemy, however, is Tryphon, who, attempting to take the kingship from Antiochus (12.39-40), deceptively captures Jonathan in Ptolemais and drives his people back

212.   Cf. the 100,000 + 20,000 soldiers Antiochus V Eupator and Lysias brought against Beth-zur and Jerusalem (1 Macc. 6.30).

to Jerusalem (12.39-51). As Ptolemais had been Jonathan's place of honour, it now becomes his place of disgrace. So much for friendship with Rome.

5. *1 Maccabees: Utopia's Realization?*

Our third hero, Simon, faces a situation resembling former transitional periods. Without a leader, Israel is threatened by 'the nations round about them', a mighty army on its doorstep and a people filled with fear (12.53–13.9). This time, however, Simon and Absalom son of Jonathan, march out *from* Jerusalem, which they have fortified, to fight the nations, who 'have gathered together out of hatred to destroy' them (13.6, 10-11). They do not defeat Tryphon, who comes from Ptolemais with a great army, and with Jonathan as hostage and bargaining chip, but facing difficulties,[213] Tryphon kills Jonathan on his way to Gilead and retreats to 'his country' where he kills Antiochus and makes himself king (13.32). Simon fortifies the fortresses in Judaea and allies himself with Demetrius, whose weakness makes possible a great diplomatic victory (13.33-40). The Jews are freed for the first time from 'the yoke of the Gentiles' in 143–142 BCE (13.41), in which year the people began to write in their documents and contracts, 'In the first year of Simon the great high priest and commander and leader of the Jews' (13.42). Now it is time to be gracious towards the inhabitants of Gezer and those in the citadel, whom he spares, which David had not (2 Sam. 5.8). Having forced them to leave, he and his own family settle therein (13.43-53),[214] as David had also done (2 Sam. 5.9).

As Media and Persia had been Antiochus IV's fate, it also becomes Demetrius II's, when he brings his troops there to 'secure help' for his war against Tryphon. Imprisoned by Arsaces king of Persia in 139 BCE (from which he is not to leave before 129), Judaea has peace in Simon's lifetime (14.4).

The period which follows is best characterized as the peaceful reign of a victorious and righteous Davidic–Solomonic–Hezekian king, fulfilling expectations of enlarging the country (14.5-6), cleansing it from internal and external enemies (14.7, 13, 14), bringing home captives (14.7), making the land fruitful (14.8) and peaceful (14.1, 8, 11-13) (re-)establishing joy (14.11), law (14.14) and the temple cult (14.15):[215]

> The land had rest all the days of Simon.[216]
> He sought the good of his nation;[217]

213.   Resistance and snow (1 Macc. 13.20-22); cf. Ps. 68.15.

214.   Josephus, *War* 1.50: 'He also got the garrison under and demolished the citadel'; cf. *Ant.* 13.215-17, which says that Simon demolished the citadel and levelled the mountain, after which the temple was the highest of all the buildings.

215.   The poem has the form of a classic victory hymn known from a variety of ancient Near Eastern texts, praising the deeds of the sovereign; cf. Thompson, 'Holy War at the Center of Biblical Theology'; Hjelm and Thompson, 'The Victory Song of Merneptah'; Thompson, 'A Testimony of the Good King' (forthcoming); *idem*, in *The Messiah Myth: The Near Eastern Roots of Jesus and David* (New York: Basic Books; London: Jonathan Cape, forthcoming).

216.   Cf. 1 Kgs 5.5: Solomon; 2 Kgs 20.19 and Isa. 39.8: Hezekiah; 2 Macc. 3.1: Onias.

217.   Cf. the characterization of Onias in 2 Macc. 4.5.

his rule was pleasing to them,
  as was the honour shown him, all his days.[218]
To crown all his honours he took Joppa for a harbour,
  and opened a way to the isles of the sea.
He extended the borders of his nation,
  and gained full control of the country.
He gathered a host of captives;[219]
  he ruled over Gazara and Beth-zur and the citadel,
and he removed its uncleanness from it;[220]
  and there was none to oppose him.[221]
They tilled their land in peace;
  the ground gave its increase,
  and the trees of the plains their fruit.[222]
Old men sat in the streets;[223]
  they all talked together of good things,
  and the youths put on splendid military attire.
He supplied the towns with food,
  and furnished them with the means of defence (ἐν σκεύεσιν ὀχυρώσεως),[224]
  until his renown spread to the ends of the earth.
He established peace in the land,
  and Israel rejoiced with great joy.[225]
All the people sat under their own vines and fig trees,[226]
  and there was none to make them afraid.[227]
No one was left in the land to fight them,
  and the kings were crushed in those days.[228]
He gave help to all the humble (τοὺς ταπεινοὺς) among his people;[229]
  he sought out the law,[230]

218. Cf. 1 Kgs 5.14; 2 Chron. 32.32; Sir. 47.6
219. Cf. Jer. 23.8; Ezek. 28.25; 34.13; 36.24; Mic. 4.4.
220. For the parallels of the cleansing of the *Akra* (1 Macc. 13) with the cleansing of the temple (1 Macc. 4), showing Simon as the worthy successor of his brother Judas, whom he surpasses, see Sievers, *Hasmoneans*, pp. 114-15.
221. Cf. 2 Sam. 7.11.
222. Cf. Lev. 25.18; 26.5; Isa. 1.19; Ezek. 28.25-26; 34.27; 36.30; Amos 9.14.
223. Cf. Zech. 4.4.
224. 1 Macc. 13.33; cf. 10.11; 13.10, 52; 14.37; cf. the fortified towns of Solomon (2 Chron. 8.1-6); of Rehabeam (2 Chron. 11.5-12); of Asa (2 Chron. 14.5-7); of Jehoshaphat (2 Chron. 17.12-13); of Uzziah (2 Chron. 9–10); of Jotam (2 Chron. 27.4); of Hezekiah (2 Chron. 32.28-29); Isa. 22.10; Ezek. 36.35.
225. Cf. Isa. 9.2, 6; 49.13; 66.10.
226. Cf. 1 Kgs 5.5; Jer. 23.6; 33.16; 49.38; Mic. 4.4; Zech. 3.10.
227. Cf. 2 Sam. 7.10-11.
228. Cf. Ps. 2's 'coronation' hymn for the king on Zion; see also Pss. 68.13-15; 105.14; 135.10; 136.17-18; 149.8; Isa. 14.9-10; 41.2
229. The 'poor-man's song' is a standard element of victory hymns; cf. Ps. 72.4, 12-14; Isa. 11.4; 49.9, 13; 66.2. See T.L. Thompson, 'Jerusalem as the City of God's Kingdom: Common Tropes in the Bible and the Ancient Near East', in S. Khadra Jayyusi (ed.), *Islamic Studies: Special Issue on Jerusalem* 40/3-4 (2001), pp. 631-47, and *The Messiah Myth*.
230. Cf. 2 Chron. 31.4: Hezekiah; 36.26: Josiah.

and did away with all the renegades and outlaws (ἄνομον και πονηρόν).[231]
He made the sanctuary glorious,
and added to the vessels of the sanctuary.[232]

While the peace of the classic victory song is eternal, this song celebrates peace in
Simon's lifetime only. The paradise-like land with plenty of food is prepared for
war as the young put on 'splendid military attire', the towns are 'supplied with food'
and 'furnished with means of defence' (14.9-10), and the king's 'renown is spread
to the ends of the earth' (14.10). Albeit the eulogy reflects eschatological visions of
a 'new Jerusalem', the author does not suggest that 'ploughshares be transformed
into pruning hooks' or that 'young people dance in the streets' (Jer. 31.13; Zech.
8.5). Neither does he suggest that 'foreigners' or 'Ephraim as sons of Jacob' come
to Jerusalem. The Zion of 1 Maccabees is not an ideal and holy Jerusalem as abode
for Yahweh's holy people. It is the king's city, liberated by the 'priest-kings', the
sons of Mattathias (1 Macc. 14.29-37), whose deeds our author praises. Thus the
story must go on; there are still many wars to fight.

Elected by *all* the people (14.25-28, 41-46)—as also David had been—and pub-
licly exposing the record of the deeds of Simon and his brothers on bronze tablets
put up on pillars on Mt Zion (14.27, 48-49), any resistance to Simon's (and that of
his sons; 14.25, 49) priestly and royal authority is liable to punishment (14.43-45).
As Solomon's renown reached the farthest corners of the world, so the renown of
this great high priest and Ethnarch of the Jews reached as far as Rome and Sparta,
who were pleased to renew their former leagues of friendship (14.16-24; 15.15-24).
As Solomon's renown and alliance caused him trouble, our author also links this
renewal of alliance with the announcement of bad tidings, as he had formerly done.
This time the bad news comes in the image of Antiochus VII, brother of Demetrius
II. Reclaiming his father's kingdom, he 'allies' himself with Simon (15.1-10),
defeats Tryphon (15.1-14, 25, 37, 39), sends one of his 'friends', Athenobius, to
Simon to reclaim Joppe, Gezer, the citadel and Jerusalem, as well as taxes from
conquered areas (14.28-30). Since Simon is not willing either to give up the cities
or to pay Antiochus the requested monetary reimbursement, the king threatens him
with war. Athenobius then comes to Jerusalem, where he sees the king's treasures,
which Simon declares are his own, as he also declares the conquered areas as
belonging to his ancestors (15.31-35). Antiochus, who is busy pursuing Tryphon,
sends now a second time, his commander-in-chief, Cendebeus, against Simon. From
Jamnia, 'he began to provoke the people and invade Judaea and take the people
captive and kill them' (15.40).

Because Simon has become old, the scenario leaves something for his sons John
and Judas (16.1-3) and his son-in-Law, Ptolemy son of Abubus (16.11), to do.
Having camped with the army for the night in Modeïn ([*sic*] 16.4), they meet
Cendebeus, whom they defeat. John pursues him to Kedron and Azotus, while leaving his brother Judas hurt on the battlefield. As in the case of Jonathan, whose real

---

231. Cf. 1 Macc. 1.15; Isa. 9.16; Ps. 9.4-7.
232. Cf. 1 Kgs 7.51: David; 15.15: Asa.

enemy was not Demetrius but Tryphon, Simon's real enemy is not Demetrius's brother, but his own son-in-Law, Ptolemy, who deceptively has Simon and his sons Mattathias and Judas killed at a banquet in his little stronghold at Jericho (16.11-17). Having sought the king's support, he further attempts to kill John in Gezer and conquer Jerusalem and the Temple Mount (16.18-20). Closing his narrative with John's killing of Ptolemy's men, who have come to kill him, and with a reference to John's exploits, the author of 1 Maccabees has implicitly presented documentation proving the worthiness of Simon's sons as his true successors, and especially given support to John Hyrcanus' claim to the throne.

As the Saul–David–Solomon narratives illustrate Solomon's way to power in competition with other claimants, 1 Maccabees begins in a family of five 'brothers', who through successive fights, victories and defeats with external and internal opposition, ends in a single 'true' claimant to the throne. The reiterative patterns employed by the author render his narrative as interpretative sequences of events, with each ruler facing his own set of problems, which, however, displays a great similarity to problems already dealt with by his predecessors. Resembling biblical narrative, the opposition to the royal prerogatives of the Hasmonaeans does not come from other royal families; it comes from priests supported by 'lawless' and 'ungodly' men of Israel. In the course of events, these priests are removed from the scene, without defiling the hands of our story's heroes, who otherwise do not hesitate to remove their rivals' anonymous supporters. Paralleling biblical narrative, the removal of (high) priests does not lead to the establishment of another ruling priestly house, but to a priest-king (Jonathan in 1 Macc. 10.20 and Simon in 13.36), appointed first by Seleucid rulers, who take the role of Yahweh and the prophet, and secondly by the people (14.41-43).[233] As David's path to the throne is littered with the corpses of Saul's three sons, so Simon's path to the throne lays open for him at the disappearance of two of Jonathan's sons (13.16-19). As Solomon's way to the throne is paved with the removal of three of his father's sons (Amnon, Absalom, Adonijah), so John Hyrcanus' succession in the high priesthood comes after his older brother Judas has been wounded in battle (16.9) and his father and two other brothers have been killed by Simon's son in law Ptolemy the son of Abubus (16.11-17), who also sought to kill John (16.19-22).

In Josephus, John was accounted 'the rule of the nation, the office of high-priest and the gift of prophecy'; his sons, however, did not have 'their father's good fortune' (Josephus, *Ant.* 13.299-300). Neither had Samuel's sons the qualifications of their father (1 Sam. 8.1-3). Even a discussion of the high priesthood vs. kingship, introducing the loyalty of the Sadducees against disloyal Pharisees (*Ant.* 13.288-300), anticipates the decision of Aristobolus son of John Hyrcanus, to transform the government into a formal kingdom (*Ant.* 13.301).

Structurally, 1 Maccabees' line of development from father (Matthatias, guardian of the Law), conqueror (Judas), judge (Jonathan) to priest-king (Jonathan, Simon, John) parallels so closely the composition of biblical narrative, that only one, if

---

233.   They bear the title of 'high priest', but they act as kings and their ideal seems to have been the Roman 'democracy', although they institute hereditary leadership; cf. 1 Macc. 8.16; 14.49.

any, of such parallel traditions is likely to reflect historical reality. Moving from a line of five brothers and their children to one line and one heir, whose sovereignty is challenged by John's brother-in law's desire for the throne, reiterates too closely the Solomon–Rehoboam transition, in which Jeroboam, an Ephraimite, given his own area of responsibility (1 Kgs 11.28), as also Ptolemy had been (1 Macc. 16.11), has the role of revolting against the king (1 Kgs 11.26). 'Taking' most of his kingdom, Jeroboam forces Rehoboam to retreat to Jerusalem and Judah (1 Kgs 12.18), as also John did, when threatened by Ptolemy (Josephus, *Ant*. 13.229). In Josephus' further elaboration of the story, he has John Hyrcanus 'shut up' in Jerusalem at the attack of Antiochus VII Sidetes (*Ant*. 13.236-41), playing the role of Shishak in 2 Chronicles 12's story about Rehoboam. In both narratives, the city is saved because of piety to the Deity (*Ant*. 13.241-43; 2 Chron. 12.7). Its kings, however, become subjects of the foreign ruler (*Ant*. 13.246-47; 2 Chron. 12.8-9).

John Hyrcanus' re-conquest of lost areas after the death of Antiochus, with whom Ptolemy had allied himself (1 Macc. 16.18), his campaigns against Syrian, Ammonite, Moabite, Ephraimite and Edomite cities (Josephus, *Ant*. 13.254-57), his renewal of friendship with Rome (*Ant*. 13.259-66), and the 'reappearance' of King Demetrius II (*Ant*. 13.253, 267) reiterate narrative patterns intensely. In this series of conquests, however, two events are exceptional. The first is Hyrcanus' conquests of Shechem and Gerizim and 'the nation of the Cuthaeans' (i.e. the Samaritans), whose temple 'was now laid waste'[234] (13.256). The second is his conquest of Idumean towns and their forced conversion to 'the Jewish way of living' (13.257). Both events have support in a Jerusalemite cult centralization program, similar to Josiah's reform. As Josiah reigned for 31 years (2 Kgs 22.1; cf. 2 Chron. 34.1), so Hyrcanus 'administered the government' for 31 years, having peace in most of his lifetime, after he had settled the internal sedition created by disagreements between Pharisees and Sadducees (Josephus, *Ant*. 13.299), the latter supporting Hyrcanus' appointment as high priest. According to Samaritan tradition, Hyrcanus furthermore sought to reconcile himself with the Samaritans (*AF*, ch. XXIX, p. 113).

After John's death, a new set of events puts first his eldest son Aristobolus on the throne as king. After having reigned for less than a year, he is succeeded by his brother Alexander Jannai, who, in turn, is succeeded by his wife Alexandra Salome. Finally, we find the sons of Alexander, Aristobolus II and Hyrcanus II, fighting over the throne when Pompey comes and divides the kingdom.

---

234. Josephus' language is ambiguous here, since the expression συνέβη δὲ τὸν ναὸν τοῦτον ἔρημον can mean that the temple 'was deserted', as Whiston's translation has it. This ambiguity of language reflects well Josephus' biblical tradition, which for instance in Isa. 24.10, 12, makes the city of emptiness a desert, with broken walls and cries in the streets. In contrast, Josephus' language is crystal clear when he relates the order to destroy the Oniad temple, using the verb καθειρέω (cf. *War* 7.421). However, according to *War* 7.433-36, the Oniad temple was not destroyed but stripped of its treasures and closed (ἀποκλείω)! That Josephus does not relate any temple destruction in his parallel account in *War* 1.63 must also be taken into consideration. Could it be that the Samaritan temple was not destroyed in accordance with Samaritan tradition (*AF*, ch. XXIX, p. 113), in which destruction of the altar and the temple, built by 'Abdāl the high priest, was the work of a Jewish king Simon (*AF*, ch. XXIV, p. 87; cf. Chapter 4 n. 350)?

6. *2 Maccabees: Divine Election of Jerusalem as Yahweh's Abode and Judas as a Worthy Theocratic Leader*

While 1 Maccabees gives witness to the royal worthiness of the Hasmonaeans, 2 Maccabees concentrates on their, and especially Judas', priestly worthiness as true interpreter and follower of the Law. It has been argued that 2 Maccabees favours Judas against 'his brothers' or expresses an opposition to the Hasmonaean high priesthood because of the seemingly negative references to his brothers, which are in contrast to the positive portrait of Onias.[235] Drawing a line, however, from Jeremiah and Nehemiah to Jonathan (2 Macc. 1.23; 2.1), and another from Jeremiah and Onias to Judas (3.1; 15.14-16), it seems more likely that our author has established continuity, which in 1 Maccabees had been made on the basis of genealogy.

The introduction to Judas in the preface to Jason's work (2 Macc. 1–2) presents him as a keeper of tradition, mentioning his re-collection of the 'books', which have been lost during the war (2.13-14; cf. 1 Macc. 1.56-57; 12.9), as had also Nehemiah 'collected the books about the kings and prophets, the writings of David and letters of kings about votive offerings' (2.13). The reference to former tradition, using Jeremiah as a bridge between the pre-exilic and post-exilic Jewish people in Jerusalem (2 Macc. 2.1-13; cf. 1.19), creates its antiquity and documents that the Jerusalem of Nehemiah stood in a continuous tradition of Law and temple: as Moses (2.4, 8, 10, 11), so Solomon (2.8, 9, 10, 12). A dissonance, however, appears, since Jeremiah handed over the Law (τὸν νόμον), which 'should not depart from their hearths', to those going into exile (2.2-3). While, according to 1 Macc. 1.56-57, it is 'the Law' and 'the covenant', which are forbidden, and in 2 Macc. 2.22 it is the 'laws that were about to be abolished', it is 'the books about the kings and prophets, the writings of David and letters of kings about votive offerings' which our author implies are the lost books collected first by Nehemiah and later by Judas (2 Macc. 2.13-14). It might be telling that he does not have an Ezra bringing the Law from Babylon. It went with those exiled (2.2) and it might be implied that it came back with the returnees, such as found in Samaritan tradition (*AF*, ch. XVI, p. 63). The books mentioned (2.13) are those which are not authorised by the Samaritans. Presenting Judas as actually also relying on the 'sacred' literature, our author initiates his first and last battle by reading from the 'holy book' (2 Macc. 8.23) and from the 'law and the prophets' (15.9). Since neither Jeremiah nor Nehemiah are presented as possessing the high priestly office (2 Macc. 1.21; 2.1, 4), but act as preservers of tradition more zealously than any priests of their time, Judas' acts afford him a position to which more legitimate high priests will show themselves unworthy, as the story goes on.

The continuation of the introduction summarizes:

> the story of Judas Maccabaeus and his brothers and of the purification of the greatest temple (τοῦ ἱεροῦ τοῦ μεγίστου) and dedication of the altar, and of the wars

---

235. E.g. Goldstein, *II Maccabees*, pp. 17-18; *idem*, 'Biblical Promises and 1 and 2 Maccabees', p. 87; Nodet, *Origins of Judaism*, p. 204.

against Antiochus Epiphanes and his son Eupator, and the appearances (ἐπιφα-νείας) which came from heaven[236] to those who strove zealously on behalf of Judaism (ὑπὲρ τοῦ Ιουδαϊσμοῦ), so that, though few in number, they seized the whole land and pursued barbarian hordes, and recovered the temple famous throughout the world and freed the city and restored the laws that were about to be abolished, because the Lord with great kindness was gracious to them. (2.19-22)

Furnishing Judas' achievements with divine intervention as a reply to his confidence in God,[237] whose mercy had turned away his wrath,[238] our author has brought documentation of his elective legitimacy.

The pre-history of the Maccabaean revolt, caused and kept alive by priestly quarrels, occupies the main interest of the narratives that the author of 2 Maccabees has 'selected' and adumbrated from Jason's five books. His chronological anchor is the reigns of Seleucus IV, Antiochus IV and V, until the defeat of the Seleucid general, Nicanor around 161 BCE. The first and last high priest mentioned is Onias, who is said to be pious and faithful towards the Law (3.1). His qualities as high priest are not expressed by genealogy, but by conduct (15.12). Placed within this framework are the stories of the impious deeds of claimants to the high priestly office—Jason (Onias' brother), Menelaus (and his brother Lysimachus) and Alcimus[239]—contrasted to the pious conduct of Judas, whom Onias and Jeremiah appoint as divine warrior (15.14-16) and whose zeal for the temple and the Law is demonstrated through narrative discourse.

Two families are involved: the high priest Onias with his brother Jason on the one side and the captain of the temple Simon with his brothers Menelaus and Lysimachus on the other. It begins with a discussion about the administration of the city market and ends in a massacre of the city, the defilement of the temple and a transference of the high priesthood to the family of Bilga to which Simon and Menelaus belong.[240] When Simon does not succeed in establishing an agreement about the city market, he first accuses Onias of withholding temple treasures from taxation (2 Macc. 3.6), next of preventing a thorough inspection by the king's chancellor, Heliodorus, and of conspiracy (4.1-2; cf. 3.8-40). This 'slander' certainly contrasts Onias' reputation of being pious and honoured even by 'Seleucus, King of Asia' (IV Philopator 187–175), which helps settle the matter in a peaceful way during Seleucus' reign (4.1-7).

236. E.g. 2 Macc. 3.24-30; 10.29-30; 11.8-10 (and 15.12-16).
237. 2 Macc. 8.2-5, 16-24, 29-30, 35-36; 10.14-18, 24-31, 38; 11.1-12; 12.5-37; 13.9-23; 14.15-18; 15.6-34.
238. 2 Macc. 8.5; cf. 1.8; 7.38.
239. Of these, 1 Maccabees mentions only Alcimus.
240. LXX reads 'tribe of Benjamin', which probably is incorrect. Bilga is preserved in *Vetus Latina* and Armenian versions, and *m. Suk.* 5.8 condemns the tribe of Bilga forever from serving at the altar; cf. M. Hengel, *Judaism and Hellenism* (repr.; London: Xpress Reprints, 1996 [1981]), p. 270. Grabbe, *Judaism*, pp. 277-78, following Tcthericover, *Hellenistic Civilization*, pp. 403-404, argues for an unnecessary variant reading, Balga, mentioned as a priestly family in Neh. 12.5, 18— which, however, reads Bilga in the *BHS*.

When the king dies, Onias' brother Jason takes advantage of the situation and obtains the high priesthood by offering King Antiochus IV Epiphanes a huge sum of money (4.7-9). Jason introduces Hellenistic customs and leads astray both people and priests (4.10-15).[241] Since it had become customary to buy the priestly office, Menelaus next outbids Jason with 300 hundred talents of silver, thus obtaining the office 'without any qualification for the high priesthood, but having the hot temper of a cruel tyrant and the rage of a savage wild beast' (4.23-25).

Menelaus' 'rule' from 172–162 BCE is marked by cruelty and corruption. With the aid of his brother Lysimachus and his co-conspirator Andronicus (a general in the army of Antiochus), he robs the temple of its treasures (4.27-32) and has Onias killed in Daphne near Antioch when he objects to the robbery (4.33-34). Summoned to the king because of these matters, he bribes Ptolemy son of Dorymenes, to persuade the king to acquit him of the charges against him (4.45-50). Succeeding in his bribing, Menelaus continues in office.

Jason, however, who had fled to the country of the Ammonites, has not given up hopes of regaining the priesthood. When false rumours arise that Antiochus has died in Egypt, he hastens to Jerusalem with a small army, makes a quick assault on the city and forces Menelaus to fly to the citadel. When Jason continues to slaughter his fellow citizens, his fortune is reversed. He is driven back and the result is a miserable ending. For the city and for the Jews, the event becomes a catastrophe. Antiochus, who thought that Jason was leading a general uprising, returns in fury. Aided by Menelaus, he massacres the population, defiles the temple and puts the city under Seleucid administration, politically as well as religiously. As a consequence of this constitutional change, he instates governors to afflict the people at Jerusalem and at Gerizim, leaving Menelaus in office and treating 'his fellow citizens worse than the others' (5.22-23).[242] The king furthermore sends an Athenian senator to compel the Jews to forsake the laws of God and to pollute the temple in Jerusalem 'and call it by the name of Zeus Olympios and that on Gerizim by the name of Zeus Xenios [the Hospitable Zeus], as is appropriate to the people living there' (6.1-2).[243]

The atrocities and the liberation of the temple, intertwined in stories about martyrdom, fates of kings, governors, armies and alliances, parallel narratives in 1 Maccabees, but more explicitly presenting Judas as divine warrior, carrying out

---

241. This Hellenization of Jerusalem seems not have been due to any asserted (E. Schürer, *History of the Jewish People* [3 vols.; Edinburgh: T. & T. Clark, 1973–87 (ed. and translated from the German, *Geschichte des judischen Volkes im Zeitalter Jesu Christi* [3 vols.; Leipzig: J.C. Hinrichs, 1885])], I, pp. 147-48) increase of Antiochus' Hellenizing policy, which can not be supported in general (Grabbe, *Judaism*, pp. 248-49), but coincides with Antiochus' rule only because of Jason's appointment and his application for Jerusalem to become a Greek *polis* (2 Macc. 4.9), a status which the city held until 168 BCE. Hellenization, as such, seems not to have caused any great concern for the Jewish population, and it was not until Menelaus and his associates' plundering of the temple treasures that the people rioted (Grabbe, *Judaism*, pp. 280-81).

242. Cf. 1 Macc. 1.52, mentioning only Judaea.

243. Not mentioned in 1 Maccabees. Josephus (*Ant.* 12.237-64 [255-63]) used the passage in his efforts to discriminate against the Samaritans; see my *Samaritans and Early Judaism*, pp. 207-12.

the will of the Almighty God. Having removed Menealus from the scene, by having him executed by the king (13.4-8), our author introduces Alcimus, 'who had formerly been high priest, but had defiled himself' (2 Macc. 14.3). He now wants to have Demetrius aiding him in regaining the office (14.4-10). His efforts to have Judas killed (14.19, 13) end in a victory for Judas, whom Nicanor appoints as high priest instead of Alcimus (14.23-26). Alcimus' complaint to Demetrius, however, leads to his request to Nicanor to send Judas to Antioch as prisoner (14.26-27). Obedient to the king's order, Nicanor fails Judas, attacks him (on a Sabbath?), but is killed (15.27-28). Of Alcimus' further fate our author is not concerned, but he seems to imply that the office went to Judas.[244] Since he crushed his 'enemies' (15.26-28; cf. 15.16) with Jeremiah's sword mediated by Onias (15.14-16),[245] and was found worthy of victory (cf. 15.21), his priestly prerogatives as successor to the pious Onias have been thus established. As Eli transferred authority to Samuel, so Onias transfers authority to Judas.

Combining a glorification of the city and the temple, which the Persian king, at the time of Nehemiah (1.34),[246] and the Asian king, Seleucus IV (3.3), had already declared holy and honoured, with a submission to its authority by their adversaries—Heliodorus (3.35-39), Antiochus IV (9.16) and V (13.23)—the temple's status as *the* place (ὁ τόπος) chosen by God[247] is strongly advocated.

Jerusalem's implicit competitors are the Jewish congregations in Egypt (1.10)[248] and at Gerizim (5.22-23; 6.1-2), both of which are not presented as having participated in the Hasmonaean revolt. According to Josephus' unreliable presentation, they either appeared as a result of the uprising (Heliopolis/Leontopolis) or were subdued and eventually removed (Gerizim) by the Hasmonaeans. While cult centralization is not part of our author's explicit argument, he implies that Jerusalem's temple is superior to other temples (cf. 2.19; 3.12; 5.15; 14.13, 31), and that 'all Israel' shares the wish of returning to Jerusalem (1.26-27; 2.18), to be 'planted there' (καταφύτευσον)[249] in God's holy place (εἰς τὸν τόπον τὸν ἅγιόν σου),[250] 'as said by Moses' (1.29; cf. Exod. 15.17). He thus might share Jeremiah, Ezekiel and

---

244. Cf. also Josephus, *Ant.* 12.414: 'When Alcimus was dead the people bestowed the High Priesthood on Judas'. Nodet, *Origins of Judaism*, who does not take 2 Macc. 14.23-26 into account and follows the chronology of 1 Macc. 9.54-57 (Alcimus died after Judas), finds Josephus' statement 'absurd in the context of unyielding Seleucid pressure'.

245. Cf. 1 Macc. 4.36 ('our enemies are crushed'), and 3.12 (Appolonius' sword, which Judas takes in his first fight).

246. A variant of the 'fireproof' motif of 2 Macc. 1.19-36, in which narrative it is 'the place' (i.e. Jerusalem), which is declared sacred and the king exchanging many gifts with those persons, whom he favoured (i.e. Nehemiah and his associates, v. 35).

247. Cf. 2 Macc. 1.29, with reference to Moses; 2.8, with reference to Moses and Solomon; 5.19-20, with allusion to Deut. 12.5; 2 Macc. 14.35, with allusion to 1 Kgs 8.27

248. Sievers, *Hasmoneans*, p. 7: 'The implicit criticism of the Oniad temple in Leontopolis has been recognised by many scholars'. For a different opinion, see D. Arenhoevel, *Die Theokratie nach dem 1. und 2. Makkabäerbuch* (Walberberger Studien, Theologische Reihe, 3; Mainz: Grünewald, 1967), pp. 100-102.

249. Cf. LXX 2 Sam. 7.10; Jer. 24.6; 38.29 = MT Jer. 31.29.

250. Cf. LXX Isa. 60.13; 2 Macc. 8.17.

Chronicles' wish of reconciling Israel's people in Jerusalem. Although the Hasmonaeans fought to realize that dream, their efforts remained as unsuccessful as had Hezekiah and Josiah's. Rather than creating unity, the policy of the Hasmonaeans fostered opposition groups and parties, some of which kept eschatological hopes of glory for Zion-Jerusalem alive. Others advocated even more strongly preservation of ancient traditions and cult places.

Chapter 7

CONCLUSION: THE PLACE YAHWEH HAS CHOSEN

My examination of discussions about cult places has shown that Deuteronomy's ambiguity about 'the place Yahweh will choose' has had a great influence in the formation of biblical and extra-biblical books. While in biblical literature reference to this discussion is implicit, in Samaritan tradition and Josephus such reference is explicit. In each, the discussion takes place in the Diaspora, related either to a return from the Babylonian exile or to questions of allegiance to either Jerusalem or Gerizim, which the Jewish and Samaritan congregations in Egypt seek to settle. Since independence is not part of our authors' worldview, the quarrels take place in front of the regents of empires, whether Persian, Greek or Egyptian. Related to Persian and Greek rulership are biblical and extra-biblical narratives about temple-building activities in Palestine, while the context for the temple in Heliopolis is set within the sphere of Ptolemaic–Seleucid competition over hegemony.

This dependency contrasts sharply with the Deuteronomistic and Chronistic stories about the independent Kingdom of David's Israel, whose city and royal house Yahweh has chosen. The explicitness with which the term בחר ('to choose') is applied to the kings Saul (1 Sam. 10.24; 12.13), David (1 Kgs 8.16; 11.34; cf. 1 Sam. 16.1, 8-13; 2 Sam. 6.21) and Solomon (1 Chron. 28.6) contrasts with the language applied to Yahweh's raising of Jeroboam and Basha as kings, expressed in the verbs לקח ('to take', 1 Kgs 11.37) רום ('to raise') and נתן ('to give', 1 Kgs 14.7; 16.2), but never in the verb בחר. Even Jehu is not chosen, but anointed (2 Kgs 9.6). The choice of David is a choice among several options: Saul (2 Sam. 6.21; cf. 1 Sam. 15.28), the house of Saul (2 Sam. 2.8-3.1) and David's seven brothers (1 Sam. 16.6-10). A summary is offered in 1 Chron. 28.4-10 of these options in David's transference of the kingship to his son Solomon, whom Yahweh has elected among David's many sons as king of Israel and builder of the temple. Five times is the verb בחר used for the election of David (v. 4), Judah (v. 4) and Solomon (vv. 5-6, 10). The election of David in Psalms is an election of the David of the narratives. The competition is set between David–Judah and Ephraim–Joseph (Ps. 78.67-70) or between David and the kings of the world (Ps. 89.4, 20-28).

In Deutero-Isaiah, it is Jacob-Israel, which has been elected (Isa. 41.8-9, 24; 43.10; 44.1-2; 45.4; 49.7).[1] Other occurrences of the term in Isaiah relate to Yahweh's re-election of Israel (Isa. 14.1) and to religious and patronage issues

---

1.   Cf. also Ezek. 20.5; Pss. 47.5; 105.6, 43 (Abraham, see also Neh. 9.7); 106.5-6 (the people, see Deut. 4.37; 7.6-7; 10.15; 14.2; Pss. 135.4).

(1.29; 40.20; 56.4; 58.5-6; 65.12; 66.3-4). The competition expressed in the ideology of election regarding the kingships and kingdoms of Israel and Judah is argued implicitly in Isaiah's Ahaz and Hezekiah narratives, which demonstrate the sovereignty of the house of David and Jerusalem. In Jer. 33.14-26, traditions are brought together in Yahweh's recollection of his election of the Levites[2] and the Davidides (v. 24) and a future restoration of Israel, Judah and Jerusalem under the supremacy of the Davidic king, who shall reign over the descendants of Abraham, Isaac and Jacob. In Hag. 2.23, it is Zerubbabel, who is not called a Davidic king, who is elected.

As the Davidic kingship is chosen in competition with other candidates and claimants, so is the place for Yahweh's abode chosen in competition with other places, all of which are given temporary existence as were the Israelite kings. Reflective of the discussion implicit in Deuteronomy 12's utterance about the place Yahweh chooses, which in the MT is held in an imperfect form (vv. 5, 11, 14, 21 and 26),[3] against the perfect tense found in SP's Deut. 12.5, 11, 14,[4] the authors of Samuels–Kings and Chronicles are eager to point out exactly when this choice is made. Thus Yahweh's election of David is prior to his request of a house, since he did not ask any of the tribes of Israel to build him 'a house of cedar' (בית ארזים, 2 Sam. 7.5-7 par. 1 Chron. 17.6-7).[5] The establishment of David's house takes place before David's son builds Yahweh's house (2 Sam. 7.11-13). In the inauguration narratives on 1 Kings and 2 Chronicles, references to Yahweh's choice relate to the city (לא־בחרתי בעיר שבטי ישראל),[6] which in Chronicles is mentioned by name and given equal status with David:

ואבחר בירושלם להיות שמי שם ואבחר בדוד להיות על־עמי ישראל

…but I have chosen Jerusalem as the place for my name and I have chosen David to reign over my people Israel. (2 Chron. 6.6)[7]

Both are elected, as is the temple Solomon has built:

ובחרתי במקום הזה לי לבית זבח

…and I have chosen this place to for myself as a house of sacrifice. (2 Chron. 7.12; cf. v. 16)[8]

2.   Cf. Deut. 21.5.
3.   Cf. also Deut. 14.23, 24; 15.20; 16.2, 6, 7, 11, 15; 17.8, 10; 31.11.
4.   Cf. also Deut. 31.11 in the SP, while the remaining occurrences in the SP's Deuteronomy appear in imperfect as in the Masoretic text.
5.   The mention of cedar reflects David's house of cedar (2 Sam. 7.2 par. 1 Chron. 17.1), but also Moses' tent sanctuary, in which Yahweh will live (ישכנתי בתוכם, Exod. 25.8), elements of which are not made of cedar but acacia (עצי שטים, Exod. 25; 26; 27; 30; 36; 37; 38 [26 times]; Deut. 10.3). In the Pentateuch, apart from Num. 24.6, cedar is used for purification only; see, for example, Lev. 14.4, 6, 49, 51, 52; Num. 19.6. In Ezra 3.7, cedars are brought from Lebanon as permitted by Cyrus. Ezek. 40–48 does not specify the wood used for the temple.
6.   Cf. 1 Kgs 8.16; 2 Chron. 6.5-6.
7.   The Dead Sea Scrolls and the LXX indicate that 2 Kings' variant is secondary to Chronicles; cf. Abegg, Flint and Ulrich, *The Dead Sea Scrolls Bible*, p. 264.
8.   Hjelm, *Samaritans and Early Judaism*, p. 92.

In contrast, no such distinct language is found in 1 Kgs 9.2's variant.

The intentionality of Deuteronomy's ambiguity both reflects and is a precondition for exactly such implicit narrative discourse, which establishes Yahweh's choice through prophetic interpretation as we have seen in Chapters 4–5. Having established the kingship and the place, a defence of Yahweh's choices is our authors' concern. Thus Yahweh's decisions regarding David and Jerusalem are still valid when part of Israel rejects his choices in favour of other kings and places (1 Kgs 11.13, 36; 14.21). The remnant created thereby is given the task of defending Yahweh's choice against their desire of challenging his authority. In Kings (2 Kgs 23.27; cf. 21.11-15), this leads to Yahweh's rejection of the city and temple he has elected

ומאסתי את־העיר אשר בחרתי את־ירושלם ואת־הבית אשר אמרתי יהיה שמי שם

> And I have rejected the city, which I have chosen, Jerusalem and the temple about which I said: 'my name shall be there'.

In Chronicles, however, the people, the city and the temple are destroyed, though not formally rejected (2 Chron. 36.16-20).[9] In this biblical discourse on 'election'— 'rejection or purification'—and 'taken back' theology, creation of a remnant connects the pre-exilic Israel with the Israel of our authors in a 'return' theology's didactic admonition to keep the commandments of the Law. Neither participated in the 'events' described.

The Israel of narrative is the Judah of the past, which in the books of Kings shares the fate of 'Israel rejected'. While Israel is replaced by other peoples, no such 'event' takes place in Judah.[10] While the sentiment of the Josiah narrative— that Jerusalem should also be rejected—belongs to the narrative discourse of the books of Kings, the Hezekiah narrative breaks that marked compositional pattern and brings in a different perspective: a counter-message promising the survival of a remnant for Jerusalem at the disappearance of Ephraim/Israel. While Israel has rejected the Law and the prophets, Judah's King Manasseh and Amon left Yahweh, but Josiah renewed the Yahweh cult. This cult is not said to have been abandoned again. Although Josiah's sons and grandson did evil in the eyes of Yahweh, it is Manasseh's sin which causes the rejection. Compositionally, this places the Josiah narrative's reinstatement of the Law and the cult on a par with the Hezekiah narrative's remnant, both of which testify that those returning from exile have traditions with which to return. The Law Ezra brings to Jerusalem demonstrably implies the Mosaic Law given to the fathers and not a new invention from Persia. In 2 Macc. 2.2, Jeremiah gives 'the law' to the exiled, while in *AF* (ch. XVI, p. 65), Nebuchadnezzar brings it to Nineveh and it is brought back by the returning Samaritans led by Sanballat and 'Abdāl, the high priest (*AF*, ch. XX, p. 78).

---

9. Cf. 2 Chron. 33.7-13's anticipation of atonement, repentance, forgiveness and purification, which are the exile's purpose; Isa. 40 (v. 2); Jer. 33 (v. 6); Ezek. 20 (vv. 39-44); Dan. 9 (v. 24); Hos. 2–3 (2.16–3.5) and Amos 9 (vv. 8–15).

10. Cf., however, the occupied land and city in Neh. 9 and Lamentations'; the 'people from Persia' in *AF*, ch. XVI, p. 65, and 'Edomites' in Obadiah and 1 Esd. 4.45.

While the closure of 2 Kings leaves open the possibility that David's house has a remnant with which to begin, Jeremiah's (and Chronicles') hope for a future of the Davidic kingship does (do) not reckon any of the sons of Jehoiachin (Jer. 22.30). The righteous Davidic king, mentioned in Jer. 23.5 and 33.15, hardly refers to Zedekiah, although the name bears allusions to him ([11]והקמתי לדוד צמח צדיק, 'and I will raise up a righteous branch of David's line'). The sprout, with which Yahweh will re-establish his covenant, does not come from the cursed Davidic line, it comes from David, thus implying a mental return to the unified kingdom of the past, which our author knows from tradition.[12] Echoing the rules of David and Solomon, this king shall establish 'justice and righteousness on earth' (ועשה משפט וצדקה בארץ), Judah will be saved and Israel will dwell in safety (בימיו תושע יהודה וישראל[13] ישכן לבטח, Jer. 23.5; cf. 33.15-16). Jeremiah's re-creation of Yahweh's people, brought home in the image of the Patriarchs (33.26), rather than Moses, implies that the new covenant becomes based on traditions about David and the Patriarchs rather than Moses. Replacing the Israelites' exodus from Egypt, the returnees shall come from the north (3.18; 23.7-8), as had also Abraham and Jacob (cf. Deut. 26.5). Implicitly marking the exodus tradition with its tribal divisiveness as the failed exodus, Jeremiah and Ezekiel (ch. 37) offer Jerusalem as a new beginning for the descendants of Abraham, Isaac and Jacob (Jer. 33.26; Ezek. 37.25).[14]

In the Ezra–Nehemiah narratives we learn that this solution can turn out as wrong as had the Jerusalem of the Davidides in the past. Ancestors, whether real or created by tradition, are not as easily transformed into loving brothers as our authors might have hoped. The unification of Israel in Jerusalem is as contradictory as it is impossible.

The viability of such discussions about traditions and cult place in extra-biblical literature of the third century BCE to the second century CE, suggests that our biblical texts and Samaritan traditions also reflect these post-exilic discussions rather than any pre-exilic establishment of a Davidic kingdom. The image of such a unified kingdom, to whose authority everyone shall be subjected, is held up as a negating reflex of the divisiveness that characterizes the world in which our authors live. The biblical canon's implied problem of establishing Abraham's heir is not an easy problem to solve, when several candidates appear on the scene.[15] The divisiveness related to tribal relations presented already in the Abraham narrative, continued in Jacob and Esau's fights over blessing and inheritance and reiterated in the sons of Jacob's anticipation of Joseph's and Judah's struggle for sovereignty, reflects the tribal and geographical divisions, which are our authors' problem. The implicit reality of our texts reflects the biblical books of Joshua–Judges rather than 2 Samuel.

---

11. Jer. 33.15: צדקה.

12. We see here a similar connection of Judah's first and last kings as found also in extra-biblical and Samaritan literature.

13. LXXS: καὶ Ιερουσαλημ; Jer. 33.16: וירושלם.

14. Ezekiel mentions only Jacob.

15. Hjelm, 'Brothers Fighting Brothers'.

While in the Pentateuch Joseph prevails over Judah, in Samuel–Kings Judah is given the sovereign's role. In the institution of kingship, the story moves once again from diversity to unity: from the twelve judges to the one king. Kingship, however, does not solve the basic problem: Who shall rule, when there is more than one candidate and more than one region? The position given in succession to King Saul, from the tribe of Benjamin, the youngest son of Jacob,[16] to David and Solomon, both from the tribe of Judah, the fourth son of Jacob,[17] increases antagonisms. Although the narrative seeks to give the impression that the Davidic kingship finally united the tribes, this 'unity' was not created by resolving former disagreements. Solomon's peaceful reign from Dan to Beersheba was one of exception rather than normality (1 Kgs 5.4-5) and everyday life did not long secure Israel and Judah's peoples under shading branches of fig and wine. Dispersion lies in wait as the story reverses itself paradigmatically. Two 'brothers' fighting over the now divided territory, within the land, in a struggle for the role of the true Israel. Judah's king Rehoboam son of Solomon, fights against Israel's king Jeroboam son of Nebat, an Ephraimite from the tribe of Joseph. Although Joseph is the second youngest son of Jacob (Gen. 30.24; 46.19; 49.22), he is given the role of the firstborn (Gen. 47.27–48.4) and receives a variation on the blessing given to Jacob (Gen. 27.27-29; cf. Gen. 49.22-26).[18]

While in the Pentateuch Jacob had only one blessing, in the books of Kings Jeroboam is given the possibility of receiving Yahweh's conditional blessing from the outset, as had David's sons. His failure to fulfil Yahweh's conditions leads to the rejection of his house, while similar failure does not lead to such an expeditious rejection of David's house. In a synchronic narrative setting, Ephraim/Israel, its kingship and its people, are rejected by Yahweh because of their conduct—their unfaithfulness towards Yahweh—while Judah is temporarily spared because of David's faithfulness. This judgment of 'the faithless Israel' is dramatically spelled out and made paradigmatic for the narrative as a whole. The implicit question about sovereignty is not so much 'Who belongs to the lineage of firstborn?', but 'Who will show himself to be the true Israel?' The logic of the Deuteronomistic History's narrative relates to the tribe of Joseph's non-reception of an unconditional promise. Its parallel is the Shechem covenant of Joshua 24.

---

16. Gen. 35.16-19, 24. Similar to Benjamin's role of securing the continuity from father to son in place of either Joseph or Judah, Saul is presented as a transitional figure, whose incorporation of the roles of priest, prophet and king leads to his rejection in the narrative's attempt at separating these roles. Cf. also Shiloh's transitional role in creating continuity between the Mosaic priesthood of the past and David's priesthood of the future mediated by the prophet, who also transfers legal authority from priest to king.

17. Gen. 29.35; 35.23; 46.12; 49.8.

18. Extending this line of firstborn, the blessing also comes to include Joseph's sons Ephraim and Manasseh, second- and firstborn (Deut. 33.13-17), who for their part have their status exchanged in yet another variant of the Esau–Jacob narrative. We here remember that Joseph and his son Ephraim are also given the role of firstborn in psalmodic and prophetic literature, while Judah never had it.

While such a competitive mode pervades our traditions, they are best character-ized as illustrative interpretations of theological doctrines. Yahweh's decision that only the place(s) he chooses is (are) fit for worship has generated narratives, which legitimate the sovereignty of some places against others. The discourse is not progressive, though its surface makes it appear as if it were. Biblical literature's reworking of the past in typological narrative, which implies a rejection of that past,[19] has created dissonance between various sections, various books and between the Pentateuch and the historical books. Examination of such dissonance has been pertinent to the present study. The hypothesis of Van Seters and others of a late Yahwist (J–E, in fact) based on the Deuteronomistic History, and Galling, Römer and Schmid's hypothesis of an autochthonous Patriarch tradition vs. an Exodus–Moses tradition, have wide-ranging implications for literary as well as historical research. Although Van Seters argues that the Yahwist's history from the creation to the death of Moses was not intended to supersede the Deuteronomistic History,[20] the hermeneutical implication is that his late Yahwist, in fact, supersedes his Deuteronomist. Whether one accepts Van Seters' argument as an explanation of a theological development of inner religio-political discussions over cult and belief or my assertion that two separate groups (Samaritans and Jews) argue for each their own perspective, supersessionism lies at the roots of such disparate traditions.

The questioning of the validity of an alleged second-century distinctive Samari-tanism, derived from a common 'Jewish' matrix,[21] also challenges assumptions about the existence of a tribal Israel, stemming from one eponym in ancient times and sharing a common history down to the establishment of the cult in Shiloh or Jeroboam's division of the Davidic kingdom, as claimed in Masoretic and Samaritan traditions. Contrary to Josephus and biblical scholarship's assertion of a development of the Samaritan cult out of Jerusalem, Jewish and Samaritan tradition agree that Jerusalem's cult had moved from the north to the south. The movement is reflected literarily in the so-called Deuteronomistic History's denigration of 'former' cult places: Shechem, Bethel, Gilgal, Shiloh, Nob and Gibeon. The deni-gration serves the promotion of David's move to Jerusalem and of Jerusalem's struggle for sovereignty. While in biblical tradition, *all* Israel participated in the transference of the cult to Jerusalem, in Samaritan tradition, most Samaritans never took part in that movement. Having established the cult in Shechem/Gerizim-Bethel in the second year after their entrance into the Promised Land, Samaritans remained in that place continuously, except when forced into exile, from whence they returned more than once.

It is within the tension of an alleged seventh- to sixth-century BCE 'biblical' and a third-century BCE to second-century CE 'extra-biblical' discussion that Samaritan history and tradition can add to our knowledge of hidden motives and themes in traditions, which we call 'Jewish' or 'Jewish-Christian'. The silencing of Samaritan voices, which our scholarly tradition has inherited from Josephus' degradation of

---

19. Thompson, *Origin Tradition of Ancient Israel*, p. 158.
20. Van Seters, 'Joshua 24 & the Problem of Tradition'.
21. Hjelm, *Samaritans and Early Judaism*.

the Samaritan existence at a time, when, in fact, these numbered as many as the Jews themselves, with whom they shared the traditions about the Patriarchs, Moses, Exodus, Joshua and the land, has been crucial to scholarly research. Albeit most of the Samaritan manuscripts date from mediaeval times, I hope to have demonstrated that their validity as witnesses to tradition and redaction-historical problems should not be too readily dismissed.

The placement of the Mosaic Law between the Patriarchs and the fathers of the desert generation suggests that these traditions can be read either in a continuum or in opposition. One might, however, benefit from viewing these traditions as governed by both concentric and linear principles.

We thus find in both Samaritan and Masoretic tradition a Hexateuchal continuum: from promise to fulfilment or from Shechem to Shechem, which the LXX's 'replacement' of Shechem with Shiloh does not have. This 'replacement' rather underscores a text tradition, which points forward to Samuel–Kings' replacement of the cult in Shiloh with that in Jerusalem, such as is found also in Jeremiah and *Eupolemus*. While Samaritan tradition never replaces Shechem/Gerizim-Bethel with other cult places, its continuum, from (Ur) Haran to Shechem/Gerizim-Bethel to Haran, takes the form in Masoretic canonical tradition of geographical linear progression: from (Ur) Haran to Shechem to Shiloh to Jerusalem to Babylon. Within this narrative progression we find another continuum: from Egypt to Egypt, which in Samaritan tradition is argued explicitly on Deut. 28.68, while in Masoretic tradition Egypt's role is ambiguous—a place of refuge (Jeremiah and 2 Kings) and punishment (Hosea). The alleged continuum is thus not quite as obvious in Masoretic tradition as it is argued by Galling, Römer and Schmid.

While Noth's projection of a Deuteronomistic History made sense within the form of continuous narrative, there are considerable problems with the increasing attempts of establishing Noth's Deuteronomistic History without Noth's 'Tetrateuch'. Where does Deuteronomy begin? Or does it begin? Albeit tradition and redaction critics base their arguments on either a late dating of Tetrateuch themes in the Former and Latter Prophets or on pre-Tetrateuch/pre-Yahwist sources, they have not given evidence that these are, in fact, additions or pre-texts to the Masoretic Tetrateuch. A systematic and thorough examination of the matter should, in fact, include a removal of all of JE and P material from the Deuteronomistic History and not what modern taste seems comfortable with. Since dismissing a passage, while retaining it in the text, is deceptive, this physically abrogated DtrH should then be compared with other books of the Hebrew Bible, especially Jeremiah. Which Jeremiah should we then choose, or should we choose them all? According to the rabbis, however, Jeremiah only wrote Kings. Did they get that idea from an observation that Kings share more similarities with Deuteronomy than do 1 and 2 Samuel, which, however, are closer to the Tetrateuch?[22] If the books of Kings are prior to J (E) and P, are 1 and 2 Samuel written after Kings and after J, E or P? And what about Chronicles' seemingly lesser 'knowledge' of Yahwistic themes or of the books of Joshua and Judges, which apart from genealogies are

---

22. Von Rad, *Deuteronomium-Studien*, p. 61.

absent from Chronicles. Before Joshua–2 Kings received its final form, at some point between the first and tenth century CE, there was not such an apparently uniform text as Joshua–2 Kings.

We need to explore further, the redaction and reception history of each of the Former Prophets before we can write the redaction history of scholars' 'Deuteronomistic History'. We also need to explore further Auld's hypothesis that 'Samuel–Kings, like Chronicles, are part commentary and part radical extension of a pre-existing narrative of the house of David',[23] whatever form this story might have had. Here, I do not think that Auld's shared text can count as an original source.[24] We must furthermore question our historicist allegation that the Latter Prophets lived in the eighth to the fifth centuries, particularly because this allegation fits Wellhausen's dictum 'from Prophets to Law'. It does not, however, fit new theories of redaction history.

Although the argument for a Deuteronomistic History was based on style, its foundation is the assumption that the Law book found by Josiah was Deuteronomy. Now, Josiah's reform in 2 Kings 23 is based on both Levitical Law (P; Lev. 14) about a house contaminated by leprosy (2 Kgs 23.4-14)[25] and Deuteronomic Law about cult centralization (23.16-20). If the 'Leviticus' part were added at a later time, cult centralization must have taken priority over cult control. The incorporation of this part, however, should have demanded some rewriting of the whole paragraph, since vv. 4-20 function chiastically in creating Jerusalem as the only place left for proper worship. But 2 Kings does not specify which Book of the Law was found and the narrative betrays several implications. First, the tradition about the hidden law in the temple is one found also in Samaritan tradition about the copy of the Law, which Eli brought from Gerizim. Second, the cleansing of the house, as if it were contaminated with leprosy, echoes Samaritan nicknaming of Jerusalem's temple: *Beit Miktesh Kifna* ('a house of leprosy'). The impurity of the temple is not only inherent to the Josiah narrative, but is a frequent characterization of the Second Temple in Pseudepigraphic literature, in which only the first and the coming temple are declared pure. Third, the 'use' of 'the Law' in Josiah's reform might serve as a purposeful demonstration of which Law book Josiah found as well as legitimizing his acts.[26]

While Jerusalem's linear narrative progression in Samuel–2 Kings might be viewed as being in opposition to a Hexateuchal continuum, the possibility nevertheless remains of reading the linear progression of Genesis–2 Kings, either in the form of a salvation or fall narrative or as a reworking of past traditions (the so-called DtrH) to a new understanding, without rejecting that past entirely.[27]

23. Auld, 'Reading Joshua After Kings', p. 106.

24. Auld, *Kings Without Privilege*.

25. L. Shedletsky, 'Priestly and Deuteronomic Traditions in the Composition of II Kings 22–23' (unpublished paper delivered at the SBL National Meeting, Toronto, 2002), who argues that the narrative is basically a pre-P account with Deuteronomistic additions.

26. Hoffmann, *Reform und Reformen*, has clearly demonstrated that Deuteronomy alone cannot carry the perspectives of a DtrH.

27. Van Seters, *Prologue to History*, p. 332.

However, as this past is not made explicit in any way by the Yahwist, J's dissonance with the Former and Latter Prophets—Isaiah, Jeremiah and Ezekiel, who
advance a synthesis, placing David in the roles of the Patriarchs *and* Moses—is not
one that can be dismissed.

The tension which our traditions have set between Moses and the prophets and
between the prophets and kings led to an examination of the roles of Moses and
David in competition and supplement, as well as an investigation of the question:
'With whom does Yahweh speak?' The main result of this research is that Yahweh
speaks with both David and Moses, that David is presented as not having a Mosaic
Law, but as having instituted justice and righteousness, and that the prophets are
given authoritative status over the king, conveying the will of God. Thus David's
transference of the Mosaic Law to Solomon (1 Kgs 3) carries with it another transference: that of the behaviour of David, both of which became parameters for the
judgment of kings and people in the books of Kings. In canonical chronology,
David's role serves to illustrate the king's dependency on the Law and its interpreters, whether it be an implied written Mosaic Law or a message conveyed by
prophets. In narrative chronology, however, the author has presented King David
as separated from past institutions: temple, priesthood and law. Compositionally,
even David's transgressions (2 Sam. 9–24) appear after he has instituted 'Law and
Justice'. In such composition, David's reign is best characterized as a creation of
something new. And we must ask whether 1–2 Samuel is, in fact, creating an
autochthonous tradition, paralleling the Yahwist's autochthonous tradition, rather
than being part of an Exodus tradition.

The visions for the 'new' that David has created are not reflected in Kings'
selection of Judah, but in the wish of Chronicles, Jeremiah and Ezekiel for a unification of Israel's tribes, a recapture of a long-vanished past, a golden age of unity
under a Davidic prince. In Isaiah and Jeremiah this is couched in Zion ideology's
expectation of sovereignty with Jerusalem at the centre of the world from which
place teaching shall go forth. Although the books of Samuel and Kings 'know' the
term 'Zion', it has become clear that Zion ideology does not belong to either the
Deuteronomistic or Chronistic History or to any alleged Yahweh Zebaoth cult of an
eleventh- to tenth-century Davidic monarchy, however much David might be seen
to have established the cult in Jerusalem. These elements of Zion ideology are
primarily literary, stemming from the Prophets and Psalms. The examination also
revealed that the judgment formulae in the books of Kings belong to its compositional narrative structure and not to alleged redactions. The judgment structure
might have been taken over from Chronicles, but that has not been thoroughly
examined, just as Chronicles' tradition-historical relationship to the Former
Prophets has not undergone extensive investigation. Examination of intertextual
relationships in the Hebrew Bible and the preference by extra-biblical traditions of
Chronicles rather than Joshua–2 Kings challenge the priority of the Masoretic
Joshua–2 Kings. The matter, however, needs more investigation.

Within the canonical tradition, Judges–2 Kings' markedly supersessionistic and
competitive character in its Jerusalem-oriented replacement of 'Pentateuch' traditions is not shared in the Yahwist's support of multiple cult places, none of which

are placed in Jerusalem.[28] While both these traditions are assumed to belong to a remote pre-exilic/exilic past and essentially to have stemmed from groups with shared Jerusalem-oriented interests, extra-biblical writings from the third century BCE onward testify to the viability of their implicit discussions at a time when other cult places were a challenge to the idea of a centralized cult (in Jerusalem). Whether Deut. 12.13-19 belongs to a first edition of the book, condoning 'multiple (or movable) shrines', which in a later edition came to connote a single, unique location,[29] or whether the contrast is set against the uncontrolled cult of the foreigners,[30] the Deuteronomistic History's defence of a single place[31] resembles extra-biblical literature's establishment of Jerusalem as the chosen place.

While the Pentateuch in its final form became a common work, acceptable to all groups because of its implied ambiguity, the Deuteronomistic History's favouring of David and Jerusalem has a rejection of competitive groups as its implied argument. Its implied historical context is not the Iron Age kingdoms of Israel and Judah, but the competition over cult places, such as we know from the third–second century BCE onwards. Based on characters and events related to the 'Hasmonaean' struggle for Judaean hegemony, our author(s) completed a work in which imperial unity is mirrored against devastating factionalism. Related to this composition, however not at its base, is a Zion ideology, the fulfilment of which we do not find in the Masoretic Hebrew Bible. In this larger composition, Zion is primarily an ideal, a divine abode, while Jerusalem is ephemeral and rejectable.

The realization of Zion expectations is merely an exception, which we find in 1 Maccabees. The search for such a realization, however, has revealed that reiterative history is a literary principle in both biblical and extra-biblical literature, related not only to themes but also to composition. As the writers of Hasmonaean matters hardly have anything to tell about their heroes that is not reflected in the narratives about Jerusalem's kings in the Former Prophets and Chronicles, one must question the historical value of each of these texts. Ascribing historicity to all these variants is highly unscientific and sorting out degrees of credibility is a hazardous enterprise. Whether based on traditions about the Patriarchs and Moses as in *Jubilees*, traditions about Jewish kings as in *Eupolemus*, 1 Maccabees, *Liber Josuae* and *AF* in Samaritan tradition, or a conflation of several traditions as in Josephus' promotion of Jerusalem against Gerizim and Heliopolis, preferences for Jerusalem do not leave the possibility open that other shrines should share its status.

---

28. Hjelm, *Samaritans and Early Judaism*, pp. 138-52 (151); Schwartz, *The Curse of Cain*, pp. 109-16.
29. Halpern, 'Centralising Formula' p. 26.
30. Hjelm, 'Cult Centralisation', p. 299.
31. Halpern, 'Centralising Formula', pp. 32-34.

BIBLIOGRAPHY

Abegg, M., P. Flint and E. Ulrich, *The Dead Sea Scrolls Bible: The Oldest Known Bible. Translated For the First Time into English* (San Francisco: HarperSanFrancisco, 1999).

Abel, F.-M., *Géographie de la Palestine* (2 vols.; Paris: J. Gabalda, 1933–38).

—*Les Livres des Maccabées* (Paris: J. Gabalda, 1949).

Aberbach, M., and L. Smolar, 'Aaron, Jeroboam, and the Golden Calves', *JBL* 86 (1962), pp. 129-40.

Ackroyd, P.R., *Israel under Babylon and Persia* (The New Clarendon Bible: Old Testament, 4; Oxford: Clarendon Press, 1970).

—'Isaiah I–XII: Presentation of a Prophet', in J.A. Emerton *et al.* (eds.), *Congress Volume: Göttingen 1977* (VTSup, 29; Leiden: E.J. Brill, 1978), pp. 16-48.

—'Isaiah 36–39: Structure and Function', in J.R. Nellis *et al.* (eds.), *Von Kanaan bis Kerala* (Festschrift J.P.M. Van der Ploeg; AOAT, 211; Neukirchen–Vluyn: Neukirchener Verlag, 1982), pp. 3-21 (repr. in *Studies in the Religious Tradition of the Old Testament* [London: SCM Press, 1987], pp. 105-20).

Adler, E.N., and M. Seligsohn, 'Une nouvelle chronique samaritaine', *REJ* 44 (1902), pp. 188-222; *REJ* 45 (1902), pp. 70-98, 223-54; *REJ* 46 (1903), pp. 123-46.

—*Une nouvelle chronique samaritaine/Texte samaritaine transcrit et édité pour le première fois avec une traduction française par Elkan-Nathan Adler et M. Séligsohn* (Paris: Librairie Durlacher, 1903).

Ahlström, G.W., *The History of Ancient Palestine from the Palaeolithic Period to Alexander's Conquest* (ed. D.V. Edelman; JSOTSup, 146; Sheffield: JSOT Press, 1993).

—*Psalm 89: Eine Liturgie aus dem Ritual des leidenden Königs* (Lund: Håkan Ohlssons Boktryckeri, 1959).

Albertz, R., *Religionsgeschichte Israels in alttestamentlicher Zeit* (Göttingen: Vandenhoeck & Ruprecht, 1992).

Albrektson, B., *History and the Gods: An Essay on the Idea of Historical Events as Divine Manifestations in the Ancient Near East and in Israel* (Lund: C.W.K. Gleerup, 1967).

Albright, W.F., 'New Israelite and Pre-Israelite Sites: The Spring Trip of 1929', *BASOR* 35 (1929), pp. 1-14.

Alt, A., *Kleine Schriften* (3 vols.; Munich: Beck, 1953).

Alter, R., *The Art of Biblical Narrative* (London: Allen & Unwin, 1981).

—*The David Story: A Translation with Commentary of 1 and 2 Samuel* (New York: W.W. Norton, 1999).

Anderson, B.W., 'The Apocalyptic Rendering of the Isaiah Tradition', in J. Neusner *et al.* (eds.), *The Social World of Formative Christianity and Judaism: Essays in Tribute to Howard Clark Kee* (Philadelphia: Fortress Press, 1988), pp. 17-38.

Anderson, G.A., 'Intentional and Unintentional Sin in the Dead Sea Scrolls', in D.P. Wright, D.N. Freedman and A. Hurvitz (eds.), *Pomegranates and Golden Bells: Studies in Biblical, Jewish, and Near Eastern Ritual, Law, and Literature in Honor of Jacob Milgrom* (Winona Lake, IN: Eisenbrauns, 1995), pp. 49-64.

Anderson, H., '3 Maccabees', in *OTP*, II, pp. 509-29.

Arenhoevel, D., *Die Theokratie nach dem 1. und 2. Makkabäerbuch* (Walberberger Studien, Theologische Reihe, 3; Mainz: Grünewald, 1967).

Arnold, P.M., 'Mizpah', in *ABD*, IV, pp. 879-81.

Attridge, H.W., 'Historiography', in Stone (ed.), *Jewish Writings of the Second Temple Period*, pp. 157-84.

Auld, A.G., 'The Deuteronomists and the Former Prophets', in Shearing and McKenzie (eds.), *Those Elusive Deuteronomists*, pp. 116-26.

—*Joshua Retold: Synoptic Perspectives* (Edinburgh: T. & T. Clark, 1998).

—'Joshua: The Hebrew and Greek Texts', in *idem, Joshua Retold*, pp. 7-18 (rev. version of a paper given at the 1977 SOTS Cambridge Summer Meeting, published in J.A. Emerton [ed.], *Studies in the Historical Books of the Old Testament* [VTSup, 30; Leiden: E.J. Brill, 1979], pp. 1-14).

—*Kings Without Privilege: David and Moses in the Story of the Bible's Kings* (Edinburgh: T. & T. Clark, 1994).

—'Prophets through the Looking Glass: Between Writings and Moses', *JSOT* 27 (1983), pp. 3-23.

—'Reading Joshua after Kings', in *idem, Joshua Retold*, pp. 102-12 (first published in J. Davies, G. Harvey and W.G.E. Watson [eds.], *Words Remembered, Texts Renewed: Essays in Honour of John F.A. Sawyer* [JSOTSup, 195; Sheffield: Sheffield Academic Press, 1995], pp. 161-81).

—'Samuel and Genesis: Some Questions of Van Seters's "Yahwist"', in McKenzie and Römer (eds.), *Rethinking the Foundations*, pp. 23-32.

—'Textual and Literary Studies in the Book of Joshua', in *idem, Joshua Retold*, pp. 19-24 (first published in *ZAW* 90 [1978], pp. 412-17).

—'What Makes Judges Deuteronomistic', in *idem, Joshua Retold*, pp. 120-26.

Bächli, O., *Amphiktyonie im Alten Testament: Forschungsgeschichtliche Studie zur Hypothese von Martin Noth* (Theologische Zeitschrift Sonderband, 6; Basel: Fr. Reinhardt Verlag, 1977).

Baillet, M., Review of Macdonald, *Samaritan Chronicle No. II*, *RB* 7 (1970), pp. 592-602.

Barrick, W.B., 'On the Meaning of בֵּית־הַבָּמוֹת/בֵּית־הַ and בָּתֵּי־הַבָּמוֹת and the Composition of the Kings History', *JBL* 115 (1996), pp. 621-42.

Barstad, H.M., 'Lebte Deuterojesaja in Judäa?', *NorTT* 83 (1982), pp. 77-87.

—*The Myth of the Empty Land: A Study of the History and Archaeology of Judah During the 'Exilic' Period* (Oslo: Scandinavian University Press, 1996).

—'The Strange Fear of the Bible: Some Reflections on the "Bibliophobia" in Recent Ancient Israelite Historiography', in L.L. Grabbe (ed.), *Leading Captivity Captive: The 'Exile' as History and Ideology* (ESHM, 2; JSOTSup, 278; Sheffield: Sheffield Academic Press, 1998), pp. 120-27.

—The Understanding of the Prophets in Deuteronomy', *SJOT* 8 (1994), pp. 236-51.

Barth, H., *Die Jesaja-Worte in der Josiazeit: Israel und Assur als Thema einer produktiven Neuinterpretation der Jesajaüberlieferung* (WMANT, 48; Neukirchen–Vluyn: Neukirchener Verlag, 1977).

Bartlett, J.R., 'Edom in the Nonprophetical Corpus', in Edelman (ed.), *You Shall Not Abhor*, pp. 13-21.

Becking, B., 'Chronology: A Skeleton without Flesh? Sennacherib's Campaign as a Case-Study', in Grabbe (ed.), *Like a Bird in a Cage*, pp. 46-72.

—*The Fall of Samaria: An Historical and Archaeological Study* (Leiden: E.J. Brill, 1992).

Ben-Ḥayyim, Z., 'The Language of Tibåt Mårqe and Its Time', in Tal and Florentin (eds.), *Proceedings of the First International Congress of the Société d'Études Samaritaines*, pp. 331-45.

—*The Literary and Oral Tradition of Hebrew and Aramaic amongst the Samaritans* (5 vols.; Jerusalem: The Academy of the Hebrew Language, 1957–77 [Hebrew]).

—'A Samaritan Text of the Former Prophets?', *Lešonénu* 35 (1970), pp. 293-302.

Ben-Ḥayyim, Z. (with assistance from A. Tal), *A Grammar of Samaritan Hebrew: Based on the Recitation of the Law in Comparison with the Tiberian and Other Jewish Traditions* (Jerusalem: Hebrew University Press, rev. edn, 2000 [first published in Hebrew as עברית וארמית נוסח שמרון [Jerusalem: The Academy of the Hebrew Language, 1977] [the Hebrew version is the fifth volume of *The Literary and Oral Tradition of Hebrew and Aramaic amongst the Samaritans* (listed above)]).

Ben Zvi, E., 'Who Wrote the Speech of Rabshakeh and When?', *JBL* 109 (1990), pp. 79-92.

—'Malleability and Its Limits: Sennacherib's Campaign Against Judah as a Case Study', in Grabbe (ed.), *Like a Bird in a Cage*, pp. 73-105.

Bergren, R.V., *The Prophets and the Law* (Cincinnati: Hebrew Union College Press, 1974).

Beuken, W.A.M., 'Isa 56.9–57.13—An Example of the Isaianic Legacy of Trito-Isaiah, in J.W. Henten *et al.* (eds.), *Tradition and Reinterpretation in Jewish and Early Christian Literature* (Festschrift J.C.H. Lebram; Leiden: E.J. Brill, 1986), pp. 48-64.

—*Isaiah. II. Isaiah 28–39* (Leuven: Peeters, 2000).

—'Isaiah Chapters LXV–LXVI: Trito-Isaiah and the Closure of the Book of Isaiah', in J.A. Emerton (ed.), *Congress Volume: Leuven 1989* (VTSup, 43; Leiden: E.J. Brill, 1991), pp. 204-21.

—*Jesaja IIIA* (POT, Nijkerk: Callenbach, 1989).

—'The Main Theme of Trito-Isaiah "The Servants of YHWH"', *JSOT* 47 (1990), pp. 67-87.

Biddle, M.E., *A Redaction History of Jeremiah 2.1–4.2* (AThANT, 77; Zürich: Theologischer Verlag, 1990).

Bickerman, E.J., *Der Gott der Makkabäer: Untersuchung über Sinn und Ursprung der makkabäischen Erhebung* (Berlin: Schocken Books, 1937 [Eng. trans.: *The God of the Maccabees: Studies on the Meaning and Origin of the Maccabaean Revolt* [SJLA, 32; Leiden: E.J. Brill, 1979]).

Binger, T., *Asherah, Goddesses in Ugarit, Israel and the Old Testament* (CIS, 2; JSOTSup, 232; Sheffield: Sheffield Academic Press, 1997).

—'Fighting the Dragon: Another Look at the Theme in the Ugaritic Texts', *SJOT* 6 (1992), pp. 139-49.

Blenkinsopp, J., 'Deuteronomic Contribution to the Narrative in Genesis–Numbers: A Test Case', in Shearing and McKenzie (eds.), *Those Elusive Deuteronomists*, pp. 84-115.

—*Ezra–Nehemiah: A Commentary* (OTL; Philadelphia: Westminster Press, 1988).

—*A History of Prophecy in Israel: From Settlement in the Land to the Hellenistic Period* (Philadelphia: Westminster Press, 1983).

—*Isaiah 1–39: A New Translation With Introduction and Commentary* (AB 19; New York: Doubleday, 2000).

—*The Pentateuch: An Introduction to the First Five Books of the Bible* (Garden City, NY: Doubleday, 1992).

—*Sage, Priest, Prophet: Religious and Intellectual Leadership in ancient Israel* (Louisville, KY: Westminster/John Knox Press, 1995).

—'The Servant and the Servants in Isaiah and the Formation of the Book', in Broyles and Evans (eds.), *Writing & Reading the Scroll of Isaiah*, I, pp. 169-75.

Blum, E., *Studien zur Komposition des Pentateuchs* (BZAW, 189; Berlin: W. de Gruyter, 1990).

Bóid, I.R.M., *Principles of Samaritan Halachah* (Leiden: E.J. Brill, 1989).

Boling, R.G., 'Judges, Book of ', in *ABD*, III, pp. 1107-17.

Boorer, S., *The Promise of the Land as Oath: A Key to the Formation of the Pentateuch* (BZAW, 205; Berlin: W. de Gruyter, 1992).

Bowman, J., *Samaritan Documents Relating to their History, Religion and Life* (Pittsburgh: Pickwick Press, 1977).

—*Transcript of the Original Text of the Samaritan Chronicle Tolidah* (Leeds: University of Leeds Press, 1954).

Brekelmans, C., 'Deuteronomic Influence in Isaiah 1–12', in Vermeylen (ed.), *The book of Isaiah*, pp. 167-76.

Brettler, M., '2 Kings 24.13-14 as History', *CBQ* 53 (1991), pp. 541-52.

Bright, J., 'Isaiah I', in M. Black and H.H. Rowley (eds.), *Peake's Commentary on the Bible* (London: Thomas Nelson, 1962).

Brooke, G.J. (ed.), *New Qumran Texts and Studies: Proceedings of the First Meeting of the International Organization for Qumran Studies, Paris 1992* (Leiden: E.J. Brill, 1994).

Brooke, G.J., and B. Lindars (eds.), *Septuagint, Scrolls and Cognate Writings* (SCS, 33; Atlanta, GA: Scholars Press, 1992).

Broyles, C.C., and C.A. Evans (eds.), *A History of Israel* (Philadelphia: Westminster Press, 1959 [2nd edn: London: SCM Press, 1972]).

—*Writing and Reading the Scroll of Isaiah: Studies of an Interpretive Tradition* (VTSup, 70/1; Leiden: E.J. Brill, 1997).

Brunneau, P., 'Les Israélites de Délos et la juiverie délienne', *Bulletin de Correspondance Hellénique* 106 (1982), pp. 465-504.

Buhl, M.-L., and S. Holm-Nielsen, *Shiloh—The Danish Excavations at Tall Sailun, Palestine, in 1926, 1929, 1932 and 1963: the Pre-Hellenistic Remains* (Copenhagen: The National Museum of Denmark, 1969).

Bunimowitz, S., and I. Finkelstein, 'Pottery', in I. Finkelstein, S. Bunimowitz and Z. Lederman (eds.), *Shiloh: The Archaeology of a Biblical Site* (Tel Aviv: Institute of Archaeology of Tel Aviv University, 1993), pp. 81-196.

Campbell, A.F., 'Martin Noth and the Deuteronomistic History', in McKenzie and Graham (eds.), *The History of Israel's Traditions*, pp. 31-62.

—*Of Prophets and Kings: A Late Ninth-Century Document (1 Samuel 1–2 Kings 10)* (CBQMS, 17; Washington: Catholic Biblical Association of America, 1986).

Campbell, E.F., 'Shechem', in Stern (ed.), *The New Encyclopedia of Archaeological Excavations*, IV, pp. 1345-54.

Carlson, R.A., *David, the Chosen King: A Traditio-Historical Approach to the Second Book of Samuel* (Stockholm: Almqvist & Wiksell, 1964).

Carr, D.M., 'Reading Isaiah from Beginning (Isaiah 1) to End (Isaiah 65–66): Multiple Modern Possibilities', in Melugin and Sweeney (eds.), *New Visions of Isaiah*, pp. 188-218.

—'What Can We Say about the Tradition History of Isaiah? A Response to Christopher Seitz's *Zion's Final Destiny*', in Lovering (ed.), *Society of Biblical Literature Seminar Papers 1992*, pp. 583-97.

Carroll, R.P., 'Blindsight and the Vision Thing: Blindness and Insight in the Book of Isaiah', in Broyles and Evans (eds.), *Writing and Reading the Scroll of Isaiah*, pp. 79-93.

—*Jeremiah* (Sheffield: JSOT Press, 1989 [repr. 1993, Sheffield: Sheffield Academic Press])

—*Jeremiah: A Commentary* (London: SCM Press, 1986).

—'Psalm LXXVIII: Vestiges of a Tribal Polemic', *VT* 21 (1971), pp. 133-50.

Cazelles, H., 'Jeremiah and Deuteronomy', in Perdue and Kovacs (eds.), *A Prophet to the Nations*, pp. 89-111.

Charlesworth, J.H., *Graphic Concordance to the Dead Sea Scrolls* (Tübingen: J.C.B. Mohr [Paul Siebeck], 1991).

Childs, B.S., 'The Enemy from the North and the Chaos Tradition', *JBL* 78 (1959), pp. 187-98 (repr. in Perdue and Kovacs [eds.], *A Prophet to the Nations*, pp. 151-61).

—*Introduction to the Old Testament as Scripture* (Philadelphia: Fortress Press, 1979).

—*Isaiah and the Assyrian Crisis* (SBT, 2/3; London: SCM Press, 1967).

Clements, R.E., 'Beyond Tradition-History: Deutero-Isaianic Development of First Isaiah's Themes', *JSOT* 31 (1985), pp. 95-113.

—*God and Temple* (Philadelphia: Fortress Press, 1965).

—*Isaiah 1–39* (NCB; Grand Rapids: Eerdmans; London: Marshall, Morgan & Scott, 1980).

—'Isaiah 14.22-27: A Central Passage Reconsidered', in Vermeylen (ed.), *The Book of Isaiah*, pp. 253- 62.

—*Isaiah and the Deliverance of Jerusalem: A Study of the Interpretation of Prophecy in the Old Testament* (JSOTSup, 13; Sheffield: JSOT Press, 1980).

—'The Prophecies of Isaiah and the Fall of Jerusalem in 587 BC', *VT* 30 (1980), pp. 421-36.

—'The Prophecies of Isaiah to Hezekiah Concerning Sennacherib: 2 Kings 19.21-34 // Isa. 37.22-35', in R. Liwak and S. Wagner (eds.), *Prophetie und geschichtliche Wirklichkeit im alten Israel: Festschrift für Siegfried Hermann zum 65. Geburtstag* (Cologne: W. Kohlhammer, 1991), pp. 65-78.

—'The Unity of the Book of Isaiah', *Int* 36 (1982), pp. 117-29.

Clancy, F., 'The Date of LXX', *SJOT* 16/2 (2002), pp. 207-25.

Clifford, R.J., *The Cosmic Mountain in Canaan and the Old Testament* (Cambridge, MA: Harvard University Press, 1972).

—'In Zion and David a New Beginning: An Interpretation of Psalm 78', in Halpern and Levenson (eds.), *Traditions in Transformation*, pp. 121-41.

—'Isaiah, Book of (Second Isaiah)', in *ABD*, III, pp. 490-501.

Clines, J.A. (ed.), *The Dictionary of Classical Hebrew* (Sheffield: Sheffield Academic Press, 1995–).

Coats, G.W., *Moses, Heroic Man, Man of God* (JSOTSup, 57; Sheffield: JSOT Press, 1988).

Cogan, M., *Imperialism and Religion: Assyria, Judah and Israel in the Eight and Seventh Centuries BCE* (SBLMS, 19; Missoula, MT: Scholars Press, 1974).

Cogan, M., and H. Tadmor, *II Kings: A New Translation With Introduction and Commentary* (AB, 11; 2 vols., Garden City, NY: Doubleday, 1988).

Coggins, R.J., *Samaritans and Jews: The Origins of Samaritanism Reconsidered* (Oxford: Basil Blackwell, 1975).

—'What Does "Deuteronomistic" Mean?', in Shearing and McKenzie (eds.), *Those Elusive Deuteronomists*, pp. 22-35.

Cohn, R.L., *The Shape of Sacred Space: Four Biblical Studies* (AAR Studies in Religion; Philadelphia: Scholars Press, 1981).

—'Convention and Creativity in the Books of Kings: The Case of the Dying Monarch', *CBQ* 47 (1985), pp. 603-16.

Cohen, J.M., *A Samaritan Chronicle: A Source-Critical Analysis of the Life and Time of the Great Samaritan Reformer, Baba Rabbah* (Leiden: E.J. Brill, 1981).

Collins, J.J., 'Messianism in the Maccabean Period', in Neusner, Green and Frerichs (eds.), *Judaism and Their Messiahs*, pp. 97-109.

Collins, N., '281 BCE: The Year of the Translation of the Pentateuch into Greek Under Ptolemy II', in Brooke and Lindars (eds.), *Septuagint, Scrolls and Cognate Writings*, pp. 403-503.

Conrad, E.W., 'Reading Isaiah and the Twelve as Prophetic Books, in Broyles and Evans (eds.), *Writing and Reading the Scroll of Isaiah*, pp. 3-17.

—'The Royal Narratives and the Structure of the Book of Isaiah', *JSOT* 41 (1988), pp. 67-81.

Cooke, G.A., *The Book of Ezekiel* (ICC; repr., Edinburgh: T. & T. Clark, 1970 [1936]).

Crane, O.T., *The Samaritan Chronicle, or the Book of Joshua the Son of Nun* (New York: John B. Alden, 1890).

Crenshaw, J.L., '*YHWH Ṣebaôt Šemô*: A Form-Critical Analysis', *ZAW* 81 (1969), pp. 156-75.

Cross, F.M., *Canaanite Myth and Hebrew Epic: Essays in the History of the Religion of Israel* (Cambridge, MA: Yale University Press, 1973).

Crown, A.D., 'Another Look at Samaritan Origins', in Crown and Davey (eds.), *New Samaritan Studies of the Société d'Études Samaritaines*, pp. 133-55.

—*A Bibliography of the Samaritans* (London: Scarecrow Press, 2nd edn, 1993 [1984]).

—'The Date and Authenticity of the Samaritan Hebrew Book of Joshua as Seen in Its Territorial Allotments', *PEQ* 96 (1974), pp. 79-100 (repr. with 'Addendum 1986', in Dexinger and Pummer [eds.], *Die Samaritaner*, pp. 281-311).

—'New Light on the Inter-Relationships of Samaritan Chronicles from Some Manuscripts in the John Rylands Library', *BJRL* 54 (1972), pp. 282-313; *BJRL* 55 (1973), pp. 86-111.

—'Redating the Schism between the Judeans and the Samaritans', *JQR* 82 (1991), pp. 17-50.

—*Samaritan Scribes and Manuscripts* (Texts and Studies in Ancient Judaism, 80; Tübingen: J.C.B. Mohr [Paul Siebeck], 2001).

Crown, A.D. (ed.), *The Samaritans* (Tübingen: J.C.B. Mohr [Paul Siebeck] 1989).

Crown, A.D., and L. Davey (eds.), *New Samaritan Studies of the Société d'Études Samaritaines*. III-IV. *Essays in Honour of G.D. Sixdenier* (Studies in Judaica, 5; Sydney: Mandelbaum Publishing, 1995).

Dalglish, E.R., 'Bethel (Deity)', in *ABD*, I, pp. 706-10.

Darr, K.F., 'No Strength to Deliver: A Contextual Analysis of Hezekiah's Proverb in Isaiah 37.3b', in Melugin and Sweeney (eds.), *New Visions of Isaiah*, pp. 219-56.

Daviau, P.M.M., J.W. Wevers and M. Weigl (eds.), *The World of the Aramaeans: Studies in Honour of Paul-Eugène Dion* (JSOTSup, 324-36; 3 vols., Sheffield: Sheffield Academic Press, 2001).

Davies, P.R., *In Search of 'Ancient Israel'* (JSOTSup, 148; Sheffield: Sheffield Academic Press, 1992).

—*Scribes and Schools: The Canonization of the Hebrew Scriptures* (Louisville, KY: Westminster/John Knox Press, 1998).

Davis, E., 'Ezra', in *EncJud*, VI, p. 1106.

Day, J., 'Ashera in the Hebrew Bible and Northwest Semitic Literature', *JBL* 105 (1986), pp. 385-408.

—'Dragon and Sea, God's Conflict With', in *ABD*, II, pp. 228-31.

—*God's Conflict With the Dragon and the Sea: Echoes of a Canaanite Myth in the Old Testament* (Cambridge: Cambridge University Press, 1985).

— 'Leviathan', in *ABD*, IV, pp. 295-96.

Debus, J., *Die Sünde Jeroboams: Studien zur Darstellung Jeroboams und der Geschichte des Nordreichs in der deuteronomistischen Geschichtsschreibung* (FRLANT, 93; Göttingen: Vandenhoeck & Ruprecht, 1967).

De Jong, S., 'Hizkia en Zedekia: Over de verhouding van 2 Kon. 18.17–19.37/Jes. 36–37 tot Jer. 37.1-10', *ACEBT* 5 (1984), pp. 135-46.

De Troyer, K., 'A Lost Hebrew Vorlage? A Closer Look at the Temple Builder in 1 Esdras', in idem, *Rewriting the Sacred Text*, pp. 91-126.

—'A Pre-Masoretic Biblical Text: The Final Touches to an Old Joshua', in *idem, Rewriting the Sacred Text*, pp. 29-58.

—*Rewriting the Sacred Text: What the Old Greek Texts Tell Us about the Literary Growth of the Bible* (Text Critical Studies, 4; Atlanta: SBL, 2003)

Deutsch, R., 'Lasting Impressions: New Bullae Reveal Egyptian-Style Emblems on Judah's Royal Seals', in *BAR* 28/4 (2002), pp. 42-51, 60-62.

Dexinger, F., *Der Taheb: Ein 'messianischer' Heilsbringer der Samaritaner* (Salzburg: Otto Müller, 1986).

Dexinger, F., and R. Pummer (eds.), *Die Samaritaner* (Wege der Forschung, 604; Darmstadt: Wissenschaftliche Buchgesellschaft, 1992).

Dhorme, P., *Les Livres de Samuel* (Paris: J. Gabalda, 1910).

Dietrich, W., 'History and Law: Deuteronomistic Historiography and Deuteronomic Law exemplified in the Passage from the Period of the Judges to the Monarchical Period', in de Pury, Römer and Macchi (eds.), *Israel Constructs its History*, pp. 315-42.

—*Jesaja und die Politik* (Munich: Chr. Kaiser Verlag, 1976).

—*Prophetie und Geschichte: Eine redaktionsgeschichtliche Untersuchung zum deuteronomistischen Geschichtswerk* (FRLANT, 108; Göttingen: Vandenhoeck & Ruprecht, 1972).

Dietrich, W., and T. Naumann, *Die Samuelbücher* (Darmstadt: Wissenschaftliche Buchgesellschaft, 1995).

Dimant, D., 'Qumran Sectarian Literature', in Stone (ed.), *Jewish Writings of the Second Temple Period*, pp. 483-50.

Dion, P.-E., *Les Araméens à l'âge du fer: histoire politique et structures sociales* (EBib, NS 34; Paris: J. Gabalda, 1997).

Dodd, C.H., *The Bible and the Greeks* (London: Hodder & Stoughton, 1935).

Donner, H., *Israel unter den Völkern* (VTSup, 11; Leiden: E.J. Brill, 1964), pp. 30-38.

Doran, R., 'Pseudo-Eupolemus: A New Translation and Introduction', in *OTP*, II, pp. 873-82.

Dozeman, T.B., *God on the Mountain: A Study of Redaction, Theology and Canon in Exodus 19-24* (SBLMS, 37; Atlanta: Scholars Press, 1989).

Duhm, B., *Das Buch Jesaia* (HKAT, 3.1; Göttingen: Vandenhoeck & Ruprecht, 1892).

Edelman, D.V., 'The Meaning of *qiṭṭer*', *VT* 35 (1985), pp. 395-404.

Edelman, D.V. (ed.), *The Fabric of History: Text, Artefact and Israel's Past* (JSOTSup, 127; Sheffield: JSOT Press, 1991).

—*You Shall Not Abhor an Edomite for He is Your Brother: Edom and Seir in History and Tradition* (Archaeology and Biblical Studies, 3; Atlanta: Scholars Press, 1995).

Eidevall, G., *Grapes in the Desert: Metaphors, Models, and Themes in Hosea 4–14* (CBOTS, 43; Stockholm: Almqvist & Wiksell, 1996).

Eissfeldt, O., 'Jahwe Zebaoth' in R. Sellheim and F. Maass (eds.), *Otto Eissfeldt, Kleine Schriften* [6 vols.; Tübingen: J.C.B. Mohr (Paul Siebeck), 1962–79], III, pp. 103-23 (first published in *Miscellanea Academica Berolinensia* II.2 [1950], pp. 128-50).

—'Stammesage und Novelle in den Geschichten von Jakob und von seinen Söhnen', in Schmidt *et al.* (eds.), *Eucharisterion*, pp. 56-77.

Emerton, J.A., 'Did Ezra Go to Jerusalem in 428 B.C.?', *JTS* 17 (1966), pp. 1-19.

Eph'al, I., 'The Samarian(s) in Assyrian Sources', in M. Cogan, and I. Eph'al (eds.), *Ah, Assyria, Studies in Assyrian History and Ancient Near Eastern Historiography Presented to Hayim Tadmor* (Jerusalem: Magnes Press, 1991), pp. 36-45.

—The "Samaritans" in the Assyrian Sources', in E. Stern and H. Eshel (eds.), *The Samaritans* (ספר השומרונים) (Jerusalem: Yad Ben-Zvi Press, 2002 [Hebrew]), pp. 34-44.

Eshel, H., 'The Prayer of Joseph: A Papyrus from Masada and the Samaritan Temple in Argarizin', *Zion* 56 (1991), pp. 125-36 (Hebrew).

Ewald, H., *Geschichte des Volkes Israel* (8 vols.; Göttingen: Dietrichsche Buchhandlung, 32nd edn, 1864–66).

Eynikel, E., *The Reform of King Josiah and the Composition of the Deuteronomic History* (OTS, 33; Leiden: E.J. Brill, 1996).

Fallon, F., 'Eupolemus', in *OTP*, II, pp. 861-72.

Finkelstein, I., *The Archaeology of the Israelite Settlement* (Jerusalem: Israel Exploration Society, 1988).

—'The History and Archaeology of Shiloh from the Middle Bronze Age II to Iron Age II', in I. Finkelstein, S. Bunimowitz and Z. Lederman (eds.), *Shiloh: The Archaeology of a Biblical Site* (Tel Aviv: Institute of Archaeology of Tel Aviv University, 1993), pp. 371-93.

—'Shiloh, 1981', *IEJ* 32 (1982), pp. 148-50.

—'Shiloh, 1982', *IEJ* 33 (1983), pp. 123-26.

Finkelstein, I., and N.A. Silberman, *The Bible Unearthed: Archaeology's New Vision of Ancient Israel and the Origin of Its Sacred Texts* (New York: Free Press, 2001).

Fish, T., 'War and Religion in Ancient Mesopotamia', *BJRL* 23 (1937), pp. 387-402.

Fishbane, M., 'Torah and Tradition', in D.A. Knight (ed.), *Tradition and Theology in the Old Testament* (London: SPCK, 1977), pp. 275-300.

Fitzmeyer, J.A., 'The Sacrifice of Isaac in Qumran Literature', *Bib* 83 (2002), pp. 211-29.

Florentin, M., ' "Shomronit": A Grammatical Description and Lexical Characterization' (unpublished PhD dissertation, Tel Aviv University, 1989 [Hebrew]).

—*The Tulida, A Samaritan Chronicle: Text, Translation, Commentary* (Jerusalem: Yad Izhak Ben-Zvi, 1999 [Hebrew]).

Fohrer, G., *Das Buch Jesaja. II. Kapitel 24–39* (Züricher Bibelkommentare; Zürich: Zwingli Verlag, 1960 [2nd edn, 1967]).

—*Einleitung in das Alte Testament* (Heidelberg: Quelle, 1965).

Fossum, J., 'Dove', in *DDD²*, pp. 500-504.

—'Samaritan Demiurgical Traditions and the Alleged Dove Cult of the Samaritans', in R. van den Broeck and M.J. Vermaseren (eds.), *Studies in Gnosticism and Hellenistic Religions* (EPRO, 91; Leiden: E.J. Brill, 1981), pp. 143-60.

Friedman, R.E., *The Exile and Biblical Narrative: The Formation of the Deuteronomistic and Priestly Works* (HSM, 22; Chico, CA: Scholars Press, 1981),

—'From Egypt to Egypt: Dtr¹ and Dtr²', in Halpern and Levenson (eds.), *Traditions in Transformation*, pp. 167-92.

—'Torah (Pentateuch)', in *ABD*, VI, pp. 605-21.

Friis, H., *Die Bedingungen für die Errichtung des Davidischen Reichs in Israel und seiner Umwelt* (Dielheimer Blätter zum Alten Testament Beiheft, 6; Heidelberg: B.J. Diebner & C. Nauerth, 1986).

—'Eksilet og den israelitiske historieopfattelse', *DTT* 38 (1975), pp. 1-16.

Galambush, J., *Jerusalem in the Book of Ezekiel: The City as Yahweh's Wife* (SBLDS, 130; Atlanta: Scholars Press, 1992).

Galling, K., *Die Erwählungstraditionen Israels* (Giessen: Alfred Töpelmann, 1928).

—'Bethel und Gilgal', *ZDPV* 66 (1943), pp. 140-55; *ZDPV* 67 (1945), pp. 21-42.

Galter, H.D., 'Hubur', in *DDD*², pp. 816-17.

Garbini, G., *History & Ideology in Ancient Israel* (London: SCM Press, 1988).

Garsiel, M., *The First Book of Samuel: A Literary Study of Comparative Structures, Analogies and Parallels* (Jerusalem: Revivim Publishing House, 1985 [Hebrew original: Jerusalem: Revivim Publishing House, 1983]).

Gaster, M., *The Asatir: The Samaritan Book of the 'Secrets of Moses' Together with the Pitron or Samaritan Commentary and the Samaritan story of the Death of Moses* (Oriental Translation Fund, NS 26; London: The Royal Asiatic Society, 1927).

—'Das Buch Josua in hebräisch-samaritanischer Rezension: Entdeckt und sum ersten Male herausgegeben', *ZDMG* 62/2/3 (1908), 207-79, 475-549.

—'On the Newly Discovered Samaritan Book of Joshua', *JRAS* (1908), pp. 795-809.

—*The Samaritans: Their History, Doctrines and Literature* (London: Oxford University Press, 1925 [repr. in 1976 and 1980]).

Gesenius, W., *Der Prophet Jesaja* (3 vols.; Leipzig: F.C.W. Vogel, 1821).

Gieselmann, B., 'Die sogenannte josianische Reform in der gegenwärtigen Forschung', *ZAW* 106 (1994), pp. 223-42.

Gitay, Y., *Isaiah and his Audience: The Structure and Meaning of Isaiah 1–12* (Assen: Van Gorcum, 1991).

—'Isaiah and the Syro-Ephraimite War', in Vermeylen (ed.), *The Book of Isaiah*, pp. 216-30.

Glazier-McDonald, B., 'Edom in the Prophetical Corpus', in Edelman (ed.), *You Shall Not Abhor*, pp. 23-32.

Gleis, M., *Die Bamah* (BZAW, 251; Berlin: W. de Gruyter, 1997).

Goldberg, J., 'Two Assyrian Campaigns against Hezekiah and Later Eight Century Biblical Chronology', *Bib* 80/3 (1999), pp. 360-90.

Goldstein, J.A., *I Maccabees: A New Translation with Introduction and Commentary* (AB, 41; Garden City NY: Doubleday, 1977).

—*II Maccabees: A New Translation with Introduction and Commentary* (AB, 41A; Garden City, NY: Doubleday, 1983).

—'How the Authors of 1 and 2 Maccabees Treated the "Messianic Promises"', in Neusner, Green and Frerichs (eds.), *Judaism and Their Messiahs*, pp. 69-96.

Gonçalves, F.J., '2 Rois 18.13–20.19 par. Isaïe 36–39. Encore une fois, lequel des deux livres fut le premier?', in J.-M. Auwers and A. Wénin (eds.), *Lectures et relectures de la Bible* (Festschrift P.-M. Bogaert; BETL, 144; Leuven: Leuven University Press, 1999), pp. 27-55.

—*L'expédition de Sennachérib en Palestine dans la littérature hébraïque ancienne* (Paris: J. Gabalda, 1986).

Grabbe, L.L., *Judaism from Cyrus to Hadrian* (2 vols.; Minneapolis: Fortress Press, 1992).

Grabbe, L.L. (ed.), *Can a History of Israel Be Written?* (ESHM, 1; JSOTSup, 245; Sheffield: Sheffield Academic Press, 1997).

—*Like a Bird in a Cage: The Invasion of Sennacherib in 701 BCE* (ESHM, 4; London: Sheffield Academic Press, 2003).

Grayson, A.K., 'Assyrian Rule of Conquered Territory in Ancient Western Asia', *CANE* (1995), pp. 959-68.

Green, A., 'Ancient Mesopotamian Religious Iconography', in *CANE*, pp. 1837-45.

Greenspoon, L.J., 'The Qumran Fragments of Joshua: Which Puzzle Are They Part Of and Where Do They Fit?', in Brooke and Lindars (eds.), *Septuagint, Scrolls and Cognate Writings*, pp. 159-94.

Gressmann, H., *Altorientalische Bilder zum Alten Testament* (Berlin: W. de Gruyter, 1926).

—*Altorientalische Texte zum Alten Testament* (Berlin: W. de Gruyter, 1927).

—'Sage und Geschichte in den Patriarchenerzählungen', *ZAW* 30 (1910), pp. 1-34.

—'Ursprung und Entwicklung in den Patriarchenerzählungen', in Schmidt *et al.* (eds.), *Eucharisterion*, pp. 1-55.

Gunkel, H., *Genesis: übersetzt und erklärt* (Göttinger Handkommentar zum Alten Testament, I.1; Göttingen: Vandenhoeck & Ruprecht, 1901).

Gunkel, H. (with a contribution from H. Zimmern), *Schöpfung und Chaos in Urzeit und Endzeit: Eine religionsgeschichtliche Untersuchung über Gen 1 und Ap Joh 12* (Göttingen: Vandenhoeck & Ruprecht, 1895).

Gunneweg, A.H.J., 'Anmerkungen und Anfragen zur neueren Pentateuchforschung', *ThR* 50 (1985), pp. 107-31.

Hall, B., 'From John Hyrcanus to Baba Rabbah', in Crown (ed.), *The Samaritans*, pp. 32-54.

Hallbäck, G., and J. Strange (eds.), *Bibel og historieskrivning* (FBE, 10; Copenhagen: Museum Tusculanum, 1999).

Halpern, B., 'The Centralisation Formula in Deuteronomy', *VT* 31 (1981), pp. 20-38.

Halpern, B., and J.D. Levenson (eds.), *Traditions in Transformation: Turning Points in Biblical Faith* (Winona Lake, IN: Eisenbrauns, 1981).

Hanhart, R., *Studien zur Septuaginta und zum hellenistischen Judentum* (Tübingen: J.C.B. Mohr [Paul Siebeck], 1999).

Hanson, P., *The Dawn of Apocalyptic: The Historical and Sociological Roots of Jewish Apocalyptic Eschatology* (Philadelphia: Fortress Press, 1989).

Hardmeier, C., *Prophetie im Streit vor dem Untergang Judas: Erzählkommunikative Studien zur Entstehungssituation der Jesaja- und Jeremiaerzählungen in II Reg 18–20 und Jer 37–40* (BZAW, 187; Berlin: W. de Gruyter, 1990).

Harrak, A., 'Tales About Sennacherib: the Contribution of the Syriac Sources', in Daviau, Wevers and Weigl (eds.), *The World of the Aramaeans*, III, pp. 168-89.

Hayes, J.H., 'The Traditions of Zion's Inviolability', *JBL* 82 (1963), pp. 419-26.

Hengel, M., *Judentum und Hellenismus: Studien zu ihrer Begegnung unter besonderer Berücksichtigung Palästinas bis zur Mitte des 2.Jh.s v. Chr* (Tübingen: J.C.B. Mohr [Paul Siebeck], 2nd edn, 1973 [1969]) (published in English as *Judaism and Hellenism* [London: Xpress Reprints, 1996 (1981)]).

Hjelm, I., 'Brothers Fighting Brothers: Jewish and Samaritan Ethnocentrism in Tradition and History', in Thompson (ed.), *Jerusalem in Ancient History and Tradition*, pp. 197-222.

—'Cult Centralization as a Device of Cult Control', *SJOT* 13/2 (1999), pp. 298-309.

—'The Hezekiah Narrative as a Foundation Myth for Jerusalem's Rise to Sovereignty', in Jayyusi (ed.), *Islamic Studies*, pp. 661-74.

—*The Samaritans and Early Judaism: A Literary Analysis* (CIS, 7; JSOTSup, 303; Sheffield: Sheffield Academic Press, 2000).

—'What Do Samaritans and Jews Have in Common? Recent Trends in Samaritan Studies', *CBR* 3.1 (2004), pp. 9-62.

Hjelm, I., and T.L. Thompson, 'The Victory Song of Merneptah, Israel and the People of Palestine', *JSOT* 27.1 (2002), pp. 3-18.

Hoffmann, H.-D., *Reform und Reformen: Untersuchungen zu einem Grundthema der deuteronomistischen Geschichtsschreibung* (AThANT, 66; Zürich: Theologischer Verlag, 1980).

Högenhaven, J., *Den gamle pagt: en introduktion til den nyere debat om pagten i det Gamle Testamente* (Tekst og Tolkning, 8; Copenhagen: Akademisk Forlag, 1989).

—'Historien om profeterne: nogle bemærkninger om de gammeltestamentlige profetbøger som historieskrivning', in Hallbäck and Strange (eds.), *Bibel og historieskrivning*, pp. 103-15.

Holm-Nielsen, S., 'Silo—endnu engang', *SEÅ* 54 (1989), pp. 80-89.

Holladay, W.L., *Jeremiah 1: A Commentary on the Book of the Prophet Jeremiah 1–25* (Philadelphia: Fortress Press, 1986).

Holloway, S.W., 'Distaff, Crutch or Chain Gang: The Curse of the House of Joab in 2 Sam. 3.29', *VT* 37 (1987), pp. 370–75.

Holt, E.K., *Prophesying the Past: The Use of Israel's History in the Book of Hosea* (JSOTSup, 194; Sheffield: Sheffield Academic Press, 1995).

House, P.R. (ed.), *Beyond Form Criticism: Essays in Old Testament Literary Criticism* (Winona Lake, IN: Eisenbrauns, 1992).

Houtman, C., *Inleiding in de Pentateuch* (Kampen: Kok, 1980) (German translation: *Der Pentateuch: Die Geschichte seiner Erforschung neben einer Auswertung* [Kampen: Kok, 1994]).

Howard, D.M., Jr, 'A Contextual Reading of Psalms 90–94', in J.C. McCann (ed.), *The Shape and Shaping of the Psalter* (JSOTSup, 159; Sheffield: JSOT Press, 1993), pp. 108-23.

Hurwitz, A., '"Diachronic Chiasm" in Biblical Hebrew', in B. Uffenheimer (ed.), *Bible and Jewish History: Studies in Bible and Jewish History Dedicated to the Memory of Jacob Liver* (Tel Aviv: University of Tel Aviv, 1971 [Hebrew]), pp. 248-55.

Hyatt, J.P., 'Jeremiah and Deuteronomy', in Perdue and Kovacs (eds.), *A Prophet to the Nations*, pp. 113-27.

Irvine, S.A., *Isaiah, Ahaz, and the Syro-Ephraimitic Crisis* (SBLDS, 123; Atlanta: Scholars Press, 1990).

Ishida, T., *The Royal Dynasties in Ancient Israel: A Study on the Formation and Development of Royal–Dynastic Ideology* (Berlin: W. de Gruyter, 1977).

Isser, S.J., *The Dositheans: A Samaritan Sect in Late Antiquity* (Leiden: E.J. Brill, 1976).

Jayyusi, S.K. (ed.), *Islamic Studies: Special Issue on Jerusalem* 40/3-4 (2001).

Jellinek, A., *Beit ha Midrash. Sammlungen kleiner Midrashim und Vermischter Abhandlungen aus der ältern jüdischen Literatur* (6 vols., Jerusalem: Bamberger & Wahrmann, 3rd rev. edn, 1967 [1853]).

Jenkins, A.K., 'Hezekiah's Fourteenth Year: A New Interpretation of 2 Kings XVIII 13–XIX 37', *VT* 26 (1976), pp. 284-98.

Jepsen, A., 'אמן', in *ThWAT*, I, pp. 314-47.

—*Die Quellen des Königbuches* (Halle: Max Niemeyer, 1953).

Johnson, A.R., *Sacral Kingship in Ancient Israel* (Cardiff: University of Wales, 1955 [2nd edn, 1962]).

Jones, G.H., *I and II Kings* (2 vols.; Grand Rapids: Eerdmans, 1984).

Joüon, P., SJ, and T. Muraoka, *A Grammar of Biblical Hebrew* (2 vols.; Rome: Editrice Pontificio Istituto Biblica, 1991).

Juynboll, T.G.J., *Chronicon samaritanum, arabice conscriptum, cui titulus est Liber Josuae. Ex unico cod. Scalegieri* (Leiden: S. & J. Luchtmans, 1848) (published in English as *The Samaritan Chronicle, or the Book of Joshua the Son of Nun* [trans. O.T. Crane; New York: John B. Alden 1890]).

Kahle, P., 'Zum hebräischen Buch Josua der Samaritaner', *ZDMG* 62/3 (1908), pp. 550-51.

Kaiser, O., *Das Buch des Propheten Jesaja: Kapitel 1–12: Übersetzt und erklärt* (Göttingen: Vandenhoeck & Ruprecht, 5th rev. edn. 1981).

—*Der Prophet Jesaja: Kapitel 13–39: Übersetzt und erklärt* (Göttingen: Vandenhoeck & Ruprecht, 1973).

Kalimi, I., and J.D. Purvis, 'The Hiding of the Temple Vessels in Jewish and Samaritan Literature', *CBQ* 56.4 (1994), pp. 679-85.

Kang, S.-M., *Divine War in the Old Testament and in the Ancient Near East* (Berlin: W. de Gruyter, 1989).

Kempinski, A., 'Shiloh', in Stern (ed.), *The New Encyclopedia of Archaeological Excavations*, IV, pp. 1364-66.

Keulen, P.S.F. van, *Manasseh Through the Eyes of the Deuteronomists: The Manasseh Account (2 Kings 21.1-18) and the Final Chapters of the Deuteronomistic History* (OTS, 38; Leiden: E.J. Brill, 1996).

Kiesow, K., *Exodustexte im Jesajabuch: Literarkritische und motivgeschichtliche Analysen* (OBO, 24; Göttingen: Vandenhoeck & Ruprecht, 1979).

Kippenberg, H.G., *Garizim un Synagoge: Traditionsgeschichtliche Untersuchungen zur samaritanischen Religion der aramäischen Periode* (Berlin: W. de Gruyter, 1971).

Kjaer, H., 'The Danish Excavation of Shiloh', *PEFQS* (1929), pp. 202-13.

—'The Excavations of Shiloh 1929', *JPOS* 10 (1930), pp. 87-104.

—'Shiloh: A Summary Report of the Second Danish Excavation, 1929', *PEFQS* (1931), pp. 71-88.

Klein, H., 'Freude an Rezin: Ein versuch, mit dem Text Jes. viii 6 ohne Konjektur auszukommen', *VT* 30 (1980), pp. 229-33.

Klein, R.W., *I Samuel* (WBC, 10: Waco, TX: Word Books, 1983).

Knauf, E.A., 'Meunim', in *ABD*, IV, pp. 801-802.

Knoppers, G.N., *Two Nations Under God: The Deuteronomistic History of Solomon and the Dual Monarchies* (HSM, 52; 2 vols.; Atlanta: Scholars Press, 1993).

Koehler, L., and W. Baumgartner, *The Hebrew and Aramaic Lexicon of the Old Testament* (subsequently revised by W. Baumgartner and J.J. Stamm with assistance from B. Hartmann *et al.*) (5 vols.; Leiden: E.J. Brill, 1994–2000).

Koopmans, W.T., *Joshua 24 as Poetic Narrative* (JSOTSup, 93; Sheffield: JSOT Press, 1990).

Kotter, W.R., 'Gilgal', in *ABD*, II, pp. 1022-24.

Kraus, H.-J., 'Gilgal: Ein Beitrag zur Kulgusgeschichte Israels', *VT* 1 (1951), pp. 181-98.

—*Psalmen* (BKAT, 15/1; Neukirchen–Vluyn: Neukirchener Verlag, 2nd edn, 1961).

—*Theologie der Psalmen* (BKAT, 15/3; Neukirchen–Vluyn: Neukirchener Verlag, 1979).

Kugler, R.A., 'The Deuteronomists and the Latter Prophets', in Shearing and McKenzie (eds.), *Those Elusive Deuteronomists*, pp. 127-44.

Kutscher, E.Y., *A History of the Hebrew Language* (Jerusalem: Magnes Press, 1982).

—*The Language and Linguistic Background of the Isaiah Scroll (1QIsa^a)* (Leiden: E.J. Brill, 1974).

Laato, A., *About Zion I Will Not Be Silent: The Book of Isaiah as an Ideological Unity* (CBOTS, 44; Stockholm: Almqvist & Wiksell, 1998).

—'Hezekiah and the Assyrian Crisis in 701 B.C.', *SJOT* 2 (1987), pp. 49-68.

—*The Servant of Yahweh and Cyrus: A Reinterpretation of the Exilic Messianic Programme in Isaiah 40–55* (CBOTS, 35; Stockholm: Almqvist & Wiksell, 1992).

—*A Star is Rising: The Historical Development of the Old Testament Royal Ideology and the Rise of the Jewish Messianic Expectations* (Atlanta: Scholars Press, 1997).

—*Who Is Immanuel? The Rise and Foundering of Isaiah's Messianic Expectations* (Åbo: Åbo Academy Press, 1988).

Labahn, A., 'Metaphor and Intertextuality: "Daughter of Zion" as a Test Case', *SJOT* 17/1 (2003), pp. 49-67.

Labat, R., *Le caractère religieux de la royauté assyro-babylonienne* (Paris: Librairie d'amérique et d'orient adrien-maisonneuve, 1929).

Landersdorfer, S., 'Das Priesterkönigtum von Salem', *JSOR* 9 (1925), pp. 203-16.

Leichty, E., 'Esarhaddon, King of Assyria', in *CANE*, II, pp. 949-58.

Lemaire, A., 'Vers l'histoire de la rédaction des livres des Rois', *ZAW* 98 (1986), pp. 221-36.

Lemche, N.P., *Ancient Israel: A New History of Israelite Society* (The Biblical Seminar, 5; Sheffield: JSOT Press, 1988).

—*The Canaanites and Their Land: The Idea of Canaan in the Old Testament* (JSOTSup, 110; Sheffield: JSOT Press, 1991).

—*Early Israel: Anthropological and Historical Studies on the Israelite Society Before the Monarchy* (Leiden: E.J. Brill, 1985).

—'The God of Hosea', in E. Ulrich, J.W. Wright, R.P. Carroll and P.R. Davies (eds.), *Priests, Prophets and Scribes: Essays on the Formation and Heritage of Second Temple Judaism in Honour of Joseph Blenkinsopp* (JSOTSup, 149; Sheffield: Sheffield Academic Press, 1992), pp. 241-57.

—'Good and Bad in History: The Greek Connection', in McKenzie and Römer (eds.), *Rethinking the Foundations*, pp. 127-40.

—*Israel i Dommertiden: En oversigt over diskussionen om Martin Noths 'Das system des zwölf Stämme Israels'* (Tekst og Tolkning, 4; Copenhagen: G.E.C. Gad, 1972).

—*The Israelites in History and Tradition* (Louisville, KY: Westminster/John Knox Press). 1998).

—'Mysteriet om det forsvundne tempel: Overleveringen om Shilos ødelæggelse i Jer. 7.12-14', *SEÅ* 54 (1989), pp. 118-26.

—'Prægnant tid i Det Gamle Testamente', in G. Hallbäck and N.P. Lemche (eds.), *'Tiden' i bibelsk belysning* (FBE, 11: Copenhagen: Museum Tusculanum, 2001), pp. 29-47.

—*Die Vorgeschichte Israels: Von den Anfangen bis zum Ausgang des 13. Jahrhunderts v. Chr.* (Biblische Enzyklopädie, 1; Stuttgart: W. Kohlhammer, 1996) (published in English as *Prelude to Israel's past: Background and Beginnings of Israelite History and Identity* [Peabody, MA: Hendrickson, 1998]).

Levenson, J.D., *Sinai and Zion: An Entry into the Jewish Bible* (San Francisco: HarperSanFrancisco, 1987).

—'Zion Traditions', in *ABD*, VI, pp. 1098-302.

Levin, C., *Der Jahwist* (FRLANT, 157; Göttingen: Vandenhoeck & Ruprecht, 1993).

Levine, L.D., *Two Neo-Assyrian Stelae from Iran* (Toronto: Royal Orientario Museum, 1972).

Lewis, J.P., 'Flood', in *ABD*, II, pp. 798-803.

Lichtenstein, H., 'Die Fastenrolle, eine Untersuchung zur jüdisch-hellenistischen Geschichte', *HUCA* 8-9 (1931–32), pp. 257-352.

Limburg, J., 'Psalms, Book of', in *ABD*, V, pp. 523-36.

Liverani, M., 'The Ideology of the Assyrian Empire', in M.T. Larsen (ed.), *Power and Propaganda: A Symposium on Ancient Empires* (Mesopotamia, Copenhagen Studies in Assyriology, 7; Copenhagen: Akademisk Forlag, 1979), pp. 297-317.

—*Prestige and Interest: International Relations in the Near East ca. 1600–1100 B.C.* (HANE/S, 1; Padova: Sargon, 1990).

Liverani, M. (ed.), *Guerra santa e guerra giusta dal mondo antico alla prima età moderna*, *Studi Storici* 43/3 (Rome: Carocci editore, 2002).

Long, B.O., *1 Kings* (FOTL, 9; Grand Rapids: Eerdmans, 1984).

—*2 Kings* (FOTL, 10; Grand Rapids: Eerdmans, 1991).

Loretz, O., *Ugarit und die Bibel: Kanaanäische Götter und Religion im Alten Testament* (Darmstadt: Wissenschaftliche Buchgesellschaft, 1990).

Lovering, E.H. (ed.), *Society of Biblical Literature Seminar Papers 1992* (Atlanta: Scholars Press, 1992).

Lowy, S. *The Principles of Samaritan Bible Exegesis* (Leiden: E.J. Brill, 1977).

Lubetski, M., 'King Hezekiah's Seal Revisited', *BAR* 27/4 (2001), pp. 44-51, 59.

Luckenbill, D.D., *Ancient Records of Assyria and Babylonia* (2 vols.; Chicago: Chicago Press, 1927 [repr., New York: Greenwood Press, 1968]).

Lutz, H.-M., *Jahwe, Jerusalem und die Völker: zur Vorgeschichte von Sach 12,1-8 und 14,1-5* (WMANT, 27; Neukirchen–Vluyn: Neukirchener Verlag, 1968).

Lyon, D.G., *Keilschrifttext Sargon's, königs von Assyrien (722–705 v.Chr.)* (Leipzig:, 1883).

Macchi, J.-D., *Les Samaritains: Histoire d'une légende: Israël et la province de Samarie* (Le Monde de la Bible, 30; Geneva: Labor et Fides, 1994).

Macdonald, J., *Samaritan Chronicle No. II (or: Sepher Ha-Yamim) From Joshua to Nebuchadnezzar* (Berlin: W. de Gruyter, 1969).

Machinist, P., 'The Crisis of History in the Study of Jewish Origins' (paper given at the closing session of the congress, 'The Origins of the Jewish People and Contemporary Biblical Scholarship', held in Chicago, 18 October 1999).

Macintosh, A.A., *A Critical and Exegetical Commentary on Hosea* (Edinburgh: T. & T. Clark, 1997).

Macuch, R., 'Samaritan Languages: Samaritan Hebrew, Samaritan Aramaic', in Crown (ed.), *The Samaritans*, pp. 531-84.

Magen, I., 'Excavations at Mt-Gerizim—A Temple City', *Qadmoniot* 23 (1989), pp. 70-96.

—'A Fortified Town of the Hellenistic Period on Mount Gerizim', *Qadmoniot* 19 (1986), pp. 91-101.

—'Gerizim Mount', in Stern (ed.), *The New Encyclopedia of Archaeological Excavations*, II, pp. 484-92.

—'Mount Gerizim and the Samaritans', in F. Manns, *et al.* (eds.), *Early Christianity in Context: Monuments and Documents* (Jerusalem: The Franciscan Printing Press, 1993), pp. 91-147.

—'Mt. Gerizim—A Temple City', *Qadmoniot* 33/2 (120) (2000), pp. 74-118 (Hebrew).

Magen, Y., H. Misgav and L. Tsefania, *Mount Gerizim Excavations. I. The Aramaic, Hebrew and Samaritan Inscriptions* (English translations by E. Levin and M. Guggenheimer; Judea and Samaria Publications, 2; Jerusalem: Staff Officer of Archaeology, Civil Administration of Judea and Samaria, 2004 [Hebrew and English]).

Maier, J., *Das altisraelitische Ladeheiligtum* (BZAW, 93; Berlin: Alfred Töpelmann, 1965).

Martens, K., 'With a Strong Hand and an Outstretched Arm', *SJOT* 15/1 (2001), pp. 123-41.

McCarter, P. Kyle, Jr, *I Samuel: A New Translation with Introduction, Notes and Commentary* (AB, 8; New York: Doubleday, 1980).

—*II Samuel: A New Translation with Introduction, Notes and Commentary* (AB, 9; New York: Doubleday, 1984).

McCormick, C.M., 'From Box to Throne: A New Study of the Development of the Ark Tradition' (unpublished paper delivered at the SBL National Meeting, Nashville, 2000).

McCullough, W.S., 'Serpent', in *IDB*, III, pp. 289-91.

McKay, J.W., *Religion in Judah under the Assyrians, 732–609 B.C.* (SBT, 2.26; London: SCM Press, 1973).

McKenzie, J.L., *Second Isaiah: Introduction, Translation and Notes* (AB, 20; Garden City, NY: Doubleday, 1968).

McKenzie, S.L., 'The Books of Kings in the Deuteronomistic History', in McKenzie and Graham (eds.), *The History of Israel's Traditions*, pp. 281-307.

—'Deuteronomistic History', in *ABD*, II, pp. 160-68.

—*The Trouble With Kings: The Composition of the Books of Kings in the Deuteronomistic History* (VTSup, 42; Leiden: E.J. Brill, 1991).

McKenzie, S.L., and M.P. Graham (eds.), *The History of Israel's Traditions: The Heritage of Martin Noth* (JSOTSup, 182; Sheffield: Sheffield Academic Press, 1994)

McKenzie, S.L., and T. Römer (eds.), *Rethinking the Foundations: Historiography in the Ancient World and in the Bible: Essays in Honour of John Van Seters* (Berlin: W. de Gruyter, 2000).

Meissner, B., *Babylonien und Assyrien* (2 vols.; Heidelberg: C. Winters/Universitätsbuchhandlung, 1920–25).

Melugin, R.F., 'Figurative Speech and the Reading of Isaiah 1 as Scripture', in Melugin and Sweeney (eds.), *New Visions of Isaiah*, pp. 282-305.

—*The Formation of Isaiah 40–55* (BZAW, 141; Berlin: W. de Gruyter, 1976).

Melugin, R.F., and M.A. Sweeney (eds.), *New Visions of Isaiah* (JSOTSup, 214; Sheffield: Sheffield Academic Press, 1996).

Mendels, D., '"Creative History History" in the Hellenistic Near East in the Third and Second Centuries BCE: The Jewish Case', *JSP* 2 (1988), pp. 13-20.

—*The Land of Israel as a Political Concept in Hasmonean Literature* (Tübingen: J.C.B. Mohr, 1987).

—*The Rise and Fall of Jewish Nationalism* (New York: Doubleday, 1992).

Mettinger, T.N.D., *The Dethronement of Sabaoth: Studies in the Shem and Kabod Theologies* (CBOTS, 18; Lund: C.W.K. Gleerup, 1982).

—'In Search of the Hidden Structure: YHWH as King in Isaiah 40–55', in Broyles and Evans (eds.), *Writing & Reading the Scroll of Isaiah*, I, pp. 143-54.

—'Yahweh Zebaoth', in *DDD*[2], pp. 920-24.

Mikolášek, A. 'Les Samaritains Gardiens de la Loi contre les Prophètes', *Communio Viatorum* 12 (1969), pp. 139-48.

—'Silo et Salem à Sichem', in Tal and Florentin (eds.), *Proceedings of the First International Congress of the Société d'Études Samaritaines*, pp. 79-80.

Milgrom, J., *Leviticus 1–16: A New translation with Introduction and Commentary* (AB, 3; New York: Doubleday, 1991).

Milik, J.T. (with the collaboration of M. Black), *The Books of Enoch: Aramaic Fragments of Qumran Cave 4* (Oxford: Clarendon Press, 1976).

Miscall, P.D., *Isaiah* (Sheffield: JSOT Press).

Montgomery, J.A., *The Samaritans: The Earliest Jewish Sect—Their History, Theology and Literature* (Philadelphia: John C. Winston, 1907 [repr.: New York: Ktav, 1968]).

Moor, J.C., de, *An Anthology of Religious Texts From Ugarit* (Leiden: E.J. Brill, 1987).

Mor, M., 'The Samaritans and the Bar-Kokhbah Revolt', in Crown (ed.), *The Samaritans*, pp. 19-31.

Mowinckel, S., 'Die Komposition des deuterojesajanischen Buches', *ZAW* 49 (1931), pp. 87-112, 242-60.

—*The Psalms in Israel's Worship* (trans. D.R. Ap-Thomas; Oxford: Basil Blackwell, 1962).

Muilenburg, J., 'Form Criticism and Beyond', *JBL* 88 (1969), pp. 1-18.

—'The Site of Ancient Gilgal', *BASOR* 140 (1955), pp. 11-27.

Mulder, M.J., *1 Kings 1–11* (Leuven: Peeters, 1998).

Mullen, E.T., *Ethnic Myths and Pentateuchal Foundations: A New Approach to the Formation of the Pentateuch* (Atlanta, GA: Scholars Press, 1997).

Murray, D.F., *Divine Prerogative and Royal Pretension: Pragmatics, Poetics and Polemics in a Narrative Sequence about David (2 Samuel 5.17–7.29)* (JSOTSup, 264; Sheffield: Sheffield Academic Press, 1998).

—'Of All the Years the Hopes—or Fears? Jehoiachin in Babylon (2 Kgs 25.27-30), *JBL* 120/2 (2001), pp. 245-65.

Müller, M., *The First Bible of the Church: A Plea for the Septuagint* (CIS, 1; JSOTSup, 206; Sheffield: Sheffield Academic Press, 1996).

Na'aman, N., 'The Kingdom of Judah under Josiah', *Tel Aviv* 18 (1991), pp. 3-71.

—'New Light on Hezekiah's Second Prophetic Story (2 Kings 19,9b-35)', *Bib* 81 (2000), pp. 393-402.

—'Population Changes in Palestine Following Assyrian Deportations', *Cathedra* 54 (1988), pp. 43-63 (Hebrew).

Naveh, J., and I. Magen, 'Aramaic and Hebrew Inscriptions of the Second Century BCE at Mount Gerizim', *Atiqot* 32 (1997), pp. 9-17.

Nelson, R.D., *The Double Redaction of the Deuteronomistic History* (JSOTSup, 18; Sheffield: JSOT Press, 1981).

—Review of C. Hardmeier, *Prophetie im Streit vor dem Untergang Judas: Erzählkommunikative Studien zur Entstehungssituation der Jesaja und Jeremiaerzählungen in II Reg 18–20 und Jer 37–40* (BZAW, 187; Berlin: W. de Gruyter, 1990), *CBQ* 55 (1993), pp. 337-38.

Neusner, J., W.S. Green and E.S. Frerichs (eds.), *Judaism and Their Messiahs at the Turn of the Christian Era* (Cambridge: Cambridge University Press, 1987).

Nickelsburg, G.W.E., *Jewish Literature Between the Bible and the Mishnah: A Historical and Literary Introduction* (London: SCM Press, 1981).

—'The Bible Rewritten and Expanded', in Stone (ed.), *Jewish Writings of the Second Temple Period*, pp. 89-156.

Nicholson, E.W., *God and His People: Covenant and Theology in the Old Testament* (Oxford: Clarendon Press, 1986).

—*The Pentateuch in the Twentieth Century: The Legacy of Julius Wellhausen* (Oxford: Clarendon Press, 1998).

Niehr, H., 'The Constitutive Principles for Establishing Justice and Order in Northwest Semitic Societies with Special Reference to Ancient Israel and Judah', *Sonderdruck aus: Zeitschrift für Altorientalische und biblische Rechtsgeschichte* 3 (1977), pp. 112-30.

Nielsen, E., *Shechem: A Traditio-Historical Investigation* (Copenhagen: G.E.C. Gad, 1955).

Nielsen, F.A.J., 'The Exodus Story According to Ezekiel the Tragedian and the Exodus Manuscripts from Qumran: A Study of the Early History of the Book of Exodus' (unpublished PhD dissertation, University of Copenhagen, 2000).

—*The Tragedy in History: Herodotus and the Deuteronomistic History* (CIS, 4; JSOTSup, 251; Sheffield: Sheffield Academic Press, 1997).

Niessen, F., *Eine Samaritanische Version des Buches Yehošuaʻ und die Šobak Erzählung: Die Samaritanische Chronik Nr. II, Handschrift 2: JR(G) 1168 = Ryl. Sam. MS 259, Folio 8b-53a* (Texte und Studien zur Orientalistik, 12; Hildesheim: Georg Olms, 2000).

Nodet, E., *A Search for the Origins of Judaism: From Joshua to the Mishnah* (JSOTSup, 248; Sheffield: Sheffield Academic Press, 1997 [a revised English version of *Essai sur les origines du Judaïsme: de Josue aux Pharisiens* (Paris: Les Edition du Cerf, 1992)]).

Nöldeke, T., 'Assyrios, Syrios, Syros', *Hermes* 5 (1871), pp. 443-68.

Norin, S.I.L., *Er spaltete das Meer: die Auszugsüberlieferung in Psalmen und Kult des alten Israel* (CBOTS, 9; Lund: C.W.K. Gleerup, 1977).

—'An Important Kennicott Reading in 2 Kings xviii 13', *VT* 32 (1982), pp. 337-38.

Noth, M., *Überlieferungsgeschichtliche Studien: Die sammelnden und bearbeitenden Geschichtswerke im Alten Testament* (Tübingen: Max Niemeyer, 3rd edn, 1967 [1943]).

—*Das zweite Buch Mose: Exodus* (ATD, 5; Göttingen: Vandenhoeck & Ruprecht, 5th edn, 1973 [1959]).

O'Brien, M.A., *The Deuteronomistic History Hypothesis: A Reassessment* (OBO, 92; Göttingen: Vandenhoeck & Ruprecht, 1989).

Oded, B., *Mass Deportations and Deportees in the Neo-Assyrian Empire* (Wiesbaden: Reichert, 1979).

—*War, Peace and Empire: Justifications for War in Assyrian Royal Inscriptions* (Wiesbaden: Reichert, 1992).

Ollenburger, C., *Zion the City of the Great King: A Theological Symbol of the Jerusalem Cult* (JSOTSup, 41; Sheffield: JSOT Press, 1987).

Olofsson, S., *God Is My Rock: A Study of Translation Technique and Theological Exegesis in the Septuagint* (CBOTS, 31; Stockholm: Almqvist & Wiksell, 1990).

Otto, E., 'El und Jhwh in Jerusalem', *VT* 30 (1980), pp. 316-29.

—*Das Mazzotfest in Gilgal* (BWANT, 107; Stuttgart: W. Kohlhammer, 1975).

—'Stehen wir vor einem Umbruch in der Pentateuchkritik?', *Verkündigung und Forschung* 22/2 (1977), pp. 82-98.

Pakkala, J., *Intolerant Monolatry in the Deuteronomistic History* (Publications of the Finnish Exegetical Society, 76; Göttingen: Vandenhoeck & Ruprecht, 1999).

—'The Original Meaning of Jeroboam's Calves' (unpublished paper delivered at the SBL International Meeting, Rome, 2001).

Parry D.W., and E. Qimron, *The Great Isaiah Scroll (1QIsa^a): A New Edition* (Leiden: E.J. Brill, 1999).

Peckham, B., 'The Composition of Deuteronomy 5–11', in C.L. Meyers, and M. O'Connor (eds.), *The Word of the Lord Shall Go Forth: Essays in Honor of David Noel Freedman in Celebration of His Sixtieth Birthday* (Winona Lake, IN: Eisenbrauns, 1983), pp. 217-40.

—*The Composition of the Deuteronomistic History* (HSM, 35; Atlanta: Scholars Press, 1985).

Perdue, L.G., and B.W. Kovacs (eds.), *A Prophet to the Nations: Essays in Jeremiah Studies* (Winona Lake, IN: Eisenbrauns, 1984).

Perlitt, L., *Bundestheologie im Alten Testament* (WMANT, 36; Neukirchen–Vluyn: Neukirchener Verlag, 1969).

Pfeiffer, R.H., *History of the New Testament Times with an Introduction to the Apocrypha* (New York: Harper & Brothers, 1949).

Philips, A., 'Nebalah—A Term for Serious Disorderly and Unruly Conduct', *VT* 25 (1975), pp. 237-41.

Polzin, R., *David and the Deuteronomist: A Literary Study of the Deuteronomic History*, III (3 vols.; Bloomington: Indiana University Press, 1993).

—*Moses and the Deuteronomist: A Literary Study of the Deuteronomic History* (3 vols.; New York: Seabury Press, 1980).

Porteous, N.W., 'Jerusalem–Zion: "The Growth of a Symbol"', in A. Kuschke (ed.), *Verbannung und Heimkehr: Beiträge zur Geschichte und Theologie Israels im 6. und 5. Jahrhundert v. Chr.* (Tübingen: J.C.B. Mohr [Paul Siebeck], 1961), pp. 235-52.

Provan, I.W., *Hezekiah and the Books of Kings: A Contribution to the Debate about the Composition of the Deuteronomistic History* (Berlin: W. de Gruyter, 1988).

Pummer, R., 'Samaritan Material Remains', in Crown (ed.), *The Samaritans*, pp. 135-77.

—'Einführung in den stand der Samaritanerforschung', in Dexinger and Pummer (eds.), *Die Samaritaner*, pp. 1-66.

Pury, A. de, *Promesse divine et légende cultuelle dans le cycle de Jacob: Genèse 28 et les traditions patriarchales* (2 vols.; Paris: J. Gabalda, 1975).

Pury, A. de, T. Römer and J.-D. Macchi (eds.), *Israel Constructs its History: Deuteronomistic Historiography in Recent Research* (JSOTSup, 306; Sheffield: Sheffield Academic Press, 2000) (first published as *Israël construit son histoire. L'historiographie deutéronomiste à la lumière des recherches récentes* [Le Monde de la Bible, 34; Geneva: Labor et Fides, 1996]).

Rad, G. von, *Deuteronomium: Studien* (FRLANT 58; Göttingen: Vandenhoeck & Ruprecht, 1948).

—*Die deuteronomische Geschichtsteologie in den Königsbüchern* (FRLANT, 40; Göttingen: Vandenhoeck & Ruprecht, 1947).

—*Theologie des Alten Testament* (2 vols.; Munich: Chr. Kaiser Verlag, 1957–60) (published in English as *Old Testament Theology* [2 vols.; New York: Harper, 1962–65]).

Ramsey, G.W., *The Quest for the Historical Israel* (London: SCM Press, 1981).

Rappaport, U., 'Reflections of the Origins of the Samaritans', in Y. Ben-Artzi, I. Bartal and E. Reiner (eds.), *Studies in Geography and History in Honour of Yehoshua Ben-Arieh* (Jerusalem: Magnes Press, 1999), pp. 10-19.

Rawlinson, H.C., *The Cuneiform Inscriptions of Western Asia* (5 vols., London: n.p., 1861–84).

Rendtorff, R., 'The Book of Isaiah: A Complex Unity: Synchronic and Diachronic Reading', in Melugin and Sweeney (eds.), *New Visions of Isaiah*, pp. 32-49 (an updated and revised version of 'The Book of Isaiah: A Complex Unity—Synchronic and Diachronic Reading', in E.H. Lovering, Jr [ed.], *Society of Biblical Literature Seminar Papers 1991* [Atlanta: Scholars Press, 1991], pp. 8-20).

—'Martin Noth and Tradition Criticism', in McKenzie and Graham (eds.), *The History of Israel's Traditions*, pp. 91-100.

—*Theologie des Alten Testaments: Ein kanonischer Entwurf* (Neukirchen–Vluyn: Neukirchener Verlag, 1998).

—*Das überlieferungsgeschichtliche Problem des Pentateuchs* (BZAW, 147; Berlin: W. de Gruyter, 1977).

Ribichini, S., 'Baetyl βαίτυλος', in *DDD²*, pp. 157-59.

Ringgren, H., 'רשׁע', in *ThWAT*, VII, pp. 675-83.

Rist, M., 'Enoch', in *IDB*, II, p. 103.

Roberts, J.J.M., 'The Davidic Origin of the Zion Tradition', *JBL* 92 (1973), pp. 329-44.

—'The Zion Tradition in Solomon's Temple' (unpublished paper delivered at the SBL National Meeting Paper, Boston, 1999).

Robinson, A., 'Zion and Ṣāphôn in Psalm XLVIII 3', *VT* 24 (1974), pp. 118-23.

Rofé, A., 'The Arrangement of the Book of Jeremiah', *ZAW* 101 (1989), pp. 390-98.

—'The Editing of the Book of Joshua in the Light of 4QJoshᵃ', in Brooke (ed.), *New Qumran Texts and Studies*, pp. 73-80.

—'The End of the Book of Joshua according to the Septuagint', *Henoch* 4 (1982), pp. 17-36.

—'Ephraimite versus Deuteronomistic History', in G.N. Knoppers and J.G. McConville (eds.), *Reconsidering Israel and Judah: Recent Studies on the Deuteronomistic History* (Winona Lake, IN: Eisenbrauns, 2000), pp. 462-74.

Rohland, E., 'Die Bedeutung der Erwählungstraditionen Israels für die eschatologie der alttestamentlichen Propheten' (unpublished PhD dissertation, University of Heidelberg, 1965).

Röllig, W., 'Bethel', in *DDD¹*, pp. 331-34.

Römer, T., 'Bernd-Jörg Diebner und die "Spätdatierung" der Pentateuch—und der historischen Traditionen der Hebräischen Bibel', *DBAT* 30 (eds. C. Nauerth and R. Grieshammer, *Begegnungen Bernd Jörg Diebner zum 60. Geburtstag am 8. Mai 1999*) (1999), pp. 151-55.

—'Is there a Deuteronomistic Redaction in the Book of Jeremiah?', in de Pury, Römer and Macchi (eds.), *Israel Constructs its History*, pp. 399-421.

—*Israels Väter: Untersuchungen zur Väterthematik im Deuteronomium und in der Deuteronomistischen Tradition* (OBO, 99; Freiburg: Universitätsverlag; Göttingen: Vandenhoeck & Ruprecht, 1990).

Römer, T., and A. de Pury, 'Deuteronomistic Historiography (DH): History of Research and Debated Issues', in de Pury, Römer and Macchi (eds.), *Israel Constructs its History*, pp. 24-143.

Rose, M., *Deuteronomist und Jahwist: Untersuchungen zu den Berührungspunkten beider Literaturwerke* (AThANT, 67; Zürich: Theologischer Verlag, 1981).

Rothschild, J.P., and G.D. Sixdenier (eds.), *Targum exégèse et philology, chroniques: Communication présentées à la table ronde internationale 'Les Manuscrits samaritains. Problèmes et méthodes' (Paris 7–9 octobre 1985)* (Leuven: Peeters, 1988).

Rowley, H.H., 'The Chronological Order of Ezra and Nehemiah', in *idem, The Servant of the Lord and Other Essays on the Old Testament* (London: Lutterworth Press, 1952), pp. 129-60.

—*Men of God: Studies in Old Testament History and Prophecy* (London: Thomas Nelson, 1963).

—'Sanballat and the Samaritan Temple', *BJRL* 38 (1955–56), pp. 166-98 (repr. in *idem, Men of God*, pp. 246-76).

Rudman, D., 'Is Rabshakeh also Among the Prophets? A Rhetorical Study of 2 Kings XVIII 17–35', *VTQ* 50/1 (2000), pp. 100-10.

Saggs, H.W.F., *The Encounter With the Divine in Mesopotamia and Israel* (London: Athlone Press, 1978).

—*The Might that Was Assyria* (London: Sidgwick & Jackson, 1984).

Sáenz-Badillos, A., *A History of the Hebrew Language* (trans. J. Elwolde; Cambridge: Cambridge University Press, 1997).

Sasson, J.M., 'Bovine Symbol in the Exodus Narrative', *VT* 18 (1968), pp. 380-87.

Schley, D.G., 'Joab', in *ABD*, III, pp. 852-54.

—*Shiloh: A Biblical City in Tradition and History* (JSOTSup, 63; Sheffield: JSOT Press, 1989).

Schiffman, L.H., *Reclaiming the Dead Sea Scrolls: The History of Judaism, the Background of Christianity, the Lost Library of Qumran* (Philadelphia: The Jewish Publication Society, 1994).

Schmid, H., 'Jahwe und die Kulttraditionen von Jerusalem', *ZAW* 26 (1955), pp. 168-98.

Schmid, H.H., *Der sogenannte Jahwist: Beobachtungen und Fragen zur Pentateuchforschung* (Zürich: Theologischer Verlag, 1976).

—'Vers une théologie du Pentateuque', in A. de Pury (ed.), *Le Pentateuque en question* (Geneva: Labor et Fides, 1989), pp. 361-86.

Schmid, K., *Erzväter und Exodus: Untersuchungen zur doppelten Begründung der Ursprünge Israels innerhalb der Geschichtsbücher des Alten Testaments* (WMANT, 81; Neukirchen–Vluyn: Neukirchener Verlag, 1999).

Schmidt, H. *et al.* (eds.), *Eucharisterion: Festschrift Hermann Gunkel* (FRLANT, 36; Göttingen: Vandenhoeck & Ruprecht, 1923).

Schmidt, W., 'Jerusalemer El-Traditionen bei Jesaja, ein religionsgeschichtliche Vergleich zum Vorstellungskreis der göttlichen Königtums', *ZRGG* 16 (1964), pp. 302-13.

Schreiner, J., *Sion-Jerusalem, Jahwes Königssitz: Theologie der heiligen Stadt im alten Testament* (StANT, 7; Munich: Kösel, 1963).

Schuller, E., '4Q372.1, A Text about Joseph', *Revue de Qumran* 14 (1990), pp. 349-76.

Schur, N., *History of the Samaritans* (Beiträge zur Erforschung des Alten Testamentes und des antiken Judentums, 18; Frankfurt: Peter Lang, 1989).

Schürer, E., *History of the Jewish People* (3 vols.; Edinburgh: T. & T. Clark, 1973–87 [ed. and trans. from the German, *Geschichte des judischen Volkes im Zeitalter Jesu Christi* (3 vols.; Leipzig: J.C. Hinrichs, 1885)]).

Schwartz, R.M., *The Curse of Cain: The Violent Legacy of Monotheism* (Chicago: University of Chicago Press, 1997).

Segni, L. Di, 'The Church of Mary Theotokos on Mount Gerizim: The Inscriptions', in G.C. Bottini *et al.* (eds.), *Christian Archaeology in the Holy Land: New Discoveries: Archaeological Essays in Honor of Vigilio C. Corbo* (Collectio Maior, 36; Jerusalem: Franciscan Printing Press, 1990), pp. 343-50.

Seitz, C.R., 'Isaiah 1–66: Making Sense of the Whole', in *idem* (ed.), *Reading and Preaching the Book of Isaiah* (Philadelphia: Fortress Press, 1988), pp. 105-26.

—'Mose als Prophet: Redaktionsthemen und Gesamtstruktur des Jeremiasbuches', *BZ* 34 (1990), pp. 234-45.

—Review of C. Hardmeier, *Prophetie im Streit vor dem Untergang Judas: Erzählkom-munikative Studien zur Entstehungssituation der Jesaja und Jeremiaerzählungen in II Reg 18–20 und Jer 37–40* (BZAW, 187; Berlin: W. de Gruyter, 1990) (repr. in *JBL* 110 [1991], pp. 511-12).

—*Zion's Final Destiny: The Development of the Book of Isaiah: A Reassessment of Isaiah 36–39* (Minneapolis: Fortress Press, 1991).

Sellin, D.E., *Gilgal: Ein Beitrag zur Geschichte der Einwanderung Israels in Palästina* (Leipzig: Deichert, 1917).

Shea, W.H., 'Jerusalem Under Siege: Did Sennacherib Attack Twice?', *BAR* 25/6 (1999), pp. 36-44, 64.

—'Sennacherib's Second Palestinian Campaign', *JBL* 104 (1985), pp. 401-18.

Shearing, L.S., and S.L. McKenzie (eds.), *Those Elusive Deuteronomists: The Phenomenon of Pan-Deuteronomism* (JSOTSup, 268; Sheffield: Sheffield Academic Press, 1999).

Shedletsky, L., 'Priestly and Deuteronomic Traditions in the Composition of II Kings 22–23' (unpublished paper delivered at the SBL National Meeting, Toronto, 2002).

Shehadeh, H., 'The Arabic of the Samaritans and its Importance', in Crown and Davey (eds.), *New Samaritan Studies of the Société d'Études Samaritaines*, pp. 551-75.

—'The Groups of the Samaritan Manuscripts of the Arabic Translation of the Pentateuch', in Rothschild, and Sixdenier (eds.), *Études samaritaines Pentateuque*, pp. 205-17.

Sheppard, G.T., 'The Book of Isaiah: Competing Structures According to a Late Modern Description of Its Shape and Scope', in Lovering (ed.), *Society of Biblical Literature Seminar Papers 1992*, pp. 549-82.

Shiloh, Y., Review of Marie-Louise Buhl and Svend Holm-Nielsen, *Shiloh—The Danish Excavations at Tall Sailun, Palestine, in 1926, 1929, 1932 and 1963: The Pre-Hellenis-tic Remains* (Copenhagen: The National Museum of Denmark, 1969), *IEJ* 21 (1971), pp. 67-69.

Sievers, J., *The Hasmoneans and Their Supporters: From Mattathias to the Death of John Hyrcanus I* (Studies in the History of Judaism, 6; Atlanta: Scholars Press, 1990).

Skehan, P.W., and A.A. Di Lella, *The Wisdom of Ben Sira: A New Translation, with Notes, Introduction and Commentary* (AB, 39; Garden City, NY: Doubleday, 1987).

Smelik, K.A.D., 'Distortion of Old Testament Prophecy: The Purpose of Isaiah xxxvi and xxxvii', *OTS* 24 (1986), pp. 70-93.

Smend, R., 'Das Gesetz un die Völker: Ein Beitrag zur deuteronomischen Redaktionsgeschichte', in H.W. Wolff (ed.), *Probleme biblischer Theologie: Gerhard von Rad zum 70. Geburtstag* (Munich: Chr. Kaiser Verlag, 1971), pp. 494-509.

Smith, M., *Palestinian Parties and Politics that Shaped the Old Testament* (London: SCM Press, 2nd corrected edn, 1987).

Smith, M.S., 'Myth and Mythmaking in Canaan and Ancient Israel', in *CANE* (1995), III, pp. 2031-41.

Smith, R.H., 'Abram and Melchizedek (Gen 14.18-20)', *ZAW* 77 (1965), pp. 129-53.

Soden, W. von, *Akkadisches Handwörterbuch: unter Benutzung des lexikalisches Nachlassen von Bruno Meissner/bearb. von W von Soden* (3 vols.; Wiesbaden: Otto Harrassowitz, 1965–81).

Soggin, J.A., *An Introduction to the History of Israel and Judah* (3rd edn [1984: *A History of Israel*; 2nd rev. edn 1993: *An Introduction to the History of Israel and Judah*] translated from the Italian: *Introduzione alla Storia d'Israele e di Guida* [Brescia: Paideia Editrice, 1998]; London: SCM Press, 1999).

—*Joshua: A Commentary* (London: SCM Press, 1972).

—*Judges: A Commentary* (London: SCM Press, 2nd edn, 1987 [1981]).

Sparks, K.L., *Ethnicity and Identity in Ancient Israel: Prolegomena to the Study of Ethnic Sentiments and Their Expression in the Hebrew Bible* (Winona Lake, IN: Eisenbrauns, 1998).

Spieckermann, H., *Juda unter Assur in der Sargonidenzeit* (FRLANT, 129; Göttingen: Vandenhoeck & Ruprecht, 1982).

Spiro, A., *Samaritans, Tobiads, and Judahites in Pseudo-Philo: Use and Abuse of the Bible by Polemicists and Doctrinaires* (New York: American Academy for Jewish Research, 1951) (repr. from *Proceedings of the American Academy for Jewish Research* 20 [1951], pp. 279-335).

Spykerboer, H.C., 'Isaiah 55.1–5: The Climax of Deutero-Isaiah: An Invitation to Come to the New Jerusalem', in Vermeylen (ed.), *The Book of Isaiah*, pp. 357-59.

Stade, B., 'Miscellen', *ZAW* 6 (1886), pp. 122-88.

Steck, O.H., *Bereitete Heimkehr: Jesaja 35 als redaktionelle Brücke zwischen dem Ersten und dem Zweiten Jesaja* (SBS, 121; Stuttgart: Katholisches Bibelwerk, 1985).

—'Tritojesaja im Jesajabuch', in Vermeylen (ed.), *The Book of Isaiah*, pp. 361-406.

Stenhouse, P., 'Chronicles of the Samaritans', in A.D. Crown, R. Pummer and A. Tal (eds.), *A Companion to Samaritan Studies* (Tübingen: J.C.B. Mohr, 1993), pp. 50-53.

—'The Kitāb al Tarīkh of Abū 'l-Fath: New Edition' (unpublished PhD dissertation, University of Sydney, 1980 [Arabic and English]).

—*The Kitāb al Tarīkh of Abū 'l-Fath: Translated into English with Notes* (Sydney: The Mandelbaum Trust, University of Sydney, 1985).

—'The Reliability of the Chronicle of Abū 'l-Fath, with Special reference to the Dating of Baba Rabba', in Rothschild and Sixdenier (eds.), *Études samaritaines Pentateuque*, pp. 233-57.

—'Samaritan Chronicles', in Crown (ed.), *The Samaritans*, pp. 218–65.

Stern, E., *Archaeology of the Land of the Bible*. II. *The Assyrian, Babylonian and Persian Periods (732–33.2 BCE)* (Anchor Bible Reference Library; New York: Doubleday, 2001).

Stern, E. (ed.), *The New Encyclopedia of Archaeological Excavations in the Holy Land* (4 vols.; New York: Simon & Schuster, 1993).

Stern, M., *Greek and Latin Authors on Jews and Judaism* (3 vols.; Jerusalem: Israel Academy of Sciences and Humanities, 1974–84).

—'The Jews in Greek and Latin Literature', in S. Safrai and M. Stern *et al.* (eds.), *The Jewish People in the First Century* (CRINT, II.2; Assen: Van Gorcum, 1976), pp. 1101-59.

Sternberg, M., 'The Bible's Art of Persuasion: Ideology, Rhetoric, and Poetics in Saul's Fall', in House (ed.), *Beyond Form Criticism*, pp. 234-71.

Stoebe, H.J., *Das Erste Buch Samuelis* (Kommentar zum Alten Testament 8.1; Gütersloh: Gütersloher Verlagshaus/Gerd Mohn, 1993).

Stolz, F., *Strukturen und Figuren im Kult von Jerusalem, Studien zur altorientalischen vor- und frühisraelitischen Religion* (BZAW, 118; Berlin: W. de Gruyter, 1970).

Stone, M.E., 'Apocalyptic Literature', in *idem* (ed.), *Jewish Writings of the Second Temple Period*, pp. 383-441.

Stone, M.E. (ed.), *Jewish Writings of the Second Temple Period: Apocrypha, Pseudepigrapha, Qumran Sectarian Writings, Philo, Josephus* (CRINT 2, II; Assen: Van Gorcum: Philadelphia: Fortress Press, 1984).

Strange, J., 'Arkaeologisk syntese og historieskrivning', in Hallbäck and Strange (eds.), *Bibel og historieskrivning*, pp. 43-57.

—*Bibelatlas* (Copenhagen: Det Danske Bibelselskab, 1998).

—'The Book of Joshua: A Hasmonaean Manifesto?', in A. Lemaire and B. Otzen (eds.), *History and Traditions of Early Israel* (VTSup, 50; Leiden: E.J. Brill, 1993), pp. 136-41.

—'The Book of Joshua: Origin and Dating', *SJOT* 16/1 (2002), pp. 44-51.

Stulman, L., 'Insiders and Outsiders in the Book of Jeremiah: Shifts in Symbolic Arrangements', *JSOT* 66 (1995), pp. 65-85.

Sweeney, M.A., 'The Book of Isaiah as Prophetic Torah', in Melugin and Sweeney (eds.), *New Visions of Isaiah*, pp. 50-67.

—'The Book of Isaiah in Recent Research', *CR:BS* 1 (1993), pp. 141-62.

—*Isaiah 1–4 and the Post-Exilic Understanding of the Isaianic Tradition* (BZAW, 171; Berlin: W. de Gruyter, 1988).

—*Isaiah 1–39, with an Introduction to Prophetic Literature* (FOTL, 16; Grand Rapids: Eerdmans, 1996).

Tal, A., and M. Florentin (eds.), *Proceedings of the First International Congress of the Société d'Études Samaritaines Tel Aviv, April 11-13, 1988* (Tel Aviv: Chaim Rosenberg School of Jewish Studies, Tel Aviv University, 1991).

Tcherikover, V., *Hellenistic Civilization and the Jews* (New York: Atheneum, 1975).

Tengström, S., *Die Hexateucherzählung: eine literaturgeschichtliche Studie* (CBOTS, 7; Lund, C.W.K. Gleerup, 1976).

—'Moses and the Prophets in the Deuteronomistic History', *SJOT* 8/2 (1994), pp. 257-66.

Thompson, M.E.W., *Situation and Theology: Old Testament Interpretations of the Syro-Ephraimite War* (Prophets and Historians Series, 1; Sheffield: Almond Press, 1982).

Thompson, T.L., *The Bible in History: How Writers Create a Past* (London: Jonathan Cape, 1999) (published in America as *The Mythic Past: Biblical Archaeology and the Myth of Israel* [New York: Basic Books, 1999]).

—*Early History of the Israelite People: From the Written and Archaeological Sources* (SHANE, 8, Leiden: E.J. Brill, 3rd edn, 2000 [1992]).

—'From the Mouth of Babes, Strength: Psalm 8 and the Book of Isaiah', *SJOT* 16/2 (2002), pp. 226-45.

—*The Historicity of the Patriarchal Narratives: The Quest for the Historical Abraham* (BZAW, 133; Berlin: W. de Gruyter, 1974 [Scranton: Trinity International Press, 3rd edn, 2002).

—'Historiography in the Pentateuch: Twenty-Five Years After Historicity', *SJOT* 13/2 (1999), pp. 258-83.

—'A History of Palestine: The Debate', *Journal of Palestinian Archaeology* II/1 (2001), pp. 18-24.

—'Holy War at the Center of Biblical Theology: *Shalom* and the Cleansing of Jerusalem', in *idem* [ed.], *Jerusalem in Ancient History and Tradition*, pp. 223-57 (first published as 'La Guerra santa al centro della teologia Biblica. "Shalom" e la purificazione di Gerusalemme', in M. Liverani [ed.], *Guerra santa e guerra giusta dal mondo antico alla prima età moderna* [Studi Storici, 43/3; Rome: Carocci editore, 2002], pp. 661-92).

—'An Introduction: Can a History of Ancient Jerusalem and Palestine Be Written?', in *idem* (ed.), *Jerusalem in Ancient History and Tradition*, pp. 1-15.

—'Jerusalem as the City of God's Kingdom: Common Tropes in the Bible and the Ancient Near East', in Jayyusi (ed.), *Islamic Studies*, pp. 631-47.

—'Kingship and the Wrath of God: or Teaching Humility', *RB* 109 (2002), pp. 161-96.

—*The Messiah Myth: The Near Eastern Roots of Jesus and David* (New York: Basic Books; London: Jonathan Cape, forthcoming).

—*The Origin Tradition of Ancient Israel: The Literary Formation of Genesis and Exodus 1–23* (JSOTSup, 55; Sheffield: JSOT Press, 1987).

—'A Testimony of the Good King: Reading the Mesha Stela', in L.L. Grabbe (ed.) (ESHM, 6; London/New York: T. & T. Clark International, forthcoming).

—'Text, Context and Referent in Israelite Historiography', in Edelman (ed.), *The Fabric of History*, pp. 65-92.

—'Tradition and History: The Scholarship of Van Seters', in McKenzie and Römer (eds.), *Rethinking the Foundations*, pp. 9-21.

—'Why Talk about the Past? The Bible Epic and Historiography', in P.R. Davies (ed.), *The Origins of the Jewish People and Contemporary Biblical Scholarship* (forthcoming).

Thompson, T.L. (ed.), *Jerusalem in Ancient History and Tradition* (CIS, 13; JSOTSup, 381; London/New York: T. & T. Clark International, 2003).

Thornton, T., 'Anti-Samaritan Exegesis Reflected in Josephus' Retelling of Deuteronomy, Joshua and Judges', *JTS* 47 (1996), pp. 125-30.

Tiller, P.A., *A Commentary on the Animal Apocalypse of 1 Enoch* (Early Judaism and Its Literature, 4; Atlanta: Scholars Press, 1993).

Toorn, K. van der, 'Anat-Yahu, Some Other Deities, and the Jews of Elephantine', *Numen* 39 (1992), pp. 80-101.

—'Euphrates', in *DDD*[1], pp. 594-99.

Torrey, C.C., *The Second Isaiah: A New Interpretation* (New York: Charles Scribner's Sons, 1928).

Tov, E., *The Book of Baruch* (SBLTT; Missoula, MT: Scholars Press, 1975).

—'Exegetical Notes on the Hebrew Vorlage of the LXX of Jeremiah 27 (34)', *ZAW* 91 (1971), pp. 73-93.

—'Scribal Practices Reflected in the Texts From the Judaean Desert', in P.W. Flint and J.C. VanderKam (eds.), *The Dead Sea Scrolls After Fifty Years: A Comprehensive Assessment* (2 vols.; Leiden: E.J. Brill, 1998–99), pp. 403-29.

—*The Septuagint Translation of Jeremiah and Baruch: A Discussion of an Early Revision of the LXX of Jeremiah 29–52 and Baruch 1.1–3.8* (HSM, 8; Missoula, MT: Scholars Press, 1976).

—*Textual Criticism of the Hebrew Bible* (Minneapolis: Fortress Press, 1992).

Tronier, H., 'Apokalyptikkens historiefilosofi: Erkendelse og historiekonstruktion i Dyre-apokalypsen, Første Enoks Bog 85–89', in Hallbäck and Strange (eds.), *Bibel og histori-eskrivning*, pp. 140-61.

Tsedaka, B., '480 Stone Inscriptions and 13,000 Coins Ranging from the Persian to the Roman Period Were discovered in Ancient Luza on Mount Gerizim', *A.B.- The Samaritan News* 845-47 (2003), pp. 136-37 (Eng. trans. L. Bernstein).

—*The History of the Samaritans Due to Their Own Sources: From Joshua to the Year 2000 AD* (forthcoming [Hebrew]).

—'The Origin of the Samaritans From the Children of Israel: The Quarrel Between the High Priest Ozzi and the Priest Eli', *A.B.- The Samaritan News* 801-803 (2001), pp. 23-33 (Hebrew).

—*A Summary of the History of the Israelite-Samaritans* (Holon: A.B. Institute of Samaritan Studies Press, 2000 [Hebrew]).

Uehlinger, C., 'Nisroch, נסרך', in *DDD*[1], pp. 1186-90.

Ulrich, E,. '4QJosh[a] and Joshua's First Altar in the Promised Land', in Brooke (ed.), *New Qumran Texts and Studies*, pp. 89-104.

—'4QJosh[a] (Pls. XXXII-XXXIV), in E. Ulrich and F.M Cross (eds.), *DJD* XIV (1995), pp. 143-52.

—*The Dead Sea Scrolls and the Origins of the Bible* (Grand Rapids: Eerdmans, 1999).

Van Seters, J., *Abraham in History and Tradition* (New Haven: Yale University Press, 1975).

—*In Search of History: Historiography in the Ancient World and the Origins of Biblical History* (New Haven: Yale University Press, 1983).

—'Is There Evidence of a Dtr Redaction in the Sinai Pericope (Exodus 19–24, 32–34)', in Shearing and McKenzie (eds.), *Those Elusive Deuteronomists*, pp. 160-70.

—'Joshua 24 & the Problem of Tradition in the Old Testament', in W.B. Barrick and J.R. Spencer (eds.), *In the Shelter of Elyon: Essays on Ancient Literature in Honour of G.W. Ahlström* (JSOTSup, 31; Sheffield: JSOT Press, 1984), pp. 139-58.

—*The Life of Moses: The Yahwist as Historian in Exodus–Numbers* (Kampen: Kok Pharos, 1994).

—*Prologue to History: The Yahwist as Historian in Genesis* (Louisville, KY: Westminster/John Knox Press, 1992).

Vanel, A., 'Ṭâbe'él en Is. vii et le roi Tubail de Tyr', in G.W. Anderson (ed.), *Studies on Prophecy: A Collection of Twelve Papers* (VTSup, 26; Leiden: E.J. Brill, 1974), pp. 17-24.

Vanoni, G., 'Beobachtungen zur deuteronomistischen Terminologie in 2 Kön 23,25–25,30', in N. Lohfink (ed.), *Das Deuteronomium: Entstehung, Gestalt und Botschaft* (Leuven: Leuven University Press, 1985), pp. 357-62.

Veijola, T., *Die ewige Dynastie. David und die Entstehung seiner Dynastie nach der deuter-onomistichen Darstellung* (AASF, B, 193; Helsinki: Academia Scientiarum Fennicae, 1975).

—*Das Königtum in der Beurteilung der deuteronomischen Historiographie* (AASF, B, 198; Helsinki: Academia Scientiarum Fennica, 1977).

Vermeylen, J., *Du prophète Isaïe à l'apocalyptique* (2 vols.; EBib; Paris: J. Gabalda, 1977–78).

—'L'Unité du livre d'Isaïe', in *idem* (ed.), *The Book of Isaiah*, pp. 11-53.

Vermeylen, J. (ed.), *The Book of Isaiah: Le Livre d'Isaïe: Les Oracles et leurs relectures. Unité et complexité de l'ouvrage* (BETL, 81; Leuven: Leuven University Press, 1989).

Vilmar, E., *Abulfathi Annales Samaritani* (Gothae: F.A. Perthes, 1865).

Vorländer, H., *Die Entstehungszeit des jehowistischen Geschichtswerkes* (Europäische Hochschulschriften, Series 23, 109; Frankfurt: Peter Lang, 1978).

Wacholder, B.Z., *Eupolemus: A Study of Judaeo-Greek Literature* (Cincinnati: Hebrew Union College Press, 1974).

—'Historiography of Qumran: The Sons of Zadok and Their Enemies', in F.H. Cryer and T.L Thompson (eds.), *Qumran between the Old and New Testaments* (CIS, 6; JSOTSup, 290; Sheffield: Sheffield Academic Press, 1998), pp. 347-77.

—' "Pseudo-Eupolemus" Two Greek Fragments on the Life of Abraham', *HUCA* 34 (1963), pp. 83-113.

Wächter, L., 'Salem bei Sichem', *ZDPV* 84 (1968), pp. 63-72.

Wakeman, M.K., *God's Battle With the Monster: A Study in Biblical Imagery* (Leiden: E.J. Brill, 1973).

Wanke, G., *Die Zionstheologie der Korachiten: In ihrem Traditionsgeschichtlichen Zusammenhang* (BZAW, 97; Berlin: Alfred Töpelmann, 1966).

Watts, J.D.W., *Isaiah 34–66* (WBC, 25; Waco, TX: Word Books, 1987).

Wedel, G., 'Abū l-Ḥasan aṣ- Ṣuri's *Kitāb aṭ-Ṭabbaḥ*: Results of the Edition, Translation and Commentary of Half of the Book', in Tal and Florentin (eds.), *Proceedings of the First International Congress of the Société d'Études Samaritaines*, pp. 305-12.

Weinfeld, M., *Deuteronomy and the Deuteronomic School* (Oxford: Clarendon Press, 1972).

Weippert, H., 'Die "deuteronomistischen" Beurteilung der Könige von Israel und Juda und das Problem der Redaktion der Königsbücher', *Bib* 53 (1972), pp. 301-39.

Weippert, M., '"Heiliger Krieg" in Israel und Assyrien', in *idem*, *Jahwe und die anderen Götter: Studien zur Religionsgeschichte des antiken Israel in ihrem syrisch-plästinischen Kontext* (FAT, 18; Tübingen: J.C.B. Mohr [Paul Siebeck], 1997), pp. 71-97.

Wellhausen, J., *Die Composition des Hexateuchs und der historischen Bücher des Alten Testaments* (Berlin: Georg Reimer, 1899).

—*Israelitische und jüdische Geschichte* (Berlin: Georg Reimer, 4th edn, 1901 [1887]).

—*Prolegomena zur Geschichte Israels* (Berlin: W. de Gruyter, 1885).

Wenham, G.J., *Genesis 16–50* (WBC, 2; Waco, TX: Word Books, 1994).

West, M., 'Looking for the Poem: Reflections on the Current and Future Status of the Study of Biblical Hebrew Poetry', in House (ed.), *Beyond Form Criticism*, pp. 423-32.

Whitelam, K.W., 'The Defence of David', *JSOT* 29 (1984), pp. 61-87.

—*The Just King: Monarchical Judicial Authority in Ancient Israel* (JSOTSup, 12; Sheffield: JSOT Press, 1979).

Whybray, R.N., *The Making of the Pentateuch: A Methodological Study* (JSOTSup, 53; Sheffield: JSOT Press, 1987).

Wildberger, H., 'Gottesnahmen und Gottesepitheta bei Jesaja', in *idem*, *Jahwe und sein Volk*, pp. 219-48.

—*Jahwe und sein Volk: Gesammelte Aufsätze zum Alten Testament* (TBAT, 66; Munich: Chr. Kaiser Verlag, 1979).

— *Jesaja 1–12* (BKAT, 10/1; Neukirchen–Vluyn: Neukirchener Verlag, 2nd edn, 1980 [1972]).

—*Jesaja 28–39* (BKAT, 10/3; Neukirchen–Vluyn: Neukirchener Verlag, 1982).

—'Jesajas Verständnis der Geschichte', in *idem*, *Jahwe und sein Volk*, pp. 75-109.

Wilson, R.R., 'Who Was the Deuteronomist? (Who Was Not the Deuteronomist?): Reflections on Pan-Deuteronomism', in Shearing and McKenzie (eds.), *Those Elusive Deuteronomists*, pp. 67-82.

Winckler, H., *Die Keilschrifttexte Sargons* (Leipzig: Eduard Pfeiffer, 1889).

Wintermute, O.S., 'Jubilees: A New Translation and Introduction', in *OTP* II, pp. 35-142.

Wolff, H.W., *Dodekapropheton 1: Hosea* (BKAT, 14/1; Neukirchen–Vluyn: Neukirchener Verlag, 1961).

—'Das Kerygma des deuteronomistichen Geschichtswerk', *ZAW* 73 (1961), pp. 171-86.

Wright, G.E., 'The Samaritans at Shechem', *HTR* 55 (1962), pp. 357-66.

—*Shechem: The Biography of a Biblical City* (New York: McGraw–Hill, 1965).

Würthwein, E., *Die Bücher der Könige. 1. Kön. 17–2. Kön. 25: Übersetzt und erklärt* (ATD, 11,2; Göttingen: Vandenhoeck & Ruprecht, 1984).

—'Jesaja 7,1-9', in *Theologie als Glaubenswagnis: Festschrift K. Heim zum 80. Geburtstag* (Hamburg: Furche-Verlag, 1954), pp. 47-63 (repr. as 'Jesaja 7,1-9: Ein Beitrag zu dem Thema: Prophetie und Politik', in *idem*, *Wort und Existens: Studien zum Alten Testament* [Göttingen: Vandenhoeck & Ruprecht, 1970], pp. 127-43).

Wyatt, N., 'Calf', in *DDD*[2], pp. 180-82.

Yahuda, A.S., 'Über die Unechtheit des Samaritanischen Josuabuches', *Sitzungsberichte der Berliner Akademie des Wissenschaftes* 39 (1908), pp. 887-914.

—'Zum Samaritanischen Josua: eine Erklärung', *ZDMG* 62/4 (1908), p. 754.

Yellin, D., 'A Book of Joshua or a Sepher Hayamim', *Jerusalem Yearbook* 7.7 (1908).

—'Das Buch Josua der Samaritaner in hebräisch', *Jerusalem Yearbook* 6.2 (ed. A.M. Luncz) (1902), pp. 138-55; 6.3 (1903), pp. 203-205 (Hebrew).

Younger, K. Lawson, Jr, *Ancient Conquest Accounts: A Study in Near Eastern and Biblical History Writing* (JSOTSup, 98; Sheffield: JSOT Press, 1990).

Zaccagnini, C., 'Breath of Life and Water to Drink', in L. Milano (ed.), *Drinking in Ancient Societies, History and Culture of Drinks in the Ancient Near East: Papers of a Symposium Held in Rome, May 17-19, 1990* (HANE/S, 6; Padova: Sargon, 1994), pp. 347-60.

Zangenberg, J., *Frühes Christentum in Samarien: Topographische und traditionsgeschichtliche Studien zu den Samarientexten im Johannesevangelium* (Texte und Arbeiten zum Neutestamentlichen Zeitalter, 27; Tübingen: Francke Verlag, 1998).

—*ΣΑΜΑΡΕΙΑ: Antike Quellen zur Geschichte und Kultur der Samaritaner in deutscher Übersetzung* (TANZ, 15; Tübingen: Francke Verlag, 1994).

Zimmerli, W., *Ezekiel 2* (Philadelphia: Fortress Press, 1983).

Zobel, H.-J., 'צבאות', in *ThWAT*, VI, pp. 876-91.

Zobel, K., *Prophetie und Deuteronomium: Die Rezeption prophetischer Theologie durch das Deuteronomium* (Berlin: W. de Gruyter, 1992).

Zsengellér, J., *Gerizim as Israel: Northern Tradition of the Old Testament and the Early History of the Samaritans* (Utrechtse Theologische Reeks, 38; Utrecht: University of Utrecht Press, 1998).

INDEXES

INDEX OF REFERENCES

INDEX OF AUTHORS